Iris Murdoch, Philosopher

Iris Murdoch was a professional philosopher before she was a professional novelist and her work was brave, brilliant, and independent. She first made her name for her challenges to Gilbert Ryle and behaviourism, and later for her book on Sartre (1953), but she had the greatest impact with her work in moral philosophy—and especially *The Sovereignty of Good* (1970). She turned expectantly from British linguistic philosophy to continental existentialism, but was dissatisfied there too; she devised a philosophy and a style of philosophy that were distinctively her own. Murdoch aimed to draw out the implications, for metaphysics and the conception of the world, of rejecting the standard dichotomy of language into the 'descriptive' and the 'emotive'. She aimed, in Wittgensteinian spirit, to describe the phenomena of moral thinking more accurately than those who emphasized behaviour and language in the style of R. M. Hare. This 'empiricist' task could be achieved, Murdoch thought, only with help from the idealist tradition of Kant, Hegel, and Bradley. And she combined with this a moral psychology, or theory of motivation, that went back to Plato but was influenced by Freud and Simone Weil. Murdoch's impact can be seen in the moral philosophy of John McDowell and, in different ways, in Richard Rorty and Charles Taylor, as well as in the recent movements under the headings of moral realism, particularism, moral perception, and virtue theory.

This volume brings together essays by critics and admirers of Murdoch's work, and includes a long Introduction on Murdoch's career, reception, and achievement. It also contains a previously unpublished chapter from the book on Heidegger that Murdoch had been working on shortly before her death, and a Memoir by her husband John Bayley. It gives not only an introduction to Murdoch's important philosophical life and work, but also a picture of British philosophy in one of its heydays and at an important moment of transition.

Justin Broackes is Professor of Philosophy at Brown University.

Iris Murdoch, Philosopher

A Collection of Essays

Edited by Justin Broackes

OXFORD
UNIVERSITY PRESS

OXFORD
UNIVERSITY PRESS

Great Clarendon Street, Oxford OX2 6DP

Oxford University Press is a department of the University of Oxford.
It furthers the University's objective of excellence in research, scholarship,
and education by publishing worldwide.

Oxford is a registered trade mark of Oxford University Press
in the UK and in certain other countries

© the several contributors 2012

The moral rights of the authors have been asserted

First published 2012
First published in paperback 2014

All rights reserved. No part of this publication may be reproduced,
stored in a retrieval system, or transmitted, in any form or by any means,
without the prior permission in writing of Oxford University Press,
or as expressly permitted by law, by licence or under terms agreed with the appropriate
reprographics rights organization. Enquiries concerning reproduction
outside the scope of the above should be sent to the Rights Department,
Oxford University Press, at the address above

Published in the United States of America by Oxford University Press
198 Madison Avenue, New York, NY 10016, United States of America

You must not circulate this work in any other form
and you must impose this same condition on any acquirer

British Library Cataloguing in Publication Data
Data available

Library of Congress Cataloging in Publication Data
Data available

ISBN 978-0-19-928990-5 (Hbk)
ISBN 978-0-19-870120-0 (Pbk)

Preface

Iris Murdoch's philosophical reputation is still, fifty years after she reached her prime, at a formative stage. When some years ago the Philosophy Department at Brown University was considering the idea of putting on a Murdoch conference, my impression was that for most of us (myself included) Murdoch was a rather vague figure one might connect with existentialism and aesthetics. Her philosophy was perhaps likely to be of only moderate interest to us; but it might appeal more to a wider group, we benignly supposed, including undergraduates and people in other departments. And there were signs of some significant philosophers talking about her too, though we didn't know quite what they were debating.

But what—or, in case one might almost be embarrassed at the directness of the question—what *exactly*, did Murdoch say?

This was a question that I, and I think others in the discussion, could not pretend to answer. I could, however, admit to having read, or read part of, *The Sovereignty of Good*. People looked surprised and delighted—perhaps slightly as if I had confessed a secret interest in Gurdjieff or that I had learned Danish to read Kierkegaard. (I didn't tell people that it had been in my first week of undergraduate Moral Philosophy—for a tutorial with John McDowell on Fact and Value and Reason and Desire, for which I had undergone the trial of reading Hume, Moore, Hare, Searle, Mackie, Nagel, Foot, and Murdoch. I had had the impression of understanding something of all the others and next to nothing of Murdoch.) 'It's good,' I said, uncertainly. By the strange ways of academic accident, this was qualification enough. I ended up running the conference, together with two colleagues no doubt better qualified than me.

This collection of essays is, though rather indirectly, the result of that conference. It is, I hope, a way of showing that Murdoch is of importance and interest to the same people as read the moral philosophy of Kant and Plato or Philippa Foot and John McDowell. The Introduction is an attempt to do a better job than I could before, of saying what Murdoch said, and why. Having fallen more or less by accident into the job, I have had a lot of work to do. What I have learned has surprised me. Murdoch's main achievements are, I think, not particularly in what she had to say about existentialism or aesthetics, nor in her early philosophy of mind—though those things are substantial enough—but in her moral philosophy and the correlative metaphysics. Her recurring concerns—like those of Kant and Plato—are with the discovery of our own nature as beings capable (very variously, but improvably) of reasoning and moral attention, and, correlatively, with the conception of the (moral and other) nature of the world, of which we are rather imperfectly conscious. What Murdoch had to say on those topics is never going to be easy; but as an interpretative tradition builds up and there are more and better guides available, I hope that new readers will be able to find their way around more easily, to see what's there and what they can do with it. It has been a delight to study her work.

Many of the papers of this volume had an ancestor that was presented in the Murdoch conference at Brown in 2001; others are entirely new. I am particularly grateful to John Bayley for graciously permitting the publication of a chapter from the book on Heidegger that Iris Murdoch left unfinished, as well as for his own contribution to the volume. Peter Conradi has been a generous supporter of the project. I must thank all the contributors not only for their work, but also for their endurance during the time it has taken me to bring our work to completion. Peter Momtchiloff, Catherine Berry, Eleanor Collins, and Carla Hodge, editors at OUP, have been models of interest, guidance, and well-timed demand; and Joe Soave has been a terrific copy-editor with a difficult text. I am lucky to have had Steven Yamamoto as Research Assistant: the hard work of preparing the Index was his. Robert Lacey and others at HarperCollins helped, when the cover photo needed some technical assistance. I would particularly like to thank Mark Shapiro, a former student of Philosophy at Brown and now a benefactor of it, who first suggested the idea of the conference, and who most generously supported it. And above all I would like to thank John McDowell: who, over weeks and months of tutorials, first guided me in moral philosophy and gave me the beginnings of what understanding I have developed of Murdoch since I returned to her, more or less accidentally, over twenty years later. There are things he said in that first tutorial that I believe I understood for the first time just a few months ago.

Contents

Abbreviations

Abbreviations for Murdoch's own writings, and a few other important works, are given below. Any other abbreviations are normally explained on their first occurrence in any of the essays. References are given, where possible, to the reprints of Murdoch's philosophical works in the collection *Existentialists and Mystics* (1997), edited by Peter J. Conradi. For the three essays (IP, OGG and SGC) that make up *The Sovereignty of Good*, page references are given both to the 1970 book publication and to the reprints in *Existentialists and Mystics* (1997), separated by a forward slash.

AD   'Against Dryness' (1961), E&M 287–95

Ak.   Kant, *Gesammelte Schriften herausgegeben von der Königlich Preußischen Akademie der Wissenschaften*, 1st division, 9 vols. (1902–23)

BP   *The Black Prince* (1973; Penguin, 1975)

DPR   'The Darkness of Practical Reason' (1966), E&M 193–202

E&M   *Existentialists and Mystics* (1997), edited by Peter J. Conradi

E&I   'Ethics and the Imagination', *Irish Theological Quarterly*, vol. 52, 1986, 92

EPM   'The Existentialist Political Myth' (1952), E&M 130–45

F&S   *The Fire and the Sun* (1977), E&M 386–463

FFE   *The Flight from the Enchanter* (1956; Penguin, 1962)

FTC   *From a Tiny Corner in the House of Fiction: Conversations with Iris Murdoch* (2003), edited by Gillian Dooley

GMS   Kant, *Grundlegung zur Metaphysik der Sitten* (1785): *Groundwork of the Metaphysics of Morals*. Page numbers refer to vol. 4 of the Ak. edition

HMD   'Hegel in Modern Dress' (1957), E&M 146–50

HT   'A House of Theory' (1958), E&M 171–87

IML   Peter J. Conradi, *Iris Murdoch: A Life* (2001)

IP   'The Idea of Perfection' (1964), SG 1–45, E&M 299–336

KpV   Kant, *Kritik der praktischen Vernunft* (1788), *Critique of Practical Reason*. Page numbers refer to vol. 5 of the Ak. edition

KV   'Knowing the Void' (1956), E&M 157–60

MDH   'The Moral Decision about Homosexuality', *Man and Society*, 7 (Summer 1964), 3–6

M&E   'Metaphysics and Ethics' (1957), E&M 59–76

MGM   *Metaphysics as a Guide to Morals* (1992)

NM   'The Novelist as a Metaphysician' (1950), E&M 101–7

NP   'Nostalgia for the Particular' (1952), E&M 43–58

OGG	'On "God" and "Good"' (1969), SG 46–76, E&M 337–62
PAS	*Proceedings of the Aristotelian Society*
PASS	*Proceedings of the Aristotelian Society* Supplementary Volume
PI	Wittgenstein, *Philosophical Investigations* (1953), tr. G. E. M. Anscombe
Rep.	Plato, *Republic*
S&G	'The Sublime and the Good' (1959), E&M 205–21
SBR	'The Sublime and the Beautiful Revisited' (1959), E&M 261–86
SE	*Standard Edition of the Complete Psychological Works of Sigmund Freud*, ed. James Strachey, 24 vols. (1953–1966)
SG	*The Sovereignty of Good* (1970)
SGC	'The Sovereignty of Good over other Concepts' (1967), SG 77–104, E&M 363–85
SRR	*Sartre: Romantic Rationalist* (1953; 1987)
TA	Hampshire, *Thought and Action* (1959)
T&L	'Thinking and Language' (1951), E&M 33–42
UN	*Under the Net* (1954; Penguin, 1960)
VCM	'Vision and Choice in Morality' (PASS 1956, 32–58), repr. (with omissions) in E&M 76–98

When line numbers as well as page numbers are given, they follow a full stop or point: thus IP 29.19/320.11 refers to 'The Idea of Perfection', page 29 line 19 in *The Sovereignty of Good* (1970) and page 320 line 11 in *Existentialists and Mystics* (1997). There is also a later edition of *The Sovereignty of Good* (2001): pp. 1–104 of the 1970 edition correspond to pp. 1–101 in the 2001 edition.

Notes on Contributors

MARIA ANTONACCIO is a professor of religion at Bucknell University. She is the author of *Picturing the Human: The Moral Thought of Iris Murdoch* (Oxford University Press, 2000), co-editor of *Iris Murdoch and the Search for Human Goodness* (University of Chicago Press, 1996), and has published numerous essays on topics in moral theory and religious ethics.

CARLA BAGNOLI is Full Professor of Philosophy at the University of Wisconsin-Milwaukee. She has written three monographs on moral dilemmas and the authority of morality, and articles on constructivism, emotions, autonomy, and humanitarian intervention. Her research project concerns the objective and subjective aspects of practical reason.

JOHN BAYLEY is an Emeritus Fellow of St Catherine's College, Oxford; he was Tutorial Fellow of New College from 1955 to 1974 and Warton Professor of English Literature from 1974 to 1992. He and Iris Murdoch were married on 14 August 1956. His books include *The Romantic Survival* (1956), *The Characters of Love* (1961), *Tolstoy and the Novel* (1966), and *Housman's Poems* (1992), and the novels *In Another Country* (1954), *Alice* (1994), *The Queer Captain* (1995), and *George's Lair* (1996). He is the author of *Iris: A Memoir* (1998), *Iris and the Friends: A Year of Memories* (1999), and *Widower's House* (2001).

LAWRENCE BLUM is Professor of Philosophy and Distinguished Professor of Liberal Arts and Education at the University of Massachusetts, Boston. He specializes in moral philosophy, moral psychology, moral education, race studies, and philosophy of education. His most recent book is the award-winning *"I'm Not a Racist, But . . . ": The Moral Quandary of Race* (Cornell University Press, 2002).

JUSTIN BROACKES is Professor of Philosophy at Brown University. He works particularly on 17th and 18th century philosophy and the history and theory of perception and colour. His special interests include colour blindness, the notion of substance and its fate in the modern period, and the metaphysics of abstract objects.

BRIDGET CLARKE received her Ph.D. in Philosophy from the University of Pittsburgh in 2003. She was assistant professor at Williams College from 2003 to 2006 and is currently assistant professor at the University of Montana. She has published pieces on Aristotle's ethics, Descartes's *Meditations*, Murdoch's ethics, and recent work in the ethics of virtue. What connects these writings is an interest in how classical conceptions of virtue and reason might help us to develop a compelling account of moral objectivity.

PETER J. CONRADI, Emeritus Professor of English at Kingston University, is the author of many books, including *Iris Murdoch: The Saint and the Artist* and *Iris Murdoch: A Life*, and the editor of Murdoch's *Existentialists and Mystics* and *A Writer at War*. His recent books include *Going Buddhist* and *At the Bright Hem of God: Radnorshire Pastoral*.

ROGER CRISP is Uehiro Fellow and Tutor in Philosophy at St Anne's College and Professor of Moral Philosophy at the University of Oxford. He is author of *Mill on Utilitarianism*

(Routledge, 1997) and *Reasons and the Good* (Clarendon Press, 2006), and, with Michael Slote, edited *Virtue Ethics* (Oxford University Press, 1997).

A. E. DENHAM is a Senior Research Fellow and sometime Tutorial Fellow in Philosophy at St Anne's College, Oxford, where she held the post formerly occupied by Iris Murdoch. She is also a member of the Departments of Philosophy and Political Economy at Tulane University. Denham's research is principally concerned with issues in the theory of value, including aesthetics, ethics, and moral psychology. Her abiding interest in the interaction of emotion and cognition in evaluative thought is reflected in her publications on moral judgment and imagination, metaphor, and the philosophy of music. Denham lives in New Orleans and East Sussex.

JULIA DRIVER is Professor of Philosophy at Washington University in St. Louis. She received her Ph.D. in Philosophy from Johns Hopkins University. She is the author of *Uneasy Virtue* (Cambridge University Press, 2001), *Ethics: the Fundamentals* (Blackwell, 2006), and is currently completing a book manuscript, *Consequentialism*. She has also published articles in normative ethical theory and moral psychology in a variety of journals.

MARGARET HOLLAND is an Associate Professor of Philosophy at the University of Northern Iowa. Her research focuses on moral psychology and morally problematic truth-telling.

RICHARD MORAN is Brian D. Young Professor of Philosophy at Harvard University. He is the author of *Authority and Estrangement: An Essay on Self-Knowledge*, and various articles on human action, speech and testimony, metaphor, and imagination.

MARTHA NUSSBAUM is Ernst Freund Distinguished Service Professor of Law and Ethics at the University of Chicago, appointed in Law, Philosophy, and Divinity. Her most recent book is *Not For Profit: Why Democracy Needs the Humanities*.

Introduction

Justin Broackes

For fifteen years, from 1948 to 1963, Iris Murdoch was a Tutorial Fellow in Philosophy at St Anne's College, Oxford.* She was both brilliant and, I think, immediately recognized as such. By the time her first published novel *Under the Net* appeared in 1954, she had already produced a small book on *Sartre* (1953), two substantial papers at the Aristotelian Society, and some reviews for *Mind*—as well as a couple of radio talks on existentialism and an ambitious piece on existentialist politics for the *Socratic Digest*. At opposite ends of her work, she was both a thoroughly professional combatant—debating with Ryle whether he had underestimated the notion of 'private' experience—and a cultural commentator of wide range and socialist sympathies—enquiring, for example, with Lukács, Oakeshott, and Merleau-Ponty whether Existentialist politics were an adolescent evasion, whereas Marxism and capitalism in their different ways at least had the recommendation of being 'an incarnation of ideas and values' (EPM 142). For a good ten years, Murdoch was a philosopher who wrote novels, not a novelist who taught—or had taught—philosophy. And her work in moral philosophy—beginning with two articles in the mid-1950s and culminating in the three papers that were collected together as *The Sovereignty of Good* (1970)—was important, difficult, and distinctive. It rejected the approach to morality of the two dominant movements of the time—Anglo-American 'analytical philosophy', with its emphasis on language and behaviour, and Continental existentialism—and opened up a third path. Murdoch proposed a form of moral realism, allowing the world to contain such things as the courage of an individual person or the meanness of some petty act—something like 'moral facts' (VCM 54/95), conceived as *what meets the eye of a just and loving moral perceiver*. She argued for this with a broadly Wittgensteinian approach, in opposition to a narrower method that (as in R. M. Hare) looked to behaviour and linguistic analysis to delimit the nature of morality. And Murdoch combined with this a moral psychology (what today might be called a theory of

* For comments, advice, and conversation, I am grateful to Melissa Barry, David Charles, Peter J. Conradi, Roger Crisp, James Dreier, Ivan Gaskell, Dana Howard, Mark Jenkins, Charles Larmore, David Matthews, David Robjant, Barbara Sattler, Dominic Scott, Jenifer Wakelyn, Kenneth Winkler, and Steven Yamamoto.

motivation and practical reasoning) and a conception of a training in the virtues that went back to Plato. Surprisingly perhaps for a kind of moral realist, she was also a great believer in historical and individual differences in moral perception and conception, and in the difficulty and duty of working for mutual understanding, enlargement of view, and (where a part of our conceptual repertoire itself embodies an injustice) conceptual reform—something more radical than merely changing our minds on the judgements we can already make with our present concepts. Most remarkably, perhaps, Murdoch believed—as Plato and Kant had done, but absolutely in opposition to the mainstream of her time—that moral philosophy should contribute, not just to abstract debates on the nature of morality, but to the practical question, 'How can we make ourselves morally better?' (OGG 52/342; cp. SGC 83/368.) But Murdoch's proposals on that question were deliberately modest: the good is distant and we know it only as seen in reflections, darkly—but we can talk of the main obstacles to perceiving it: social convention, neurosis, fantasy and, above all, the selfish ego, operating obscurely in ways we hardly understand, but which Freud and Plato so richly display for us. In this Introduction I shall say something of Murdoch's philosophical career and reception; I shall go on to introduce the ideas of her earlier papers from the 1950s and 60s and, especially, *The Sovereignty of Good*, and then, more briefly, some of her later work; I shall end with some comments to introduce the papers in this collection.

1   Biography and philosophical career

Murdoch went up to Somerville College, Oxford in 1938, at the age of 19. She appears from the start to have led a rather fabulous existence: 'Practically the very first thing I did', she reported, somewhat dramatically, later, 'was to join the Communist Party', while throwing herself into a 'hurricane of essays and proses and campaigns and committees and sherry parties and political and aesthetic arguments'.[1] She read Mods and Greats—that is, Latin and Greek, Ancient History and Philosophy—, was thrilled and terrified (and fondled) by the magisterial Eduard Fraenkel, whose Aeschylus classes she attended, and formed intellectual and passionate friendships to last a lifetime. It was a remarkable philosophical generation: Philippa Foot, Mary Midgley, and Iris Murdoch all took finals from Somerville in 1942. (Elizabeth Anscombe, at St Hugh's, had taken Greats the year before—but she and Murdoch really became friends later, particularly in 1947–48.) Murdoch and her friend Mary Midgley—at that time Mary Scrutton—were the only candidates in Greats from Somerville that year; both got Firsts, as did Philippa Bosanquet—better known, after her marriage, as Philippa

---

[1] For Murdoch's life, and a wonderfully vivid picture of these early years, see Peter J. Conradi, *Iris Murdoch: A Life* (2001, henceforth abbreviated as IML), on which I have drawn freely in this section. I quote here from Slavcho Trunski, *Grateful Bulgaria* (1979), 14, and from IML 83, which in turn quotes Murdoch from the *Badminton School Magazine* 79 (Spring–Summer 1939).

Foot—who was taking Philosophy, Politics, and Economics. Somerville at the time had no philosophy tutor, so Murdoch, Midgley, and Foot were all taught by Donald MacKinnon, the philosophy Tutor at Keble—a somewhat shambling, powerful man of extreme devotion to matters philosophical, moral, and spiritual,[2] who was to become Regius Professor of Moral Philosophy at Aberdeen (1947–60) and Norris-Hulse Professor of Divinity at Cambridge (1960–78). One might wonder at the strength and independence of this generation of women philosophers—features which Mary Midgley has linked with the relative absence of men from the student body at the time and with the unstinting attentions of their extraordinary tutor.[3]

After Oxford, Murdoch had five years in the larger world, first at the Treasury in London (1942–44) and then with the United Nations Relief and Rehabilitation Administration UNRRA (1944–46), which took her to Belgium and Austria, working in scenes of extreme destruction, injury, hunger, crime, and bereavement. It was largely the excitement of existentialism, as it reached her and many others in Belgium, that revived Murdoch's philosophical interests.[4] She met Sartre in Brussels in the autumn of 1945 after he gave a talk there (IML 215), and found him gentle and carefully attentive the next day at a *café-séance* with a series of young people 'who were dying to talk to him without having anything much to say'.[5] In the excited months that followed, she read everything of Sartre's she could lay her hands on (IML 215–6). Working with UNRRA in Innsbruck in February 1946, Murdoch also met the author Raymond Queneau, who became a friend, as well as literary model with his novel

[2] Murdoch writes, in a letter to Frank Thompson of 29 January 1942:

It's good to meet someone so extravagantly unselfish, so fantastically noble, as well as so extremely intelligent as this cove. He inspires a pure devotion. One feels vaguely one would go through fire for him, & so on. Sorry if this makes him sound like a superman. There are snags. He's perpetually on the brink of a nervous break-down.... He is perpetually making demands of one—there is a moral as well as an intellectual challenge— & there is no room for spiritual lassitude of any kind. (Quoted in Conradi, IML 123)

[3] 'Most of the men were away at the war. Classes were small, and they contained about as many women as men. The loud contests of competing male voices were not there. This was helpful, and I think it had a lot to do with allowing me, along with the other women, to be heard and work out our own ideas—an invaluable experience.... I should say that Philippa, Iris and I owed a huge debt to a wonderful male tutor who was wedded to large questions and gave us unstinted time to discuss them.' (Mary Midgley, *The Guardian*, 3 Oct. 2005.) 'Wedded' is a telling word here: MacKinnon apparently told one student that he 'had so terrible a conscience about not being in the forces [at this stage in the Second World War] that he lived in his college rooms, and left his newly-married wife living twenty or thirty yards away, working far too hard in order to justify himself'. (Conradi, IML 125) On this world of women philosophers, consider a journal entry following a trip to Oxford, when Murdoch was finishing her time at Cambridge in 1948: 'Back from Oxford. A world of women. I reflected, talking with Mary, Pip & Elizabeth [i.e. Midgley, Foot & Anscombe], how much I love them.' (Journal, 12 June 1948, IML 268)

[4] 'Everyone was in a state of frenzy about existentialism': Murdoch, in Interview with W. K. Rose (1968), repr. in G. Dooley, *From a Tiny Corner in the House of Fiction* [FTC] (2003), 20.

[5] Murdoch, Interview with Harold Hobson (1962), FTC 98.

Pierrot mon ami (1943)[6]—and who may have helped in her first successful encounters with Hegel.[7] Murdoch returned to academic life with a brief stay in Cambridge (1947–48). She arrived intending to write a Ph. D. thesis on Husserl,[8] but quickly abandoned the idea in favour of arguing about Wittgenstein. Unfortunately for Murdoch, Wittgenstein himself had just stopped lecturing and, after a Michaelmas term sabbatical, was giving up his Professorship at the end of 1947. But Murdoch met him, was supervised by John Wisdom (after a brief spell with C. D. Broad), and spent huge amounts of time in philosophical friendship with members of the Wittgenstein circle which included Yorick Smythies, Georg Kreisel, Wasfi Hijab, and Kanti Shah. Before the year was out, she had been elected to a Fellowship at St Anne's, and began teaching in the autumn of 1948.

She could hardly have been more enthusiastically received into the philosophical world. She had two reviews almost immediately in *Mind* (1950). In 1951 she appeared at the main British philosophy conference—the Joint Session of the Mind Association and the Aristotelian Society[9]—reading a paper to which A. C. Lloyd and Gilbert Ryle presented replies. Gilbert Ryle was some twenty years her senior, Waynflete Professor at Oxford since 1945, and fresh from the success of *The Concept of Mind* (1949), to which Murdoch's paper raised some forceful resistance. Murdoch's paper must have made quite an impression, for she was invited to give another Aristotelian Society talk in London less than a year later—rather exceptionally, given the way the limited number of lecture invitations are usually distributed. She published a short book on *Sartre* (1953), and another Joint Session paper, 'Vision and Choice in Morality' (1956), which was her first large-scale move into the field of moral philosophy, challenging the views of R. M. Hare. She had also talked on 'Metaphysics and Ethics' in a BBC radio series the year before (1955) on *The Nature of Metaphysics*—where she appeared in the company of H. P. Grice, P. F. Strawson, David Pears, Stuart Hampshire, Bernard Williams, Gerd Buchdahl, Patrick Gardiner, G. J. Warnock, Gilbert Ryle, Mary Warnock, and Anthony Quinton.[10] These were the most brilliant of the rising generation, appearing with

---

[6] Murdoch made a translation of Queneau's novel, though it was never published (IML 231–4), and the book was a very visible influence on her own novel *Under the Net* (1954).

[7] Queneau was the editor of Alexandre Kojève's hugely influential lectures on the *Phenomenology of Spirit*, published as an *Introduction à la lecture de Hegel* (1947)—and he gave Murdoch a copy of the book in September 1947, which she read carefully. (It is now in the Kingston University archive.) See also IML 640 n. 1. Murdoch already had Baillie's translation of the *Phenomenology* (her copy is dated Aug. 31, 1946)—and some of the fruits of her appreciative reading of it can be seen in her BBC talk, 'The Novelist as Metaphysician' (1950): esp. E&M 102–3.

[8] See the Heidegger typescript in the Iris Murdoch Archives at Kingston University, 83.

[9] For those unfamiliar with the British philosophical world, the Aristotelian Society has in practice nothing particularly to do with Aristotle: it is the society under whose aegis a series of a dozen or so talks by invited speakers are given through the academic year in London, on topics from the full range of academic philosophy; and it sponsors an annual conference, in the form of a 'Joint Session' with the Mind Association (itself more or less equivalent to the body of subscribers to the journal *Mind*), which occupies two or three days in July each year.

[10] See D. Pears, ed., *The Nature of Metaphysics* (1957). In his review of the volume, W. H. Walsh described Murdoch's piece as 'without doubt the most striking and perceptive essay in the book' (*Philosophy* 34 (1959):

Ryle their senior, and they represented the new blood of Oxford Philosophy in one of its heydays: the people who would (together with Elizabeth Anscombe and Michael Dummett) lead philosophy in Britain for the next 30 years and more. When Ved Mehta profiled Oxford intellectuals for the *New Yorker* in 1961 and 1962, after briefings in London from Ernest Gellner and Bertrand Russell (who warned him against Ryle and the heritage of Austin), he made his first visits in Oxford to Hare and to Murdoch,[11] before calling later on Warnock, Strawson, and Ayer.

Along with her St Anne's College Tutorship, Murdoch took a University Lecturership as from October 1951—adding an income of £300 per year to the £600 which came with the College Fellowship. (The older established men's colleges meanwhile offered salaries of about double.[12]) Her lectures were no bread-and-butter coverage of 'Ethical Theories' or an 'Introduction to Ethics' (Hare's topics at the time). The titles show the ambition and the development of her interests: 'Meanings, Descriptions, Thoughts' (H51),[13] 'Concepts and Images' (M51), 'Some Problems in Bradley' (T52), 'Imagination' (H53), 'Existentialist Moral Philosophy' (T53), 'The Naturalistic Fallacy' (H54), 'Analysis in Moral Philosophy' (a Graduate Class, given with Philippa Foot and Basil Mitchell, T54), 'Moral Philosophy and the Ethics of Liberalism' (H55), 'Art and Morals' (a Graduate Class with Patrick Gardiner, T55), and 'Morals and Politics' (T56 and H57).

From the later 1950s, however, one may discern Murdoch taking a more abstracted path. She did not ask for a continuation of her University Lecturership when it came up for renewal in the summer of 1957, though she continued with her college teaching.[14] (Among her pupils in 1959–60 was the 18-year old David K. Lewis, later the distinguished philosopher, visiting Oxford from Swarthmore College, accompanying his

---

53–4). In 1960, when a similar BBC Third Programme series debated *Freedom and the Will* (publ. in book form, 1963), Murdoch appeared again, in discussion with Stuart Hampshire, Patrick Gardiner, and David Pears; other broadcasts in the series were by Bernard Williams, H. L. A. Hart, P. F. Strawson, J. F. Thomson, G. J. Warnock, and Mary Warnock.

[11] Murdoch doesn't seem to have made a particularly good impression on Mehta. They talked briefly of her interests in Sartre and Kierkegaard when she worked in Belgium, and then of Wittgenstein, Anscombe, and Foot, and of existentialist challenges to the couching of morality entirely in terms of *principles*. 'As she talked on, it became clear to me that she was much more an intuitive person than an analytic one, and regarded ideas as so many precious stones in the human diadem. Unlike Hare, she found it hard to imagine the diadem locked up in an ivory tower, or like the Crown Jewels in the Tower of London' (*Fly and the Fly-Bottle: Encounters with British Intellectuals* (1963, 1965), 53). I have slightly the impression that it may have been precisely for the self-compromising charm of Crown Jewels in an ivory tower that Mehta was searching Oxford.

[12] The St Anne's advertisement inviting Applications 'for the post of Tutor (woman)...to teach Philosophy' (also 'to direct and take a share in the teaching of Latin') appeared in the *Oxford University Gazette* for 21 April 1948 (651): it offered a minimum of '£400 a year, rising to the £600 at the end of two years'. A men's college would have offered e.g. '£650 per annum initially, rising to a maximum of £1,350 per annum' (from an advertisement for a comparable post at Magdalen).

[13] M, H, and T (along the last two digits of the year) stand for the Michaelmas, Hilary, and Trinity (i.e. autumn, spring, and summer) terms of the Oxford academic year. Lecture Lists at the time were published in the *Oxford University Gazette*.

[14] I take the dates from the Oxford University Archives. Cp. also Conradi, IML 457n.

academic parents for the year.) Murdoch published two papers linking ethics and aesthetics with more general cultural criticism: 'The Sublime and the Good' (1959) and 'The Sublime and the Beautiful Revisited' (1959). They must, however, have been less noticed in philosophical circles, appearing as they did in the *Chicago Review* and the *Yale Review*. (The second had been a lecture at Yale when she was invited there for a month in the autumn of 1959. In the journal's Notes on Contributors, where others talk of their teaching and employment or institutional affiliation, we read simply: 'IRIS MURDOCH is a well-known British writer.') At the same time, she was producing a good stream of reviews of philosophical books in more general publications like the *Listener* and *Spectator*, the *New Statesman* and *Encounter*,[15] as well as the acclaimed and much-reprinted article 'A House of Theory' (1958), a manifesto for a more theoretical socialism than was evident in the Labour Party of the time.

There are people who suspect now, I think, that Murdoch was either not quite a serious and substantial philosopher or not quite a professional, recognized by her fellows. Of the seriousness and substance of her work, the remainder of this volume, will I hope be sufficient confirmation; of her professionalism and recognition, her public career in the 1950s could hardly give more evidence. Philippa Foot, who became perhaps the most admired figure in British moral philosophy, was in the first twenty years of her career no more prolific;[16] and while Foot's paper 'Moral Beliefs' (PAS 1958–59) became something of a classic, it would have been hard to tell either in 1960 or in 1970 which of the two presented a more powerful challenge to the dominant moral philosophy.[17] In *The Sovereignty of Good*, Murdoch developed what

[15] And elsewhere: not all are reprinted in E&M. There is, for example, in the *Partisan Review* (Spring 1960), a sharp discussion of Ernest Gellner's *Words and Things*, in which Murdoch talks of post-Wittgensteinian philosophy, very much as an insider.

[16] By the end of the 1950s, Foot had five main papers (*Philosophy* 1952, PASS 1954, *Philosophical Review* 1957, PAS 1958–59, *Mind* 1958); Murdoch had published three similarly academic pieces (PASS 1951, PAS 1951–52, PASS 1956), two articles on the Sublime, and the small book on *Sartre*. In the decade of the 1960s, Murdoch produced the three big papers that became *The Sovereignty of Good* (1970); Foot published three smaller but highly respected articles (PASS 1961, *Oxford Review* 1967 ('The Problem of Abortion and the Doctrine of Double Effect'), and a piece for David Pears's *David Hume: A Symposium* (1963)); and she edited the collection *Theories of Ethics* (1967). Foot gave a talk at the British Academy in 1970 ('Morality and Art') and was elected a Fellow in 1976.

[17] Murdoch's own estimate (to David Hicks, about 1945) was: 'Philippa is much the better philosopher than me' (see Conradi, IML 209). Philippa Foot, looking back later, places herself in the mainstream, and Murdoch outside it: 'We were interested in moral language, she was interested in the moral life . . . She left us, in the end' (to Conradi, IML 302). But Murdoch was, if anything, I think, the more prominent of the two in the profession in the mid-1950s: witness, along with the Aristotelian Society invitations and the series of Radio talks, e.g. her appearance with Anthony Quinton, Stuart Hampshire, and Isaiah Berlin in the 'Special Oxford number' (June 1955) of the monthly review *The Twentieth Century*, which devoted nearly 30 pages to 'Philosophy and Beliefs: A discussion between four Oxford philosophers'.

For the love and friendship between Murdoch and Foot, see Conradi's biography, from their time as undergraduates together (IML 85, 97, 127–8) to the end of Murdoch's life (593, 597). They shared a London flat in 1943–44, in Seaforth Place, near Victoria Station—with wartime shortages and night-time bombings, and transformations in their relations with the men in their lives that left an uncomfortable imprint on their own friendship (IML 142–7; 165–9, 175–9, 205, 223). There was a reconciliation in 1946–47 (IML 252–4) and Murdoch lived with Philippa and Michael Foot (the historian, not the Labour politician of the same

might be called a substantial, unified, and very distinctive overall position—the kind of thing that a new young philosopher could spend months studying and years either challenging or developing.

What is true, however, is that Murdoch had much less of an academic following, and if there was such a new young philosopher to develop and take it forward, he was not to appear until the arrival of John McDowell—particularly with his articles 'Virtue and Reason' (1979) and 'Non-Cognitivism and Rule-Following' (1981)—more than fifteen years after Murdoch herself had left the profession.[18] Philippa Foot's classic paper 'Moral Beliefs' (PAS 1958–59) was accessible, soon reprinted in other places, and would have appeared on almost any undergraduate reading list for 'Fact and Value' or some such topic. Murdoch's 'Idea of Perfection', which I think is no less of a masterpiece, appeared, by contrast, in the *Yale Review* (1964), where it was unlikely to be seen either by students or their teachers; it became part of *The Sovereignty of Good* (1970) but was otherwise, I think, not reprinted until 2001.[19] If it appeared on an undergraduate reading list at all, it might as easily—or hardly—have been classified under 'Fact and Value', 'Reason and Desire', 'Freedom', or 'Moral Perception' (itself a topic that hardly existed in 1965 as a subject for an undergraduate study), not to mention other issues which figured under no standard heading at all. And of course Murdoch's style—allusive, all-embracing, non-aligned in the cold war of analytic and continental philosophy, and, quite simply, *hard*—was going to be appreciated by few without the help of a teacher. But by the time 'The Idea of Perfection' appeared in Spring of 1964, Murdoch had already left Oxford, where she had anyway stopped

name) in her first year back in Oxford (1948–49); but the friendship seems to have been fully renewed only in 1959 after the separation of Philippa and Michael Foot (IML 430–1). Foot appears in Murdoch's fiction in various mostly intimidating guises—Paula in *The Nice and the Good* (1968) is a portrait (IML 485). They seem to have had a varying and undying love. Philippa to Iris was her 'life-long best friend' (IML 128): 'My God, I did love her', Iris said of those intense London months (to David Hicks, Nov. 1944, IML 220). Of Iris, Philippa said, 'She was the light of my life' (IML 592–3).

[18] One should mention others who took up her work about the same time or slightly later, including Richard Rorty, Hilary Putnam, and Charles Taylor—to all of whom Murdoch may have been of particular interest as showing one way for an 'analytic' philosopher to leave the fold, or at least to argue over the grazing rules. Rorty in his 1979 NEH Summer Seminar for University & College Teachers, on 'Epistemological and Moral Relativism', included *The Sovereignty of Good*, along with texts of Kuhn, Davidson, Putnam, Sellars, MacIntyre, Wiggins, Nagel, and Harman. Rorty seems (as Ken Winkler reports to me from his notes at the time) to have read Sellars (in *Science and Metaphysics*) as coming close to Murdoch on attention, community, and what it is to take up the moral point of view—or at least, as being *on the verge* of saying Murdoch-like things, but as being held prisoner by the vocabulary of analytic philosophy. From such an admirer of Sellars, these sentiments sound high praise. Putnam was, from at least the mid-1970s, a clear supporter of Murdoch's (on both 'faulty moral psychology' and the problems of Hare's attempt to disentangle 'evaluative' and 'descriptive' meaning): see Putnam, 'The Place of Facts in a World of Values' (1979; presented in 1976), and 'Objectivity and the Science/Ethics Distinction' (1990): both in *Realism with a Human Face* (1990), esp. 150, 166–8. (See also Putnam, *The Collapse of the Fact/Value Dichotomy* (2002), 35–40, 118–19, 128.) Charles Taylor, in his *Sources of the Self* (1989), explicitly presents Part I as pursuing a Murdochian project: that of retrieving modes of conception of the Good, in order to set them in relation to varying conceptions of the Self (see 3; cp. 84, 95–6). For Taylor's overall placing of Murdoch, see also his 'Iris Murdoch and Moral Philosophy', in M. Antonaccio & W. Schweiker (eds.), *Iris Murdoch and the Search for Human Goodness* (1996).

[19] It appeared in Elijah Millgram (ed.), *Varieties of Practical Reasoning* (2001).

giving university lectures more than five years before. So there was no band of tutored students to mediate her work to a larger audience. The people most likely to appreciate it were a small number of impressive near-contemporaries—like Hampshire, Anscombe, Foot, and Williams—who had a high regard for her work, but were following their own path.[20] Hare made no reply in print to the criticisms in Murdoch's 'Vision and Choice in Morality' (1956) and he seems in his publications entirely to have ignored them. (As far I can see, Hare's one mention of Murdoch is—in a discussion of universalizability—a reference to 'Miss Murdoch's delightful novel *Under the Net*'.[21]) Meanwhile, among the more general reading public, Murdoch certainly had a reputation from the *Sartre* book (1953) and her radio appearances, but the former was, actually, a rather difficult work, without showing much of what was to be her mature philosophy, and the really distinctive views argued in the radio talks may have passed by all too fast. So it is perhaps unsurprising if, by the time *The Sovereignty of Good* appeared in 1970, people thought of it as the work of a novelist who had once been a philosopher, rather than (as I think is true) a work of extreme concentration and energy, the culmination of more than a decade of sustained professional attention,[22] advancing a view of large areas of moral philosophy that was ambitious, independent and quite opposite to the philosophical fashions of the time.

It was left, I think, for John McDowell to reinvent or develop Murdoch's position, for that view to have any very definite impact on later philosophers. One might summarize the largest ideas for academic moral philosophy (remembering that other things stand out from other points of view) under five main headings:

(1) a form of moral realism or 'naturalism'—allowing into the world instances of such moral properties as humility, generosity, and courage;

(2) an anti-scientism (to escape the view that the world can be said to contain only what science tells us is there or what is clearly reducible to that);

(3) an anti-Humean moral psychology, rejecting the view that moral action is standardly to be explained as the upshot of belief plus desire (allowing, instead, e.g. that the perception of a child's need may be enough to explain a parent's attention, without our needing to posit an additional desire or 'choice' in the parent, e.g. to meet needs of some relevant kind k);[23]

---

[20] The graduate classes that Philippa Foot and Iris Murdoch gave (together with Basil Mitchell in 1954) certainly did make a mark on Bernard Williams, however, e.g. in his distinction between 'thick' and 'thin' ethical concepts. See *Ethics and the Limits of Philosophy* (1985), 218 n. 7, quoted in fn. 37 below; and the discussion of thesis (iv) in the main text below.

[21] R. M. Hare, 'Universalisability', *Proceedings of the Aristotelian Society* 55 (1954–55), 295–312, at 310—which of course antedates Murdoch's 'Vision and Choice' paper (1956).

[22] On the need for professional devotion to the subject, Murdoch was explicit. In the final sentence of 'On "God" and "Good"': 'there can be no substitute for pure, disciplined, professional speculation' (OGG 76/362).

[23] No less important, I think, is (3′) an in some sense anti-Kantian moral psychology—opposing the dualism in Kant's picture of the human being as 'an indiscernible balance between a pure rational agent and an impersonal mechanism' (OGG 54/343): with reason and will abstracted and set in opposition to our

(4) a resistance to the idea that the content of morality must be statable in the form of universal principles (allowing, instead, e.g. that it might be captured in what would ideally be *seen* or thought of each individual case by a just person)—what some people have called 'particularism';[24]

and finally,

(5) a special attention to the virtues.[25]

---

sensuous existence. Murdoch's own conception might be described as affirming in human beings the inextricability of perception and reason and will and desire, which, together and in a single realm, act in essential interconnection, upon a background of habit and inheritance (which itself has evolved through a constant interplay of forces internal and external to the person), the whole personal system being capable of operating at different levels of refinement and understanding and freedom from the selfish ego and other forces of corruption. There are many different familiar dualistic pictures: Hume opposes belief to desire; Kant divides reason and will from desire and sensuous experience; Hampshire (*Thought and Action* ch. 2) keeps 'a personal will' as a maximally protected centre of freedom, while abandoning 'thought' and reason (as being governed by public rules) to the category of the ideally automatic, and, it seems, determined (IP 40/332, cp. 4–6/302–4). Murdoch opposes to the last of these dualisms (as also to the earlier ones) a more unified conception of the person: 'Man is not a combination of an impersonal rational thinker and a personal will. He is a unified being who sees, and who desires in accordance with what he sees, and who has some continual slight control over the direction and focus of his vision' (IP 40/332; cp. OGG 47–51/338–41). Kant is, I think, for her the greatest guide—the capacities for rational and moral thought are true signs of what may properly be called freedom; but rather than those being (as at least on one reading of Kant) set in ontological and evaluative opposition to our sensual nature, they are, I think for Murdoch, supposed to take a place beside the latter in the ordinary empirical world, a world which philosophers may need to reconceive, but which ordinary people have typically understood as quite capacious enough to contain both such things.

[24] People sometimes treat the seeing of the moral character of particular things and situations as a specially Aristotelian idea (e.g. on the basis of *Nicomachean Ethics* II.2, esp. 1104a7–8); but it is no less to be found in Plato, complete with the imagery of moral perception. 'Once habituated you will see them [i.e. the obscure things back in the cave] infinitely better than the dwellers there, and you will know what each of the images is and whereof it is a semblance, because you have seen the reality of the beautiful, the just and the good' (*Rep.* VII 520c). A quite general statement of law could never in one go 'accurately encompass what is best and most just for all people' and make, so to speak, a permanently definitive prescription: 'The best thing is not that *the laws* should prevail, but rather *the kingly person who possesses wisdom*', i.e. the wise individual who knows how to rule (*Statesman* 294–6, esp. 294a).

[25] For these ideas, see e.g.:
(1) IP, and especially its use of the example of the mother M and her daughter-in-law D: if we accept that 'When M is just and loving she sees D *as she really is*' (IP 37/329, my emphasis)—and accept that what she sees is indeed there to be seen—, then we can conclude that D is in reality 'not undignified but spontaneous, not noisy but gay' and so on. (Murdoch's own term for this view is not 'realism', however, but 'naturalism' (IP 44/335).) Thus goodness is 'connected with knowledge': a good person is one who has 'a refined and honest perception of *what is really the case*, a patient and just discernment and exploration of what confronts one' (IP 38/330, my emphasis). Cp. the talk of 'moral facts' (VCM 54/95).
(2) Murdoch's examples (of repentance and M's change of view) are chosen particularly to challenge the objectivist (and scientific) conception of reality implicit in philosophers like Hampshire, for whom 'anything which is to count as a definite reality must be open to several observers' (*Thought & Action* 162; quoted at IP 5/302 and 23/317). 'What is at stake here is the liberation of morality, and of philosophy as a study of human nature, from the domination of science: or rather from the domination of inexact ideas of science which haunt philosophers and other thinkers' (IP 27/320); cp. IP 23.34–34.22/318.7–327.3, esp. 25–6/319–20, 34/326–7. See also OGG 76/362: 'it is from . . . art and ethics, that we must hope to generate concepts worthy, and also able, to guide and check the increasing power of science'.
(3) IP 34.23–42.32/327.4–334.2; OGG 55.21–56.23/345.1–35. 'Will and reason . . . are not entirely separate faculties' (IP 40/331). 'Man is not a combination of an impersonal rational thinker and a personal will. He is a

At least the first four of these can be described in fundamentally negative terms:[26] anti-non-cognitivism (to use McDowell's term), anti-scientism, anti-Humean moral psychology, and anti-universalism (if I may coin the term). And this is not accidental: they are forms of resistance to the idea that morality can be forced into one particular mould, rather than attempts to specify another mould into which to put it.[27] And in a sense, (5) has that same character too: Murdoch adds the virtues to the many things not to be omitted in moral philosophy, rather than advancing a theory of 'virtue ethics'.

One might also draw out something included in passing under (3) and (4):

> (6) an emphasis on the idea of moral *perception*, and the metaphor of *seeing* moral features of people and situations, and *seeing* what is to be done.[28]

This at once integrates and gives a place to much in Murdoch's other views. To draw out some of the connections: The idea of moral perception brings with it the idea of a moral *fact* (as *what is seen*), as in (1). If, then, we reflect on how our *particular perceptual or conceptual scheme* will influence what kinds of things we are equipped to pick out and talk about (some people talk of *sensibility* and *point of view* here, but Murdoch's interest is above all in what a person sees thanks to their particular 'scheme of concepts' (IP 32/ 325) and especially thanks to the *moral* character of those concepts (IP 24–28/318–21)): then we will find those things to include facts of kinds that one can probably

unified being who sees, and who desires in accordance with what he sees' (IP 40/332, quoted in fn. 23). We should think in terms of 'a world which is *compulsively* present to the will' (IP 39/331). 'If we picture the agent as compelled by obedience to the reality he can see, he will not be saying... "I *choose* to do this", he will be saying "This is A B C D" (normative-descriptive words), and *action will follow naturally*' (IP 42/333, my emphasis). A good thing, suitably attended to, is itself 'a source of energy' (OGG 56/345).
(4) VCM 43.27–51.18/84.22–92.2; the 'just and loving gaze directed upon an *individual* reality' (IP 34/327, my emphasis) and, in general, Murdoch's use of Weil's conception of 'attention'; but cp. also the 'turning of attention away from the particular' at SGC 101/383). See also S&G 215.
(5) The central argument of SGC, esp. 84.13–end/369.10–end.

[26] How true this is of (1) is clear from the research description that Murdoch included as part of the application for her University Lectureship in 1950 (now in the Oxford University Archives). Her ambitious project is a study of 'transcendental logic'—drawing out the implications, for metaphysics and the conception of the world, of rejecting the dichotomy of language into the 'descriptive' and the 'emotive'. The aim is to improve on Wittgenstein and Ryle—most urgently where they fail to *describe* our thinking (especially in the domains of imaginative and creative thought, moral decision, and thought about ourselves)—, taking assistance from Kant, Hegel, and Bradley: an *empiricist* task (in Murdoch's understanding of that term), which, however, has been undertaken really faithfully only by idealists. And Murdoch's starting point is the *rejection* of an imposed dichotomy between 'descriptive' and 'emotive'.

[27] For resistance to moulds, see e.g. M&E (1957): 'We should... resist the temptation to unify the picture by trying to establish, guided by our own conception of the ethical in general, what [moral] concepts *must be*.... [I]n the process important differences... may be blurred or neglected' (75). Cp. 67 and VCM 44–51/ 84–92.

[28] The very title of 'Vision and Choice in Morality' (1956) contrasts the approach of those (like Hare) who put 'choice' at the centre of morality with others (like Murdoch) who emphasize 'vision'. In SG, consider the presentation of M's change of mind ('Is not the metaphor of vision almost irresistibly suggested... ? M *looks* at D, she attends to D, she focuses her attention ' (IP 22/316–7))—and, in general, the use of Weil's conception of *attention*: 'a just and loving gaze directed upon an individual reality' (IP 34/327; cp. 37–9/329–31). See also fn. 92 below.

live happily with only given (2) some kind of anti-scientism. Such facts may include essentially *response-invoking facts*, or facts the appreciation of which is *intrinsically motivating*—in which case we would have (3) the rejection of the Humean model of motivation. Perception is, of course, also typically perception of individual things with their qualities, in a particular environment, as (4) emphasizes. And, as moral perception and its no less important complement, the *acting* upon perception (IP 43.23–9/ 334.26–31), are things that can be treated as trainable and specially valuable capacities, we have a place for something like the idea of virtue (5). Murdoch's model of morality as *perception of particulars* was therefore radically distinctive. It offered the prospect of freeing moral thinking at once from assimilation to mere feeling or passion, to intellectual intuition, to ordinary 'descriptive' judgement, and even to the issuing of prescriptions. And to the extent that the model presented itself from the start as one of *perception*, rather than of 'sensation' as conceived in the Lockean theory of secondary qualities, it was proof against confusion with some kind of projectivism. Which is not to say, of course, that it could not be attacked or challenged from the perspective of any or all of those rival conceptions: but it represented a distinctive and new conception— something that, whatever its Platonic roots, Murdoch made newly thinkable for her time by a new post-Wittgensteinian presentation.[29]

I do not know in what ways exactly one should talk of their relation, but John McDowell immersed himself at times in *The Sovereignty of Good*, reading and re-reading it with admiration, and he has described himself to Murdoch's biographer as having been 'pervasively influenced' by her (Conradi, IML 303). The five or six ideas I have singled out as distinctive of Murdoch certainly became distinctive of McDowell's moral philosophy[30]—though developed there with much else, not least a readiness (as also in David Wiggins) to allow the notion of truth to apply straightforwardly

[29] Philippa Foot was, of course, also a critic of Hare and much else in 'modern moral philosophy', but not in the same way. If her earliest articles were in some ways ambiguous, she was soon insisting on the conception of 'Morality as a System of *Hypothetical* Imperatives' (to quote the title of her 1972 paper; my emphasis)—explicitly requiring for moral motivation the additional desires that Murdoch's moral psychology wanted to do without. For that reason, the realism one might find in Foot's early work was a realism of a different kind too from that in Murdoch: Foot's moral properties were (in Hare's terms) 'descriptive', rather than, as Murdoch's might be, (in a suitable context) essentially reason-providing or (to come closer to Murdoch) *energy*-providing. On much of this, Foot later changed her mind in the direction of Murdoch and McDowell: see 'Does Moral Subjectivism Rest on a Mistake?' *Oxford Journal of Legal Studies* (1995), 4.

[30] A selection of articles would be 'Are Moral Requirements Hypothetical Imperatives?' (AMR, 1978); 'Virtue and Reason' (VR, 1979); 'Non-Cognitivism and Rule-Following' (NCRF, 1981); 'Aesthetic Value, Objectivity, and the Fabric of the World' (AVO, 1983); 'Values and Secondary Qualities' (VSQ, 1985); and 'Some Issues in Aristotle's Moral Psychology' (SIA, 1988): page numbers here refer to the reprints in his *Mind, Value & Reality* (MVR, 1998). For (1) Realism, see, e.g. NCRF and VSQ. (NCRF talks of making a space for 'realism . . . about values' (212); though McDowell later expresses a preference for the term 'anti- anti-realism' (MVR (1998), viii). For (2) Anti-Scientism: e.g. AVO §5; even a subtle non-cognitivism owes its origin to 'a philistine scientism' (VR 72). For (3) the non-Humean moral psychology: AMR §5, and e.g. NCRF §4. For (4) resistance to a requirement of codification in universal principles: VR §4; McDowell will talk also of 'the appreciation of particular cases' (68); cp. also VSQ §5 (e.g. 149), and (for Aristotle) SIA §§4–10. For (5) Virtues: see e.g. VR. For (6) Perception: VSQ; also e.g. in connection with Aristotle (*Nicomachean Ethics* 1142a23–30), SIA §5.

to moral statements. And the fundamental rationale for those views in McDowell (namely, I think, a Wittgensteinian return to taking the phenomena of moral thought and talk 'at face value') is almost exactly the same as the rationale in Murdoch.[31]

It may also be worth pointing out, however, some other themes important to Murdoch—three that made less of an impact on any later philosophers, and one that had fairly widespread acceptance and development. Perhaps not incidentally, the first three might all be counted as a matter of substantive morality no less than of meta-ethics.[32] The first is part of Murdoch's response to Hare and others who present morality as primarily a matter of *choice*, and who treat moral *disagreement*, therefore, as a matter of difference in the ways in which people 'choose' among straightforwardly surveyable alternatives. Murdoch, instead, emphasizes:

> (i) The dependence of moral thought upon *conceptual scheme*. 'I can only *choose* within the world I can *see*' (IP 37/329: my emphasis on 'choose'). A person's conceptual apparatus may restrict,[33] or enlarge—or, more importantly (since the issue is hardly one merely of *quantity*), may focus in one way, or another—the range of *options* that she is so much as in a position to recognize as available for her to choose among. The conceptual scheme may in a sense be said to determine and reveal the character of the moral *world* in which she lives.

Most remarkable perhaps are the ways in which Murdoch characterizes these conceptual schemes—with (though this is hardly a single or simple item):

> (ii) An emphasis on *difference* and *disagreement* among people in moral outlook: difference not just in application of shared concepts, but in the repertoire of concepts that different people understand and employ. Hence Murdoch's interest not just in the phenomenon of *changing one's mind* about a particular

---

[31] VCM replies to Hare's general conception of morality by encouraging us to go 'back again to the data' (VCM 97/57) and to reconsider the 'initial delineation of the field of study' (76/33): there are many cases of what surely can properly be called moral thought and talk that do not easily fit the mould of Hare's universalizability requirement or his dichotomy between descriptive and evaluative meaning. 'Why insist on forcing moral attitudes into the "universality" model when this is contrary to appearances?' (VCM 84/44). And the result of appreciating this is to see the possibility of a form of 'naturalism' (VCM 92–8/51–8). And Murdoch (like McDowell later) wishes whatever ordinary naturalism might emerge to be something like an acceptance of appearances, not a new claim to another form of systematic metaphysics. The central discussion in IP is governed by a caveat from Wittgenstein: 'Being unable—when we surrender ourselves to philosophical thought—to help saying such-and-such; being irresistibly inclined to say it—does not mean being forced into an assumption, or having an immediate perception or knowledge of a state of affairs' (Wittgenstein, PI §299, quoted at IP 16/312).

[32] Cf. 'It is here [with conceptual innovation] that description moves imperceptibly [though not necessarily objectionably, I think Murdoch wants us to understand] into moralising' (M&E 74).

[33] Note, though, whatever 'restriction' that may amount to, we must not suppose it will make it impossible for critics in a social group to see or act upon a need for conceptual innovation. On the contrary, the restriction (in moral as also in non-moral domains) may sometimes be felt as a frustration that itself serves as an impulse to 'renewal of language' (TL 36).

case; but also in the processes of *revision*, evolution, and 'deepening' of moral vocabulary and conceptual scheme (IP 29/322, 31–3/324–6); and particularly, and most remarkably, in a kind of *privacy* of understanding (IP 25–9/319–22).[34]

If we have a conception of our understanding—of moral concepts and of individual people—as being endlessly improvable in the direction of an idealized perfect understanding (Murdoch's 'idea' of perfection), we must also recognize, given our nature and our actual condition, that our own conceptions as they advance may in practice also become increasingly *private*. Our conception of love, for example—or of courage or repentance (IP 29/322, 26/320)—will vary with age and experience; and our deepest and most revelatory experiences may, in a fairly ordinary sense, be remarkably private. Even if in principle they are open to others, the number of people in a position of being suitably like-minded and well-placed and attentive enough to recognize them may in practice be small, and perhaps indeed—as those experiences accumulate in their particularity (though they will also interconnect)—increasingly small. 'Since we are

---

[34] On (i) and (ii): Morality is essentially characterized by its employment of concepts that are non-equivalent to the classifications made in science: 'Moral concepts do not move about *within* a hard world set up by science and logic. They set up, for different purposes, a different world' (IP 29/321; cp. (2) and (8) in main text). Conceptual differences—and the consequential differences in the kinds of thing we recognize in the world—are neglected by linguistic philosophy, and especially by Hare: M&E 72–3, VCM 40–3/81–3. 'We [human beings] differ not only because we select different objects out of the same world but because we see different worlds'. (VCM 41/82: different people, with different moral and other vocabularies, will discover in the worlds they 'see' different ranges of things—and may fail even to understand the classifications made by each other. Cp. (7) in main text below.) On conceptual innovation, see also VCM 42/83 ('Great philosophers coin new moral concepts and communicate new moral visions and modes of understanding.'); VCM 49–50/90–1 ('The task of moral philosophers has been to extend, as poets may extend, the limits of the language'). Existentialism has been very free to introduce new concepts (E&M 133, 152); as have Gabriel Marcel, particularly fruitfully (E&M 126–8), and Elias Canetti (E&M 190–1); cp. also HT 182.20–2. We also need an extension of our conceptual repertoire if philosophers are to find *thinkable* some suitable form of moral 'naturalism' or realism: AD 293; cp. IP 45.9–13/336.1–4. Vocabularies may bring with them substantive moral views (and this is true too, though less obviously, of the supposedly 'neutral' terms of modern moral philosophy: M&E 74); they may embody injustices. ('A smart set of concepts may be a most efficient instrument of corruption', IP 33/325; cp. also IP 3.2–3/300.31–2.) The central example of the mother and daughter-in-law in IP is, I think, meant *not* as a case where the mother merely changes the application of an unrevised set of concepts, but rather as one where the mother appreciates, perhaps dimly, the unsatisfactoriness of whole ranges of concepts she has earlier employed unreflectingly. (She says to herself, 'I am old-fashioned and conventional. I may be prejudiced and narrow-minded. I may be snobbish.' IP17/ 313.) The implication is, I think, that some more general conceptual reconfiguration takes place as the mother experiences the *difficulty* of consistently and confidently applying her initial set of concepts to the reality of the daughter-in-law before her (IP 31–4/324–6): 'We . . . *grow by looking*' (31/324). (Does it make sense, one might ask—filling in what might be one step in the mother's reflections—, for her to judge her daughter-in-law as being, *or not being*, 'insufficiently ceremonious' (IP 17/312)? What kind of ceremonious-ness would it be appropriate for her to expect from her daughter-in-law? Is the presumption of a standard here itself something that needs to be put in question?) (In Murdoch's discussion of the learning of moral concepts at IP 31–4/324–6, there are echoes, I think, of F. N. Sibley on learning aesthetic concepts: see his *Phil. Rev.* 1959 paper 'Aesthetic Concepts'.) Such reflection and conceptual revision is important also to McDowell (see e.g. *Mind and World*, 81–2; cp. 12–13, 40, 126); but when he presents it with references to the imagery of Quine (as at *Mind and World*, 13n.), Murdoch is at best, I imagine, fairly distantly in the background. (i) is a thought particularly dear to Murdoch; cp. Max Lejour in *The Unicorn* (1963): 'What we can *see* determines what we choose' (100). The thought goes back to VCM (41–3/82–4).

human historical individuals'—each of the last three words is worth weighing separately—'the movement of understanding is onward into increasing privacy' (IP 29/322). Murdoch was at odds here with a whole academic movement, which had a rather different sense of what we had to learn from the heritage of Wittgenstein.

Murdoch (like Plato and Aristotle and many Hegelians,[35] but in opposition to many academic philosophers of the mid-20th century) sees the topic of moral philosophy as not merely a matter of relatively limited issues of, say, contracts and promises, or even of 'overriding obligation', but something much wider: one might say, all that contributes to making a good life good. We may talk therefore of

(iii) The all-embracing scope of moral thought: 'The area of morals, and ergo of moral philosophy, can . . . be seen . . . as covering *the whole of our mode of living* and the *quality of our relations with the world*' (SGC 97/380, my emphasis).[36]

There is, however, one theme that did have wide and visible influence—particularly in Bernard Williams's talk of 'thick' and 'thin' ethical concepts—:

(iv) An emphasis on 'secondary' or 'specialised' words like 'rude' and 'bumptious' (or more importantly, 'generous' and 'brave'), by contrast with 'the most empty and general' moral terms, like 'good' and 'right' (IP 42/333, 23/317). The latter might seem (e.g. to Hare) applicable 'freely' at will to practically anything (subject only to a logical requirement of universalizability); but the former ('normative-descriptive words', 31/324) can surely only properly be applied to

---

[35] F. H. Bradley (in whom Murdoch had a special interest) stresses that 'our *character* . . . is within the moral sphere', and, in a sense, '*nothing* . . . falls outside of it' (my emphasis). Even our unreflective actions are evidence of our character, and that character, 'whether good or bad', is a 'second nature', which has grown and changed under the influence of past actions where we did reflect. ('Ideal morality', in Bradley's *Ethical Studies* (1876, 1927) 218–9 & n. 1.) For the breadth of application of moral consideration in Plato, one might cite not just the role of the Good as essential to the ultimate intelligibility of any and all of the Forms (*Rep.* 509a–c), but also the application of something like moral evaluation—*via* the notions of *grace* and *gracelessness*—to all or most of what we might call general culture, including musical modes, painting, weaving, embroidery, architecture, and household furnishing; see *Republic* 3, 400e–401a.

[36] Even in her 1956 article VCM, Murdoch talks of the 'moral nature' of a person's 'total vision of life, as shown in their mode of speech or silence, their choice of words, their assessments of others, their conception of their own lives, what they think attractive or praise-worthy, what they think funny': all this constitutes 'the texture of a man's being or the nature of his personal vision' (VCM 39–40/80–1). (Murdoch says that the fact that such things are *moral* matters itself shows the need for a conception of morality that is not (like the modern moral philosophers') limited to the 'choice and argument' model.) There is a rather similar protest in Anscombe at the restricted use of 'moral' for the domain merely of what one is, or could be, 'obliged or bound *by law*' to do—a restricted use that Aristotle is happily free from ('Modern moral philosophy' (1958), 5, my emphasis). Here again (as with the phrases 'modern moral philosophy' and (particularly inaccurately) 'moral psychology': see fn. 77 at start of §5 below), it turns out that Anscombe has become famously associated with a very similar idea to one that Murdoch had no less distinctively, though somewhat less dramatically, expressed in print some years before. For Murdoch's later development of the idea, see also IP 22/316 ('fabric of being'); IP 37/329 ('attention . . . continuously . . . builds up structures of value round about us. . . . The moral life . . . is something that goes on continually'); OGG 54/343 ('the tissue of that life'). Indeed: 'All just vision, even in the strictest problems of the intellect, and *a fortiori* when suffering or wickedness have to be perceived, is a moral matter' (OGG 70/357).

things fitting some relevant evidently factual characterization (though the characterization may not be readily graspable by just anyone—cf. (ii) above and (7) below).[37]

(One might compare Philippa Foot's argument that 'dangerous' is a term that can properly be applied only to things that actually have the characteristic of threatening some 'kind of serious evil such as injury or death' ('Moral Beliefs', 115)—the term 'injury', in turn, inviting further investigation.) It is particularly ascriptions of the specialized terms that are (in relevant situations) immediately motivating, in accord with the anti-Humean moral psychology of (3) above.[38]

There are some important, though lesser or more incidental, points shared by Murdoch and McDowell:

(7) the view that we are in no position to claim that a person who did not share the evaluative interest of a term would be capable of capturing ('purely descriptively') its extension;[39]

---

[37] There is an early version of the distinction in Murdoch's 'Metaphysics and Ethics' (1955, publ. 1957), 73, and in VCM 41–2/82–3; and related ideas appear in Foot's discussion of 'rude' in 'Moral Arguments' (1958) as well as of 'dangerous' in 'Moral Beliefs' (1958/59). See also thesis (7) below, and references there to Murdoch's VCM. Hampshire quietly takes up a similar distinction (as much else in Murdoch's moral philosophy: *Thought and Action* 197–214 reads as an uprooting and replanting of many of Murdoch's thoughts in an environment that is rather fundamentally at odds with them; and IP is Murdoch's attempt to put them back in the right place): 'The type of moral philosophy that considers only the use of the "purely moral terms"—e.g. "right", "good", "ought"—tends to be as vacuous and uninstructive as the type of aesthetics that isolates the purely aesthetic terms—e.g. "beautiful"' (TA 269). (Hare recognized a somewhat parallel distinction (illustrated by 'good' vs. 'tidy' and 'industrious'), but he understood it very differently: *The Language of Morals* (1952) 121.) Bernard Williams (*Ethics and the Limits of Philosophy* (1985), 140–2) talks of how 'thick' ethical concepts, like *coward, lie, brutality, gratitude*, are both 'action-guiding' and 'world-guided', and says (as in thesis (7) below) there may be no 'descriptive equivalent' that would enable just anyone to get the extension of the term right without sharing the evaluative perspective of ordinary users of the term or having some imaginative understanding of it. Williams mentions McDowell's earlier development of the point and adds that it is basically a Wittgensteinian idea. (Presumably: outsiders to a practice may be unable to 'go on' and apply the relevant terms to new cases in the way that insiders do.) 'I first heard it expressed by Philippa Foot and Iris Murdoch in a seminar in the 1950s' (ELP 218 n.7)—no doubt, the class they gave with Basil Mitchell in the spring of 1954. Williams had become a Fellow of All Souls in the year he took his BA, 1951, but then spent two years doing national service in the RAF; he returned to Oxford in 1953 and was a Fellow of New College 1954–59, before moving to London as Lecturer at UC, and then Professor at Bedford College (1964–67). A recommendation to study precise rather than dully generic evaluative terms was something of a commonplace among those who had heard, or heard much about, Wittgenstein's Lectures on Aesthetics. (And, as Anscombe said: 'It would be a great improvement, if, instead of "morally wrong", one always named a genus such as "untruthful", "unchaste", "unjust".' 'Modern Moral Philosophy', 8–9.) What was distinctive lay in what one might say about the latter terms.

[38] 'The agent will not be saying, "This is right", i.e. "I *choose* to do this" [using an "empty" term like "good" and making a "free" Hare-style "choice"], he will be saying, "This is A B C D" (normative-descriptive words), *and action will follow naturally*' (IP 42/333, my emphasis, quoted also in fn. 25).

[39] 'Communication of a new moral concept cannot necessarily be achieved by specification of factual criteria open to any observer ("Approve of *this* area!") but may involve the communication of a completely new . . . vision; and it is surely true that we cannot always *understand* other people's moral concepts' (VCM 41/82). Murdoch adds a note mentioning Foot's 1954 PASS article ('When is a Principle a Moral Principle?') 'on this and related topics'—though I have to say I have difficulty finding much in Foot's article precisely on this subject. (It may be that Murdoch had a debt to acknowledge to Foot on this, but had nothing better in

(8) rejection of the use of the term 'naturalism' for a merely scientific naturalism, when we might use the term instead in a way correlative with a broader view of nature that might include in it something like moral facts;[40]

(9) an emphasis on the idea that moral value is an irreducible kind of value that we should not aim to establish or recommend, for example, on the basis of the *usefulness* or prudential value of morality;[41]

print to refer to. The discussion of 'rudeness' in Foot's paper 'Moral Arguments' (1958) certainly develops the point; and, though it has more to say on the *inextricability* of 'descriptive' and 'evaluative' meaning than directly on the *inaccessibility* of the complex meaning of a moral term to someone lacking a suitable interest or training in its subject matter, the article does in fact end on the latter point. 'It is quite common for one man to be unable to see what the other is getting at, and this sort of misunderstanding will not always be resolvable by anything which could be called argument in the ordinary sense' ('Moral Arguments', 109).) McDowell develops the idea in 'Non-cognitivism and Rule-Following', §2. Murdoch makes the point explicitly at the level of sense and understanding; the same is mostly true, I think, of McDowell: the difficulty is with the idea that 'the extension . . . could be *mastered* independently of the special concerns . . .'; '*Understanding* why just those things belong together may essentially require *understanding* the supervening term' (NCRF 201, 202, my emphasis).

[40] 'The true naturalist . . . is one who believes that as moral beings we are immersed in a reality which transcends us and that moral progress consists in awareness of this reality and submission to its purposes' (VCM 56/96). For McDowell's development of the concept of the natural, see *Mind and World* (1994), Lecture IV and Lecture V §3; and 'Two Sorts of Naturalism' (1995). Wittgenstein, of course, stands in the background behind both Murdoch and McDowell here; but cp. also Kant's insistence on using the term *Natur* both for 'the sensuous nature of rational beings in general' and for 'the supersensuous nature of the same beings' (KpV 5:43). (KpV abbreviates Kant, *Kritik der praktischen Vernunft* (1788), *Critique of Practical Reason*. Page references are given to vol. 5 of the Akademie edition, given in the margin of modern scholarly translations.) For an earlier attempt to put 'requiredness' into the natural world broadly conceived, while acknowledging that it would have no place in a narrower conception of nature as 'a realm of *mere* existence and of *mere* facts', see Wolfgang Köhler, *The Place of Value in a World of Facts* (1938): I quote from p. 363 (my emphasis). Curiously, Kurt Koffka, another great emigré figure of Gestalt Psychology, was lecturing on Köhler's book at Oxford in the summer of 1940 (under the heading of the Philosophy lectures in the Faculty of Literae Humaniores), the term when Iris Murdoch, having done Mods in Latin and Greek, was beginning more advanced work in Philosophy and Ancient History. I have no reason to suppose that Murdoch attended Koffka's lectures—and Köhler looks for more of a scientific counterpart to underlie 'requiredness' in the world (namely, he thinks, Forces) than Murdoch (or McDowell) will later think necessary; but his book remains a remarkable challenge to positivist conceptions of reality.

[41] 'The Good has nothing to do with purpose, indeed it excludes the idea of purpose. . . . The only genuine way to be good is to be good "for nothing"' (OGG 71/358); cp. Murdoch's talk of the '*absolute* pointlessness of virtue', combined with the 'supreme importance' of it (SGC 86/371: my emphasis); 'the nakedness and aloneness of Good, its absolute for-nothingness' (SGC 92/375; cp. SGC 93.34–94.1/ 377.9–10; E&M 233.24–6). Cp. McDowell, 'Are Moral Requirements Hypothetical Imperatives?'; 'The Role of Eudaimonia in Aristotle's Ethics' §§ 12–13; 'Some Issues in Aristotle's Moral Psychology' esp. §12; 'Two Sorts of Naturalism' §2. This is another issue on which Murdoch had very different views from Philippa Foot at the time (see e.g. the last couple of pages of Foot's 'Moral Beliefs'). McDowell specifically associates the view he is recommending with D. Z. Phillips, who in 1964–65 had been saying some very striking things of a similar kind. (McDowell, 'The Role of *Eudaimonia*', 17n.; 'Are Moral Requirements Hypothetical imperatives?', 86n.) It is worth noting how good a source or kindred spirit Murdoch herself would have been here–as also Plato, in his treatment of Good as a non-hypothetical first principle (*Rep.* 510b) and, e.g. in the view that injustice does not really benefit even the possessor who 'gets away with' his injustice (*Gorgias* 472d– 479e; *Rep.* 9.591ab & ff, cp. 10.611ab). I suspect that a similar conception is to be found also in Kant's talk of duty and of Virtue as its own reward (cp. e.g. *Metaphysics of Morals*, Ak. VI.406, 482–3). The moral law is something 'in comparison and contrast to which life and its enjoyment have absolutely no worth' (KpV 5:88). For an interpretation that places Murdoch at a greater distance from Kant on this issue, however, see Crisp's essay in this volume.

and finally and, I imagine, most incidentally—and in Murdoch's case, with a strong counterbalancing influence also from Kierkegaard—:

> (10) a high view of Hegel, both as showing the importance of doing philosophy historically, and as a source of a simple direct realism.[42]

These views, however, are not particularly clear or accessible in Murdoch. (I must have read her work many times before I could have extracted anything like the list of themes I have given here.) And even where the views were clear, their presentation—sometimes essayistic, and with a promiscuity of reference and association, to religion, literature, and philosophical history in several languages, from each of which analytic philosophy was in the 1960s precisely trying to define itself by separation—all that may have given the impression to academic philosophers that those views could be either ignored or regarded with benign indifference. It was McDowell who gave them a new frame and support, in a philosophical context of his own, and showed in sustained and visible debate[43] their power in the philosophical market-place. For all his rejection of a 'coercive philosophy' that 'aims to compel an audience into accepting *theses*',[44]

---

[42] Murdoch's 'Thinking and Language' (1951) (mentioning idealists, though not Hegel in particular) proposes a conception of thought as not the representation of the *absent*, but a form of *possession*: 'If we think of conceptualising rather as the activity of grasping, or reducing to order, our situations with the help of a language which is fundamentally metaphorical, this will operate against the world-language dualism which haunts us because we are afraid of the idealists' (T&L 40). For Murdoch, as later for McDowell (*Mind and World*, 44–5, 110–11), Hegel is the true realist whom 'empiricists' (often Murdoch's word for philosophers who take things as they find them: cf. fn. 118 below) should embrace as a friend. (Hegel 'could...be considered as the first great modern empiricist; a dialectical empiricist, as opposed to, say, Hume who might be called a mechanistic empiricist. What Hegel teaches us is that we should attempt to describe phenomena' ('The Existentialist Political Myth' [EPM] (1952) 131).) In fact, 'It is almost mysterious how little Hegel is esteemed in this country. This philosopher, who, while not being the greatest, contains possibly more truth than any other, is unread and unstudied here' (EPM 146). (By the time of MGM, more than thirty years later, Hegel may be admired but should not in general be followed: he is no longer the great recognizer of phenomena but the one who takes phenomena and forces them to fit within his system. 'The most obvious objections to Hegel may indeed be to the outrageous implausibility of the whole machine; but more sinister is a lingering shadow of determinism, and the *loss of ordinary everyday truth, that is of truth*. The loss of the particular, the loss of the contingent, the loss of the individual' (MGM 490).) On Murdoch's view of the need for philosophical understanding to be historical understanding I shall have to leave discussion for another occasion.
   Kierkegaard was a constant love of Murdoch's—and an influence perhaps especially on her concerns with the particular and private and her suspicions of the systematic and universal (cf. (4) and (ii) in the main text). *Fear and Trembling* (1843) was one of her favourite books: one of only three philosophical works that she mentions (along with Plato's *Symposium* and Weil's *Attente de Dieu*) when drawing up a list of influences on her. (Journal, on her plans for a 1976 British Council talk, quoted in Conradi, IML 524n.)
[43] Particularly with Simon Blackburn and Philippa Foot: see e.g. McDowell's 'Non-Cognitivism and Rule-Following' (1981) and 'Values and Secondary Qualities' (1985), to which Blackburn replied in 'Rule-Following and Moral Realism' (1981) and 'Errors and the Phenomenology of Value' (1985); and McDowell's 'Are Moral Requirements Hypothetical imperatives?' (1978) (in response to Foot's *Phil. Rev.* 1972 paper) and 'Two Sorts of Naturalism' (1995). There are also McDowell's writings on Williams, including a Critical Notice of *Ethics and the Limits of Philosophy* for *Mind* (1986) and 'Might there be External Reasons?' (1995), with a Reply by Williams in the same volume.
[44] From McDowell's Response to Crispin Wright, in Nicholas H. Smith (ed.), *Reading McDowell on Mind and World* (London: Routledge, 2002), 291, my emphasis.

McDowell made those views in a sense inescapable: they became almost unavoidable reference points even for people who disagreed with them. And whereas Murdoch's views as put forward by Murdoch may easily have seemed 'unreceivable' in the academic world of the 1960s (there may have seemed for many people 'no way to get there from here'), McDowell, following his own very distinctive path, detached them from some of their old associations—left aside the references to religion and literature—, and set them in a new environment where they had as neighbours the mainstream 1980s debates about Wittgenstein on rule-following, Davidson on truth, and Dummett on realism: he showed, so to speak, how academic philosophers could indeed 'get there from here'. Even careful readers of McDowell, however, might easily miss the connection—there are, I think, only three references to Murdoch in his main publications[45] and there are followers of McDowell's who show not the slightest recognition of Murdoch.[46] In different ways, recent movements under the banners of Particularism, Moral Perception, Virtue Theory, and Moral Realism that connect themselves with McDowell could as truly trace their history to Murdoch—though she herself was no proponent of theoretical '-ism's'. But few of the proponents do, and many seem almost completely unaware of her.

So what happened? What particularly singled Murdoch out from her philosophical generation and resulted, after such a brilliant debut, in the relative neglect of her most striking work? Her interests in Sartre and existentialism were signs of Francophilia and a search for an alternative to the British philosophical tradition, but neither would particularly have set her against her fellows. (The young Ryle was hardly held back by his famous early interests in Meinong, Husserl, and Brentano.[47]) Sartre was, in fact, hardly a source of insight for Murdoch,[48] and it is hard, I think, to find much positive influence from him upon the distinctive aspects of her thought: indeed, the criticisms

---

[45] McDowell, nn. 35–7 in 'Virtue and Reason', as reprinted in *Mind, Value, and Reality* (1998), 72–3.

[46] Russ Shafer-Landau's *Moral Realism: A Defence* (2003)—though his realism is rather different from McDowell's—promises (on the book cover) a systematic defence of objective moral standards 'in the tradition of Plato and G. E. Moore'. It is remarkable that Murdoch, who could hardly be a more important defender of a moral realism in precisely that tradition, should receive not one mention in a 10-page bibliography that contains four entries for McDowell and four for Colin McGinn. Elijah Millgram points out ('Murdoch, Practical Reasoning, and Particularism' (2002) nn. 1 & 3; 191 in *Ethics Done Right* (2005)) that recent defenders of particularism (like Jonathan Dancy, Margaret Little, and David McNaughton) happily connect themselves with McDowell, but often make only the most casual mention of Murdoch, if any at all: 'a recent anthology titled *Moral Particularism* [ed. Brad Hooker & Margaret Little, 2000] contains only one reference to Murdoch [at 292n], and that reference gets the title of her best-known philosophical publication wrong'. A rare exception, giving Murdoch a prime role in the history, is Hilary Putnam, 'Objectivity and the Science/Ethics Distinction' (1990), 166–8; *The Collapse of the Fact/Value Dichotomy* (2002), 35, 38, esp. 62. See also J. Dancy, *Moral Reasons* (Oxford: Blackwell, 1993) ix, xii.

[47] For this stage of Ryle's philosophical development, see the fascinating letter and the introduction to it: Brian McGuinness and Charlotte Vrijen, 'First thoughts: An unpublished letter from Gilbert Ryle to H. J. Paton', *British Journal for the History of Philosophy*, 14 (2006): 747–56.

[48] 'I always loved France ... and getting back to contact with France [after the war] was very much existentialism. I met Sartre actually ... and I got hold of a copy of *L'être et le néant* when hardly anybody else had managed to get one and things like this. So that was part of that excitement ... and then somehow I began to see myself as a philosopher.... [B]ut I don't think I ever was an existentialist. I think that my

of Sartre by Gabriel Marcel that Murdoch mentions in her book[49] are a much better pointer to Murdoch's mature views than Sartre's own ideas are. In any case, a little interest in Sartre was quite domesticable in Oxford philosophy: Ryle, as editor of *Mind*, very likely himself commissioned Murdoch's reviews in 1950 of English translations of Sartre and Beauvoir; Hare (like Gellner) was perfectly professional, if condescending, in defining his views in opposition to 'the existentialist';[50] and a short book on Sartre was a perfectly proper thing for an Oxford tutor to produce, as Mary Warnock later did with her own *The Philosophy of Sartre* (1966).[51] What really changed Murdoch and set her apart was, I suspect, her reading of Simone Weil.

Murdoch reviewed *The Notebooks of Simone Weil* (tr. Arthur Wills, 1956) for *The Spectator* in November 1956, and it made, I think, a huge impact upon her. Her review was penetrating—it was a real achievement to weave together for the review a presentation of ideas so clear, expressive, and fundamental out of the six hundred pages of Weil's wandering and brilliant text. And the material that Murdoch found there was, I think, both fruitful and not at all easily domesticated in the house of Oxford philosophy. It seems to me very possible that there were three main factors that led Murdoch away from Oxford professionalism in the late 1950s: her success and delight at writing novels, the increasing impact of Hare's approach in moral philosophy—and perhaps the fact that her own very thorough criticisms (in the 1956 paper) went more or less unanswered and unacknowledged—, and, finally and above

---

objections to existentialism went right back to my first meeting with it.' Murdoch in interview with Christopher Bigsby ([1979], 1982), FTC 98.

[49] *Sartre*, 17/21/49, 25/35/63, 50/77/105, 67/104/132. (I give page references in turn to the 1953 edition (78 pp.), the 1967 edition (126 pp.) and the 1987/1989 edition (158 pp).) Cp. also Conradi, IML 270.

[50] E. A. Gellner, 'Ethics and Logic' and R. M. Hare, 'Universalisability', both in *Proceedings of the Aristotelian Society* 55 (1954–1955), 157–78 and 295–312.

[51] On the other hand, it wasn't a way to raise your standing either. 'Soft options for the girls was certainly then the general feeling' is Mary Warnock's comment on the fact that it was three women who were asked in turn (in the late 1950s) if they would contribute a volume on *Ethics Since 1900* for OUP's 'Home University Library'. And 'rather at the last minute' Warnock was called by the General Editor of that series, asking if she could add to the book a chapter on existentialism, 'to set it apart from other current histories of the subject'. Warnock's response to the challenge is instructive:

I had never read a word of Sartre... My heart sank, but I agreed to do it... So for a cold and windy summer I sat on the beach at Sandsend on the North Yorkshire coast... and I read *L'Etre et le Néant*. *I hated it, and in many ways I still do*... But I realised, at the same time, that here was a kind of philosophy completely different from the purely "second order" moral philosophy of Oxford. (Mary Warnock, *An Intelligent Person's Guide to Ethics* (1998), 12–13, my emphasis.)

Murdoch, by contrast, read Sartre with love and excitement, though 'The Idea of Perfection' is a record of disappointed expectations. Her early response to Sartre was this: 'It's the real thing—so exciting, & so sobering, to meet at last—after turning away in despair from the shallow stupid milk & water "ethics" of English "moralists" like Ross & Prichard... Nietzsche's and Schopenhauer's great big mistakes are worth infinitely more than the colourless finicky liberalism of our Rosses & Cook Wilsons' (Journal 3 Nov. 1945: Conradi, IML 216).

all, the difficulty of domesticating within the existing philosophical world the new ideas she was developing from Weil.[52]

What Murdoch found in Weil was a form of Platonism expressed with a heady religious tone.[53] To paraphrase some of the main ideas from Murdoch's own review:[54] Good is a transcendent reality, and 'Good and Evil are connected with modes of human knowledge' (e.g. the good person is one who *knows* or sees things as they are— in their moral and other aspects). The soul has lower and higher parts: 'Until we become good we are at the mercy of mechanical forces, of which "gravity" is the general image' (—we are *weighed down* by our nature—), and these forces are (as psychoanalysis indeed says) only darkly understood by us. To resist gravity is 'to *suffer* the void' (it is to *hold back from filling* a certain kind of vacuum in our existence): a task that humans can perform only with the aid of *grace*.[55] Progress in morality is a matter of 'meditation' rather than simply of action (—Murdoch will talk of the moral character of our 'consciousness' and 'states of mind'—). When we direct our attention to the good, it excites *love* in us, though we recognize that we are ultimately incapable of attaining it.[56] Suffering purifies only to the extent that it is 'pure affliction', though the sufferer is in danger of seeing in it an imaginary *consolation*. And, finally, our ideal is to pay attention to the reality outside us 'to such a point that we no longer have the choice' of what to do (to quote, as Murdoch does, from Weil (*Notebooks* 205)). I here have given more or less the core of Murdoch's report of Weil in her review (E&M 158–9) and more or less every part of it was adopted by Murdoch into her own philosophy. (We might even add (as something only glancingly mentioned in the

---

[52] The immediate cause of her leaving St Anne's in 1963 was, however, 'to free herself from a mutually obsessional attachment to a woman colleague' (Conradi, IML 457). Murdoch went on to teach as a one-day-a-week tutor at the Royal College of Art until the summer of 1967 (IML 469–76)—where she found some brilliant and congenial colleagues, but many of the students seem to have regarded the requirement to pass 'General Studies' as something between a distraction and a contemptible impediment to making art. (For a fuller picture of Murdoch's life in this world, see the fascinating memoir by David Morgan, *With Love and Rage: A Friendship with Iris Murdoch* (2010).) For the difficulty of philosophy and the impossibility of combining it properly with novel-writing: 'It really needs a lifetime of thinking about nothing else, and I do, if I've got to choose, choose the other game.' (To W. K. Rose (1968), FTC 20) 'I "do" philosophy and I teach philosophy, but philosophy is fantastically difficult and I think those who attempt to write it would probably agree that there are very few moments when they rise to the level of real philosophy' (in discussion in Caen (1978), FTC 78).

[53] For a larger view of Weil, see Peter Winch, *Simone Weil: "The Just Balance"* (Cambridge: CUP, 1989) and, on her political thought in particular, Lawrence A. Blum & Victor J. Seidler, *A Truer Liberty: Simone Weil and Marxism* (New York: Routledge, 1989).

[54] 'Knowing the Void', *The Spectator*, November 1956, repr. in E&M 157–60. It was not Murdoch's first encounter with Weil (cf. Conradi, IML 299, also 260); indeed she had given a BBC Third Programme talk on Weil five years earlier (18 Oct. 1951) as a sort of review of *Waiting on God*. But the *Notebooks* made, I think, a different and greater impact in 1956, perhaps because of the ways in which Murdoch's own philosophical interests had been developing: see the visible signs of Weil's influence in the 1959 articles S&G (at 215, though Weil is not mentioned by name) and SBR (at 270; cf. AD 293), as well as, increasingly, in IP (34/327, 40/331–332) and OGG (50/340 and *passim*)—which are in this respect quite unlike what we see in the moral philosophy of VCM and M&E from 1955–56.

[55] My emphasis on '*suffer*'. For 'gravity', see S. Weil, *Notebooks*, i.128–9, 138–9 and around; for 'the void' i.137 and around; or (more accessibly) the selections earlier collected in *Gravity and Grace* (1952) under the headings 'Gravity and Grace', 'Void and Compensation', 'To accept the void', and 'Imagination which fills the void'.

[56] For accessible selections, see *Gravity and Grace*, 'Attention and Will', 'Necessity and Obedience'.

review, but taken up later in 'On "God" and "Good"') Weil's conception of an 'energy' for good action, felt as coming from outside when we contemplate the good—in an analogue of the workings of *grace* in Christianity.[57]) The resulting combination of views is almost entirely accepted by the Murdoch of *The Sovereignty of Good*. Not wholly— Murdoch makes no particular use, I think, of the image of 'gravity', and she is, in a way, more suspicious of suffering and of other-worldliness than Weil is, and slightly more optimistic about the possibility and actual existence of everyday modest virtue. But by and large, I think, Weil's views must have struck Murdoch as a kind of philosophy that was both exceptional and important—and extremely hard to integrate into the non-religious, non-mysterious prose of English mid-century philosophy.

It was, I think, Murdoch's great achievement to see a way to transpose and develop these ideas in a form where they could be combined with the criticisms of Hare and existentialism that she had already independently developed. But it was not going to be an easy task to achieve in the pages of *Mind* or the Aristotelian Society. It was something Murdoch achieved precisely by withdrawing somewhat from the philosophical mainstream which she had entered so brilliantly a decade before—bringing to a culmination her philosophical energies in relative isolation, at a time when she had given up regular university lecturing: and publishing her philosophical masterpiece, 'The Idea of Perfection', in a general literary journal rather a long way from home.

2 Murdoch's early philosophical work: questioning behaviourism

Murdoch's first papers were the responses of a person deeply impressed with Wittgenstein to the behaviouristic tendency, for example in Ryle, to rule out any good sense for talk of 'inner experience'.

'Thinking and Language', Murdoch's first paper, presented at the Joint Session (in June 1951) was, and remains, impressive. Its main project is to investigate how far the kinds of concern Wittgenstein and Ryle pressed about the ways we learn and employ psychological language imply (as many people supposed) that there is no such thing as 'inner experience' (T&L 38). While accepting the Wittgensteinian starting point that meaning is use, Murdoch argues against drawing conclusions that oppose the idea of an 'inner life': for, she says, it is internal to the *use* of psychological terms that there is more to their reference than is verifiably present on occasions of correct usage of them.

---

[57] One might also mention as an influence on 'On "God" and "Good"' (an influence largely but not wholly accepted), Weil's idea of reviving some kind of ontological proof of God—see *La Connaissance surnaturelle* (1950), e.g. 109–10 and 313, a passage which Murdoch particularly noted (as we can see from her copy of the book, now at Kingston University): 'Even if God were an illusion from the point of view of existence, He is the sole reality from the point of view of the good. I am certain of this, since it is a definition. "God is the good" is as certain as "I exist". 'I am in truth |—here Weil echoes the words of Pascal also quoted by Heidegger (*Sein und Zeit* (1927) 139n, *Being and Time* transl. MacQuarrie & Robinson (1962) 492 (n. to 178)), and from him again re-echoed in Murdoch's chapter in the present volume, p. 102| if I tear my desire away from everything which is not a good to direct it solely towards the good, without knowing whether it exists or not' (my transl.). On Weil's influence on Murdoch, see also Conradi in his Preface to E&M, xxvii.

It is surely important that the users of mental words would [, if asked,] often indignantly deny that 'what they meant' was the overt and not the inner. Such an 'idea of meaning' [found among ordinary speakers] proves, moreover, a perfectly acceptable basis for communication, and one without which the use would sensibly alter. (Imagine a people who *really* held that what happened 'in their heads' was irrelevant to the use of words such as 'decide'.) The reaction to this should not be to denounce an illusion and suggest that the inner *is nothing*, or is at best shadowy and nameless. One should attempt a new description. (T&L 38)

Murdoch gives the excellent example from George Eliot's *Daniel Deronda*: 'when Gwendolen hesitates to throw the lifebelt to her detested husband, who subsequently drowns, it matters very much to her [when she later looks back on the event] whether or not at that moment she *intended* his death' (T&L 36, my emphasis): unspoken inner goings-on are not to be relegated, if admitted at all by the post-behaviourist philosophers, to the status of *unimportant accompaniments* of the important overt actions. On the other hand, Murdoch insists that the inner realm should not be conceived in a crudely ontological way either (T&L 39). She ends with some extremely interesting comments on the need to take thought not as 'designat[ing] absent objects', but as 'possessing' or 'grasping' present ones (T&L 40–41)—a suggestion which, together with the recognition of ways in which our mental descriptions are inescapably metaphorical, will operate, she hopes, 'against the world-language dualism which haunts us because we are afraid of the idealists' (T&L 40).

It was an astonishingly independent and brave performance: accepting the fundamental motivations of the modern thinkers like Wittgenstein and Ryle, but buying none of the standard conclusions that were commonly drawn from them.

In many ways, Murdoch's performance at the Joint Session is more interesting than Ryle's: he accepts her point that we talk of mental images, for example, and of speeches rehearsed in one's mind without being given overt expression; but where Murdoch had remarked that we seem forced to employ metaphorical descriptions for a large part of what we call thinking, Ryle replies by agreeing, but declaring this to be simply parallel to the way in which, in many other circumstances, what is called for is a 'history' rather than a blow-by-blow 'chronicle'. (When a soldier gives a report of the battle, he does not 'chronicle' how he tied his shoelaces and what his comrades said to him and when, but rather gives a 'history', for example, of what the strategy and tactics employed were.) This strikes me as replacing a rather interesting point in Murdoch— about the indispensability of metaphor (it 'is not an inexact *faute de mieux* mode of expression, it is the best possible' (T&L 39–40))—with a weaker and less plausible point. I am not at all sure that a description of a mental state which involves metaphor is much like a 'history' of a battle or anything else. It is no doubt true that when 'I was in a fog' is true, there is something more specific going on: *being in a fog* is not the fullest possible description; but it seems quite unclear that the elements of a 'best description' would in all cases (as I think Ryle wants to suggest) be able to do without metaphor or transferred usage.

The second paper, 'Nostalgia for the Particular' (PAS 1952) is harder and, I think, less successful. It considers once again the 'nostalgia for the particular' (NP 55.15, cp. T&L 36.1)—i.e. the desire to bring back and rehabilitate individual mental events after the behaviourists had banished them to the past. (Note Murdoch's stance even in her earliest work: to recall philosophers from theory to phenomena (cp. IP 1/299).) But in this paper, Murdoch allows the Rylean more success: she presents the anti-Rylean rehabilitator as having the task of defending the idea of mental events which are 'self-describing' and which are 'experiences of meaning' (NP 51)—an idea which by the end of the article is pretty much discredited (e.g. because a moving artistic experience would seem a prime candidate for the status of such an event, while the significance of such a thing actually lies *not* in the momentary experience itself but rather in its 'context' (NP 55)). My impression is that the discussion confuses two issues: whether there are mental occurrences that have meaning 'intrinsically', in that (*a*) they do not require some further 'interpretation' to give them meaning; and whether such things are 'self-describing' in that (*b*) they wear their character on their sleeve—so that anyone who had the experience would immediately know how best to describe or characterize it. But once again, Murdoch surprises us: in the last paragraph, it turns out that she accepts neither of the two sides that had seemed to be at war, but takes up a third position: we must admit 'symbolic experiences' (i.e. moments like the one she quotes from Rilke, where the 'momentary impression [of a face] involuntarily assumes the proportions of a symbol' (NP 56)), though we need not say that such experiences 'say themselves' or have 'intrinsic sense'; and we can admit inward mental events, without supposing that psychological language is solely in the business of telling us about such things (NP 58.9–10 & 12, 53.15).

3 The move to moral philosophy

In the mid-1950s Murdoch turned her attention from behaviourism about the mind in general to behaviourist and linguistic approaches to morality in particular. She presented 'Metaphysics and Ethics' for BBC Radio (Third Programme, 1955; publ. as a book contribution, 1957) and 'Vision and Choice in Morality' (PASS 1956). The latter takes the form of a thoroughly sympathetic reply to R. W. Hepburn (who later became Professor at Edinburgh), joining him in challenging Hare's prescriptivism. In many ways Murdoch dominates the Symposium, though she is officially Hepburn's respondent; and the title of the session, 'Vision and Choice in Morality', makes perfect sense as the title of her paper and almost none as title of his. Murdoch contrasts, on the one hand, the moral philosophy of Hare and others that puts 'choice' at the centre (whether it be 'choice' of 'moral principles' or the taking of a particular practical decision), with, on the other hand, views that treat morality as a matter of 'vision'. (The term is applied first to the moral outlook of an individual, the evolving 'total vision of life', against the background of which particular acts or decisions stand out (see VCM 39–40/80–82, and esp. 40.35–37/82.1–2); it is extended later also to the agent's particular judgements and decisions themselves—since Murdoch has by the end of the article introduced the notion of a *moral reality* of which moral judgements might be described as being cases of 'awareness' (VCM 56/96).) There are, on this new view, what might almost be called 'moral facts', 'observable' thanks to our possessing the appropriate 'specialised concepts' (VCM 54/94–95). From being a metaphor that might amount to little more than everyday talk of moral 'outlook' or 'perspective', the talk of vision comes to include something like awareness of particular moral facts—indeed, even more ambitiously, 'visions, inspirations or powers which emanate from a transcendental source concerning which [the thinker] is called on to make discoveries and may at present know little' (VCM 56/96). The exact nature of the reality in question is at this moment left indeterminate; and Murdoch leaves open also that the transcendental background may be something that we are, at best, entitled to '*believe*' in, but not claim knowledge of (VCM 55–56/96)—as Kant says too, of the existence of God and of freedom.

I shall pause a little over this impressive work. One sees in it, almost fully formed, though it is Murdoch's first publication in moral philosophy, many of the more ambitious themes of *The Sovereignty of Good*, advanced with care, control, and brio. And, unlike the later papers, which are not directed explicitly at Hare (even when he is clearly in the target area), it presents a comprehensive investigation of his work. The core of Hare's position can be seen as combining the approach of ordinary language philosophy with a Humean division of fact and value: there are no such things as moral facts for moral judgements to be describing or stating; ethical sentences are 'imperatives in disguise', governed by a general logic of imperatives;[58] the meaning of an evaluative term can be segmented into a 'descriptive' component (associating with the term certain purely descriptive 'criteria' chosen for its application) and an evaluative component (roughly equivalent, in the case of 'good — ', to the prescription 'Choose such things!'); finally, the key feature of moral prescriptions (unlike commands in general) is that they are universalizable: for a prescription to be treated as a moral prescription is for it to be treated as having behind it a *universal* principle (something of the form, e.g. 'All fs that are g are good', taken as equivalent to, approximately, 'Choose fs that are g!'). This is the core of the Universal Prescriptivism that took definitive form in Hare's *The Language of Morals* (1952) and his PAS paper 'Universalisability' (1955), and it remained, extended (to include a form of Utilitarianism) but only very slightly modified, as a prime orthodoxy in the English-speaking world for more than 30 years.

Hepburn argues in his paper[59] that, besides making moral claims which they treat as universalizable, people often commit themselves also to a project of making their life as a whole have a certain kind of 'meaning' or 'pattern'—making it constitute a certain kind of 'fable', to use a term from the poet Edwin Muir's autobiography *The Story and the Fable* (1940). And the commitment to make one's life conform to some such pattern

---

[58] R. M. Hare, 'Imperative Sentences', *Mind* 58 (1949), 21–39, at 23.

[59] R. W. Hepburn, 'Vision and Choice in Morality', *Proceedings of the Aristotelian Society*, Supplementary Volume 30 (1956), 14–31. Page references in parentheses in the present paragraph are to this paper.

may, Hepburn argues, be a recognizably *moral* project, even where it is not a matter of universal or universalizable maxims:

Moral criticism and control...may find expression in maxims, principles, or...as fable. For example; [*sic*] Jesus sought to 'fulfil' the Old Testament fable, partly by precept but far more by acting out 'prophetic symbolism', by parable and by the re-interpreting of religious images like the Throne of David and the Son of Man. (26)

And, as Hepburn argues, to allow such projects to be moral projects, such kinds of evaluation to be moral evaluation, need involve none of the general errors in the philosophy of mind that Hare and supporters warned us against—such as a belief in a substantial soul, or in the infallibility of introspection (22–23); nor (we might add) need it always take a religious form.

Murdoch's response is sympathetic, but she takes Hepburn to be, if anything, too generous to Hare.[60] She arranges her main points under four headings.[61] (1) Even if behaviourists are right to reject introspection as a supposedly privileged source of knowledge of our mental states, that is no reason for rejecting the kind of 'private or personal' vision of life that is quite capable of being expressed 'overtly' as well as 'inwardly' (VCM 37/78). And such outlooks are no less important to the moral life than particular practical decisions, and in some sense may be more fundamental. We must consider, not just the actions and 'choices' emphasized by Hare, but also people's 'personal attitudes':

their total vision of life, as shown in their mode of speech or silence, their choice of words, their assessments of others, their conception of their own lives, what they think attractive or praise-worthy, what they think funny: in short, the configurations of their thought which show continually in their reactions and conversation. (VCM 39/80–81)

Morality is a matter of such 'vision' as much as it is of 'choice'.

Perhaps most fundamental for the 'naturalism' that Murdoch envisages later in the paper is (2) her challenge to Hare's view of moral concepts. For Hare, the force of a moral concept for an individual user can be segmented into 'descriptive' and 'evalu-ative' meaning—in the case of 'brave', for example, (a) the specification of 'factual

---

[60] Iris Murdoch, 'Vision and Choice in Morality', *Proceedings of the Aristotelian Society*, Supplementary Volume 30 (1956): 32–58, abbreviated as VCM. Page references are given both to the original printing and (following a forward slash /) to the reprint in *Existentialists and Mystics* (1997). Where I give line numbers, these are added following a point. It is worth reading the article in the original printing: the E&M reprint aims to make Murdoch's reply to Hepburn into a self-contained article by removing references to Hepburn but otherwise leaving the text maximally unchanged; the result is that about 45 percent of the opening six pages of the original are omitted, though thankfully very little of the remainder of the article. I suspect the aim was never going to be very successfully achievable even if it was desirable. There are almost inevitable difficulties of detail (e.g. the phrase beginning 'Whereas...' at 82.8 in the reprint is actually a qualification or response not to the sentence that precedes it in E&M, but to a sentence in the original that has dropped out). But, more importantly, I suspect the basic direction of the discussion makes more sense when shown in relation to Hepburn.

[61] The discussions begin at VCM 36.4/78.22, 41.4/82.8, 43.27/84.22 and 51.19/92.3 respectively.

criteria open to any observer' for application of the term and (b) a recommendation of things meeting those criteria ('Approve of *this* area!', VCM 41/82). One criticism—and this is a point on which Murdoch and Foot were particularly influential on McDowell and Williams[62]—is that it may be impossible to find any 'purely descriptive' equivalent—graspable by people who do not share, even in imagination, an evaluative interest in the moral classification made by ordinary users of term. Far from us living all 'in the same world' (of empirical facts available to anyone), someone who lacks a certain area of moral vocabulary may in a sense live *in a different moral world* from someone who possesses it—and it may be harder, therefore, to reach agreement in moral argument, or even to comprehend disagreement, than Hare imagines when he portrays moral disagreement between two people as being either about facts or about whether or not to 'choose' to approve of some particular (descriptively identifiable) class of things or actions. A disagreement may, Murdoch argues, be more a matter of 'vision'—where one party cannot even see how the other 'goes on' to apply the term in question to new cases (to use the phrase from Wittgenstein's discussion of rule-following: PI §§139–242, e.g. at §§151, 154), or what might be the point of doing so. And that points to a further conclusion: that morality needs to be studied historically. If 'moral differences are conceptual (in the sense of being differences of vision)' (—in that what one can 'see' in Murdoch's sense depends in part on what concepts one has—), then this 'makes impossible the reduction of ethics to logic, since it suggests that morality must, to some extent at any rate, be studied historically' (VCM 43/84).[63] Even a conceptual investigation would be a study of concepts varying over time and differently available to people according to their evolving historical and (as Murdoch will later stress) personal circumstances and experience.

(3) Murdoch makes two slightly different challenges to Hare's emphasis on univer-salizability. There are cases where a person regards himself as set apart from others 'by a superiority . . . or by a curse, or some other unique destiny': if one is Napoleon, 'one does not think that everyone should do as one does oneself'. This could be forced into a universalizability model (saying 'if anyone had the same personal destiny, then . . . '); but an important difference remains: between 'moral attitudes which have this sort of personal background' and those which do not (VCM 46/86). The second challenge is perhaps more radical: there are moral outlooks that turn for guidance, not to rules with respect to repeatedly encounterable characteristics, but rather to 'parables' or 'stories', or (rather differently) to the example or guidance of an individual. 'Certain parables or stories undoubtedly owe their power to the fact that they incarnate a moral truth which is paradoxical, infinitely suggestive and open to continual reinterpretation.' (Murdoch cites the parable of the prodigal son: VCM 50/91.) 'Such stories provide, precisely through their concreteness and consequent ambiguity, sources of moral

---

[62] See above, theses (iii) and (7) in § 1 and references there.
[63] For the 'reduction of ethics to logic', cp. Hare's Preface: 'Ethics, as I conceive it, is the logical study of the language of morals' (Hare, *The Language of Morals*, iii).

inspiration which highly specific rules could not give' (VCM 50/91). There may of course be *dangers* in some such attitudes (Murdoch knows very well the comparisons Ernest Gellner had made with 'the *Fuehrerprinzip, credo quia absurdum*, and romantic love': VCM 49n/90n[64]); but there are recognizably *moral* discussions that involve such concerns ('certain idealist views, certain existentialist views, certain Catholic views', e.g. in Gabriel Marcel and Maurice Nédoncelle: VCM 47n/87n), and it cannot be right for the linguistic analysts simply to declare as outside the definition of morality things that might equally be taken as *counter-examples* to their particular definition of it. Their theory, of course, fits well enough the secular liberal conception of morality that dominates in 'modern' societies (cp. VCM 49–50/89–90, 56/96), and it may even in turn seem to give support to that liberal conception. But philosophical disease comes— as Wittgenstein warned (PI §593)—from a 'one-sided diet' of examples.

Murdoch's most radical challenge to Hare lies in (4) her conception of moral freedom. She will conclude, in brief, that freedom does not consist, as Hare believes, in the freedom to 'choose' what to apply moral concepts to (e.g. to call different things 'good' from one's parents, or to reject the evaluative 'criteria' of other people); instead it resides in the freedom 'to "deepen" or "reorganise"' our concepts or, in a process of moral evolution, to 'change' those concepts for others (VCM 55/95; cp. IP 27/321). And that point is important precisely as undercutting an argument against 'naturalism' (or against the reality of 'moral facts'): for if, as Hare believes, the agent is *free* to select with equal right whatever descriptive criteria she wishes for the application of a moral term like 'good', then there can hardly be moral facts outside us (something which would be 'observable' (VCM 54/94), and which 'moral progress' would consist in a progressive 'awareness' of (VCM 56/96)). This is Hare's reason for the 'prohibition on defining value in terms of fact' (VCM 54/94). But though the concept of *good* is thin enough that it may indeed seem associable with more or less any descriptive criteria, this is not true of the 'more specialised concepts which themselves determine a vision of the world' (VCM 54/94)—concepts like those that figure in Murdoch's later example of M & D, *vulgar, undignified* and *noisy*, or *refreshingly simple, spontaneous* and *gay* (IP 18/313): the kind that Bernard Williams later called 'thick' concepts.[65] And with them

---

[64] The phrase *credo quia absurdum* ('I believe, because it is absurd') is usually associated with Tertullian (*c.* 160–*c.* 240), though the nearest he came to saying it seems to have been '*credibile est, quia ineptum est*' ('It is credible, because it is inappropriate'), in *de Carne Christi* 5.4 (defending the view that the flesh of Christ was real, rather than phantasmic, as Marcion had claimed). The *Führerprinzip* is the idea, dominant in Nazism, that individuals in groups owe absolute obedience to a leader who holds authority over them as subordinates; leaders of the lower groups in turn owe obedience to a higher leader, in a hierarchical structure—and legitimacy and authority derive from the special character of the leader rather than (as in democratic conceptions) from her or his having been chosen by the people. Romantic love was regularly mentioned as being a commitment not subject to a requirement of universalizability: one who loves a person is not required to love her or his double, however similar they may be.

[65] Williams's examples—*coward, lie, brutality, gratitude* (ELP 140)—are in a sense more substantial than Murdoch's: one might ask indeed if the very terms that figure in M's first view of D do not need to be put into question (and not just their application)—*vulgarity* might be a notion that only made sense against a background of class conceptions that would not survive mature reflection. This would be no surprise in

the fact-value distinction seems to break down: 'fact and value merge in a quite innocuous way': 'There would, indeed, scarcely be an objection to saying that there were "moral facts"' (VCM 54/95). Our principal freedom is not the freedom 'to lift the concept off the otherwise unaltered facts and lay it down elsewhere' (i.e. to 'choose' a different set of descriptive criteria for the application of the evaluative term); it is the ability 'to "deepen" or "reorganise" the concept or change it for another one' (VCM 55/95). If there is a moral reality, then the freedom that counts is the freedom to abandon the concepts that structure a benighted moral outlook and to develop concepts better suited for 'awareness of this reality and submission to its purposes' (VCM 56/96).

At this point, this 'naturalism'—which Murdoch describes as free of *philosophical error*' (VCM 54/95) but seems to hold back from formally affirming—takes on a rather supernatural aspect. Murdoch tells us there is nothing in the 'naturalistic fallacy' argument to prevent us from *believing* in the existence of 'alleged transcendent metaphysical realities, such as God, or History, or the Church' (VCM 55/95): Murdoch's emphasis on the word '*belief*' echoes Kant's claim that he has done away with *knowledge* (e.g. of God) 'in order to make room for *faith*' or belief (G l a u b e, *Critique of Pure Reason* B xxx). The 'true naturalist'—whom Hare would call a descriptivist, and others a moral realist—is, for Murdoch, 'one who believes that as moral beings we are immersed in a reality which transcends us and that moral progress consists in awareness of this reality and submission to its purposes' (VCM 56/96, quoted in part above). Her examples of such believers are the 'Marxist' and 'certain kinds of Christian'. Murdoch conceives of this belief in a moral reality as having a rich transcendental background—something that turns out in later essays, I think, and particularly OGG, to be rather less metaphysically opulent than might at first appear.

Hare may demand and proclaim the freedom to choose at will the criteria for his moral concepts; but in the eyes of the 'naturalist', this is to fail to understand 'the truth about the universe': Hare 'imagines himself to be the source of all value', but cannot thereby *make* himself any such thing (VCM 57/97).[66]

principle to Murdoch: 'A smart set of concepts may be a most efficient instrument of corruption' (IP 33/325)—and (though precisely this point may or may not be still in the air then) the word 'common' appears as an example only a few lines later. And M's improved vision comes precisely through her recognition of herself as *old-fashioned* and maybe *snobbish* (IP 17/313). One might feel some discomfort, however, over even the second set of concepts (the ones expressing how D is seen when M has been 'moved by love or justice' (18/313) and should therefore be coming to see her 'as she really is' (37/329)): *refreshingly simple* and *delightfully youthful* are rather conspicuously relational (refreshing to people in what condition?!, one might ask, and is 'delightfully youthful' a description that could be used by anyone who was anything like the same age as the person being talked of?); and even *gay* and *spontaneous* seem rather slight to serve as main terms of a successful attempt to see the daughter-in-law 'justly' and 'lovingly' (23/317). But the general point about moral vision and moral facts is surely separable, I think, from weaknesses in Murdoch's particular illustration of it.

[66] As Foot said (setting out what one would need to establish in order to refute Stevenson and Hare): 'a man can no more decide for himself what is evidence for rightness and wrongness than he can decide what is evidence for monetary inflation or a tumour on the brain' ('Moral Arguments', 99).

Apart from the arguments under the four main headings, Murdoch makes some fine points more incidentally. She presents Liberalism as a substantial and questionable moral or political stance embedded in the supposedly 'neutral' views of Hare and his associates (VCM 42–3/83–4, 55/95); she treats a transcendental background to morality as something that philosophy must not rule out under the pretence of merely doing logic (VCM 55/96); she emphasizes—quite exceptionally in the academic environment of Ryle, Austin, and the younger generation including Hare—the importance of historical and cultural variation, both in the practices of moral thinking and in our attempts to develop a philosophy of language to tell us what 'morality' can or must involve: Hare's picture of the 'logic' of morality turns out to be the logic merely of those moral systems that fit with his own 'Liberal atheist' or 'Protestant Christian' traditions; this excludes by definitional decree the attitude of those ready to think against a transcendental background, like that of 'the Marxist' or 'certain kinds of Christian' (VCM 56/96) mentioned above. By contrast, Murdoch thinks: 'For the purposes of analysis moral philosophy should remain at the level of the *differences*',—a good Wittgensteinian injunction in a thoroughly Wittgensteinian sentence[67]—'taking the moral *forms of life* as given, and not try to *get behind them* to a single form' (VCM 57/ 97; first emphasis mine).

It is with this paper that Murdoch, I think, finds her voice. It still has the form of a respectful academic response (both to Hepburn and to Hare); but it is swelling with ideas—and a richer language—that can hardly be contained within the form.[68] It was the last paper she published in the standard annals of academic philosophy: from this point on, her reviews and her large philosophical papers appeared not in *Mind* and the *Proceedings of the Aristotelian Society* but in journals like the *Yale Review* or *Encounter*, or in collections of papers by literary or political writers rather than philosophers. It was soon afterwards that she decided to drop her University Lecturership and to reduce her

---

[67] Emphasis on differences: 'I was thinking of using as a motto for my book a quotation from *King Lear*: "I'll teach you differences."' (Wittgenstein, reported by M. O'C. Drury, in 'Conversations with Wittgenstein', in R. Rhees, ed., *Recollections of Wittgenstein* ([1981], 1984), 171.) Cp. Wittgenstein's protest at the 'one-sided diet' of philosophers who nourish their thinking with 'only one kind of example' (*Philosophical Investigations* (1953) §593; cp. 'What has to be accepted, the given, is—so one could say—forms of life', 226). For the dangers of trying to 'get behind': 'We feel as if we had to *penetrate* phenomena' (PI §90); 'This finds expression in questions as to the *essence* of language, of propositions, of thought. . . . [T]hey see in the essence, not something that already lies open to view and that becomes surveyable by a rearrangement, but something that lies beneath the surface' (PI §92).

[68] I think of Murdoch's description of 'the man who believes that moral values are visions, inspirations or powers which emanate from a transcendent source concerning which he is called on to make discoveries and may at present know little' (VCM 56/96); as also of 'moral attitudes which emphasise the inexhaustible detail of the world, the endlessness of the task of understanding, the importance of not assuming that one has got individuals and situations "taped", the connection of knowledge with love and of spiritual insight with apprehension of the unique' (VCM 46/87); and of the 'people whose fundamental belief is that we live in a world whose mystery transcends us and that morality is the exploration of that mystery in so far as it concerns each individual' (VCM 46/88; all quoted, in whole or part, at other places above).

College tutorial teaching.[69] One can only be grateful that Murdoch could be brought out of this partial retirement to give the wonderful lectures that became *The Sovereignty of Good*.

In 'Vision and Choice in Morality', a richer naturalism is presented as integral to various existing moral outlooks that, as a matter of socio-linguistic fact, a proper study of the language of morals cannot ignore, and that it can formally reject or deny only by abandoning its official stance of 'neutrality' on substantive ethical matters (e.g. as when it takes 'Liberalism' for granted: VCM 42–3/83–4, 52/93, 55/95). Murdoch does not explicitly sign up for any of these richer conceptions of morality—but she argues that some such views are available to be *believed*, if not known (VCM 55–6/96), and that the 'naturalistic fallacy' is no fallacy (VCM 52–7/92–7). Hare and his fellows may insist on the extricability of fact and value (as a doctrine supposedly in the philosophy of language) in order to maintain our freedom to choose our values. But in what sense is that a freedom that we have? Can we 'choose' our values any more than we can choose our mathematics? We may, perhaps, in some sense 'choose' our concepts; we do in a sense, 'choose' what to believe when e.g. we decide, or make a balanced judgement on the basis of certain reasons, that it is the case that p and not q; but it is far from obvious— indeed, Murdoch thinks, far from being true—that we can 'choose' our values, in the sense of ensuring, simply by 'deciding' to take things of kind k as valuable, that such things will indeed be of value in the way we have supposed.

This leaves the task of actually defending some particular form of naturalism— something which Murdoch undertakes in 'The Idea of Perfection'—and of then analyzing what kind of transcendence it really commits her to—which she does in 'On "God" and "Good"'. It turns out, I think, that the slightly mystical religious tone attached to the naturalism that is presented (though not affirmed) in 'Vision and Choice' is capable, in Murdoch's later papers, of being grounded, deflated, and rendered innocent—and accepted.

4 The 'House of Theory', aesthetics and morals

Before we find Murdoch at that point however, it is worth mentioning her political essay 'A House of Theory' and two substantial papers that take off from Kant's conception of the Sublime.

'A House of Theory' was written for *Conviction* (1958),[70] a collection of essays by a dozen 'Thoughtful Young Men' (as the dust cover put it), convinced of the impor- tance of Socialist ideas and methods, and replying to the question, 'What is wrong with the British Left—and what should be done about it?' Contributors included the political economist Peter Shore (later Minister in the governments of Harold Wilson

---

[69] Cp. Conradi, IML 457n, and see above, pp. 5–6; though the Oxford University Archives imply that her University Lecturership officially ended in 1957, rather than 1958.

[70] N. Mackenzie, ed., *Conviction* (1958), 218–33.

and Jim Callaghan), Raymond Williams (whose *Culture and Society 1780–1950* appeared that same year, 1958), Richard Hoggart (already well-known for *The Uses of Literacy* (1957)),[71] Nigel Calder (editor of the *New Scientist*, 1962–6), and Paul Johnson (editor of the *New Statesman*, 1965–70)—people who were to be leaders of the 1960s intelligentsia, and in some cases to disappoint their old admirers with their later movement to the political right.

Murdoch's paper is primarily concerned with questions of the good life for a whole society, and with how the Welfare State has (for all its achievements) not secured it (HT 183). Most of the first half of the paper is a history of the impoverishment of philosophy—and the bleaching-out from it of substantive moral and political issues in favour of the study of the logic of moral and political statements. The second half insists—in the face of a 1950s Labour Party that concentrated on Benthamite questions of technological 'efficiency'—on the need for a re-examination of *ends*, using *theory*. Socialism must 'far more frankly . . . declare itself a morality' (180; cp. 182.11, 185.16), and it must debate ends—rather than concerning itself mainly with means-end policies. Above all, the socialist movement should return to 'its original great source of inspiration and reflection', the problem of labour: the problem of 'the transformation of labour from something senseless which forms no real part of the personality of the labourer into something creative and significant' (184). And to achieve this, Murdoch proposes we should 'go back' (185)—a recurring recommendation in Murdoch, uttered confidently in her earlier days, and with more regret in later years—to, in this case, ideas shared by both the Guild Socialists and Marx.

The paper was much reprinted,[72] and its ideas and title were, rather remarkably, taken up in a manifesto for the radical American group Students for a Democratic Society (SDS): Tom Hayden (a founder and President for 1962–3, and well-known later in the anti-war and economic democracy movements) drew on C. Wright Mills and Iris Murdoch for some of the leading ideas of what became a defining statement of the movement at its 1962 Port Huron meeting.[73]

---

[71] The subtitle was: 'Aspects of working class life with special reference to publications and entertainments'; Hoggart's post at the time was Senior Staff Tutor in Literature, Department of Adult Education, University of Hull.

[72] For example, in: *Partisan Review* 26.1 (Winter 1959) 17–31; and in D. Cooperman and E. V. Walter, eds., *Power and Civilization: Political Thought in the Twentieth Century* (1962), 442–55. The first three paragraphs reappeared more recently in *The Daily Times* (Pakistan), November 18, 2003.

[73] 'We need, and the Left should provide, some refuge from the cold, open field of Benthamite empiricism, a framework, a house of theory' (Murdoch, HT 181). Tom Hayden 'picked up this imagery, coming to think of the SDS manifesto as an initial attempt to build this house.' (Ira Katznelson, 'From the street to the lecture hall: The 1960s', *Daedalus*, Winter 1997.) Early sketches of Hayden's speech talk of 'the orderly building of a house of theory' (see Kirkpatrick Sale, *SDS* (1973), 25). The version of the manifesto that I've seen does not actually contain the imagery of the 'house' (<http://www3.iath.virginia.edu/sixties/HTML_docs/Resources/Primary/Manifestos/SDS_Port_Huron.html>), but it proclaims much the same conception of work as Murdoch (as 'creative, not mechanical; . . . encouraging independence, a respect for others, a sense of dignity') and it talks very similarly of the need to turn away from the post-war technical approach of 'program without vision' instead to theoretical questions of social goals, values, and ideals. For the theory of work that is central to Murdoch's discussion, see Marx, *Grundrisse* (1857–58), tr. by M. Nicolaus

'The Sublime and the Good' (*Chicago Review*, Autumn 1959) is a beautiful example of Murdoch's power to run where others walk. The essay is in part an exposition of Kant on the Beautiful and the Sublime, and an attempt to transform Kant's theory of the latter into a more adequate conception of art in general than Kant himself achieved. But it also takes us, if briefly, to the heart of Murdoch's conception of morality. The core of the paper takes off from the wonderful moment in the Third Critique ('suggestive, indeed intoxicating', S&G 212: §59 in the *Critique of Judgement*, I presume, along with §§ 26–7) where Kant connects our experience of *Achtung*—or respect for the moral law—, with our experience of the sublime. (In both cases, we feel elation in the consciousness of our rational nature and in the demand of Reason to find our world a systematic whole—even if (faced with the moral law) we also feel pain at the thwarting of our sensuous nature, as also (faced with the very large or very powerful) we feel distress at our inability to encompass it in imagination.) Murdoch's first project is to find a theory of art that steers between Kant and Tolstoy: Kant's theory of art (which is, unfortunately, pretty much identical with his theory of beauty) must be rejected because, though it may help with the abstract beauty of a flower or a Mallarmé poem, it fails in any way to 'account for the greatness of tragedy' (S&G 211). Tolstoy's theory of art, on the other hand, must be rejected: though Tolstoy underlines the value of the expression of 'the highest and best feelings to which men have risen'—and traces those feelings particularly to our *religious* consciousness—, nonetheless he seems to leave no place for great art which is *difficult*. Is there a way to join the best of Kant with Tolstoy? Murdoch's answer lies in a important passage, which is the crux of the whole article (S&G 215–6; cp. SBR 281–3): by transferring into the theory of art the core of Kant's theory of the Sublime (which, of course, is no part of *Kant's* theory of art). The proper object of our feeling of elation at the unencompassable is not—as Kant supposes—the Alps or 'the boundless ocean in a state of tumult' (Kant, *Critique of Judgement* §28); it is the boundless variety of *free persons*, as (endlessly) *revealed by love*. And (as the companion essay SBR brings out) what that provokes, in someone seriously aware of it, is a sense not of the superiority of Reason (as in Kant) but of

---

(1973), 610–12, and Marx's note at the end of *Das Kapital* Bk. I (1867), Pt. 1 Ch. 1 §2 ('The dual Character of the Labour embodied in Commodities'). (*Das Kapital* III ch. 48 contains what, I imagine, Murdoch would regard as a less promising conception.) Marx is rebutting Adam Smith's conception of work or labour as simply the sacrifice of a certain number of hours that might otherwise, and supposedly preferably, have been rest. What Smith ignores, Marx believes, is the fact that the individual 'also needs a normal portion of work, and of the suspension of tranquillity': rather than simply being the production of goods for 'external natural urgencies', work may present itself as the freedom of realizing an aim which the individual sets for himself—as writing is for the writer. Labour may be turned into 'attractive work'—which of course is different, again, from mere amusement (*Grundrisse*, 611). Murdoch takes the 'problem of labour' here—the transformation of work from 'something senseless' to 'something creative and significant' (HT 184)—to be both a conceptual and a practical matter; and the reconception would bring with it a new understanding also of the familiar ideas of *equality*, *democracy*, and *freedom*. It may help to keep the scope and importance of such conceptual reconfiguration in mind when considering Murdoch's other comments on conceptual revision and 'deepening': cf. fn. 34 and thesis (ii) in §1 of main text above.

humility and 'the un-self-centred . . . agnosticism which goes with tolerance' (SBR 283); and it has some of the character (as in Tolstoy) of a *religious* consciousness.

The result is 'nearly but not quite' Hegel's theory of tragedy (S&G 213). Hegel treats tragedy as a conflict between two incompatible goods (e.g. those of Antigone and Creon in Sophocles—Murdoch is thinking of Hegel's *Phenomenology of Spirit*, VI.A.a); but he regards the conflict as in a sense a mere appearance due to the protagonists' partial views of the social totality. (If we understand the complete situation which encloses them both, then 'the unity of the ethical substance is given as total, and within it we see and comprehend a conflict of goods' (S&G 213).) To this Murdoch replies that it is a diminution of tragedy: if there is a human social totality, it is not one we can grasp or encompass, and conflicts in it are not so consolingly to be resolved: 'To use an awkward mixed metaphor, the circle [—the totality demanded by Reason—] must be *humanised* [—as it is in Hegel—] but it must not [as again in Hegel] be *given*' (S&G 214, my emphasis).

At this point it turns out that what Murdoch has found to be the essence of tragedy (the awareness of free individuals in conflict) is in a sense also the essence of morals:

Art and morals are, with certain provisos . . . , one. Their essence is the same. The essence of both of them is love. Love is the perception of individuals. Love is the extremely difficult realisation that something other than oneself is real. Love, and so art and morals, is the discovery of reality. What stuns us into a realisation of our supersensible destiny[74] is not, as Kant imagined, the formlessness of nature, but rather its unutterable particularity; and most particular and individual of all natural things is the mind of man. (S&G 215)

The conception of love here is almost exactly that of Simone Weil (unnamed in this article, and mentioned only in a different context in the companion piece (SBR 270); but the influence becomes increasingly explicit at AD 293, IP 34/327, and OGG 50/340). And Murdoch adds that 'the enemies of art and of morals, the enemies that is of love, are the same: social convention and neurosis' (S&G 216).

'The Sublime and the Beautiful Revisited' (*Yale Review*, December 1959) develops many of the same ideas as 'The Sublime and the Good'; but this time, Murdoch writes primarily 'as a novelist' (261) rather than a philosopher, and asks whether literature in particular can help correct the failures of the 'Liberal-democratic' conception of a person.[75] Her answer is that prose literature can indeed 'help our health': 'by not abandoning the naturalistic idea of character' (284). The paper divides into a historical

---

[74] The phrase echoes the *Critique of Judgement* §27, par. 2, where Kant talks of *das Gefühl unserer übersinnlichen Bestimmung*, 'the feeling of our supersensible vocation': in our experience of the sublime, the inadequacy of sensibility to span the overwhelmingly large (or overwhelmingly powerful, §29) itself reminds us of the supersensible powers of Reason. (Cp. also Kant's talk in the KpV of 'the sublimity of our own nature (in its vocation)' and of 'the sublimity of our own supersensuous existence' (Ak. 5:87, 88).) The Meredith translation of the *Critique of Judgement* contains, I think, a definite mistranslation, in talking of 'the feeling of the supersensible *side of our being*' (106, my emphasis).

[75] This helps explain why the article is separated from its original companion and placed in Part Six of *Existentialists and Mystics*: it is being put under the heading 'Can Literature help cure the Ills of Philosophy?'.

analysis first of *philosophical* conceptions of man, from Kant to Linguistic Empiricism and Existentialism (262–70); and then of *literature* during more or less the same period (270–80). In both domains, man has become portrayed as, for the most part, rational, free, but terribly *alone* (265, 268, 279, 288): in a sense, we have lost the conception of other people outside ourselves as *centres of meaning* for us—something we can reclaim, in part, by (in the novel) showing the reality of their consciousness (280–6). (Murdoch takes the twin failures of convention and of neurosis as the basis for a dichotomy in the domain of literature: the novels of Beauvoir are journalistic surrenders to social convention, those of Camus are hard 'crystalline' objects that surrender instead to neurosis (the other characters become an extension of the subject's consciousness (278–9; cp. 269)); what neither party displays is the *attention to the reality of other people* that is visible *par excellence* in Tolstoy (280).) And, just as in the other paper (S&G) the essence of art proved in a sense to be the essence of morals, so here, *virtue* in art (a term not much used before by Murdoch) turns out to be much the same as virtue in morality in general: in both domains, it is love, attention, recognition. 'Virtue is in this sense to be construed as knowledge, and connects us so with reality.' 'The artist is the analogon of the good man' (284).

'Against Dryness' (*Encounter*, Jan. 1961) is a compressed and short essay: it reads somewhat as a manifesto or a summary of conclusions argued elsewhere—as indeed it is. The title alludes to T. E. Hulme's comment 'We must find beauty in small dry things' (cp. SBR 273). Murdoch disagrees: what the novelist must seek to produce is not small dry objects, like the poems of Mallarmé, but, rather, things which present the great ungraspable variety of 'real people' (AD 294) in frankly contingent relations— works which should, among other things, break the 'fantasy-myths' that dominate in existentialist literature. (Echoing the distinction of 'The Sublime and the Beautiful Revisited' (278–9), the paper repeats the complaint that 20th-century novels are typically 'either crystalline or journalistic' (AD 291, 294).) The essay extends the criticisms of the two earlier papers on the Sublime (SBR and S&G) of the Liberal & Existentialist conception of man and the reality surrounding him; it complains, as had done 'A House of Theory', that the advances of a Welfare State have left us insuffi- ciently motivated towards a real *theoretical* investigation of the nature of social relations (AD 290.3–9, 293.11–12). But the paper has the distinction of explicitly invoking Simone Weil for her view that morality is 'a matter of attention, not of will' (AD 293), and of insisting on our need to cultivate concepts. 'We need more concepts than our philosophies have furnished us with' (AD 293, cp. 290). Murdoch means, I think, first, that moral progress consists not simply in taking the moral propositions already available to us and readjusting our assignment of truth values (or affirmations and rejections) to them—but rather in revising our moral concepts themselves (cp. M&E 72–4; VCM 42/83, 48/89, 55/95): making things thinkable that were not for us thinkable before. But her main point here, I think, goes further: that, as theoreticians, we need new concepts even to make sense of the idea of a *moral reality*—and for that,

Murdoch sees Simone Weil as our first guide: 'we need a new vocabulary of *attention*' (AD 293, my emphasis).

Perhaps the most remarkable statement in the essay is this:

We need to be enabled ... to picture, in a non-metaphysical, non-totalitarian and non-religious sense, the transcendence of reality. (AD 293)

(The last phrase means, I think: *the fact that reality transcends us, and the way in which it does so*, not *how WE might transcend reality*.) This is the kind of Murdochian statement that may be a delight to admirers and maddening to critics: it may sound simply unashamedly paradox-mongering, but it is meant, I think, as a first step towards a quite prosaic untying of any paradox—showing, in this case, how there is, after all, a quite straightforward conception of a moral reality that is in some sense both *transcendent* and *non-metaphysical*. It has to be said, I think, that it took Murdoch some years to give us much of an idea of what that conception might be. Increasingly from the mid-1950s she had talked of the need for a recognition or realization of 'a vast and varied reality outside ourselves' (SBR 282; cp. M&E 70)—and linked it with Simone Weil's idea that the appreciation of this reality was effected by 'love', and accompanied by humility and 'tolerance' (SBR 283). She made reference to the 'reality' neglected by both existentialists and contemporary empiricists (AD 292); she had complained, concerning the 'man' of her contemporaries, that 'Nothing transcends him' (AD 288). But one might easily wonder quite what 'reality' Murdoch had in mind as that which the mainstream was neglecting: was knowing this reality a question of knowing simply *the states of mind of other people*, or of knowing *general principles of morality*, or of knowing some *transcendent metaphysical facts*—or what? (All of which things could seem either too little or too large.) One of the remarkable achievements of 'The Idea of Perfection' was, I think, to provide a remarkably simple answer to that question: a person's knowledge of the moral reality transcending her could be knowledge of such things as that another individual is *refreshingly simple* or *spontaneous* (IP 17–18/313). The idea of a moral reality turns out to be no weirder than that of a world of people and things with *refreshing simplicity*, *spontaneity*, and other such qualities—yet it is transcendent, both in that it has an endless complexity that goes beyond whatever we may at any one time capture of it, and in that the very concepts of the moral and personal understanding in which we try to capture that world can be said themselves to have an endless 'depth': there is more to *love*, for example—and even to *simplicity* and *spontaneity*—than what figures in our partial conceptions of those things.

5   *The Sovereignty of Good*

The first essay of the collection, 'The Idea of Perfection' (presented in lecture form in 1962, published in *Yale Review*, 1964), is a paper of extraordinary range and energy. The title refers to the idea (IP 28–33/321–6) that our thinking is governed by the notion that our knowledge of an individual is 'infinitely perfectible' (23/317), as also is our knowledge of a moral concept.[76] But that idea is only one contributor to the main project of the essay itself: to attack the whole picture of 'man'—the 'moral psychology'—that dominated the 'modern moral philosophy' (4/302) of the 1950s and 1960s, and to propose an alternative.[77] Instead of thinking of the will as *creator* of value, we

---

[76] Murdoch talks of the 'Idea' of Perfection to allude, I think, to Kant's Ideas of Reason: we have no empirical conception of what it would be to reach perfection (in knowledge of persons or of moral and personal concepts), but reason is driven to count on the possibility of progress in the direction of such perfection, and it constructs what might be called the Idea of an ideal limit for it; cp. IP 31.2–3/324.2, 42.18–20/333.27–9; compare the 'Ideas of Reason' in Kant's *Critique of Pure Reason* B366 ff., B377 ff, B595–9. In Kant's moral philosophy, too, the Idea of a 'holy' will is 'a practical Idea' which serves as a model for finite rational beings to 'strive toward', though it is impossible for us to reach it: 'The utmost that finite practical reason can accomplish is to make sure of the unending progress of its maxims toward this model . . . This is virtue, and . . . it can never be perfect' (KpV Ak. 5: 32–3).

[77] The phrases 'moral psychology' and 'modern moral philosophy' (as a term for an object of attack) have become specially associated with Elizabeth Anscombe, but their usage may have at least as much to do with Murdoch. A great stream of articles by well-respected philosophers attributes to Anscombe in her article 'Modern Moral Philosophy' (1958) a demand for an 'adequate moral psychology'. (Try a Google search for 'Anscombe adequate "moral psychology"'.) One author indeed asks, 'What did Anscombe mean by moral psychology?'. Which would be an interesting question, except that the phrase 'moral psychology' is one that Anscombe never employed in that famous article—and it is equally absent from her book *Intention* (1957). (What Anscombe talks of is our need for an 'adequate *philosophy of psychology*' and an investigation of the 'concepts' of 'action', 'intention', 'pleasure', and 'wanting' ('Modern Moral Philosophy', 1 (my emphasis), 15). It is interesting, therefore, that, whereas people may wonder whether 'moral psychology' either could or should best be taken as a term for an empirical rather than conceptual investigation, Anscombe's original wording invited—indeed left room for—no such further question.) And when Anscombe needed a name other than 'philosophy of psychology' for the subject she had in mind, she usually called it 'Philosophical Psychology'—the title of three series of lectures she gave in Oxford (Hilary Term 1967) and Cambridge (Lent and Easter 1973). (See the Anscombe Bibliography by J. M. Torralba at <www.unav.es/filosofia/jmtorralba/anscombe_bibliography.htm.>) 'Philosophical Psychology' was indeed the standard term among followers of Wittgenstein (as with the series of little red books by Kenny, Geach, Malcolm, Winch under the title of 'Studies in Philosophical Psychology'). All of which makes Murdoch's repeated use of the phrase 'moral psychology' in 'Idea of Perfection' (4/301–2, 10/306, 41/332) all the more distinctive. Quite how the phrase—which Murdoch used with some force—came to be associated instead with Anscombe—who seems not to have used it at all in the places where one might expect it—is perhaps a subject worthy of further investigation. Jane Heal tells me (personal communication) that neither she nor Jonathan Lear has any memory of Anscombe's using the phrase 'moral psychology' in lectures or conversations in the early- or mid-1970s: Heal's impression is that the term was, however, common currency in Cambridge by the mid-1980s—thanks, probably, she thinks, to Bernard Williams. If so, then it is quite possible that (as with the distinction between 'thick' and 'thin' moral concepts: ELP 218 n.7) Williams was presenting his own transformation of ideas that actually derived from Murdoch and Foot in his formative years (e.g. in their joint seminar with Basil Mitchell, 1954)—and that later hearers lacked or lost trace of the earlier source. (I should mention, incidentally, that the point is not to explain the arrival of 'moral psychology' as a new phrase; the phrase was a quite ordinary one, widely used in many different ways; my interest is, rather, in how it came to be given a special charge and use, in the way that is surely found in Murdoch—and that later became associated with Anscombe. People talked much in the 1950s of the moral psychology of Cudworth, Shaftesbury, Hutcheson, and Hume; they talked of Socratic and Platonic moral psychology; C. D. Broad gave lectures in Cambridge on Moral Psychology to precede his treatment of Moral Philosophy. What I think was new was the idea that philosophers, not just in the theory of free will and determinism, and not just in the history of the subject, needed to raise as a topic for continuing debate the quite general picture of human beings, in their motivations and their cognitive and moral relations to their environment. That is the task to which Murdoch applied herself using the term 'moral psychology'; it is curious that while her contribution to it was definitely more substantial than that of Anscombe, it was Anscombe who later became almost definitively associated with the phrase.)

need to recognize the possibility of talking of *vision* and *discovery* of a moral reality external to ourselves; instead of confining the term 'morality' to questions fundamentally of external behaviour, we should recognize the importance of internal moral reflection, aimed, for example, at achieving a just *view* of another person's moral character; instead of thinking of freedom as the exercise of choice responsible to nothing outside the unconstrained will of the agent, we should recognize the ideal form of freedom as simply that of doing 'almost automatically' (37/329) things that we see genuinely to be good—where the moral work lies more in the continual activity of building up and adjusting our picture of the moral character of people and things in the world, than in the moments when a particular choice seems to need to be made. Indeed, 'If I attend properly I will have no choices and this is the ultimate condition to be aimed at' (40/331).

In broad terms, the three papers in *The Sovereignty of Good* pursue one and the same program—to substitute this new conception for the 'modern' conceptions of our moral psychology and the place of morality in the world. But the material for Murdoch's attack comes from different sources in the three papers: in 'The Idea of Perfection', the material is mainly what we find ourselves 'irresistibly inclined to say'

As for 'Modern Moral Philosophy'—as a term for an object of attack: the phrase certainly became famous from Anscombe's 1958 paper which took the phrase as its title. Murdoch's 'Idea of Perfection' (1962, 1964), with its criticism of '"the man" of modern moral philosophy' (IP 4/302) is, of course, several years later. But Murdoch had been using the phrase for some time in similarly critical terms—e.g. in her 'Metaphysics and Ethics' (1955, 1957), 64 (twice). (Cf. the same article's talk of 'the modern moral philosopher' (M&E 67, twice), and the similarly critical talk of 'modern ethics' and 'certain modern philosophers' in VCM (1956): 38/79, 42n/83n.) Both Anscombe and Murdoch quite self-consciously took modernity in philosophy—at least as it actually manifested itself—to be an obstacle to good moral philosophy. But I am inclined to say that Murdoch was the one who more thoroughly tied the problems she diagnosed to the specific condition of modernity. Anscombe traced the problems to a law-based conception of morality and the now no longer generally viable idea of 'God as a law-giver' (6), and she looked back to Aristotle for a workable alternative—so one might be forgiven for worrying that the problems alleged could be attributed to the tradition of Exodus and Deuteronomy as much as to the special conditions of modernity. Murdoch, more moderately and more plausibly, traced (in VCM) the problems to a recent linguistic philosophy that ignored much of the actual variety to be found in moral phenomena—and she developed her historical diagnosis later, talking (in IP) of scientism and (in SGC) of Romanticism—; and she recognized plenty of philosophical movements—including those of 'Thomists, Hegelians, Marxists'—as providing serious alternatives to modern non-naturalism (M&E 70). And she actually found that those innocent of philosophy were also typically innocent of the problems of non-naturalism (IP 38/330). The result, I think, is that the problems Murdoch found in Modern Moral Philosophy really deserve that name: they come from the conjunction of Modernity and Philosophy—whereas the problems Anscombe found hardly do. We cannot, I think, accept quite the diagnosis of either philosopher in its entirely. (Marxists can hardly be accused of a lack of either modernity or scientism: so the question arises how they are thought to escape the usually damaging effects of those factors. Maybe in their case a particular kind of reductionism alleviates what otherwise would have been influences toward non-naturalism.) But it seems to me that when Murdoch talks of the problems of 'modern moral philosophy' she has a fairly precise conception of the modernity and the philosophy in question and of ways to avoid or amend them; whereas Anscombe uses the phrase for a phenomenon she has not characterized as clearly, and that—as she characterizes it—is rather dubiously responsible for all that is attributed to it. It was indeed surely Anscombe who made the phrase 'Modern Moral Philosophy' famous—her 1958 paper was the object of an enormous amount of attention—; but it seems to me that Murdoch may have had a more powerful claim to the phrase and known better what to do with it.

(IP 16/312, 21/316) about ordinary cases like Murdoch's famous example of a mother changing her view of her daughter-in-law; in 'On "God" and "Good"', it is Christian ideas about prayer, transposed (with the help of Simone Weil) to fit a 'world without God' (OGG 55/344); in 'The Sovereignty of Good over other Concepts', it is Platonic ideas about beauty and the *technai* (i.e. crafts or disciplines like mathematics or language-learning), as introductions for our approach to the Good—transformed again in Murdoch's hands and supplemented with a much greater role for art than Plato recognized.

5.1 'The Idea of Perfection'

I shall concentrate here on 'The Idea of Perfection' and speak more briefly of the other two papers. Since the first is, I think, extraordinarily rich and remarkably hard to survey, I shall start with what might be called an interpretative summary of it—attempting to go section-by-section through the essay, but with some filling out of allusions and references where the detail might otherwise be hard to grasp.[78] (Comments that draw more than ordinarily on material from outside the text I shall usually put in square brackets. As elsewhere, references in the form n.m relate to page n line m in *The Sovereignty of Good* (1970) and, following a forward slash, in *Existentialists and Mystics* (1997).) Apart from an introduction and some final qualifications, the article may be divided into three parts (I, II, and III below), the first of which may in turn be divided into two (Ia and Ib):

1.1–4.8 / 299.1–301.30 *Introductory comments.* The need for a 'return' from 'theories' to 'facts' (e.g. from the modern moral philosophy of Hampshire[79] to the importance of the concept of *love* in moral philosophy and the fact that the unexamined life can be virtuous). Modern moral philosophy (despite its claims to 'neutrality') has a tendency to make certain values *inexpressible* (i.e. not allowable by the rules assigned to the language); the reasons lie in 'current philosophy of mind' and a certain picture of the soul (and of its relation to the world): 'a whole moral psychology' (4/301). Murdoch will offer 'a rival soul-picture'.

—G. E. Moore has been much admired and much criticized by recent philosophers. On almost every point where critics have 'corrected' him, Murdoch will follow not the critics, but Moore himself. (Approximately: 'Good' is not a 'movable label affixed to the world' but a quality or part of the world. There may be 'vision'—not just willing (or 'choice')—of what is good. The good may be something hard to access, not simply 'the tool of every rational man'. Moral judgement may be 'contemplative' [a matter of correctly 'seeing' the moral character of things around us], rather than always action-directed.)

[78] I draw here on a Commentary on *The Sovereignty of Good* that I am preparing.

[79] R. M. Hare's *The Language of Morals* (1952) is also a prime target, though Hare appears by name only twice in the version of IP that became part of *The Sovereignty of Good* (1970) and in E&M (1997): at 12/308 and 35/327. In the original publication (in the *Yale Review*, 1964), however, there are a couple of extra sentences that became deleted from later versions, and Hare is mentioned at the end of the second paragraph.

4.9–16.12 / 301.31–311.34 (Ia) *The dominant picture of 'man' in 'modern moral philosophy' and its basis in a 'genetic' view of meaning.*

4.9 / 301.31 There is a standard picture of man, e.g. in Hampshire's *Thought & Action*:[80]

    (1) The core of a man's existence and moral life is overt action;

    (2) imagery for describing such action typically comes from metaphors of *touch*: *moving* things around in the world;

    (3) what counts as 'real' is what meets a scientific criterion of interpersonal public recognizability;

    (4) the 'inner' is parasitic on the 'outer', and, if not linked with it, has only a 'hazy' or 'shadowy' (and derivative) existence;

    (5) action is pictured as the upshot of Will and Reason together (Will being autonomous and personal, Reason being governed by the impersonal rules of a 'public' system).

6.11 / 303.21 Hampshire's lecture 'Disposition & Memory' adds: an ideally rational man would find his motives in 'satisfying his instinctual needs' and would employ ideally accurate awareness of the objective 'features of the situation' (to maximize the efficacy of his means to those ends). An 'interminable analysis' by a psycho-analyst (i.e. an imaginary endless analysis that would supposedly reveal all of a person's past memories that might influence his actions) might make possible a deterministic prediction of the person's actions; but there would still be (Hampshire thinks) a role for 'personal verification' (i.e. for the subject to decide either to accept the analysis and prediction or to reject them). Murdoch will argue (26/ 320) that this correctly recognizes the importance of a person's history and past experience, but treats it in a fundamentally impersonal way, under the influence of 'an old-fashioned conception of science'.

7.13 / 304.15 *Comments.* On this picture, morality is like shopping (i.e. a matter of merely 'choosing' things on the basis of whatever we might will or want). (By contrast, (e.g.) a Marxist critique would be concerned with the 'right' goods (those that would meet our needs), not merely with the goods we might want or be inclined to 'choose'.) Note how:

    (6) The Will, as 'pure choice', finds its perfect expression in the 'empty' moral term 'good'—which can (at least, apparently) be applied to more or less anything at will.

This picture can be described as behaviourist, existentialist, utilitarian, and Kantian. . . . The 'keystone' of the view is (4) and the 'genetic' theory of meaning that seems to support it.

10.8 / 306.29 The view can be seen as a special application of the 'genetic' theory of meaning that generated Wittgenstein's attack on 'private' mental items. The meaning of a word must (so the Wittgensteinian argument runs) be fully mani-fested in the usage by exposure to which a learner can acquire the term. The

---

[80] I have numbered six characteristic theses of Hampshire's—and later of Murdoch's—with a view to bringing out the central matters of debate between them; but the list is selective.

meaning of a word is a matter of public usage and the following of public rules—
and 'inner' entities are (a) of 'no use' for those matters, and in any case (b) (for
either empirical or logical reasons) non-existent. Applying this to psychological
language, Wittgenstein and his followers conclude that terms like 'pain' and
'anger' can be used only in connection with overt characteristics of behaviour.
Applying it to moral language, Wittgenstein's academic followers have derived
the picture sketched above. The methods of approach have been refined; objections can be replied to. The results have been sound in destroying sense-datum
theories (cp. 25/319) and 'the misleading image of the infallible inner eye' (15/
311); but the result is the elimination of what is not public, overt, and accessible in
accordance with a scientific model of objectivity; while [in the existentialist
rhetoric of Hampshire and much Anglo-American moral philosophy] the will is
set aside ('outside the machinery' of objective nature and public rules: 16/311),
and linked with a mode of knowledge that sets it apart from ordinary natural
things:[81] it becomes 'footloose, solitary, substanceless' (16/311).

16.13–23.33 / 311.34–318.6 (Ib) *An 'alternative view': The example of M and D and what*
we would like to say but (on the standard view) cannot.

16.13 / 311.34 These are disturbing conclusions (though some will be happy with
them: 'temperament will play its part' in determining our response). Consider a
mother M who changes her view of her daughter-in-law D: she first finds D
'good-hearted' but 'unpolished and lacking in dignity and refinement', 'sometimes positively rude, always tiresomely juvenile'. But the mother reflects on
factors that may have influenced her (e.g. her own conventionality, prejudice,
narrow-mindedness, and snobbery) and makes the effort to bring a 'careful and just
attention' to the object which confronts her. And as she 'observes' or 'reflects' on D,
motivated by 'love or justice', she finds that her 'vision' of D alters: D is 'discovered' to be 'not vulgar but refreshingly simple', 'not undignified but spontaneous',
and so on. There is a morally important change in the mother's mind, but (as the
story is told) no change in her outward behaviour.

19.4 / 314.6 There are technical ways in which the existentialist-behaviourist may try to
accommodate the example while maintaining his basic view, talking e.g. of changes
in M's dispositions to behave or to talk; or insisting that the content of any 'inner'
occurrence is still fixed in terms of (i) the public meaning of the symbols the thinker
would use in expressing or reporting that occurrence; and (ii) the public rules on the

---

[81] Murdoch is thinking of Hampshire's distinction between knowledge of action from the *agent's* own
standpoint and knowledge from a '*spectator's* point of view' (*Thought & Action* 108; cp. 103–8, 174, and 275
(Postscript to the 1982 edn.)): he argues that agent's knowledge provides a kind of freedom that is immune to
being undermined by the possibility of a spectator's predictions. (See below, fn. 84.) Murdoch's implied
objection is not to the claim that there is a special form of self-knowledge; it is to the triviality and smallness of
the life of freedom that Hampshire recaptures for the self—and to the supposedly scientific requirements of
publicity and 'objective' rule-governedness, which result in a diminished conception of moral and personal
life.

significance of the employment of those symbols in particular contexts. Things can be said on both sides. But this is 'one of those exasperating moments in philosophy when one seems to be being *relentlessly prevented* from saying something which one is *irresistibly impelled* to say' (my emphasis).

22.9 / 316.29 What we *want* ('as yet without justification') to say includes:

(1′) There are acts of mental moral reflection that may not show up in overt action.

(2′) For such acts, the imagery that suggests itself is of moral *vision*.

(4′) Such acts are not 'hazy' or minor; they may connect with the whole 'fabric of being' of a person.

(6′) The content of such perceptions is particularly well expressed in our use of 'secondary moral terms' (e.g. 'rude', 'refreshingly simple'). (31–32/324 will say more about how we learn such terms; and 42/333 about how they connect more directly with action than 'good' does.[82])

(3′) The mother's activity of moral reflection does not fit Hampshire's requirements of intersubjective observability; but that is not because the activity is 'hazy' or less real, but because it is *personal* and *moral*—and the moral and personal do not (and should not be expected to) meet the requirements that Hampshire derives from his conception of science.

(5′) *Freedom* is a matter not of the Will 'leaping about', but of *progress* in *seeing justly* and *lovingly*—something that is 'infinitely perfectible'.

23.34–34.22 / 318.7–327.3 (II) *What makes moral concepts fail to fit the genetic theory and the requirement of publicly checkable application: The Perfectibility of our grasp of moral concepts and our application of them.*

23.34 / 318.7 Rather than merely prolonging a battle between these two opposed conceptions (under (Ia) and (Ib)), we need a 'change of key': a reconsideration of the idea of the real as the publicly observable—an idea which derives from 'an uncriticised conception of science'. Hume believed in hard little mental atoms; 20th-century philosophy (e.g. with Austin's attack on sense-data) has turned its back on such items in the mind, but it still keeps the idea of the *real* as the *impersonally identifiable* (approximately: what is identifiable by just anyone from just any point of view). J. L. Austin gives up on hard little ('objective') items in an internal mind-world but substitutes for them a no less objectivist conception of hard objective items in an external language-world. (And a certain reading of Wittgenstein's conception of language as rule-governed[83] persuades people that 'logic' makes such conceptions inescapable.)

---

[82] The point is one which Bernard Williams expresses by saying 'thick' moral concepts are both 'world-guided' and 'action-guiding' (ELP 141; cp. 129–30, 140–5).

[83] Murdoch has in mind what we might call impersonal objectivist interpretations of Wittgenstein, according to which following a rule would be something like executing a formula that was *publicly* stateable, in the sense of being expressible and comprehensible to just any intelligent being regardless of 'point of view'. Hampshire does indeed seem to propose this kind of conception. ('*To give a sense* to any expression which replaces "so-and-so" [in ostensive explanations in the form "This is a so-and-so"] is *to give instructions for*

25.17 / 319.15 This conception has trouble finding a place for persons and morality. There is an endless perfectibility in our knowledge of a moral term and our knowledge of an individual; and this refutes the 'genetic' view of meaning. 'Repentance may mean something different to an individual at different times in his life' (and something similar will be said of 'love' and 'courage': 28–9/322): even the *standard* (and the 'checking procedure') for a person's application of these concepts may vary with time and personal experience, rather than being constantly tied to the minimal 'public' meaning found in any 'competent' usage of the term—and the more developed understanding of the term will not be 'genetically' analysable in terms of the original usage of it.

26.19 / 320.11 Hampshire may claim that psychoanalysis is a science capable of doing justice to this 'deepening' of understanding over time: an 'ideal' analysis would bring to light all the memories that might influence a person's development (and, therefore, any development in her understanding of moral concepts and of persons). But (a) psychoanalysis is 'a muddled embryonic science' and (b) the idea of an 'ideal analysis' is a mythical one (or else derivative from the idea of what, e.g. God might see in a person's mind, which in turn derives from the idea of what is there anyway to be seen). In any case, why should science be thought to be a definitive test (for, e.g. whether a person has genuinely *repented* or not)? 'This is a *moral* question; and what is at stake here is the liberation of morality, and of philosophy as a study of human nature, from the domination of science: or rather . . . of inexact ideas of science.'

27.14 / 320.37 Existentialism responds (to the threatened domination) by giving the individual an ability to 'fly in the face of the facts'. But even a full psychoanalytical (or other scientific) explanation to M of her conduct would not *confine* her—though the reason (why her freedom would remain unconstrained) is not (a) that M can leap outside causal law (as the Existentialists want) or can act as someone 'blind' to the reasons incumbent upon her; nor (b) that, with additional knowledge, M has additional freedom (as Hampshire wants to say[84]). The reason is (c) that she uses moral concepts, which set up a 'different world' from that of science.

---

distinguishing "so-and-so's" from anything else' (Hampshire, TA 15–16, my emphasis). I take it that the terms of the instructions are intended to be governed by a requirement that applications of them be publicly establishable by just anyone.) We see how radically—in rejecting this and insisting instead on a conception of concepts and facts (and therefore, one presumes, rules) as things that may well be graspable or grasped only by people with a particular 'point of view'—Murdoch was breaking with many of her contemporaries: fighting with them over the way to develop the heritage of Wittgenstein. See also McDowell's distinction between the 'third-personal' and the 'objective', in 'Aesthetic Value, Objectivity and the Fabric of the World' §4; cf. 'Values and Secondary Qualities' §3 (last par.); 'Wittgenstein on Following a Rule' (1984), §§11, 12, 14.

[84] Ch. 3 of Hampshire's *Thought and Action* argues (among other things) for a link between freedom and knowledge: 'A man becomes more and more a *free* and responsible agent the more he at all times *knows* what he is doing' (177, my emphasis). Hampshire is keen (129–30, 173–8, 190) to defeat what might seem a threat to freedom, from scientific determinism—which Hampshire does not want to claim is false, but rather, in a curious way that draws on existentialism, itself grist to the mill of freedom. If someone presents me with an inductive prediction of some future action of mine, this is no reason to conclude that I am less free in the matter. I have a choice. If (1) I accept the prediction, then a third party will take me to be accepting the

28.9 / 321.26 What is distinctive about moral concepts by contrast with those of science?—A person's grasp of moral concepts typically deepens with experience, and experience varies from person to person and period to period. The roles of the historical individual and of perfectibility of grasp destroy the genetic theory of meaning: 'since we are human historical individuals the movement of understanding is onward into increasing privacy', though also (ultimately) 'in the direction of the ideal limit'.

29.21 / 322.30 These views are not particularly new. (They connect with Plato, and Christianity, and with talk of 'concrete universals'.[85]) They fit with the conceptions of ordinary people: they are not 'esoteric'. And they accord with one aspect of Kant (e.g. in his talk of Ideas of Reason): 'His is not the "achieved" or "given" reason which belongs with "ordinary language" and convention, nor is his man on the other hand totally unguided and alone. There exists [for Kant] a moral reality'.

31.25 / 324.22 How 'deepening' of our grasp of concepts occurs: We learn by *looking* (e.g. as M attends to D).[86] There are ways in which one person may come to understand another person's local, or contextually private, terms: through hearing uses of a term in a context of shared 'attention' to 'a common object', and (with more theoretical terms) through learning more of the other person's 'general theory'. There is no 'ordinary world of rational argument' that we can take as common among all competent speakers of a language [as Hare seems to think]; ordinary empirical privacy is a fact (along with a more distant prospect of ultimate mutual comprehensibility in principle): 'Language is far more idiosyncratic than has been admitted.' 'Human beings are obscure to each other, in certain respects which are particularly relevant to morality'.

---

inductive considerations as actually 'constitut[ing] a good *reason*' for performing or attempting the action in question; and the acceptance 'cannot disguise . . . [my] unavoidable freedom of action' (130). If, on the other hand, (2) I do not 'accept' the prediction in the way Hampshire envisages, then (he says) I cannot have any confidence in the prediction. (And the recognition of a relevant causal uniformity 'is a first step towards finding the means of *evading its effects* by trying to alter the initial conditions' (190, my emphasis).) There are difficulties. Compulsive behaviour may constitute a challenge to (1); as also may the point that inductive considerations can be stated in terms that are predictively impressive yet surely not of a kind to be taken as *reasons* for acting in the way described at all.

[85] Why or how?
(1) Plato treats our understanding of the Good, and even of the lesser virtues, as something essentially progressive; see e.g. the images of Line and Cave in *Rep.* 509c–511e and 514a–17a; and the progressive approach to the Form of Beauty in *Symposium* 210a–212a.
(2) Christianity illustrates both a kind of particularity and a kind of historicity: it places the individual Jesus as a central figure to be followed, and it implies that there are moral conceptions (whether one accepts them or not) that are only accessible to people in the accidental position of having been born into a place and time from which they can look to his example.
(3) F. H. Bradley and the British Hegelians were interested in the notion of a concrete universal, i.e. a universal not sharply separable from (nor graspable independently of) the perceptible concrete, nor from other related universals.

[86] Murdoch is using a conception of attention that (as she says at 34/327) she borrows from Simone Weil. In the present context, the idea is, I think, that, from close and just *attention* to D, M sees *both* how badly the term 'vulgar' (for example) actually fits her, *and* (more generally) how doubtfully excellent the term itself (in its unreconstructed usage) is.

34.23–42.32 / 327.4–334.2 (III) *From our new picture we can derive a better conception of Freedom and of the relation of Will and Reason.*

34.23 / 327.4 We have reached a new picture: 'the characteristic and proper mark of the active moral agent' is to direct 'a just and loving gaze . . . upon an individual reality' [i.e. in the central case, upon another person].

35.15 / 327.28 *Moral choice: a phenomenon misunderstood by the existentialists.* Modern British philosophers emphasize that, given his view of the 'facts', a person is always free in his choice of what is to be done and what to take as his 'reasons'. —But is this realistic? In some cases—with 'difficult and painful choices'—, there is indeed often a 'strange emptiness' at the moment of choosing: a sense of not being determined by reasons. To explain this phenomenon, (a) Kantian Existentialists [like Hare] say we are *free to decide our reasons*;[87] (b) the Surrealist Existentialists [like Sartre, at times] say *there are no reasons* [i.e. we must choose 'arbitrarily']; while (c) there is a tendency in extreme Existentialists (like Dostoevsky) to fall into fatalism, saying there is no free choice at all.

In fact, (d): We should pay more attention to the moral life that goes on at times *other* than the moment of choice. Choice takes place against the background of the kind of vision one has learned to have. ('I can only choose within the world I can *see*'.) *Attention* and 'moral imagination' are *continually* building our appreciation of value; so we should not be surprised 'that at crucial moments of choice most of the business of choice is already over'.[88] Acting 'almost automatically' at the moment of choice may be a sign, not of *absence* of reasons or of a place for arbitrary 'choice', but of the clarity of our *recognition* of the reasons (seeing, e.g. some particular thing that needs to be done). Thus, freedom is not 'a grandiose leaping about unimpeded at important moments', it is 'a small piecemeal business which goes on all the time'.

37.30 / 329.30 Freedom is knowledge of the reality revealed by 'just attention'. (To be free is to see what is seen by a person who sees the world with justice and

[87] In Hare's view, when a person makes a moral judgement like, e.g. 'You shouldn't smoke in this railway compartment', there stands behind it some such 'reason' or 'general principle' as 'One should not unnecessarily harm or endanger the health of children': and such 'reasons' are to be understood as universal prescriptions or imperatives chosen 'freely' by the individual. See Hare, *The Language of Morals*, 176–8, and 68–78. There is indeed some plausibility in calling such 'general principles' *reasons* when the latter term is understood in the ordinary way—as applying to more or less fundamental moral judgements, standing in a rational relation of at least partial support to a further conclusion, and themselves having their own rationale or grounding, whatever that may be. Whether they can maintain the status of being *reasons* if they are understood instead merely as universal prescriptions (e.g. 'Do not unnecessarily harm or endanger the health of children!') 'freely' chosen— perhaps on no better basis than an arbitrary whim—is, of course, highly contentious.

[88] Murdoch's point is made vividly in some wonderful comments by Tolstoy on Dostoevsky (complete with an emphasis on the role of reflection and consciousness rather than overt action):

True life does not take place where large external changes occur, where people move, collide, fight, kill one another. It takes place where hardly-at-all differentiating changes are made. / Raskolnikov's real life did not take place when he was killing the old woman or her sister. . . . / His real life took place where he was thinking about whether or not he ought to live in Petersburg, whether or not he should accept money from his mother, about questions which had nothing to do with the old woman. The decision whether or not he would kill the old woman was made then, in that animal sphere of life completely independent of reality. Those decisions were not made when he stood in front of the other woman with an axe in his hand, but rather when he was not yet acting but only thinking, when only his consciousness was active, when barely perceptible changes were taking place in that consciousness. (Leo Tolstoy, 'Why do men stupefy themselves?' (1890), extract transl. G. Gibian, in F. Dostoevsky, *Crime and Punishment*, ed. G. Gibian (1964, 1975, 1989), 487–8.)

attentiveness: who sees, e.g. that D is not undignified but spontaneous.) And—as is 'obvious' also to serious common sense—goodness is a matter of 'refined and honest perception of what is really the case': a kind of 'vision' that is not the result of merely 'opening one's eyes' but of a kind of 'moral discipline'. (Existentialist *Angst* is the Will's fright at the fact that the world is now '*compulsively* present' to it [i.e. that there are facts that, when the good person is aware of them, compel her to act accordingly], and the Will is dismayed to find it cannot be all that it had pretended to be.) Properly understood, the will becomes something like a principle of 'obedience' to (accurately perceived) reality—something that saints speak of and artists understand.

40.15 / 331.35 *Moral Psychology*. Will and Reason are, therefore, not wholly separate faculties: man is not a combination of an 'impersonal rational thinker' and a 'personal will' [i.e. of objective 'reason' and subjective 'choice', or of 'belief' and 'desire']; he is 'a unified being who sees, and who desires in accordance with what he sees'. Reality becomes 'that which is revealed to the patient eye of love' [and it includes, e.g. D's moral character, therefore, no less than her scientifically recognized qualities]. And these conceptions are not 'unfamiliar' to the ordinary person.

41.3 / 332.18 One merit of this view is that art and morality can be seen as part of a single struggle: virtue in both domains is 'selfless attention to nature'. (Cézanne strives to present the things before him in his painting, and—in his rapt attention to them— can be said to lose or forget himself, and to disappear as an ego; similarly, the moral agent strives accurately to see the moral character and needs of objects around, and—as he attends to them—his ego seems to recede: cp. OGG 59/348.)

41.30 / 333.15 *A point connecting moral language and moral psychology*: The existentialist-behaviourist has a world that is 'devoid of normative characteristics'; hence he can get along with just the 'most general and empty' terms like 'right' and 'good'— corresponding to the 'emptiness' [i.e. the unconstrainedly 'choosing' character] of the will. For Murdoch, by contrast, the work in moral thought could be done wholly by the 'secondary, specialised words' (like 'spontaneous', 'gay': cf. 18/313, 23/317, 31–2/324)—and these terms connect more immediately with action. ('Compelled by obedience to the reality he can see', the agent will say 'This is A B C D' (using 'secondary', normative-descriptive terms) and 'action will follow naturally'.)

42.13 / 333.21 *The Good*. But to say this is not 'to demote or dispense with' the term 'good'; it is to restore it to the dignity it had before G. E. Moore.[89] Good is to be understood in relation to the Real and to Love. *Goodness* is an exercise of *love* (namely, loving attention to people and things); it is a matter of obedience to *reality*

---

[89] Murdoch returns cyclically, near the end of the article, to the topics of Moore and the Good, which she introduced near the start (3/300–1). The point is presumably, that *good* in its full generality is something we will only thoroughly understand (a) *via* an understanding of its connections with the high-level concepts of *what is the case* and of *loving attention* (which connects us with what is the case) and (b) *via* an understanding of more specific types of the good, like the spontaneous and the courageous, and of the not so good, like the mean and snooty. Hare, by contrast, attempts, so to speak, to parachute direct onto the summit and to tell us what it's like—and if he connects the good with a higher-level concept it is that of *choice* (cf. OGG 58.4–10/347.5–10).

(recognizing the moral character and needs of people and things in the environment, and acting accordingly). It is indefinable, in being as various as (the different kinds of moral character to be found in) *reality*.

42.33–end / 334.3–end *Some Qualifications and Clarifications.*

At the heart of Murdoch's argument is the example of a mother M trying to get a juster view of her daughter-in-law D; it is the story of a change in 'vision' (17/313).[90] And out of it, Murdoch derives an ambitious replacement for the whole picture of mind and world presented to us in 'modern moral philosophy'.

At the first stage in Murdoch's story, the mother finds the daughter-in-law 'inclined to be pert and familiar, insufficiently ceremonious, brusque, sometimes positively rude, always tiresomely juvenile'. 'M does not like D's accent or the way D dresses. M feels that her son has married beneath him' (17/312). But the mother begins to reflect. She says to herself: 'I am old-fashioned and conventional. I may be prejudiced and narrow-minded. I may be snobbish. I am certainly jealous. Let me look again.'[91] Making an effort, she finds that 'her vision of D alters': 'D is discovered to be not vulgar but refreshingly simple, not undignified but spontaneous, not noisy but gay, not tiresomely juvenile but delightfully youthful, and so on' (17–18/313). And a main line of argument derives a kind of moral realism or 'naturalism' directly from this kind of case: for if we can take at face value M's perceptions—if we can accept Murdoch's description of the mother's change, and accept that what she sees when she sees 'justly or lovingly' (23/317) is indeed there to be seen—, then we can conclude that D is indeed ('in the world', so to speak) 'not undignified but spontaneous, not noisy but gay' and so on; and we can acknowledge the importance of something like *vision* of those characteristics.[92]

The second part of the paper proposes a more general perspective within which this view can be maintained and defended: and it raises objections to a kind of scientism that would rule it out (esp. 25–6/319–20, 33–4/326–7). Instead of allowing into reality

---

[90]   The story is sketched at 17.6–19.3/312.22–314.5; what the existentialist-behaviourist might say about it is given at 19.4–21.29/314.6–316.15, and what Murdoch herself wants to say at 21.30–23.33/316.29–318.5, with a further account of the process of moral progress in such a case at 31.25–33.11/324.22–325.35.

[91]   Note the obstacles to moral perception cited here: on other occasions, Murdoch classifies such things particularly under the headings of social 'convention' and 'neurosis' (e.g. SBR 268–9 and ff.). For more on this, see Margaret Holland's piece in the present collection.

[92]   'Is not the metaphor of vision almost irresistibly suggested ...?' (22/317). Murdoch is repeatedly explicit that such talk is, precisely, metaphorical: 'We develop language [and, in particular, moral and personal language] in the context of looking: the metaphor of vision again' (33/326). But where there is metaphor, we must not imagine that the philosopher ought to be trying to substitute some non-metaphorical description in its place: 'Metaphors are not merely peripheral decorations or even useful models, they are fundamental forms of awareness of our condition' (SGC 77/363). (The metaphor of moral seeing she traces particularly to *The Republic*: F&S 439.30: one might cite, e.g. *Rep.* 520c, quoted above in fn. 24.) I am not sure if Murdoch uses precisely the phrase 'moral perception' common in academic discussions today. But 'perception' certainly appears (as when goodness is connected with 'a refined and honest perception of what is really the case' (IP 38/330)). And 'vision' and 'moral vision' show up frequently in a variety of ways—both for a general moral outlook (e.g. M&E 71.8–9, 73.18 ('deep differences of moral vision'), VCM, *passim*, esp. 42.5–7/83.3–4) and for more particular perceptions (cp. IP 35.7–8/327.22, describing the opposition view).

only what meets a 'scientific' requirement of public observability or decidability by 'objective observers' (24/318), we should allow the world to contain all that meets the gaze of a just and loving moral perceiver.[93] If we do so, we will allow into the world cases of 'normative characteristics' (42/333)—something like the 'moral facts' of VCM (54/95)—the kinds of thing that M reports using such 'normative-descriptive' terms as 'spontaneous' and 'gay' (18/313, 22–3/317, 31/324, 41–2/333). If we do not do so, we have trouble recognizing persons in the world at all. We must learn to live with the idea that reality contains features which are accessible only to creatures with a certain kind of subjectivity or with concepts that are grasped and shared by only a limited number of people.[94] 'The idea of "objective reality" . . . undergoes important modifications when it is to be understood, not in relation to "the world described by science", but in relation to the progressing life of a person' (26/320).

At some level, the way the M and D example operates is, I think, fairly simple. But it may be worth mentioning two ways in which the argument may seem to bring its main target only gradually into focus, or to approach it from an odd angle. It may seem at first that Murdoch's prime concern is with limitations of behaviourism and those who will not give a place to the moral reflections *in M's mind*; it turns out, however, the more radical question concerns what might be called the things that M is thinking about *in the world*: D and her moral characteristics. Secondly, in the middle section of the paper, it may seem that Murdoch is using the infinite perfectibility of our understanding of a concept and a person mainly as an objection to 'genetic' or behaviouristic accounts of the content of moral concepts. It turns out, I think, that her real target is not behaviourism in particular but scientific naturalist conceptions of persons in general. The concern with infinity, which initially looks like a special objection to a particular sub-Wittgensteinian theory of meaning, turns out to be part of a larger—very Kantian—objection to the idea of the *real* as consisting merely of the *impersonally identifiable*, or merely what passes scientific tests for objective existence (23–6/318–320). I shall come back to this.

The paper is directed mainly at Stuart Hampshire—as a prime representative of 'modern moral philosophy'—along with existentialism, as what might seem the main alternative available to it.[95] The choice of Hampshire may cause some readers difficulty—

---

[93] 'What is really the case' includes 'what confronts one' as a result of a 'perfectly familiar kind of moral discipline' (IP 38/330). 'When M is just and loving she sees D as she *really* is' (37/329, my emphasis).

[94] Cf. VCM 41/82: 'Communication of a new moral concept cannot necessarily be achieved by specification of factual criteria open to any observer ("Approve of *this* area!") but may involve the communication of completely new, possibly far-reaching and coherent vision; and it is surely true that we cannot always understand other people's moral concepts'. (A fn. refers us to Philippa Foot's 'When is a principle a moral principle?' (PASS 1954).)

[95] Murdoch with deliberate irony sometimes lumps the two groups together—and talks of Hare, Hampshire, and Ayer as 'existentialist' along with Sartre (35/327). This was of course something of a slap in the face to the self-image of the anglophone philosophers. Quite apart from the fact that the analytic-continental divide had recently taken a canonical form with 'analytic' philosophers defining their positions in explicit rejection of the existentialists and those associated with them (e.g. in Carnap's and Ayer's ritualized ridicule of Heidegger's '*nichts nichtet*', 'nothing noths'), Hare had for years been taking Sartre and 'the existentialist' as a target in his arguments to show that moral statements had to be 'universalisable'. (See

both in that Hampshire's work is less familiar today, and in that he was never a writer of academic moral philosophy in the way, for example, of Hare's *Language of Morals* (1952) or C. L. Stevenson's *Ethics and Language* (1944). There are ways to mitigate the difficulties: it may be helpful to think of Hare as being the target no less than Hampshire (as indeed he sometimes was);[96] and it may be helpful to think of the target as being the familiar Humean moral philosophy with its value-free world and belief–desire psychology.[97] But the fact is that Murdoch for her larger purposes needed Hampshire as her object, in that her objections were to much more than the names of Hare and Hume would suggest: she was wanting to show the defects even of the most scientifically easy-going, forward-looking Wittgensteinianism that the academia of the time could offer. Hampshire's Wittgensteinianism still maintained an objectivist conception of persons which needed to be dislodged: and where he found a place for freedom, it was still a kind of freedom that one might call escapist[98]—by contrast with the much more Kantian conception that dominates in the final third of Murdoch's article. With Hare and Hampshire as targets, it should be unsurprising that Murdoch talks in critical terms both of neo-Kantian moral philosophy and of academic Wittgensteinian theory of meaning; but the overall direction of the whole article can be said to be deeply Kantian and Wittgensteinian. With a Wittgensteinian attention to the variety of phenomena (of moral thought), in the absence of the straitjacket of familiar theory (dividing 'descriptive' from 'evaluative'), Murdoch reaches something like a Kantian conception of persons and their moral character—only, if anything, with a greater concern than one usually sees in Kant to integrate, so to speak, the moral and the ordinary empirical aspects of our existence within a single largely-inclusive world.[99]

Murdoch employs three main kinds of argument against the dominant picture of man in modern moral philosophy. In part I of the paper (4–23/301–18) the argument runs in terms of *what we are tempted to say* about cases like the example of the mother and her daughter-in-law; in such cases we feel 'irresistibly inclined' to say things which we are 'relentlessly prevented' from saying (21/316) by the constraints of the dominant moral philosophy: we want to say, for example, that the daughter-in-law is 'discovered to be not vulgar but refreshingly simple' (17–18/313), but the common moral philosophy has no place for such moral facts or the perception of them. The argument

e.g. R. Hare, 'Universalisability', PAS 1954–55, following E. Gellner, PAS 1954–55, 157.) What Murdoch had in mind, however, were the strange and fundamental agreements which she had long been noting between the supposedly opposing camps, especially in their conceptions of 'choice' and the will: see for example 'The Novelist as Metaphysician' (1950), E&M 105, with a wonderful 'existentialist' quotation from Ayer. And in good Hegelian spirit, she attacks the two supposedly opposing camps on their common ground.

[96] See fn. 79.

[97] Locus classicus: Hume's *Treatise of Human Nature* 2.3.3 and 3.1.1 & 2.

[98] I have in mind the central argument of *Thought and Action*, 129–130 and 173–178, 190 (see fn. 84 above).

[99] 'Man is not a combination of an impersonal rational thinker and a personal will. He is a unified being who sees, and who desires in accordance with what he sees' (IP 40/332; cf. fn. 23 above). This is directed against Hampshire, not of course at Kant; but the concern to make a unified human being is constant. Cf. also, in MGM (148, 250, 320, 399, 506–7), the presentation of us as unified beings that operate at a whole variety or continuum of different levels (a view she associates, accurately, I think, but non-obviously, with Plato)—rather than being divided, so to speak, into a 'good' bit and a 'bad' bit, or a 'higher' and a 'lower'.

seems to have the form: we are irresistibly inclined to say that *p* (e.g. that M came in the end to see D to be refreshingly simple); if we can take appearances at face value, then (setting aside cases of what we might call 'local error'[100]) we can surely conclude that *p* (e.g. that D *was* refreshingly simple).[101] Of course that will leave further work to do— to check that there is no internal incoherence in the claim (e.g. that D has such characteristics), and to investigate the theory that seemed to rule it out. But provisionally and 'as yet without justification' (22/316) we can take that view.[102]

The second part of the paper (23–34/318–27) goes more deeply behind the inconclusive battle in the first part. It might seem mainly to be a direct refutation of her rivals, building on the 'idea of perfection'. The emphasis in 'modern moral philosophy' on overt action and the 'public' derives partly from a view of meaning as determined by 'genetic', historical, and 'public' factors; that view is refuted, however, Murdoch argues, by the *infinite* or *indefinite perfectibility* of our understanding of a term like 'love' or 'repentance': a person's later, richer, and often more personal and historically specific understanding of such a term can hardly be fixed by the *origin* of her understanding of it—when she had merely some ordinary conception sufficient for her to count as a basic user of the term.[103] And that undermines the general theory of meaning behind the objections of the 'modern' opponents in the first part of the article to 'private' moral thinking (e.g. when M sees that her daughter-in-law is gay and spontaneous). But Murdoch's aims are larger: she is bringing into question the modern moral philosopher's dependence on a contestable scientific conception of reality. If our world is a world only of 'hard' scientific items, then persons in their full complexity will in a sense have no place in it. 'Moral concepts do not move about within a hard world set up by science and logic. They set up, for different purposes, *a different world*' (28/321, my emphasis). Except that that is perhaps to put the point over-dramatically. In a sense the two worlds constitute a single world—containing things of rather different sorts, corresponding to the rather different character of the different ranges of concepts we use to pick them out.

The third part of the article develops from this a conception of freedom: as, ideally, acting in accordance with the moral reality that one accurately perceives. And

---

[100] 'When M is just and loving she sees D *as she really is*' (37/329, my emphasis); whereas, in her initial view of D, she viewed her with some injustice, and, I presume, did not.

[101] There is, I think, a parallel between Murdoch's argument from ordinary moral judgements (when acceptable by the ordinary standards of the discourse) to ordinary moral facts and Fregean arguments from ordinary arithmetical judgements (under similar conditions) to the existence of arithmetical objects with their arithmetical properties. (For the latter, see e.g. Dummett, *Frege: Philosophy of Language* ch. 14, esp. e.g. 497.) There is no mention of Frege in either E&M or MGM, but he was very much in the air in Murdoch's world: he was regarded (with the Russell of 1905–18) as essential to the understanding of Wittgenstein; Austin had recently translated the *Grundlagen der Arithmetik* (1950); the Geach and Black *Translations from the Philosophical Writings of Gottlob Frege* appeared in 1952 and Dummett's 'Nominalism' in 1956—and Philippa Foot indeed lectured on the *Grundlagen* in the Spring of 1952.

[102] For discussion of the relation between M's earlier and later views of D, in terms of the notion of *seeing as*, see Richard Moran in the present volume.

[103] 'It is just the presence of this idea [namely of progress or perfection] which demands an analysis of mental concepts which is different from the genetic one' (23/318).

Murdoch adds an extremely interesting argument, from the phenomenology of moral choice, which in turn is meant to add support to her earlier proposals. At a time of momentous choice one sometimes has a feeling of 'emptiness', as if there were no reasons for the choice one is making. The sense of emptiness can be read as a sign, however, not of there being no reasons operative, but of two factors: first, that a person may act almost automatically precisely because of the clarity of his recognition of what is to be done; and, what is more, the real work of reflection and 'deciding' is largely done, not, so to speak, in the heat of the moment when an action is called for, but in the background of years of constant adjustment of movement and direction, the cultivation of some things and neglect of others, that have brought the person to the present juncture in his present condition. The phenomenon of 'emptiness' is, Murdoch argues, best explained on her own conception of freedom and morality, rather than on that of her rivals—and 'a theory, whether normative or logical, is the more attractive the more it explains' (34/327). In addition, Murdoch's view—with its account of the existentialists' *Angst* as the fright of the will at the fact that it cannot be all that it pretended (in their book) to be (38–9/330–1)—explains 'why people are obsessed' with existentialist views, whereas the latter cannot explain the attractions of a view such as Murdoch's (45/336).

I shall make some comments about the arguments of the first and especially the second part of the paper; and then end by exploring how Murdoch can meet some of the suspicions that may be raised about the conception of freedom in the third part.

In the central part of the paper, Murdoch brings in the idea of perfection as her prime means of opposing the 'genetic' theory of meaning and establishing the special character of the personal and moral reality that we need to recognize. It is not, however, always clear, I think, quite which kinds of perfection Murdoch has in mind and how precisely they are supposed to contribute to the argument. Murdoch argues, for example, that knowledge of a person is always endlessly improvable, that there is always 'an inevitable imperfection' to our 'love' or 'knowledge of an individual' (28/321). This is surely true—and it may contribute to characterizing the special character of the moral and personal realm—; but it is not clear how much the point might undermine genetic or historical theories of meaning. (Would the idea that our knowledge of the shape of Mount Everest was endlessly perfectible refute a genetic view of the meaning of terms for the relevant physical measures of shape and size?) Might it not simply be that the concepts employed in describing the object needed endless reapplication at levels of indefinitely greater detail; rather than that the concepts themselves could not be captured in a 'genetic' account?

Perhaps more damaging to the genetic theory of meaning is Murdoch's point that our grasp of moral concepts undergoes a form of 'deepening' (29/322, 31/324) as we gain in experience: hence the originally grasped public meaning of a moral term will not be the whole of its meaning. The point is, I think, both correct and important. As Murdoch says, 'we have a different image of courage at forty from that which we had at twenty' (29/322; cp. VCM 50–1n/91n). On the other hand, it is not clear how much of an objection this constitutes to genetic or historical approaches to meaning: for the supporter of genetic considerations might say that the origin of the later understanding (of, say, courage) was evidently (and in his theory recognized as being) *different* from the origin of the earlier understanding. The *genesis* of the whistle-blower's mature understanding of the word 'courage' is surely different from that of the ordinary person. (As Murdoch herself says, 'what use is made of [the concepts] is partly a function of the user's *history*' (IP 26/319): and surely a genetic theory cannot be denied attention to history.) The real object of Murdoch's attack is, I think, not the historical or 'genetic' concerns of her opponents, but rather their emphasis—within the realm of 'past experience'—upon what is 'publicly available': the external rather than the internal, and what is common to a whole linguistic community rather than special to certain individuals.

Where does that leave the main argument? The issue is confused, I think, by the fact that Murdoch's overt concerns have been somewhat overtaken by events in the middle of the article. The overt issue is whether the behaviouristic theory of meaning of part I can finally be rejected—and the behaviourist objections to the recognition of M's internal and unexpressed moral reflections be definitively dislodged. The refutation of behaviouristic theories of meaning, I think, may or may not be achieved. (It depends on what we count as 'behaviourist'. Murdoch's arguments for certain kinds of somewhat 'private' moral conceptions (e.g. of courage or repentance) seem to me good; whether they constitute an objection to a theory of understanding that requires, e.g. *manifestability in principle in behaviour* seems to me more doubtful. There may be few who know what it is like to maintain the courage of a whistle-blower exposing a corporate crime (or who have a developed theological conception and experience of repentance), but one might expect them to be able to recognize each other if they talk, and, if they do, to find plenty that they could bring each other to understand of each other.) But aside from that, we should surely anyway be quite ready to allow that M can reflect silently (without telling others) on such questions as whether D is pert and familiar or spontaneous and gay—using what surely all sides would recognize to be fairly widely shared (though not culturally colourless) concepts, in ways that involve no special privacy of understanding. So it seems to me that, for the part I argument for a form of moral realism, the part II considerations about privacy and infinity are only moderately helpful. But, I suspect, they were only moderately necessary in the first place. The argument for a kind of realism (in terms of what we find it tempting to say) was already, I think, both successful and important.

When I say the original overt concerns in part II become overtaken by events, what I mean is that the considerations about infinity take on a life of their own—as characterizing the nature of the personal and the moral, and as undermining a certain kind of scientism. In that role, how well do Murdoch's considerations work? There are some remarkable parallels between her project and Donald Davidson's famous argument a few years later, in 'Mental Events', against the possibility of psychophysical laws.[104] It is the

---

[104] D. Davidson, 'Mental Events' (1970), reprinted in his *Essays on Actions and Events* (1980). The Kantian influence in Davidson should be evident too: the paper begins with a quotation from Kant's GMS on the relation of 'freedom' and 'nature' and ends with a second quotation from the same work.

interminability (i.e. *infinite continuability*) of interpretation in terms of the mental scheme that Davidson uses as an objection to the possibility of there being psychophysical laws or any reduction of mental properties to physical ones.[105] (In Murdoch's paper it is the *infinite perfectibility* of understanding that is used as an objection to any capture of moral classifications using 'impersonal' classifications governed by a 'scientific' criterion of public observability.) Davidson argues that the *rational*—like the *moral* in Murdoch, though that category is hardly distinguishable in her from the *personal* or the *human* in general (e.g. 25/319, 34/326)—cannot be captured by an approach that insists on codifiability in public rules: 'Rationality is . . . a normative notion which by its nature resists regimentation in accord with a single public standard.'[106] Many of these claims are, I think, correct and important; but it may still be disputed whether Davidson's anti-reductionist conclusion can be reached by the route that Davidson attempts. How far is it really true that our choice of a manual of interpretation for our fellows (attributing to them mental states during some past period) is always liable to being overturned by further evidence? May it not be the case that, with certain ascriptions, within certain limits of accuracy, we are actually in a position to be quite confident of many of our attributions? (Is Davidson not in danger of building his argument on a view that is tantamount to the claim that—given the infinite possibility of reinterpretation of the evidence—we have no right ever to claim knowledge of what anyone thinks about anything?) And if on the other hand we allow that we sometimes have a decently firm understanding of each other and can make decently firm attributions of mental states to others, in what way is whatever infinitude of interpretation remains an obstacle to establishing even limited coextensiveness claims between certain psychological and physical predicates? And, incidentally, are the extensions of physical predicates not themselves open to some kind of infinite refinability?[107] Yes, one might say, but not in the same way. All of which seems to me to leave us in a position where the issues can be described as difficult and unconcluded. So my own inclination is to think that an argument for realism about the mental or the moral (as in part I of Murdoch's paper) may be more secure than an argument for a definite and general irreducibility of these phenomena (as in part II). The special character of our approach to the moral (and to the mental)—via a scheme of explanation governed by constitutive ideals of rationality

---

[105] 'Beliefs and desires issue in behaviour only as modified and mediated by further beliefs and desires, attitudes and attendings, *without limit*' ('Mental Events', 219, my emphasis). 'An arbitrary choice of translation manual would be of a manual acceptable in the light of all possible evidence, and this is a choice we cannot make' (223).

[106] Davidson, 'Replies to Essays X–XII', in B. Vermazen and M. B. Hintikka, eds., *Essays on Davidson* (1985), 245. For Murdoch, 'The active "reassessing" and "redefining" which is a main characteristic of live personality often suggests and demands a checking procedure which is a function of an individual history' (IP 26/320): that is, even the yardstick against which we measure something when we judge it in moral terms, is not something that can be characterized in simple non-personal terms or even universal public terms (the 'single public standard' in Davidson's characterization).

[107] As Collingwood claims: 'There is no finality in any knowledge whatever. There is nothing about which we have any knowledge at all, about which there is not more to know.' ('Reality as History' (1935), in *The Principles of History and Other Writings* (1999), 170–208, at 189).

and excellence—is indeed radically different from the character of our approach to the physical, using the explanatory schemes of the physical sciences. Whether that means that the items and types individuated in the former types of discourse are always proof against identification with items and types individuated in the latter, seems to me less clear. But anti-scientism, in at least one form, does not depend upon it: the scientism that wishes to recommend, as our best route to understanding the mental or the moral, one that employs an explanatory system modelled on the physical sciences and turns its back on the explanatory scheme in which those ranges of phenomena have their primary home, is one that may be in danger of losing hold altogether of those phenomena. And to reach that conclusion, I think, the central argument of the second part of Murdoch's essay gives us the materials that are required.

In her review of Simone Weil's *Notebooks*, Murdoch repeats Weil's words: 'We should pay attention to such a point that we no longer have the choice.'[108] In what I have called the third part of 'The Idea of Perfection' (34.23–42.32 / 327.4–334.2), Murdoch defends Weil's view that in ideal cases, attending to the situation and its circumstances will make clear to the good agent what is to be done, without leaving any serious room for a 'choice' of other actions. Some people find strange the thought that cases presenting in some sense no choice should also be thought to be cases— indeed ideally good cases—of *freedom*.[109] This is no place to pretend to argue the issue to a conclusion. But it may be worth examining some of the reasons one might give— and answering one main objection.

Murdoch's disagreements with the existentialists on choice and freedom are some- thing of a rerun of Descartes's disagreements with the scholastics who supported the 'freedom of indifference'.[110] The freedom of 'indifference', claimed for us by the Jesuit theologian Luis de Molina (1535–1600), involved the power *indifferently* to choose an act and not to choose it.[111] (Molina argued that God's omniscience with respect to acts not yet chosen by us was therefore only *scientia conditionata* or *media*, i.e. knowledge of what each of us *would* do *if* certain conditions were to obtain—which (so it was argued) left us free indifferently to choose the action or not.) The problem that occurred to many objectors, was that, if a certain act was evidently *better* than any alternatives that presented themselves as options, then to be indifferent among those options seemed a sign not of freedom but of failure to recognize the goodness of the act in question. (After all, on Aquinas's view, 'We may call *indifferent* all those acts which are either equally good or equally bad'.[112]) The objectors proposed that freedom required 'spontaneity' rather than

---

[108] Weil, *Notebooks*, 205; quoted by Murdoch in 'Knowing the void', E&M 159.

[109] For further discussion, see Margaret Holland's essay in the present volume.

[110] E. Gilson, *La liberté chez Descartes* (1913), esp. Part II chs. 3 and 5, gives a vivid picture of the debates. I can pretend here only to give a very sketchy presentation of some of the issues. See also N. Grimaldi, *Six études sur la volonté et la liberté chez Descartes* (1988).

[111] 'Potentiam quippe liberam esse, non esse aliud quam posse indifferenter elicere hic et nunc et non elicere actum ...' Molina, *Concordia liberi arbitrii cum gratiae donis* (1588–89), 23, 4–5, 1, 7, quoted in Gilson, *Index Scolastico-Cartésien* (1913, 1979), §552.

[112] Aquinas, *Summa Theologiae* Ia IIae 32 6 ad 3.

'indifference'—performing an act willingly and without constraint, whether or not performance and non-performance of the act were indifferently choosable by us.[113]

The objectors included Gibieuf (*De libertate*, 1630), encouraged by the Cardinal de Bérulle, and Jansen (in his *Augustinus*, 1640). The similarities between the 17th-century objections to indifference and Murdoch's objections to the existentialist conceptions of freedom are remarkable. Gibieuf talks of the arrogance of those claiming separation and independence from God; Murdoch protests at the arrogance of those pretending to be independent of truth and reality—in a position just to 'choose' what is to be good or bad. Bérulle talks (as Gibieuf reports in his Dedicatio) of the supporters of *scientia media* as having invented the doctrine to flatter human reason and to raise up nature; Murdoch believed the existentialists with their 'inflated and yet empty conception of the will' (OGG 76/362) did much the same. For Gibieuf, as for Augustine, submission to grace is *freedom*[114] (and for Augustine, a perfectly good person is not even capable of choosing an evil act[115]); for Murdoch 'obedience to reality' (IP 41/332) is freedom and the true office of the will.

But what is the meaning behind this devotional language and why should we accept any of it? Descartes, I think, gives good reasons, starting from the case of theoretical reasoning. Having seen in the *cogito* that, from the fact of his own thinking, 'it follows quite evidently that I exist', would it be freedom for Descartes to be able *indifferently* to conclude that he exists and that he does not? No: it would be a mere sign of ignorance or unclarity in his thought. A free thinker will be one who believes what he sees clearly to be the case, and who is lucky enough to be suitably endowed and embedded in the world, so as to see to be the case what is in fact the case (in his own domain). And the situation is parallel with morality: a free thinker is one who acts upon what he sees clearly to be good, and who is in the happy position of being suitably endowed, trained and attentive, so as to see those things to be good that are in fact good.

If I always saw clearly what was true and good, I should never have to deliberate about the right judgement or choice; in that case, although *I should be wholly free*, it would be *impossible* for me ever to be *in a state of indifference*. (Descartes, *Meditation* 4, AT VII.58, CSM ii.40; my emphasis)[116]

---

[113] Latin *spontaneitas* has as its root meaning something like *voluntariness*: the term is cognate with the adverb *sponte*, 'willingly', 'of one's own accord'. The terms reappear in the opening paragraph of Hume's *Treatise* 3.2.2: the 'liberty of indifference' is 'that which means a negation of necessity and causes', while the 'liberty of spontaneity' is 'that which is opposed to violence'—and it is only the latter which Hume is concerned to preserve.

[114] Gilson, *La liberté chez Descartes*, 300.

[115] 'In the future life, it shall not be in [man's] power to will evil, and yet this will constitute no restriction on the freedom of his will. On the contrary, his will shall be much freer when it shall be wholly impossible for him to be the slave of sin. . . . As . . . the soul even now finds it impossible to desire unhappiness, so in future it shall be wholly impossible for it to desire sin' (*Enchiridion* 105, tr. Dods; in V. J. Bourke, *The Essential Augustine* (1964, 1974), 186).

[116] Descartes believes that God's freedom is different—a freedom of indifference; since there can be no truth and no good in any sense prior to him. In Leibniz, by contrast, God himself acts out of a recognition of what is (independently) good and true. For it is 'freedom of the highest sort, to act in perfection following sovereign reason' (*Discourse on Metaphysics* sect. 3, in Leibniz, *Philosophical Essays* (1989), tr. Ariew & Garber, 37). 'It is . . . obvious how the Author of the World can be free . . . , since he acts from a principle of wisdom or perfection. Indeed, indifference arises from ignorance, and the wiser one is, the more one is determined to do that which is most perfect' ('On the ultimate origination of things' (1697), *Philosophical Essays*, 151).

This is not the place to follow the debate over what it would take for this view and Murdoch's to be vindicated. I shall mention just one ground for suspicion of it. There is, I think, certainly something strange and—if the word is not too odd—creepy about some statements that might seem to be in this same vein. Here is the Victorian biologist T. H. Huxley:

> if some great Power would agree to make me always think what is true and do what is right, on condition of being turned into a sort of clock and wound up every morning before I got out of bed, I should instantly close with the offer. The only freedom I care about is the freedom to do right; the freedom to do wrong I am ready to part with on the cheapest terms to any one who will take it of me. (T. H. Huxley, *Method and Results: Essays* (1893) 192–3)

There is, I think, something odd and priggish about regarding with satisfaction the prospect of becoming 'a sort of clock' controlled into rectitude (and superiority over one's fellows) by some higher Being. But what makes the prospect most disquieting is, I think, the fact that Huxley's vision is of supposedly doing right and thinking the truth thanks to the great Power's daily intervention—rather than out of his own *understanding* of the matter. What Leibniz and Descartes were talking of was quite different: the power to accept truths and to will good things *because one recognized* them *as* true or good— thanks to one's own understanding, not some divine intervention. And that too is what Murdoch is proposing—not the strange and mechanical goodness in Huxley. Freedom in Murdoch is the voluntary doing of what one sees to be good because one is *rationally sensitive to* the good—capable of seeing and recognizing it for what it is.

5.2 'On "God" and "Good"'

'On "God" and "Good"' was first published as a contribution to the slightly curiously-named 'Study Group on the Foundations of Cultural Unity', and cultural unity is indeed, in a way, its main topic.[117] Its concern is with the role of moral philosophy in the general culture of the time (in particular, a culture increasingly dominated by styles of thought modelled on the physical sciences—to which varieties of existentialism were for many people the only available, and all too accepting, reply); and the essay returns repeatedly to both the attractions and the dangers of any faith in 'unity'. It begins and ends slightly with the tone of a manifesto yet to be adopted by the party: 'We need...We need...' (46/337), 'there can be no substitute for...' (76/362). But at the core there is a philosophical thesis that is bold, carefully argued and, I think, plausible. It may be clearest if set out as a parallelism between two domains:

---

[117] It appeared in Marjorie Grene, ed., *The Anatomy of Knowledge: Papers presented to the Study Group on the Foundations of Cultural Unity, Bowdoin College, 1965 and 1966* (1969). The Study Group was organized by Michael Polanyi, Edward Pols, and Marjorie Grene, with the help of grants from the Ford Foundation. Presentations included Michael Polanyi on the Hungarian Revolution and (separately) on 'The Structure of Consciousness', E. P. Wigner on the 'Epistemology of Quantum Mechanics', and Sigmund Koch (a noted opponent of 'ameaningful' (i.e. meaning-avoiding) psychology) on 'Value Properties: their Significance for Psychology, Axiology, and Science'.

Just as, in Christian theology:	*so also, in morality:*
God is an object of *prayer* (a form of loving 'attention to God'),	*Good* is an object of *loving attention*,
which may be answered by *grace* (55.8–15/344.26–33),	from which we receive *energy for good action* (63.32–4/351.33–5),
which redeems us from the *sinfulness* of human nature;	which saves us from the *selfish egotism* that Freud pointed out in the human mind (51.3–26/341.9–30).

Murdoch draws an important consequence from her core discussion: that the conception of freedom and the will in modern moral philosophy must be replaced with a new 'picture of the human personality' (66/354). (Part III of the paper (66.31–71.29/354.13–358.17) develops many of the same conclusions as the final main part of IP (34.23–42.32/327.4–334.2): see the summary below.) And the main positive argument concludes with an affirmation of the importance of the idea of Good as a 'central point of reflection': '*Good, not will*'—as the existentialists had supposed—'*is transcendent*' (69/356). The 'transcendence' here turns out to be both important and modest, as we shall see in more detail later. The *goodness* (of a person) turns out to coincide more or less with *love*—in the special sense, borrowed from Simone Weil, of *loving attention*: the ability to see things as they are, 'purely, without self', in their moral and other complexity (70/357). (SGC, by contrast, ends (102/384) with a denial that Good can be identified with love—but that is, I think, because Murdoch is no longer giving 'love' the rather idealized and extended sense that she here gives it.) And that provides another parallel between the domains of morality and religion: '*One-seeking intelligence* is the image of "faith"' (70/357, my emphasis)—the thinking of a person who searches for a unity in the diversity of the moral world is Murdoch's analogue and successor to the thinking of a person who traces all things to God.

   Murdoch has, one might say, two main tasks, one practical, one theoretical. The practical task is to answer the question, 'How can we make ourselves morally better?' (52/342). The question is a pressing one—and even to ask it is to signal a rejection of Modern Moral Philosophy, which prided itself on being 'neutral' and not 'preaching'. But it must be said that the question is more fully answered in the third essay of the group than in the second. 'On "God" and "Good"' contains a diagnosis of our need—namely, to be freed from the selfish 'fat relentless ego' (52/342)—; and Murdoch tells us what would meet that need—namely, loving attention to reality. But as to how we might in practice bring ourselves to that achievement—the question of the moral education and reorientation required actually to achieve such love—, Murdoch here tells us relatively little. It is in the third essay (SGC) that Murdoch will describe a training in the virtues on a Platonic model, moving from the appreciation of Beauty, through the development of skills or *technai*, to a deepening grasp of the moral virtues.

   The theoretical task and ultimate purpose of OGG is to establish a place for moral philosophy that is capable of surviving the challenges and ambitions of science and scientistic philosophy: 'to rescue thought about human destiny from a scientifically minded empiricism' (71/358). This task is, I think, achieved and not merely announced: if (as the core of the article argues) Good can be conceived as 'a single perfect transcendent non-representable and necessarily real object of attention' (55/344), then the object of morality is something that will elude the grasp of scientific empiricism—though not, Murdoch would say, the grasp of a more inclusive empiricism.[118] In particular, the Good, conceived in that way, seems both important and incapable of being reduced 'in, for instance, Freudian terms, or Marxist terms' (60/349)—or, Murdoch might add (given the arguments of 'The Idea of Perfection', 27–8/320–1), in the terms of a scientific physicalism. Murdoch reminds us, however, that this leaves much work to be done: 'philosophers must try to invent a terminology' in which to talk clearly of the moral world and our relation to it, and in particular to show *how* 'our natural psychology' can be *altered*—as experience seems to indicate it is—by conceptions (and, one might add, facts) that lie beyond the reach of 'scientifically minded empiricism' (71/358; cp. IP 44.35–45.13/335.31–336.4). (For example, how are we to recognize a person as being motivated by seeing a need in someone they are related to? How is it that energy can be said to come, either from religious or moral attention?) That final task is one that Murdoch begins in the present paper, and continues in 'The Sovereignty of Good over other Concepts' (OGG 71.12–29/ 358.1–13 is more or less a blueprint for the whole project of SGC): a crucial part of the conceptual apparatus will be Plato's image of the Sun as the Good.

There are two more mid-level tasks that Murdoch is no less determined to achieve, one in moral psychology and one in metaphysics. The general project might seem, so far, to be high-minded but in a sense neglectful of naturalism—in danger, indeed, of seeming shamelessly indulgent to mythic quasi-religious notions that have no obvious place in an enlightened world-picture. Murdoch is, however, determined that her enquiry should be naturalistic. The world she is investigating is 'a world without God' (55/344); but there remains the task of describing, realistically and naturalistically (though with no restriction to the terms and methods merely of natural science), for example, 'by what means' God—or, at least, thinking apparently directed toward God on the part of worshippers—'affected' worshippers, producing a phenomenon that was sometimes thought of as the enjoyment of 'grace', taken as a 'supernatural assistance to human endeavour which overcomes empirical limitations of personality' (55/344). Murdoch has no wish to talk of any supernatural activity actually having been at work in such cases; but the phenomenon of additional 'energy' in the believer is real—and Murdoch wishes to give an accurate naturalistic description of it. Her first comparison

---

[118] I have in mind Murdoch's use of the word 'empiricism' not for, e.g. Humean views on concept acquisition and the scope of knowledge, but for something like a descriptive philosophy that recognizes phenomena in all their complexity as it finds them. Hegel is, for Murdoch, 'the first great modern empiricist . . . What Hegel teaches us is that we should attempt to describe phenomena' (EPM 131, cf. fn. 42 above). This may be a mid-century usage that has only rather patchily survived: 'Empiricists are the ones who keep saying, "No, that won't do. Things are a bit more complicated than that"' (Mary Midgley, *The Owl of Minerva: A Memoir* (2005), 120).

is with falling in—or out—of love with one and the same person, in accordance with the direction of one's own attention.

> That God, attended to, is a powerful source of (often good) energy *is a psychological fact*. It is also *a psychological fact . . .* , that we can all receive moral help by focusing our attention upon things which are valuable: virtuous people, great art, perhaps . . . the idea of goodness itself. (56/345, my emphasis)

There are details here that Murdoch does not investigate. The point is not merely that thinking something to be good goes with being motivated to pursue it; it seems to involve the idea that the more attentively one considers the thing in question, the more energy one has for pursuing it. (Yes, often, one might be tempted to reply. But what about the phenomenon of being *bored* by something or someone that one still takes in some sense to be good? Here, the appearance seems to be of *more* attention being accompanied by *less* energy. A person might say: Perhaps the attention in such a case is not to the detail, or not to the detail in the right way. —But then is the phenomenon (of being energized by the Good) clearly an empirical one—or are we in danger (with the demand for the attention to be 'of the right kind' or 'in the right way') of reducing to a tautology (or hardening into a rule) what initially pretended to be an empirical claim?[119] And if so, would the scheme of description be therefore invalidated, or merely be shown to have its 'flexion' and empirical application in places and ways other than those we first thought?) Murdoch does not take up such questions, but what is clear is that she wants to treat the phenomenon firmly as an empirical phenomenon, to be described as it is. And she is surely right that there have been religious people with a kind of inner energy apparently received as an unearned response to prayer and attention—as with the many cases William James reported, also as empirical psychologist, in his carefully-named book *The Varieties of Religious Experience: A Study in Human Nature* (1902). That such phenomena are sometimes morally ambiguous is well-known to Murdoch. (Note the phrase 'often good' at 56/345.) And we might ask—as Murdoch does not—how much such cases may or may not have in common with surely dubious phenomena like, for example, the strength of mind of people described as anorectic, obsessive, or fanatic. But Murdoch may still be right—and I think is—in her description of the religious cases as being of a kind with those that are at work in cases of moral attention to the good.

The other more mid-level project that Murdoch adopts is that of giving what might be called a deliberately modest account of the 'transcendence' of the good. It is, Murdoch believes, integral to our conception of the good that it is in some sense a

---

[119] I am here alluding to Wittgensteinian ideas that were very much in the air at the time Murdoch was writing. A (later published) *locus classicus*: Wittgenstein, *Remarks on the Foundations of Mathematics* (3rd edn., 1978) VI.22 ('it is as if we had hardened the empirical proposition into a rule'); *On Certainty* (1969) §96. Anthony Flew calls the move 'going into a *Conventionalist Sulk*' and '*The No-True-Briton* (or *what have you*)-*Move*' and convicts Hume of making it with his principle that all ideas are derived from impressions: see A. Flew, *Hume's Philosophy of Belief* (1961), ch. 2, esp. 25–6. See also H. Putnam, 'The Analytic and the Synthetic' (1962), in his *Mind, Language and Reality, Philosophical Papers*, vol. 2, (1975), 33–69.

conception of something transcendent. But in which sense? Murdoch gives us a modest answer, something that a naturalist (though perhaps not a simple scientific naturalist) would have no trouble acknowledging. Her conception could be described, I think, as both realist and deflationary—designed to show both that we are entitled to accept the existence or reality (in the appropriate sense) of a transcendent Good and that this existence or reality is less demanding than critics may have suspected. The Good, she says, 'lies always *beyond*, and it is from this beyond that it exercises its authority' (62/350, my emphasis). And the 'beyondness' of the Good turns out to amount to something like this: goodness is the characteristic property of *ideally accurate* perception; always *beyond*, or more than, what we find in the partial instances we encounter of it;[120] and *beyond*, or more than, what we grasp in our partial conceptions of it; and not open to simple reduction.

Here, rather than a full summary, is a slightly simplified interpretative summary, bringing out the central themes and arguments:

46.1 / 337.1 (I) *Introduction.* We have needs in moral philosophy: to recognize certain values; and for a moral psychology that would speak of the ego and connect it with virtue (recognizing the self as it really is, and speaking of how it might ideally be). Existentialism is a popular philosophy, but it is unrealistic, over-optimistic, and 'the purveyor of certain false values' (especially, sincerity and a misconceived variety of freedom). We have an inflated conception of ourselves; we have lost the idea of a (moral) reality external to ourselves; we have forgotten our own selfishness. In modern conceptions of the self [e.g. like Hampshire's], the 'will' is preserved as a centre of pure freedom, while 'belief' and 'reasoning' are surrendered to a pseudo-scientific determinism. There is a hostility to the actual self and the faculties of the self; the will has become oddly insubstantial, and isolated from the ordinary empirical psyche. [For Murdoch's response on these last issues, see also IP 40.15–41.2/331.35–332.17. 'Man is not a combination of an impersonal rational thinker and a personal will. He is a unified being who sees and who desires in accordance with what he sees' (IP 40/332).]

50.18 / 340.28 *A problem diagnosed.* The 'unambitious and optimistic' modern philosophical picture of man is unrealistic: it ignores Freud's understanding of the mind as 'an egocentric system of quasi-mechanical energy', prone to fantasy more than reason, objectivity and unselfishness.

54.24 / 344.9 (II) Are there *techniques to purify* and *reorient* this 'energy which is naturally selfish'? Plato had one answer [namely, personal love, in our first steps in an ascent to a vision of Beauty: *Symposium*, 209e–212a]; religion has recommended *prayer* [which will be explained as a *loving attention to God*]; Murdoch will suggest another answer [namely, *loving attention to the good*].

---

[120] The point needs some care in statement. A poorly-drawn circle is an imperfect instance of, none the less, perfect circularity, and we may clearly enough find it to be so. So: perfect circularity is not *beyond* what is found (imperfectly instantiated) in it, but it is *beyond* what is found (perfectly instantiated) in it.

55.7 / 344.26 The notion of *God* was the notion of 'a single perfect transcendent non-representable and necessarily real object of attention'; Murdoch will argue that moral philosophy should 'attempt to retain' a concept which has the same characteristics (namely, the concept of *Good*). Prayer is (in Christian theology) loving attention to God, to which the 'supernatural assistance' of grace may be the response. [Similarly, loving attention to the Good may supply us with a kind of additional 'energy' for good action.] We will investigate the traditional object of this attention and 'by what means' it affected its worshippers.

Good, like God, is:

55.21 / 345.1 (*a*) *an object of attention* that is a source of energy. But there is 'nothing odd or mystical about this': focusing on an object is 'natural' to human beings, and when the object is God, it is a 'psychological fact' that '(often good) energy' results. It is, similarly, a 'psychological fact' that 'we can all receive moral help by focusing our attention upon things which are valuable'.

56.24 / 345.36 (*b*) *unitary*. (False belief in unity may certainly be dangerous. But consider Courage and Justice: there is an interconnection and ultimate unity among the virtues.)

58.11 / 347.11 (*c*) *transcendent*. (Beauty can be said in some sense to be transcendent: even if the statue is broken, still 'something has not suffered from decay and mortality'. But this gives us no model as yet for understanding how Good may be said to be transcendent: our sense that there is something 'separate' and 'behind' the multifarious cases of (more or less) good action.)

61.14 / 349.32 (*d*) *perfect* and (*e*) *necessary*. Is the idea of a perfect (or absolute) good important to us? Yes. 'A deep understanding of any field of human activity . . . involves an increasing revelation of *degrees* of excellence' (my emphasis). And we take it that there is—and *must* be—such a thing as *perfect* good (rather than merely relations of better and worse): *unmixed love* goes out only to what is seen as *unmixed good* [and, Murdoch supposes, we take it that there is such a thing as unmixed love].

63.3 / 351.8 The status of these claims. (Approximately: they are an unpacking of what is integral to our experience-informed conception of Good—rather as the ontological argument is an unpacking of what is integral to the believer's experience-informed conception of God. —In saying that Good exists we must 'avoid any heavy *material* connotation of the misleading word "exist" ' (my emphasis); but we take it that the claim of existence is a matter of more than mere 'subjective conviction of certainty' on the thinker's part.)

64.8 / 352.5 (*f*) *real* (or, as it turns out: connected with *realism* and perception of the real). What does this come to? Art is the 'clue': the appreciation of beauty is 'a completely adequate entry into . . . the good life, since it *is* the checking of selfishness in the interest of seeing the real'. Similarly, the necessity of the good is '*an aspect of the kind of necessity involved in any technique for exhibiting fact*' [i.e. we *need* the idea of *ideally good* perception in the same way as—with any case of (re)presenting or 'exhibiting' facts—we *need* the idea of an *ideally accurate* presentation of those facts].

Goodness is not perceptible in the way that *beauty* is and its 'transcendence' is more puzzling (60.5–20/348.30–349.6). But we now have a good sense for this talk of *transcendence*: goodness is the characteristic property of *ideally accurate* perception (66.3–7/353.25–29); infinitely refinable *beyond* whatever provisional grasp we may ever have of it (62.20–24/350.30–34); and not susceptible of simple reduction (60.33–61.2/349.17–21).

66.20 / 354.3 Love is the faculty that takes us to the *real* [i.e. loving attention to things leads us to see them as they really are].

66.31 / 354.13 (III) *A new 'picture of human personality'* is emerging:

1. The freedom we need is 'freedom from fantasy' (something to counteract our egotistical self): the ability realistically to *see* [sc. what is morally and non-morally the case]. *Love* is what provides that liberation from fantasy.

2. Sincerity and self-knowledge are not (as existentialism supposed) particularly important.

3. Clarity of moral vision is easily corrupted by sado-masochism, and suffering mistaken for purification.

68.31 / 355.38 Further questions about Good; further work to be done.

71.30 / 358.18 (IV) *Final issues*:

72.3 / 358.25 1. Objection: What if 'none of it is true'?! Answer: 'There is . . . something in the serious attempt to look compassionately at human things which automatically suggests that "there is more than this".'

73.33 / 360.9 2. Is this just a view for an 'élite of mystics'? —No. Some sort of *mysticism* is indeed (even after the disappearance of religion) the proper 'background' to morals—namely, 'a non-dogmatic . . . faith in the reality of the Good, occasionally connected with experience'. But that is not something for an élite: 'We are *all* capable of criticising, modifying and extending the area of strict obligation which we have inherited' (my emphasis).

72.27 / 360.34 3. Status of the argument.

75.13 / 361.15 4. Ordinary personal love will not help: it is too possessive and mechanical to be a place of vision. Art shows us that the highest love is impersonal.

75.34 / 361.34 5. Two Assumptions of the argument could be challenged (namely, that 'there is no God', and that influence of religion is waning); but Murdoch is sure of her criticism of recent philosophies, especially in their inflated conception of the will. Though philosophy is not as important as art for the survival of the human race, we need 'pure, disciplined, professional speculation' to generate concepts suitable to check the growing power of science.

How exactly does Murdoch's core argument work? I shall try to describe the basic structure; the issues are of importance, I think, both in themselves and for understanding the way in which Murdoch can be described as a Platonist. (This is, I think, the first paper in which Murdoch can be said to speak as a kind of Platonist: in IP she spoke as a follower of Simone Weil, but she took her agreements with Plato to be fairly commonplace (29/322). In OGG she acknowledges her debt to Weil (50/340), and talks again of her more ordinary agreements with Plato (51/341). But Plato has now become a constant reference point (60/348, 67/354 (with Socrates's daemon), 68/355, 70/356–7, 75/361); Murdoch talks now in Platonic terms of virtues (57/346), of *technai* (65/353), and of the sun as a metaphor for the Good (70/357): she echoes Plato (e.g. on the unity of the virtues (56/346) and on the 'reorientation' of attention (56–7/345)), even while apparently talking in her own voice. And 70.1–3/356.36–8 is an echo of *Republic* 505e.) Murdoch's fundamental topic is the Good and the moral psychology of (thought about) the Good—in particular its magnetic power, attracting those who attend to it, while in turn providing a kind of energy to them. And she explores it by looking at a traditional conception of God, and the rather similar psychology of (thought about) God. Murdoch's method is to take in turn a series of attributes ascribed to God, and to explore the sense in which they can be attributed also to Good. Good, like God, can be said to be an object of attention, unitary, transcendent, perfect and necessary, and real. (Being '*non-representable*' (55/344) turns out to be much the same as being indefinable, which in turn appears under the heading of 'transcendence': the former feature will therefore be traced to the fact that the ideal Good is in some sense *beyond our grasp*.)

Murdoch's list of attributes of God is not, I think, meant to be taken as a definitive characterization of God. Indeed, if those attributes had been intended as definitive, Murdoch could hardly have recommended a faith in the reality of something that she thought possessed them all (namely, Good), while refusing a commitment to the reality of God (74/360).[121]

Murdoch takes the various attributes in turn. There is relatively little difficulty over the first two. Good is, indeed, fairly obviously (if it is an object of thought at all) (*a*) an *object of attention*—and this is one reason why it can do the job of turning us away from the egoistic self: the human mind is such that we cannot simply drop an old attachment (to the self) without finding another object for it. (It is worth noting, however, that we are told later in the paper that 'the Good itself is not visible' (70/357): we see other things 'in its light' (62/350, cp. SGC 92/376), rather than seeing the Good directly. SGC 101/383 will take a different view on this.) Murdoch argues that the Good is (*b*) *unitary* by arguing a version of Plato's thesis of the unity of the virtues (famously defended in the *Protagoras*, 328d–334c): we can have a full grasp of even one of the virtues only if we have a grasp of all of them—the virtue of courage, for example, if it is to be distinct from mere recklessness, will involve the ability to distinguish which dangers are worth facing and which are not—which itself requires other virtues,

---

[121] Murdoch is discussing what remains of the techniques of religion 'in a world without God' (55/344), while remaining, I think, at this point uncommitted on whether our world is or is not definitely a world of that type. (For example, 'Whether [analytic philosophers] are right [in their objections to an ontological argument] about "God" I leave aside' (63/351).) In SGC, by contrast, Murdoch says straightforwardly that there is, in her view, 'no God in the traditional sense' (79/365).

including that of justice. Courage in its highest forms involves the 'other' virtues: 'The best kind of courage' is 'steadfast, calm, temperate, intelligent, loving' (57/346), where what might at first have seemed to be *other* virtues—steadfastness, calmness, temperance, intelligence, love—turn out to be aspects of the same general moral capacity.

When Murdoch argues that the Good is also (*c*) 'transcendent', (*d*) 'perfect' and (*e*) 'necessary', and (*f*) 'real', however, we need to ask quite what these attributes amount to. Murdoch's first main step in dealing with the first of them is to propose: 'One might start from the assertion that morality, goodness, is a form of *realism*' (59/347)—that is, that *being good* is a kind of *seeing things as they really are*. And a person who attends to things outside himself, will attend less to the self within. But how exactly does that amount or lead to a form of *transcendence*? Murdoch alludes to a way in which beauty in art has a kind of transcendence:

> The statue is broken, the flower fades, the experience ceases, but something has not suffered from decay and mortality. (59/348)

But while this is interesting in itself, Murdoch points out that the good is not visible or experienceable in the same way as beauty is; and therefore (though I am not sure that the reason given really constitutes a relevant obstacle) she rejects the idea of using the transcendence of the beautiful as a model for the transcendence of the good.

At this point Murdoch takes up the attributes of (*d*) *perfection* and (*e*) *necessity*, as a kind of interlude, having not yet finished with transcendence. The idea of a *perfect* goodness is, she says, important to us—in that the deep understanding of any human activity, like e.g. painting, requires the sense of *degrees* of goodness; and (if I read Murdoch's rather Kantian implications correctly) we need the idea of *perfect* goodness since *unmixed* love (the idea of which we surely recognize) can only be directed to what is *unmixedly*—or perfectly—good. While in some sense providing *order* (i.e. serving as a standard against which different things can be seen as good to differing degrees), this idea of perfect goodness is indefinable:

> It is in its nature that we cannot get it taped [i.e. measured up or defined]. This is the true sense of the indefinability of the good, which was given a vulgar sense by Moore and his followers. It lies always *beyond* and it is from this *beyond* that it exercises its authority. (62/350, my emphasis)

Whatever good we may conceive, we can apparently conceive of there being yet other goods *beyond*—other things that are yet better—though *how* exactly better, in which ways, we may be unable to specify. This seems to me both very likely true and in a sense remarkably modest—but it is already to bring us to a kind of transcendence for the Good. (See also SGC 93/376 on the 'non-metaphysical meaning of the idea of transcendence to which philosophers have so constantly resorted'.) Whatever may be the varieties of goodness that we already grasp, we can conceive of there being yet higher varieties, and may even in some way feel dimly aware of some of them. This partial grasp may influence our judgements and our moral progress—and (as was argued in IP) we form for ourselves the idea of an ideal limit for such a progression:

an Idea or Form of Good, or goodness in its highest perfection. And it would be very possible to fill out Murdoch's argument by adding a neo-Fregean readiness to allow the existence of properties as abstract objects—in which case, this *goodness* obscurely grasped by us would be one such abstract object. There would be such a thing as Goodness, transcendent in the sense of being *beyond our full grasp*, as well as being not dependent for its existence upon its being instantiated by things in the material world. We would have a fairly robust form of Platonism.[122]

This seems to me a form of Platonism that is both interesting and plausible—though (especially perhaps for those either attracted or repelled by some of more high-sounding talk in Plato or Murdoch) it may seem oddly modest. I am not sure how far exactly it coincides with the Platonism that Murdoch herself wants. It would treat the existence of *goodness* as generally no stranger than, for example, the existence of *circularity*—though there would of course be differences between the properties themselves: the existence would be secured by the truth of such simple and surely widely acceptable statements as 'there is a feature that these plates and those wheels all pretty decently instantiate, but which that figure you've just drawn falls far short of' and 'there is a feature—namely goodness—that Bill constantly aims to instantiate, but is sadly aware of falling far short of'. Quine's criteria of ontological commitment would count anyone prepared to make such statements seriously as committed to the existence of the corresponding properties; and many people would find such statements no harder in principle to accept than more ordinary statements that mention more ordinary properties—like 'this clock has the annoying property of losing 5 minutes a day'. We would certainly need to convince ourselves that the use of such terms was coherent. And Frege would emphasize the need for such terms to be connected with criteria of identity to specify the conditions under which a newly-presented item was

---

[122] Modern interpreters often read Plato as giving Forms the role of being (1) *kinds, properties,* or *universals* (e.g. *justice, health*) with an existence and nature independent of any instances of them, and the role of being (2) *paradigms,* in the image of which particular things can be thought of as made (e.g. the Couch, cf. *Rep.* 596a, 598d). (Note, e.g. Plato's easy transition between 'equality' (the property), and 'the equal itself' or 'the equals themselves' (the paradigm) at *Phaedo* 74c1, 74a10).) Many critics doubt whether any one thing can play these two roles—but the failure of the attempt to yoke them both together might leave open the still fundamentally Platonic project of showing the coherence of a belief in Forms of the first and (perhaps separately and in addition) Forms of the second kind. There are many versions of such projects—my sympathies are mainly with developments of Platonism in Frege's philosophy of mathematics, and more recently in Michael Dummett and Crispin Wright—which would, if valid, I think, provide for the introduction of property terms no less than for the Fregean introduction of number terms and direction terms in accordance with something like a contextual definition. See Frege, *Grundlagen der Arithmetik* (1884), esp. §§62–5, and e.g. Dummett, *Frege: Philosophy of Language* (1973), chs. 4 and 14, and Wright, *Frege's Conception of Numbers as Objects* (1983). The issues are of course contentious, but if there is promise in these projects, there is promise in a Platonic belief in goodness or in the Good—provided, at least, that there is a coherent usage of the predicate 'good'. I shall here put most weight on (1) rather than (2): the conception of *goodness* as a *property* independent of the existence of any actual instances of it. I shall bracket here the issue of the ways in which 'good' in moral contexts might be 'attributive' in Geach's sense. To the extent that it is, the implication would be that goodness was not an ordinary first-level property (with *objects* constituting its extension) but something like a mixed-level property (with *objects* taken with a certain *kind* constituting its extension).

identical with any such purported property. But one way or another, there are plausible arguments, I believe—though of course the matter is controversial—for the recognition of such abstract objects. And to find some such view in Murdoch would not be particularly odd—she was close to the surge of interest in Frege in the 1950s, and I have already found similarities between her arguments for a kind of moral realism and Fregean arguments for realism about numbers.[123]

But the fact is that what Murdoch says about the Good is not entirely parallel to what the Fregeans say about numbers. The Fregean would treat 'Goodness' as literally a name, and Goodness as literally a thing named by it. But while Murdoch talks of the Good as existing, she has a definite reluctance to talk of goodness as literally (even in the Fregeans' deliberately colourless sense) a thing. (She talks of 'the *metaphor* of "thing"' that we employ when we talk of Plato's sun—or Goodness—as a thing (SGC 92/376, my emphasis).) She warns against 'any heavy material connotation of the misleading word "exist"', if we talk of the existence of goodness (64/351)—whereas a Fregean would take material existence to be obviously not in question for a category of item (namely a property) that never had any aspiration to being material; and a Fregean would find nothing 'misleading' about the word 'exist' in itself. Murdoch's view has a resemblance to a Fregean view, but it is in a way more deliberately non-committal: it may indeed be more genuinely Wittgensteinian—in that it works hard at an understanding of the *transcendence* that, Murdoch believes, really is integral to the concept of Goodness; whereas a commitment to the *existence* of Goodness *as a thing* might seem to Murdoch in danger of being groundless philosophical theorizing—something with no fundamental basis or importance in our use of the language of goodness.[124] But for all the differences, Murdoch's project remains close to that of the Fregean: she wishes to show the innocence of talk of the transcendent existence of goodness, while giving it an interpretation, according to which it demands no more for its truth than is secured by the existence and character of the material world with all that we find in it. It is a view that combines realism with a mildly deflationary conception of what such realism amounts to.

I shall pass quickly over a challenge Murdoch considers and her reply to it. What if it were merely that it was psychologically helpful to us to act 'as if' all this were true—'as if' there were a Good? It is here that a fifth attribute comes into play: (e) necessity. Murdoch's answer seems to be (following the model of some versions of the ontological argument for the existence of God) that we may be able to say that it is *part of the concept* of Good that there is *certainly* such a thing as Good, and that 'we must receive a return when good is sincerely desired' (63/351)—which is, I suppose, a version of the

---

[123] See also fn. 101 above on Frege in connection with the realism of IP.

[124] Cf. also Murdoch's use in IP (16/312) of Wittgenstein's remark (PI §299): 'Being unable—when we surrender ourselves to philosophical thought—to help saying such-and-such . . . does not mean being forced into an assumption, or having an immediate perception or knowledge of a state of affairs' That is, I think: we should take seriously what we feel 'irresistibly inclined' to say, but we should not to pretend to read off from it some theoretical metaphysical fact-structure.

principle that in some sense virtue is its own reward. If so, then we can deduce from our having the very concept of Good that there is, necessarily, indeed, such a thing as the Good.[125] In any case Murdoch thinks the conviction of the existence of (ideal) Good, on the part of one who has the concept of Good, is surely more than its being 'as if' there were such a thing. But though Murdoch seems tempted indeed by this kind of usage of something like an ontological argument—and might even say it was valid as applied to her own conception of Good—, she does, I think, not want to place any special weight on it, or assert that it is true of everyone's conception of Good. She is well aware of questions about 'what status' should be given to such claims; and having raised them, she consciously leaves them unanswered.

At this point Murdoch comes, finally, to the attribute of (f) 'reality'—or realism. Murdoch deals with something that is not, I think, quite what she had earlier advertised. We were told at the outset that the Good would be shown to be—as God was traditionally taken to be—an object of attention, unitary, transcendent, perfect, necessary, and 'real' (55/344). We might expect Murdoch, therefore, to talk now of the *reality* of the Good in some sense: of the *existence of goodness*, or of its *thing-like character* (as a thing or *res*), or of its *causal efficacy* (if, as some people wish, we were to say that something was real only if it had, in some sense, causal power). Murdoch does not do so. She has things to say on all of those matters elsewhere.[126] But when she comes to the last of her list of attributes here, what she talks of is something different— and of no less importance for her general moral psychology—: namely, the '*realism*' that is the ability to *see things as they are*.

Murdoch talks of this realism first in the domain of art, and then in morality. Art is, Murdoch argues, clearly and importantly an enterprise calling for realism, both in the artist and (though differently) in the consumer of art. Good art requires, in both parties, the ability to see things with 'exactness and good vision': 'unsentimental, detached, unselfish, objective attention' (65–6/353). Murdoch treats this as a guide to the realism that is fundamental also to morality: 'a similar exactness', she says, is called for.[127] And

---

[125]   A suspicious reader might say this provides necessity of the consequence, not of the consequent: the argument would imply, of necessity, that the Good existed, rather than implying that the Good was a necessary existent (as traditionally, God had been thought of as being). That may or may not be true. There may be specially modest versions of the ontological argument that conclude from the concept of a (perhaps merely contingently existing) God to the existence of such an item; but traditional versions start with a concept of God that is already the concept of a necessary being. It would seem open to Murdoch, either to draw in her horns and claim merely what we might call the a priori existence of the Good (claiming only necessity of consequence); or (more ambitiously) to say that the concept of the Good implicit in her moral thinking was from the start the concept of something that exists necessarily if it can be said to exist at all.

[126]   The ontological argument with Good is meant to secure (for those who have a notion of Good such as Murdoch's) the existence of the Good—though we must avoid 'any heavy material connotation' of the word 'exist' (63–4/351). Murdoch reminds us later that we treat 'the Good' as a name of a thing, as well as using 'good' as a predicate (SGC 93/376). And she has talked of the Good as 'a magnetic but inexhaustible reality' (IP 42/333)—in some sense treating it as something that exerts an influence upon (and provides an 'energy' to) those who turn their attention to it (e.g. 56/345).

[127]   On fantasy in bad art, realistic vision in good art, and the way the latter is a model for accuracy in moral vision, see also SGC 85.12–88.18/370.3–372.27, and my discussion of SGC below.

there follow two sentences of great importance for Murdoch's thought and extraordinary—perhaps maddening—difficulty:

I would suggest that the authority of the Good seems to us something necessary because the realism (ability to perceive reality) required for goodness is a kind of intellectual ability to perceive what is true, which is, automatically, at the same time a suppression of self. *The necessity of the good is then an aspect of the kind of necessity involved in any technique for exhibiting fact.* (66/353)

What this means, I think, is this. Anything that claims to 'exhibit' or represent facts may be assessed as being better or worse at doing so. The necessity of the good is the necessity of the notion of the ideally good (or ideally accurate) representation (or presentation, or perception or 'exhibiting') of things with their various features—something which will include, in the case of moral perception, the perception of those things' moral character. Such ideal goodness in 'representing or exhibiting' things is beyond our capacity as benighted human beings either to instantiate or to grasp perfectly in detail—but it is a goodness that in some sense we are committed to recognizing as the ultimate excellence. It is the goodness of the perfect moral perceiver. And, as the first of the two quoted sentences implies, the ability to attend to what is the case outside oneself will bring with it a reduced attention to oneself. Thus, to repeat:

The necessity of the good is . . . an aspect of the kind of necessity involved in any technique for exhibiting fact. (66/353)

But it is only 'an aspect', perhaps, in that there may be other dimensions of assessment of the representing or 'exhibiting' of fact (e.g. as being polite or not, or relevant or not); or, perhaps, in that moral properties constitute only one of many ranges of properties that may figure in such representings or exhibitings. (The '*authority* of the Good seems to us necessary', in that it seems to us necessary that *the Good has the right to tell us what to do or think*—and that, in turn, is traced to the surely (with suitable qualifications) necessary idea that one should think what is the case.)

Murdoch's view might seem liable to a rather dangerous—actually Platonic—objection. Announcing near the end of *Republic* VI the 'longer path' (504cd) that we will have take in order to learn about the Good and complete our understanding of the virtues, Socrates starts out (505b–d) by dismissing the view of the 'cleverer thinkers' (*kompsoteroi*) who might imagine that we could define the Good simply as *knowledge* (*phronēsis*). The objection is that if we ask these thinkers *which* variety of knowledge the relevant knowledge needs to be, they end up saying it is knowledge *of the Good*:— which is circular and uninformative, given our existing difficulty in saying what Good itself is. Murdoch's proposal—that the Good is something like *accuracy* or *realism* in the exhibiting of fact—might seem very close to the view of the 'cleverer thinkers', and liable to the same objection. But Murdoch's view is, I think, deliberately different—she actually intends the relevant *accuracy* to be, not knowledge merely (and circularly) of what is good, but knowledge literally of anything: accuracy in the presentation of any fact is a good, whatever the fact may be. 'All just vision, even in the strictest problems of the intellect, and *a fortiori* when suffering or wickedness have to be perceived, is a moral matter' (70/357).

This seems to me very true—but it may now be liable to a new objection: that it does justice at most to one among several roles that we need the notion of Good to play. Murdoch's proposal may allow us to identify goodness as a feature *of the moral observer*. But what about goodness as it figures elsewhere in the world: in what that observer sees? If, for example, a person chooses something because it seems good, then what is this feature, goodness, that the thing in question seems to have? It can hardly be the goodness of *accurately* '*exhibiting*' or representing fact. Murdoch has, one might say, told us about goodness of *vision* or goodness in *an observer*, but not of the goodness in the *observed*.

Murdoch again, I think, would have a reply. We do indeed use the word 'good' both for agents and for the things that they choose. But there are at least some philosophers who believe this second usage to be either mistaken or derivative. In Kant's view, it is impossible to think of anything 'which can be taken as good without qualification, except a *good will*' (GMS 4.393). If we find truth in the scholastic formula *nihil appetimus, nisi sub ratione boni* ('we desire nothing except under the form of the good'), it is only if we also recognize that 'the concept of good and evil is not defined *prior* to the moral law' (KpV 5:62; see generally 5:59ff., esp. 62–3): if we apply 'good' to things or actions rather than to persons and the will, it is in a secondary sense—as we might, for example, apply 'good' to such actions as a person performs when he is acting in accord with the moral law. And Murdoch herself may take a similar view of 'good' as having its primary application only in the domain of persons. (Her comment that 'nothing in life is of any value except the attempt to be virtuous' (SGC 87/371) may suggest this.) Whether this is ultimately correct is a topic I cannot take further here. But we might ask: if goodness is the quite general (and one might say colourless) quality of *accuracy* in perception or 'presentation', then in what sense can it be the crowning excellence that the Platonist, and Murdoch herself in the final essay of the volume, would like it to be? Perhaps the reply will be that goodness—like truth—is something the varieties of which are going to be in a sense more interesting than the general quality itself. Or perhaps one might say that it is only as approached *via* an understanding of its sub-varieties—the accurate seeing that constitutes wisdom, the accurate seeing that constitutes bravery, the accurate seeing that constitutes justice—and only as understood to subsume them all, that goodness will be something that we can have a more than formal and colourless understanding of. If so, then there will be both a deep Platonism and a deep Kantianism to Murdoch's very deliberately modest metaphysics.[128]

---

[128] This may be the view Murdoch reaches near the end of SGC (98/380–1, 102/383–4), where she seems to retreat from the claim that goodness can be identified with general accuracy in 'presentation'—or indeed with love—both of which had figured so strongly in OGG. Such *general accuracy* would, I suppose, be equivalent to *truth*—and Murdoch argues that truth cannot be identified with the Good: 'Even the concept of Truth has its ambiguities and it is really only of Good that we can say "it is the trial of itself and needs no other touch"' (SGC 98/381). Love is similarly denied to be identical with the Good—in that there are forms of love that are not good. The departure from Murdoch's earlier views is perhaps smaller in the case of love

I shall say little about the third part of the essay (66.31–71.29 / 358.18–354.12): from the metaphysics that Murdoch has been elaborating, she sees a new 'picture of human personality' emerging (66/354). The freedom we need is 'freedom from fantasy', i.e. the freedom to see reality as it is. *Love* (i.e. loving attention to reality) is what provides that liberation; sincerity and self-knowledge are not (as existentialism supposed) particularly important. I shall not attempt to add to the comments I have already made in discussing the last main part of IP.

5.3 'The Sovereignty of Good over other Concepts'

'The Sovereignty of Good over other Concepts' argues precisely what its title slightly unobviously implies: that the notion of the Good is central in morality and moral philosophy, and sovereign or supreme over all others.[129] As well as offering a reading of the imagery of the fire and the sun in Plato's Cave, Murdoch argues that good is indefinable and (as part of her reading of Plato's Line image) that good provides 'unity' among the concepts of morality and other things. But there are other projects as well. The importance of *virtue*—and, above all, of the virtues at work in *accurate perception* of an independent and respected reality—is first recognized in the experience of art and the intellectual disciplines, and then seen to play a similar role in morality. And one can see the whole paper as constituting an argument against a picture of human beings and the origin of value that Murdoch labels Romanticism (82–3/367–8; cf. 84–5/369). Very roughly, the Romantic picture sees the individual as *creating* values by choice and will; Murdoch's opposing picture sees the individual as *discovering* value in things outside—if he is not impeded by the seductive warmth of the *self*. Whereas Murdoch's object of attack in 'The Idea of Perfection' was presented as a philosophical movement—the 'existentialist-behaviourist type of moral psychology' (10/306)—, much the same picture of human beings and the origin of value is presented now as a phenomenon in the general artistic culture of the previous two centuries.

It is worth mentioning that the whole paper has a religious and high metaphysical tone, though in a context that is intended, I think, to be wholly secular. Murdoch talks of 'the spiritual life' (90/374) and of us as 'spiritual creatures' (103/384) and of true morality as 'a sort of unesoteric mysticism' (92/376). But this, like the recurrent Platonic language, is, I believe, intended to be given a thoroughly unmetaphysical— or, at least, a minimally and entirely unfrighteningly metaphysical—interpretation. We are spiritual creatures simply in that we have, in Kant's sense, a 'supersensible nature': we are creatures with an ability to think, with varying degrees of success, about things

---

(in that the love that is 'capable of infinite degradation and . . . the source of our greatest errors' in SGC (103/384) can surely only be a homonym of the love that was the *loving attention* of Simone Weil, emphasized in the earlier essays). But there is certainly a deliberately greater and more independent role given to the Good in SGC than in OGG.

[129] The image is Plato's: the Good is said to 'rule' or 'be sovereign over' (*basileuein*) the intelligible realm (*Republic* VI 509d). By contrast, for the existentialist, 'The sovereign moral concept is *freedom*', or, in a sense, courage and *the will* (SGC 80/366, my emphasis).

as being *right* or not and *reasonable* or not.[130] If we talk of the Good as a *thing*, we must remember that this is a metaphor (94/377), though an important one; if we talk of the Good as *transcendent*, this means something like *beyond the veil of selfish consciousness*, and *infinitely beyond our own limited conceptions* (93/376–7)—we are not talking of it as an object in a heavenly realm of 'transcendent' items, but (as OGG also has argued) simply as a property, the nature and extension of which will always go beyond what we human beings find instantiated in our environment, and beyond what we can precisely grasp and define. The language flies high, but Murdoch wants our feet to stay firmly on the ground. And this is not the result simply of a fondness for grand language: it is part of Murdoch's conviction that such imagery is particularly apt and more or less irreplaceable in its powers.[131] Murdoch had earlier looked specially at our talk of attention to the good as *giving* an *energy* (OGG 55–6/345, 71/358); the present essay concentrates more on the metaphors of *turning* and *progressive advance*, of *shadow* and *reality* and *light* in Plato's Cave and Line. Humeans, no less than anyone else, of course have their own imagery too—talking, for example, of 'strength' of will, or of the 'force' of a desire for an end being 'channelled' into subsidiary desires for means. To favour one form of imagery to the exclusion of another may be to make certain kinds of moral claim and understanding almost unthinkable. And Murdoch is concerned to win back some of what the dominant idioms of modern philosophy have left us almost unable to think. But she is, perhaps above all, excited at the thought that reviving the Platonic idioms may put us also in a position to answer the fundamental question, 'How can we make ourselves better?' (78/364). The answer will turn out to be: by turning away from the self and the illusions it promotes and turning to the reality of the world around us, thanks to a progressive education in the virtues. And that education—in which the enjoyment of natural beauty and the study of works of art and *technai* (or 'disciplines') really does prepare us for morality—is one that will help us improve not only in our practice but also in our theoretical and metaphysical understanding.

Here is a summary of the paper.

77.1 / 363.1 *Introduction.* The importance of metaphor [e.g. the metaphors of Cave, Fire and Sun in Plato]. In moral philosophy, (1) we need a realistic account of human nature; and (2) (since we cannot avoid commending something), we need to commend a worthy ideal—and face the question 'How can we make ourselves better?' [The answer will be: by the acquisition of the virtues, approached through the study of Beauty and the *technai*.]

---

[130] For Kant's distinction between our 'sensible nature' and our 'supersensible nature', see, e.g. *Critique of Practical Reason* (KpV) 5: 43–4.

[131] The point again is a Kantian one: Kant talks very vividly of the importance of metaphor even for our theoretical knowledge, in the case of things that cannot be literally pictured: *Critique of Judgement* §59 (Ak. 5:351–4)—a passage that Murdoch knew well (and had echoed earlier in her talk of art as 'an excellent analogy of morals' at OGG 59/348).

78.20 / 364.13 Two assumptions of the argument:

1. That human beings are naturally selfish, prone to fantasy and 'reluctant to face unpleasant realities';
2. That life has no external point or *telos*; there is 'no God in the traditional sense of that term'.[132]

79.28 / 365.13 (I) *The post-Kantian conception of Man—and an alternative.*

On the post-Kantian view (from Kant through Nietzsche to Existentialism), the will is 'creator of value', and the 'sovereign moral concept' is freedom (together with courage, will and power). There are distinctive (and, IM thinks, dangerous) emotions in this Romantic conception: *Achtung* (Kant's 'respect' for the moral law, which becomes a kind of 'suffering pride' accompanying our recognition of duty); Kant's experience of the Sublime (which impresses on us both our smallness in material nature and the greatness of our rational powers); *Angst* (in existentialism); and the tendency to find a 'thrill' and illusory 'consolation' in suffering and death.

83.4 / 368.8 There is an *alternative* conception, held by 'the ordinary man', especially in religious thinking: states of mind (and not just actions) matter and they differ in quality (i.e. in excellence); selfishness can blind us to much of what is around (including the moral character of people). Counteracting this selfishness will yield a more accurate consciousness of others and promote virtue in us; improvements in 'quality of consciousness' can provide a new 'energy for good action'.

84.13 / 369.10 (II) *An 'argument against . . . "Romanticism"' (84/369): some materials for a 'training' in 'virtue' (86/371).*[133]

(A1) *Beauty in nature* is the 'most accessible' place of moral change. Beauty in nature improves the quality of our experience. It turns us away from 'selfish care' and yields 'a self-forgetful pleasure in the sheer alien pointless existence of animals, birds, stones and trees'. ('There is nothing now but kestrel.')

85.12 / 370.3 (A2) *Beauty in art.* Art is 'the most educational of all human activities'. Much art is self-consoling fantasy. But good art (partly because of its form) gives delight at the 'independent existence of what is excellent', and it is 'totally opposed to selfish obsession'. It displays the virtues employed by the artist in creating it. But most

---

[132] This will contribute to the later claim that, in some sense, the only order to be found is *order at the level of thought* or *formal structure*—not in the ordinary empirical world itself. Murdoch finds that good art shows this (87/371–2); as in part does philosophy (with the interconnection of the Good with other Forms: esp. 94–7/377–80). The point is, obviously enough, not meant to exclude what one might call *causal order* or regularity in the world—indeed Murdoch emphatically places such regularity there (under the headings of 'chance' and 'necessity': 79/365; cf. OGG 71/357, 74/360). What it excludes is any supernatural providence from outside the world and any intrinsic order of *rational structure* or purpose within it.

[133] How can what follows be both of these things? How can setting out the elements of a practical moral training be supposed also to change our view on the metaphysics of the relation of 'man' to world? Perhaps: in giving ourselves an account of how the details of the training operate, we find ourselves making use of notions from the non-Romantic explanatory scheme, and thereby discover for ourselves the importance of those notions. And it may be easier to see the ways in which value attaches to things in the world (and to see that it is not as envisaged by the Romantic) when looking at the domains of art and the *technai* than if we start with the case of morality: as points (1)–(6) under the heading of (A2) *Beauty in art* illustrate.

importantly, it shows the way in which 'virtue is *tied on* to the human condition': (1) Art—like virtue and morality—is *absolutely* pointless, but still [so to speak, 'from the inside'] supremely important. (2) Art reveals the *unsystematic detail* of the world, but with a sense of *unity* or form. (3) Art gives us a 'truthful image of the human condition' in what is perhaps 'the only context in which many of us are capable of contemplating it at all'. And it does so (4) thanks to the 'clear realistic vision' of the artist, which is essentially 'both pity and justice'. (5) Art shows death (i.e. the ultimate finality of our existence) without false consolation. (6) It shows the importance of the notions of 'hierarchy' (i.e. degrees of excellence) and 'authority' (i.e. there being objects outside us that may legitimately command our attention or recognition in relevant ways).

88.19 / 372.28 (B) *The technai*. Plato preferred *mathematics* to the experience of beauty in nature or art (A1 and A2) as a preparation for higher thought (and the understanding of the Good), but IM will take as her example of a *technē* the case of learning Russian. We find the same virtues at work there as in morality (e.g. justice, truthfulness, humility, respect for a reality outside oneself); and they are 'more simply on display' in a *technē*. We see that 'Attention is rewarded by a knowledge of reality'. And we see how the virtues are *interconnected* (e.g. accuracy, justice, and love shade into each other). But the *technai* are only 'introductory images of the spiritual life'—they do not yield the whole of virtue.

90.20 / 374.16 (C) *General morality*. Let us make a closer approach to the Good.
—Summary of the particular points that beauty and the *technai* have taught us about the nature and operation of virtue. It may be hard to see that virtue operates similarly in the domain of *Morality*. We are tempted to think morality is a question of 'personal will' rather than 'attentive study'. Yet here too [as with (3) and (4) in the case of Art, and similarly in the case of learning Russian], faced with difficult moral questions, we find that 'the love which brings the right answer is an exercise of justice and realism and really looking'. Good action depends on the *justice* of our modes of *vision* and on the *quality* of our habitual attachments.

92.5 / 375.29 (III) *The concept of Good* ties together (A), (B), and (C). The 'true morality' has its source in an 'unconsoled love of the Good', which may also be called a sort of 'unesoteric mysticism'. (That is, it arises from love of the Good—which in OGG was specially linked with attention and accuracy of perception—, unaccompanied by illusory 'consolations' (e.g. about an afterlife, or the wiping out of sin by suffering, or an externally-set purpose to the world). It is *mystical* in involving (as in mystical religion) 'a non-dogmatic essentially unformulated faith [in this case, in the reality of the Good], occasionally connected with experience'. It is *unesoteric* in being available and 'essentially the same' for all (OGG 74/360).) To explain the Good, Plato uses the image of the Sun [*Republic* VI–VII, 506b & ff.].

92.24 / 376.7 *Plato's Metaphor of the 'Sun'*: Coming out of the Cave [*Rep.* 516ab], we see things in the light of the sun (i.e. we see the Forms thanks to their relation to the Good); the Sun itself (representing the Good) is the last and hardest thing we come to see.

Murdoch interprets this: —We naturally talk of the Good as, metaphorically, a *thing*. (Indeed: the term 'good' has substantive as well as predicative uses.) —Goodness is a matter of *perfection* (a distant ideal), something we are far from possessing or seeing; but we can sense its *direction* (we have a sense of some things as being *better than* others, and of what differences make for such betterness). —The *self* is 'a place of illusion' (attention to the self produces error about self and other things); goodness is a matter of seeing the *unself*: 'to see and respond to the real world in the light of a virtuous consciousness'. —Goodness is *transcendent*, in being a matter of (1) going *beyond* our selves and (2) going *beyond* our erroneous perceptions of other things—that being, for us, (3) an *infinite* task which we could always do yet better.

94.14 / 377.22 *The concept of the Good is i. unifying*: Plato's Line (*Rep.* 509c–511e) pictures the soul as rising through four stages of enlightenment to the Good, and then descending again [511b], revisiting the Forms she had previously had only an imperfect conception of. *Only when we have grasped the Good* do we see the nature of the other concepts and how they *relate* to each other. —This seems true: we come to see the *connections* among the virtues (e.g. *courage* turns out to be 'a particular operation of *wisdom* and *love*'); we reconceive the nature of freedom, or of humility. But goodness is 'for use in politics and in the market place': so this (*conceptual* understanding) must also be combined with attention to the random detail of the everyday world. (There is a 'return to the cave': *Rep.* 520c.) This combination of 'random detail' [in the world] and 'intuited unity' [at the level of thought] is found also in (A2) art and (B) intellectual work. The highest under-standing of any particular subject involves knowing its place in 'the whole of . . . life'. We may be 'specialised' in our virtues (and may have (at least the beginnings of) some virtues without others); but there is a 'shadowy unachieved unity' among the moral and other concepts and it is the concept Good that provides it.

97.24 / 380.12 *And ii. indefinable*: One reason for claiming Good to be indefinable is 'logical': (i) No definition of Good as X (e.g. as Love or Truth) will work without specifying the sub-variety of X that is relevant; and with that (if we say, e.g. *good* love) we refer again (circularly) to the notion of Good. [Cf. Plato, *Rep.* VI 505b–d.] Another consideration is: (ii) that there is no such thing as being good without qualification, but only being a good *f* or a good *g* (for some kind *f* or *g*). And some [e.g. Hare] take this to show that 'good' is in itself virtually contentless: a mere 'general adjective of commendation' attachable (subject to universalizability requirements) to *anything*. But (IM replies): excellence has a kind of unity; and . . . [the remainder of the article will give further reasons against the view that 'good' is an empty term].

99.6 / 381.20 *We find the idea of Good mysterious* [and therefore indefinable]:
partly because
i. The world is chancy and aimless;
ii. we are distant from the Good;. and blinded by self; and
iii. it is difficult to look at the sun [i.e. the Good]. (There are dangers of masochism and worship of false suns.)

100.25 / 382.29 The *fire* in Plato's cave is a false sun: we may interpret it as symbolizing *the self*. Some newly-released prisoners may become fascinated with *the self* that was source of the old shadows they used to think were real, and advance no further.

But (101.23 / 383.20) *there is a place for 'a sort of contemplation of the Good'*: 'an attempt to look right away from self towards a distant transcendent perfection, a source of uncontaminated energy'. And this may be what helps most, when difficulties [in practical life] seem insoluble.

102.2 / 383.33 *Concluding remarks: Connections of Good with (a) Love and (b) Humility:* Even if Good is indefinable, is it specially close to certain other concepts? Not especially to Freedom, Reason, Happiness, Courage, or History [championed variously by neo-Kantians, utilitarians, existentialists, and Hegel]. However,

(a) Goodness and Love are close, though not the same. Personal love is usually 'self-assertive' and 'capable of infinite degradation'. But Love shows 'that we are spiritual creatures, attracted by excellence and made for the Good'.

(b) The Good man is a humble man: 'because he sees himself as nothing, [he] can see other things as they are'. Humility too is not the same thing as Goodness. But the humble man is, perhaps, 'the kind of man who is most likely of all to *become* good' (my emphasis).

Before the main argument, Murdoch sets out two main assumptions and a brief sketch of the Romantic post-Kantian conception of man that will be the object of her attack. The presentation is extremely compressed: but I shall be selective, even so, in order to bring out just a couple of points. The two assumptions are, first, that human beings are 'naturally selfish' and prone to the avoidance of reality (78/364);[134] and, secondly, that our existence has no externally-set purpose or point: there is no prospect of an afterlife and 'no God in the traditional sense' (79/364–5). These assumptions interlock: perhaps prime among the realities that we are prone to pretend to escape is that of the sheer conclusiveness of death (82–3/367–8). It is a mark of at least some[135] of the more unrealistic manifestations of the Romantic conception of the self to mythologize death in such a way that it would be something thrilling and almost to be yearned for. (Murdoch is thinking of Wagnerian *Liebestod* and—with the 'sublime emotions and . . . image of tortured freedom' (83/368)—, no doubt, of Heidegger.) It will turn out later (87/371–2) that 'good art' is capable of a much greater realism in the recognition of death. (Murdoch is thinking particularly of Tolstoy and of Shakespearean tragedy.[136]) And their realism (i.e. their facing of reality) is integral to their goodness: the avoidance of any deceptive appearance of providential plan, the acceptance of the finality of death, the avoidance of false consolation.

---

[134] On Murdoch's conception of this, it may be helpful to look back at Murdoch's slightly fuller presentation of what is 'true and important in Freudian theory' at OGG 51/341.

[135] Not all, evidently: in Hare, for example, there are few signs of it. But the issue is still an important one. Murdoch's target is the Romantic conception of the self both in a narrower (more literarily prominent) form and in a broader (often more academic and less dramatic) form. Her attention is in this essay mostly on the former, but the general argument is directed no less at the latter.

[136] MGM ch. 5 continues the investigation.

It is interesting that, both in the opening characterization of human psychology and in the later parts of the paper, Murdoch talks in terms that echo Freudian psychology—particularly, with the notions of fantasy, form, and reality.[137] And they supply her with a language in which some important Platonic ideas can be given a more evidently *this-worldly* form. Plato talks of our need to turn from *appearances* to *realities*—in the first instance, it seems, from everyday things to Forms. Murdoch talks of our need to turn from *fantasy* to *reality*—where the reality is now the reality of the world around us, in its moral and other complexity. (Murdoch puts the matter in terms that echo Freudian talk of fantasy and reality, though in the end her conception of that everyday reality is no doubt richer (and more morally contentful) than Freud's own conception.) And this presentation is, Murdoch would say, not a departure from Plato, but entirely of a piece with his overall philosophy: knowledge of the Forms is of course a crowning achievement, and Murdoch is not going to turn her back upon it; but one of the ultimate ends of the guardians' training is to ensure that, back in the obscurity of ordinary life, they can clearly see and accurately judge the moral character of ordinary phenomena (*Rep.* 520bc). And for them to do so is for the city to be governed by people 'with waking minds, and not as most cities now are, which are inhabited and ruled darkly as in a dream by men who fight one another for shadows' (520d). So, one might say, even in Plato's own imagery, to be 'awake', for a human being, is not to live merely in the world of Forms, but to live in the concrete world where we find ourselves, with a clear awareness both of sensible things and of Forms, in their exact character, each as they are.[138]

---

[137] OGG 51/341 contains a good summary of what Murdoch accepts from Freudian theory, and Freud is clearly in Murdoch's mind when she refers to 'modern psychology' at 78/364. For the similarity between Murdoch and Freud in expression and conception, consider, e.g. Murdoch: 'It is true that human beings cannot bear much reality' (OGG 64/352; with a nod, also, to T. S. Eliot in 'Burnt Norton', *Four Quartets*). Freud: human beings 'cannot subsist on the scanty satisfaction which they can extort from reality' (*Introductory Lectures on Psycho-Analysis* (1917), SE 16:372). For Freud's views on the reality principle, the pleasure principle, and phantasy (as the Standard Edition prints the term), see, e.g. Freud, 'Formulations on the Two Principles of Mental Functioning' (1911), SE 12: 218–26 (with section (6) on Art); and 'Beyond the Pleasure Principle' (1920), SE 18: 7–64, esp. §1. On phantasy, art, and the role of form, see, e.g. Freud, *Introductory Lectures* (1916–17) ch. 23, SE 16: 358–77, esp. 375–7; and 'Creative Writers and Day-Dreaming' (1908), SE 9: 143–53. Murdoch had long talked of social convention and neurosis as 'the enemies of art and of morals' (S&G 216; cf. SBR 268–71; see §2 of main text above) and it is worth noting how extremely well the detail of Freud's largely cognitive conception of neurosis connects with Murdoch's realist conception of morality. For Freud neurosis involves a 'loosening of the relation to reality', indeed a 'loss of reality'. (See, e.g. 'The Loss of Reality in Neurosis and Psychosis' (1924), SE 19: 183, repr. in S. Freud, *The Essentials of Psycho-Analysis*, selected by Anna Freud (1986), 568.) Freud's reality is not Murdoch's, but with Murdoch's enrichment of reality to include the moral, we can see how Freudian neurosis (now taken in a correspondingly broader sense) would become one of the principal forms of moral failing: the inability to face the world in its true moral and other character. And a kind of cognitive courage would be correspondingly a principal virtue: the ability to face the world sanely and without fear (cf. DPR 201). See also Margaret Holland's essay in the present volume.

[138] Cf. Plato's characterization of the philosopher whose life is a 'waking' life: he is 'the man whose thought recognizes a beauty in itself, and is able to distinguish that self-beautiful and the things that participate in it, and neither supposes the participants to be it nor it the participants' (*Rep.* V 476cd). To be 'awake' is to recognize participants and Forms each as what they are—not to attend only to the latter category of item.

In its treatment of art the present essay also echoes Freudian language and ideas. Freud presents art—or at least ordinary, run-of-the-mill art[139]—as arising out of fantasy[140] combined with form so as to yield pleasure and consolation to the reader, and in turn worldly success to the artist. As the *Introductory Lectures* describes the process:[141] The artist takes the material of his 'day-dreams' and fantasy, removes 'what is too personal about them and repels strangers', and 'tone[s] them down so that they do not easily reveal their origin from proscribed sources'. He *forms* and shapes his material 'until it becomes a faithful image of his phantasy', and he attaches to it 'so large a yield of pleasure . . . that . . . repressions are outweighed and lifted [or removed, *aufgehoben*] by it'. The result is that readers or viewers can derive '*consolation* and alleviation' [*Trost und Linderung*, my emphasis[142]] from 'their own sources of pleasure in their unconscious which have become inaccessible to them'. (Note: it is their own unconscious drives that are, apparently, gratified in the fiction.) The artist thereby earns their gratitude and admiration—thus achieving '*through* his phantasy' (i.e. by the publication of the fantasy transformed) 'what originally he had achieved only *in* his phantasy'—namely, 'honour, power and the love of women'. Murdoch treats this model as accurate enough in the case of bad art. ('A great deal of art . . . actually is self-consoling fantasy' (85/370).) But there is such a thing as good art, which, far from indulging fantasy actually presents us with a more accurate and realistic image of the human condition: 'Good art *reveals* what we are usually too selfish and too timid to recognise . . . together with a sense of unity and form' (86/371, my emphasis). It '*resists* absorption into the selfish dream life of the consciousness' (86/370, my emphasis).

I shall not examine each stage of the central argument. The crucial transition, from the *technai* to *morality*, takes place with the words:

That virtue operates in exactly the same kind of way in the central area of morality is less easy to perceive. . . . Yet is the situation really so different? . . . The love which brings the right answer is an exercise of justice and realism and really *looking*. (91/375)

Murdoch here gives us more or less the core of her conception of morality: the core of what we have recognized in the cases of the experience of beauty and art and in the

---

[139] 'Creative Writers and Day-Dreaming', explains that the account is supposed to fit 'not the writers most highly esteemed by the critics, but the less pretentious authors of novels, romances and short stories, who nevertheless have the widest and most eager circle of readers of both sexes' (SE 9: 149).

[140] For example:

If, at the end of one chapter of my story, I leave the hero unconscious and bleeding from severe wounds, I am sure to find him at the beginning of the next being carefully nursed and on the way to recovery . . . The fact that all the women in the novel invariably fall in love with the hero can hardly be looked on as a portrayal of reality, but it is easily understood as a necessary constitutent of a day-dream. (Freud, 'Creative Writers and Day-Dreaming', SE 9: 149–50.)

[141] Freud, *Introductory Lectures* ch. 23, SE 16:376–7.

[142] For Murdoch's distrust of consolation, see, e.g. SGC 79/364 (the psyche 'constantly seeks consolation'), 82/367 (the consoling power of purgatory), 83/368 (prayer and sacraments ' "misused" . . . as mere instruments of consolation'), 85/370 ('a great deal of art . . . is self-consoling fantasy', quoted below in main text), 87/371 ('Any story . . . consoles us since it imposes pattern'), etc.

learning of a language, which also can be carried over into the case of morality. The key ideas are those of *perception*, *reality*, and *virtue*. In some sense, none of these receives fundamental examination in the present paper, though they are all used, developed, and set in relation. If we want further examination of the notions of reality and perception, we probably do best to look back at 'The Idea of Perfection': the reality we are to become aware of is the reality of such moral facts as that the daughter-in-law in Murdoch's example is 'not vulgar but refreshingly simple, not undignified but spontaneous' (IP 17–18/313): it is a reality that has expanded beyond the 'reality' of the scientific view to include something like moral facts.

That morality involves virtue, and that the key virtues are—as in the domains of art and the *technai*—justice, realism, and really *looking*, exercised in a form that constitutes love, are claims that invite further attention; but I shall have to leave a fuller consideration for another time. There are several remarkable things in Murdoch's treatment— that she puts the emphasis on *virtues*, rather than simply right action; and that, among virtues, she puts the emphasis on virtues *of perception* and *attention* rather than, so to speak, of execution. I believe a good defence can be mounted for the former feature. The latter feature can perhaps be explained as the outcome, not of an undervaluing of action in itself, but of a moral psychology that makes action particularly readily follow from the suitably focussed consciousness.[143]

With Murdoch's interpretation of the Cave itself, perhaps the most puzzling question is whether one can accept her proposal to read the fire in the cave as symbolizing the self, 'the old unregenerate psyche, that great source of energy and warmth' (100/382). There are certainly attractions to the reading: if one looks, for example, at the various attempts to explain justice at the start of the *Republic*—both Thrasymachus's and Glaukon's at the start of book II—, they couch their explanation in terms of advantage of self or group of selves. ('And each form of government enacts the laws with a view to *its own advantage*', 338e. 'Those who lack the power to avoid [the suffering of injustice] and to seize [the committing of injustice] determine that it is *for their profit* to make a compact with one another', 358e–359a.) With such accounts, it can easily seem that benefit for the self is what lies behind all appearances of morality and is the smart thing to cite in philosophical explanation of it. And only with much work will we be able to see that such advantage for the self—while a fascinating and even philosophically interesting thing—is a pale imitation of the larger Good of which we may find in ourselves—perhaps to our surprise—a more or less developable latent conception. Finally, it may be worth raising a question related to the arguments near the end of the paper about the uniqueness and, one might say, aloneness of the Good. Good is, Murdoch now wants to say, something *other than*, and greater than, either Love or Truth (97–8/380)—even in the sense of ideally accurate presentation or 'exhibiting' of fact. There are questions one could raise about what exactly, in that

---

[143] e.g. 'he will be saying, "This is A B C D" . . . , and action will follow naturally' (IP 42/333): 'true vision occasions right conduct' (OGG 66/353).

case, the Good is and what more we might say about it. Understandably enough, given that Murdoch, like the rest of us, finds herself at an 'immense distance' from this object (99/381), she undertakes to offer little by way of positive characterization of the Good that she has in mind—though she tells us there is (despite her earlier doubts: OGG 70/357) such a thing as 'a sort of contemplation' of the Good (101/383). But even while modesty recommends itself on that matter, a larger question arises about one central project of the three essays that make up this very remarkable collection. 'On "God" and "Good"' aimed at exhibiting the transcendence of the Good as something that could be thoroughly untroublesome for open-minded metaphysicians. To that end, Murdoch's procedure was to give a mildly deflationary account—with a 'beyond-ness' that was interesting and important, but no more troublesome than the 'beyond-ness' of ideally good perception. There is now, however, a new difficulty. If the final suggestions of 'The Sovereignty of Good over other Concepts' can be sustained, then there may be more to the Good than the earlier metaphysics of 'On "God" and "Good"' recognized—and we may have to search for a more substantial account of what its transcendence amounts to, and how we can justify ourselves in believing in it.

6 Murdoch's afterthoughts—what remained to be done

Even if it is an achievement of *The Sovereignty of Good* to show how a form of moral realism might be thinkable which talks of moral perception and virtue, and even if it is a strength to show that such ideas can be presented as very much in harmony with everyday appearances and ordinarily reflective thought, still, a Hegelian might say that it was very undialectical of Murdoch not to have talked about *how we ever got to a point* where it seemed such things could be said at all. For example: if we persuade ourselves that we can and must be good 'for nothing' (OGG 71/358; cp. SGC 92/375), how did we reach that point? How did we come to talk as if desires and pleasures were, so to speak, nothing to do with it? Or if not nothing to do with it, then only derivatively or incidentally to do with it? What is the connection between, on the one hand, the virtues and the good, and, on the other, human pleasures and wants, and the contin-gencies of our existence, social organization, and taste?

Some sort of disquiet set in with Murdoch herself. By 1968 she was declaring herself 'profoundly bored with my thoughts, notably with the whole long (ten years long at least) train which led up to "The Sovereignty of Good". Not that I think this is all "wrong" but I just sense it as fearfully *limited* and partial' (quoted in Conradi, IML 501).

Christopher Cornford (Dean of General Studies when Murdoch taught at the Royal College of Art) complained: 'her account of human nature & the good isn't apparently historical' (IML 501). That is, I think, precisely right: it is not *apparently* historical; but Murdoch's own Hegelian (and Marxist) sympathies would have made her well aware of the unfinished business on those matters. There is something like a transcendental deduction of a right to talk of the reality of the Good as she conceives it (in OGG, and later in MGM, chs. 13 and 14), though some may find that it makes only a rather modest contribution to confirming confidence on the matter; but there is nothing resembling a historical deduction, in Hegelian, or even Humean, spirit, investigating how we got into a position where we could claim such a right.

Further unfinished business, I think, arises with Murdoch's talk of us both as discovering value and as 'introducing' it into the world. I shall present a couple of quotations and admit that they indicate problems that are not explicitly solved in her work.

First, a passage from Murdoch's 1966 review of Hampshire's *Freedom of the Individual*, which seems to talk as if we in some sense *create* moral reality:[144]

> Hampshire's sharp distinctions of active and passive, reason and will, break down because *a constructive activity of imagination and attention 'introduces' value into the world which we confront.* We have *already* partly willed our world when we come to look at it; and we must admit moral responsibility for this 'fabricated' world, however difficult it may be to control the process of fabrication. *On such a view it will be impossible to separate 'pure freedom'* [as emphasized by the existentialist] *as a value untouched by secondary values.* (DPR 201; Murdoch's emphasis on the last sentence, other emphases mine.)

By contrast, consider the following passage which stresses instead the conception of the world as something that already has meanings that we must learn to recognize:

> we enter a world where there are things which we *discover* and these things are discovered, not *invented*. . . . [The bourgeoisie with the kinds of view that so disgusted Sartre] should be stirred up and made to realize that they don't have to believe these things; they choose to believe them, they ought to criticize what they are doing instinctively. But I don't think that this suggests [as the only possible philosophical image, that of somebody who is simply *inventing* his values [as in Sartre], because *discovery* about the world is very closely connected with the evolution of the moral person and I think the word *discovery* is very much in place here. One is just not *inventing* it out of oneself, one is *finding it out* for instance by observing other people, and from art and from all sorts of sources. (Interview with Bigsby, FTC 109–10.)

I think one clue to reconciling these passages is to see that Murdoch's fundamental point in the review of Hampshire is that we do not first encounter, so to speak, pure non-evaluative facts and then upon that basis make 'free' moral decisions about what is or is not valuable, right, good, etc; rather, the world we encounter, if we are going to have any plausible basis for moral decision at all, is already a world conceived in certain moral terms. (Thinking of it in terms of 'secondary' value-concepts (such as rudeness or spontaneity) will be inescapable.) If so, then this passage is certainly not proposing the view that we invent or project values and meanings onto the meaning-free things in the world: rather, it is the view that when we look at the world, the world we find will be one in which we already seem to see meanings and values to which we are attuned. Murdoch may seem to make the process sound oddly accidental and contentious, however, when she says that 'the constructive activity of imagination and attention "introduces" value into the world' and that we have already in part 'willed' our world

---

[144] Carla Bagnoli discusses this passage in her contribution to the present volume.

as soon as we come to look at it. It may be that, while it sounds suspiciously as though she was talking empirically of minds as constructing moral reality, Murdoch is making a kind of Kantian point about the transcendental construction of reality, parallel to Kant's talk of the role of the imagination in synthesis; and—as for the talk of 'willing' the world, which surely should not be Murdoch's general term for the employment of some received moral scheme—it may be that, as Murdoch is putting her point as a criticism to Hampshire, she puts it in terms that he will most easily recognize, at the price of some betrayal of her own view.

Besides, there may be a further way to reconcile the passages. At any one time, we approach the world with a certain set of moral concepts, which will partly determine what we are capable of recognizing and seeing there; these concepts may be excellent, or they may be tools of corruption, embodying oppressive or false conceptions; in the latter kind of case, it is for us to try to adjust the concepts—as, in any case, we may always aim to improve both our general conceptual moral scheme and the particular judgements we make employing it: at no time do we see a pure value-free reality; but we may at one stage see a world tinged with false values, and with luck, we may come to see the world, or a part of it, in, as we might say, something closer to its true colours. It might be said that in the false colour world the false colours were in some sense literally our invention, though with misleading concepts we may still in certain ways approximate or track truths, though only under a disguise. It would not be true to say that the colours of the true colour world were literally our invention—on the contrary, it would be a matter of discovery which concepts are required for that true colour conception, and the particular truths that we came to believe using those concepts would be another kind of discovery. Such, I think, is a partial reconciliation of Murdoch's claims.[145] It raises, of course, further questions—for example, about the right to talk of the conception or perception of the world in its true (moral) colours.

What Murdoch attempted from the late 1960s or so, was to go back to low level life and basic needs.

In her journal for 6 January 1969 she says: 'I used to think Good was more important than free because political freedom cd look after itself, theoretically at any rate. Now— perhaps it is goodness that can look after itself?' (IML 502). She came to think that *behind virtue* there was something more fundamental: the everyday needs of human beings for food and shelter and, no doubt, for clothing and health:

When I was young I thought ... that freedom was the thing. Later on I felt that virtue was the thing. Now I begin to suspect that freedom and virtue are concepts which ought to be pinned into place by some more fundamental thinking about a proper quality of human life which begins at the food and shelter level. ('Existentialists and Mystics' (1970), E&M 231)

---

[145] 'The painter and the writer confront ... a reality which is *alien* and at the same time something which *they are bestowing meaning* upon.' But, Murdoch believes, 'the *otherness* of nature is a more important part of the image': 'We bestow significance but we also constantly test it and we incorporate the tests, the tests of truth, in the work itself' ('Art is the Imitation of Nature' (1978), E&M 257, my emphases).

She could have taken Plato too as an ally in this conception:[146] the difference is that Plato thought that this provided a substructure from which grew a conception of the good that could contain elements incomprehensible merely in terms of that foundation; whereas Murdoch was now deliberately turning her back on what she saw as 'mystical' in such conceptions, as also on existentialism, and was treating as her new third way a sort of combination of utilitarianism and 'militant liberalism' (E&M 231).

She was much relieved to have left St Anne's. ('How lonely I was all those years with———'. (——— is a fellow-tutor, with whom she had ended a long and difficult affair: IML 459.)) But there were moments of a more general crisis of confidence in her work. She seems to have been deeply wounded by what may have been a misunderstanding or mishearing, when, one day over lunch, Frederic Samson, a dear colleague of hers at the Royal College of Art, seemed to have said he thought her novels no good. 'I live so near to despair about my work: why go on?' she wrote in her Journal (IML 482). Her faith in her work did indeed regularly depart and return 'for no reason' (Journal: IML 483). But a more general and more particular disappointment seems to have begun to set in too, both with the cultural world of this time and with the adequacy of her response to it. Some friends suspected that she was becoming reactionary (IML 495–6).

The paper 'Existentialists and Mystics' (1970; E&M 221–34) takes up many of the views of 'On "God" and "Good"' (1966), but with a rather strange reversal of confidence in them. In the 1966 paper Murdoch rejects existentialism in favour of an unashamedly 'mystical' approach to the good. ('The background to morals is properly some sort of mysticism' (OGG 74/360).) But the 1970 paper treats 'mysticism' as itself a position to be renounced (and as already overtaken, indeed, in the dominant artistic culture: 227–31)—in favour of a more utilitarian and '*naturalistic*' philosophy that emphasizes that 'what is valuable is food and shelter and work and peace' (230). Murdoch does not exactly reject the earlier concern with virtue of OGG (and SGC), but she presents it as valid only to the extent that it is grounded in more utilitarian thinking 'which *begins* at the food and shelter level' (231).

I have to say that this later article seems to me a sad case of needless regret: it ends up joining forces with those who reject the idea of 'an unachieved area of real good, making positive spiritual demands upon the human soul', as being simply 'the last stage of a very long illusion' (229)—though the former idea is almost exactly what Murdoch herself had been defending in OGG.[147] 'Perhaps Wittgenstein is right' (232), she laments in the 1970 article, in thinking that 'talking about ethics' is 'running fruitlessly against the boundaries of language', and that there is even 'something fundamentally incoherent and unimaginable in the whole idea of goodness' (229).[148] Murdoch gives,

---

[146] 'The origin of the city . . . is to be found in the fact that we do not severally suffice for our own needs . . . Now the first and chief of our needs is the provision of food for existence and life. . . . The second is housing and the third is clothing and that sort of thing' (*Rep.* II 369b–d).

[147] OGG advocates 'some sort of mysticism, if by this is meant a non-dogmatic essentially unformulated faith in the reality of the Good' (74/360).

[148] Murdoch is thinking of Wittgenstein's 'Lecture on Ethics', *Philosophical Review* (1965), esp. the final paragraph, and *Wittgenstein and the Vienna Circle* (1979), recorded by F. Waismann, 68 (quoted by Murdoch at MGM 29).

I believe, no very substantial reasons for abandoning her earlier views. The fact that general culture had recently moved on from the 'mystical' perspective, she could hardly have taken seriously as a main argument for the philosophical weakness of that perspective; and when she mentions masochism as the 'chief temptation' (227) of the mystical novel, it is not at all clear that she has any right to take this as inevitable (if she did)—rather than as simply a danger that needs to be, and can be, avoided, as OGG had actually argued (68/355). It is clear that Murdoch, in the late 1960s, came to have serious doubts about the sufficiency of her earlier views: she saw (quite properly, I think) the need for talk of virtue and the good to be, in some sense, *grounded* in issues of basic need; but when she succumbed to the inclination altogether to abandon talk of the reality of the Good, together with her earlier 'non-dogmatic mysticism', she gave us, I believe, no very solid reason to follow her.

'Salvation by Words' (1972) makes some strong statements on the power of, quite literally, words; but it is, I think, less tight, less clear in direction, and, above all, less idealistic than the work from the decade before: it speaks more with a tone of slightly defensive disappointment than in the manifesto spirit that characterized much of *The Sovereignty of Good*. 'There is a deep crisis of confidence in the very idea of art as the making of completed statements', she says (E&M 236). But she may have seen that crisis from a little too close up. The mid-1960s students of the Royal College of Art—as prone as any to that aspect of Art School culture that is defiantly resistant to being forced to do anything other than make art—were never going to be the best audience for Murdoch's novels or for her philosophy. And meanwhile it may have been hard—having left teaching in Oxford for very good reason—to see the larger philosophical world that might indeed have been more receptive.

She had long before thought of herself as wanting to 'look back' or 'return' us to facts that we had been blinded to by recent theory. ('Reflection . . . is return to the facts' (M&E 69). 'We need to return from the self-centred concept of sincerity to the other-centred concept of truth' (AD 293). 'Philosophy has in a sense to keep trying to return to the beginning . . . I wish in this discussion to attempt a movement of return' (IP 299, cp. 332).) But in 'Art is the Imitation of Nature' (1978), the tone is different: Murdoch seems to present her concerns as simply 'old-fashioned'—a term that appears three times in two pages, to characterize things she holds dear.[149] Having earlier had the stance of a newcomer advocating the merits of a return to truths unjustly neglected by her elders, she was coming to take on a role more like that of one elder defending the things beloved of her fellows. But there had been, I think, no principled need to veer away from the ideas most beloved in her earlier writing. And there were reasons indeed for resisting the crisis of confidence, if such it was: this was in fact just the time

---

[149] E&M 254–5: 'such speculations may seem simple-minded and perhaps old-fashioned'; 'the old-fashioned mimetic paradigm'; 'what one might call, to use those old-fashioned words, nature, reality, the world'.

when McDowell was developing or reinventing Murdochian ideas in Oxford seminars before a certainly receptive audience.

There is a further story to tell about Murdoch's philosophical development from the late 1970s. She published *The Fire and the Sun* (1977) and the two 'Platonic dialogues' of *Acastos* (1986); she gave the Gifford Lectures in Edinburgh in 1982, which later became the important book *Metaphysics as a Guide to Morals* (1992). And she returned again and again to the topic of Heidegger, writing in the late 1980s a very large part of a book on him, of which I am delighted to be able to include a chapter here.

The Fire and the Sun appeared as a short book (1977) and was later incorporated within *Existentialists and Mystics* (1997). Its main topic is not—or not immediately—the imagery and subject matter of the Cave in the *Republic*. It is a study, as the subtitle puts it, of 'Why Plato Banished the Artists'. One answer is metaphysical: because of the inferior status of the mimetic art as a copy of a copy of the Forms. Another answer is political: the avoidance of certain kind of supposedly undesirable unruliness. But Murdoch argues that Plato's fundamental reason was deeper: that he wanted to promote, in a sense, a *religious* conception of life–and art, as he envisaged it, seemed incompatible with that (F&S 443–9). Murdoch has much sympathy with this. (She talks with sympathy of the rejection of images in many religions and of the crudely materializing influence that representational art had in Christianity, the religion that most unashamedly promoted it (447–8).) But she does not in the end accept Plato's view. She replies (449–63) with an extended defence of art in her own voice: arguing that, even by Platonic standards, it should be valued for its role, in a sense, in connecting us with truth and reality. She explains how there is such a thing as good art, and good art can be good for human beings (453–62: the argument is a development of SGC 87–8/371–2). The prescription for art is in fact the same as the prescription for philosophical dialectic: 'Overcome personal fantasy and egoistic anxiety and self-indulgent day-dream. Order and separate and distinguish the world justly' (F&S 455). I shall add only that the discussion—of Forms (406–14) and of beauty (414–23) as well as of art—shows a deep understanding, I think, of Plato: but one which is presented in a perhaps deceptively direct style that may have the effect that it is only those who already know most about him that will have much chance of appreciating the perceptiveness and philosophical drive of Murdoch's discussion.

The scope and ambition of *Metaphysics as a Guide to Morals* (MGM) are huge, and to sustain them would have been the work of a philosopher of first rank at the very height of her powers, bringing to conclusion decades of sustained and detailed work. Murdoch was, I think, a philosopher of first rank, but by the time it appeared, she was in her seventies and it had been more than three decades since she had been a regular university lecturer; she had written in the meantime some twenty novels of generally increasing complexity. She worked the material up many times over, through several thousands of manuscript pages that are now at the University of Iowa. It would be no dishonour if a person of her stature was in the circumstances somewhat overtaken by the magnitude of the task. Whether this in fact was the case, however, I feel unsure how to judge. I have read much of the book many times over, without yet feeling much confidence that I have the measure of it. But recently my view has certainly changed. There is a widespread view that much of the book is in a sense unfinished, with chapters ending inconclusively, or trailing off into quotations unintegrated with the main argument. There is a rather opposing view, that the kind of reflection proposed in the book and the manner of its presentation are actually well-suited to each other: a sort of open-texture in the book's construction answering to the openness of the philosophical approach that Murdoch was both calling for and displaying. My own experience with recent readings has been not only of increasing admiration and understanding, but also of a much greater unity and tightness of argument in individual chapters and the whole work. Many things that had once seemed only accidentally attached now seem to me to have a very solid relation to the whole. But I can only reserve judgement on how far with more study the process would continue and what kind of unity I would find in the work.

The book is certainly a difficult one—and the way the publishers have designed it multiplies the difficulties.[150] There are difficulties in Murdoch's style of argument: she often tells us, in a sense, not that things might be *this* way, they might be *that* way, and *these* are her reasons for thinking that they are *this* way rather than *that*—but simply, that they are the way in question. The result is that the landscape can seem rather *flat* (in the sense of Wittgenstein's remarks about logic in the *Tractatus*): as though everything were on the same level. (It also removes some of the sport for ordinary philosophers: like children, we like to be given alternatives and to see if we can resist the choices proposed.) There are certainly reasons given, but often it is only a person who already has a good understanding of the general structure of Murdoch's thought who will know what is meant as a basis for what, what is merely an incidental illustration, and what are the main conclusions. And even knowing the intended relations, it may take real work to make out what the route from the one to the other is meant to be; and one may have to clear the path oneself. There is a difficulty in some of the sketches of large tracts of philosophical history (like ch. 2 on the Fact/Value distinction and chs. 6 and 8 as 'a sort of history of the concept of consciousness' (231)) in seeing what Murdoch means as the presentation of an already generally-recognized landscape, and what as substantial recharting of the terrain. (The trick for the reader is, I think, to assume nothing is quite as you'd thought, to read every quotation with care, and to attempt to skim nothing.) There are sentences that demand the most careful reading, occurring in the course of a sub-point midway through an incidental discussion: the constancy of concentration makes the task sometimes a tiring one. But as I do the work, the book

---

[150] This book which so much needs to be worked on, scribbled over, flicked back and forth through, was published with features that constantly frustrate such aims. The book has no running chapter headings to use in finding one's way around. The Allen Lane hardback has rough-cut pages of slightly different widths which fall through one's fingers in clumps. The paperback has tiny margins. Some of this, I presume, is the result of the publisher trying to fit a lot of text into 500 pages or so; but the squeezing is a little strange, in that the paperback has ended up actually less wide, less tall, and less thick than *Existentialists and Mystics*.

seems to me only increasingly rewarding, increasingly well-structured, and increasingly successful in almost every way.[151]

I shall describe what I think is the central line of argument. For more detailed discussion I recommend Maria Antonaccio's contribution to the present volume and Stephen Mulhall's study in another place.[152]

The central project of the book can be seen as a sort of transcendental argument for the reality of Good. Supposing Thrasymachus says 'there is *nothing* deep' (MGM 238, my emphasis)—i.e. that there is nothing deeper to morality than our ordinary selfish desires and interests—; how are we to reply? Murdoch's answer has, I think, two main parts. The first (developed mainly in ch. 8) is to show that our ordinary experience and consciousness manifests occasions where we display our commitment to a richer conception of goodness. The second is to show that that commitment is not to be rejected as illusion (chs. 13–14, summarized at 508–10). In the Ontological Argument our *concept* of God is taken to imply the *existence* of God. There are problems with the argument in the case of God. (The conception of an existent God is in a sense self-contradictory, so Murdoch argues, in being actually the conception of an imperfect thing: 'No existing thing could be what we have meant by God. Any existing God would be less than God' (508).) But a parallel argument can be used, Murdoch believes, in the case of Good: it turns out that our concept of Good in a sense implies the existence of its referent. In the absence of some deeper incoherence coming to light in the very idea, we may be confident of the reality of Good.

At the first stage, we find in ourselves a conception of Good. (This is an empirical discovery, perhaps to our great surprise.) At the second (by logical reflection, 'internal' to the mind) we conclude to the reality (in the relevant manner) of the Good of which we started with only a conception. (The inference might be compared with conclusions drawn from existence-involving senses: If one finds oneself making any judgements at all involving the notion of water, then (given something like Putnam's externalism about the reference of 'water') one can conclude to the existence ('in the world') of water.[153]) The first stage is close to the kind of reflection we find in

---

[151] I am inclined to say, though, that it might have been helpful to have an Analytical Table of Contents at the start of the book enabling one to survey the main lines of argument in each chapter. And I have sometimes wondered if incidental points (as well as longer bibliographic references) inserted within the main text would not have gone better into footnotes. I don't know what Murdoch's wishes in the present case might have been; but her practice in her earlier maturity (as one can see from the manuscripts of 'The Idea of Perfection' at Iowa) includes the use of sometimes quite extensive philosophical footnotes that later—no doubt to fit the dictates of publishing—were simply inserted (without any special topping and tailing) as additional paragraphs into the course of the main text. The result is usually to produce something that may be superficially more attractive for those who are not reading the text, but which is definitely more indigestible for those who are.

[152] Stephen Mulhall, 'Constructing a Hall of Reflection: Perfectionist Edification in Iris Murdoch's *Metaphysics as a Guide to Morals*', *Philosophy* 72 (1997), 219–39.

[153] Whether and in what ways such inferences might be acceptable is a delicate and debated matter: see, for example, Michael McKinsey, 'Anti-individualism and privileged access', *Analysis* 51 (1991), 9–16, and the essays by Martin Davies and Bill Brewer in Paul Boghossian and Christopher Peacocke, eds., *New Essays on the A Priori* (Oxford: Clarendon Press, 2000).

Kant: when the cheating gambler, though he is winning at cards, catches himself saying to himself 'I am a worthless man', he shows in his judgement a recognition of a kind of value other than that of his pecuniary winnings (KpV 5: 37)—a recognition he may be surprised or indeed resistant to admit to himself. Murdoch explores the 'ubiquity of value' as it shows up in our consciousness—our thought is constantly coloured (that not being a term for the introduction of mere appearance) with the evaluation of things around—and we can see this in a novelist's description (167, 250). And the conception of Good that we find ourselves to operate with is not merely a conception of an easily- or even hardly-attained success: we leave a constant place for further perfecting. Even when 'rescued or changed by a meeting with a very good person, we do not assume that he is sinless' (509).

What kind of a thing is this goodness that we have proved? A Platonic idea or something in the world? In a sense both, though Murdoch's emphasis is mostly on the latter, and especially the very varying degrees in which goodness is present in the world. And what is it that is present when goodness is present? Primarily, accuracy in a person's cognition or perception of her world. This may be thought of as the goodness of 'pure cognition' (to use a phrase from Katsuki Sekida's writings on Buddhism)—free of egoistic illusion and subject-object opposition (241–6). It may be thought of as the 'animal attentiveness' that Rilke spoke of in Cézanne—marked by objective vigilance and consciousness without self-consciousness (246–7). But, in committing ourselves to such a goodness, we are not committing ourselves to a Husserlian essence (250), nor to a Goodness that inhabits a Platonic heaven conceived as parallel to the Christian heaven. ('There is no Platonic "elsewhere", similar to the Christian "elsewhere"' (399).) The goodness in question is just 'a penetration toward the true, real, aspects of the ordinary world' (250): Murdoch's emphasis is on the word *ordinary*. And the goodness is no very strange thing: it is the characteristic of a mind that sees things in the ordinary environment as they are. Goodness is therefore a quality of consciousness—a 'quality' in two senses: an *excellence* and a *characteristic* or property, possessed in varying degrees by us. So *consciousness*, as a phenomenon in the world, not only proves our possession of a conception of goodness; it also provides more or less imperfect instances of it in the ordinary empirical world. And for the further elaboration of this enthusias- tically embodied, and sometimes rather sexual conception of the mind in relation to the world, Murdoch invokes Plato, both in his metaphysics and in his conception of the soul as capable of operating at a constantly changing variety of different heights or 'levels'. (Murdoch is thinking of the succession of kinds of thinking in the Line and the Cave (*Rep.* 509c–511e, 514a–18b), and of the person advancing from the love of one particular beautiful person to a grasp of beauty itself in the *Symposium* (210a–212a) (MGM 16).) Knowledge is sexualized—a sort of ideal union—; sex is epistemicized—a form of ideal comprehension. 'Sex', indeed, can be not merely an 'image' of 'spiritual- ity' but actually its 'substance' (MGM 16).

If the argument for the reality of goodness constitutes the main part of the central path of the book, I should mention that the path extends both further back and further forward—back in a historical discussion of the dichotomy of Fact and Value (ch. 2) and forward with the elaboration of a kind of practical morality for our own rather low-level existence, that Murdoch wants us to derive from the conception of Good and to use to supplement it. (The morality has as its main headings 'Axioms', 'Duties', and 'Eros' (chs. 10–12, 17); and it encounters—as a challenge for which a place must be found—the Void of Simone Weil (ch. 18).) And a little aside from the main path, or perhaps on a parallel path or a broadening of it, there is a large, but I think subsidiary, discussion of art. As morality must have some reply to its Thrasymachus, art—especially in its claims to produce things with a kind of meaning, unity, and truth—must respond to its own sceptics and deniers, especially, in this case, to Derrida's post-structuralism.

'My whole argument can be read as moral philosophy', Murdoch says (481); but she adds (appropriately enough in a series of Gifford Lectures) that her treatment also has something of the 'dimension' of 'religion' (481). (Lord Gifford's bequest was to endow lectures at Glasgow, Aberdeen, Edinburgh, and St Andrews to 'promote and diffuse the study of Natural Theology in the widest sense of the term'.) 'Holiness and reverence' are 'not the exclusive property of believers' (484–5). The word 'Religion' is not to be tied exclusively to belief in a God. 'Religion is', in Murdoch's own proposed definition, 'the *attachment* to an ultimate and fundamental demand, the demand or urge that we become truthful and compassionate and wise, it *is* the *love* of that demand' (146). And if religion is conceived in that way, then even those who try to flee religion may find that they are no more able to do so than to flee their own selves.

The title of the book alludes to a question at its heart: 'How can metaphysics be a guide to morals?' (146). What Murdoch means, I think, is: how can a large and general picture of the mind and world in relation to each other be a guide to morals? Murdoch's reply is, I think: both helpfully and importantly. With a conception of the good as ideal accuracy of perception of one's environment, it is not hard to see how there can be (more or less imperfect instances of) such a thing in the world, and not hard to see how we might try to cultivate it. For those of us (i.e. all of us) who do not perceive immediately and accurately, Murdoch has given some fuller elaboration of what a practical morality should involve. Meanwhile, the metaphysical conception of value—and even the conception of the good as 'magnetic' and of ourselves as (with suitable endowment and training) magneto-sensitive—may be presented as merely theoretical philosophical description; but it may also, I think, be capable of aiding and supporting the practice of morality itself.[154] A clear-headed conception of the metaphysics of morals may prevent certain kinds of evasion that arise precisely from theoretical or meta-theoretical cleverness; the conception of the good as 'attractive' may itself make it easier for us to be attracted by it; the treatment of needs and moral

---

[154] Whether the higher-level metaphysics of morality really does have any essential implications for lower-level morality is of course a disputed matter: for some views that tend in the opposite direction to Murdoch's, see, e.g. J. L. Mackie, *Ethics* (1977), ch. 1 §§2–3, and Simon Blackburn, 'Must we weep for sentimentalism?', in J. Dreier, ed., *Contemporary Debates in Moral Theory* (2006).

relations as things with the same kind of reality in the world as persons themselves may itself make their inescapability clearer. For these reasons and more, Murdoch is, I think, entitled to conclude that a metaphysics close to that which she has presented has not only a large chance of being enduringly defensible but also a large chance of being a help and guide to morality itself in those who pay attention to it.

7 Essays in this volume

The papers in this collection focus mainly on *The Sovereignty of Good*, while looking more briefly before and after. The first three papers frame this main work. Peter Conradi describes Murdoch's own biographical route into philosophy and some of the ways in which the real philosophical figures of Yorick Smithies and Elias Canetti found their way into the early novels. Martha Nussbaum examines the ways in which *The Black Prince* contains signs both of Platonic and Dantesque conceptions of sexual love: love may be seen as a route to the contemplation of the good or instead as a 'fog' (*caligine*, Purgatorio xi.30) impeding clarity of vision. From the detail of *The Black Prince* itself, Nussbaum argues that the book's general sympathy is more with the Platonic conception; she adds, however, that it is in a sense the *artwork* rather than the *man* that is uplifted by personal love: it is 'the artwork, or the artist as creator of the artwork' who attains moral virtue and the ability to see another person truly, whereas 'the man never gets this far—until he is . . . left in solitude to write his story'. That is, the novel seems to present a real limitation to the idea of personal love effecting a lifting of the soul on the model one might find in Plato's *Symposium*. The philosophical conception that emerges here in the novel is important in itself; but it is interesting also, I think, in coinciding almost exactly with what Murdoch explicitly says in one of her philosophical essays: 'human love is normally too profoundly possessive . . . to be a place of vision' (OGG 75/ 361). It is the more 'impersonal' love found in the production and enjoyment of *art* that is our true introduction to the good—something that Plato himself failed to recognize. The coincidence between what Nussbaum finds in the novel and what we are explicitly told in Murdoch's philosophical essays is perhaps worth remarking, in view of the fact that Murdoch herself professed an 'absolute horror of putting theories or "philosophical ideas" as such into my novels' (E&M 19). One may wonder if the horror was as strong as she pretended. (As John Bayley says, also in this volume: 'she several times said . . . that she tried to keep philosophy out of [the novels]. But it seemed to me always to get in' (116).) In the third paper, Maria Antonaccio gives a broad introduction to Murdoch's philosophical work—not only to *The Sovereignty of Good* and the other essays collected in *Existentialists and Mystics*, but also to the later book *Metaphysics as a Guide to Morals*. She discusses the influences upon Murdoch and the impact of her work upon other thinkers.

The central group of four papers studies fundamental issues in Murdoch's essays. Richard Moran examines Murdoch's attacks on existentialism for injustice in her presentation, and argues that the rival view which Murdoch promotes in fact incorporates many existentialist ideas. The moral work that the mother-in-law performs in the famous example of M and D, for example, shows, he argues, a sense in which we need to *take responsibility* for our stance toward objects in the world outside—an idea that is stressed by existentialists, and that Murdoch can be seen as taking up from them. (On this issue, Murdoch's comments in the Interview with Bigsby quoted in Section 6 above (shortly after the flag for fn. 144) might count—with the existentialist phrase 'they *choose* to believe them' (my emphasis)—as interesting support for Moran's case.) The paper raises, I think, large questions about what that responsibility, in turn, might amount to. Carla Bagnoli's paper looks both at the attack on the existentialist-behaviourist picture, and at the picture of moral life that Murdoch wants to substitute for it. Among the issues she raises is the particularly interesting question, in what way Murdoch wants us to recognize value as actually 'in the world'. On Bagnoli's interpretation, Murdoch's view is a genuine alternative to both 'moral realism' and 'noncognitivism': the view cannot be a moral realism, since Murdoch herself says 'the constructive activity of imagination and attention "introduces" value into the world' (DPR 201). If value is to be found in the world, it is only because in some sense we have put it there ourselves. Bagnoli also makes the interesting challenge that though Murdoch talks (with allusions to Hegel) of the essentially historical nature of our grasp of moral concepts, she fails to consider the life of the individual within the context of social institutions. Bridget Clarke, in her wide-ranging essay, considers Murdoch's use of the notion of moral perception, and takes up various challenges made by Barbara Herman. Herman argues, for example, that those who talk of a perceptual moral sensitivity need to provide for some manner or means by which that sensitivity itself can be criticized and revised—and, she believes, that additional critical method will have to make use of *principles*. Clarke considers some interesting cases of obstacles to moral perception, both individual and social in origin; and, building on some proposals of Marilyn Frye's, investigates ways to identify the moral lack of perception involved in forms of sexism. Margaret Holland takes up a closely related topic in her paper. Murdoch tells us that 'social convention' and 'neurosis' are the primary obstacles to accurate moral perception (e.g. SBR 268–71). Holland investigates what these obstacles might amount to, and, in particular, how they sometimes operate in combination—as seems to happen, for example, in the case of opposition to homosexuality, something analyzed by Murdoch herself in a little-known paper of 1964. Holland also examines Murdoch's 'seemingly paradoxical' conception of freedom: that we have freedom when without obstacles we perceive what is right, when action follows perception 'almost automatically' (IP 37/329), and ideally we have 'no choices' (IP 40/331).

The four papers that follow consider what might be called fundamental ideas that perhaps lie slightly aside from the main line of argumentation in Murdoch's most famous papers. Roger Crisp sees in Murdoch a notion of special moral value that is not captured in the theories of Aristotle, Kant, or utilitarianism—the kind of value which can be seen in, for instance, the self-sacrificing work of Magda Trocmé, trying to help Jewish refugees in Vichy France. The difficulty for the Aristotelian, Kantian, and Utilitarian concerns not the beneficence of Magda Trocmé (which is easily enough recognized by them), but her self-sacrifice; and it is indeed hard, on many conceptions, to give proper recognition to the value that seems to attach to such self-sacrifice. But, as Crisp argues, Murdoch does indeed have a morality that can give a place to such things—in her conception of morality as *sui generis* and irreducible, as well as being of supreme importance and demandingness. Julia Driver's paper is a vigorous reply to the moral particularism in Murdoch's 'Vision and Choice in Morality' (1956)—that is, to Murdoch's view that moral claims need not meet the requirement of universalizability promoted, for example, by Hare. Driver distinguishes three forms of particularism, all of which she ascribes to Murdoch; she raises objections to the first two but grants a portion of the third idea. Lawrence Blum examines the important role that Murdoch gives to visual metaphors (like those of *attention*, *looking*, and *seeing*). He argues that Murdoch's usage of such terms is inadequate consistently to mark the distinctions that she needs; and he traces part of the problem to her belief in the Good as 'magnetic'. In the final two sections of his paper, he criticizes Murdoch for concentrating on personal rather than social obstacles to moral perception, and brings out the oddity of her statement that 'If I attend properly I will have no choices' (IP 40/331)—apparently leaving no place for deliberation. In the final paper of the volume, A. E. Denham looks at the implications of some recent studies of the psychology of psychopaths for the question of the relation between cognitive and affective states and for Murdoch's moral psychology. She considers the work of James Blair and others, who have claimed that psychopaths show no deficit in their 'mindreading' of other people, but only in their emotional and motivational responses to them—which might seem to undermine such views as Murdoch's, that seeing the character and needs of others is internally connected with being motivated to act appropriately toward them. But, Denham argues, neither the facts nor the interpretation on this point are clear. Even if in experimental situations psychopaths show normal enough cognitive recognition of relatively 'cool' mental states in other people, it remains open that they may have some impairment in cognitive identification of other people's 'hot' emotions, such as fear or sadness, in extreme situations. And in any case, even if representing another's point of view requires 'feeling with and for' him, it may also be true that 'feeling with and for' him requires representing his point of view. If that is correct, Denham argues, then there is no need to take it that the relevant feeling and representing are (in Humean terms) 'distinct existences', and the challenge from psychopaths to Murdoch's view—and generally to internalist theories of motivation—can be averted.

Many of the contributors touch on similar issues from different, indeed conflicting, points of view. Several of the authors discuss the famous example of M and D.[155] In my

---

[155] Of many others who have discussed the case I might mention Mary Midgley, in 'The Objection to Systematic Humbug', *Philosophy* 53 (1978), at 165; Maria Antonaccio, *Picturing the Human* (2000), esp. 86–95; and Christopher Mole, Samantha Vice, and Maria Antonaccio in their contributions to Anne Rowe (ed.), *Iris Murdoch: A Reassessment* (2007). Hilary Putnam alludes to it in *The Collapse . . .*, 109, 118–19, 128; as does Martha Nussbaum in *Love's Knowledge* (1990), 46 & n., 151 & n (and cp. 142). There has been something of an explosion of philosophical work on Murdoch more generally. Of recent publications, I might also

own Introduction, for example, I have tended to read Murdoch as treating only the later perceptions of M as being 'just', and being perceptions of D 'as she really is' (IP 37/329). Moran, on the other hand, treats it as a case of aspect shift where what is 'seen' first and what is 'seen' later by M are both '*there to be seen*' (193). (The issue is, however, I think, far from being a simple disagreement. There are forms of injustice that consist not in the falsehood of a judgement but in the weight given it or the inappropriateness or other failing of the terms of assessment. It is surely true, as Moran points out, that M was not merely 'under some *illusion*'—or even simply *mistaken*—'when she saw this young woman as somewhat vulgar or juvenile' (193). The change required is a different one from the avoiding of simple falsehood.) To take another issue: Blum criticizes Murdoch for focussing on 'individual psychology', 'with very little appreciation of the social and cultural forms of the distorting images that block an appreciation of... other human beings' (317). Margaret Holland and Bridget Clarke, by contrast, find ways in which Murdoch's explicit concern with the dangers of 'social convention' (e.g. S&G 216) faces up to serious social and cultural forces— even if not, perhaps, to all the kinds and varieties of such forces that Blum brings to the fore.

There is a recurring question, what exactly the Platonism and transcendence that Murdoch talks of really comes to. Two contributors agree in finding some kind of more mundane, rather than 'other-worldly', force given to such talk by Murdoch. Crisp suggests (without claiming 'strong evidence' on precisely this point) that Murdoch may have regarded talk of the Form of the Good, as also perhaps the apparatus of religion, as being 'useful metaphors' for 'a more mundane, but nevertheless important, notion of moral value' (289). Holland takes the 'transcendence' of the Good in Murdoch (by contrast with Plato) to involve only the idea that 'goodness' requires 'reaching out toward non-self aspects of the world, particularly other persons' (257). And the reading of 'On "God" and "Good"' in the present Introduction contains another attempt, in part, at much the same question.

8 Conclusion

Iris was in Greek myth the daughter of Thaumas ('Wonder') and Electra ('the shining one'; cf. ἤλεκτρον, *amber*).[156] She was a personification of the rainbow, and, more generally, of that relation between heaven and earth, between gods and human beings,

mention Marije Altorf, *Iris Murdoch and the Art of Imagining* (2008), Kate Larson, '*Everything Important is to do with Passion': Iris Murdoch's Concept of Love and its Platonic Origin* (2009), Megan Laverty, *Iris Murdoch's Ethics* (2007), Patricia J. O'Connor, *To Love the Good: The Moral Philosophy of Iris Murdoch* (1996), Heather Widdows, *The Moral Vision of Iris Murdoch* (2005), Sonja Zuba, *Iris Murdoch's Contemporary Retrieval of Plato* (2009), and the work of David Robjant and others. Two earlier works that might too easily be missed, but which show a rare acquaintance with their subject, are Basil Mitchell, *Morality: Religious and Secular* (1980), esp. ch. 5, and Guy Backus, *Iris Murdoch: The Novelist as Philosopher, the Philosopher as Novelist; 'The Unicorn' as a Philosophical Novel* (1986).

[156] Hesiod, *Theogony* 266 (with West's notes), 780, 784; Homer, *Iliad* 3.121, 8.397ff (Iris as messenger from Zeus), 'swift footed' (2.786, 5.368, 13.195 etc.), 'storm-footed' (24.77 & 159), and 'wind-footed' (24.95); associated with the rainbow (11.27, 17.547).

that the rainbow represents. She was responsible, like Hermes, for carrying messages from the gods. In Plato's *Theaetetus*, Iris is Philosophy herself.[157] As a classicist and reader of Plato, keeping myth alive in both her novels and her life,[158] and ready to be painted in the portrait by Tom Phillips as the foreground to Titian's *Flaying of Marsyas*,[159] Murdoch must have known well these roles. And the call to make philosophy a mediation between something like heaven and earth was an expectation that she found a rare way to answer. The work that became *The Sovereignty of Good* was in many ways unique—it aimed to recall philosophy from theory (in particular, a crudely linguistic theory of morals and a scientistic conception of reality) to some of the actual facts of morality; but it actually made possible a revolution in moral theory, the consequences of which (accepted by some, rejected by others) have certainly not run their course. Its span reaches from the ordinarily mundane to a Platonic conception of the Good that is ambitious but modest enough, I think, to be literally believable. Murdoch claims that morality has in the past always been connected with religion, and religion in turn with mysticism (OGG 74/360): her task is to maintain the connections of morality with the mystical, in a world that no longer has religion as middle term. This task was effected with a historical scope that started in dialogue with Existentialism and Oxford Philosophy, and then reached back to the traditions of Plato and Christianity, Kant and Wittgenstein, and that led her forward to something that seemed close to Buddhism—all this being developed within a broad historical outlook that carried (especially in earlier days) the imprint of Hegel, as well as some of the contrary influence of Kierkegaard. It was a large project, but it came to seem to its author too small: and she seems sometimes to have had her doubts about it, even as a part of the truth. My own view is that she underestimated her achievement, and the philosophical world may have done so too.

---

[157] Plato, *Theaetetus* 155d: philosophy starts from wonder, 'and the man who said Iris was the daughter of Thaumas [i.e. Wonder] seems to have been doing his genealogy not at all badly' (tr. McDowell).

[158] 'The "Black Prince," of course, is Apollo—most critics who reviewed the book in England didn't appear to realise this' (FTC 76–7). In a 1984 interview with Simon Price, Murdoch tells of her own experience of something like a miracle at Delphi, the home of Apollo. A huge winged beetle was crashing around the hotel dining room, causing consternation among the guests. The waiters flapped their napkins, trying to kill it. 'So I willed it to come to *me* and it came and it landed on me just *here* (on her chest), and I took it outside and released it' (FTC 148). In Murdoch's own mythology, Apollo is not (as in Nietzsche) the god of light and reason, he is 'a most terrible murderer and rapist': he is a terrible god, but also 'a great artist and thinker and a great source of life', and Dionysus is regarded 'in a sense as a part of Apollo's mind' (FTC 153).

[159] The satyr Marsyas is being skinned alive for his failure to outdo on the flute (or pipes) the beauty of Apollo on the lyre. The story (which shows up in four of Murdoch's novels) is not just one of hubristic ambition punished. In Dante—and Renaissance painters—, Marsyas's punishment is also a divine liberation: Apollo is to be read as extracting the soul of Marsyas from the sheath of his limbs (*sì come quando Marsïa traesti / de la vagina de le membra sue*), releasing him for visions that bodily encumberment would prevent (*Paradiso* I, 19–20). Cf. also Mary Kinzie's Introduction to *The Sea, The Sea* (Penguin, 2001).

Sein und Zeit: Pursuit of Being
from *Heidegger*

Iris Murdoch

Heidegger's book *Being and Time* (*Sein und Zeit*) starts with a quotation from Plato, *Sophist* 244A. 'For manifestly you have long been aware of what you mean when you use the expression "being". We, however, who used to think we understood it, have now become perplexed.' *Being and Time* was first published in 1927 when Heidegger was comparatively young, but most of his numerous and important later writings can be seen as developments from these early ideas. This book raises for us in a new and challenging form questions about metaphysical philosophy and therefore (a related question) about empiricism. Derrida calls Heidegger the last metaphysician, whose work signals the end of philosophy, the particular mode of reflection invented by the Greeks. On page 26: 6 of *Being and Time* Heidegger again refers to the *Sophist*, 242C, where the Socratic figure, the Eleatic Stranger, complains that Parmenides and others, when discussing the nature of real things (τὰ ὄντα), have 'told us a story (μύθος, myth) as if we were children'. (Note: in references to pages of *Being and Time* the first number is that of the English edition, the second that of the later German editions, conveniently provided in the English text.) Plato here indicates pre-Socratic speculations (by Parmenides, Pherecydes, Heraclitus, Empedocles) about whether reality is one, or whether it 'consists of' two things, or principles, which are at war, or else in harmony, or perhaps three, and so on. Such picturesque manufacture of pseudo-entities, Heidegger tells us, must be avoided if we are to understand the problem of Being. The philosophers, Plato's Stranger goes on to say (at 243A, not quoted by Heidegger) fail to consider 'the majority of people, like ourselves', and do not care 'whether their arguments carry us along'. Plato here implicitly distinguishes his own use of myth, as explanatory metaphor, occurring within philosophical argument, from the fairy tales of his predecessors. He also suggests that philosophy should not be obscure personal fantasy, but clarified reflection capable of convincing a qualified 'majority'. If we try to test Heidegger, and Plato himself, against such requirements we raise questions, especially important now in our newly sceptical age, about metaphysics, empiricism, and the place of moral philosophy, and of religion. Can an empiricist be a metaphysician? Can the myths and pictures of traditional metaphysics be restated without loss in ordinary language, is this a fair criterion? Must a moral philosopher be a metaphysician? How does religion relate to theology? Can undogmatic 'religious views' be a part of philosophy? Can, or should, philosophy now be modest, unsystematic, concerned with conceptual problems here and there, morally neutral, unaware of religion? What sort of thinking is philosophical thinking? Would one rather be damned with Schopenhauer, Bradley, Collingwood, and Simone Weil, than saved with Prichard, Ross, Hare, Toulmin, Rorty, and Parfit?

Philosophers criticise, undermine, modify, reject previous philosophers, philosophical geniuses establish entirely new beginnings. One must see what a philosopher is rejecting. Hegel spoke of getting back 'to the things themselves', and he criticised previous metaphysical systems for losing 'the living nature of concrete fact'. (Preface to *Phenomenology.*[1]) Husserl also wanted to get back, by a form of scientific intuition, 'to the things themselves', to a form of thinking which is prior to all thinking. The two philosophers in the twentieth century who have most deeply disturbed philosophical thinking are Wittgenstein and Heidegger. It is a sad, interesting comment on the general state of philosophy that there are so few thinkers who are equally interested in both. The world of philosophy seems to be divided into two kingdoms, each one unaware (or if aware contemptuous) of the other. This need not be so, since although they differ so much in style, they have some important fundamental ideas in common. For instance, both could claim that they have brought to an end the era of 'the metaphysical subject', who was invented by Descartes and deified by Hegel. What makes reading Wittgenstein so different from and, contrary to what might at first appear, more difficult than, reading Heidegger, is that Wittgenstein is not interested in philosophical history, in 'the Greeks' or 'the tradition' or in carefully placing himself in relation to carefully criticised predecessors. He is well aware of the problems that matter to him, but the names of other philosophers rarely appear in his writings; and (I am told) he did not in fact read very much philosophy, or very much anything. Whereas Heidegger is an omniscient scholar, fascinated by other philosophers and by his difference from them. He was also deeply interested in religion, was a theological student, and lived, when younger, and in a sense all his life, 'inside religion'. Whereas Wittgenstein's remarks on the subject are those of a brilliant outsider. Influences on Heidegger, apart from the Greeks, include the Christian mystics, Hölderlin, Hegel, Kierkegaard, Nietzsche, Husserl, Scheler, Zen, and Tao. Both Heidegger and Wittgenstein, the former explicitly, put the future of philosophy into question. What Heidegger calls 'the old metaphysical quest for security' is now seen to be in vain. An essay (1962) of Heidegger has the title 'The End of Philosophy and the Task of Thinking'. By philosophy, Heidegger means (Greek) metaphysics. Derrida called

[1] 'The living nature of concrete fact': G. W. Hegel, *Phenomenology of Spirit*, tr. J. B. Baillie (London: S. Sonnenschein, 1910, rev. 1931), Preface §51. Post-Kantian 'Philosophy of Nature' performs feats of fine-sounding but vacuous labelling, but 'It has lost hold of the living nature of concrete fact' (*das lebendige Wesen der Sache*). (This and other footnotes are added by the present editor, JB.)

Heidegger the last metaphysician. Well, what is philosophy to do? It is certainly not a science, nor can it be a theology, though it should certainly be aware of religion. Are 'philosophers' now just very intelligent general thinkers? (Was Simone Weil a philosopher?) Could one 'translate' Heidegger's philosophy into 'ordinary language', and would that still be philosophy? Must moral philosophy now be the fundamental form of philosophy? Well briefed empiricists should enter into this fray.

Metaphysics, which is about 'everything' and involves some degree of system, may be contrasted with what was once called in Cambridge the 'fire station' view of philosophy, that is the contention that the philosopher has no positive general role but as it were sits at home waiting for conceptual problems to be brought to him by, for instance, biologists, physicists, psychologists, doctors, artists, politicians. In order to enlighten those muddled people the philosopher must also be capable of detecting and removing conceptual confusion in the works of former philosophers. Some thinkers in the Wittgensteinian tradition might argue that empiricism should now limit itself to this, certainly not unimportant, role. Was Wittgenstein an empiricist? He certainly dealt, in a general and systematic *manner*, with the oldest problems of philosophy. If someone says, we must start from scratch, Wittgenstein says, 'But how do we get back to scratch?' Heidegger wonders, how do we get back to the 'the things themselves'? Are these objects, or a mode of being, or what? Heidegger's innovations, the ideas which make his philosophy revolutionary, concern the starting point of philosophical thought (which he removes from the traditional subject), they also concern time, contingency, states of mind. He aims to renew the western tradition of thought by returning to Greek sources, to Plato and Aristotle, but also beyond them to the pre-Socratics, to find, in these earliest reflections, elements which we have more lately (for instance since Schopenhauer) rediscovered through an awareness of Buddhism and 'oriental religion'. The most fundamental move is the retirement of the old metaphysical subject, held in common by Descartes and Hegel. (Wittgenstein, with less fuss, also retires this figure.) Heidegger uses the term *Dasein*, 'being there', to indicate, in the most general and initially vague sense, human awareness, consciousness, something there. Dasein is also primordially Being-in-the-World. It is its world. In Heidegger's argument initial concepts often appear 'vaguely', or 'roughly' or 'provisionally', *zunächst und zumeist*, translated in *Being and Time* as 'proximally and for the most part'. This terminology is introduced on page 25: 6, and explained more fully on page 422: 370. That is, he wishes to indicate matters (not exactly things) of which we are certainly aware, but which we cannot exactly 'give an account of'. (Compare Wittgenstein's quotation from St Augustine *Confessions* I.8 with which he opens the *Philosophical Investigations*.[2]) The account of such matters will be offered to us in due course. The starting point, Dasein, must be grasped at

---

[2] Wittgenstein's *Philosophical Investigations* (Oxford: Basil Blackwell, 1953), §1, opens with a quotation from Augustine's *Confessions* I.viii (13). In translation, the passage begins: 'When they (my elders) named some object, and accordingly moved towards something, I saw this and I grasped that the thing was called by the sound they uttered when they meant to point it out.'

once as a being-there which is *not* in the traditional philosophical, or common-sense, sense a subject, *not* an entity 'outside' which objects exist whose 'reality' must then be proved. 'The "scandal of philosophy" is not that this proof has yet to be given, but that *such proofs are expected and attempted again and again*. Such expectations, aims, and demands arise from our ontologically inadequate way of starting... If Dasein is understood correctly, it defies such proofs, because in its Being it already *is* what subsequent proofs deem necessary to demonstrate for it' (249: 205). Dasein (the German term is used in English translation) is then not a secluded Cartesian subject, nor is it a Kantian subject, or a (dialectical) Hegelian subject. It is not a subject, or an 'individual' or an entity, but rather a sort of relation, or world-awareness, or being-there of a world. (Wittgenstein, again without fuss, and in terms of the nature of language, makes the same move, *Tractatus* 5.62 and following and *Investigations passim*.) The 'world' of this 'awareness' is essentially contingent, its Being-in-the-World (*In-der-Welt-Sein*) is accidental. Dasein is thrown, *geworfen*, into an accidental (and so limited, temporal, historical) scene. It is surrounded by an indefinite beyond. Dasein is (partly, proximally) describable in terms of its states of mind: moods, anxieties, fears. G. E. Moore was interested in 'states of mind' and thought (rightly) that we ought to have good ones, but he assumed that we knew what states of mind were, and did not make any radical use or offer any radical account of the concept. Heidegger reasonably claims (178: 139) that 'the basic ontological Interpretation of the affective life in general has been able to make scarcely one forward step worthy of mention since Aristotle. On the contrary, affects and feelings come under the theme of psychological phenomena, functioning as a third class of these, usually along with ideation and volition. They sink to the level of accompanying phenomena.' (And, one might add, become the property of novelists.) Heidegger goes on to say that it has been a merit of 'phenomenological research that it has again brought these phenomena more unrestrictedly into our sight. Not only that: Scheler, accepting the challenges of Augustine and Pascal, has guided the problematic to a consideration of how acts which "represent" and acts which "take an interest" are interconnected in their foundations. But even here the existential-ontological foundations of the phenomenon of the act in general are admittedly still obscure' [178: 139].[3] Heidegger's footnote on this passage quotes from Pascal's *Pensées*: '*Et de là vient qu'au lieu qu'en parlant des choses humaines on dit qu'il faut les connaître avant que de les aimer... les saints au contraire disent en parlant des choses divines qu'il faut les aimer pour les connaître, et qu'on n'entre dans la vérité que par la charité.*'[4] In human matters, one must know before one loves, in divine matters one must love in

---

[3] Page references in square brackets are inserted by the present editor. All other cases of square brackets go back to Murdoch's original text.

[4] 'And hence it happens that whereas, in speaking of human matters, we say that one must know them before loving them ..., the saints on the contrary say, in speaking of divine matters, that one must love them in order to know them, and that one enters into truth only by charity.' Blaise Pascal, *Opuscules et Pensées*, ed. Léon Brunschvicg (Paris: Hachette, 6th edn., 1912), 185, my transl. The passage actually comes not from one of the *Pensées* but from *De l'esprit géométrique*, one of the *Opuscules*. The ellipsis is Murdoch's: Heidegger quotes Pascal without omission.

order to know. Also from Augustine *Contra Faustum*: *non intratur in veritatem, nisi per charitatem*.[5] Truth is only entered through charity. Anselm's *inveniam amando*, and *credo ut intelligam*[6] might have been quoted to the same effect. Heidegger here notices, and at once abandons, an idea of immense importance, that of the moral content of cognition and the ubiquity of evaluation. (He himself says later that 'the divine' is everywhere.) The implication of his lack of interest is that at an 'everyday' level, proximally and for the most part, human life has no in-built moral aspect. In his system, moral insight or inspiration is a later, or farther, or special, or specialised, narrowly defined, achievement. Sartrian existentialism and the morality of Marxism also display this pattern. I shall return to these matters.

Heidegger's central and most important and interesting image is that of a 'clearing' (*Lichtung*), to be thought of for example as a clearing in a forest. Heidegger, lover of the Black Forest, entitled a later work *Holzwege*, woodland paths. Dasein is not a thing, but more like an open space, or absence, which permits or encourages manifestations of Being. Only in human existence, consciousness, is Being disclosed. Dasein, in making a clearing, retires, so that something else which is can advance and be manifest. Not 'to the things themselves', but rather 'let things be'. In a ceaseless process Being is revealed, is retained, then sinks back into undisclosedness or disguise. Entities, beings, exist only as thus given to a consciousness, their *presence* requires a corresponding *absence* or withdrawal. Heidegger also said: man is the shepherd of Being. We must distinguish then between beings, entities which appear, and Being, which is that from which, or by which, they are given, and as (roughly) what surrounds Dasein on every side. Dasein is thus a relationship with, or servant of, Being. Heidegger emphasises that his imagery is not that of Hegelian idealism. That what is, is for a consciousness, is common ground. But Heidegger holds no theory of a transcendent systematised order of spiritual reality, or true knowledge, which it is man's proper destiny to realise. The word 'Being', in Heidegger's parlance, indicates the infinite availability of beings to each Dasein, 'thrown' as it is into contingent surroundings, where it always confronts 'more' and 'other'. '*Being is the t r a n c e n d e n s pure and simple*' (62: 38). *This* is what must be taken as absolutely primary; and not the old metaphysical subject who was always busy constructing, or argumentatively seeking, or dialectically pouncing upon, the objects of which its 'external world' was to consist.

Dasein is at first described in its everyday (*alltäglich*), provisional, incomplete, not yet authentic, ordinary state. (In which, as I shall argue, Heidegger portrays it as curiously bereft of values.) Dasein is to be thought of as initially 'fallen', though not from any

---

[5] Augustine, *Contra Faustum Manichaeum* (J.-P. Migne, *Patrologia Latina* (Paris: Migne, 1844–55), vol. VIII) XXXII.18, translated by Murdoch in the sentence that follows.

[6] Murdoch quotes from two famous lines in the *Proslogion*: 'inveniam amando, amem inveniendo' ('May I find [you, Lord] by loving [you]; may I love [you] by finding [you]') and 'neque enim quaero intelligere ut credam, sed credo ut intelligam' ('For also, I do not seek to understand in order to believe, but I believe in order to understand', my transl.). See e.g. M. J. Charlesworth, tr., *St. Anselm's Proslogion*...(Oxford: Clarendon Press, 1965), ch. 1, p. 114.

prior state. Everyday Dasein, the fuzzy confused state of our ordinary awareness, is analysed by Heidegger in terms of various structural levels. Primary structures, constitutive of being the 'there', are understanding (*Verständnis*) and state of mind (*Befindlichkeit*, how we 'find' ourselves). Mood (*Stimmung*) characterises both states of mind, and also understanding as primary cognition. Fear, for instance, is a mode of state of mind. Dasein's fundamental and ubiquitous form of apprehension is described as care (*Sorge*) or concern (*Besorgen*), our restless practical state of being concerned with our world, which is also a sense of contingency and mortality. Although Heidegger admits (178: 138) that 'the different modes of state-of-mind and the ways in which they are interconnected in their foundations cannot be interpreted within the problematic of the present investigation', and that the 'existential-ontological foundations' of such phenomena remain obscure, he takes considerable trouble to attempt a fundamental analysis of our 'awareness' or 'consciousness' in terms of concepts such as those mentioned above. Such an analysis, it seems to me, cannot but be arbitrary, and in this case is designed by Heidegger to offer a primary support, in 'inauthentic' being, for his later theory of 'authentic' being, which consists of higher and enlightened forms of what are already represented as fundamental structures. A good novelist can more accurately describe these fugitive aspects of the human condition, but of course that is not philosophy, and the novelist too has his formal purposes. We here touch on fundamental problems in moral philosophy (that is, in philosophy). *Being and Time* does not contain enough *examples*. Plato and Kant are more generous with these. We may also contrast, with Heidegger's purposive, carefully moulded, system-oriented concepts, the idea of 'attention' as presented by Simone Weil. Heidegger admits his debt to Kierkegaard, and has made his own the concept of *Angst*, translated by Macquarrie and Robinson in the established English edition of *Being and Time* as 'anxiety', though elsewhere in discussions of Heidegger, as in the first translations of Kierkegaard's work into English, as 'dread'. Heidegger's use of *Angst* moves between both senses, since he makes of this experience a sort of messenger or guide between inauthentic and authentic states. It may be argued that the concept does better work in the picturesque 'stories' of Kierkegaard, than in the grand syntheses of Heidegger, or of Sartre.

The concept of Dasein, as starting point, transcends the old dualism of subject and object, and also (with that) outmodes the (from a Heideggerian point of view mechanical) Hegelian dialectic. There is the continual movement or 'play' of presence and absence as beings, manifestations of Being, come and go. Being is not a thing, but an infinite possibility of manifestation, and in this sense a transcendent presence. Each Dasein, as it *responds* to Being and enables its manifestation as beings, creates its own world. (Not unlike Wittgenstein's 'world'.) This world however may be filled with illusions, constant temptations to error. 'Being-in-the-world is in itself *tempting* [*versucherisch*]' [221: 177]. A prime temptation is represented by *They*: public opinion, conformity, society. 'Idle talk and the way things have been publicly interpreted' [221: 177]. Heidegger often refers to the effect of idle talk (*Gerede*) and curiosity and ambiguity, whereby Dasein's Being towards its world, toward others, and towards itself is 'in a mode of groundless floating' (221: 177). However he also 'excuses' this condition. 'The expression "idle talk" is not to be used here in a disparaging sense' (211: 167). Everyday chatter is not necessarily bad though it may lack authenticity. 'But the inauthenticity of Dasein does not signify any "less" Being or any "lower" degree of Being. Rather it is the case that even in its fullest concretion Dasein can be characterised by inauthenticity—when busy, when excited, when interested, when ready for enjoyment' (68: 43). This is a point at which we may wish to question Heidegger's account, which often in fact seems realistic and capable of being explained equally well without philosophical jargon. Of course 'everyday chatter', or 'gossip', though unreflective or time-wasting or frivolous is, if not malicious etc., not something 'bad', but rather something natural and even, as a form of relaxation, useful. On the other hand it is not a manifestation of human greatness or virtue. All right; but in Heidegger's system the distinction (yet to be discussed) between what he calls authentic (*eigentlich*) and inauthentic in effect leaves the ordinary world of human activity, when we are busy, interested, enjoying something, without any signs of moral activity or moral orientation. When we are interested we may be, for good or ill, learning something, when we are busy we may be telling lies or telling the truth, what we enjoy may be right or wrong. There is a kind of contempt for human existence if not in some way 'exalted' implied in Heidegger's condescension toward *Gerede* and similar 'inauthentic' activities. His account, perpetually, suggests that value, moral orientation, virtue, exists only at a level markedly above that of the everyday. So it is not even worth examining the idea of *Gerede*, which Heidegger does use in a disparaging sense but also denies that he does.

Another set of concepts which are expressive of Heidegger's general view concern what he calls *Zeug*, a word which may be translated as tools, or 'stuff', (he has the stuff he needs, or also he has the stuff, or makings, of a soldier) but is best, as Heidegger uses it, put into English as 'equipment' or 'gear'. 'Equipment is essentially "something in order to ..."' 'In the "in-order-to" as a structure there lies an assignment or reference [*Verweisung*] of something to something' (97: 68). In describing our intentional grasp of our world Heidegger makes a distinction which corresponds rather roughly to that between the practical and the theoretical. The distinction is set out however in a more complicated manner (98: 69), as one between what is ready-to-hand (*zuhanden*) and what is *present-at-hand* (*vorhanden*). 'Readiness-to-hand is the way in which entities as they are "in themselves" are defined ontologico-categorially. Yet only by reason of something present-at-hand is there anything ready-to-hand. Does it follow, however, granting this thesis for the nonce, that readiness-to-hand is ontologically founded upon presence-to-hand?' (101: 71) A hammer, for instance, may be either used or considered. Using is, in some general sense, more basic and immediate than considering. However 'practical' behaviour is not 'sightless', it involves circumspection (*Umsicht*), quick everyday 'looking around'. 'Our concernful absorption in whatever work-world lies closest to us' (101: 71). Readiness-to-hand is not, Heidegger emphasises, a 'subjective colouring' given to 'some world-stuff which is proximally present-at-hand in itself'. Entities are not theoretically known and then used. Heidegger has already explained (88: 61) that cognition, knowledge is as it were a secondary or prompted movement of basic Dasein. We do not instantly or by definition 'know' the world which we are 'living'. 'Perception is consummated when one *addresses* oneself to something as something and *discusses* it as such. This amounts to interpretation in the broadest sense' (89: 62). Theoretical behaviour, which is described at 99: 69 as 'looking without circumspection', that is without the apt sense of context involved in ready-to-hand behaviour, is a matter of using rules and constructing a method. In understanding this part of Heidegger's argument we are not just required to think of 'honest peasants' (though Heidegger often thinks of them) or the instinctive tool-using of primitive man or simple craftsmen; we are to realise that all Daseins inhabit (experience, make-to-be) a precognitive, and prelinguistic, world which demands or prompts interpretation. 'Dasein is never to be defined ontologically by regarding it as life (in an ontologically indefinite manner) plus something else.' It is originally 'primitive' in the sense of being primordially absorbed in 'phenomena' (75–76: 50–51). This is, for Heidegger, a difficult piece of system-building wherein, it seems to me, his new phenomenology does not justify itself. He rightly indicates the importance of conceiving, philosophically, of fundamental (pre-linguistic, sub-conceptual) levels of consciousness, and of evading old philosophical 'problems of knowledge'. Heidegger's concept of Dasein as in this sense 'deep' contrasts favourably not only with the Cartesian metaphysical subject, but with the smart linguistic subject of Derrida's structuralism.

That which is ontically closest and well known is ontologically the farthest and not known at all; and its ontological signification is constantly overlooked. When Augustine asks: '*Quid autem propinquius meipso mihi?*'[7] and must answer: '*ego certe laboro hic et laboro in meipso: factus sum mihi terra difficultatis et sudoris nimii*', this applies not only to the ontical and pre-ontological opaqueness of Dasein but even more to the ontological task which lies ahead; for not only must this entity not be missed in that kind of Being in which it is phenomenally closest, but it must be made accessible by a positive characterisation. (69: 43–4)

(Augustine: 'But what is closer to me than myself?' He asks this question in the course of a discussion of memory and recognition, which might be described as 'Wittgensteinian' in tone, and in course of which he has already cried out, 'Most certainly, Lord, I labour upon this [problem] and within myself: I have made myself into a land of difficulty and exceeding sweat'. *Confessions* X 16. Both Heidegger and Wittgenstein recognise in Augustine a great empirically minded philosopher whose voice sounds most aptly today.) However it is one thing to point to that deep, close, area which must not be overlooked, it is another to give it a 'positive characterisation'; this may, in my

---

[7] This sentence and the one that follows are translated by Murdoch a few lines below: 'But what is closer...?' and 'Most certainly...'. See Augustine, *Confessions* X.xvi (25), e.g. tr. H. Chadwick (Oxford: Oxford University Press, 1992).

SEIN UND ZEIT: PURSUIT OF BEING 101

view, be done more profitably by lengthy, and not system-dominated, discussion in non-jargon ordinary language, without, for instance, the use of the word 'ontological'. ('Ontological', concerned with the philosophical problem of Being, is to be distinguished from 'ontic', meaning, in a more ordinary sense, concerned with existent beings in a common-sense manner.) Much of Heidegger's early (proximal) machinery is designed to fill out the coming contrast, mediated by his concept of truth, between inauthentic and authentic being. The values of everyday Dasein appear to be those of *Gerede* and 'They', said casually by Heidegger not to be thought of in a disparaging sense. There is, it is true, a distinction between good and bad moods (175: 136). 'The "bare mood" discloses the "there" more primordially, but correspondingly it *closes* it *off* more stubbornly than any *not*-perceiving. / This is shown in *bad moods*. In these, Dasein becomes blind to itself, the environment with which it is concerned veils itself, the circumspection of concern goes astray.' This sounds like a promising description of ordinary selfish untruthful behaviour, but is not explored as such by Heidegger, who treats these distinctions as if they concerned 'low-level' psychological conditions, unconnected with the really important moral orientations. He does not clarify a relation of value (morality) to his distinction of ready-to-hand and present-at-hand, except in so far as he treats the former as primary. The distinction is in any case a clumsy one. Circumspection already includes theory. Heidegger speaks of a switch from *Zuhandenheit* to *Vorhandenheit* as capable of 'refreshing' the former. The emphasis on the use of tools seems arbitrary, and smacks of ethnology, which Heidegger explicitly wishes to exclude. The change from using things to looking at them need not exclusively suggest adopting a theoretical, in the sense of unpractical or idle, attitude. It can on the contrary suggest a more understanding, reflective, respectful, evaluative attitude. This is a case of Heidegger's jargon being, at a crucial point, distinctly unhelpful.

As I said above, Heidegger's concept of truth mediates the relationships between the ordinary less-evolved unenlightened everyday being of Dasein, and its authentic enlightened being; and, as it may seem, in order to glorify the contrast, Heidegger unobtrusively downgrades *Alltäglichkeit*, everydayness, by treating its various manifestations as quasi-factual and unworthy of being paid the compliment of discriminating moral criticism.

Many of Heidegger's fundamental ideas join together in his concept of truth. In explaining 'phenomenology' (59: 35) Heidegger tells us that Being is not a set of entities or beings but is the Being of entities, and that this Being can be 'covered up so extensively that it becomes forgotten and no question arises about it or about its meaning. Thus that which demands that it become a phenomenon and which demands this in a distinctive sense and in terms of its ownmost content as a thing, is what phenomenology has taken into its grasp thematically as its object . . . Only as phenomenology is ontology possible' [59–60: 35]. Moreover, what is to become a phenomenon can be hidden, covered-up, in various ways. Trust is a matter of uncovering, disclosure. There are different levels of disclosure. Any Dasein is a

disclosing, a making of a space or clearing (*Lichtung*) for the appearance of a phenomenon, whose demand or claim is thereby met. Dasein is described by Heidegger as
primordially in truth and untruth. Consciousness is consciousness of something (starting point of Husserl), any perception makes something be, seeing sees colours, in this
sense perception is always true. This is *not*, as Heidegger's further argument shows, an
introduction to a phenomenalist sense datum theory of knowledge. Perception as
something which may be distinguished from cognition, is not to be taken as providing
original elements out of which cognition is to be constructed. A more general primary
concept here is mood (*Stimmung*), Dasein is always attuned to something. 'Dasein
always has some mood . . . having a mood brings Being to its "there" ' (173: 134). 'The
possibilities of disclosure which belong to cognition reach far too short a way compared
with the primordial disclosure belonging to moods.' Heidegger adds that 'a mood of
elation can alleviate the manifest burden of Being; that such a mood is possible also
discloses the burdensome nature of Dasein, even while it alleviates the burden'.
Heidegger here, playing with his own powerful imagery, offers us a picture of
Dasein *burdened* by meeting the *demands* or *claims* of Being. So, 'there' and 'mood'
are, as disclosure, basic forms of truth, although at the same time what is disclosed may
be untrue as being disguised or distorted, for instance when something is 'seen as'
something else. Language (capable of truth and untruth) has its 'ontological "*locus*" . . . in
Dasein's state of Being' (210: 168). Heidegger who has much to say about language, is
not a 'linguistic philosopher' in the sense of either Wittgenstein or, *mutatis mutandis*,
Derrida. So, any disclosure is a sort of truth, but may be untrue (disguised) truth,
involving distortions and mistakes or sheer unformulated vaguenesses which may be of
many kinds.

Heidegger's theory of truth, which he says goes back to ancient Greek sources,
avoiding the errors of later epistemology, is designed to preclude the idea, held by some
philosophers and by common sense, that truth is agreement, correspondence, *adaequatio, ὁμοίωσις*.

To say that an assertion 'is true' signifies that it uncovers the entity as it is in itself. Such an
assertion asserts, points out, 'lets' the entity 'be seen' (ἀπόφανσις) in its uncoveredness. The
Being-true (truth) of the assertion must be understood as Being-uncovering [*Entdeckend-sein*].
Thus truth has by no means the structure of an agreement between knowing and the object in
the sense of a likening of one entity (the subject) to another (the object).

Being-true as Being-uncovering is in turn ontologically possible only on the basis of Being-in-
the-world. The latter phenomenon, which we have known as a basic state of Dasein, is the
foundation for the primordial phenomenon of truth . . .

'Being-true' ('truth') is[8] Being-uncovering. But is not this a highly arbitrary way to define
'truth'? By such drastic ways of defining this concept we may succeed in eliminating the idea of
agreement from the conception of truth. Must we not pay for this dubious gain by plunging the
'good' old tradition into nullity? But while our definition is seemingly *arbitrary* it contains only

---

[8] Macquarrie & Robinson: means.

the *necessary* interpretation of what was primordially surmised in the *oldest* tradition of ancient philosophy and even understood in a pre-phenomenological manner. If a λόγος as ἀπόφανσις is to be true, its being-true is ἀληθεύειν in the manner of ἀποφαίνεσθαι—of taking entities out of their hiddenness and letting them be seen in their unhiddenness (their uncoveredness). [261–2: 218–9]

Heidegger then goes on to attribute this view of truth, as a showing of 'entities in the "how" of their uncoveredness', to Aristotle and Heraclitus. (The translators also suggest 'to-be-uncovering' as a possible translation of *Entdeckend-sein*.) Philosophers who have been wondering whether truth is correspondence or coherence may breathe a sigh of relief when a finger is pointed in a more fundamental direction. Wittgenstein too pointed in this direction (*Tractatus* 5.63 and following[9]).

I am my world. The thinking, presenting subject; there is no such thing . . . The subject does not belong to the world but it is a limit of the world. Where *in* the world is a metaphysical subject to be noted? . . . From nothing in the field of sight can it be concluded that it is seen from an eye. This is connected with the fact that no part of our experience is also *a priori*. Everything we see could also be otherwise . . . There is therefore really a sense in which in philosophy we can talk of a non-psychological I. The I occurs in philosophy through the fact that the 'world is my world'.

(Much of the *Philosophical Investigations* is an unassertive raking over of implications of these concise remarks.) Heidegger's Dasein too is *thrown* into a contingent world, where everything it sees could be otherwise; the world is its world, it is its world. This is the move, mentioned above, which was to eliminate the 'scandalous' philosophical 'problem' about how the subject constructed his objective surroundings. But how does this affect truth and the 'good old' conviction that 'the cat is on the mat' is true if, and only if, the cat is on the mat? This is one of many points where one wishes that Heidegger would explain his machinery in ordinary language. Wittgenstein's elegant terseness, in both *Tractatus* and *Investigations* also often seems wilful.

Heidegger explains his 'Greek sources' by reference to certain words (concepts). The Greek word ἀλήθεια means 'truth' as opposed to a lie, and also to mere appearance, or to sham. ἀληθινός means, of men, truthful, trustworthy, or of things, genuine, real. (*Republic* 499C, true philosophy, genuine philosophy.[10]) ἀληθής means unconcealed, so true, real, not false, or apparent. Heraclitus: ἀληθὲς τὸ μὴ λῆθον.[11] (Truth is what is

---

[9] L. Wittgenstein, *Tractatus Logico-Philosophicus*, tr. C. K. Ogdon (London: Routledge & Kegan Paul, 1922).

[10] 499B–C is the place where Socrates says that neither city nor polity nor man will become perfect until philosophers become rulers or else 'a true passion for true philosophy' takes possession of the present rulers or their sons.

[11] The Greek phrase here (translated by Murdoch in the parenthesis that follows) is not found in Heraclitus, nor is it ascribed to him by Heidegger in *Being and Time*—though it would fit with Heidegger's understanding of the etymology and of Heraclitus. Heidegger (262: 219) does mention (though he does not quote) one relevant Heraclitus fragment (Diels-Krantz B1) as showing the connection of the *truth* of a *logos* with *uncoveredness*. In Barnes's translation, the fragment ends: 'Other men fail to notice [τοὺς δὲ ἄλλους . . . λανθάνει] what they do when they are awake, just as they forget what they do when asleep' (J. Barnes, *Early Greek Philosophy* (Harmondsworth: Penguin, 1987), 101).

not hidden.) The verb λανθάνω, or λήθω, or λάθω, means to escape notice, to be unknown or hidden. (Compare Latin *latens* hidden, *lateo* to lie hid, and English latent.) λήθη (*Lethe*) is forgetfulness, forgetting. Heidegger is suggesting to us that truth should be seen revelation, as emergence. Being is hidden, Dasein makes it to be unhidden. This is the fundamental idea upon which we should concentrate rather than speaking of 'judgements' being 'true' in the sense of either corresponding to some external entity or structure, or cohering with some system of ideas. In this context Heidegger introduces the powerful and disputed word λόγος (*logos*).

Both realism and idealism have—with equal thoroughness—missed the meaning of the Greek conception of truth, in terms of which only the possibility of something like a 'doctrine of ideas' can be understood as philosophical *knowledge*.

And because the function of the λόγος lies in merely letting something be, in *letting* entities be *perceived*, λόγος can signify the *reason* [*Vernunft*]. And because, moreover, λόγος is used not only with the signification of λέγειν but also with that of λεγόμενον (that which is exhibited, as such), and because the latter is nothing else than the ὑποκείμενον which, as present-at-hand, already lies at the *bottom* of any procedure of addressing oneself to it or discussing it, λόγος *quâ* λεγόμενον means the ground, the *ratio*. And finally because λόγος as λεγόμενον can also signify that which as something to which one addresses oneself, becomes visible in its relation to something in its 'relatedness', λόγος acquires the signification of relation and relationship. (58: 34)

Heidegger here connects λόγος with λέγειν. According to Liddell and Scott's Lexicon, λόγος means primarily word, also thought (as inner word), also saying, sentence, proposition. λέγειν means primarily lay, also pick out, gather, also speak, say, tell. λεγόμενον then means what is laid, picked out, or said. ὑπόκειμαι means to lie under, or underlie. So Heidegger means that λόγος as any discourse, and as picking out or disclosing, may be thought of, in primordial, or developed sense, as a use of the faculty of reason. It can also, as producing a λεγόμενον (something picked out) which is also (as laid or lying there) an underlying foundation, be seen as reason in the sense of ground, or justification. And, since a λεγόμενον, something visible or attended to, must be seen in its context, in its relatedness to other things, λόγος can also mean relation. The Greeks, both in their pre-philosophical and their philosophical ways of interpreting Dasein, 'defined the essence of man as ζῷον λόγον ἔχον.[12] The later way of interpreting this definition of man in the sense of the *animal rationale*, "something living which has reason", is not indeed "false", but it covers up the phenomenal basis for this definition of Dasein. Man shows himself as the entity which talks, and this talk is a fundamental part of his world discovery' (208: 165). 'And only because the function of λόγος as ἀπόφανσις [declaring, showing] lies in letting something be seen by pointing it out, can the λόγος have the structural form of σύνθεσις [putting together]. Here "synthesis" does not mean a binding and linking together of representations, a manipulation of psychical occurrences where the "problem" arises of how these bindings, as something

---

[12] i.e. *animal possessing logos*.

inside, agree with something physical outside. Here the συν has a purely apophantical signification and means letting something be seen in its *togetherness* [*Beisammen*] with something—letting it be seen *as* something. / Furthermore, because the λόγος is a letting-something-be-seen [as something[13]], it can *therefore* be true or false. But here everything depends on our steering clear of any conception of truth which is construed in the sense of "agreement" ' (56: 33). Moreover we must keep in mind that what is hidden, or relapses and gets covered up, or shows itself in a disguised form, 'is not just this entity or that, but rather the Being of entities' [59: 35].

It may be helpful here to attempt some separation of the items in Heidegger's philosophy which are blended together in his view of truth. There are the fundamental concepts of Dasein and Being. The idea of Dasein is the radical move, the new starting point, which avoids the old philosophical problems about the relation of subject and object, inner and outer. This move is also made, differently, by Wittgenstein. The concept of Being, indeed the 'problem' of Being in this new form is another matter, it belongs especially to Heidegger, and I shall discuss it further later. This seems to me to be a piece of metaphysics in a different sense of 'metaphysics' from what we find for instance in the *Tractatus*. Further items: Heidegger's theory of quality, or texture of consciousness. As I have argued earlier, I think such theorising is important and welcome in philosophy. However Heidegger's concepts and distinctions in this field seem to me too much influenced by an idea of phenomenology as a definite philosophical method, and also by Heidegger's final metaphysical aims, especially his prime desire to establish 'the authentic' as against the 'inauthentic'. To put it crudely, Heidegger wishes to exalt his own 'hero' to use a word which recurs at intervals in his writings. In speaking of consciousness, for instance in what has been quoted above, about perception, and synthesis, he rightly emphasises the unclarified, yet 'there', nature of much perception (seeing is seeing colours), and how all awareness, whether distinct or not, is a seeing of things in their 'togetherness', we already and fundamentally 'see as'. We do not have to struggle with philosophical problems about how we construct concepts of things or a 'world' out of primal items 'in the mind'. Here again, Wittgenstein has moved us out of that dilemma. 'Seeing as' is discussed at length in the later part of the *Investigations*, where it seems to me that Wittgenstein makes unnecessary difficulties for himself by brooding on ambiguous visual figures (duck-rabbit etc.). In a sense all seeing is seeing as. In another sense we raise problems of what 'interpretation' is and is like, which may or may not lead us out of philosophy. Here many questions may arise; for instance about 'experience' of 'value', which I shall return to later. But these are different problems, which do not affect the philosophical insight that removes the old inner-outer dilemma. To proceed. Heidegger's theory of 'moods', another philosophical way of characterising consciousness, is a more dubious and arbitrary matter. I like the idea of speaking, in philosophy, about moods. But what

---

[13] Inserted by Murdoch.

exactly is a mood? In reading novels we have no trouble with the concept. A systematic use of the idea in philosophical writing can seem arbitrary. Here again Heidegger (it seems to me) creates his primary ('descriptive') concepts with a view to his later (evaluative) ends. Heidegger suggests that we are always in a mood. Is a mood then any state of mind? Care (*Sorge*) seems to be omnipresent, as Dasein's concern (*Besorgen*) with its world. Anxiety (*Angst*) is ubiquitous, but seems capable of a lower and a higher form. There is also guilt (*Schuld*), which we may be more or less aware of, and of course fear, which may be a kind of unreflective Angst. A whole battery of psychological terms fill in the picture of Dasein's awareness: circumspection, foresight (*Vorsicht*, also *Vorgriff*, *Vorhabe*) as consciousness of time, curiosity (*Neugier*) as an ingredient of *Gerede*, and so on. It is interesting that the concepts of 'love' and 'loving' are not made use of. 'Love' is mentioned in a footnote (note iv, 235: 190) as a Christian theological concept, together with repentance. In the same note Heidegger observes that the concepts of anxiety and fear have never, except in the writings of Luther and Kierkegaard, been analysed by theologians. Heidegger, though he makes his own special use of the idea of guilt, does not discuss repentance, or remorse. I think it is, in general, very difficult to create, for philosophical purposes, any *systematic structure* out of the innumerable concepts which may be used to characterise states of mind. On the other hand it is important, I think essential, in philosophy, to handle these great ambiguous ideas, doing the best one can with them in particular contexts. Philosophy should be able to do this. Heidegger's relegation of 'love' and 'repentance' to the province of Christian theology, outside the wide general area of human existence, is certainly interesting.

Finally, to return more precisely to the question of what is truth, and whether it is *adaequatio intellectus et rei*, and what this means anyway. (258: 215 following) Heidegger asks 'Is the ontological meaning of the relation between Real and ideal ($\mu\acute{\epsilon}\theta\epsilon\xi\iota\varsigma$) something about which we must not inquire? . . . Why should this not be a legitimate question? Is it accidental that no headway has been made with this problem in over two thousand years? Has the question already been perverted in the very way it has been approached—in the ontologically unclarified separation of the Real and the ideal?' By 'Real' and 'ideal' Heidegger indicates the general tendency (in philosophy and common sense) to separate an idea in the mind from a real thing in the world and (in philosophy) to work away subsequently to relate these. Heidegger's theory of truth is based in the concept of Dasein as already and fundamentally a 'knowing'. (Heidegger's view owes, as he indicates, something to Husserl's concept of intentionality—but 'corrects' Husserl's idealism.) An assertion is not demonstrated or confirmed by 'an agreement of knowing with its object, still less of the psychical with the physical; but neither is it an agreement between "contents of consciousness" among themselves'. The concept of truth must be understood through the concept of disclosure. Dasein as disclosure of Being is 'in the truth'. Primordially, truth is the pointing out or disclosing of Being. As such, 'disclosedness is constituted by state-of-mind, understanding and discourse'. Heidegger has already distinguished a vague unreflective level of awareness (one might say like Plato's *eikasia*[14]) from a more articulate or thoughtful awareness. 'Uncovering is a way of Being for Being-in-the-world. Circumspective concern, or even that concern in which we tarry and look at something, uncovers entities within the world. They are "true" in a second sense. What is primarily "true"—that is, uncovering—is Dasein. Truth in the second sense does not mean Being-uncovering [or to-be-uncovering] but Being-uncovered (uncoveredness).' Heidegger then allows a primary sense of truth, and a 'second sense', which is based upon the conditions postulated for the first, and which bears more resemblance to the common-sense concept. One might even speak here (though I think Heidegger does not use the term) of degrees of truth, as degrees of access to reality (Being). Truth is an area of achievement. 'To say that an assertion "*is true*" [in the second sense] signifies that it uncovers the entity as it is in itself. Such an assertion asserts, points out, lets the entity "be seen" (ἀπόφανσις) in its uncoveredness. The *Being-true* (*truth*) of the assertion must be understood as *Being-uncovering*' [261: 218]. (Or to-be-uncovering, *Entdeckend-sein*.) So, to remove the idea slightly from Heidegger's language, a truthful Dasein is a state of mind in which Being is disclosed as entities uncovered as they are in themselves. What they are 'in themselves', how they are tested as being such, and what the phrase can mean in various contexts is left unclear. I think this is fair enough. Heidegger is speaking of something fundamental to the idea of truth. Methods of verification are another matter. In Heidegger's picture, truthfulness, tendency to disclose things as they really are, is a state of being, a state of mind. To one brought up in the empiricist Wittgensteinian tradition this account must sound 'psychologistic', though it certainly avoids and precludes the old errors. It may also be seen as moralistic, in that it implies that there are, in respect of truthfulness, good and bad states of mind. We may compare and contrast Heidegger's radical treatment of the old problem with that of Wittgenstein. The knot is cut with picturesque ruthlessness at the beginning of the *Tractatus*. Propositions are pictures of facts; what a picture must have in common with reality in order to represent it, rightly or falsely, is its form of representation, its pictorial form. Language represents, corresponds to, the world. But the structure of this relation is and must be invisible. The picture cannot represent its form of representation (or projection), it cannot place itself outside its form of representation (2.172, 174). The same matter is approached, in a different tone, in the *Philosophical Investigations* 435–6.

If it is asked: 'How do sentences manage to represent?', the answer might be, 'Don't you know? You certainly see it when you use them.' For nothing is concealed. How do sentences do it? Don't you know? For nothing is hidden. But given this answer, 'But you know how sentences do it, for nothing is concealed' one would like to retort, 'Yes, but it all goes by so quick, and I should like to see it as it were laid open to view.'

Here it is easy to get into that dead-end in philosophy, where one believes that the difficulty of the task consists in this: our having to describe phenomena which are hard to get hold of, the

[14] *eikasia: image-thought, picture-thinking*, the lowest of the four types of thought in Plato's Line (*Republic* VI 509c–11e, at 511e, cp. 534a).

present experience which slips quickly by, or something of the kind. Where we find ordinary language too crude, and it looks as if we were having to do, not with the phenomena of every-day, but with ones that 'easily elude us, and in their coming to be and passing away, produce those others as an average effect.' (Augustine: *Manifestissima et usitatissima sunt, et eadem rusus nimis latent, et nova est inventio eorum.*[15])

Wittgenstein, and this is characteristic of him, reaches to what is essential and does not offer or contain in what he says any further, latent, yet to be developed, persuasions or world pictures. The last part of the *Tractatus*, though said by its author to be most important, is certainly enobled by what has gone before, but can be separated from it. One does not have to 'buy' the last part as well. Other observations about morality and the world in general turn up as isolated remarks or epigrams. Perhaps Wittgenstein comes near to a thought of Heidegger's when he says, 'No one *can* speak the truth, if he has still not mastered himself. He *cannot* speak it—but not because he is not yet clever enough. The truth can be spoken only by someone who is already *at home* in it; not by someone who still lives in falsehood and reaches out from falsehood towards truth on just one occasion' (*Vermischte Bemerkungen*, translated as *Culture and Value*,[16] p. 35). This of course is to speak of the virtue of truthfulness, not of the philosophical problem of truth. Heidegger's metaphysic connects these together. The essence of truth is the unconcealment which meets the claims of Being. Authentic Dasein meets these claims properly.

Morality, value, appears in Heidegger's argument at two levels. At the lower level the structures are established which are to give access to, or be transformed into aspects of, the higher level. In *Being and Time* Heidegger proceeds to explain the higher (authentic) level in the later pages, and also in his later writing, elaborated his views of goodness or enlightenment. Value of some kind must be thought of as belonging to the everyday. Our 'world', Being as we disclose it, has, primordially, meanings, including value-meanings. 'In interpreting we do not, so to speak, throw a "significa-tion" over some naked thing which is present-at-hand (*vorhanden*), we do not stick a value on it; but when something within-the-world is encountered as such, the thing in question already has an involvement which is disclosed in our understanding of the world, and this involvement is one which gets laid out (*herausgelegt*) by the inter-pretation' (190–91: 150). So, Heidegger's primal move, his concept of Dasein in-the-world, precludes, by-passes, not only the problem of how the subject reaches the object, but also the problem of how values become attached to facts. Both the old subject-object distinction, and the old fact-value distinction are excluded from the

---

[15] 'These usages [e.g. "*How long ago* did he say that?" and "*The time* this syllable takes *is twice* the time that simple, short one takes'] are utterly manifest and ordinary. And yet those same things lie deeply hidden, and the discovery of them is new.' (Augustine, *Confessions* XI.xxii (28), my transl.) The Latin for 'lie . . . hidden' (*latent*) is the cue for Wittgenstein's counter-blast 'Nothing is hidden'—and it is picked up in the line of Murdoch's that follows: 'Wittgenstein . . . does not offer . . . latent . . . persuasions.'

[16] L. Wittgenstein, *Culture and Value*, ed. G. H. von Wright, in collaboration with Heikki Nyman, tr. Peter Winch (Blackwell, 1980).

start. 'An interpretation is never a presuppositionless apprehending of something presented to us' [191–2: 150]. Interpretation at the ordinary level is likely to be dominated by *Gerede* and 'they'. 'We take pleasure and enjoy ourselves as *they* take pleasure; we read, see and judge about literature and art as *they* see and judge' [164: 126–7].

Distantiality, averageness and levelling down as ways of Being for the 'they', constitute what we know as publicness [*die Offentlichkeit*]. Publicness proximally controls every way in which the world and Dasein get interpreted and it is always right—not because there is some distinction and primary relationship-of-Being in which it is related to 'Things' or because it avails itself of some transparency on the part of Dasein which it has explicitly appropriated, but because it is insensitive to every difference of level and of genuineness and thus never gets to the heart of the matter [*auf die Sachen*]. By publicness everything gets obscured and what has thus been covered up gets passed off as something familiar and accessible to everyone. (165: 127)

'Publicness' and 'they' are 'right' however, and not necessarily to be thought of in a disparaging way, in the same sense in which any state of Dasein is somehow 'in the truth', that is, something is grasped as an object of care and concern. Heidegger quotes (242: 197) a Latin fable about Cura (Care, *Sorge*), telling how Care who originally shaped man out of clay, was given possession of him while he lived, although earth provided his material and Jupiter his spirit. Heidegger's *Sorge* may be thought of as a humbler but not less energetic force than Plato's Eros. We are busy restless curious creatures, always getting the world in some way or other; and it may be that *Sorge* will drive us on from the everyday getting-by values which are 'right' in their own way, and not to be 'disparaged', toward something higher. Dasein is also of course immersed in, composed of, time. Foresight, memory, time-grasp (*Vorgriff, Vorhabe*), history, tradition, colour, provide the presuppositions which belong to primary Dasein. How far local and historical limitations can, in understanding and interpreting the world, be overcome is a problem which can receive no general solution. There is no one 'definite ideal of knowledge'. 'An entity for which, as Being-in-the-world, its Being is itself an issue, has, ontologically, a circular structure' (194–5: 152–3).

Editorial Note & Acknowledgments

The basis for this publication is the typescript now in the Iris Murdoch archive at Kingston University, but I have compared it also with the manuscript in the Library of the University of Iowa. I am very grateful to Anne Rowe and the librarians of the Iris Murdoch Archive at Kingston University and to Sidney F. Huttner and Katherine J. Hodson in the department of Special Collections at the Library of the University of Iowa for their help and permission to use their copy. I would like to thank John Bayley for giving permission to publish the piece from these sources and Peter Conradi for his advice and encouragement.

Peter Conradi has supplied a short note:

Iris Murdoch gave Heidegger's *Sein und Zeit* to the tormented Carel in her 1967 novel *The Time of the Angels*, and in *The Sovereignty of Good* referred to Heidegger as 'possibly . . . Lucifer in person'.

The evidence concerning her first encounters with Heidegger is mixed. By 1993 she seems to have believed that she had first encountered *Sein und Zeit* in Macquarrie and Robinson's translation in 1965. However, there are at least three indications of an earlier interest from the time of her late twenties. She mentions Heidegger in a letter to David Hicks in October 1945 (*A Writer at War*, 245), her 1947/8 journal reports that she discussed Heidegger while at Cambridge, and Gilbert Ryle (who had reviewed the book in 1929) lent her *Sein und Zeit* in March 1949.

It seems that in November 1993, Iris Murdoch arranged to have typed up some manuscripts for a projected book, *Heidegger*, to be dedicated to Stanley Rosen. After attempting to edit the typescript, Iris Murdoch decided that, although she had been working on this intermittently for six years, it was no good and should be abandoned. The book was apparently intended to comprise five sections: '*Sein und Zeit*: Pursuit of Being'; 'Death'; 'Heidegger'; 'Notes on Heidegger'; 'The Pursuit of Being: Notes upon Heidegger'.

A mixture of frustration at her loss of power and the confusion of the illness that followed prevented her from editing the typescript. Her admirers, too, will be frustrated that she could not fulfil her ambition—which evidently included addressing the question of why Heidegger and Plato alike were attracted to tyrants. What follows here is—despite its blanks—the most coherent section—the first. Its strength, eloquence and cogency allow it to stand by itself, as well as to suggest something of what we have lost.

There is no obvious best way to edit this material. It is a work caught literally in progress, half-corrected. It occupies sheets 1–26 of the full 224-sheet typescript on Heidegger, and the first 35 sheets (numbered 1025–1059) of the approximately 269-sheet manuscript (with sheets numbered 1025 to 1293 and some supplementary sheets inserted within the sequence). The manuscript is written mainly on just one side of each sheet, but with comments and additions intended for a recto page sometimes inserted on the facing verso of the previous sheet. The continuous numbering of the manuscript pages dates from a time when Murdoch was working on the text as a whole—and it indicates that the five sections were being intended to form a continuous sequence. What is published here is the whole of the first of what seem to be five sections (though what follows as the second section—with the heading 'Death'—is rather more definitely separated off in the TS than in the original MS). The section, as we have it, appears, from the manuscript, to have originally been the later part of a larger discussion, the first part of which came to be deleted: the opening lines of sheet 1025 continue mid-sentence from an earlier sheet, but they are crossed out, and what was once simply a new paragraph in an earlier plan becomes the opening of the present section—with headings being added in the margin area at the top of the page: 'HEIDEGGER', 'Pursuit of Being', and 'Sein und Zeit' (along with 'Thoughts about Heidegger', which did not make it into the Typescript version). I know nothing of what has become of sheets 1024 and earlier.

The manuscript of the present section (sheets 1025 to 1059) carries dates at various points suggesting it was being written in mid-June 1987. (The third and longest section, 'Heidegger', occupying sheets 1069–1186, seems to have been written in various spurts, in December 1988, January-February 1989, and June and later that same year.) It seems that in 1993, after the appearance of *Metaphysics as a Guide to Morals* (1992) and *The Green Knight* (1993), Murdoch had these Heidegger manuscripts typed up. She did a partial correction of the typescript that came back (marked 'WPXS - 18th November 1993 . . . HEIDEGGER - IRIS MURDOCH' as a running footer on every page, as if from a typing agency). Murdoch wrote in the Greek where the typist had left a string of asterisks, corrected mistypings, modified a phrase here and there. She caught some big errors ('medical' for 'radical'; the loss of 21 words at the end of the first quotation from (178: 139)); but evidently not all. The word 'defies' in the manuscript appears in the typescript as 'deifies', '*au contraire*' as '*au contaire*', and 'states of mind' as 'stages of mind'. It seems clear that there are many remaining typist's errors that the author would have corrected if she had noticed them—as, for example, at the place where nine words have dropped out, no doubt because the typist's eye has jumped from a word in the manuscript to a repetition of the same word a line below.

On the other hand, it would not be right to take the manuscript instead as a basis rather than the typescript: there are corrections inserted in Murdoch's hand into the typescript that evidently supersede the original manuscript. My general policy has been to follow the typescript, but making modifications in the light of the earlier manuscript where the typist seems to have made a mistake.

How much further should an editor go? A finished typescript will normally later be subjected to a publisher's copy-editing—e.g. checking spelling, punctuation and styles of quotation, querying or adjusting repetitions and unclarities of expression—as indeed happened (notwithstanding Murdoch's notorious dislike of the copy-editor's pencil) with her earlier philosophical publications. But one could go too far imposing such changes on the present text: this is not a finished typescript and to give it the superficial form of something wholly tidy and finished might invite it to be judged by inappropriate standards. The very process of publication gives an author occasion for reconsidering details and even matters of substance—which Murdoch did not have available to her in the present case. On the other hand, to publish the typescript with the most obvious superficial slips might satisfy antiquarian interests but would surely impede philosophical understanding.

The text here is a compromise. The main point of publication in the present volume must be, I think, to make more of Murdoch's philosophical work available to a philosophical audience, rather than to contribute to the study of her manuscript and typescript methods. To this end, there is perhaps a good model to follow: that of *Metaphysics as a Guide to Morals*. The Acknowledgments (p. 513) thank five people for, variously, nursing it into print, scanning every page and making suggestions, scholarly copy-editing, and typing and re-typing the 'seemingly endless text'. The result may not be precisely what Murdoch, with world enough and time, and absolutely at the height of her powers, would have produced. But it is certainly more fairly presented with some editorial interventions than simply, so to speak, as a typescript. That is the model I have attempted to follow in the present publication. The result is a compromise, evidently not quite finished, but something that I have found, like her earlier works, to get better and better the more I reread it.

I have made small corrections to what are clearly typing errors. I have inserted Greek accents where necessary. (Murdoch inserts them on some words but not others.) For some of the quotations from Heidegger, Murdoch inserts page references; I have supplied references for the other quotations, placed in square brackets. Murdoch's quotations from Heidegger are based on the translation of *Sein und Zeit* by John Macquarrie and Edward Robinson: *Being and Time* (1962, 1967). I have corrected some small discrepancies from Macquarrie and Robinson that are, I think, accidental and that might be confusing. But I have left untouched some larger deviations that may have been deliberate on her part—including Murdoch's ignoring of the capital letter for, e.g. 'Interpreted' and 'Object', and differences over inverted commas and italics. (She has 'in a disparaging sense' where Macquarrie and Robinson have 'in a 'disparaging' signification' (211: 167).) Where, within a quotation from Heidegger, square brackets occur, they are exactly as in Murdoch's typescript: some are insertions by Murdoch, others go back to the translation she is quoting and are insertions by Macquarrie and Robinson. I have taken the longest quotations and set them off as blocks, removing the quotation marks at beginning and end (and, in the case of the long quotations from *Being and Time* 261–2: 218–9 and 58: 34, inserting paragraph-breaks, as in the original being quoted). I have in two places inserted a slash (/), to mark a paragraph division in the middle of a passage from Heidegger which Murdoch quotes without a break.

Where Greek appeared in the original manuscript, the typist has placed a sequence of asterisks as a place-holder. Murdoch has corrected the typescript, inserting the Greek by hand, but only up to p. 17 of the TS (the second line of p. 104 in the present edition). From 'λήθη (*Lethe*) is forgetfulness ...', the insertions are my own, checked against the manuscript.

There is one place (TS p. 17; corresponding to p. 104 here) where a sentence from Heidegger is quoted twice. (The first sentence of the block quotation from (58: 34) is quoted in the TS also one sentence earlier (following 'system of ideas.'): the duplication comes from a revision having been inserted in the MS on an additional sheet, without the necessary adjustment being made on the previous sheet.) And at one point (the earlier quotation from (101: 71)), the typist—in the process of dealing with a quotation that Murdoch has written into the top margin of the MS for insertion into the text below—has inserted also what seems to be an instruction of Murdoch's to herself ('*Quote* 101: 71'). I have deleted this and supplied an ordinary page reference to follow the quotation. OUP conventions have been followed on quotation marks, and on the relative positioning of parenthetical page-references and punctuation marks. There are a couple of places where I have corrected what seemed a small slip, e.g. where a word seems to have dropped out, and have inserted a couple of commas.

All footnotes are added by the present editor.

Justin Broackes

Iris on Safari: A Personal Record

John Bayley

Iris always enjoyed travelling on what might be called 'business', and we always travelled together. Sometimes we were on an assignment for the British Council, in the spacious days when the Council had more funds to spend, and could afford to despatch flying cultural missions of various kinds. In this way we visited, at one time or another, Australia, New Zealand, Egypt, Israel, Turkey (Istanbul only), Romania, Poland, Yugoslavia, Hungary, and Berlin. At all these places we gave talks, sometimes together, but more often with Iris on philosophy, and me on poetry, the novel, or something like that. (A favourite phrase of Iris's always spoken, in the Irish way, 'Somting like dat'.)

When I had a chance I used to sit secretly in at the back of Iris's talk, and without really understanding much of anything, I used to sit marvelling at her clear and forceful exposition: just the way she talked. Unlike most professional and accomplished lecturers, she never tried to lighten the atmosphere, or to make a joke. Her seriousness was lucid, and in some way reassuring to her audience, and even flattering. Like me, I think most of her audiences simply enjoyed hearing her speak—speak rather than talk, for she had a way of finding the words as if they had never existed before. This made her audience follow them closely, and with a kind of excitement. (Why I always tried to keep my presence secret, incidentally, was because Iris preferred me not to attend her talks. I knew this, though she never said so. I think she felt that our life together was so different from other things—professional things—that she did, that her instinct was to keep the two as far apart as possible.)

But where Iris really excelled was not as a talker or lecturer but in the discussion and question time which followed. Here, she was really in her element. When this took place one saw what a peerless teacher she must have been, as indeed was testified by all her St Anne's college students, many of whom went on to become what Iris called 'pals for life'. With the exception of the occasional Jesuit, whom she delighted in, these pupils whom she taught, both at St Anne's and later on in London, at the Royal College of Art, had little or no gift for philosophy at all. My own boredom threshold where the subject is concerned being very low indeed, I marvelled at Iris's ability to make them not only interested but deeply absorbed by what she tried to teach them.

And it was the same with these discussions and question times when we visited abroad. There always seemed to be a great access of animation, and a sudden enthusiasm for whatever philosophical topic had been the subject of Iris's discourse. She smiled at every questioner, and seemed to take him or her, figuratively speaking, to her bosom. But it was all done so quietly and naturally and without any suggestion of histrionic intent.

So it was, at least, until an occasion in May 1995 when we were taking part at a conference in Israel, at the University of the Negev. Iris seemed suddenly to lose her way, and to lose the words that were usually both so kindly and so well-considered. The audience became restive, and presently some people began to get up and walk out. Iris did not seem to notice, or to feel bothered at all, and when I asked her afterwards how she felt things had gone, she seemed to feel all had been quite normal. That was the year her last novel *Jackson's Dilemma* came out, and she had often said to me that she didn't feel she would ever write another, but I put this down to a temporary discouragement—it had happened before—or to some form of writer's block. The condition of Alzheimer's was not confirmed by a brain-scan for another year and a half.

Although we hardly ever talked about her novels, she several times said, to me and to others, that she tried to keep philosophy out of them. But it seemed to me always to get in, in some form, often through Iris's fascination with *power*, and particularly the power that some individuals could exercise over others. Nietzsche and Heidegger were very much in the background of her literary as well as her philosophical imagination, and she had herself experienced what it was like to submit voluntarily to the power exercised by a wholly remarkable individual – in her case the writer and *Dichter* Elias Canetti. But cheerfulness, as the philosophical aspirant is supposed to have said to Dr Johnson, would keep breaking in. Iris seemed so cheerful, innocent, and happy in her home life that I could barely understand or even imagine the sort of experiences she had been through before we were married.

Iris never said in so many words that she hated power, although it is an underlying theme in so many of her most powerful novels. She opposed it to what her oldest and dearest friend, Philippa Foot—whom she often said was a '*real* philosopher, not like me'—has called 'Natural Goodness'. She was good herself in the most absolute way; and I frequently felt amazed at the contrast between her own goodness and the powers of the imagination that produced her novels. I once said to her: 'Could Shakespeare have been a good man, do you think?' She was amused, then thoughtful, and finally said: 'I don't see why not.' I quoted *Paradise Lost*, where Adam observes that 'evil into the mind of God or man may come and go'. She said: 'That's just it . . . Shakespeare's imaginative powers covered everything, and there's more evil in "everything" than good. But why shouldn't he have been good in himself and as a man?' She strongly, even passionately, believed that the man and the writer were two different things, or rather two different people; and once when I quoted to her Robert Lowell, the poet's, words about

'One life, one writing', she said, quite sharply for her, 'Well, too bad for Robert Lowell.' It is only fair to add that when we met Lowell in Oxford she was completely charmed by him, and saw him several times after that in London: he almost became a 'pal'. (Hawthorne, incidentally, would be a perfect example of a happy cheerful good man with an extraordinarily rich, dark, and disquieting imagination. No 'One life, one writing' there?)

Although she was such a good teacher and 'discusser', Iris for some strange reason extremely disliked reading aloud, even though (or could it be because?) she had loved her adored father reading stories like *Treasure Island* to her when she was six or seven years old. We never read aloud to each other at home; but if I found something funny in the paper, or in what I was reading (it might well have been in a novel by Barbara Pym, to whose writing I was, and am, very much addicted), I would rush upstairs to read it to Iris, who never in the least minded being disturbed by me, in this way, while she was engaged in her own writing.

After Iris became ill with Alzheimer's, I tried once or twice reading something to her, it might be from her once favourite *Tale of Gengi* or *The Lord of the Rings*, but it made her so unhappy that I very soon gave it up. In any case it was not long before she passed the point where books meant anything to her at all; and if a friend produced a novel of hers and asked her to sign it 'Iris', which for a long time she could still do, she would look at it with what seemed like amused curiosity, and smile her always delightful smile.

'Natural goodness' remained, manifesting itself. Before dementia set in Iris had a lively interest in any concept of 'God', although from her mid-30s onward she held no sort of religious belief. Buddhism attracted her, and she loved to talk with two friends who were practising Buddhists, Peter Conradi and his partner, Jim O'Neill. But although God did not exist for her as a supreme value, the Good very much did. I remember her once having a discussion with her old friend Philippa about whether animals could be naturally good. Iris, as I remember, was sure that they could be. And her own last days showed that Goodness can survive and triumph over any degree of sickness, failing, and dementia. In those last days this triumph of the Good in Iris was for me, as I witnessed it, itself transcendental.

1

Holy Fool and Magus: The Uses of Discipleship in *Under the Net* and *The Flight from the Enchanter**

Peter J. Conradi

1

In late June 1942, Isobel Henderson, ancient History tutor at Somerville, arranged a dinner party in a smart Oxford restaurant for Iris Murdoch and Mary Midgley, her only 'Greats' finalists that year. Both girls had won Firsts and Henderson wished to reward them. She accordingly invited two distinguished sages to entertain the girls: J. B. Trend, Mozart-scholar, translator, musicologist, and the polymath A. L. Rowse. Iris and Mary were very tired, and quite willing to be interested, but Rowse showed off, ate up the available space, was conceited and self-centred, and this exhausted and confused them. 'Did we learn something new this evening?' Mary asked Iris, as they stumbled home through the moon-lit black-out on St Giles.

'O Yes, I think so,' declared Iris . . . '*Trend is a good man and Rowse is a bad man.*' At which exact but grotesquely unfashionable judgement we both fell about laughing . . . helplessly.[1]

Mary thought Iris's diagnosis was 'dead right' and that it put the evening in perspective. It was a great relief to her to have Iris's Manichaean or allegorical perspective. Already during this, her Marxist period, Murdoch's view of the world was remote from that of contemporary philosophy.

Oxford philosophy, she was increasingly to feel, in the very epoch of Stalin and Hitler, tended to evacuate the ideas of Good and Evil and render them idle functions of the choosing will. It was at its driest, Iris Murdoch noted, morality being treated as a special subject dealt with by various technical devices '(emotive utterances, imperatives etc).

---

* For further details on some of the topics of this essay, please see Peter J. Conradi, *Iris Murdoch: A Life* (Harper Collins, 2001), from which some of the present article is developed.
[1] M. Midgley, *The Owl of Minerva: A Memoir* (Routledge, 2005), 126.

Factual language was firmly separated from value language, and value was insubstantial,'[2] the moral agent reduced to an isolated will and intellect choosing afresh and *ex nihilo*, moment by moment. This picture, she felt, was not merely excessively individualistic, but inaccurate and wrong, diminishing or leaving out of account the inner life. It offered no convincing way of distinguishing Trend from Rowse, the good from the mediocre man.

Midgley's, Murdoch's, and also Philippa Foot's philosophy tutor from 1940 was Donald MacKinnon, who, though he had then published very little, influenced all three. They thought him a rare example of a good man as well as someone whose teaching illuminated the idea of virtue. MacKinnon would in 1960 be appointed to the Norris-Hulse chair of Divinity at Cambridge. The title of his inaugural lecture— 'Borderlands of Theology'—is evocative. Philosophy and theology are somehow to be brought back together. MacKinnon believed that those thinkers especially are to be commended who 'live out . . . the consequences of [their own] attitude of mind', moral philosophy being the study of 'what in the last resort can only be lived', a central tenet of *The Sovereignty of Good*.[3]

A decade or so after Finals, and Murdoch's first two novels both concern the anxiety of influence and, in their different ways, address the importance of good and bad philosophies. *Under the Net* has a man who is unconsciously good at its heart; *The Flight from the Enchanter* concerns a man who is power-driven and thus (in Murdoch's terms) bad. Both Hugo Belfounder and Mischa Fox are philosopher-kings, or priest-kings, who dominate those whom they meet; but do so very differently.

Murdoch always hated being discussed as a 'philosophical novelist'. It sounded to her, I suspect, both doctrinaire and schematic. Ideas-in-art, she would say, must suffer a sea-change, and so at the heart of a good novel, she felt, should be a vital spiritual struggle implicating both writer and reader: thus her demons often possess the best tunes. Without such struggle, literature proper would give way to propaganda. Sartre's *Nausea* she believed to be the only successful philosophical novel of the twentieth century, and while Roquentin's plight in that book was that of a philosopher, K's in *The Castle* was by happy contrast 'that of everyman'. Kafka's model, not Sartre's, she strongly implies, is the one she wishes to follow.

Kafka, she noted,[4] was one who sees the forces at work in the world more clearly than we, and so can 'prophecy'. He always mattered greatly. She hoped to be influenced by him, and probably saw him as, very broadly speaking, a religious writer.

---

[2] S. Aldwinckle, *Christ's Shadow in Plato's Cave: A Meditation on the Substance of Love* (Amate Press, Oxford, 1990), with foreword by Murdoch.

[3] MacKinnon felt that if life must bear witness to philosophy, then enquiry into the 'good life' still matters; those who call ethics a 'bogus subject' are usually posturing, and 'the kind of mystery which tends to gather round . . . notions of good and evil' cannot easily be dispelled. (See Donald M. MacKinnon, 'Evil and Personal Responsibility' and 'The Crux of Morality', *The Listener*, 18 March 1948, pp. 457–9 and 16 December 1948, pp. 926–7.) His thinking points towards attitudes IM would later adopt wholesale.

[4] In her *Sartre, Romantic Rationalist* (1953), *passim*.

She would have minded the label 'religious novelist' far less than 'philosophical novelist', and it is to the essentially religious mysteries of good and evil that she applies herself in all her fiction, including the two novels I shall discuss here. These novels look forward to later ones featuring courts, cabals, or covens, within which the themes of discipleship or apprenticeship are crucial; a topic I'll return briefly to at the end. It is extraordinary and perhaps instructive, that critics have, over fifty years, explored almost every other issue in Murdoch's work except this one.[5]

To early critics such as A. S. Byatt, Murdoch's first novels were partly notable for being so different from any other fiction being written at the time; but also notable for being so different one from another. *Under the Net* is picaresque, *The Flight from the Enchanter* a dark fantasy, *The Sandcastle* a romance, while *The Bell* explored the religious sense in a post-Christian world. Despite their seeming to belong to different worlds of generic discourse, biography suggests a kinship between these fictions. Both *Under the Net* and *The Flight from the Enchanter* (like *The Bell*) have a court-structure. And at the centre of each court is a character based in real life on a thinker who influenced his friends and disciples, and who compelled Murdoch imaginatively. The theme recurs throughout her work.

2

Iris Murdoch first met Raymond Queneau[6] on the 16 February 1946 in Innsbruck, where she was working in the refugee camps for UNRRA. Soon she wrote to Queneau of the '*question de chercher un maître, problème important et dangereux*'. Apprenticeship can unlock new talent, and this 'important and dangerous' problem of finding

---

[5] The collocation 'court, coven, cabal' first occurs, I believe, in George Steiner's introduction to my edition of Murdoch's *Existentialists and Mystics* (1997). The similarities between *Under the Net* and *Flight* were first pointed out to me by Mary Midgley in c. 2002. It struck her that the heroes of both need to outgrow those who dominate them.

[6] Her meeting with the 'very avant-garde' Queneau was one that she had long hoped for: 'Part of me wants to be Raymond Queneau, another wants to be Thomas Mann.' She had introduced her war-time flat-mate Philippa Foot to *Pierrot mon ami* (1943)—probably one of the books brought back for her from liberated Paris in 1944—which both read in French with enthusiasm. In December 1945 the book-seller Ernest Collet, back in Brussels after a trip to Paris, was trying to help secure her translation rights for Queneau's novels and she noted with excitement that Queneau 'wants to see me'. She had long desired this meeting. She was planning to translate Queneau's *Pierrot mon ami* first and secure permission later, though 'I'm not sure my obscene vocabulary is large enough in English'. IM's 'not wholly successful' translation of *Pierrot* probably remained unfinished. The playful iconoclasm and audacious linguistic fireworks of his brilliant comic writing posed problems. Nonetheless Queneau influenced her first published novel *Under the Net*, not least in the form of the narrator-hero.

Under the Net tries to copy Queneau's *Pierrot mon ami* and Beckett's *Murphy*, a book Denis Healey introduced her to at Oxford in 1938. These two novels are among Jake's few—and treasured—possessions. *Under the Net* resembles neither. Its humour is very different from the owlish pedantry of *Murphy*. True, like Queneau's *Pierrot mon ami*, it concerns *petites gens* and is picaresque and unexpected. But its marvellously lyrical evocations of London and of Paris, its wit and endless comic invention, its philosophic theme yet lightness of touch, resemble neither. For more on IM's relations to Queneau, see my *Iris Murdoch: A Life*, 384.

an adequate literary and/or philosophic master absorbed her life, her philosophic quest, and her novels alike.

She dedicated *Under the Net* to Queneau. Its hero, Jake Donaghue was translating the French novelist, Breteuil, just as Murdoch had translated Queneau's *Pierrot mon ami*— and, again like Murdoch—was about to abandon translation and turn into a novelist in his/her own right: the writer and publisher John Lehmann turned down her translation of *Pierrot mon ami* in 1949. Both IM (it is simplest to refer to her) and Jake are Irish Londoners with 'shattered nerves', who after leaving the Young Communist League are now politically disaffected. The form of male first-person narrative liberated her in *Under the Net*. She had hit upon an idiom in which she felt instinctively at home, and to which she would return in many later fictions, which enabled her to speak confidently through a masculine 'mask'. It was also a way of championing that inner life philosophers then neglected: IM's conviction that Sartre, Wittgenstein, Ryle, and Ayer all (differently) undervalued the inner life might—perhaps—be answered by a first person narrative that displayed the potency, strangeness, and consequentiality of that inner life. And the perhaps paradoxical idea that fiction might, *mutatis mutandis*, help in correcting the ills of philosophy, abounds in her early essays.[7]

London is a real presence in this as in her other books, almost another character. Jake reflects that Dave Gellner, being Jewish, could afford to live off the Goldhawk Road— a 'contingent address'—whereas he was not sure that he could. The address in the notebooks for *Under the Net*—her parental home 4 Eastbourne Road—is a Chiswick address contingent, as the novel jokes, 'to the point of nausea'.

In her journals she calls it a 'a philosophical adventure story': the title alludes to Wittgenstein's *Tractatus* 6.341, the net of discourse behind which the world's particulars hide, which can separate us from our world, yet simultaneously connect us. Sartre is here too; but where *Nausea* presented the contingency of the world as the enemy, *Under the Net* presents some healing surrender to its otherness as a precondition for happiness and creativity alike. The instrument of Jake's education is Hugo Belfounder. Many linked him to Wittgenstein, and were not wholly misled: both have Central European origins, a tormented love-life, a care for their boots, give up their fortune, are associated with hospital-work, employ the word 'decent' as high commendation. But so keenly did Wittgenstein's own disciples and pupils emulate him, even to his Austrian accent[8]—that when Wittgenstein gave a lecture at Cornell, Sir Peter Strawson recalled that one student asked 'Who is that old man imitating Norman Malcolm?'

One year after returning from Austria in 1947, IM had won a Sarah Smithson studentship in philosophy at Newnham College, Cambridge. Although she recorded thinking of studying the philosophy of Husserl, she is remembered that year as talking

[7] See *Existentialists and Mystics*, passim, but especially 'Against Dryness' and 'The Sublime and the Beautiful Revisited'.
[8] For Anscombe's Austrian accent, see Mary Warnock, *A Memoir: People and Places* (London: Duckworth, 2000), 60.

and asking 'incessantly' about Wittgenstein.[9] She had arrived too late, to her bitter regret, to listen to him lecture: in the summer prior to her going up, Wittgenstein had resigned his chair as from December 31st, keeping his rooms for one last Sabbatical term, and that Christmas decamped to Ireland. Since IM could not sit at the feet of the Master, she listened carefully[10] to a dozen or so who had been close to him: especially Wasfi Hijab, Kanti Shah, and Georg Kreisel. Hijab even dreamed of Wittgenstein at night. They had a single topic: 'Wittgenstein, Wittgenstein, and Wittgenstein'.

3

Three weeks after arriving in Cambridge she met Wittgenstein. Trinity, where she frequently was, had been Wittgenstein's College, more off than on, since 1912. Anscombe, Wittgenstein's premier pupil, would translate, and give IM a copy of his *Investigations*, the revolutionary handbook of the second phase of his thinking, only in May 1953. Meanwhile his *Brown* and *Blue Books* were circulating in type-written form, like Samizdat literature behind the Iron Curtain, and generating a comparable excitement. IM had mentioned Wittgenstein to Frank Thompson in a letter of 5 July 1943, and had talked about him with Anscombe in 1944. After some preliminary 'devastating' skirmishing with Anscombe, who, with John Wisdom, might effect an entree, IM met him on Thursday 23 October 1947. He had two empty narrow barracks-like rooms, K.10 in Whewell's Court, at the top of a gothic tower, with no books or bathroom,[11] only two deck chairs and a camp bed. She thought him very good-looking, rather small, with a sharpish, intent, alert face and 'those very piercing eyes. He had a trampish sort of appearance.' He said to IM: 'It's as if I have an apple tree in my garden & everyone is carting away the apples & sending them all over the world. And you ask: may I have an apple from your tree.' IM remarked, 'Yes, but I'm never sure when I'm given an apple whether it really *is* from your tree.' 'True. I should say tho' they are not good apples' and 'What's the good of having one philosophical discussion? It's like having one piano lesson.' He famously did not think women, in any case, could do philosophy; 'men are foul, but women are viler' he would remark.[12] Anscombe was an honorary male.

His extraordinary directness of approach, the absence of any paraphernalia or conventional framework, his denuded setting, all unnerved IM. There was a naked confrontation of personalities. She met him once more, never got to know him well, always thought of him with awe and alarm. Wittgenstein and the differently alarming and influential Austin, she later said, were 'the most extraordinary men among us'.[13]

[9] John Vinelott at Queen's reading Moral Sciences 1946–50 witnessed these discussions. Other participants were Stephen Toulmin, Norman Malcolm, John Wisdom, Peter Minkus.
[10] Letter to Author from Stephen Toulmin, Feb. 2000, and interview with Hijab, 13 February 2000.
[11] B. McGuinness, *Wittgenstein, A Life: Young Ludwig* (1889–1921) (London, 1988), 131.
[12] Kreisel, Conversation with Author 4 March 1998.
[13] Ved Mehta, *Fly and the Flybottle* (1963; Penguin, 1965), 52.

Since she was too late to hear him lecture, his influence reached her mainly through disciples such as Elizabeth Anscombe and Yorick Smythies whose personal style ('authenticity') and philosophic style were seen to coincide.

The ruthless authenticity of Elizabeth makes me feel more & more ashamed of the vague self-indulgent way in which I have been philosophizing. I must make a tremendous effort if I am to get any sort of philosophical clarity or truth out of the sea of fascinating dramatic, psychological, moral & other ideas in which I've been immersed.[14]

One week after meeting him, while reading the *Brown Book*, she asked: 'What are the main points of the Wittgenstein revolution?... What's happening? The solidity seems to go. "We act like automatons much of the time." True in a way.' Her focus was not on the discontinuities between early and later Wittgenstein but on the effect of his philosophy generally on our conception of ourselves. He had an excessive suspicion of the inner life.[15] Two days later, she asked herself, 'Will I admit I acted like automaton? I might—.' This message she found also in Freud: that we, and our motives, are dark to ourselves. 'I am obscure to myself. I don't coincide with my life. (*This* is basis of metaphysics)' she wrote on November 4th, noting on the same day that 'Julian of Norwich[16] is just as self-certifying as Wittgenstein'. And she criticized Wittgenstein's as 'a world without magic' objecting from the first to the division he pressed between fact and value: 'Our imagination is immediately & continuously at work on our experience. There are no "brute data".'[17]

IM saw Wittgenstein first as numinous; later as demonic. She dreamt of him all her life (never of Sartre). She gave *Tractatus* aphorisms to the mystical and unsatisfactory character Nigel in *Bruno's Dream*, and started *Nuns and Soldiers* teasingly: '"Wittgenstein –". "Yes?" said the Count.' Part of what doubtless fascinated her was the way he commandeered his students' lives, humiliated and sometimes excommunicated them. She wrote to Queneau on 6 November 1947 that the atmosphere around Wittgenstein was 'emotional and esoteric';[18] and, much later spoke of him as evil: he had abandoned old friends, 'harshly criticized Jewish refugee-philosophers'—probably his combative ex-disciple Friedrich Waismann—ruined careers by telling promising students to give up philosophy—including Smythies.[19] Wittgenstein, she later noted, could, like

---

[14] Journal, 25 July 1947.

[15] Peter Strawson, Conversation with Author 11 March 99. That Murdoch continued in this belief, found strange by Philippa Foot, is shown by ch. 9 in her *Metaphysics as a Guide to Morals*, entitled "Wittgenstein and the Inner Life".

[16] Dame Julian of Norwich, the 14th century mystic and anchoress was important to Murdoch. The Norwich chapel in which she conducted her long retreat, destroyed by enemy action in 1942, was restored and rededicated on 8 May 1953. The phrase 'All shall be well, and all manner of thing shall be well', from Dame Julian's still vivid and energetic and much-loved *Revelations of Divine Love*, is repeated—often ironically—in many Murdoch novels.

[17] Journal, 17 November 1947.

[18] Journal, 6 November 1947.

[19] So she told Sir John Vinelott in 1993. See, also, Jeffrey Meyers, *Privileged Moments: Encounters with Writers* (Wisconsin, 2000).

Kreisel, 'destroy the very inward part of someone's self-respect'.[20] He was ferocious and destructive. Yet she continued to admire his obstinate and at times difficult lucidity, which influenced Oxford analytical philosophy generally, and is observable in her own best work.

Hugo Belfounder in *Under the Net* is in fact a portrait of Wittgenstein's star-pupil from 1937, Yorick Smythies, often the only person allowed to take notes in Wittgenstein's lectures,[21] and one of many disciples Wittgenstein had dissuaded from pursuing a philosophical career. 'What a poor image of Yorick Hugo Belfounder is! But this is unkind to Hugo. The fault is mine.' IM noted. Smythies is recalled as resembling a cross between Hamlet and the grave-digger, thin, stooped, myopic, tall, pure-of-heart, given to the slow catechizing that Wittgenstein favoured as a method of investigation, and to strange abstinences. He had, aged five, put up a notice on the nursery door: 'Keep out! Am reading Plotinus.' Close friends use of him precisely the same parlance as IM of Hugo: he was 'totally truthful',[22] to the point of wild eccentricity. Like Hugo, Yorick in real life was divided between two women-loves, (neither of whom resembled Anna or Sadie Quentin). Like Hugo, who ends apprenticed to a Nottingham watchmaker, Yorick wished to become a bus conductor but, IM noted, was the only person in the history of the bus company to fail the theory test; they muddled him with complex situations so that he could not give the correct change.[23] When he accidentally pressed part of the ticket-punching gadget which conductors wore around their necks, 'great sausages' of rolled-up tickets came spewing out. During his single driving-lesson the instructor left the car as Yorick drove on and off the pavement.

Though IM in 1977 wrote to Chatto[24] pleading for a philosophical work by Yorick to be taken seriously by them, his only known publication is a review of Russell's *History of Western Philosophy*, a book he feared would encourage slip-shod thinking.[25] He lived mainly as a librarian; Wittgenstein 's testimonial for him in this job is a warm one. Yorick for IM was a wise counsellor, quick, sensitive, humorous, an excellent listener. When he died in 1980, she wrote his death into the novel she was then composing, *The Philosopher's Pupil*, where Hugo leaves his clocks to 'that writer-chap'—in other words to Jake Donaghue. Before this he suffered a schizophrenic break-down, which caused him to hide behind trees, making strange utterances ('Soft soap'; 'Heil Hitler'). Like Anscombe, Smythies was a Catholic convert and pacifist. A record of conversations with Yorick kept by his friend Peter Daniel from 1952, at the time Murdoch was writing him into *Under the Net*, makes clear Yorick's wide culture,

[20] 29 January 1968.
[21] Ludwig Wittgenstein, *Cambridge Letters*, ed. B. McGuinness and G. H. von Wright (Oxford, 1995), 305.
[22] Barry Pink, a friend from Cambridge in c.1934, 10 August 1998; also Peter Daniel, March 1998.
[23] Polly Smythies, January 1998; Peter Daniel explains they asked him trick questions.
[24] Reading University archive, 1 December 1977.
[25] *The Changing World*, No 1, Summer 1947, 72–81.

his wholly original views, his religious passion, his belief that ordinary consciousness is unfree since enslaved to sin, his attraction to Buddhism (when a film of *Under the Net* was discussed in 1956, IM proposed to simplify the philosophy by making this Buddhist),[26] his preoccupation with the question of saintliness. He believed in human 'transformation'. He wished we had recorded conversations between a saint and an ordinary worldly person. The kindest and most charitable Christians he met were his fellow-inmates in the mental hospital. Saints, though suffering, were still happy. He found *The Cloud of Unknowing* helpful. He was not so unworldly as to be unable to see that many Oxford dons were bored and jealous. He took snuff.

IM shared his concern with sin and saintliness, and his love of the great mystics; also of Kafka; and Murasaki's *Tale of the Genji*. Yorick helped IM through a number of emotional crises. The wise or holy fool Hugo, in the book, cuts through Jake's illusions about who-loves-whom, but also, by his very mode-of-being, reawakens in Jake a humility and—a related matter—sense of wonder. The novel concerns a re-enchantment of the ordinary, the redemption of particulars, a re-christening of the eyes. Hugo stands in this process for the puritan ideal of silence, to which art must of neccesity be opposed, but by which it may also be refreshed; Jake for the necessary compromises of art.

In July 1953, after completing the novel, she paddled Yorick Smythies in her canoe as far as 'The Plough' at Wolvercote.

a long conversation in which Y. was more like Hugo than it's possible to imagine. A diary couldn't but be 'a lie'. All art was a lie. Only the Bible was not a fabrication. Chaucer, Dante? Perhaps Chaucer was all right . . . I said, some people's trade is writing, & if it's possible to sin in it, this doesn't differentiate it from any other trade. Y. said—it's different because it involves judging. He agreed later perhaps this only differentiated it from simple manual jobs. All others were 'tainted' in some similar way! I said too—there must be people who try to purify ideas & speech. You advocate some terrible dichotomy—tainted speech or silence.

In *Under the Net* Jake writes up such conversations with Hugo as a pretentious dialogue called *The Silencer*, while Anna Quentin who loves Hugo, creates an equally silent Mime theatre in Hammersmith out of his influence. Being pure-of-heart and nobly un-self-conscious, Hugo, who lives without self-image, is unable to recognize these reflections. The quarrel between Hugo and Jake is IM's first of many treatments in her work of the frutiful war beween the 'saint and the artist'—for 'artist' read 'arch-individualist'.[27] She thought the novel immature. Jake and Hugo are together for only half-an-hour during the entire book, and what Hugo is engaged in is not immediate to the reader, remaining in the realm of theory.

---

[26] Clive Donner, 'I once met Iris Murdoch', *The Oldie*, September 1999, 15.
[27] See my *Iris Murdoch: The Saint and the Artist*, passim.

4

The Flight from the Enchanter invents its own complex poetic rhetoric that brings together feminism, Hitler, and the confusion of pity with power. The source of this rhetoric is the novel's philosoper-king Mischa Fox, named for his cunning, and based upon Elias Canetti, the book's dedicatee, with whom Murdoch began a liaison in January 1953 that was lastingly important to her and to her art. 'Don't you think Canetti is exactly like God?' the wife of the then French Cultural attaché Mme Mayer was asked; to which she riposted, 'Yes. But is God like Canetti?'[28] The story shocked him.

He was born in Ruschuk in Bulgaria in 1905, with Ladino, the medieval Spanish spoken by Sephardi Jews his first language. His intense pride in this patrician inheritance marked a life rich in further displacements. His polyglot merchant father moved the family to Didsbury, Manchester, from 1911, where he learned English and French; at the age of eight, in Vienna, his gifted, possessive mother obliged him with a fiercely cruel singleness of will, in weeks, to learn German. Knowing many languages is one way of not being tied to any single identity; as an adult he similarly travelled on a Nansen passport, invented for citizens displaced by the Treaties of 1919.[29] Though schooled in Lausanne and Zurich, and having sojourned in Berlin, Vienna remained the capital of his interior universe, and German its chosen tongue.

At the time that Iris Murdoch met Canetti, around 1951, his habits of working late at night, then moving nomadically—'as if hunted'[30]—between a variety of neatly book-lined safe-houses, including a seedy flat at no. 14 Crawford Street and another in Compayne Gardens belonging to his official mistress Marie-Louise von Motesiczky but used by his wife Veza, were well-established. He visited friends separately and kept them apart, living a double, sometimes a triple life, holding court in the coffee-shops of Hampstead which recreated a lost 'Mittel-Europa'. When IM was asked how he fitted his wife into his busy round of visits, IM replied airily, 'Oh, he sees her at 4 in the afternoon'.[31] Both Canetti and Veza insisted she be treated with all the respect due to a Wife Number One in a classical Chinese household: 'Canetti can have as many mistresses as he likes, I don't care, for I am Veza Canetti, and no one else can call themselves that.'

His 1935 novel *Die Blendung* was translated during the war by Veronica Wedgwood and published to acclaim in 1946 as *Auto da Fé* (and in the USA as *The Tower of Babel*). The book is a Georg Grosz-like black comedy of justified paranoia. Susan Sontag, whose brilliant championing of his work helped win him the Nobel Prize for Literature[32] noted that it was impossible not to regard the derangement of its monomaniac

---

[28] K. Raine, *Autobiographies* (London, 1991), 297.
[29] Honor Frost, Conversation with Author, 16 February 1998.
[30] Allan Forbes's description on the telephone, 21 September 1999; and letter 23 December 1999.
[31] Source: Anne Hamburger. Mary Douglas recalls his speaking of Veza as 'schizophrenic'.
[32] Sontag was told by two people in Stockholm, one a publisher, the second a writer who went on to become a member of the Swedish Academy, that her *New York Review of Books* (*NYRB*) essay was 'most

hero, the book-man Kien, as other than a variation on his author's most cherished exaggerations; that it is animated by an exceptionally inventive, delirious, hatred of women; Canetti's mother predicted that women would worship him for his misogyny; an accurate prediction.

Canetti appeared to be proud of IM and would often claim to have been her discoverer; if he helped 'make' her a writer, it was not quite in the manner that he assumed: an *argument* with him is latent throughout. Canetti claimed to Kathleen Raine, whom he felt, was too starry-eyed to understand, to have introduced IM to an understanding of evil: Iris Murdoch 'respected' evil, Raine not. Through Canetti she discovered something about the workings of power, and her own complicity in this. If so it made her a better writer. Many of her best novels have Canetti somewhere behind them, too. Canetti, in one of his 'transformations' is present within or behind every male enchanter-figure of Murdoch's novels, from *Flight* and *A Fairly Honourable Defeat* to *The Sea, The Sea*. Later power-figures such as Charles Arrowby and Julius King are better-realized than Fox; they help—retrospectively—illuminate Mischa Fox.

5

Canetti, an acclaimed writer and accomplished listener, attracted what Murdoch called 'apostles' or—like Fox—'creatures'. Though distinctly a man of the Left politically, he had a great respect for power and a liking for the affluent and patrician; there were hostess-patrons—the author Gladys Huntingdon, with whose family off Hyde Park he at first lived in 1939; Diana Spearman on Lord North Street, associated with the periodical *Time and Tide*; Flora Solomon in Mayfair, once mistress to Kerensky. He arrived knowing no one. Ten years later he consorted with 'painters, cabinet ministers, sculptors, intellectuals, film actresses'.[33] The artist Milein Cosman and her husband the musicologist Hans Keller were neighbours and friends of Canetti's. So were the writers Bernice Rubens and Rudi Nassauer. Gwenda David, literary 'scout' for Viking, lived at no. 44 Well Walk. At no. 21, were Clement Glock, who painted scenery at Covent Garden, and her husband William Glock, future head of music at the BBC. The poet Kathleen Raine and the brothers Gavin and Sir Aymer Maxwell were other 'apostles'. Perhaps Aymer and Flora Solomon helped support Canetti. Raine obsessively and unhappily loved the predominantly homosexual Gavin Maxwell, author of *Ring of Bright Water*, and *both* employed Canetti as their *confident* and counsellor.[34] It was Aymer who first called him 'The Master'. Gavin Maxwell: 'None of us needs Canetti as much as Canetti needs us.' As at court, not everyone stayed in favour. Carol Stewart: 'He *ruled* over both men and women.'

---

influential' in putting Canetti at the top of the list for the 1981 Nobel prize. [Fax, dated December 1998 from SS's assistant Benedict Yeoman.] Sontag and Canetti never met.

[33] Allan Forbes, letter, 23 December 1999.

[34] See Raine, op cit, and Douglas Botting, *Gavin Maxwell: A Life* (London, 1993).

He was (partly) intensely secretive. He had lived part-time for eleven years with his second wife and baby daughter in Zurich before his long-term London mistress of thirty years, the painter Marie-Louise von Motesiczky learnt of the extent of the change in his situation. He was also jealous, paranoiac, and a mythomaniac who, in the words of one friend 'loved creating and undoing human relations and toying with people, watching their relations as a scientist might watch his white mice', a description that recalls or looks forward to the character of Julius in *A Fairly Honourable Defeat*. The same friend—Susie Ovadia (*née* Benedikt)—watched Canetti drill her sister Friedl Benedikt in preparation for a grand party, probably at the William Glocks. She had never before sat through such a detailed set of instructions, of war-like strategies and tactics. It was like Clausewitz, Friedl acting delighted lieutenant to Canetti's dictator.

What is most disturbing in Canetti often rests on a confusion of life and literature. He seemed to belong inside a novel, as when he claimed that the English bored him, because they were 'not wicked enough'. Raine observed that he had 'studied evil more closely' than she, that he had 'specialised in it'. She also saw him as a puppet-master who lacked any sense of the sacred, and thought himself invisible. Not for nothing are the characters in *Auto da Fé* tormented worms.

6

The war-writings of Canetti and of two other friends of Murdoch, and of one another bear out the truism that the 20th century, our world is the work of Hitler. Franz Steiner started his Doctorate on *Slavery* in 1939 as an atonement for and attempt accurately to apprehend the Holocaust, in which his family perished; Günther Adler wrote his monumental and pioneering *Theresienstadt 1941–45*, completed in 1948, scrutinizing the Nazi machinery of genocide—transports, administrative structures, accomodation, diet, health with a systematic eye (1955). And Canetti at the outbreak of war abjured all other creative writing and devoted himself exclusively to writing his parallel study of the phenomenon of Mass behaviour, *Crowds and Power*.[35] In the copy of *Crowds and Power* Canetti gave Adler, returnee from Auschwitz, he wrote, 'To Günther, who experienced what I wrote about'.

In Canetti the emphasis on power and victimhood fell differently. Canetti wrote in German feeling that the Germans had had so much taken away from them, 'it was not right that they should lose their language too'.[36] He might have enjoyed the savage quip that the Germans would never be able to forgive the Jews for Auschwitz. Many saw in *Crowds and Power* 'a message of forgiveness from a Jewish writer to the German people'.[37] Others wondered whether he had earned by suffering the 'right' to offer

[35] See Adler and Fardon's Introduction to Franz Baerman Steiner, *Selected Writings*, edited by Jeremy Adler and Richard Fardon (New York: Berghahn Books, 1999).

[36] Carol Graham-Harrison (Carol Stewart), English translator of *Crowds and Power*, 31 December 1997.

[37] Mary Douglas, Letter to Author; and Susan Sontag, 'Mind as Passion', *New York Review of Books*, 25 September 1980, 47–52, passim.

such forgiveness? His authority to speak for a whole culture was that of the *Dichter* or authoritative 'seer' who owns all available truth. That this is a convention actively mistrusted by the English was probably one reason he resented them and their accursed 'modesty', and forbade publication of his biographies in Britain.

One comes away from *Crowds and Power* overwhelmed by the reduction of the entire panorama of human history to what Lenin termed 'Who: Whom': the triumph of survivors who delight in cruelty. Canetti's own brief piety at the end about being 'against power' reads feebly. He has offered no analysis of how the power instinct—whose tenacity over millennia he spent twenty years remorselessly demonstrating—can be attenuated. Here is history reduced to slaughterhouse, blood-lust, will-to-power. The secret mythologies upon which all human affairs permanently rest are joy-in-killing, and delight-in-power.[38]

7

Canetti's qualities, positive and negative, are so contradictory that it is hard to see how they belong within the same person. No accident that, when Murdoch portrayed him in *Flight*, she gave him one brown and one blue eye and then, to boot, divided him into two: cunning Mischa Fox, effortlessly superior, and god-like, and Calvin Blick, his Smerdyakov-like double, manipulative and wicked. Iris Murdoch remarked early in 1953 to Canetti, 'Whatever I shall do you will have foreseen it and understood it even before I have myself', a sentence that gets echoed in—and embodied in the very title of—*The Flight from the Enchanter* where the leaves that appear to be fleeing from Shelley's *West Wind* are in fact driven by that wind, 'like ghosts from an enchanter fleeing'.

Mischa Fox's only public act of power consists in his buying up the Suffragette paper *The Artemis*. The novel itself never explains why, though Fox is described as 'not, to put it mildly, a supporter of female emancipation' [173]. He secretly wishes, we are to surmise, not to enfranchise so much as to disenfranchise—if not to enslave—women.

It is the main point of *The Flight from the Enchanter* that those enslaved to Mischa Fox—men as well as women—are enslaved voluntarily. The 'alien god' can rule only because his creatures surrender their will. As Virginia Woolf once noted: 'Hitlers are bred by slaves'. The karmic 'blame' of power is in Murdoch's view thus shared between bully and victim, it rests on an act of collusion, and the victims of power, as she expressed this in *The Unicorn*, are 'infected' too passing on the virus to others. Much

---

[38] With disarming apparent candour: 'I would have a purer relationship to Machiavelli if I were not also interested in power; here my path crosses his in a complicated and intimate way. For me, power still is evil absolute.' (Elias Canetti, *Notes from Hampstead: The writer's notes, 1954–1971*, tr. John Hargraves (New York: Farrar, Straus and Giroux, 1998), 8–9.) That he acted consistently as a *Macht-Mensch*—one who seeks, consolidates, and hangs onto power—renders such high-minded protestations mainly rhetorical.

that is monstrous in Canetti is symptomatic, or so the novels imply, of what is monstrous in all of us, and in our century.

8

The final draft was finished in February 1955, when Murdoch was increasingly drawn to John Bayley and her relations with Canetti unresolved. Fox's power—like Shelley's 'unseen presence'—is literally inexplicable. If there are literary antecedents, one might be Thomas Mann's 1931 short story *Mario the Magician*, an anti-Hitlerite fable where a conjuror-hypnotist bewitches his audience, and the voluntary enslavement of that audience is as blameworthy as are the manipulations of the Magician himself.

No one knows Fox's age, what country he comes from, or can fathom his apparent omniscience. Rainborough stands in for all Fox's 'creatures' in asking anxiously, 'Did he say anything about me?' Annette, like the younger IM, positively wills her enslavement to him, suffering the illusion that she can thereby 'liberate [his] soul from captivity' [221]; while Rosa, like an older and wiser IM, dislikes his assertions of power and finds the 'strength to flee . . . the demon' [242]. Nina, captive to her fear of him, finally escapes not to Australia as she plans, but by throwing herself out of the window to her death.

The Flight from the Enchanter opens with a meditation on the vulnerability of all monsters. Annette thinks of Dante's poor condemned minotaur in the twelfth canto of *The Inferno*. 'Why should the poor minotaur be suffering in hell?' He hadn't *asked* to be born a monster. This softens our judgement on Mischa Fox: monsters deserve our pity. Yet monsters, the novel also suggests, are bred out of an ambiguity within the experience of pity itself, which may be corrupted into cruelty and power. The inward nature of that protective anxiety which Fox, (like Canetti), recorded especially about the fate of animals[39] is closely examined in the novel.

Fox is a mystery-man whom, since Canetti was then poor, Iris Murdoch disguises as wealthy and because wealth can fascinate as a power-source. We forget that he is a newspaper magnate: the point is never developed. He is given Canetti's moustache, and also one blue and one brown eye, pointing to a divided and double nature, is 'famous for being famous'. Much is merely stated of him—that he is 'capable of enormous cruelty', that the 'sight of little independent things annoys him'—he wants them in his power; that he is capable of taking a careful revenge after ten years, that he has collected around London 'dozens of enslaved beings' waiting to do his will whom, as Saward observes, he drives mad; that his parties are carefully constructed plots for the forcing of various dramas; that, dragon-like, he eats up young girls and, for Rosa, is sometimes the 'very figure of evil'.

---

[39] Canetti, *The Human Province* (Picador, 1986), 32 ('Why do animals suffer death? What is their original sin?') and *passim*.

Little of his power-broking, his 'oriental magic'—or his philosophy—are actually shown. The best scene has him arriving unannounced at Rainborough's when the latter in panic has shut away young Annette, bare-breasted, in a cupboard. Fox talks, with a poetry both sinister and interminable, about the protean and malleable nature of women and their need to be broken; his *Schadenfreude*, both towards Rainborough whose predicament he surely intuits, and towards women, is simultaneously comical and disturbing. Fox takes pleasure in disquieting others.

The crisis of the novel, also both funny and sinister, is a Dostoevskian *skandal*, a party in Mischa's palazzo where a gold-fish bowl gets smashed and a fish, by mistake, 'saved' in a decanter of gin. His inviting Agnes Casement is typical of Canetti, who was adept both at discovering his friends' secrets, and also of paying attention in social gatherings to the least probable guest.

Murdoch solves the aesthetic problem that Canetti/Fox is morally mixed, at a time when she was in thrall to Canetti, by giving Fox a wicked double, Calvin Blick, who is 'the dark half of Mischa Fox's mind. That's how Mischa can be so innocent.' Blick argues that reality 'is a cipher with many solutions, all of them right ones', a view Carol Stewart recalls as close to Canetti's, and is opposed in this foggy relativism by the good Peter Saward, who argues on the final page by contrast for a humble striving towards truths which may be unreachable. Saward plays saint to Misha's artist, as necessary to the others as an object of contemplation and speculation as the cunning Fox himself. Evil (in Fox) and Good (in Saward) embody forces half-independent of society, the drama of whose opposition is the secret dynamo of the novelistic world.

The novel memorably distances its tone—surreal (Annette swinging from the chandelier), lightly comic, Lewis-Carroll-like, fantastic,—from its grim subject matter. The worst we know of Mischa Fox, reputed to cry when reading the newspapers, is that when a boy he killed a kitten. 'If the gods kill us, it is not for their sport, but because we fill them with such intolerable compassion, a sort of nausea', he comments. Hitler, mentioned once only, who killed those he had rendered piteous by uprooting, is a real presence. When Fox asks Peter whether he does not feel that everything in the universe requires his protection, 'Even this matchbox', Peter demurs, observing how close in Mischa lie the springs of pity and of cruelty. Murdoch's work, of course, abounds too in attempts to rescue trapped birds, fishes, animals . . .

Canetti's own writings are tender towards animals, and memorable when encountering what is maimed or not whole—the anonymous human sack at the end of *The Voices of Marrakesh* that produces a single note; the young paralyzed cripple Thomas Marek whose mother pushes him around on a wagon, whom he befriends near Vienna in his *Memoirs*. He liked to rescue those 'in extremis'. Here a bird with only one foot (in real life sighted by IM with Momigliano at Kew) fascinates Mischa. How will it manage in a storm? *Flight* examines the connexions between pity and power, and between sentimentality and cruelty, like Pound in Canto XXX. Rainborough is predator to Annette, victim to Agnes Casement; but most play both victim and predator. Only Peter Saward and Annette's mother stand outside the web of enslavement, which reaches one comic apogee in the persecutions the old Suffragette Mrs Wingfield visits on her companion Miss Foy: 'Would you say old Foy was a virgin? . . . She isn't !' Agnes Casement too, who nearly swallows Rainborough whole, shows Iris Murdoch's consistent refusal ever to depict women purely as victims.

9

These two philosopher-kings—Hugo and Fox—differ in their relation to their apostles. Hugo does not recognize his own reflection either in *The Silencer* or in Anna's Mime theatre. Anna and Jake—both based on IM herself—are Hugo's chief or only disciples. Perhaps like Yorick Smythies, Hugo so lacks a self-image that he cannot grasp that Anna and Jake could be his disciples.

Mischa Fox in *The Flight from the Enchanter* by contrast influences everyone except Peter Saward, whose immunity to Fox's power-broking is a leading sign of his virtue. Mischa wishes everyone into a subordinate relation with him, and recognizes *only* disciples. While Hugo/Yorick refused a life-myth, Fox/Canetti is a mythomaniac. Hugo suspected narrative and stories and feared their ambiguous power, Fox/Blick revels in the relativity of stories.

Thus *Under the Net* and *Flight* are both concerned with truth. 'Annandine', the persona of Hugo invented by Jake, says that all stories are lies. Yet truth matters to him.[40] 'Only the greatest men can speak and still be truthful' he avers.

Blick, Fox's *alter ego* in *Flight* says by contrast: 'You will never know the truth, and you will read the signs in accordance with your deepest wishes. That is what we humans always have to do. Reality is a cipher with many solutions, all of them right ones.'[41] The novel implicitly rejects Blick's relativism.

When Rosa flees Mischa in Italy towards the end of *Flight*, Iris Murdoch was enacting her own symbolic liberation from Canetti, one which in real life she had not yet, when completing composition in early 1955, achieved. This took one further calendar year. The objectivity she could display in her fiction was something she had not achieved in her life. Hence, precisely, one value to her of her art.

Just as Rosa outgrew Mischa, so, too, Jake outgrew Hugo, or—which comes to the same thing—assimilated Hugo's wisdom so that he no longer needed its originator. These themes of discipleship, and of the Hegelian 'Master/slave' relation never lost their interest or topicality for her. Her first two published novels look forward to later ones such as *The Unicorn, The Sea The Sea, The Good Apprentice, The Message to the Planet, The Philosopher's Pupil, The Green Knight*: all present courts, cabals, or covens, within which the investigation of the themes of discipleship and apprenticeship continue to be crucial. All contain 'Masters' whose virtue—or lack of it—and whose relations with truth, we are invited to assess, and vicariously to experience.

[40] UN 80–1: 'We must be ruled by the situation itself and this is unutterably particular. Indeed it is something to which we can never get close enough, however hard we may try as it were to crawl under the net.'
[41] Paperback, 278.

2

'Faint with Secret Knowledge': Love and Vision in Murdoch's *The Black Prince**

Martha Nussbaum

1 Blinding joy

Bradley Pearson, unsuccessful writer, age 58, sits with Julian Baffin, student, age nineteen, in the restaurant on the top of London's Post Office Tower. Recalling the evening, many years later, he writes that it was a moment of 'blinding joy'. 'It was as if stars were exploding in front of my eyes so that I literally could not see.' His breathing was rapid; 'a quiet and perhaps outwardly imperceptible shuddering possessed my whole frame' (238). His legs 'ached and throbbed', his knees were weak, and a feeling of giddiness fills his body, locating itself primarily in the genitals. Those, he recalls, were some of the physical symptoms:

They can readily be sketched in words. But how to convey the rapture of the mind, as it mingles with the body, draws apart into itself, and mingles again, in a wild and yet graceful dance? The sense of being absolutely in the right and longed-for place is fixed and guaranteed by every ray in the universe . . . Consciousness half swoons with its sense of humble delighted privilege while keen sight, in between the explosions of the stars, devours every detail of the real presence. I am

---

* As readers will see, this paper is a relative of my 'Love and Vision: Iris Murdoch on Eros and the Individual', in *Iris Murdoch and the Search for Human Goodness*, ed. M. Antonaccio and W. Schweiker (Chicago: University of Chicago Press, 1996), 29–53. What is the same is the positioning of Murdoch between Plato and Dante and the argument that the novel lies closer to Plato. But this paper, unlike the earlier one, focuses on *The Black Prince*. alone and offers a more detailed reading of it that differs in some respects from the briefer reading in the earlier paper, particularly in focusing on the novel's form and on the many indications that Bradley is unreliable. The present paper's concluding section, about the vision of the artist, and Murdoch's relation to Proust, is altogether new. The present paper has also been drawn upon in part for the Introduction to the Penguin edition of *The Black Prince*. The material reworked is acknowledged as: 'Introduction' by Martha C. Nussbaum, copyright © 2003 by Martha C. Nussbaum from *The Black Prince* by Iris Murdoch. Used by permission of Viking Penguin, a division of Penguin Group (USA) Inc.

here now, you are here now, we are here now. To see her among others, straying like a divine form among mortals, is to become faint with secret knowledge. (239)[1]

In this artful retrospective description of the blinding force of new erotic love, Bradley alludes, as several times elsewhere in his narrative, to Plato's *Phaedrus*. He depicts his passion as moment of blinding light and sudden vision, vision of a form of goodness and beauty from which mortal eyes are typically cut off. Many of the specific touches in the passage are clear allusions to the experience of the lover in the *Phaedrus*, confronted with the sight of a young man who truly possesses beauty. Bradley thus suggests that his love offers a kind of insight into the truth of the world that we can hardly attain otherwise. As we shall see, he develops this idea extensively in the narrative as a whole.

But there are also countervailing indications, suggestions that Bradley's erotic vision is a kind of self-centered illusion that does not really offer any insight into any real thing or person outside the ego itself. Consider, first of all, the sheer literariness of his description. If the experience is really so like the experience described in Plato, this does not necessarily inspire our confidence that it really yields true vision of Julian Baffin, or of any goodness or beauty residing in her. People who model their experiences on works that they admire are all too likely to be egocentric lovers, seeking to cast the beloved into a scenario dreamed up inside their own fantasy.

Consider, too, the fact that Bradley himself expresses doubts about the quality of his insight. Only a few days before, he believes that he may be falling in love with Julian's mother Rachel, and he asks himself: is this really love, or is it 'just nothing, . . . the transient embarrassment of an elderly puritan who had for a very long time had no adventures at all' (142)? Especially in view of his rapid switch from mother to daughter, one might well ask the same question of his subsequent attachment. When we do so, we need to consider the fact that Bradley has been embarrassingly impotent with the mother, and has repeatedly become successfully aroused in the presence of the daughter. Anxiety about sexual performance is a major motif in the story he tells, and one that undermines to some extent our confidence in the other-directedness of his vision.

Consider, further, the fact that Julian herself believes that Bradley does not really care to know anything about her. Much though she loves him, she repeatedly accuses him of egoism of vision: '"You talk as if there was nobody here but you . . . You don't seem to know me at all. Are you sure it's *me* you love?"' (264–5). And indeed, the Bradley depicted in those scenes is so intensely focused on his own inner states that it seems quite true that the sufferings and experiences of Julian are not quite real to him—something that even his description of his vision suggests, with its mention of a joy that is 'blinding'.

Consider, finally, the form of the novel as a whole. Most of the novel is Bradley's narrative of his love and its tragi-comic denouement. In that sense the novel is unusual

[1]   All references to *The Black Prince* are to the Penguin edition of 1975.

in Murdoch's oeuvre: rarely does she show so much confidence in a single character, yield so much of the world of the novel to that character's eyes. The story told by Bradley is endorsed in many respects by the mysterious Editor who writes a Foreword and a Postscript to his manuscript, and who signs himself P. Loxias. And yet there are also signs that Bradley is not to be altogether trusted: for his narrative is followed by four commentaries by other participants in the story: Rachel Baffin, Julian Baffin, Bradley's ex-wife Christian, and Francis Marloe the psychiatrist, Christian's brother. All four reject parts of the narrative as fantasy or worse, and all depict Bradley as an unreliable and self-centered narrator. Julian, in particular, says that Bradley's art is egoistic and false because it is too much inspired by personal erotic passion; although there was love between them, Bradley's words do not describe it.

So: is love a source of insight into a kind of goodness and beauty that we can, perhaps, grasp in no other way? Or is it a source of egoistic fog and delusion?

Iris Murdoch was a major moral philosopher. More than any other figure of her generation, she challenged us to think better about the moral significance of the imagination, and of the inner moral work that we perform when we try to see another person clearly. These ideas have influenced moral philosophy through her books *The Sovereignty of Good*, *The Fire and the Sun*, and *Metaphysics as a Guide to Morals*, books that are now central in the revival of interest in an ethics of virtue, an ethics concerned not just with action and rules of duty, but with the attempt to perfect one's inner world, removing egoism and seeking clear vision of others. But of course Murdoch's philosophical contribution does not reside only in her overtly philosophical texts. Her novels should not be seen as tracts or theoretical arguments for a position, a fact she continually emphasized: for this would make them, perhaps, accomplices to our manifold attempts to flee the real, to obscure our sight with generalities. But, as she openly acknowledged in *Metaphysics*, the novel is itself an ethical form, dedicated to true vision. Her novels are thus rightly seen as meditations on human love and virtue, in which the complex intelligence of the author, at once both skeptical and loving toward her characters, illuminates the structure of the whole in a way that invites the reader to look for connections with the more overtly meditative texts.

My plan in this paper is to look closely at just one novel, *The Black Prince*, to see what its complex structure suggests about one of Murdoch's major philosophical themes, the relationship between erotic love and the true vision of other people. I shall begin by introducing two philosophical views that are clearly present in the novel, the views of love in Plato's *Phaedrus* and in Dante's *Commedia*. By invesigating tensions between them, I shall pose some questions about the novel that I shall then attempt to answer, through a close reading of its story of anxiety, love, and vision. Having come up with an account of where the novel stands between these two conflicting texts, I shall then make things much more complex by suggesting that we must distinguish the question about the moral potential of erotic love from a question about the moral potential of art inspired by erotic love. I shall suggest, in concluding, that, though the novel lies closer to Plato, in the end, than to Dante, it is not because erotic love itself supplies the superior vision; it is because the erotic work of art supplies that vision. And that conclusion in turn will suggest another: that Murdoch may actually be less close to Plato, here, than she is to Proust, for whom true vision of particular people is never actually possible, because all real-life love is marred by possessiveness, and all art uses mere people as material for the construction of the artwork.

2 Blindness and longing

We live bereft of sight and filled with yearning. Cut off from the vision of the good that was ours in another world, we seek to return to that world and that knowledge. In our striving, beauty, and the body's erotic response to the sight of beauty, play a central role, since, as Socrates says,

sight is for us the sharpest of the bodily senses. It does not see wisdom—for indeed wisdom would give rise to awesome erotic longing, if it did enter our field of vision and provide a clear likeness of itself, and so too the other objects of our erotic longing. But as things are, only beauty has that lot, to be the most evident and the most erotically arousing. (*Phaedrus* 250D)

Those whose vision of the good is dim respond obtusely to their own sexual arousal, giving themselves to pleasure and seeking only the physical gratification of procreation or of superficial sexual release (250E).[2] Their arousal itself, Plato suggests, is superficial, focusing on the surface of the bodily form and failing to honor the divine beauty within.[3] But in those who remain closer to the other world the sight of sexual love pierces deeper, catching glimpses of the soul's beauty in the form and features of the body (see 252E7–253A1). For such people, sexual arousal is a seismic upheaval of the entire soul, whose terrifying disruption of habitual order brings with it a turning toward the good. The sight of the beautiful beloved brings a shudder of awe, which mysteriously turns to a sweating and fever, as the stream of beauty entering through the eyes waters the parched roots of the soul's wings. The wings now begin to grow 'over the entire form of the soul' (251B): they belong, that is, to the soul's emotions and bodily desires, as well as to its intellect. And now, indeed, the soul 'boils and throbs as a whole', with a feeling like the throbbing in the gums of a teething child when a tooth is about to come through. Madness prevents sleep; the soul is riven between joy and anguish. But when at last the beloved is in the lover's presence, the soul of the lover 'channels the stream of desire into herself as through an irrigation trench, releasing the pent-up waters. Then she has a respite from her stings and agonies, and reaps the fruit of the sweetest pleasure this life offers' (251E).

---

[2] For my account of the diverse scholarly interpretations of this difficult sentence, and my own argument, see 'Platonic Love and Colorado Law', in my *Sex and Social Justice* (New York: Oxford University Press, 1999).

[3] 250E3: 'he does not revere it when he sees it'.

Plato's extraordinary description, with its mixed images of irrigation, of teething, of boiling, of stinging—and with its complex and culturally bold sexual intimations of both activity and receptivity, in which irrigating oneself with the water of the loved one's beauty brings the summit of pleasure[4]—is, we have no doubt, a description of a certain type of personal erotic love, a love in which the body's response to the sight of a beautiful body is linked in mysterious ways with a deeper yearning for the soul that inhabits the body, and for the vision of the good that this soul appears to offer. This passage has been important to Iris Murdoch in quite a few of her writings, both fictional and philosophical. It has a central place in the argument of *The Fire and the Sun*, receives frequent discussion in *Metaphysics as a Guide to Morals*, and underlies the plot and action of *The Black Prince* (see especially 210, 239, 349).

The passage as a whole appears to make four claims about sexual love:

(1) Love of this sort is a crucial, apparently even a necessary, source of *motivation* for the soul in its search for the vision of the good. Without the unique role of beauty and sight, without the upheaval of sense occasioned by the physical presence of the beloved, the soul does not search for the good, and remains in a parched and depleted condition.

(2) Love of this sort is a crucial source of *vision*—vision both of the beloved person and of the external impersonal good, the two being closely linked. The passage makes it clear that the discovery of the inner divinity and the nature of the beloved person, and the generous loving actions inspired by this discovery (see 253B, 255B) would not have taken place without the violent erotic reaction of the *whole* soul, therefore not without its sexuality; and sexuality itself, operating as it does here in concert with the emotions and the intellect[5], serves the person as a reliable indicator of the presence of the good. The passage also argues that although direct unmediated arousal by the good is conceivable it is not empirically possible; as we are, we need the body's response to beauty to stimulate our vision and send it searching for goodness. Blind sexual love is very common, and Plato acknowledges it. But obtuse reasoning is also common; and Plato argues here that reasoning will always be obtuse, unless it is guided by erotic love.

(3) Sexual love is not simply a starting point for the mind in its search for the good, but a lifelong accompaniment to that search. Plato's highest contemplative lovers do forgo full intercourse, on account of Plato's view that that intense

[4] For sensitive comment on the sexual imagery of the passage, see K. J. Dover, *Greek Homosexuality* (Cambridge, MA: Harvard University Press, second edition 1989), 162–4; for more specific comments on the validation of erotic receptivity, and its culturally anomalous status, see my 'Reply to David Halperin', *Proceedings of the Boston Area Colloquium for Ancient Philosophy* 4 (1989), 53–72, and chapter 7 of *The Fragility of Goodness* (Cambridge: Cambridge University Press, 1986, updated edition 2001). The language of 'reaping the fruit of pleasure' is suggestive of orgasmic pleasure, in the poetic language of Plato's time.

[5] I do not mean to imply that there is no tension among these elements; clearly Plato believes that there is, and I shall return to this point. For an excellent discussion of the entire passage, and especially of this tension, see A. Price, *Love and Friendship in Plato and Aristotle* (Oxford: Clarendon Press, 1989).

degree of bodily pleasure would obscure the soul's vision. But they regularly indulge their sexual desire in caresses that stop short of intercourse. And the many couples who continue to have full intercourse will be rewarded by the gods in the afterlife 'on account of their erotic love'; they will spend a 'blessed life wandering around in the light with one another', and will regain their wings, with similar plumage (256DE). Plato never suggests that the sexual element in their desire should itself be forgone; in fact, he strongly suggests that it remains throughout life an important component of the search for goodness, both in itself and in one another. In fact, in a culturally remarkable move, he imagines the beloved himself conceiving a reciprocal desire (*anterôs*) for the lover, and depicts this desire as an important part of the younger person's spiritual development.[6]

(4) In erotic love of the best sort, the lovers see and acknowledge one another's individuality, in two ways: (a) They acknowledge one another as *agents*, each striving toward the good. A respect for the separate agency or freedom of the beloved, and a wish to foster it, is a big part of what differentiates this generous love from the jealous and possessive loves against which the beloved young person has so frequently been warned (253B, 255B). (b) They acknowledge one another's *qualitative specificity*, in the sense that their love is all about a true perception of and desire for the specific 'divinity', or pattern of aspiration, that they discern in the beloved, knowing its presence through its bodily traces.

As we have already seen, Bradley Pearson situates his love in relation to this text, and clearly wishes to claim for it the insight ascribed to the good sort of love in the text. In view of the doubts we have already raised, however, let us now investigate a different view of love, no less central to Murdoch's thinking.

3 The fog of the world

Dante has passed through the flame that disciplines the lustful, the purifying flame of the Angel of Chastity, whose song is 'Beati mundo corde', 'Happy are the pure in heart.'[7] The last P, the last sign of sin, has been stricken from his brow. Now, as he stands in the Earthly Paradise, the Heavenly Pageant halts before him, as the Prophets sing the passionate words of the *Song of Solomon*: 'Come with me from Lebanon, my bride.' These words are passionate: and yet it is clear that theirs, like Dante's, is a passion

[6] See David Halperin, 'Plato on Erotic Reciprocity', *Classical Antiquity* 5 (1986): 60–80, and Nussbaum, 'Eros and the Wise: the Stoic Response to a Cultural Dilemma', *Oxford Studies in Ancient Philosophy* 13 (1995), 231–67.

[7] See Nussbaum, '"Beatrice's Dante: Loving the Individual?"', in *Virtue, Love, and Form: Essays in Memory of Gregory Vlastos*, ed. Terence Irwin and Martha C. Nussbaum, *Apeiron* 26 (1993), numbers 3 and 4, at 161–78; and now see the related ch. 12 of *Upheavals of Thought: The Intelligence of Emotions* (Cambridge: Cambridge University Press, fall 2001).

from which sexual lust has been entirely purged away. And now, from that chariot, from within a cloud of flowers, a lady appears before Dante, her veil the white of Christian faith, her cloak the green of hope, her gown the flame red of Christian love. This lady is not unknown to Dante, nor he to her:

> My soul—such years had passed since last it saw
> that lady and stood trembling in her presence,
> stupefied, and overcome by awe—
> now, by some power that shone from her above
> the reach and witness of my mortal eyes,
> felt the full mastery of enduring love.[8]

Turning to Virgil, Dante now quotes Virgil's own lines, lines said by Dido when she recognizes that her love for Aeneas is the 'same love' that she felt for her dead husband Sychaeus: 'I recognize the tokens of the ancient flame', 'Conosco i segni del antica fiamma.'[9] These words of recognition strike the reader as profoundly ambiguous: for if Dante's passion is characterized by shuddering and trembling, by intense erotic longing, and by an upheaval of the soul as intense as the upheaval that shakes the lover in the *Phaedrus*, there is also a very real sense in which it cannot possibly be 'the ancient flame', given that flame itself has removed the sexual heat that once suffused it, and given that flame, in Beatrice's gown, now symbolizes a Christian love purified of bodily desire. It is at this point, as Beatrice addresses him, that Dante's own name occurs for the first and only time in the poem:

> Dante, do not weep yet, though Virgil goes.
> Do not weep yet, for soon another wound
> shall make you weep far hotter tears than those!
> Look at me well. I am she. I am Beatrice.
> How dared you make your way to this high mountain?
> Did you not know that here man lives in bliss?[10]

Now, at the moment when Dante is purified of sin, he is addressed by his own name—as if only now were he being seen and loved in all his individuality. And the object of his passion, she who sees him with loving particularity of vision, she too emphasizes the full individuality in which she stands before him. 'Ben son, ben son Beatrice', 'I really am, I really am Beatrice.' The emphatic linking of the name with its rhyme, 'felice', 'blessed', indicates, once again, that it is in the context of Christian salvation that individuality is most truly seen and loved.

[8] Dante, *Purgatorio* (*Purg.*) XXX.34 ff., trans. Ciardi, except in l. 36, where I have replaced Ciardi's 'stupefied by the power of holy awe', since no word corresponding to 'holy' appears in the original, and it seems wrong to suggest that Dante's youthful love for Beatrice was already holy.
[9] Virg. Aen. IV.23, agnosco veteris vestigia flammae.
[10] *Purg.* 55–7, 73–5. The literal translation of l. 73 is 'Really look—I really am, I really am Beatrice.'

It is evident that this perception of individuality could not have taken place before the purification of sin. For, as Dante so elaborately shows his reader, 'the world is blind' ('lo mondo è cieco', *Purg.* XVI.66). The manifold lures of the world—including fame, honor, money, and sexual gratification—create a 'fog' around the sight of the individual[11], blocking him from truly perceiving other individuals, and to a great extent from being truly perceived. The sins that are purged in Purgatory are all different forms of false love, in which the soul has taken an excessive interest in objects that are not the worthy or true objects of its love. These false loves get between the individual and a love of persons, who are worthy objects of love. In pride, for example, one attends only to one's own standing; this leads to a failure to notice the needs of those one loves. In envy, one fixes on the possessions or standing of others, again failing to notice who they are and what they need. In anger one is filled with resentment at slights to oneself, and so cannot fully attend to the particular history and needs of another. In sloth and gluttony, one's absorption in one's own comfort and gratification make one slow to go to another's need. Lust, finally, is also seen as a deformation of individual love. The suggestion is that the lustful, focusing as they do on their own bodily pleasure and excitement, are imperfectly able to notice and respond to the needs of the person whom they love, or even to take in their full particularity. A person who is seen as a vessel of pleasure is not seen truly for what he or she *is*. Dante's reader would recall that Paolo and Francesca, though together in love for all eternity, do not exactly see one another's individual specificity. He speaks of her as a 'bella persona', a 'beautiful form',—and she notices that this bodiliy form is hers no longer. She sees him as a source of 'piacer', and calls him 'costui', 'that one'. Never in her long speech does she mention his name. Nor does either recognize the other as a center of agency and freedom: their love delights in the thought of mutual surrender and passivity.

If, then, we take this passage of the *Purgatorio* in its context, we find it yielding four theses about sexual love, which do not seem easy to reconcile with the claims of the *Phaedrus*:

(1) Sexual response to the bodily beauty of another decreases motivation to pursue the vision of the good (*and* of the individuality of the person) by binding the mind to a false object of love.

(2) Sexual love, like other sins, creates a kind of egoistic 'fog' around the lover, impeding his vision of the reality of the other, and of the good.

(3) Even if sexual desire cannot be avoided as one stage in human life, love must be purified of bodily desire before true vision of the other person, or of the good, can be achieved—and this means, as well, before the best form of human love and beneficence can be achieved.

---

[11] *Purg.* XI.30: 'purgando la caligine del mondo'.

(4) Sexual love is incapable of fully attending adequately either to the agency or the qualitative specificity of the object of love. It prefers to conceive of its object as passive, surrendering, and as a seat of superficial pleasantness.

These claims conflict with the claims of the *Phaedrus*. One might attempt to resolve the conflict by saying that some cases of sexual love have *Phaedrus* properties and some have the properties that Dante notes. Plato himself lends support to this strategy, since the *Phaedrus* prominently recognizes cases of sexual love that *are* superficial in vision, that do not lead to an accurate view either of the beloved or of the good. But Dante's argument will not admit this reconciling strategy. He makes it very clear that in even the best cases of human sexual love—and we must suppose that his own love of Beatrice is a pretty good case—the sexual element in the love is an impediment and a source of delusion. True sight is recovered the far side of the purifying flames. And if one never had lust in the first place one would be much better off as a perceiver and lover.

My puzzle is that the Dantean view of sexual love is also a Murdochian view. Murdoch, more than any other contemporary ethical thinker, has made us vividly aware of the many stratagems by which the ego wraps itself in a cozy self-serving fog that prevents exit to the reality of the other. Her catalogue of sins, in fact, closely resembles Dante's. In the famous example of the mother and daughter-in-law in *The Sovereignty of Good*, it is envy and perhaps also sexual jealousy that causes the mother-in-law to focus on the superficial and unattractive traits of her daughter-in-law. M's effort to see D truly is an inner moral effort that could usefully be compared to the discipline undergone by Dante's souls in Purgatory. For if to Sartre 'l'enfer c'est les autres', hell is other people, for Murdoch, by contrast, hell is being walled up inside one's own fat cozy ego without means of egress to the other or to the good; heaven is the place of true and selfless vision; and purgatory the place of moral effort that attempts to deliver us from the one to the other.

It is frequently suggested, both in Murdoch's philosophical works and in her novels, that sexual desire, and the bodily component in love, are sins in the Dantean sense, that is, sources of egoistic self-delusion and self-immersion that persistently come between us and the reality of those we love. And if that is so, if, that is, it is so pervasively, then Murdoch cannot endorse the entirety of Plato's vision in the *Phaedrus* as a story about how we recover our wings. She can endorse the special role Plato gives to the sight of beauty, and she can argue that the bodily response to beauty plays a crucial role in motivation and in vision. But she cannot hold that the sexual ferment the *Phaedrus* actually describes is a valuable part of the search for truth, far less, as Plato strongly suggests, a necessary part.

4 Anxiety and madness

Let us now return to Bradley and Julian. There are, as I have said, many indications in the novel that Bradley is a Dantean sinner, his love an egoistic fog. Although his love initially makes him overflow with feelings of love and generosity toward everyone in his surroundings, these generous feelings are quickly supplanted by the pain of anxiety, by jealousy and possessiveness, and especially, after the two arrive at the country retreat where Bradley had initially planned a solitary vacation, by overwhelming and obsessive concern about sexual performance. The novel lets us see clearly that this last concern does indeed blind Bradley to important truths about his world. In the grip of the idea that he must finally make love successfully to Julian, he allows himself to conceal from Julian, and to distance from his own thoughts, the news of his sister Priscilla's suicide, a death for which he is in part responsible because of the neglect induced by his passion. He does not think seriously enough of Julian's real emotions to recognize that she will be devastated and profoundly shocked when she realizes that she has just been making love to a man who has just received the news of his sister's death, but who has concealed it in order to go to bed with her. Erotic anxiety and vanity do, here, defeat the real vision of the beloved. Bradley also does not recognize the importance to Julian of his other lie, about his age. (He says he is in his forties, rather than fifty-eight; when her father reveals the truth, her romantic attraction to Bradley is seriously undercut, though whether more by the lying or by the truth it is hard to say.)

As I have also noted, the four narratives at the novel's end all convict Bradley of various forms of egoistic illusion. For Christian, Bradley is a humorless Puritan whose infatuation with Julian was a crude attempt to conceal from himself the fact that he was really in love with Christian. As for the love between them, 'it was obviously mostly in his mind' (395). For Francis Marloe, psychoanalyst, Bradley's story is just one more confirmation of the truth of Freudian theory. Bradley is in the grip of a childhood ambivalence toward his mother, passionately desiring her but also hating her for her infidelity to him; therefore he fears women and is homosexual. The fact that he is physically most aroused by Julian when she is dressed up as Hamlet is just one detail that confirms, for Francis, the essential truth that Bradley is pursuing a childhood fantasy. For Rachel, Bradley is plainly in love with her all along. His story about Julian is just a silly fiction. 'His great "passion" for her is a typical dream-up' (405), resulting from a sadomasochistic fantasy of doom and separation. For Julian, now married to the teenage boyfriend with whom she had just broken up before the affair with Bradley, there was something like love between them, but it is a great mistake on Bradley's part to think that eros can reveal the truth. 'Love is concerned with possession and vindication of self', Art with 'truth in its least pleasant and useful and therefore most truthful form' (410). Eros is thus a corrupter of art, incapable of telling truth. His words therefore cannot truthfully describe the love between them.

These are the doubts. Now we must consider the other side of the ledger. We should notice, first, that Bradley's claims for the truth and value of erotic vision are claims that Murdoch makes in her own voice, with similar allusion to Plato, in *Metaphysics as a Guide to Morals*:[12]

Love, as the fruit and overflow of spirit. Plato's visions may seem far away from the mess of ordinary loving, but they shed light, we can understand. Falling in love is for many people their most intense experience, bringing with it a quasi-religious certainty, and most disturbing because it shifts the centre of the world from ourself to another place. A love relationship can occasion extreme selfishness and possessive violence, the attempt to dominate that other place so that it be no longer separate; or it can prompt a process of unselfing wherein the lover learns to see, and cherish and respect, what is not himself. There are many aspects to this teaching; for instance, letting the beloved go with a good grace, knowing when and how to give up, when to express love by silence or by clearing off. This negative heroism may be very enlightening, aided by the palpable satisfaction of having behaved well when one desired to behave otherwise! (*M* 16–17)

Here Murdoch grants that erotic love has a potential for violence and extreme selfishness; but she insists that it is also the greatest source many people can ever have of an experience of being forced out of their own ego, by the sheer blazing power of another person, toward the vision of something true outside the self. Nor is this an isolated passage. In another novel of the same period, *The Sacred and Profane Love Machine*, a similar reflection occurs, not in the thought of any particular character, but, so to speak, in the author's own voice:

Intense mutual erotic love, love which involves with the flesh all the most refined sexual being of the spirit, which reveals and perhaps even *ex nihilo* creates spirit as sex, is comparatively rare in this inconvenient world. This love presents itself as such a dizzily lofty value that even to speak of 'enjoying' it seems a sacrilege. It is something to be undergone upon one's knees. And where it exists it cannot but shed a blazing light of justification upon its own scene, a light which can leave the rest of the world dark indeed. (SPLM, 261)

Here again, Murdoch depicts erotic love as a rare source of vision and illumination. These passages suggest that we ought to return to the novel, prepared to see Bradley Pearson as a more complex figure than the pathetic self-deluded character depicted by the four Postscripts.

And indeed, to the reader of the entire novel, it is really the four postscript writers, rather than Bradley, who emerge as Dantean sinners. Each one is thoroughly obsessed with the self, to the extent that they misrepresent the world in quite comical ways. (When we say 'misrepresent' we are, of course, trusting Bradley, but then he gives us so much more, in terms of human vision and insight, than the thin flat worlds of the Postscripts. These narratives are so thin, so transparently self-serving, that they just *cannot* be true: they wear their egoism on their face.) Christian, while in some ways generous and full of an admirable energy, is essentially vain and mercenary, totally lacking in any sense of the spiritual side of life. (It's no surprise, since she has lived so

[12] Iris Murdoch, *Metaphysics as a Guide to Morals* (New York: Allen Lane, The Penguin Press, 1992).

long in America.) Her very incomprehension about the value of art betrays her; and her comic conviction that Bradley is in love with her convicts her further. Francis is moving in his affection for his old friend; but he sees the world through the lens of a simplifying universal theory, always a Murdochian sin, and for this reason cannot really comprehend the complex reality of an individual person. Rachel has staked her whole life on a series of lies about Bradley and herself. (She has trapped Bradley into taking the rap for her murder of her husband, understanding that his love of Julian will prevent him from telling the truth and saving himself.) The closest we get in Murdoch to thoroughgoing evil is in characters like Rachel, so profoundly deceptive and self-deceptive that the reality of other people simply ceases to exist for them. As Bradley observes, evil is rarely the result of a 'conscious leering evil intent'. Much more often it is 'the product of a semi-deliberate inattention, a sort of swooning relationship to time' (189).

Of the four narrators, Julian is the saddest, so shell-shocked by the events involving her mother, father, and lover that she has retreated from people into a kind of austere anti-erotic art that cannot, we feel (and Loxias confirms), be very much good as art. So, rather than undercutting Bradley, the poverty of the four Postscripts actually illumin-ates, by contrast, all that is rich, generous, and true in the vision of the world from which most of the novel is narrated.

When we return to Bradley with this contrast in mind, we discover that much of his story enacts, in fact, the story of the lovers in the *Phaedrus*. For years, the center of Bradley's world has been himself: his sterility as an artist, his envious friendship with Arnold Baffin, the successful popular writer. His passion for Julian opens his eyes, and allows his art, ultimately, to see truth—as the mysterious editor of his manuscript remarks, vindicating Bradley against the older Julian's denunciation of the erotic element in art. 'Of course it [sc. art] is to do with truth', Loxias writes, 'it makes truth. But to that anything can open its eyes. Erotic love can' (414). Anxiety and envy have closed Bradley in, but passion opens his eyes, permitting him to see all the figures of the novel in the variegated and richly human way in which they appear before us.

In fact, as he looks back on his love, Bradley persuasively articulates a very Platonic and also a very Murdochian theory of vice and illumination that seems a pretty good explanation of what happens to him. In general he argues, we do not see others truly. Our anxious personal emotions 'cloud the view, and so far from isolating the particular, draw generality and even theory in their train' (81). Egoistic anxiety is the root of all the vices:

Anxiety most of all characterizes the human animal. This is perhaps the most general name for all the vices at a certain mean level of their operation. It is a kind of cupidity, a kind of fear, a kind of envy, a kind of hate. Now, a favoured recluse, I can, as anxiety diminishes, measure both my freedom and my previous servitude. Fortunate are they who are even sufficiently aware of this problem to make the smallest efforts to check this dimming preoccupation . . . The natural tendency of the human soul is towards the protection of the ego. (183)

Because of anxiety, Bradley suggests, we cannot see other particular people too precisely; their sharp particularity would be too threatening, would give us too much pain. (Here Bradley's, and Murdoch's, ideas about vision lie close to those of Proust, a comparison to which I shall return.) We therefore 'defend ourselves by descriptions and tame the world by generalizing' (82). This crude vision of people and things is an essential prelude to evil: 'When we do ill we anaesthetize our imagination. Doubtless this is, for most people, a prerequisite of doing ill, and indeed a part of it' (170). In general, the mind of an everyday human being is like one of the souls in Plato's cave, nourished by comforting shadows (192, 208, 285). (We are clearly to connect this insight with the comic description of the novels of Arnold Baffin, crude farragos of philosophical theory and exotic generality.)

Love, Bradley now argues, is for most people the only force powerful enough to break the grip of the anxious ego. The lover is 'dazzled by emergence from the cave' (208). In the blinding joy of the vision of beauty, the lover attains a wonderful loss of self, and something like the regrowing of the wings that Plato's *Phaedrus* describes. Erotic love gives Bradley wings of joy, a sense of the blotting out of self, a turning away from customary fears:

A common though not invariable early phase of this madness, the one in fact through which I had just been passing, is a false loss of self, which can be so extreme that all fear of pain, all sense of time (time is anxiety, is fear) is utterly blotted out. The sensation itself of loving, the contemplation of the existence of the beloved, is an end in itself. (244)

Now of course anxiety may, and does, arise in the context of love. The self more or less inevitably returns, revives (209, 244). In fact, 'The presence of the loved one is perhaps always accompanied by anxiety' (238). But, continues Bradley, 'this one grain of darkness cannot be accounted a blemish. It graces the present moment with a kind of violence which makes an ecstasy of time' (238). Anxiety and love are antagonists, not accomplices, and love is the only force powerful enough to prevail against the anxious ego. Because we are imperfect, the triumph of love, and its vision, are also imperfect. Bradley's love is, in this way, marred by jealousy, by sexual anxiety, and by a failure to imagine Julian's distress at Priscilla's death.

Nonetheless, it is evident that Bradley is freed from egoistic self-preoccupation, to the extent to which he is, thanks only to the intensity of his desire, not in spite of it. His experience of love does include the virtuous actions Murdoch names—letting the beloved go with good grace, knowing when to give up, behaving well when one wishes to behave otherwise. In fact, although he does not praise himself, we understand well that love has brought him to a virtuous action extreme in its consequences—for it is clearly for Julian's sake that he conceals the true facts concerning her mother's murder of her father, and takes the conviction and sentence with staggering courage. It is also thanks to love that he becomes a real artist: for we are to think that the manuscript we read is his first humanly rich and truly perceptive work of art. It is subtitled 'A Celebration of Love', and its editor, P. A. Loxias, is a proxy for the god Apollo himself.

There are certainly doubts about the vision inherent in Bradley's love. We wonder, for example, how truly he sees Julian, when he sees her as a 'divine form straying among mortals'. The fact is that she is a confused adolescent girl, in some respects very ordinary. So is he seeing her, or is he seeing *through* her to something general that she merely instantiates? These are worries about Plato and Murdoch's Platonism, however, not doubts about the extent to which *The Black Prince* is, indeed, Platonic. And surely, Bradley would reply, to see the divinity in Julian is a truer sort of vision than the cramped mean-spirited vision of Rachel and Arnold Baffin, who treat her dismissively as an ordinary not very interesting girl. Love sees truly, in part, because it *does* see divinity rather than the muddled everyday.

Surely, then, despite all the imperfections of Bradley's love for Julian, the Platonism of Murdoch's 'Celebration' of the erotic has the last word. In her Postscript Julian, grown older but hardly wiser, expresses the anti-Platonic view: true vision is 'very very cold'. 'Erotic love never inispires art. Or only bad art.' 'Love is concerned with possession and vindication of self. Art with neither. To mix up art with Eros, however black, is the most subtle and corrupting mistake an artist can commit' (410). Love, she argues, is inherently narcissistic, antithetical therefore to the outward-reaching truth-directed vision of good art (411). This view of the world and of Bradley Pearson is, however, repudiated—first of all, internally, since the self-conscious arty prose of Julian Belling rings false, gives us the sense of a stunted personality and imagination. More important, it is repudiated by Loxias himself, who makes fun of her 'very *literary* piece', and asserts that erotic love *can* open the lover's eyes to the truth.

5   The erotic work of art

The novel's picture of *eros* is, then, more Platonic than Dantean, though it complicates Platonism with a complex diagnosis of the roots of self-avoidance. Through sexual love Bradley does find himself jolted out of himself, prepared to search, at least, for the real good that is in the world and the reality of its people. Through erotic love, again, he becomes capable of real art. But now we arrive at a deep problem: that of the relationship of erotic love to the erotic work of art. For this is a love story, to be sure. But it is also, very self-consciously, an art story, whose culmination is not the love itself, but the turning of love into art. And although there may be Platonism and Platonic vision in the love story, it is Bradley the artist who very artfully constructs his story as a Platonic story.

Had we only Bradley's narration, we would still need to consider this issue—just as, in Dickens's *David Copperfield*, we need to understand that the quality of mind that narrates the entire story—and not just the happy husband of the novel's internal ending—is who David has become, a personality more erotic and complex, more generous and truly loving, than his husbandly self. But in *The Black Prince* the theme of art's relationship to life is signalled to us again and again—by casting Bradley as a blocked and unsuccessful writer for whom Eros opens the door to erotic expression, by the constant self-conscious allusions to the process of narrating his life story, by his Foreword, with its literary self-consciousness about style and form, and, above all, by the Editor's Foreword and Postscript, which are given authority by the name of the mysterious editor, P. Loxias, obviously the god Apollo himself. I have said that one of the worries with which the scene in the Post Office Tower inspires us is a worry about the literary artfulness with which it is narrated: can anything this carefully constructed actually contain a loving vision of a particular beloved?

We must ask two closely related Proustian questions, then, about art and life in this book. First, if there is a true and generous vision of Julian Baffin in this book, whose vision is it? That of Bradley the lover, or that of Bradley the recollecting artist? Would a true vision of an individual be possible to someone who is a lover without being, later, an artist of his love? Second, if the vision that animates the text and that is given Apollo's authority belongs to the artist, not the lover, or to the lover only insofar as he retains, in his solitary life of art, traces of his former loves, what does this say about the role of Julian the real woman in the work before us? Is there, after all, anything like a true vision of a particular woman here, or is the particular awkward reality simply source-material for the creation of a work that goes beyond her? To put this question in other terms, is the vision of the artist a vision that loves real people, or one that appropriates them for its own creative ends?

To the first question, I believe we must reply that the vision that is validated in the work is the vision of Bradley the recollecting artist. The proof of the truth of his vision is in the story he tells, so rich and variegated and deep, by contrast to the crudeness of the four Postscripts. And repeatedly he draws attention to moments of illusion, anxiety, and error in Bradley the man, in such a way that we do not ever have stable confidence in the vision of the man as he goes through his bewildering adventures. We do acknowledge that eros has opened his eyes; but the fruit of that initial experience, the fruit that is really valuable, is the work of art before us, and the vision that it contains. As he says in his own Postscript, 'The book had to come into being because of Julian, and because of the book Julian had to be . . . This is her deification and incidentally her immortality. It is my gift to her and my final possession of her' (389). Only in the work of art has Bradley finally shaken off fog and anxiety, and his love of his teacher and friend Loxias is, in the end, the enveloping love story of the work.

What this means, too, is that it is the artwork, or the artist as creator of the artwork, who possesses moral virtue and the capacity to see another truly that is the essence of Murdochian virtue. The man never gets this far—until he is separated from all human society by imprisonment, left in solitude to write his own love story. (Here we arrive at a theme central to the art of Henry James, one of the novelists whom Murdoch most admired.)

Thus the Murdoch of the novel seems to agree with Proust's narrator, who holds that our loves must be studied by reflection in a condition of detachment from love, before the literary work of art that recaptures them can ever come into being. The vision of love itself is inherently unstable and inconstant. Only through the life of art do we ever succeed in possessing all that we have loved, in the sense that only then does our mind embrace the past experience with unerring specificity and sureness.[13] Proust adds, in a way that Murdoch would very likely endorse, that in this way works of art are otherworldly exemplars of virtue, for they show a clarity of vision to which in real life, distracted by jealousy and anxiety, we never attain.[14]

This being the case, we must now ask our second Proustian question: where in the erotic work of art is the real-life loved one? For Proust, the work of art must rest on a series of experiences, because it is only as the result of several distinct experiences of love that we can successfully extract the 'general form' of our love:

[T]he writer, in order to achieve volume and substance, in order to attain to generality and, so far as literature can, to reality, needs to have seen many churches in order to paint one church and for the portrayal of a single sentiment requires many individuals. (III.945, Kilmartin translation)

Indeed, 'infidelity toward the individual' is a prerequisite of the appropriate creative posture (945). The artist is delighted not by this or that particular love, but by a general form of love and desire that emerges from all the concrete experiences, in the unity of one portion of her past with another: for he 'is nourished only by the essences of things', in these alone he finds her 'sustenance and delight' (III.905). Reaching back to a particular love in memory, the artist will now view the beloved as a model who has 'quite simply been posing for the artist at the very moment when, much against his will, they made him suffer most' (939). And in this way, in the very process of causing her pain, the beloved has brought her stone 'for the building of the monument' that is his narrative artwork (941).

In other words, returning to our original questions about the perception of individuality, Proust's view entails that the artist's vision never fully sees either another person's particularity or another person's agency. Particularity is submerged in the search for essences, for the general form of our own love; agency is cast aside in order to make of the loved one a mere artist's model, a stone for the building of the monument. Indeed, Proust holds that nobody sees the particular, ever: not artists, because they delight in general forms, not ordinary people because they are blind and obtuse. There is but one exception. The only contact we have with the particularity and agency of

---

[13] I discuss these aspects of Proust in chapter 10 of *Upheavals of Thought*.

[14] Consider the following passage, after the death of Bergotte the writer:

All that we can say is that everything is arranged in this life as though we entered it carrying a burden of obligations contracted in a former life; there is no reason inherent in the conditions of life on this earth that can make us consider ourselves obliged to do good, to be kind and thoughtful, even to be polite . . . All these obligations, which have no sanction in our present life, seem to belong to a different world, a world based on kindness, scrupulousness, self-sacrifice, a world entirely different from this one and which we leave in order to be born on this earth, before perhaps returning there to live once again beneath the sway of those unknown laws which we obeyed because we bore their precepts in our hearts. (III.186)

another person is, in fact, in our relationship with the literary work of art: for the artist does succeed in capturing in his text his own particularity and agency, and through that lens we have access, the only access we will ever have, to the reality of someone else's mind.[15]

Now I believe that Murdoch is in many respects less austere than Proust, as is the novel she has written. She does not suggest, that is, that the artist must abstain from dwelling on the particular loved one in order to search for general forms, and she represents Bradley as obsessed with the memory of just one beloved, Julian, rather than as engaged in a search for essences through the recovery of several previous loves. Julian, in consequence, appears in the text with a clarity and specificity that is always denied Albertine, whose individuating traits fluctuate inconstantly through the novel. Loxias's account of art, moreover, seems more inclusive and generous than that of Proust, more open to the idea that art can contain the messiness of a real particular. In *Metaphysics*, similarly, Murdoch stresses that art (unlike moral theory, she says) can tell the truth about 'the whole entity' the human being (*M* 492), with all the idiosyncrasy and contingency that characterize a real life. It does so in large part by being funny, since the funny is 'a great redeeming place of ordinary frailty' (*M* 91).

So the case is not simple. And yet, I believe that there is reason to see in *The Black Prince* the Proustian view that the main point of the particular loved one is to be served up in the work of art. Given that the work, and not ordinary life, contains the vision of truth, what else could Bradley say? Julian, as he well says, had to be in order for the novel to be, and it is in the novel that she most is. Even though it is also true that the novel is inspired by her and could not be without her (something that may not be true for Albertine), nonetheless, her real being is ultimately of interest primarily insofar as it does contribute to the vision of the work. And thus it really does seem that Bradley's love for her sees through her to something else, something that, while about her and dedicated to her, and in a way more her than her, is in a way also not her.

I connect these vague anxieties about the novel, very tentatively, to my personal experience of Iris Murdoch. I did not know Murdoch well. I met her when I gave a speech in her honor at the New York Art Club in around 1985, and she then invited me to lunch at the house in Charlbury Road, Oxford where she and John Bayley lived at that time. I went round to the house, very nervous and awkward, and sat for two hours being scrutinized, as I felt it, by her sharp probing eyes. We talked about Proust and Henry James, about postmodernism and current developments in ethical thought, about Charles Taylor, whom she admired, and R. M. Hare, whom she did not.

---

[15] An artist's style, writes the narrator:

is the revelation, which by direct and conscious methods would be impossible, of the qualitative difference, the uniqueness of the fashion in which the world appears to each one of us, a difference which, if there were no art, would remain for ever the secret of every individual. Through art alone are we able to emerge from ourselves, to know what another person sees of a universe which is not the same as our own and of which, without art, the landscapes would remain as unknown to us as those that may exist on the moon. (931–2)

All the while, I felt that her very intense gaze went, as it were, straight through me, to something that was not me at all, but to which I was somehow related. More than once I had a Julian-like thought: 'You don't really see *me*'—especially when, being a great lover of food, I found myself offered only two items, neither of which I could eat—a very fatty paté, which I hate, and a plateful of cherries, to which I have an allergy. (In desperation, I ate some cherries and was sick for the rest of the day.) No cognizance was taken of these facts, and I was too embarrassed and in awe to ask whether there might be anything else in the house. She fixed me with her eyes and went on, eating paté absent-mindedly with her fingers. Above all I cannot forget those eyes, and the way they attended to something of immense importance that was, as I say, not exactly outside of me, and that was perhaps more real than me, but that was not precisely me either. Nor can I ever forget the essential mysteriousness of her face, so much more alive than most people, so blazing with uncompromising passion, so intent upon things that were not exactly in the room. (This quality of mysteriousness is brought out more beautifully than I ever could by Bayley in his *Elegy for Iris*.)

If the gaze of art is in this way both intent on the person and at the same time intent on the creative work that appropriates and goes beyond the person, the question is whether this gaze can ever be, in the fullest sense, a humanly loving gaze. Why not? It sees more truly than most loving people see. I had no doubt, for example, that Murdoch could have described me, after an hour, far more precisely than any lover of mine after some years. In that sense Proust seems right when he says that art is the fully-lived life, life without patches of deadness and obtuseness. But I think that there is something more to loving vision than just seeing. There is, for example, a willingness to permit oneself to be seen. There is also a willingness to stop seeing, to close one's eyes before the loved one's imperfections. There is also a willingness to be, for a time, an animal or even a plant, relinquishing the sharpness of creative alertness before the presence of a beloved body. Does the artist's vision have about it these aspects of vulnerability, silence, and grace? Or does the artist's eye, like an eagle's soaring above us, look down with something like disdain at the muddled animal interactions of human beings with one another, so obtuse and so lacking in nuance?

I connect these vague thoughts with John Bayley's moving description of his strange feeling of bodily and emotional closeness to Murdoch in her last days, a closeness made possible, he speculates, only because the element of sharp mysteriousness was no longer present.

But I believe that *The Black Prince* in the end knows and embraces all this too—and that its endorsement of the vision of art is qualified by a very explicit awareness of the limits of that vision. Although both Bradley and Loxias seem at times to claim that art can contain the whole of a life, Bradley's most genuinely loving moment is one in which he yields before the elusive reality of the real Julian, acknowledging that she has a being that is not encompassed by his work:

And I would not wish it to seem at the end that I have, in my own sequestered happiness, somehow forgotten the real being of those who have figured as my characters . . . And Julian. I do not, my darling girl, however passionately and intensely my thought has worked upon your being, really imagine that I invented you. Eternally you escape my embrace. Art cannot assimilate you nor thought digest you. I do not now know, or want to know, anything about your life. For me, you have gone into the dark. Yet elsewhere I realize, and I meditate upon this knowledge, that you laugh, you cry, you read books and cook meals and yawn and lie perhaps in someone's arms. This knowledge too may I never deny, and may I never forget how in the humble hard time-ridden reality of my life I loved you. That love remains, Julian, not diminished though changing, a love with a very clear and a very faithful memory. It causes me on the whole remarkably little pain. Only sometimes at night when I think that you live now and are somewhere, I shed tears. (392)

And this means that there is a real sense in which the conclusion of the love story, and of its celebration of love, is written in the silence after this conclusion, and in the artist's solitary and for once inarticulate tears.

3

The Virtues of Metaphysics: A Review of Iris Murdoch's Philosophical Writings*

Maria Antonaccio

1 Introduction

That Iris Murdoch's moral thought is significant for contemporary ethics should, by now, require little argument. Murdoch's work has been appropriated by numerous scholars in ethics at least since the publication of *The Sovereignty of Good* in 1970.[1] Thinkers as diverse as Charles Taylor, Susan Wolf, and Martha Nussbaum (in philosophy) and William Schweiker and Stanley Hauerwas (in religious ethics) have made use of central insights from her thought in advancing their own constructive agenda. More generally, Murdoch's philosophical influence resonates in several prominent strands of contemporary ethics, including the emphasis on the role of vision and imagination in moral reasoning, the renewed interest in moral psychology, the turn to literature and narrative ethics, the combination of moral particularism and the critique of Enlightenment rationality, and the appeals of postmodernists to 'the other' as the locus of human ethical obligation. In all of these areas, Murdoch's essays, including some written as far back as the 1950s, have been prescient in anticipating many recent trends in ethics.

Yet remarkably, Murdoch's philosophy has, with few exceptions, been cited only in passing, even by those who acknowledge a profound debt to her work.[2] This neglect is all the more striking given the fact that the twenty-six novels constituting her literary

* An earlier version of this essay appeared in the *Journal of Religious Ethics*, 29, 2 (Summer 2001): 309–35. The author gratefully acknowledges the permission of Blackwell Publishers to reprint portions of the original essay here.
[1] Iris Murdoch, *The Sovereignty of Good* [SG] (London: Routledge & Kegan Paul, 1970).
[2] See especially Charles Taylor's *Sources of the Self: The Making of the Modern Identity* [SS] (Cambridge, Mass.: Harvard University Press, 1989) and Susan Wolf, *Freedom Within Reason* (New York: Oxford University Press, 1990).

corpus have been the subject of critical monographs for nearly three decades and continue to be closely studied for their religious and philosophical idea-play.[3] In contrast, the critical and appreciative assessment of Murdoch's contribution to moral philosophy and religious ethics, roughly fifty years after the start of her career and more than a decade after her death, has just begun.[4]

2 A complex legacy

There are several possible reasons for the lack of sustained attention to Murdoch's philosophy. In the first place, careful study of her thought has been hampered by the fact that, until fairly recently, her essays were scattered among philosophical and literary journals to which scholars had only limited or inconvenient access.[5] In addition, the disparate character of many of Murdoch's writings (which range from densely argued treatises on analytic philosophy, existentialism, and literary and political theory to more occasional pieces on art, religion, and culture) makes them difficult to interpret through a single disciplinary lens or in light of any obvious systematic plan. It may also be the case that Murdoch's decision, in 1968, to leave an academic position in philosophy at Oxford to pursue a full-time literary career has led scholars and critics to focus more on her novels than on the philosophical works which she continued to produce concurrently.

There may, however, be deeper reasons for the critical neglect—reasons related to the dominant intellectual trends in ethics in the second half of the twentieth century. Although her thought has been instrumental in some of the key movements in contemporary ethics, the precise nature of Murdoch's contribution to current thought is often difficult to determine or confounds expectations. Consider, for example, her influence in the area of moral psychology. As Charles Mathewes has noted, Murdoch's call for a 'working philosophical psychology' (E&M 337) was part of a larger trend in post-World War II philosophical ethics, as ethicists sought to fashion a thicker, more concrete description of moral agency and practical reasoning through the recovery of Aristotle and ancient ethics generally.[6] This trend has produced a vast philosophical

[3] The major critical monographs on Murdoch's fiction are A. S. Byatt, *Degrees of Freedom: The Novels of Iris Murdoch* (London: Chatto & Windus and New York: Barnes & Noble, 1965); Elizabeth Dipple, *Iris Murdoch: Work for the Spirit* (Chicago: University of Chicago Press, 1982), Peter J. Conradi, *Iris Murdoch: The Saint and the Artist* (London: Macmillan, 1986, 1989), 3rd edn. under the title *The Saint and the Artist: A Study of the Fiction of Iris Murdoch* (London: HarperCollins, 2001); David J. Gordon, *Iris Murdoch's Fables of Unselfing* (Columbia, Mo.: University of Missouri Press, 1995). See also the work of Barbara Stevens Heusel, esp. *Patterned Aimlessness: Iris Murdoch's Novels of the 1970s and 1980s* (Athens, Ga.: University of Georgia Press, 1995) and Bran J. Nichol, *Iris Murdoch: The Retrospective Fiction* (New York: Palgrave Macmillan, 2004).

[4] See my *Picturing the Human: The Moral Thought of Iris Murdoch* [PH] (New York: Oxford University Press, 2000) and my *A Philosophy to Live By: Engaging Iris Murdoch*, forthcoming from Oxford University Press in 2012.

[5] The publication of a collection of Murdoch's essays has gone a long way in helping to remedy this situation. See Peter J. Conradi (ed.), *Existentialists and Mystics: Writings on Philosophy and Literature* [E&M] (London: Chatto & Windus, 1997; New York: Allen Lane, 1998; Penguin, 1999).

[6] Charles T. Mathewes, 'Agency, Nature, Transcendence, and Moralism: A Review of Recent Work in Moral Psychology'. *Journal of Religious Ethics* 28.2 (Summer 2000): 298.

literature on moral psychology since the 1970s, in large part due to the efforts of Murdoch, Elizabeth Anscombe, and others.[7] Yet it is important to emphasize that Murdoch did *not* (as Anscombe did and many others have done since) retrieve Aristotle in her quest for a working philosophical psychology. As is well known, her moral psychology and theory of virtue derive their primary inspiration from Plato.

Moreover, unlike much contemporary philosophical work in moral psychology, Murdoch's work remained hospitable to the insights of Western theology (notwith-standing her rejection of the concept of God) and other religious traditions, such as Buddhism. In fact, her account of moral psychology and moral-spiritual change, which describes the arduousness of the psyche's effort to move from appearance to reality (from egoistic illusion to a vision of the Good), cannot easily be accommodated within the framework of tradition-constituted rationality and its dominant motif of habitu-ation.[8] Given her divergence from the dominant neo-Aristotelianism of contemporary moral theory and religious ethics, it is perhaps not surprising that, despite her influence in putting moral psychology back on the agenda of ethics, Murdoch's thought might seem out of step in what she described as an 'anti-metaphysical' and 'untheological' time—a time in which Plato is often dismissed as an arch-foundationalist, metaphysics is seen as a 'totalizing' discourse, and religious thought is increasingly driven to seek refuge in the discourse of traditions and narratively constituted communities. Her influence persists nonetheless.

In current debates over the literary turn in ethics, the critical reception of Murdoch's work manifests a similar complexity. On the one hand, she has often been seen as an advocate of the literary turn.[9] Her own work as a novelist and her comment that 'literature is a way to picture and understand moral situations' (E&M 326) are often cited in support of this view, and understandably so. Yet it is surely misguided to claim, as some have, that Murdoch's critique of Kantian rationalism and her appreciation for the particular make her an 'anti-theorist' who renounced the generality and compre-hensiveness of theory in favor of a thoroughgoing contextualism. If anything, Murdoch revitalized moral theory by appealing to the imaginative possibilities implicit in metaphysical theorizing.[10] Even so, the fact that an unapologetically Platonic and metaphysical thinker could be appropriated by contemporary critics of 'theory' testifies both to the fecundity of Murdoch's thought and the difficulty of interpreting it through any straightforward conceptual lens.

---

[7] See 'Modern Moral Philosophy' (*Philosophy* 33 (1958): 1–19), repr. in Roger Crisp and Michael Slote (eds.), *Virtue Ethics* (Oxford: Oxford University Press, 1997), 26–44.

[8] I have developed this point in 'Moral Change and the Magnetism of the Good'. *Annual of the Society of Christian Ethics* 20 (2000): 143–64.

[9] For an example of this characterization of Murdoch's thought, see Geoffrey Harpham, *Getting it Right: Language, Literature, and Ethics* (Chicago: University of Chicago Press, 1992), 159.

[10] For further treatment of this point, see my essay, 'The Consolations of Literature'. *Journal of Religion* 80.4 (October 2000): 615–44.

In narrative ethics, too, Murdoch's insistence on the role of language and perception in moral agency has provided important theoretical support. This is nowhere more evident than in the early work of Hauerwas, whose creative appropriation of Murdoch's philosophy for a Christian ethics of character in the 1970s helped transmit her work to a wide range of religious ethicists and other scholars.[11] Drawing not only from *The Sovereignty of Good,* but also from essays of hers which were largely unknown to the American audience at the time, Hauerwas highlighted what he took to be the Wittgensteinian elements of Murdoch's theory of language. The role she assigned to language in the formation of moral sensibility, the priority of vision over the act of moral choice and decision, and the dependence of moral vision on particular contexts of attention were marshaled into the service of a narrative ethic of Christian moral formation. More recently (and despite his wry admission of having made a career out of 'stealing' from her), Hauerwas has distanced himself from Murdoch's thought.[12] This is not surprising, given their vastly different metaphysical, philosophical, and religious commitments; what is surprising is that it took Hauerwas so long to notice the incompatibility. However, the force of Murdoch's best insights has always made them attractive even to thinkers whose basic assumptions differ from her own.

These brief examples of the critical reception of Murdoch's work suggest that anyone who wishes to take the measure of her contribution to contemporary thought must come to terms both with her unmistakable influence and with the complexity of her intellectual legacy. Fortunately, a more productive period of Murdoch scholarship may now be underway, thanks, in part, to two books that have the distinctive merit of displaying the full range of Murdoch's interests and moral concerns, both as a philosopher and as a cultural critic. *Existentialists and Mystics: Writings on Philosophy and Literature,* edited by Peter J. Conradi, represents the first collection of Murdoch's philosophical writings in a single volume. In addition to providing convenient access to the major essays and reprinting *The Sovereignty of Good, The Fire and the Sun,* and *Acastos* in their entirety, the book offers a developmental reading of Murdoch's thought by organizing the essays into six major time periods, each devoted to a particular unifying theme or concern. *Metaphysics as a Guide to Morals*[13] is a revised version of Murdoch's 1982 Gifford Lectures at the University of Edinburgh, and it offers the closest thing we have to a Murdochian 'system', although the avoidance of system is itself a central feature of the book's argument.

Given their nearly comprehensive scope, assessing the content of these two volumes is tantamount to reviewing the whole of Murdoch's philosophical corpus. Obviously,

[11] Stanley Hauerwas, *Vision and Virtue: Essays in Christian Ethics* (Notre Dame, Ind.: University of Notre Dame Press, 1974); see esp. 30–47.

[12] See Hauerwas's provocative essay, 'Murdochian Muddles: Can we Get Through Them If God Does Not Exist?' in Maria Antonaccio and William Schweiker (eds.), *Iris Murdoch and the Search for Human Goodness* [SHG] (Chicago: University of Chicago Press, 1996).

[13] Iris Murdoch, *Metaphysics as a Guide to Morals* (New York: Allen Lane/Penguin Press, 1992), hereafter abbreviated as MGM.

an adequate assessment of such a substantial body of philosophical work is not possible in these limited pages. Nevertheless, I will try to offer a concise account of Murdoch's thought as a whole.[14] I will begin by noting three areas in which Murdoch's insights have permeated contemporary ethical thought, using Taylor's work as a reference point. I will then consider the two books in relation to some of the more familiar insights of *The Sovereignty of Good*. In the final section, I will outline some of the constructive implications of her philosophy for current and future ethics.

3 Murdoch and contemporary ethics

Of all the contemporary thinkers who have cited Murdoch as an inspiration for their own work, perhaps none is more significant than Taylor. Having been a student of Murdoch at Oxford, Taylor has produced a body of work that bears numerous marks of his teacher's influence (both direct and indirect). As a result, several of Murdoch's most influential insights have reached a wider audience of thinkers in moral philosophy and religious ethics through the prism of Taylor's work. Three areas of Murdoch's thought have been especially significant for Taylor and for current thought generally: 1) her effort to extend the domain of ethics beyond a narrow focus on obligatory action ('morality' strictly speaking), 2) her retrieval of the notion that consciousness is 'the fundamental mode or form of human moral being' (MGM 171), and the corresponding claim that consciousness is inherently evaluative in nature, and 3) her affirmation of a reflexive relation between consciousness and language in the face of contemporary claims for the primacy of language over consciousness. I will comment on each of these below in order to set the context for Murdoch's significance.

3.1 Extending the domain of ethics

In 'Iris Murdoch and Moral Philosophy', an essay which pays tribute to his former teacher, Taylor notes that Murdoch 'was criticizing the narrowness of moral philosophy well before the present counterwave' of neo-Aristotelians and neo-Nietzscheans—although not on entirely the same grounds.[15] Like a host of recent thinkers such as Bernard Williams and Martha Nussbaum, Murdoch sought to extend the domain of the ethical beyond constricted notions of obligation ('what it is right to do') in order to encompass ideas of the good life and 'what it is good to be' (SHG 5). In initiating the transition from the narrow 'corral' of morality to the wider 'field' of ethics (the image is Taylor's), Murdoch helped shape debates over the priority of the right or the good in ethics, ongoing discussions of the nature of the self in liberal political theory, and corresponding debates in religious ethics regarding the constitution of moral identity and the nature of practical reasoning.

---

[14] For my book-length treatment of Murdoch's thought, see PH.
[15] This essay was published in Antonaccio and Schweiker (eds.), *Iris Murdoch and the Search for Human Goodness* [SHG]; the quotation is from p. 5.

Yet unlike many of her fellow critics of modern moral theory both past and present, Murdoch was persistent in arguing for the necessity of a metaphysical conception of ethics. This makes it difficult to categorize her unequivocally as a moral particularist, virtue ethicist, or anti-theorist, as these terms are usually understood. Although Murdoch was acutely aware of the historical nature of moral claims and concepts, she did not take the historicist turn represented by thinkers such as Alasdair MacIntyre and, indeed, by Taylor himself in *Sources of the Self*. Rather, Murdoch attempted to rescue a notion of metaphysics that could provide a general account of human existence while still doing justice to 'the great *variety* of the concepts that make up a morality' (E&M 73, emphasis in original). Her metaphysical method proceeds by way of conceptual analysis of various 'pictures' of the human (which she understood are themselves historical), rather than by way of a narrative description of the self and its goods over time.

3.2 *The evaluative nature of consciousness*

The second insight from Murdoch's philosophy that Taylor develops in his own work is her claim that the notion of consciousness should be central to moral theory and that consciousness is inseparable from some idea of the good. In *Sources of the Self*, his study of the making of the modern identity, Taylor gives prominent place to Murdoch's notion of the good as 'the object of our love or allegiance' and the 'privileged focus of attention or will' (SS 3). In contrast to modern moral theory, whose constriction of the ethical to the domain of obligation rendered it inarticulate about 'higher goods', Murdoch's work provides an exemplary account of how such moral sources may still function in modernity by pointing to something 'the contemplation, respect, or love of which enables us to get closer to what is good' (SS 95–96). In contrast to a view of the moral agent in which 'the focus is on the principles, or injunctions, or standards which guide *action*, while visions of the good are altogether neglected' (SS 84, emphasis in original), Murdoch reinstated an older Platonic (and Augustinian) insight that what we do is conditioned by what we love and by the direction of our attention. Taylor develops this insight at length, arguing that such a vision, though deeply suppressed in modernity, may still be available to us through the language of 'personal resonance', if not in a vision of 'ontic logos' (SS 534). In short, despite modernity's 'inarticulacy' about higher goods and their bearing on moral identity, Taylor insists that 'selfhood and the good, or in another way selfhood and morality, turn out to be inextricably intertwined themes' (SS 3).

This claim about the value-laden character of human consciousness may be the most significant point of contact between Murdoch's thought and Taylor's. Both defend this point by challenging the extent to which modern ethical theory has adopted some of the assumptions and aspirations of natural science. In his collected papers, Taylor develops a critique of what he calls the reductive 'naturalism' of modern ethics. Naturalism rests on 'the paradigm status accorded to the natural sciences as the models for the sciences of man'.[16] By attempting to expunge the first-person standpoint and 'give an account of things in absolute terms', naturalism fails to recognize a crucial feature of human agency: our experience of ourselves as 'self-interpreting agents' who see things against a background of 'strong evaluations' (PHS 2–3). Taylor argues that human identity is constituted by a framework of questions about value—by distinctions, commitments, and attachments that delimit a moral world and constitute our self-understanding. 'To be a full human agent, to be a person or a self in the ordinary meaning', he writes, 'is to exist in a space defined by distinctions of worth. A self is a being for whom certain questions of categoric value have arisen, and received at least partial answers . . . [T]his is not just a contingent fact about human agents, but is essential to what we would understand and recognize as full, normal human agency' (PHS 3).

Taylor's critique of naturalism owes much to Murdoch's thought, if only implicitly. In her landmark essay, 'Metaphysics and Ethics', Murdoch argues that human beings are constituted by their own self-understanding: 'Man is a creature who makes pictures of himself and then comes to resemble the picture' (E&M 75), she writes. Because of this, 'it is not possible in principle to translate propositions about men making decisions and formulating viewpoints into the neutral languages of natural science' (E&M 342). Rather, she held, moral philosophy must take into account the peculiar capacity of human beings to reflect on themselves, to imagine who they are and who they might become by forming and revising their ideas about themselves in relation to certain evaluative 'pictures' (or ideas of the good). As a result of this critique, Murdoch developed an ethics of vision built on the fundamental analogy between art and ethics, where moral rationality is more like the perceptive vision of the artist than the rational objectivity of the scientist (as Taylor's account of naturalism supposes). In doing so, she not only shifted the 'root metaphor' of practical reasoning from science to art, but also undermined one of the cornerstones of analytic ethics—its assumption of logical and ethical neutrality. In Murdoch's view, moral theorizing 'is an activity whose purpose and justification are *moral*' (E&M 180, emphasis added). That is, it is carried out by human beings who are engaged in the process of forming themselves in relation to their own ideals. Its method, accordingly, should eschew logical neutrality and enter 'the cloudy and shifting domain of the concepts which men live by' (E&M 74). This kind of conceptual analysis was the purview of metaphysics as Murdoch understood it.

3.3 Language and agency

In a period in which language has become, as Murdoch notes, 'a prime philosophical concept' (MGM 153), Taylor's and Murdoch's works illuminated the role of language

---

[16] See Taylor, *Philosophy and the Human Sciences: Philosophical Papers*, vol. 2 [PHS] (Cambridge: Cambridge University Press). The quotation is from p. 2. Taylor's use of the term 'naturalism' in this context must be distinguished from ethical naturalism, which does not necessarily embrace the value-neutral epistemology of the natural sciences.

in human agency. The ascendancy of language in our contemporary self-understanding has been noted by Seyla Benhabib, who argues that a defining feature of postmodernism is that '*the paradigm of language has replaced the paradigm of consciousness*' in philosophical reflection.[17] As a result, 'the focus is no longer on the epistemic subject or on the private contents of its consciousness but on the public, signifying activities of a collection of subjects'.[18] Among those who embrace the new paradigm, the notion of autonomous agency has been largely replaced by a decentered subjectivity in which the self is understood as an 'effect' of the linguistic system. Language no longer plays a mediating role between self and world, but becomes, in Murdoch's words, 'a vast system or sign structure whereby meaning is determined by a mutual relationship of signs which transcends the localized talk of individual speakers' (MGM 188).

Both Taylor and Murdoch have consistently resisted postmodernism's 'inflation' of language, though in different ways.[19] Taylor accepts what he calls the 'expressive' view of language—that is, he sees language not as a 'simple instrument which ought in principle to be fully in our control and oversight' but 'more like a medium in which we are plunged, and which we cannot fully plumb' (SS 238). However, in contrast to more subjectivist forms of expressivism, Taylor favors the view that what comes to expression in language is not merely the self but a way of being in the world related to a speech community. This view 'tries to go beyond subjectivism' by seeing language as a way of 'responding to the reality in which we are set, in which we are included of course, but which is not reducible to our experience of it'.[20] For Murdoch, more so than for Taylor, what is at stake in the debate over language is the status of the individual as agent. Whereas Taylor seems to grant the social and linguistic constitution of identity, Murdoch was more circumspect. A persistent defender of the idea of the individual, she worried that the tendency to dissolve consciousness into language would concurrently degrade the status of the individual as a responsible moral agent. Although she accepted the idea that language constitutes an order of public meanings and is learned in particular communities, she insisted that 'statements are made, propositions are uttered, by individual incarnate persons in particular extra-linguistic situations, and it is in the whole of this larger context that our familiar and essential concepts of *truth* and *truthfulness* live and work' (MGM 194, emphasis in original). In short, she held that human beings are creative *users* of language, and not simply participants in or 'discursive effects' of a linguistic system. Despite these differences, both Taylor and Murdoch are alike in their determination to preserve the sense of a reality that is not reducible to our experience of it, though both have acknowledged

---

[17] Seyla Benhabib, *Situating the Self: Gender, Community and Postmodernism in Contemporary Ethics* (New York: Routledge, 1992), 208, emphasis in original.

[18] Ibid., 208.

[19] The phrase is William Schweiker's. See his essay 'Consciousness and the Good: Schleiermacher and Contemporary Theological Ethics'. *Theology Today* 56.2 (July 1999): 180–96.

[20] See Taylor's valuable collection of papers on this theme, *Language and Human Agency: Philosophical Papers*, vol. 1 (Cambridge: Cambridge University Press, 1985), 235.

that we have access to this reality only through the mediations of language and consciousness. For this reason, both may be considered 'reflexive' moral realists.[21]

Having presented some of the ways in which Murdoch's thought has entered contemporary ethics, I want to turn now to a discussion of *Existentialists and Mystics* and *Metaphysics as a Guide to Morals*. It will become evident that each of the aspects of Murdoch's thought just noted—her critique of the ethics of obligation, her retrieval of the notion of consciousness, and her defense of consciousness against the primacy of language—are present in her writings in one form or another from the very beginning.

4 Existentialists and Mystics

An editor seeking to collect the writings of any complex and productive thinker faces numerous questions regarding the selection, arrangement, and interpretation of his or her materials. The task is particularly challenging in the case of a thinker like Murdoch, whose disparate writings make her thought difficult to present coherently, especially to a general audience. In *Existentialists and Mystics*, Conradi (who is author of a critical monograph on Murdoch's novels as well as the first biography of Murdoch) has succeeded admirably in this task. He has included not only Murdoch's major essays and several of her longer monographs, but several well-chosen reviews and lectures as well, and he has arranged them in an intelligent sequence which suggests successive, overlapping stages in Murdoch's development as a thinker.

Part 1 opens with an interview between Murdoch and Bryan Magee on the subject of 'Literature and Philosophy'. The volume then proceeds through six additional 'rubrics' that successively chart Murdoch's early preoccupation with issues in analytic philosophy (Part 2, 'Nostalgia for the Particular'), her deep critical engagement with existentialism (Part 3, 'Encountering Existentialism'), her recognition of the importance of theory, especially in the realm of politics (Part 4 'The Need for Theory'), her movement towards the articulation of a religious sensibility (Part 5, 'Towards a Practical Mysticism'), her impassioned defense of the value of the individual in art and ethics (Part 6, 'Can Literature Help Cure the Ills of Philosophy?'), and her extended conversation with the thought of Plato (Part 7, 'Re-Reading Plato'). Each section of the book begins with an epigram from Murdoch's work that effectively captures the theme under discussion. Taken as a whole, the arrangement of the materials presents a plausible and insightful narrative of the major phases of Murdoch's philosophy. Elements of this narrative are further elaborated in a helpful introductory preface by Conradi and a substantive foreword by the eminent critic George Steiner.

Like the arrangement of its materials, the title of the volume, taken from the title of an essay published in 1970, also expresses an editorial decision. Conradi intends the

---

[21] The term is William Schweiker's. See his *Responsibility and Christian Ethics* (Cambridge: Cambridge University Press, 1995). I have adopted this terminology in my interpretation of Murdoch's moral realism in PH.

opposition between existentialist and mystic to stand as the guiding principle for the volume and for Murdoch's thought as a whole. So vital is this distinction, the editor contends, that 'a crude and simplified account of [Murdoch's] thinking might identify existentialism with the self-centred picture of moral choice as a "leap of the will", mysticism with the other-centred picture of moral choice as dependent on the agent's ability to look' (E&M xxiv). Although such a characterization of Murdoch's thought would not be entirely inaccurate (see her essay 'Vision and Choice in Morality'), the prominence given to the opposition between existentialist and mystic in the conception of the volume may be misleading. It signals the editor's view that existentialism was the 'principal ideological opponent' against which Murdoch set herself, and it leads to the characterization of Murdoch's religious sensibility as a 'practical mysticism' that was similar to utilitarianism in its 'immersion in the real world' of human suffering and human need (E&M xxii–xxiv).

While no serious reader of Murdoch's philosophy could deny that existentialism was one of her 'principal opponents', it seems more balanced to suggest that Murdoch's attitude toward existentialism remained ambivalent.[22] This ambivalence was rooted in the fact that Murdoch sympathized deeply with what she regarded as Jean-Paul Sartre's underlying liberal assumptions about the value of the individual and individual freedom, even though she believed that his philosophy failed to provide the conceptual resources necessary to support those values. After World War II, like many members of her generation, Murdoch was drawn to the moral and political passion of existentialism, its 'ethic of resistance' against political and social tyranny. Sartre's picture of 'the heroic consciousness, the individual self, inalienably and ineluctably free, challengingly confront[ing] the "given", in the form of existing society, history, tradition, other people',[23] was a picture that resonated with the experience of many people in Europe in the aftermath of the war. Murdoch's concern for the integrity of the individual was forged in this political and cultural context, and she remained deeply preoccupied with the problem of freedom as it pertained to the irreducibility of the individual to any form of totality. (These themes come to the fore in *Metaphysics as a Guide to Morals*.)

4.1 Tensions in Murdoch's theory of religion

Conradi's identification of Murdoch's position with the 'mystical' side of the existentialist/mystic opposition contains ambiguities as well. It is undeniable that Murdoch became increasingly preoccupied with religion, and it is true that she used the terminology of mysticism to refer to the attempt to preserve a consciousness of the good in an age when God could longer be taken for granted. In contrast to the existentialist hero of twentieth-century literature, who was 'the new version of the romantic man, the man of power, abandoned by God, struggling on bravely, sincerely

---

[22] For an interpretation of Murdoch's relation to Sartre, see PH, esp. chap. 3.

[23] Iris Murdoch, *Sartre, Romantic Rationalist* (1953); reissued with a new Introduction (London: Chatto & Windus/New York: Viking, 1987; Penguin, 1989), 9–10.

and alone', the mystical hero was 'the new version of the man of faith, believing in goodness without religious guarantees, guilty, muddled, yet not without hope' (E&M 227). She described the latter as 'the man who has given up traditional religion but is still haunted by a sense of the reality and unity of some of sort of spiritual world. The imagery here is an imagery of height and distance' (E&M 227). Both Conradi and Steiner contend in their introductory essays that Murdoch was compelled to embrace a more 'practical' version of this mysticism, one less focused on the magnetic and remote reality of the Good, more attuned to the here-and-now. Because she was thus driven to think in a more immediate way about human needs, such as 'food and shelter, and work and peace' (E&M 230), she associated, in certain contexts, this kind of mysticism with utilitarianism—a philosophy, she noted, that was perfectly suited to an age of 'vanishing [metaphysical] backgrounds' (E&M 232).

Yet to characterize Murdoch's religious sensibility wholly in these terms (as the title of Part 5 'Toward a Practical Mysticism' suggests) does not do justice, in my view, to the more metaphysical aspects of her thinking about religion. In particular, it does not account for the view she expressed in *Acastos,* and later developed at length in *Metaphysics as a Guide to Morals,* that religion is about what is 'deep' and 'absolute' in human life. We see here a tension in Murdoch's thought, which she referred to elsewhere as 'the two-way movement in philosophy' between metaphysics and empiricism. The empirical element is represented in this context by practical mysticism, an 'untheory' (in Murdoch's phrase) which holds that 'human good is something which lies in the foreground of life and not in its background. It is not a flickering of will-power, nor a citadel of esoteric virtue, but a good quality of human life: and we know, naturally, where to *begin* thinking about this' (E&M 231, emphasis in original). The metaphysical element in Murdoch's thought, however, insists that religion is more than this: it is ontological. In a phrase Murdoch borrows from the theologian Paul Tillich, religious represents 'the unconditional element in reason and reality', and, hence, the unconditional claim of morality on human life. Thus, religion lies not merely in the practical foreground of human life (along with immediate human needs like 'food and shelter, and work and peace') but also in the ontological background. As the character Plato says in the dialogue 'above the Gods' in *Acastos,* 'Religion is the love and worship of the good, and that's the real basis of morality' (E&M 519). It is 'beyond us, it's more real than us, we have to come to it and let it change us, religion is spiritual change, *absolute* spiritual change' (E&M 514, emphasis in original).

Rather than characterize Murdoch as a practical mystic, therefore, I would argue that her thought contained both of these types of thinking about the good; the more immediate, practical, empirical element is constantly held in tension with the more distant, 'esoteric', metaphysical element. The dialectic between metaphysics and empiricism in Murdoch's thought might be put this way: metaphysics without empiricism may be unable to effect good in the world; but empiricism without metaphysics severs the connection of morality to some unconditional or absolute background. In my judgment, it is the latter problem more than the former that preoccupied Murdoch in her thinking about religion.[24] Fortunately, because this volume contains texts that represent both sides of this dialectic, the reader has the necessary resources at hand to assess the role of religion and mysticism in Murdoch's work. Moreover, Murdoch herself made the dialectic of metaphysics and empiricism a major theme of *Metaphysics as a Guide to Morals*.

Despite Conradi's somewhat misleading equation of Murdoch's position with that of the practical mystic, his choice of the epigram for the volume as a whole successfully reveals the heart of Murdoch's ethics: 'Man is a creature who makes pictures of himself, and then comes to resemble the picture.' This statement from her essay 'Metaphysics and Ethics' articulates the crucial assumption underlying her metaphysical ethic: that ethics is properly the study of human beings in the process of moral transformation. But the statement also directs our attention toward one of the most vexing problems in Murdoch scholarship: how to characterize the relation between her philosophical and literary work. Without engaging this question in detail here, I will simply note that any reader of Murdoch's philosophy is bound to recognize its deeply literary character, just as any reader of her novels cannot fail to observe their constant philosophical pre-occupations. Conradi calls attention to the deep interpenetration of philosophy and literature in Murdoch's thought by placing her interview on this subject with Bryan Magee first, and by including two essays (in Part 6) that exemplify her use of literary figures and trends as an instrument of philosophical diagnosis. He also reprints in Part 7 the full text of *The Fire and the Sun: Why Plato Banished the Artists*, ostensibly the most relevant text in Murdoch's corpus on the so-called ancient quarrel.

4.2 Murdoch as a philosopher of culture

Turning our attention now from the arrangement of the volume to its substantive content, we might ask what a reader who comes to *Existentialists and Mystics* from *The Sovereignty of Good* (or perhaps the novels) stands to gain. Although there are far too many benefits to summarize easily, I will note three areas in which readers may meet a somewhat unexpected Murdoch in these pages.

First, readers may be struck by the depth and breadth of Murdoch's competence in both analytic ethics (including linguistic analysis and logical positivism) and continental philosophy (including existentialism and phenomenology), as well as her facility in sorting out technical philosophical debates early in her career. The list of renowned philosophers with whom Murdoch conversed, both in print and in life, include A. J. Ayer, R. M. Hare, Stuart Hampshire, Anthony Quinton, Elizabeth Anscombe, Gabriel Marcel, Jean-Paul Sartre, Simone de Beauvoir, Elias Canetti, Isaiah Berlin, and Michael Oakeshott (among others). The essays in Part 2 in particular illuminate the intellectual context in which Murdoch first threw down the gauntlet to modern moral theory (and

---

[24] For a detailed analysis of the tension between metaphysics and empiricism as an organizing principle both of Murdoch's philosophy and her theory of the novel, see my essay 'Form and Contingency in Iris Murdoch's Ethics' in SHG, 110–37.

indeed to some of her own colleagues at Oxford) by challenging both the elimination of metaphysics from ethics and the constricted view of moral language and moral agency represented in the method of linguistic analysis. In spite of her criticisms, however, we also meet a philosopher who was herself trained at Oxford and Cambridge and who, as Conradi notes, 'admires the lucidity of analytic philosophy, and masters this clarity early' (E&M xxvi).

Readers may also be surprised to discover how profoundly Murdoch immersed herself in the politics of post-World War II Europe. This is evident both in the essays that display her close engagement with existentialism (which she often portrayed as a rival to Marxism) and in certain of her essays on the need for theory. Readers who have come to regard Murdoch primarily as a kindly novelist or saint-like figure urging us to 'be good', or who think of her ethics largely in terms of the famous example of the mother and daughter-in-law from *The Sovereignty of Good* (see E&M 312–318) may be surprised by an essay like 'The Existentialist Political Myth', where she asks: 'What form . . . can a metaphysics of social democracy take in a world such as ours where it is increasingly impossible to think in terms of the *Contrat Social?*' (E&M 140). Similarly, in 'A House of Theory', Murdoch investigates the causes of the decline of the socialist movement in England, noting that 'we have not mended our society since its mutila-tion by nineteenth-century industrialism' and arguing for a revitalization of a socialist theory of labor (E&M 183–184). The vibrancy and moral passion of these political writings show us a Murdoch who was not only an academic philosopher and novelist, but also a cultural critic and public intellectual.

This leads me to note a third and related insight that this collection makes possible. Murdoch emerges here as a kind of philosopher of culture—one who sees not only philosophy, but art, politics, religion, literature, science, and other human activities as different modes of 'picturing' human life. The task of moral philosophy *qua* metaphys-ics, in her view, is to evaluate the products of these diverse forms of human imagination in terms of the ideals and concepts they advance for the guidance of human life. I have already noted that Murdoch used such a method with respect to literature. In 'The Sublime and the Beautiful Revisited', for example, she traced a common problem for twentieth-century literature and politics—the difficulty of portraying and valuing individuals—to underlying tensions in the history of thought. In doing so, she enlarged our understanding of some of the internal tensions of the culture that produced both liberalism and romanticism, Immanuel Kant and G. W. F. Hegel, existentialists and empiricists, and the accompanying literary forms of each. Murdoch's approach in these disputes suggests a cultural hermeneutic which has applications beyond the spheres of literature and philosophy in which she chiefly employed them, a point to which I will return.

In sum, the reader who absorbs the wealth of insights available in *Existentialists and Mystics* will gain a much richer appreciation of Murdoch's philosophical achievement and may begin, thanks to the careful work of the editor, to grasp the recurring patterns and persisting concerns that characterize her thought. However, what may still be missing is a clear understanding of how (or whether) the diverse elements of Murdoch's philosophy fit into any kind of systematic or comprehensive whole. For that, we must turn to *Metaphysics as a Guide to Morals*.

5 *Metaphysics as a Guide to Morals*

Metaphysics as a Guide to Morals was Murdoch's last and longest published philosophical work. It appeared nearly a quarter-century after *The Sovereignty of Good* and a full decade after Murdoch first delivered the Gifford lectures on which the book is based. Although it is the closest thing we will ever have to a systematic statement of Murdoch's ethics, its meandering narrative is one of the first things one notices about it. The reader is confronted not with a recognizably systematic metaphysical treatise, but rather with something resembling an extended monologue or the author's stream of consciousness. It is full of detailed reflection and analysis, but also dense with seemingly random associations, humorous asides, and profound insights. Paragraphs frequently run on for pages, rarely sticking to one topic, but rather pursuing connections to other thinkers and ideas as they occur and then abandoning them abruptly. Even the chapter divisions, which in the table of contents seem orderly and distinct, are more arbitrary in the actual reading; the topics and themes under discussion in one chapter seem to burst their boundaries and run into the next.

Yet the book does not lack coherence. A definite structure and formal pattern undergird the fluid stream of analysis, observation, and comment. The argument is cumulative and depends on an implicit ordering of the book's nineteen chapters into three thematic clusters that exemplify Murdoch's life-long concerns: art, morality, and religion. These themes may not be immediately obvious, and some chapters admittedly fit these rubrics more clearly than others. Nevertheless, the first third of the book is devoted, roughly, to the theme of art (chapters 1–5), the second third, to the idea of moral selfhood or consciousness (chapters 6–12), and the final third, to religion and the idea of the good (chapters 13–18).

Not surprisingly, the chapters on consciousness occupy the center of the book, testifying to the essential role this concept plays in Murdoch's ethics. Chapters 6 and 8, devoted to the theme of 'Consciousness and Thought', defend the moral status of the idea of consciousness from diverse threats in the history of thought. Two other chapters take up specific challenges to the idea of consciousness or the inner life from thinkers in the continental and analytic traditions, specifically Jacques Derrida (chapter 7) and Ludwig Wittgenstein (chapter 9). Taken together, these chapters exemplify Murdoch's insistence that consciousness is the fundamental mode of moral being.

5.1 *Obligation as integral to an account of consciousness*

A systematic impulse is also present in Murdoch's attempt to give a comprehensive account of the central elements of morality and their relation to one another. Despite her earlier critique of the ethics of obligation as excessively narrow, she avoided any comparable one-sidedness here. *Metaphysics as a Guide to Morals* is emphatically *not* limited to the 'ethics of vision' but also contains a theory of duty or obligation. It treats the explicitly public aspects of morality (the relations between persons and their conduct toward one another) through the analysis of categories like love, respect, will, duty, obligation, and freedom. It also explores the phenomena of personal morality (the good of individuals) through the analysis of terms related to consciousness, illusion, eros, egoism, attention, and imagination. Finally, it presents a normative theory of the good of human life, often in conjunction with an analysis of religious categories and images such as the notions of God, void, and the ontological proof.

From the perspective of Murdoch's earlier writings, it is particularly noteworthy that Murdoch chose to treat her theory of duty or obligation in the midst of her defense of consciousness. She included chapters on will and duty (chapter 10) and morals and politics (chapter 12) in this section of the book, with the imagination (chapter 11) mediating between them. This placement suggests, among other things, that Murdoch considered matters of obligation and public conduct to be integral to an account of consciousness rather than ancillary to it—as one might have expected from her long-standing emphasis on the inner life and moral vision. Indeed, one of the characteristic features of this book is the way it holds conceptual opposites—such as will and vision, duty and eros, politics and morality, public and private—in complex tension.

Such structural observations shed new light on familiar ideas in Murdoch's philosophy, and they compel one to return to her earlier work to test the new insights against one's previous understanding. What one discovers is that the text is not as much a rambling monologue as it initially seems; the experience of reading it is actually dialogical and intertextual. In its constant circling back to themes, images, and occasionally even verbatim phrases from Murdoch's other works, the book is an echo chamber in which her entire philosophy comes into play through the mutual resonances (and sometimes dissonances) among her ideas. A similar dialogical quality is present in Murdoch's numerous references to other texts, traditions, and thinkers, including recurring philosophical figures (for example, Plato, Kant, Hume, Hegel, Kierkegaard, Mill, Sartre, Wittgenstein, Schopenhauer, Hobbes), Christian thinkers and mystics (for example, Anselm, Augustine, Meister Eckhart, Julian of Norwich, St. Paul, St. Matthew), as well as Buddhist thinkers. In this sense, the structure of the book is less architectonic than the title (which sounds vaguely Kantian) suggests, and more sprawlingly capacious—recalling to mind an image Murdoch associated with Plato's writings: 'a huge hall of reflection full of light and space and fresh air, in which ideas and intuitions can be unsystematically nurtured' (MGM 422).

The distinctive structural features of the book make it difficult, if not impossible, to separate issues of 'form' from issues of 'content'. In fact, the book is permeated with what Murdoch called (in *The Sovereignty of Good*) 'the two-way movement in philosophy, a movement towards the building of elaborate theories, and a move back again towards the consideration of simple and obvious facts' (E&M 299). This movement cuts across the form-content distinction and provides a crucial hermeneutical principle that illuminates not only the structure of this book but Murdoch's entire philosophy. This principle allows us to redescribe (if not resolve) certain tensions or dilemmas in Murdoch's thought that I noted earlier. In what follows, I show how this principle bears on three central aspects of her moral theory: metaphysics, individual consciousness, and the idea of the good. In each case, Murdoch's underlying systematic interests become clear.

5.2 Metaphysics and empiricism

According to Murdoch,

[t]he problem about philosophy, and about life, is how to relate large impressive illuminating general conceptions to the mundane ('messing about') details of ordinary personal private existence . . . How do the generalisations of philosophers connect with what I am doing in my day-to-day and moment-to-moment pilgrimage, how can metaphysics be a guide to morals? (MGM 146)

This question captures the two countervailing impulses of Murdoch's own philosophical imagination. As we have seen, Murdoch is often read as a critic of 'theory' in spite of her insistence on the necessity of metaphysical theorizing, and she is often read as a moral particularist in spite of her concern to offer a general account of the good of human life. By stating the central question in this way, Murdoch confronted two impulses in her own thought while she also thematized a more general philosophical problem.

Although the conundrum Murdoch was pondering might be called by many names (for example, the problem of the one and the many, the tension between form and contingency, the contrast between universality and particularity, and so forth), Murdoch chose to refer to it by means of the distinction I noted earlier between metaphysics and empiricism. Metaphysics, as she described it in this book, is chiefly a 'one-making' endeavor. It seeks to impose unity on a mass of detailed perceptions about human life in order to provide a guide to moral reflection. Great metaphysicians are thinkers who erect large conceptual structures that attempt to hold everything together and to highlight certain unconditional features of human life. Empiricism, on the other hand, is an unsystematic attention to varied ideas and perceptions that does not rely on any large-scale theoretical framework. 'In general', Murdoch wrote, 'empiricism is one essential aspect of good philosophy, just as utilitarianism is one essential aspect of good moral philosophy. It represents what must not be ignored. It remembers the contingent' (236). Murdoch described the two-way movement between these two elements of philosophy as follows:

Philosophy is perpetually in tension between empiricism and metaphysics, between, one might say, Moore and McTaggart. This argument can take place within the same philosopher. Religion moves similarly between simplicity and elaboration, puritanism and its opposite (to which many names may be given). There are times for piecemeal analysis, modesty and commonsense, and other times for ambitious synthesis and the aspiring and edifying charm of lofty and intricate structures. (MGM 211)

This dialectic clarifies the tension noted earlier between the metaphysical impulse of the traditional mystic, who strives to retain a consciousness of the good in spite of its seeming remoteness from human life, and the empirical, utilitarian impulse of the 'practical' mystic, who worries less about theorizing and more about embodying goodness in concrete acts that respond to human need. Murdoch's complex conception of metaphysical unity enacted in this book attempts to account for both of these elements in a single moral theory. There is, in short, a two-way movement between 'theory' (or metaphysics) and its negation (that is, 'untheory' or void).

5.3 Defending the individual

Murdoch's insistence on the need for both kinds of reflection is related to her concern for the status and value of the individual, a theme that was present from the very beginning of her career, as numerous essays included in *Existentialists and Mystics* attest (see, for example, 'Against Dryness' and 'The Sublime and the Beautiful Revisited'). In fact, Murdoch's enduring project can be seen as an attempt to retrieve a metaphysical framework for the moral life, while defending the value and irreducibility of the individual. This was not merely an interesting formal problem for her (that is, a question of how to construct an adequate theory) but a moral and political matter as well.[25] As an Administrative Officer with the United Nations Relief and Rehabilitation Administration, Murdoch worked in refugee camps after World War II and had witnessed first-hand the devastating effects of totalitarian political forces on human lives. As a philosopher at Oxford and Cambridge, she had studied the thought of neo-Hegelian philosophers such as F. H. Bradley, who seemed to diminish the reality of the individual person. As a novelist and critic, she had observed the rise of Symbolist trends in modern poetry and literature, trends that seemed to question the importance of the portrayal of character in literature. In the face of such powerful cultural expressions of the idea that 'only the whole is real', Murdoch insisted, in language which resonates intentionally with Kierkegaard's protest against Hegel, that the particular and individual were paradigmatic of the real.

Against this background, the question of the value and reality of the individual emerges in *Metaphysics as a Guide to Morals* as the central issue in the tug-of-war between metaphysics and empiricism. Although Murdoch accepted the need for a general theory of morality and human existence, she was concerned that the 'one-making' impulse of metaphysical systems might, in the end, 'lose' the individual in the system. The entire book may be read as an argument in defense of 'a conception of the idiosyncratic individual as valuable per se' (MGM 364) in the context of a

---

[25] It is also an aesthetic problem. Murdoch noted that a novelist creating the work of art faces a problem analogous to that of the metaphysician constructing a theoretical framework. See my 'Form and Contingency in Iris Murdoch's Ethics' in SHG.

metaphysical framework that remains, somehow, non-systematic and non-totalizing. Indeed, Murdoch argued that the danger of 'totalizing' philosophies, whether based on the thought of Marx or Hegel or poststructuralist views of language is precisely that they fail to maintain the reality of the individual in the face of the determinism of historical progress, the network of linguistic systems, or the totality of social or class relations. The problem addressed in Murdoch's later work is no longer the problem of the heroic voluntarism of the existentialist self, bravely rejecting the conventional world and bound by no other authority than his or her own value-creating will; it is rather the problem of the 'displacement' of the individual into some 'supra-personal whole' that renders individual consciousness invisible (MGM 153).

Murdoch concentrated her defense of the individual on recovering a description of the mind or consciousness as a bearer of value or moral being and not merely as a neutral surveyor of the facts (as it is considered to be in the 'naturalism' that Taylor criticizes). In the face of contemporary philosophies that appeared 'to render problematic the commonsense conception of the individual self as moral centre or substance', Murdoch retrieved the inner region of consciousness as a moral domain which is essential to our conception of the individual (MGM 153). In arguing that 'consciousness or self-being [is] the fundamental mode or form of moral being (MGM 171), Murdoch challenged those positions (exemplified by Kant and Sartre) that tend to reduce moral subjectivity to a unitary faculty such as reason or the will, the operations of which then become the exclusive focus of ethics, as well as those positions (exemplified by Hegel, Wittgenstein, and Derrida) that tend to reduce the being of the self to a mere cipher in a larger network or totality (whether linguistic or social) that is considered the authoritative source of reality and value. However different these two dominant views of moral subjectivity might be, Murdoch believed them to be alike in their reductive treatment of the moral self. That is, they constrict the areas of our moral being to something less than the complex of consciousness, which includes a range of states of mind that bear on both will and reason and serve to distinguish selves from one another. As the distinct mode of human selfhood and individuality, consciousness, Murdoch insisted, is a complex whole whose unity cannot adequately be represented by reason or will and whose particularity cannot be diminished to being a mere function in a larger network.

5.4 The ontological proof

I turn, finally, to the third major aspect of Murdoch's moral theory, the idea of the good. In her essay 'On "God" and "Good"' ([OGG], in SG), Murdoch had argued that philosophy and religion traditionally shared a common goal, the defeat of the ego by fostering techniques to overcome selfishness and to enlarge one's perception of reality. In contrast, modern moral philosophy had become 'egocentric': 'Our picture of ourselves has become too grand, we have isolated, and identified ourselves with, an unrealistic conception of will, we have lost the vision of reality separate from ourselves, and we have no adequate conception of original sin' (OGG 47). Given this diagnosis,

Murdoch's contention was that moral philosophy 'should attempt to retain a central concept which has all [the] characteristics' traditionally associated with God as a transformative object of attention, such as unity, perfection, transcendence, non-representability, and necessary existence (OGG 55). The most appropriate proof for such a concept, she noted, would be some form of the ontological proof, which was not a proof strictly speaking but rather a 'clear assertion of faith' designed to show that the concept of God 'contains the certainty of its own reality' (OGG 63). Murdoch returned to this major theme of 'On "God" and "Good"' many years later, in *Metaphysics as a Guide to Morals*, by offering a more careful and detailed analysis of what the ontological proof would look like if its subject were the idea of the Good rather than God. In two remarkable chapters (chapters 13 and 14), she drew from diverse resources in the history of thought (especially Plato and Anselm, but also Augustine, Descartes, Kant, and others), to reconstruct the proof as a way of demonstrating the kind of certainty that she attributed to the idea of the good, and the necessary relation that obtained between the idea of the good and the structure of human consciousness.[26]

In keeping with the hermeneutical principle I have been tracing, Murdoch presented two arguments for the concept of the good, one transcendental and one empirical, and she related them to two corresponding aspects of consciousness: a 'one-making' aspect, which seeks to unify disparate phenomena, and a discriminating or 'particularizing' aspect, which apprehends distinctions and detail. Thus the dialectic between metaphysics and empiricism reappears in the structure of Murdoch's ontological proof. In its first, transcendental aspect, Murdoch repeatedly described the Good using Plato's image of the sun: human life is lived under the aspect of the Good, or in its light. The Good does not represent any particular being or value, but is rather the ground or source of all being and value; it is not a thing we see directly, but that which makes seeing possible; it is not an object of knowledge, but the condition of the possibility for knowledge. Murdoch expressed this aspect of the Good by saying that 'there is something about moral value which adheres essentially to the conception of being human, and cannot be detached; and we may express this by saying that it is not accidental, does not exist contingently, is above being'(MGM 426).[27]

The transcendental Good has its corollary, according to Murdoch, in the one-making aspect of human consciousness. 'The unity and fundamental reality of

---

[26] I have analyzed Murdoch's use of Plato, Anselm, and Kant in her reconstruction of the proof in 'Imagining the Good: Iris Murdoch's Godless Theology'. *Annual of the Society of Christian Ethics* 16 (1996): 223–42.

[27] It is worth noting that Murdoch had already implicitly acknowledged the transcendental aspect of the Good in 'The Sovereignty of Good over other Concepts':

We see the world in light of the Good, but what is the Good itself? The source of vision is not in the ordinary sense seen . . . Asking what Good is not like asking what Truth is or what Courage is, since in explaining the latter the idea of Good must enter in, it is that in the light of which the explanation must proceed. (SGC 98/380)

goodness is an image and support of the unity and fundamental reality of the individual', which is rooted in consciousness as the bearer of our moral being (MGM 427). As a transcendental notion, the Good represents the background condition for every act of cognition, perception, or evaluation. In the one-making light of the Good, all of human experience is morally 'colored'. Thus, the transcendental aspect of the Good is directly related to Murdoch's emphasis on moral perception. In her view, human beings do not *impose* value on a morally neutral world of facts by an act of will; rather, the world is already constituted as a moral world through our perception, which is a function of the ordinary operation of consciousness. In the light of the transcendental Good, therefore, all perception is moral perception.

The second aspect of Murdoch's theory of the Good is an empirical argument about how the concept of Good operates in our cognitive truth-seeking activities. The argument appeals to our experience of gradations or degrees of value through which we gradually come to apprehend the idea of the most perfect as the ideal end-point in a series. We learn about the Good through 'reflection upon our ordinary perceptions of what is valuable, what it is like to seek what is true or just in intellectual or personal situations, or to scrutinize and direct our affections' (MGM 398). This empirical argument coheres with Murdoch's analysis of the progressive, truth-seeking nature of consciousness as possessed of rankings or qualitative distinctions of value. Murdoch's claim is that perception is not only carried out against a transcendental background of value, but also is progressive in its attempt to make discriminations of value in relation to an implicit ideal of perfection. This pilgrimage from appearance to reality is carried on in every serious exercise of understanding. In intellectual studies, work, art, and human relations, we learn to distinguish gradations of value in relation to the real. In this respect, the whole of our cognitive experience furnishes us with evidence of the idea of perfection.[28]

In the twofold structure of her ontological proof, Murdoch unified the countervailing impulses of metaphysics and empiricism under a single principle of the Good. The Good is at once transcendental (providing the conditions for our consciousness of value in the world), and it also orients us towards perfection (providing the standard for the evaluation of particular values in the moment-to-moment pilgrimage of consciousness). By affirming such a correlation between self and good through the reflexive structure of the proof, Murdoch, in effect, claimed that consciousness itself is internally structured by a notion of value or the Good. This claim cut sharply against the modern

---

[28] Again, it is worth noting Murdoch had already implicitly acknowledged this empirical argument for the Good in 'On "God" and "Good"', where she argued that:

A deep understanding of any field of human activity (painting, for instance) involves an increasing revelation of degrees of excellence and often a revelation of there being in fact little that is very good and nothing that is perfect. Increasing understanding of human conduct operates in a similar way. We come to perceive scales, distances, standards, and may incline to see as less than excellent what previously were prepared to 'let by'... The idea of perfection works thus within a field of study, producing in increasing sense of direction. (OGG 61–62/350)

naturalistic assumption that moral rationality is essentially 'value-neutral' up until the point at which the agent chooses. Instead, for Murdoch, metaphysics *guides* morals by helping us to picture the way in which morality and evaluation are omnipresent in human life.

Consciousness *au fond* and *ab initio* must contain an element of truth-seeking through which it is also evaluated. In this sense, some cognitions are purer than others; but we cannot descend by any unitary 'scientific' or systematic method below the levels at which, in various ways, we test truth and reflect upon moral understanding. (MGM 241–242)

That is, consciousness is unified in its 'one-making' and 'truth-seeking' aspects under an idea of moral value (that is, the Good) that is present in the very activity of consciousness itself.

The complex metaphysical unity that Murdoch managed to achieve in her correlation of consciousness and the Good is counterbalanced (and perhaps destabilized) by another deep formal pattern in the book that keeps her metaphysics from final closure. This pattern is revealed in the progression of themes from the first chapter, called 'Conceptions of Unity. Art', to the penultimate chapter, titled 'Void'. This progression suggests the familiar problematic of the theological *via negativa* in its movement from art to void, from the production of images to their negation, from appearance to reality, and from theory to its undoing. In other words, for all of her sophisticated theorizing about the good, Murdoch reinstated her initial paradox of metaphysics and empiricism at the end of the book in order to remind us of what always escapes theory: the intractable and contingent reality of individual human fates. In an effort to avoid what she recognized as the consoling effects of any attempt to impose unity on a reality that is, at bottom, 'chancy and incomplete', Murdoch returned in her penultimate chapter to empirical facts that resist theorizing: 'The average inhabitant of the planet is probably without hope and starving', she wrote. 'Can one go on talking about a spiritual source and an absolute good if a majority of human kind is debarred from it?' (MGM 498, 489).

Such a view may indeed compel one to forgo metaphysics and to adopt, as Conradi has argued, a more 'practical mysticism' concerned with immediate and concrete human needs. Murdoch herself seemed to suggest as much when she voiced an imagined objection to her own position: 'Someone may say . . . any cult of personal spirituality or "goodness", presented as fundamental reality, is merely selfish pleasure in disguise, and all we can do which is in any way decent is to alleviate suffering whenever we come across it' (MGM 498). However, Murdoch did not, in my judgment, unambiguously embrace this conclusion—the ultimate chapter is titled 'Metaphysics' not 'Void', Nevertheless, the contrast between this dense, talkative work and the silence and emptiness of 'void' suggests that any theory of the good must acknowledge the reality of the good's apparent absence in many human lives.

6 Resources for moral reflection

This paper has presented a reading of Murdoch's philosophy and its significance for contemporary ethics through a detailed analysis of two major volumes of her writings. In doing so, I hope I have substantiated my initial claim that Murdoch's moral thought is more multivalent than many interpreters have allowed. The two books I have discussed go a long way toward making possible a deeper critical appreciation of her work. It remains for me to identify what I take to be the constructive contribution of Murdoch's thought to future ethics. There are, in my judgment, at least three areas in which Murdoch's thought offers important resources for moral reflection: her work helps us recover the moral subject from both linguistic and materialistic reductions; her approach to moral psychology contains a significant opening to social and political questions; and her theory of the imagination suggests a method for engaging in a critical hermeneutics of culture.

6.1 Against reductionism

In one form or another, as I noted earlier, the call for a retrieval of moral psychology has been a feature of moral inquiry at least since the 1950s, when Murdoch, Anscombe, and others first questioned the dominance of the ethics of obligatory action. Since then, issues of moral psychology and moral formation have been championed by virtue ethicists, narrative ethicists, communitarians, and moral development theorists. However, a retrieval of moral psychology on Murdochian grounds would distinguish itself from these positions by taking issue with two broad trends in recent ethics.

First, it would challenge the ascendancy of the idea of language in contemporary ethics. As I noted earlier, there has been an inflation of claims about language in recent thought (including claims about narrative and tradition) with the result that the idea of language or the linguistic community has replaced consciousness as the primary paradigm for speaking about moral agency. Paradoxically, the return to moral psychology and moral formation has, in this respect, often resulted in a *loss* of the psychic dimension of ethics in favor of a socio-linguistic analysis of how moral identity is formed in communities of ethical practice.[29] This is one example of the way that the neglect of the inner life of consciousness to which Murdoch called attention in analytic ethics several decades ago persists in other, less obvious forms in current ethics. On the other hand (and this is the second trend a Murdochian ethics would challenge), even those thinkers who explicitly defend the place of consciousness in ethics often do so in ways that could be considered self-defeating. For example, current attempts to explain moral consciousness on the basis of cognitive science often threaten to swallow the normative dimension of ethics in an empirical analysis of the brain's mental functioning.[30]

---

[29] For more on this point, see my 'Moral Change and the Magnetism of the Good'.

[30] As Virginia Held has argued: 'We already know that to have moral beliefs requires a brain . . . But what we think persons ought to do . . . is a normative question that no amount of further knowledge of how the brain works can address'. See Held, 'Whose Agency? Ethics versus Cognitive Science' in Larry May, Marilyn

Although any adequate contemporary moral psychology cannot deny either the formative role of language in human agency, or the material and biophysical conditions on which consciousness depends, a reconstruction of moral psychology seeking to extend Murdoch's insights in the current context would affirm both that 1) consciousness is capable of transcending, in some measure, the conditions of its own social and linguistic formation and that 2) an apprehension of value is an ineradicable feature of conscious perception and requires something other than a scientific or materialist explanation. The challenges entailed in defending Murdoch's recovery of consciousness against reductive maneuvers grounded in the empirical sciences are substantial, but Murdoch herself anticipated them long ago. 'If a scientifically minded empiricism is not to swallow up the study of ethics completely', she wrote, 'philosophers must try to show how our natural psychology can be altered by conceptions which lie beyond its range' (E&M 358). That is why Murdoch believed that every moral psychology presupposes a metaphysics—a theory that takes value as basic to the kind of creatures human beings are. Precisely *because* we are valuing creatures, she believed, ethics requires a different moral ontology than the empiricism of 'the world described by science' (E&M 320).[31]

6.2 Moral psychology and political ethics

Despite her success in putting issues of moral psychology back on the agenda of ethics, some have faulted Murdoch for failing to develop an adequate theory of social and political justice that would function as the counterpart to her moral psychology.[32] While there may be some merit to this charge, such critics may have underestimated the extent of Murdoch's social and political concern because they may have been unaware (until recently) of how many of Murdoch's essays are taken up with questions relevant to political theory. It is also possible that they have been looking for Murdoch's politics in the wrong places.

In contrast to the approach of a liberal theorist like John Rawls, for example, whose theory of justice focused on establishing the conditions and procedures necessary for social cooperation, Murdoch addressed these social conditions at a more basic level: at

Friedman, and Andy Clark (eds.), *Mind and Morals: Essays on Ethics and Cognitive Science* (Cambridge, Mass.: MIT Press, 1996), 74.

[31] For an initial attempt to develop a moral psychology based on the premises of what Murdoch called a 'non-dogmatic naturalism', see my essay, 'Picturing the Soul: Moral Psychology and the Recovery of the Emotions'. *Ethical Theory and Moral Practice* 4 (2001): 127–41.

[32] Martha Nussbaum (despite her deep admiration for other aspects of Murdoch's thought), has suggested that Murdoch's emphasis on moral psychology and her concern to defend the moral status of the inner life of persons caused her to 'veer sharply away from [questions of social justice], and even to suggest that in the end . . . the only important things was each person's struggle for self-perfection'. See 'When She Was Good', her review of Peter Conradi's *Iris Murdoch: A Life* (*New Republic*, 31 December 2001: 28–34). For related criticisms, see Alan Jacobs, 'The Liberal Neoplatonist?' in *First Things* 89 (January 1999): 57–61 and Stuart Hampshire, 'The Pleasures of Iris Murdoch' in *The New York Review of Books*, 48, 18 (15 November 2001): 24–6.

the level of how individuals *regard* each other, including the distortions and limitations that often attend their perceptions of themselves and of others. Murdoch treated one of the central questions of modern political liberalism, 'How can we generate a just political system that allows for multiple conceptions of the good without devolving into violence or social chaos?' as a moral psychological question, 'What does it mean to take up a distinctively "liberal" attitude toward others?' Murdoch's answer to this question, in effect, was that liberal tolerance requires a properly ordered soul or psyche, one that is prepared to set aside its own self-interest and egoistic perception in order to see others as valuable in themselves.[33]

When seen in the wider context of Murdoch's writings on liberalism, therefore, the process of 'unselfing' that plays such a dominant role in *The Sovereignty of Good* is not simply a practice of individual self-betterment. It can also be read as the moral precondition for liberal tolerance and respect for others. The distinctive conjunction of Platonic and liberal insights in Murdoch's thought suggests that we need to pay closer attention to the underlying moral psychology presupposed in the political ethics of liberalism.

6.3 Imagination and critical moral perception

A final area in which Murdoch's thought provides constructive resources is the centrality of the imagination to practical moral reasoning. Several contemporary thinkers—Jonathan Glover, Richard Kearney, and Martha Nussbaum, among others—have pursued this possibility. Murdoch did not conceive imagination to be simply an aesthetic activity, narrowly associated with the creative genius of the artist, not did she consider it to be an 'unreasoning' capacity concerned with the expression of feeling rather than with knowledge. In contrast to a broadly Kantian view of practical reasoning, where the will chooses a course of action based on a rational evaluation of a set of morally neutral facts, Murdoch insisted that the imagination plays a significant role in practical reasoning by shaping our initial conception of the so-called facts from which we choose. In this sense, the imagination is not peripheral to moral reasoning; it is a semi-figurative or 'picturing' activity of the mind that is deeply at work in moral cognition.

A further implication of this insight is that Murdoch's theory of the imagination contains an implicit hermeneutics of culture. The imagination is at the core of what she described as the reflexive capacity to 'make pictures' of ourselves, and then come to resemble the picture. In this process of value creation, human beings build up a perception of 'how things are' and then project those evaluations outward into the cultural world, where they acquire the status of an objective social fact, forming the givens of our cultural life and shaping what we regard as the available choices and possibilities. Murdoch's contention that the imagination has a hand in *creating* the world

---

[33] I have attempted to give an account of Murdoch's 'liberal Platonism' at some length in 'The Moral and Political Imagination of Iris Murdoch'. *Notizie di Politeia* XVIII, 66 (2002): 22–50.

in which we choose may surprise those who tend to read her as a strict moral realist and poses certain puzzles that I have explored elsewhere.[34] But the point I want to stress here is the implications of this fact for cultural criticism.

Because of the work of imagination in building up the world in which we choose, we are in her view partially complicit in our own perceptions of what the world is like. This makes us responsible for our ways of seeing and their practical consequences. 'We are obscure to ourselves', Murdoch writes, 'because the world we see already contains our values and we may not be aware of the slow delicate processes of imagination and will which have put those values there' (E&M 200). Because of this, 'the good and evil that we dream of may be more incarnate than we realise in the world within which we choose' (E&M 200). The constructive implication of this insight is that moral psychology, as Murdoch developed it, cannot simply limit itself to the examination of inner psychic processes; it must also include an analysis of the creative externalization of psychic processes in the socio-cultural world. It is not only *individuals*, therefore, who need to purify their moral vision, but *societies* as well. A cultural hermeneutic along Murdochian lines would serve the ends of critique by scrutinizing the imaginative processes by which human beings invest values in the social-cultural order, and by unmasking the distortions in that process that prevent a truthful vision of reality and destroy the basis for a just and tolerant respect for other persons.

In one of her early political essays, Murdoch urged the development of a form of social and political analysis that 'would enable those of us who are not experts to pick up the fact of our situation in a reflective, organized, and argumentative way ... [and] give us what Shelley called the power to imagine what we know' (E&M 181). She felt keenly the dangers of a predicament in which technical knowledge of social issues on the part of 'experts' had outstripped the ability of ordinary people to conceptualize human problems and to imagine a solution. 'It is not true', she wrote that 'everyone knows what is wrong with our society' and differs only over a simple choice of solutions. What we see as wrong, and our ability to express what is wrong in a profound, subtle, and organized way, will influence our conception of a solution as well as providing us with the energy to seek it (E&M 183).

This is precisely what Murdoch tried to offer us in presenting a theory of the imagination as both a moral and political necessity, and in her insistence that the way we *see* the world—embodied in our religion, art, politics, culture, and more—is a moral activity in its own right, and one worthy of our sustained moral and critical attention.

---

[34] This is why I have interpreted Murdoch as a 'reflexive' moralist. See PH, esp. chap. 5.

4

Iris Murdoch and Existentialism*

Richard Moran

It is not unusual for even the very greatest polemics to proceed through some unfairness toward what they attack, indeed to draw strength from the very distortions which they impose upon their targets. In the same way that a good caricature of a person's face enables us to see something that we feel was genuinely there to be seen all along, a conviction that persists in the face of, and may indeed be sustained by, our ongoing sense of the discrepancy between the picture and the reality. Some such distortion may be necessary in order to point to or make visible a feature that is perfectly present, but is obscured by the mass of other details. In the case of ideas and systems of thought there is an additional reason for a positive concern with distortion, and that is that we do not encounter ideas in a social or intellectual void. Rather, they come to us through their admirers, detractors, followers, and opponents. The social and intellectual reception and dissemination of Plato, or Marx, or the Bible are now and forever part of the meaning of those texts, and this remains true however demonstrable it may be that their reception involves a large distortion of what is actually there in those texts. To concern oneself with them must also be to concern oneself with what both their advocates and opponents have made of them, and in this or that context this image may be of greater social and intellectual importance than the question of strictly 'correct' readings.

And of course for no contemporary school of philosophy has the social and cultural milieu of its reception been more important to its identity as a trend of thought than in the case of Existentialism, particularly in its French, Sartrean form. Today, of course, it has been a fact of intellectual life within the Academy for over thirty years that Existentialism has no friends, and is probably even more fully dead on the Continent these days than it ever was within the Anglo-Saxon establishment. And even when figures like Nietzsche or Heidegger are given respectful philosophical attention today, it seems a requirement of such attention that we first be told that this interest is sharply divorced from any association with Existentialism as such. (I can't speak for the

* This paper was originally delivered at the conference, 'Iris Murdoch, Philosopher' held at Brown University, in April 2001. I am grateful to comments from those present at the conference, in particular Carla Bagnoli, Justin Broackes, and Martha Nussbaum.

situation in Europe, but in the USA anyway a peculiar feature of the institutional oblivion of Existentialism *within* professional philosophy is that this has not made any difference to its hold on the imagination of youth during that same thirty years. For some, such a fact will only serve to confirm its oblivion.) Iris Murdoch encountered Sartre's Existentialism at the height of its cultural fashion and influence, and as one of its first and most important expositors in English, she played a crucial role in bringing these ideas out of the realm of posture and fashion and into the realm of serious thought. And much of her later thought involved a self-conscious distancing of herself from these beginnings, culminating in the sustained criticism of Existentialism contained in *The Sovereignty of Good*.

I hope it will be understood as a form of praise if I characterize Iris Murdoch's book *The Sovereignty of Good* as a polemic. It is a passionate rejection of an entire climate of opinion and a deep-seated conception of the practice of philosophy in general and of moral philosophy in particular. But what is rejected there is more than a particular way of conducting a certain form of scholarly business, or a particular conception of the subject matter. Rather, in *Sovereignty* she is rejecting a conception of ourselves which can be found in movies, popular songs, and forms of romantic life as much as in works of philosophy. It exists as a style and an attitude much more than simply a theory. What is Murdoch's target here, then?

It is an idea of the person which emphasizes his status as an agent, one who deliberates, chooses, and acts. It is a picture that emphasizes sincerity and purity of motive, but which also, curiously, has no real place for the 'inner life', in that the meaning and moral importance of what we do is restricted to the overt, publicly observable act. It denies the existence of genuine objective value but endows the person with the super-human ability to invest features of the world with value, by the simple exertion of his arbitrary and unconstrained will.

This presents us with a familiar image of 'Existentialist Man', and no one will have a livelier appreciation than Murdoch herself of how much caricature is involved in this picture. In her hands the caricature is hardly born of a superficial acquaintance with the texts in question.[1] Rather, in *Sovereignty* and elsewhere the caricature has a positive philosophical point, and a complex one. For she wants to examine living ideas in their actual social and intellectual setting, and to look at how such ideas function in the life and culture of actual human beings. For this purpose the caricature itself is a genuine datum, of just as serious a claim on our philosophical attention as the actual texts of *Concluding Unscientific Postscript* or *Being and Nothingness*. At the time she wrote *Sovereignty* (roughly 1964–1970) 'existentialism' still survived as a cultural phenomenon, a style of life and literature, and a political stance. Her concern here is not exclusively, or even centrally, with a doctrine existing in books. And if the caricature itself has had its

---

[1] Murdoch is the author of the first book-length study of Sartre in English: *Sartre: Romantic Rationalist* (1953; with a new Introduction, 1987).

attractions for otherwise thoughtful people, then it will be worth the philosopher's trouble to investigate and criticize the sources of that attraction.

A further reason for choosing this simplified and exaggerated figure as her target is that she is interested in how *certain* ideas with an Existentialist pedigree combine with a conception of moral discourse from a very different tradition of philosophy—British analytic empiricism—to produce an unstable but still pervasive model for moral thinking that is not only mistaken, but which functions to make it difficult to so much as imagine an alternative to it.[2] Even for those who disagree with her conclusions, or even resist the entire drift of her thought, the reason for gratitude to *The Sovereignty of Good* and related essays (especially 'Vision and Choice in Morality' (1956)) is their resoluteness about breaking the grip of such restrictions on our thinking, and expanding the field of the philosophically imaginable. But at the same time, I want to argue that, in addition to the genuine virtues of Murdoch's very broad-brush approach to the traditions of thought she characterizes as 'Existentialist', especially in their social setting, the distortions she imposes on this thought ill-serve the presentation of her *own* thinking, and indeed may prevent the deeper reception of what is most powerful and important in Murdoch's own thought.

A familiar story we are told about Murdoch's intellectual development is that, while she was one of the first and best interpreters of (Sartrean) Existentialism in the 1950s and 1960, she soon came to see through its political and intellectual barrenness, finding her way to a deeper engagement with the more contemplative ideals of Plato and Simone Weil (among others).[3] The encounter with Sartre was a youthful indiscretion, or an adventure we can admire and even learn from, but a decidedly wrong turn nonetheless. I think this story is wrong about Existentialism and misleading about the direction and content of Murdoch's thinking. To the contrary, I would argue that we reach a better appreciation of many of the distinctive features of her thought about action, vision, and the ideals of life by seeing them as responses to and creative elaborations of characteristic Existentialist ideas. This is not a matter of either denying her originality or of simply dragging a philosopher back to her sources. Instead, I want to suggest that the broad cultural repudiation of Existentialism since the 1970s, dismissing it for its faddishness and doing so on the basis of no more than a faddish acquaintance with its texts, stands between us and a deeper understanding of Murdoch's own thought. Downplaying this inheritance prevents us from appreciating just what kind of philosophical work is being done by the characteristically Murdo-

---

[2] On p. 2 of *The Sovereignty of Good* (Routledge, 1970) Murdoch speaks of 'a kind of Newspeak which makes certain values non-expressible' (IP 2/300). Except where indicated otherwise, all quotations from Murdoch are from this book. The individual essays 'The Idea of Perfection' and 'On "God" and "Good"' are abbreviated as IP and OGG respectively, followed by page numbers referring both to the 1970 edition and to the reprintings in *Existentialists and Mystics* [E&M], edited by Peter Conradi (1997; Penguin, 1999).

[3] See, for instance, Peter Conradi's introduction to *Existentialists and Mystics*, where he says that, 'for reasons already touched upon, it was felt necessary fully to document Murdoch's growing scepticism and hostility towards existentialism' (E&M xxviii), and 'It is hard to escape the conclusion that by the late 1970s Iris Murdoch had helped to render existentialism out of date.'

chian emphasis on such themes as the sheer pervasiveness of morality in life, the rejection of the atomistic picture of actions as particulars, the metaphor of vision itself and the idea of struggle in connection with seeing clearly, the centrality of emotion and *attention*, and the neglect of these cognitive attitudes in contemporary moral philosophy, the emergence from the drag of solipsism and egoism, and the moral activity of thinking itself.

Naturally any such reading as I am proposing will have to deal with the various more or less explicit statements of repudiation in the text of Murdoch's work. The essay 'On "God" and "Good"' (part 2 of *The Sovereignty of Good*) opens with the announcement 'I shall argue that existentialism is not, and cannot by tinkering be made, the philosophy we need' (OGG 46/337). What Murdoch herself does with Existentialism can certainly not be described as 'tinkering', and of course nor can it be seen as anything like adoption. What she plainly does is criticize it, searchingly and severely, but at the same time as she represses the words of Existentialist philosophers themselves, along with her own debt to them, and substitutes a very different creation in their place. As mentioned earlier, Murdoch's target in both *Sovereignty* and the early essay 'Vision and Choice in Morality' (1956) is something of an amalgamation, and not restricted to Existentialism *per se*. For she is interested in an image of the moral situation of the person which settles at the intersection of several currents of thought, three currents in particular:

The very powerful image with which we are here presented is behaviourist, existentialist, and utilitarian in a sense which unites these three conceptions. It is behaviourist in its connection of the meaning and being of action with the publicly observable, it is existentialist in its elimination of the substantial self and its emphasis on the solitary omnipotent will, and it is utilitarian in its assumption that morality is and can only be concerned with public acts. (IP 8–9/305)

In part, the justification for this amalgamation lies in the legitimate interest in the reception of Existentialism within a certain familiar intellectual milieu, one which combines these diverse streams of thought. And this same interest may explain the nearly total neglect in *Sovereignty* of citation from any of the actual *texts* associated with Existentialism. For certain purposes our philosophical interest may well be in something 'existentialist-sounding' rather than anything actually defended by Sartre, Kierkegaard, or others. But there are obvious dangers in this 'assimilating' approach nonetheless. For of course, to take one example, the existentialists themselves are anything but behaviorist, either in their understanding of consciousness or their conception of the meaning of human action, nor could any of them be understood as utilitarians, even in the very restricted sense given by Murdoch above. The danger here is not really one of misrepresentation of these thinkers, since it is reasonable to hope that no one would actually be misled so as to ascribe such positions to Sartre, Nietzsche, Kierkegaard, or Heidegger, but rather that we fail to see that in criticizing this or that element of this combined image, Murdoch is resourcefully deploying several of the defining insights of certain Existentialists themselves. Or so I hope to show.

Let me give more detail to the picture Murdoch is opposing. In 'Vision and Choice in Morality' (VCM), the distillation of this combined image is referred to as the 'choice and argument' model of moral discourse (VCM 81).[4]

On this view, the moral life of the individual is a series of overt choices which take place in a series of specifiable situations. (VCM 77)

These overt choices are where all the moral action takes place. Some action or other is required of us, and we need to know which way to go. We weigh up the relevant facts as best we can, but since no set of mere facts can themselves entail a moral or otherwise evaluative conclusion, the aftermath of this weighing procedure can only be an exercise of pure, unconstrained Freedom. For all the facts together leave the question of value wide open. Goodness itself, being openly and unapologetically evaluative, cannot be an object of knowledge or contemplation on this view, since it is not to be found anywhere among the facts. So although deliberation concerns itself exclusively with the facts, and deliberation is undertaken only in order to determine one's choice, the choice itself must ultimately hang free of this deliberation. This may seem puzzling for the agent, and it should seem so. For if deliberation still leaves the question raised as open as before, why should anyone bother with deliberating about the question in the first place? This picture makes deliberation seem pointless for the agent. But this conclusion is thought to be the only way both to avoid a troublesome metaphysics of value, and to secure the complete freedom and responsibility of the moral agent. In criticizing this picture of the situation of choice, Murdoch makes one of her best deflating characterizations of the general 'choice and argument' model:

On this view one might say that morality is assimilated to a visit to a shop. I enter the shop in a condition of totally responsible freedom, I objectively estimate the features of the goods, and I choose. (IP 8/305)

So, the moral consumer picks and chooses among possible acts or values, unconstrained by anything in 'the facts' themselves, and the moral import or meaning of this transaction is exhausted by the question of what ends up in the shopping cart, the cashier at the check-out counter having no concern with whatever 'private goings-on' may have preceded this selection. As Murdoch goes on to say, 'Both as act and reason, shopping is public. Will does not bear upon reason, so the "inner life" is not to be thought of as a moral sphere' (IP 8/305).

In this way the 'choice and argument' model simultaneously inflates the human will to super-human proportions, while also leaving the inner life entirely out of the moral equation. And the role of *thinking* in guiding or influencing choice becomes quite mysterious since on this view there is no possibility of a cognitive or contemplative relation to good and bad, those words having been stripped of any descriptive or factual meaning (which is all that proper thinking has to work on). And this in turn means that

---

[4] Citations from Murdoch's essays are from the collection *Existentialists and Mystics*.

at the moment of selection the choosing will is isolated from the world, including whatever of the flesh and blood person belongs to the world, for the world is the world of the facts, and we've already seen how the will defines itself by its independence from them.

At this point, Murdoch asks, 'If we are so strangely separate from the world at moments of choice are we really choosing at all, are we right indeed to identify *ourselves* with this giddy empty will?' (IP 36/328). And indeed, the difficulties in *seeing ourselves* in this disorienting picture of our freedom can lead to a skepticism about the coherence of the idea of any freedom at all. We oscillate then between the idea of an arbitrary unhinged will and an idea of complete determinism or fatalism. It is at this point that Murdoch introduces her substitution of a contrary ideal, the ideal of *attention*.

Do we really have to choose between an image of total freedom and an image of total determinism? Can we not give a more balanced and illuminating account of the matter? I suggest we can if we simply introduce into the picture the idea of *attention*, or looking, of which I was speaking above. I can only choose within the world I can *see*, in the moral sense of 'see' which implies that clear vision is a result of moral imagination and moral effort. (IP 36–7/328–9)

The contrary ideal is presented as rejecting the identification of morality with the realm of *action*, and insistence on other moral values which the 'choice and argument' model threatens not simply to downplay, but to make altogether 'non-expressible' (IP 2/300). The metaphor of vision which she goes on to develop in her celebrated example of the woman's change of view about her daughter-in-law is intended to give substance to this more 'contemplative' 'vision-oriented' ideal, specifically with respect to the idea that the Good itself can be pictured not as a matter of one's simple choosing, but as the object of genuine apprehension of something real outside oneself. Contrary to the tradition she is attacking, value and the good are in truth genuine qualities we seek contact with, and not simply the reification of our otherwise unconstrained recommendations, prescriptions, or expressions of mere feeling. (Throughout *Sovereignty*, the Prescriptivism of Richard Hare and the Emotivism of A. J. Ayer and others are the central objects of her attack, which she assimilates to the common element of non-naturalism in Kant and Existentialism.) Hence the apprehension of value as something real can be seen not in the awarding of the empty predicate 'good' to some course of action, but rather in the sustained attention to the more descriptive but still evaluative qualities we perceive under the heading of such terms as 'the spiteful remark', 'the sweet disposition', and 'the prim and the prissy'. The picture of attention is also meant to displace a familiar atomistic picture of moral change itself, as if it were something made possible by isolated acts of instantaneous conscious choice. For attention, by contrast, is in its very nature answerable to something outside oneself, and the action of attention does not produce its results instantly or by fiat, but is rather part of the arduous, progressive, piecemeal business of moral growth. In sum, Murdoch's metaphor of vision is presented as a correction to the exclusive concentration in moral thought on action and agency, *particularly* as this agency is depicted in Existentialism, in favor of the ideas of vision, attention, and progressive focusing on the Real outside oneself.

Let's first briefly take up a few separate points of Murdoch's criticism of this picture, considered as a critique of Existentialism. First, it would be difficult to make a case for seeing any of the major Existentialists as wedded to the fact/value distinction that is the cornerstone of the argument above which establishes the 'choice and argument' model. Instead, it is a classic (or notorious) Existentialist thesis, in thinkers as diverse as Nietzsche, Kierkegaard, Heidegger, and Sartre that the facts we apprehend and which serve as premises in our arguments exist for us as colored by our concerns; that it is the individual's defining and inescapable *orientation* in the world, and the values which are given expression in that orientation, which makes facts as such available to him. Even more than most philosophical currents, Existentialism arises as a reactive movement of thought (a stance embodied in the familiar Existentialist figure of rebellion), and the common ground of its diverse figures is much more apparent in what they oppose than in any positive theses they may defend. And in this regard one could hardly identify a more central unifying theme than their various rejections of any positivist idea of 'fact' which defines it in opposition to the 'evaluative'. So while it is certainly possible, for instance, to criticize Nietzsche on the idea of knowledge as will-to-power, or Kierkegaard on the task of becoming subjective, or Heidegger on the worldhood of the world announcing itself through Dasein's structure of care, it is *not* possible to see these central ideas of theirs as anything but rejections of the fact/value distinction as it functions in Murdoch's reconstruction of the 'choice and argument' model. And as mentioned before, no one could reasonably accuse *these* writers, of all people, of restricting moral attention to single, overt, and public actions, and leaving out of account the moral importance of the 'inner life', including emotional life and habits of attention.

(Indeed, I would argue that it is from within a broadly Existentialist framework that we can break the hold of another opposition which Murdoch seeks to overcome: seeing any 'serious' or 'cognitive' moral change in the person as grounded exclusively in a change of *belief*, with the rest of mental life confined to mere sensations, and thus lacking any understanding of the moral difference made by such things as changes in attitude, feeling, attention, or habits of thought. —But more on that in a moment.)

What about the picture of the will, especially in its Sartrean presentation, doesn't that take us back to the 'choice and argument' model, the free but anxious moral consumer? And doesn't this represent both a wildly unrealistic picture of the powers of the will, as well as but a different version of the same restriction of moral attention to *actions*, even though here the relevant action is not restricted to what is publicly observable?

It will reward us to tread a bit carefully here. In particular I want to consider this question (of the Sartrean will) in connection with Murdoch's extended example from *Sovereignty* of the mother-in-law's change of vision, which is introduced as a corrective to the 'choice and argument' model and the Sartrean Existentialist's apotheosis of the empty will. Murdoch carefully sets up the case so that there need be no difference at all in overt behavior, with the mother-in-law M behaving beautifully toward D throughout, both before and after her change of view. In addition, the example is devised so that there need be no change in the daughter-in-law's behavior either; hence the case is constructed so that it is, in a perfectly straightforward sense, *the same facts* about D that are being responded to both before and after M's change of vision. At first,

M finds D quite a good-hearted girl, but while not exactly common yet certainly unpolished and lacking in dignity and refinement. D is inclined to be pert and familiar, insufficiently ceremonious, brusque, sometimes positively rude, always tiresomely juvenile. (IP 17/312)

Later,

D is discovered to be not vulgar but refreshingly simple, not undignified but spontaneous, not noisy but gay, not tiresomely juvenile but delightfully youthful, and so on. And as I say, *ex hypothesi*, M's outward behaviour, beautiful from the start, in no way alters. (IP 17–18/313)

This sort of change is in its own way simple and familiar. Such transformations can be momentous, but they need not be; indeed in a given case such a change of attitude can be the sort of thing that passes unnoticed by the very people involved, and it has certainly passed beneath the notice of most moral philosophers. We would have reason to be grateful to Murdoch if she had done nothing more than force this characteristic moral phenomenon on our attention. Let me note just two things about it right away. First, in carefully setting up the case so as to involve no overt change in the behavior of either party, Murdoch not only focuses our attention on the 'inner' events of M's change of view, but also shows that the change in question is of the sort that Wittgenstein describes as a 'change of aspect'.[5] A central part of the intrigue of the examples of the duck-rabbit or the 'fallen' triangle is that the viewer is aware at one and the same time that *nothing* has changed in the configuration of lines, and yet that *everything* has changed in their physiognomy, in what they immediately convey to him. That is, the duck-rabbit is importantly *not* a visual illusion. The *experience* of it is not like that of, say, a line appearing to move when we know it is stationary, or a straight line appearing to bend when seen against a certain background. These are illusions, even though the person doesn't have to be taken in by them to experience them. In contrast to this, when the figure seen as a duck switches to being seen as a rabbit there is no *illusion* that what one is looking at has altered in any way, not even an illusion one fails to be taken in by.[6] In Murdoch's case, M is continuously aware that nothing has altered

---

[5] *Philosophical Investigations*, Part Two. Translated by G. E. M. Anscombe (Basil Blackwell, 1953).

[6] The distinction I have in mind can perhaps best be brought out by considering a single case that may exhibit *both* phenomena, visual illusion *and* 'aspect change'. So, for instance, the outline drawing of a box whose three-dimensional projection allows for seeing it with one of its corners advancing toward the viewer and the other receding, or the other way around. There is visual illusion in the appearance of three-dimensionality, in the experience of advancing and receding (which is not to say that the viewer fails to recognize it as a visual illusion). But when the viewer switches from seeing one facet of it as advancing to seeing it as receding, there is change of aspect but no (additional) visual illusion, for the experience is *not* as if

in D's behavior. Instead she is now seeing the very same behavior under a different aspect. M is not under any illusion that anything in D herself has altered, nor must she see either her previous view or her current one as deceptive in any way. When she saw her under the aspect of the noisy and juvenile she was seeing something real too; though her vision of her was certainly limited and constricted in various ways.

The second thing I want to point out here is that although the example is introduced to develop Murdoch's counter-ideal of vision and attention, as against the emphasis on the self as *agent* (IP 3/301), when we look closer we see that the metaphor of vision is not in any simple *opposition* to the idea of action, but in fact contains it. Indeed it is the morally difficult *activity* of imagination that Murdoch uses the metaphor of vision to draw our attention to, not a matter of passive receptivity, but rather the endless effort to see clearly (IP 36–7/328–9). In describing the change in how M sees her daughter-in-law, Murdoch insists that 'M has in the interim been *active*, she has been *doing* something' (IP 19/314, her emphases). So, contrary to the impression we might have received before, the metaphor of vision is not intended as competitor to the picture of the self as agent, but is rather in the service of rejecting a particular impoverished picture of agency itself, in favor of a deeper one.[7]

I would argue further that, not only is the metaphor of vision itself the development of a richer, as well as more realistic, picture of agency, but that the resources being developed here are themselves characteristically Existentialist ones. This will seem strange, since if there is one thing Murdoch is consistent in her rejection of it is the 'giddy empty will' (IP 36/328), the 'footloose, solitary, substanceless will' (IP 16/311) that is supposed to be the fulcrum on which the entire Existentialist drama turns. In particular, it is the *isolation* of the will or the choosing self that she finds to be the common error of both Existentialism and Logical Empiricism.

Immense care is taken to picture the will as isolated. It is isolated from belief, from reason, from feeling, and is yet the essential center of the self. It is separated from belief so that the authority of reason, which manufactures belief, may be entire and so that responsibility for action may be entire as well. (IP 8/304–5)

But what exactly is the force of the idea of 'isolation' here? We have already seen that the isolation of the choosing, valuing will from the world of fact and argument is foreign to the Existentialist picture of the place of value in the world. And as far as arbitrariness goes, even Sartre himself is frequently at pains to deny that the will as he

the array of lines actually changed, not even an illusion one is aware of as such. The visual experience is of the array of lines remaining *unchanged* throughout the change of aspect.

[7] See IP 22/316–7 for further emphasis on forms of agency which are *left out* of the picture she opposes: 'The analysis pictures M as defined "from the outside in": M's individuality lies in her will, understood as her "movements". The analysis makes no sense of M as continually active, as making progress, or of her inner acts as belonging to her or forming part of a continuous fabric of being: it is precisely critical of metaphors such as "fabric of being". Yet can we do without such metaphors here? Further, is not the metaphor of vision almost irresistibly suggested to anyone who, without philosophical prejudice, wishes to describe the situation?'

pictures it is unconstrained or removed from its situatedness in the world. In the long course of *Being and Nothingness* he surely does say a number of provocative and unqualified things about freedom, but he also says

> Thus we do not intend here to speak of anything arbitrary or capricious . . . This does not mean that I am free to get up or to sit down, to enter or to go out, to flee or to face danger—if one means by freedom here a pure capricious, unlawful, gratuitous, and incomprehensible contingency. (BN 453/584)[8]

At the same time it cannot be denied that there is something absolute in Sartre's conception of freedom or, as I would rather put it, in the aspect of freedom that interests him. (And, I hope to show, this aspect is also what Murdoch is exploring in the example of M and her daughter-in-law.) For our purposes here, this aspect of freedom can perhaps best be indicated by means of a set of slogans familiar from the literature of Existentialism. So for instance, we are told that the person is always engaged in some *situation* or other (or rather an interlocking set of situations); that the person does not exist and then somehow come to *acquire* a situation, but is always already to be found within one. And to be in a situation is for the person to *orient* himself (or herself) in one way or another toward it, whether in resolve to change, resignation, satisfaction, or resentment. And complementary to the slogan that there is no alternative to being in some situation or other, toward which one orients oneself one way or another, is the insistence that there is always more than one possible, defensible form for this orientation to take. The fate of situatedness as such is not escapable, but at the same time the situation does not itself dictate one's orientation to it. Hence the complementary thought could be phrased in the slogan: Every situation has its possibilities; there are different possibilities of response *within* any situation.

From this vantage, we can begin to make out a Sartrean conception of freedom as both finite and unbounded. It is finite in the ordinary sense that anyone's freedom is limited in various ways, that we exist with capacities and in situations that are only partially of our own choosing. And at the same time it is unbounded in the sense that there is always room for a variety of possible ways that the person may orient himself toward these capacities and situations, these very finitudes. The 'facticities' which make up my situation may be said to be 'given', but there is always the question of what the person makes of them, and that is his or her own business. Consider the analogy with one's bodily posture. One is always in *some* position or other, whether standing, sitting down, leaning against, or whatever. And insofar as the person is free to move, and hence has other positions open to him, the fact of his being in *this* one posture rather than another may be said to represent a choice on his part, if only the default choice to

---

[8] All citations from Sartre are from *Being and Nothingness*, translated by Hazel Barnes, (Philosophical Library, New York, 1956), abbreviated as BN. There are two established paginations, with 638 pages (New York, 1956; London, 1957, 1969) or with 811 pages (New York, 1966): I give references to them both, separated by a slash/.

leave well enough alone. Further, any particular posture, such as sitting, will itself be something that will necessarily manifest itself in some *particular* way or other, hence not simply 'sitting down' *simpliciter*, but sitting in some manner, whether as perched on the chair, or slouching into it, or otherwise sitting in it in some way or other. Hence the body cannot avoid being in some posture or other, and there will always be more than one possibility here, and *within* any such general posture there will be more than one way of orienting oneself towards *it*. And along both these dimensions, the position of the body expresses something of the person, whether the person's will, or his desire, his concern or lack of concern, his care or carelessness.

And if one's situation includes a daughter-in-law, then one will be oriented toward her in one way or another, and since there will not be only one possible way of relating to her, and no single description exhausts who this person is, the very *particular* ways in which one sees and relates to her will also be expressions of oneself that one is answerable for. The mother-in-law will necessarily 'take in' this new presence in her life in certain terms and not in others, and will respond to the qualities she sees in her with certain attitudes and not others. These attitudes toward D do no *befall* her any more than do the particularities of her physical posture. Just as the person's physical stance expresses his orientation in space and directedness toward the objects that confront him, so the person's attitudes represent his orientation toward the persons and situations which concern him. At no point does the person find that there is only one possible posture open to him, only one way of physically orienting himself to the spatial world. That would be to annul the very concept of adopting some posture. It is true that a person who is paralyzed or tied fast to a chair does not *choose* the position his body is in; that field of possibilities may be said to be closed to him, and for that very reason his being either laid out or propped up is not any *posture* of his at all. In a similar way, it only makes sense to speak of a person's *attitude* toward something insofar as it is understood that this represents a particular assessment of one sort or another, an assessment that might have gone differently and which might yet go differently upon subsequent reflection. Any attitude is partial with respect to the richness and complexity of what experience presents us with, and this partiality is something the person is answerable for. An attitude that did not position itself with respect to other conceivable ones would not be an attitude at all. It is for these reasons that the words 'posture' and 'attitude' can be synonymous in certain contexts because they both denote dimensions of assessment to which the person is necessarily subject, one way or another, insofar as he is a thinking and acting being at all. And a person's particular posture or attitude counts as an *expression* of the person because in both cases the particular orientation he adopts is partial with respect to the total field of possibilities, and hence is something which persists subject to the person's reasons and commitments, and other attitudes.

What I meant earlier by the 'absolute' aspect of freedom in Sartre and other Existentialists can perhaps be brought into focus by this comparison. When he says that my physical posture always represents a *choice* of mine, he is not claiming absurdly that there are no limits to how I can move my body or that there are not dramatic differences between people in what they can accomplish physically. I cannot simply pick and choose any position or movement I might wish for myself. But at the same time, within my quite limited powers, at any given moment there are an infinity of movements and positions open to me, and my adoption of the particular one of them that is mine at the moment represents a choice of mine. It might have been otherwise, in countless possible ways, and the fact that it is this way with me rather than otherwise is something that expresses my reasons, concerns, and commitments, as well as my sense of what is not worth bothering with (which I am also responsible for). This is not an idea that is beyond philosophical criticism (or philosophical defense, for that matter), but it is an idea of a different logical order from the claim that the scope of the will is absolute in the sense that nothing is beyond its power.[9]

The analogous idea with respect to the attitudes is, again, not the absurd claim that no attitude toward the situation is closed to me, or that all particular attitudes are on a par with respect to their reasonableness, or that one can simply pick and choose whatever attitude one would most 'like'. Rather, the idea is that any particular attitude toward a person or situation is partial with respect to other possible ones, and hence represents a selection from this totality. This is clear enough even when Sartre indulges in provocative claims like 'I cannot be crippled without choosing myself as crippled' (BN 328/432), which he immediately glosses by saying 'This means that I choose the way in which I constitute my disability (as "unbearable", "humiliating", "to be hidden", "to be revealed to all", "an object of pride", "the justification for my failures", etc.).' Hence he is distinguishing what he means by 'choosing' here from either the bizarre thought that the person somehow chooses *to be* crippled, or the idea that just any arbitrary response to this facticity will make sense or be available to the person. Rather the thought is that even a drastic constraint like this one necessarily provides room for more than one possible orientation from the person, and that as with posture, even *within* one particular attitude there will be more than one way of adopting it and inhabiting *it* (that is, his pride or his humiliation will itself take particular forms). This scope for the person's own commitment is an aspect of the rationality of attitudes, not a denial of it. For even what we refer to as the 'rational *compulsion*' toward a particular attitude is not like the physical compulsion of being dropped from the roof, since the former critically involves the person's endorsement of the compelling reasons demanding his assent.

Murdoch presents the example of the mother-in-law to illustrate what she takes to be not only missing but suppressed in the 'choice and argument' model or moral discourse. Earlier I drew attention to the relation between the change in view she undergoes and the idea of 'aspect switching' in order to underscore that it is part of

---

[9] Cf. *Being and Nothingness*, 529/677: 'Although I have at my disposal an infinity of ways of assuming my being-for-others, *I am not able not to assume it*. We find here again that condemnation to freedom which we defined above as *facticity* . . . . Whether in fury, hate, pride, shame, disheartened refusal or joyous demand, it is necessary for me to choose to be what I am.'

Murdoch's point in this example that the mother-in-law is described as responding to the same qualities in her daughter-in-law when she goes from seeing her as 'undignified' to seeing her as 'spontaneous', etc. The example is carefully constructed to illustrate something quite different from the case where such a change of view is prompted by realizing some previously unknown fact that makes all the difference, or when one realizes that one simply misinterpreted the situation altogether. For the mother-in-law was not under some *illusion* when she saw this young woman as somewhat vulgar or juvenile, not if the word 'illusion' is understood to mean that those qualities were not, after all, *there to be seen* in her behavior. Her failure, as Murdoch describes it, was a failure of vision and attention and imagination. What is wrong in her previous apprehension of this person is not that she sees something that isn't there, but that she fails to realize that her view of these very qualities is partial, incomplete, and hence potentially unfair, and kept in place by her own limited imagination and sympathies. What she comes to see, and what makes her change possible, is that there is more than one possible response to these very qualities, and that it is her business, a matter of the engagement of her own capacities, what her orientation to those qualities is to be. This is not a complete description of the conditions of moral progress, and in other cases the change in question may require the *repudiation* of one's initial view of the other person, as not being merely partial but as being *wrong* or distorted. But the acknowledgement of this capacity is a requirement of any such progress. What the construction of Murdoch's example enables us to see, I take it, is that a certain kind of moral progress does not require that one's previous view is seen as mistaken or false to the facts, but rather that it is a partial view of those facts, and that one can pass beyond it into a view that is deeper or more encompassing, from which perspective one's earlier view is seen not so much false as irrelevant or unworthy.

To put this point in more explicitly Existentialist terms, the more fundamental error the mother-in-law corrects in herself is that of seeing the attributes of her daughter-in-law as *facticities*, to see her as 'pert and familiar, brusque and juvenile' in the same way that Sartre's inkwell is round, solid, and black (BN 59/102). Before she can so much as undertake the activity of thought which Murdoch describes, and ultimately see (something like) those very same qualities as now 'not vulgar but refreshingly simple, not undignified but spontaneous' she must affirm a kind of responsibility for her attitudes, to see them as *her own* in the sense of seeing them as the expression of her *orientation* to her daughter-in-law, and seeing the question of her orientation to her as *up to her* and not simply dictated by the facts of the situation. Her original perception of her as vulgar and juvenile is something she is not the passive victim of, not something that simply befalls her like a rash, but rather something that it is her business either to continue with, to affirm, or to revoke. What she encounters, and what makes her change of vision possible, is the defining Existentialist insight that the person always has a '*say*' in how he orients himself toward the situation that confronts him, that this is not decided for him, although in the playing out of the situation it will inevitably be decided one way or another.

In this way the very metaphor of vision which Murdoch begins by opposing to the exclusive attention to freedom and action in the tradition she is attacking is in fact a metaphor of the very dimension of action that Existentialists like Sartre and Kierke-gaard are fairly obsessive in insisting on. Neither for them nor for Murdoch is the sort of change undergone by the mother-in-law 'an arbitrary leap of the giddy isolated will'. Nor is it an 'empty self' which makes this movement of thought, but rather a fully situated self using all the resources at its disposal, and which is refusing to reify or take for granted the given attitudes with which it approaches the situation.

We could call this self 'empty' only in the following sense: when it confronts such a situation calling for thought, the ideal it holds itself to is that any core belief or other attitude is sustained in the self only by the continued endorsement of the self. (This is the sense of Sartre's slogan 'There is no inertia in consciousness' (BN 61/104).) Nothing survives for free; any part of the self may at some point have to hold itself open to the test provided by its encounters with the world, including of course the world of others. This self is 'empty' only in the sense that Neurath's ship is empty, composed of nothing that might not somehow need to be replaced, but which nonetheless manages to keep afloat and complete its journey. The mother-in-law's self is not one which is empty or rudderless, but one which does not objectify its own experiences and attitudes and project them as fixed properties of the people it encounters. Seen in these terms, this effort just *is* the struggle against what Murdoch describes as the 'fat, relentless ego' (OGG 52/342): this ego is fat because in its self-satisfaction it stores up and accumulates its impressions, prejudices, and habits of thought and rather than risk finding them inadequate compared to the actual multi-plicity of life, instead spreads this accumulated life-material upon experience, upon others, until this accumulation of its own personal history and culture is all that can fall within its range of vision.

We need a place for the role of freedom here to do justice to the sense of *struggle* that Murdoch rightly emphasizes in the story of the work of *attention*, and coming to a new appreciation of something or someone (IP 22/316–7). And, I would argue, we have to make sense of the 'activity' involved here in order to make sense of those *confrontations* between different selves, when one person needs or demands a new response from someone else with whose regard they are entwined, as in the need for forgiveness, or remorse, or a change of heart. Such changes cannot be accomplished magically or arbitrarily, but at the same time they are among the things that can be *asked* of us on occasion, and when that happens we are being asked to *do* something. The concept of 'attention' which Murdoch offers us in this context is rich and multivalent in ways that make it especially appropriate here, for to *attend to* some matter also means to assume responsibility for it, to take charge of it (as when I attend to the inadequacy of my response to what I did). And when its object is a particular *person*, 'attending' also means to accompany, to be present to, or to serve. It is this same density of meaning in the idea of attention that the Existentialist draws in aligning the concepts of consciousness as attention, which in turn means that consciousness is to be understood within the categories of care, concern, and responsibility.

I'll conclude with one final look at the place of choice within Existentialism. Murdoch is rightly suspicious of any picture of the moral life that concentrates on isolated dramatic moments of decision, especially when this is at the cost of attention to the background that makes such instants moments of decision at all. (That would be like what Wittgenstein describes as trying to 'make out what the word "checkmate" meant by close observation of the last move of some game of chess'. *Philosophical Investigations*, § 316.) And in *Sovereignty* she says:

> The existentialist picture of choice whether it be surrealist or rational, seems unrealistic, overoptimistic, romantic, because it ignores what appears at least to be a sort of continuous background with a life of its own; and it is surely in the tissue of that life that the secrets of good and evil are to be found. (OGG 54/343–4)
>
> If we ignore the prior work of attention and notice only the emptiness of the moment of choice we are likely to identify freedom with the outward movement since there is nothing else to identify it with. But if we consider what the work of attention is like, how continuously it goes on, and how imperceptibly it builds up structures of value round about us, we shall not be surprised that at crucial moments of choice most of the business of choosing is already over. This does not imply that we are not free, certainly not. But it implies that the exercise of our freedom is a small piecemeal business which goes on all the time and not a grandiose leaping about unimpeded at important moments. The moral life, on this view, is something that goes on continually, not something that is switched off in between the occurrence of explicit moral choices. (IP 37/329)

While agreeing wholeheartedly with her positive point here, I would still disagree with her choice of targets. For it is because of what I referred to earlier as the 'unbounded' aspect of human freedom, the fact that the person always orients himself one way or another toward both his capacities and obstacles, that the Existentialist sees an element of choice in all the continuities and discontinuities of a person's gestures, postures, and attitudes, as well as in their explicit decisions. In this we can see Murdoch's insistence on the sheer pervasiveness of the moral dimension in human life, in the 'fabric of being' that makes up the background of any explicit decisions we make, and the gradual, piecemeal change that makes up what may be genuinely momentous in the soul's progress.

And it is this very dimension of life, and its implications for the situation of choice, that Kierkegaard, for instance, is developing in a classic statement of a characteristic Existentialist *ethos*, one which I think Murdoch's own formulations help us to hear better, and thus to see how much the same are the illusions concerning agency which their writings seek to undo. I can't do better than conclude with this passage, without commentary, since Kierkegaard's very language here picks up so many of the themes that Murdoch is at pains to stress, thus highlighting the concerns of both of them, and showing how much is lost by divorcing Murdoch's thought from its Existentialist heritage.

For an instant it may seem as if the things between which a choice is to be made lie outside of the chooser, that he stands in no relationship to it, that he can preserve a state of indifference over against it. This is the instant of deliberation, but this, like the Platonic instant, has no existence, least of all in the abstract sense in which you would hold it fast, and the longer one stares at it the less it exists. That which has to be chosen stands in the deepest relationship to the chooser, and when it is a question of a choice involving a life problem the individual must naturally be living in the meantime, and hence, it comes about that the longer he postpones the choice the easier it is for him to alter its character notwithstanding that he is constantly deliberating and deliberating and believes that thereby he is holding the alternatives distinctly apart. . . . One sees then, that the inner drift of the personality leaves no time for thought experiments, that it constantly hastens onward and in one way or another posits this alternative or that, making the choice more difficult the next instant because what has thus been posited must be revoked. Think of the captain on his ship at the instant when it has to come about. He will perhaps be able to say, 'I can either do this or that'; but in case he is not a pretty poor navigator he will be aware at the same time that the ship is all the while making its usual headway, and that therefore it is only an instant when it is indifferent whether he does this or that. So it is with a man. If he forgets to take account of the headway, there comes at last an instant when there no longer is any question of an either/or, not because he has chosen but because he has neglected to choose, which is equivalent to saying, because others have chosen for him, because he has lost his self. . . .

For to think that for an instant one can keep one's personality a blank, or that strictly speaking one can break off and bring to a halt the course of the personal life, is a delusion. The personality is already interested in the choice before one chooses, and when the choice is postponed the personality chooses unconsciously, or the choice is made by obscure powers within it. (Kierkegaard, *Either/Or*, 'Equilibrium Between the Aesthetical and the Ethical in the Composition of the Personality', vol. 2, 167–8 (translated by Walter Lowrie, Princeton University Press, 1959).)

5

The Exploration of Moral Life*

Carla Bagnoli

The most distinctive feature of Murdoch's philosophical project is her attempt to reclaim the exploration of moral life as a legitimate topic of philosophical investigation. In contrast to the predominant focus on action and decision, she argues that 'what we require is a renewed sense of the difficulty and complexity of the moral life and the opacity of persons. We need more concepts in terms of which to picture the substance of our being' (AD 293).[1] I shall argue that to fully appreciate the novelty of this proposal we need to recognize some elements of continuity with analytic methods of philosophical inquiry and themes that belong to continental traditions. On Murdoch's view, the most important question facing moral philosophy is that of whether and how we can become better persons. In order to describe moral progress and failure, struggle and ascent, we need ethical concepts capable of capturing mental events such as change in mind, self-examination, and redescription. These concepts are presently unavailable, and this lack seriously undermines our attempts to understand the phenomena of morality. Because of this conceptual loss, we succumb to the mistaken idea that moral life coincides with its scattered outer manifestations, i.e. public acts. Instead, Murdoch tells us that 'the moral life . . . is something that goes on continually, not

* This paper is a distant ancestor of my comment to Richard Moran's 'Vision, Choice, and Existentialism', presented at a Conference on Iris Murdoch Philosopher, at Brown University, 2001. I am especially grateful to Richard Moran for his stimulating paper, and for the opportunity to start a conversation with him which lasts to these days. I owe thanks to Justin Broackes for his detailed and perceptive comments, and to Luca Ferrero, Elijah Millgram, Terry Pinkard, Julius Sensat, and to an anonymous referee of Oxford University Press for their precious suggestions.
[1] Abbreviations for Murdoch's essays are as follows. AD: 'Against Dryness' (1961). DPR: 'The Darkness of Practical Reason' (1966). EPM: 'The Existentialist Political Myth' (1952). HMD: 'Hegel in Modern Dress' (1957). HT: 'A House of Theory' (1958). M&E: 'Metaphysics and Ethics' (1957). NM: 'The Novelist as a Metaphysician' (1950). NP: 'Nostalgia for the Particular' (1952). S&G: 'The Sublime and the Good' (1959). SBR: 'The Sublime and the Beautiful Revisited' (1959). TL: 'Thinking and Language' (1951). VCM: 'Vision and Choice in Morality' (1956). Page references are given to the reprintings in *Existentialists and Mystics* [E&M], ed. P. J. Conradi (1997). In the case of M&E and VCM, page references (preceding a forward slash/) are in addition given to the original printings: 'Metaphysics and Ethics', in D. F. Pears (ed.), *The Nature of Metaphysics* (London: Macmillan, 1957) and 'Vision and Choice in Morality', *Proceedings of the Aristotelian Society*, Supplementary Vol. 30 (1956), 32–58.

something that is switched off in between the occurrence of explicit moral choices' (SG 37/329).[2]

Murdoch's point is that we need to conceive the locus of agency more broadly if we want to understand the complicated machinery of action. But perhaps more importantly, she points out that we may be morally active while entertaining a contemplative attitude, which does not issue in action. The grain of moral life, she argues, is constituted by the continuous imaginative constructions of our mind; it is there that our individuality resides. To be able to fruitfully explore and fully explicate the nature of moral life, contemporary philosophy needs to reclaim a richer moral vocabulary and elaborate a developmental model of agency capable of accounting not only for episodic changes but also for the kinds of failures and achievements that make sense only within a conception of the life of a person that appreciates progress and history.

Some fifty years after Murdoch first raised these issues, we are still very much in need of the words, the concepts, and—most importantly—a detailed developmental model of agency necessary to properly account for moral life. Or so I shall argue.

1 Reclaiming the words

Murdoch's contribution to moral philosophy has principally been read as providing a trenchant critique of ethics in the analytic tradition. This reading is not inaccurate, as Murdoch rejects many of the supposedly indisputable methodological assumptions of analytic ethics. Her complaint is that with logical positivism ethics becomes a peripheral discipline, virtually ejected from the domain of philosophy. She mounts a powerful attack on ordinary language philosophy as dry, shallow, superficial, and incapable of capturing what really matters. In Murdoch's view, this narrow approach to ethics marks the apex of the ineluctable historical process of modernity, which is not confined to the circle of Oxford scholars. It begins as an attempt to emancipate philosophy from the obscurities of metaphysics, and it ends up dispensing with any hypotheses about human nature and the mind (VCM 34/77, SG 48–50/339–40).[3]

In 'Metaphysics and Ethics', Murdoch denounces the unfortunate effects that this philosophical move has on moral philosophy, and in particular on the ways in which we are supposed to think of the study of morals. The mind seems resistant to any serious philosophical treatment, it is suggested, because it is 'particular' and 'individual',

---

[2] Murdoch, *The Sovereignty of Good* [SG], (London: Routledge, 1970). Page references, separated by a forward slash/, are given both to the 1970 edition and to the reprintings in *Existentialists and Mystics*.

[3] Murdoch attacks logical positivism, ordinary language philosophy, and various forms of non-cognitivism. While these movements significantly differ from one another, they all undertake the task of avoiding metaphysical commitments, and consider language as the starting point of philosophical investigation, hence restricting ethics to a peculiar form of meta-ethics. This complaint was not uncommon, see e.g. D. M. MacKinnon, 'Things and Persons', *Proceedings of the Aristotelian Society*, Supplementary Vol. 22 (1948), John Wisdom, *Philosophy and Psychoanalysis,* (Oxford: Blackwell, 1953). For a historical reconstruction of the intellectual circles at Oxford, and the lasting influence that MacKinnon and Wisdom apparently exerted on Murdoch, see Mario Ricciardi, 'Philosophy, Literature, and Life', *Notizie di Politeia*, 66 (2002), 5–21.

i.e. the domain of the private. Introspection is a dubious method, and the minds of others escape philosophical investigation. Hence, it is further argued, to be free from metaphysics, ethics needs to restrict itself to what is visible and manifest, the sphere of action. This restriction is paired with a view of moral language as expressive or persuasive (M&E 102–103/61–2).[4] Subsequent refinements of the Emotivist view of moral language from A. J. Ayer, to C. L. Stevenson and R. M. Hare develop the project of eliminating metaphysics from ethics (M&E 105/63). By the end of this process, ethics discards metaphysical concepts such as 'will', and psychological concepts such as 'moral feelings': 'It is pictured without any transcendent background' (M&E 105/63) and it does without moral psychology and philosophy of mind. Part of Murdoch's argument is that this apparently anti-metaphysical restriction is in fact a moral move, dictated by the Liberal preoccupation not to attach any given morality to the fabric of the world; hence, it is neither a logical nor a neutral philosophical move (M&E 108–110/65–6; VCM 57/97).[5] But my concern here is to bring to light the reasons why the philosophical/moral move that removes the mind from morality and morality from the world have pernicious consequences on the inquiry of morality.

Murdoch's claim in this respect is that the separation of ethics from any hypotheses about human nature, the mind and its workings, not only narrows the scope of philosophical inquiry to observable patterns of behavior, but it also deprives moral philosophers of the appropriate means for carrying on their investigation. This separation precludes the exploration of important moral phenomena, such as moral achievements and moral failures, moral differences and disagreements. To appreciate this aspect of Murdoch's critique of non-cognitivist views of moral language we need to place it in its context.

On close inspection, it appears that Murdoch's critique of the linguistic approach in 'Vision and Choice in Morality' is not meant to discard the analytic method, but to reclaim it and deploy it more radically. She thinks of language as a starting point for furthering our understanding of moral phenomena, in a way that is in fact quite compatible with, and inconceivable without, certain trends of philosophy of language that prevailed by the end of the fifties, thanks to Wittgenstein and J. L. Austin. Arguably, Austin's philosophy of language is more congenial to Murdoch's agenda than Wittgenstein's. According to Murdoch, non-cognitivists (such as R. M. Hare, A. J. Ayer, and Stuart Hampshire) mistakenly appropriate Wittgenstein's argument for the logical impossibility of private language in order to force the mind out of the proper domain of philosophical investigation (SG 12/308).[6] To avoid any metaphysical commitments, philosophers renounce any attempt to figure out the

---

[4] Murdoch explicitly refers to Stevenson's conception of moral language and attributes to him the view that reference to the mind is nothing but reference to 'observable actions and patterns of behaviour', M&E 103/61. The same criticism is formulated against Hare, see M&E 104–5/62–3.

[5] Murdoch's point is that this allegedly neutral position hides a moral (Liberal) conviction, see Cora Diamond, before '"We are Perpetually Moralists": Iris Murdoch, Fact and Value' [WPM], in Maria Antonaccio and W. Schweiker (eds.) *Iris Murdoch and the Search for Human Goodness*, (Chicago: University of Chicago Press, 1996), 79–109.

[6] She refers to Richard M. Hare *The Language of Morals* [LM], (Oxford: Oxford University Press, 1952).

mind, its workings and its relations to agency, and instead they merely present 'a relaxed picture of mediocre achievements' (SG 50/340). Ordinary language speaks of ordinary people and reveals ordinary conduct. Moral life becomes an outcast concept. By contrast, Murdoch suggests that we should ask: 'What is a good man like? How can we make ourselves better? *Can* we make ourselves better? These are questions the philosopher should try to answer' (SG 52/342). 'Ethics should not be merely an analysis of ordinary mediocre conduct, it should be a hypothesis about good conduct and about how this can be achieved' (SG 78/364, see also SG 45/335–6, 52–53/342–3).

Murdoch denounces the severe limitations of the linguistic approach to morality, but she does not set it aside. What she is opposing is a misuse of analysis, and one that embodies an objectionable philosophical agenda, namely, the analysis of moral language as reducible to the non-cognitivist formula: description plus evaluation, facts plus prescriptions.[7] Fear of metaphysics lures analytic philosophers into non-cognitivism, and as a consequence, they are at loss for words for describing important moral phenomena.

Murdoch's fierce attack on the non-cognitivist approach to ordinary moral language can be fully appreciated only in the light of a conception of language as revealing certain realities.[8] Precisely because there is an important link between moral language and moral phenomena, we need to use the analytic method in order to explore, that is, articulate, elucidate, explicate, and reconstruct, instead of reproducing what goes on at the surface of phenomena.[9] The task of reclaiming the words to account for moral phenomenology is never only descriptive; e.g. it does not consist of giving a full description or a comprehensive analysis of inner phenomena, but in offering plausible articulations and reconstructions of them, and thus in making new places for reflection. Because this process of reconstruction is inevitably normative and evaluative, Murdoch prefers to talk of 'explorations' rather than 'analysis'.[10] Explorations are not neutral (in ways in which analysis is purported to be) but normative and imaginative. That is,

---

[7] 'When we consider here the role of language in illuminating situations, how insufficient seems the notion of linguistic moral philosophy as the elaboration of the evaluative-descriptive formula', VCM 49/90.

[8] In fact, she is quite right that 'the emotive theory of ethics was not created as the result of a patient scrutiny of ethical propositions. It arose largely as the by-product of a theory of meaning whose most proper application was in other fields', M&E 102/61.

[9] On the nature of the analysis of ordinary language, see Hare's LM and Stanley Cavell, 'Must We Mean What We Say?', in Vere Chappell (ed.), *Ordinary Language*, (Englewood Cliffs: Prentice Hall, 1964), 75–112.

[10] 'I have argued that in so far as ethics sets out to be analysis rather than exploration it can attain only a precarious neutrality, like that of history, and not the pure neutrality of logic. This will also imply that ethics is in certain important respects discontinuous with the rest of philosophy ... Ethics surely is in fact, as it has always *mutatis mutandis* been, both exploration and analysis', VCM 58/98. To this, it should be added that on Murdoch's view descriptions and analyses of moral realities are inexhaustible, for reasons that will emerge in section 6. On this latter point, compare Stuart Hampshire, *Thought and Action* [TA], (London: Chatto and Windus, 1959), 21.

explorations require us to be perceptive of but also to force the bounds of ordinary language, and to be creative in order to be more discerning.[11]

These remarks remind one of a famous passage of J. L. Austin's 'A Plea for Excuses', where Austin remarks that proceeding from ordinary language involves examining *what we should say when,* and so why and what should mean by it'.[12] In this account of the linguistic approach, analysis has significant normative implications. For Austin, words are tools to be used, among other things, to gain awareness of realities:

When we examine what we should say when, what words should we use in what situation, we are looking again not *merely* at words (or 'meanings', whatever they may be) but also at the realities we use the words to talk about: we are using a sharpened awareness of the words to sharpen our perception of, though not as the final arbiter of, the phenomena.[13]

Ordinary language is, for Murdoch as for Austin, a starting point for the investigation of moral phenomena, but it is not the last word. It is to be studied carefully but finally overridden.[14] Since words help us sharpen our perception of realities, a loss of words is a loss of awareness;[15] hence, the necessity to come up with a new moral vocabulary, a novel array of metaphors and concepts, to acquire an understanding or deepen our awareness of moral phenomena.

Murdoch insists on the plurality of individual moral visions and urges philosophers to appreciate such variety and recognize that moral language relates to complex and various phenomena, sometimes inaccessible. However, her project must not be understood as a retrieval of metaphysics; to reclaim the language of moral psychology is not necessarily a metaphysical enterprise and does not make morality ineffable and mysterious.[16] The phenomena, which Murdoch endeavors to explore, are mundane and ordinary phenomena, yet the task of explicating and exploring them is not trivial. Phenomena such as moral progress and failure, however familiar, are difficult to examine; this is not because they belong in the mind, and the mind is hazy and unutterable, but because they are individual and concrete experiences (SG 23/317).

---

[11] 'Great philosophers coin new moral concepts and communicate new moral visions and modes of understanding', VCM 42/83.
[12] J. L. Austin, 'A Plea for Excuses' [PE], in *Philosophical Papers*, (Oxford, Clarendon Press, 1961, 1970, 1979), 175–204, at 181.
[13] Austin, PE 182. See also Hampshire, TA 11–25.
[14] As Austin eloquently puts it: 'It is necessary first to be careful with, but also brutal with, to torture, to fake and to override, ordinary language', Austin, PE 186.
[15] SG 34/326. Compare Austin, PE 182. Reference to ways of sharpening our perception of reality should not be taken to mean that for Austin sentences are used to report on facts either truly or falsely, see Alice Crary, 'The Happy Truth: J. L. Austin's *How to Do Things with Words*', *Inquiry* 45 (2002), 59–80. As it will appear as my argument proceeds, this is not Murdoch's claim either.
[16] As Murdoch notices, some continental philosophers carry out the exploration of the mind without any metaphysical pretensions, VCM 58/97–8. It could be misleading to characterize Murdoch's project to study moral life as a retrieval of a (realistic) metaphysics because reclaiming the concepts to account for the mind is not necessarily a metaphysical project, and does not necessarily imply any queer metaphysics; compare Maria Antonaccio, 'The Moral and Political Imagination of Iris Murdoch' [MPI], *Notizie di Politeia* 66 (2002), 22–50.

It is this feature of moral experience, its concreteness and individuality, which demands philosophical investigation, for which we must gain a richer moral vocabulary and rely on an understanding of ethical concepts different than the one suggested by non-cognitivism. We must, that is, reclaim the concepts necessary to account for moral thinking as a mental activity.

2 The locus of moral agency

A depleted moral vocabulary suits an impoverished conception of moral agency, which equates moral activity with an outward performance. Call this the 'behaviorist' model of agency. The merits of this model are apparent: it makes no suspicious reference to the elusive mind, it requires no queer metaphysical entities, and it coheres with a simple psychology. The simplicity of this minimalist model explains its fortune in some quarters. For Murdoch, instead, it is empirically mistaken, poorly defended, and morally objectionable. It is empirically mistaken because moral agents clearly do much more than performing, and they hardly regard themselves as mere executors of their actions; hence, the model is too poor to properly account for how people are.

As for the philosophical soundness of its basic tenets, the fundamental argument in support of the behaviorist model is that the 'inner' is parasitic on and subordinate to the 'outer': we know the inner via our knowledge of the outer. Mental events are reconstructed genetically, that is, via the events they have produced. Curiously, it is Wittgenstein's argument against private language that offers the grounds for defending the behaviorist model.[17] Wittgenstein holds that meaning is not a private operation of the mind, but it presupposes a complicated web of shared practices. According to Murdoch, this argument encourages the philosophical move that, by stressing our reliance on practices we share with others, banishes the mind from the domain of philosophical investigation. The mind is private and individual, hence mysterious and inaccessible. By contrast, the sphere of action is manifested and public, and thus actions become the sole object of moral appraisal and philosophical concern. By this route, mental life becomes a 'shadow of life in public', hence moral life is reduced to a public performance (SG 7/304).

Two metaphors are designed to represent the behaviorist view: the metaphor of choice and that of movement. Emphasis on choice is meant to capture the solitary moment of the decision. It tells us that to be an agent it takes only a giddy will. More importantly, the will is not a metaphysical concept any longer; it merely is its outward and public counterpart. The metaphor of movement tells us that actions are not different than any other event in the world: they are changes of some sort, which any observer can detect. Both metaphors suggest that moral activity must be public.

---

[17] As Murdoch clarifies, this was not the argument's intended effect, see SG 12/308. See also SG 11–3/ 307–9 and ff.

For Murdoch, actions are assigned this privileged status because of their *public* nature. This qualification is used in three different senses, which are worth distinguishing in order to identify the different polemical targets at which Murdoch aims. First, actions are public as opposed to *private* events in one's mind because they are accessible, manifest and outward performances, observable from the outside, like movements. Second, actions are public as opposed to *idiosyncratic*, in that their meaning is governed by rules, in virtue of a public symbolic system, against the background of shared practices, hence understandable to anyone. Third, actions are public as opposed to *individual*; unlike thoughts and imaginings, which are the mark of individuality, actions can be anybody's.

Murdoch traces a very complicated ancestry for this model of agency, which includes quite improbable suspects, such as Kant and Sartre. As Richard Moran forcefully argues, to understand Murdoch's originality we need to revisit her relation to Existentialism. In emphasizing important elements of continuity between the existentialist and Murdoch's account of agency, Moran insists on the account of moral change as a kind of re-orientation.[18] My purpose is to take up Moran's argument by reconsidering Murdoch's recurrent remark that the behaviorist model is Kantian in spirit (EPM 134, DPR 195, SG 48–50/338–40). I shall not offer a rejoinder to Murdoch's uncharitable claims about Kantian and Existentialist ethics.[19] Rather, what I want to emphasize is that Murdoch's critique of the kinds of misunderstanding, which she characterizes as 'the last dry distilment of Kant's view of the world' (SG 48), has a distinctive Hegelian flavor.[20]

In fact, Murdoch openly attacks Sartre because he remains Kantian, despite his promise of an examination of consciousness, a superficial display of a dramatic Hegelian psychology (M&E 102–103/61; EPM 132; HT 177; DPR 195). In refusing to investigate the historicity of individuals, Sartre disappointed Murdoch's Hegelian expectations: 'Our existence as historical entities and as members of society is quickly shuffled aside. Our "fundamental dilemma" is seen as that of a solitary being' (HMD 149; SBR 268). On her account, this is a failure to appreciate the complications of moral

---

[18] See Richard Moran, 'Iris Murdoch and Existentialism', this volume. SG 55–6/344–5, 78/364. Interestingly, Murdoch herself acknowledges Existentialism among the sources of the metaphor of vision, see VCM 46–7/87. But she has in mind Kierkegaard (rather than Sartre): 'It is Kierkegaard who most specifically . . . displays the transformation of an idealist philosophy into a phenomenology of individual moral struggle', VCM 47n5/87n†.

[19] Moran is right that Murdoch shows the verve of the polemist rather than the accuracy of the scholar, and often she offers no more than a caricature of Kant and Sartre. However, at least in the case of Kant, this caricature is enjoying a remarkable fortune in current debates, (quite surprisingly, given the recent outpouring of Kantian scholarship). I explore Murdoch's complex relation to Kant's conception of agency in my 'Respect and Loving Attention' [RLA], *Canadian Journal of Philosophy*, 33 (2003), 483–516.

[20] Textual evidence supports my claim that Murdoch thinks of the exploration of moral life as a Hegelian theme; see especially EPM 131–2. Murdoch complains that while Hegel 'contains possibly more truth than any other, is unread and unstudied here', and that the investigation of human consciousness is a subject which no longer exists in British philosophy (HMD 146; see also 148).

life, and in particular, its individual and historical nature, the fact that freedom is not the presumption of morality, but a piecemeal and everyday achievement.

If unfair when directed against Kantian and Existentialist ethics, these objections have legitimacy against the non-cognitivist 'quandary ethics', the view that the aim of ethical theory is to provide us with a decision procedure to resolve practical puzzles and disagreements.[21] Preoccupied with this sole normative task, non-cognitivism adopts a simplified account of moral language, and an impoverished account of agency, which prevents it from addressing the most important moral phenomena, such as difference, change, and progress. Murdoch's critique can be reformulated by saying that out of fear of metaphysics, non-cognitivism refrains from exploring the complexity of moral activity and fails to allow for mutual recognition.

3 The machinery of action and the bounds of deliberation

On the behaviorist model, actions are 'instances of moving things about in the public world' (SG 5/302). The metaphor of movement suits well a conception of moral activity that reduces moral agency to its executive aspect: doing things, bringing about something, and producing a visible change that can be tracked from the outside (SG 5–7/302–4, 12/308).[22] Being morally active is equivalent to plumping and performing.

This unflattering characterization is well deserved by non-cognitivists. Non-cognitivists like Hare are preoccupied to show that moral disagreements and conflicts are all amenable to rational resolution, and they aim to prove that actions could be rationally justified.[23] Their view is that ethics is practically relevant if it is action-guiding, capable of determining how we should act; hence, moral language is conveniently understood as primarily prescriptive or expressive. This sort of non-cognitivism does not allow for complications in the machinery of actions, and encourages a view of deliberation as a decision procedure. More importantly, 'decision' does not have any

---

[21] In VCM and M&E, the behaviorist model is said to characterize non-cognitivism; in SG the critique is extended to Existentialists. Interestingly, however, Murdoch often recognizes Sartre's superiority over non-cognivitists like C. Stevenson, see e.g. M&E 106/63–4. I borrow the qualification 'quandary ethics' from E. Pincoffs, 'Quandary Ethics', *Mind* 80 (1971), 552–71. This cursory characterization fits non-cognitivism and, in particular, R. M. Hare who thought of himself as a Kantian, see M&E 104–5/62–3.

[22] I take the term 'executive aspect' from Austin, PE 193.

[23] Ayer defends Emotivism on the ground that it can explain why moral disagreement resists rational resolution, see A. J. Ayer *Language, Truth, and Logic*, (London: Gollancz, 1936, 1946), chapter 6. However, later variations of non-cognitivism attempt to show that moral disagreements can be resolved via rational argumentation, although not all can, see C. L. Stevenson, *Ethics and Language* [EL] (New Haven Yale University Press, 1944), Stephen Toulmin, *An Examination of the Place of Reason in Ethics*, (Cambridge: University Press, 1950), and R. M. Hare, *Freedom and Reason* (Oxford: Clarendon Press, 1963). In particular, Hare argues that universal prescriptivism vindicates the rational basis of morality. He thinks that his theory has an advantage over Intuitionism and early Emotivism exactly because it allows us to resolve rationally most moral disagreements. The preoccupation to resolve moral conflicts rationally is crucial to Hare's philosophical investigation, especially in his later works, and remains an important feature of current versions of expressivism.

further 'inner structure; it *is* its outer structure' (SG 13/309). There is nothing behind and before a decision, except a public and universally accessible procedure, which issues action at a given moment. An agent who decides but does not act on her decision either is insincere or does not understand the logic of moral language (See SG 21/315–6).[24]

Contrary to this view, Murdoch insists on the importance of recognizing the continuity between the executive and non-executive aspects of moral activity, which include mental processes like thinking and rethinking, considering and reconsidering, imagining and theorizing, in a word: deliberating. In Murdoch's argument, the metaphor of vision is opposed to the metaphor of choice and movement, which characterizes the behaviorist model of agency. But this oppositional use of the metaphors is part of a polemical strategy. Murdoch never denies the moral significance of action, and more importantly, she is extremely careful in acknowledging the continuity between vision and choice, the deliberative and executive aspects of agency. In this respect, Murdoch's main point against the behaviorist model is that it does not recognize the continuity between vision and choice, it isolates the moment of choice from the process of moral thinking, and thus it dissociates the performance of actions from the inner workings of imagination, which precede and follows actions.

Even Hampshire's *Thought and Action*, whose principal aim is to relate moral philosophy to philosophy of mind, and thus seems a promising ally to Murdoch, does not escape this critique. He prefers the metaphor of movement to that of vision because he wants to separate the moment of perception from action. In his view, thoughts are relevant and different from daydreaming only to the extent that they issue in action.[25] Hence, being active means manipulating and handling; touch, rather than vision, is the sense with which we act.

Murdoch objects that for the sake of illustrating the nature of moral activity the metaphor of movement is misleading because it fails to recognize the continuity

[24] These remarks seem to be directed to Hampshire, TA and Hare, LM; Hare subsequently changed view about the stringency of these logical features of moral language.

[25] Murdoch's assessment of Hampshire might be seen as strikingly unfair, as Hampshire is attempting to restore the mind and its workings to their legitimate place in philosophical debate, and recognize dignity to ethics. Like Murdoch, he is sensitive to the inexhaustible descriptions of realities, and holds that the world is open to conceptual rearrangements; see Hampshire, TA especially pp. 21, 40. But on her view, he rejects a broad conception of moral activity, and he is mainly concerned with action as movement. Murdoch's reaction might be provoked by passages like the following: 'No sense can be given to the notion of a situation and a point of view, if the perceiver is not thought as a self-moving object among other objects', Hampshire, TA 41, see also TA 46–7. For Hampshire, the paradigm of activity is manipulation, and the object is defined by the range of manipulations, hence his predilection for the metaphor of touch rather than vision; see Hampshire, TA 48–9, 52. He is also very interested in separating the stage of perception from the stage of action: 'In handling and manipulating, we are not so much perceiving as acting. We often identify things as things of a certain kind by the particular pattern of action and reaction in our physical dealing with them ... Action and perception are in this way necessarily complementary and cannot be assimilated to each other', Hampshire, TA 52. However, the contrast with Murdoch's agenda is exaggerated, and in fact depends on a disagreement concerning the scope and bounds of deliberation, see e.g. Hampshire, TA 219–22. Compare SG 19/314.

between executive and non-executive aspects of agency, and it obscures the fact that a good choice depends on good evaluation and adequate perception of the situation (SG 54–56/344–5, 62/350, 66/353–4, DPR 199, 201). Moral failures are often the results of misperception, thoughtlessness, and lack of imagination, rather than failure in intelligence and planning (VCM 54–56/94–6. Compare Austin, PE 194). We choose in the right way because we have come to see the situation in the right way. Thus, there is an important continuity between appreciating, planning, resolving, and executing an action.

In an apparently similar fashion, Austin maps the many departments into which the business of doing actions is organized, and emphasizes that there is a crucial stage, too often overlooked, that takes place before the execution of an action, namely, the *appreciation* of the situation. At this stage, 'we are required to cast our intelligence into such a form, under such heads and with such weights attached, that our equally excellent principles can be brought to bear on it properly, in a way to yield a right answer' (Austin, PE 194). Unlike Hampshire, Austin recognizes appreciation as a stage that pertains to the machinery of action. It might seem that Murdoch's purpose is similar to Austin's, that is, directed to complicate the machinery of action, but in fact she makes a more radical claim.

Murdoch's point is not only that we should endorse a more complicated and sophisticated model of agency that recognizes appreciation as a stage in the machinery of action. By opposing the metaphors of choice and movement, she also means to emphasize that action is continuous with a process of deliberation that should be recognized as cognitive and conceptual (SG 90–91/374–5). Therefore, for Murdoch, to insist that there is continuity between the executive and non-executive aspects of agency is also to insist on the continuity between cognitive and affective aspects of agency. It is to argue that moral deliberation is a cognitive activity of understanding reality, hence not limited to what we do. The appreciation of a situation is not merely the stage that precedes and prepares to a good performance. In fact, sometimes we deliberate not in order to figure out what to do, but to understand better what we face. Murdoch's radical claim is that one can be morally active while entertaining a contemplative attitude, while doing nothing; or rather she argues that 'imagining is *doing*, it is a sort of personal exploring' (DPR 199. See also SG 19/314, 5/302–3).

This suggests that we should revisit not only the machinery of action, but also the conception of the bounds of deliberation. On the behaviorist model, the upshot of moral deliberation is an outward event. A thought that does not issue in action is unaccountable and inaccessible; we have no means to explore it. To the contrary, Murdoch argues that the upshot of moral deliberation might be a redescription of the situation, a new more accurate vision of it.

This case is vividly illustrated by the famous example of the mother-in-law, a sensitive and imaginative woman who resents her daughter-in-law for her lack of manners, but then she reflects on her hostility towards D, until gradually her vision of

D alters. This alteration can be accounted for in terms of the different descriptive accounts that M gives before and after deliberation. At first, she regarded D as unceremonious and tiresomely juvenile. Eventually M considers D as refreshingly simple and delightfully youthful. But the result of this alteration can be also accounted for in terms of the different attitudes that M entertains toward D: changing from hostility to loving attention, from jealousy to kind regard. The result of D's deliberation is not an action, but a redescription that comes with a novel attitude toward D.

The behaviorist model lacks the resources to account for this example of deliberation in which there is no outward alternation. M conducts herself properly before and after the change;[26] hence, her change escapes the behaviorist model. Such a model conceives of the scope of deliberation very narrowly, and neglects to investigate the role of emotions, attitudes, and redescriptions. For the behaviorist, the role of emotions and attitudes is mainly expressive and instrumental: at best, they are ancillary to deliberation, help us perform an action, and trigger our motivation—when they are not simply disturbances. Descriptions are neutral representations of publicly available facts, the given starting point of our deliberation about what to do. A different picture of deliberation, which includes emotions and descriptions within its bounds, suggests also a different conception of the loci and sources of values. In this alternative picture, attitudes and emotions are modes of valuing, and therefore not only expressive (as the non-cognitivist has it) but also, and more importantly, perceptive of value. Descriptions are representative but rarely neutral: they are rich modes of envisioning reality.

4 The loci and sources of value

Murdoch's project to dethrone the non-cognitivist view of deliberation is thus tantamount to deposing also its conception of value. The same philosophical attitude that expunges any reference to states of mind from the philosophical investigation of morality and reduces the moral life to silence also motivates the non-cognitivist view that value is a function of the will, which operates in an otherwise valueless world.[27]

Although there are more venerable and ancient sources for the metaphor of vision, in reviving this metaphor Murdoch carries forward G. E. Moore's legacy (VCM 46–47/86–87, 47n5/87n†). *The Sovereignty of Good* opens with the acknowledgement that 'Moore is as it were, the frame of the picture' (SG 3/300). In 'Against Dryness', she remarks that Moore 'reinstated the concept of experience' and 'directed attention away from the mechanics of action towards the inner life' (AD 290). It is, thus, to focus on moral life and internal experience that Murdoch appropriates the intuitionist

[26] 'In M's case, however, since there is no outward alteration of structure to correspond to the alleged inner change, no sequence of outer events of which the inner can claim to be shadows, it is dubious whether any sense can be given here to the Idea of "activity"', SG 21/316.

[27] This is also a Kantian thesis: 'Much modern philosophy (existentialist and analytical) follows Kant here: since value has clearly no place in the empirical world it must be given another kind of importance by being attached directly to the operation of the human will', DPR 195, see also SG 49–50/340–1, EPM 134.

metaphor of vision. Like Moore, she denies that value is a function of the will, and argues that one can be active while entertaining a contemplative attitude.[28] Like Moore, she considers 'good' the sovereign concept in morality rather than duty, obligation, or virtue. And like Moore, she thinks that good is indefinable, inexhaustible, and magnetic (SG 42/333).[29] But she treads these themes very differently from Moore, and the resulting picture is quite original.

Murdoch retrieves the intuitionist metaphor of vision in order to characterize the locus of value, but also its sources. In her view, descriptions are bearers of value, and their purpose is to represent reality. But representation is a rare moral achievement, a difficult reconstruction of reality. The moral exercise of describing reality is different from simply mirroring a reality that is before us. Rather, it is a constructive and hence normative task. To carry on this task, we have to use concepts and interpret. Interpretation is a kind of cognitive activity that goes on perpetually, and it constitutes the basic activity of moral thinking. It is the *constructive activity of imagination [that] "introduces" value into the world which we confront. We have already partly willed our world when we come to look at it; and we must admit moral responsibility for this fabricated world'* (DPR 201).[30] We actively participate in the normative reconstruction of reality; the exploration of reality is both an evaluative and cognitive activity.

Because of the metaphor of vision and the talk of reality, it is easier to locate Murdoch's disagreement with non-cognitivism than with realism. For the same reason, it is tempting to classify her view as realistic. In fact, her view is a genuine alternative both to moral realism and non-cognitivism, or so I will argue. The matter of contention ultimately concerns the nature of concepts.

Murdoch's argument against the non-cognitivist view of ethical concepts and moral thinking is straightforward. On the non-cognitivist view, moral thinking is logically independent of describing because ethical concepts are descriptively unanchored. There is no logical limit to what can be considered morally, and ethical concepts can be used by anybody with the same prescriptive or emotive meaning regardless of the substantive morality they hold. On this view, ethical concepts can be applied to just about anything; they can be laid as rings on any portion of reality, as Murdoch says. These claims are based on the assumption that ethical concepts can be decomposed into

---

[28] To fully appreciate this analogy with Moore, it would be worthwhile to consider Moore's exchange with Paton: H. J. Paton, 'The Alleged Independence of Goodness', in P. A. Schilpp (ed.), *The Philosophy of G. E. Moore*, (Evanston, Chicago: Northwestern University, 1942), 111–34, G. E. Moore, 'Replies to my Critics', in *The Philosophy of G. E. Moore*, 616–18.

[29] The term 'magnetic' is not Moore's, but Stevenson's. Stevenson speculated that the main idea of non-cognitivism was implicit in Moore's thinking: 'non-natural property should be taken as an invisible shadow cast by confusion on emotive meaning', Stevenson, EL 109. For Stevenson, the hypothesis of non-naturalness obscurely and confusedly alludes to what he calls 'magnetism': a feature of ethical judgment such that 'a person who recognizes X to be good must ipso facto acquire a stronger tendency to act in its favour than he otherwise would have had', Stevenson, EL 72.

[30] Compare SG 40/331–2. Imagination is understood as a mode of attention, hence not as a totally free creation. For an alternative interpretation of the relation between imagination and moral realism in Murdoch, see Sabina Lovibond, *Realism and Imagination in Ethics* (Oxford: Blackwell, 1983), sections 41–4, 46, 48.

cognitive and conative elements. To accept this presumption is to admit that it is always possible to master an ethical concept by isolating the cognitive content of this concept from the attitude attached to it.

Murdoch argues that this view of ethical concepts is mistaken, and it engenders a narrow conception of the scope of moral activity. In order to give justice to the idea that thinking and doing alike constitute moral activity, we need to conceive of concepts 'as deep moral configurations of the world, rather than as lines drawn round separable factual areas' (VCM 55/95, see also 54/94). On this alternative view of concepts, the distinction between value and fact cannot be characterized as a logical gap because 'then there will be no facts "behind them" for them to be erroneously defined in terms of' (VCM 55/95). The logical distinction between facts and values is spurious not because evaluating implies that we select certain facts as relevant and salient, but because we cannot describe without (at the same time) evaluating. Describing and evaluating are both conceptual and cognitive activities.

However, to reject the view that there is a logical gap between fact and value is not to deny that evaluating and describing are different activities. Rather than being logical, the relation between facts and values is what I shall call 'hermeneutic'. We see certain facts *as* significant; in evaluating, we interpret something as deserving attention and concern. The salience of some facts is not something we find already in the world, nor is it a function of our will, a matter of mere preference. By interpreting the facts, we attach some meaning, we make them normative, and thus through our conceptual and cognitive activity we transform them into values. This claim does not imply that our interpretations are *ex nihilo* creations of values. On the contrary, our imagination is exercised against the background of shared practices, and in virtue of a specific kind of sensibility. The role of imagination is to make us join reality, not to concoct one. Nonetheless, we do need to interpret reality, and our interpretations are normative reconstructions, that is, imaginative ways to see the world.[31] To insist on this element of interpretation is to emphasize that our seeing the world as it is is a *doing*, that is, something of our making, and for which we are responsible. Values are anchored to the world through the workings of our mind,[32] although they are not mere invertions. Thus, it would be misleading to admit of a normative reality before and independently of our moral thinking. For the same reason, as Murdoch explains, to hold that values are descriptively anchored is not to say that they are queer ontological entities:

On the alternative view I have suggested, facts and values merge in a quite innocuous way. There would, indeed, scarcely be an objection to saying that there were 'moral facts' in the sense of

---

[31] For a similar conception of value, and a similar attack on non-cognitivist views about the source of value, see David Wiggins, 'Truth, Invention, and the Meaning of Life' [TIML], in *Needs, Values, Truth* (Blackwell: London, 1987), 87–138.

[32] 'The value concepts are here patently tied on to the world, they are stretched as it were between the truth-seeking mind and the world, they are not moving about on their own as adjuncts of the personal will. The authority of morals is the authority of truth, that is of reality', SG 90/374.

moral interpretations of situations where the moral concept in question determines what the situation is, and if the concept is withdrawn we are not left with the same situation or the same facts. (VCM 54/94)

Contrary to non-cognitivism, then, Murdoch argues that moral language is representational and descriptive. This claim might seem sufficient to label her view as realistic. But then, she argues, representation and accurate description are not given: they are *achieved*. This is where Murdoch differs from standard versions of moral realism.[33] In its standard formulation, moral realism holds that moral properties are genuine properties in the sense that they are neither constituted by nor dependent on the availability of a characteristic human response. Contrary to standard moral realism, Murdoch holds that we are responsible for moral reality, which is partly dependent on our normative activity of exploration, interpretation, and reconstruction. Hence, the kind of realism that Murdoch elaborates is not the platonic kind of realism usually attributed to Moore. Nor is it the kind of dogmatic naturalism advocated by Philippa Foot.[34] For Murdoch there are no normative realities if we do not participate in their perception of them, and there is no interesting objective reality independently of the workings of our mind. Reality is not already normative before we enter the scene; rather, it is *made* normative through the operations of our mind, the constructive work of imagination, and the patient and humble exercise of attention.[35]

The search for truth is never a kind of 'tracking', as the standard realist claims. It is always a kind of participation, a rather difficult kind of participation which involves the mind.[36] We do not merely happen to encounter reality; we are responsible for this

[33] Moral realism is the view that there are moral facts or moral properties, which are real features of reality and independent of our mind. On a weak variation, moral realism is not committed to the view that moral properties are independent of our awareness of them. It is a matter of dispute whether weak moral realism is a self-standing form of realism and a genuine alternative to both standard realism and anti-realism; see Jonathan Dancy, 'Two Conceptions of Moral Realism', *Proceedings of the Aristotelian Society*, Supp. Vol. 60 (1986), 167–87, Carla Bagnoli, 'Moral Constructivism: A Phenomenological Argument' [MC], *Topoi* 21 (2002), 125–38. Therefore, I shall refer only to standard moral realism. If we use this standard formulation of moral realism, Moore is a realist but Murdoch is not: in her view, moral facts are genuine features of reality but they are not independent of the kind of mind, sensibility, and history evaluators have. Murdoch's insight about the nature of moral concepts is developed by John McDowell, 'Values and Secondary Qualities' [VSQ], in Ted Honderich (ed.), *Morality and Objectivity* (London: Routledge, 1985), 110–29.

[34] Compare Philippa Foot 'When is a Principle a Moral Principle?' *Proceedings of the Aristotelian Society*, Supplementary Volume 28 (1954), 95–110. On the qualifications of naturalism, see also Wiggins TIML 87–138, and John McDowell, 'Two Sorts of Naturalism' [TSN], in Rosalind Hursthouse, G. Lawrence, and Warren Quinn (eds.) *Virtues and Reasons* (Oxford, Clarendon, 1995), 149–79. On the differences between Murdoch's view and neo-Aristotelian forms of naturalism, see Elijah Millgram, 'Inhaltsreiche ethische Begriffe und die Unterscheidung zwischen Tatsachen und Werten', in C. Fehige and G. Meggle (eds.), *Zum moralischen Denken* (Frankfurt am Main: Suhrkamp, 1995), 354–88, and M. McLean, 'On Muffling Murdoch', *Ratio*, 13 (2000), 191–8.

[35] It seems to me that in order to capture this view about the need of meaningful normative interpretations, the metaphor of construction is more useful than the realist metaphor of discovery and the non-cognitivist metaphors of invention and creation; see Bagnoli MC.

[36] This remark applies to reality in general; see Murdoch, *Metaphysics as a Guide to Morals* [MGM], (London: Chatto & Windus, 1992).

encounter. We can fail at it, and we do fail quite often. But this failure is genuinely a moral *and* cognitive failure, different from a failure in copying, tracking, or reproducing an independent reality. In fact, Murdoch says explicitly that the realist notion of 'copying' is a category mistake (MGM 11). In the search for truth we are guided by an ideal. Referring to an ideal or original pattern does not amount to an imitation of the model itself or of some chosen instantiation (example) of it, but to

an inspired interpretation into the realm of practical life of a deep and certain moral insight. . . . *Imitatio Christi* does not work simply by suggesting that everyone should give away his money, or wondering how Christ should vote. The Demiurge (mythical creator) in Plato's *Timaeus* 'copying' the Forms (spiritual ideas) in order to create the world, interprets them into an entirely different medium. (MGM 11)

More than a 'creator', then, the Demiurge is a constructor.[37]

Murdoch's plea for metaphysics is thus not a plea for acknowledgment of an independent moral reality. It is, rather, an invitation to reclaim the concepts that neo-positivism expunged from our vocabulary. We only need the appropriate concepts to be morally guided; we do not need prefabricated moral properties for whose reality we bear no responsibility. The realist is right that some perceptions are more accurate than others and that reality is independent of ourselves. The realist is also right that in order to perceive reality correctly we should be aptly equipped. But that reality is independent of our *selves* does not mean that it is independent of our *minds*. Rather, it means that the effort to search for truth amounts to the effort to emancipate our minds from our selfish fantasies.

We are aptly equipped not because we are endowed with a faculty to detect an independent moral reality, but because we can rely on a good moral ideal and an adequate set of moral concepts. This is all the cognitive equipment we need for moral insight.[38] A corollary of this view is that being deprived of adequate moral concepts we are also deprived of moral insight. But it would be a mistake to evince that concepts are the mere instruments by which we detect an external reality. Concepts are not fixed and abstract entities, or rings that select portions of reality. Murdoch's point is that the necessity of these concepts can be forced on us by our own experience (MGM 415). In order to make our experience intelligible we formulate the need for adequate concepts. The need for concepts is thus perceived *simultaneously* with the urgency and

---

[37] I insist on the utility of the metaphor of 'construction', but I am not attributing to Murdoch any specific form of Constructivism. Interestingly, Antonaccio notices a similarity between Rawls' usage of 'devices of representation' and Murdoch's example of 'imaginative theorizing'. She writes: 'his use of such constructs is not entirely incompatible with the essentially figurative and metaphorical cast of metaphysics as Murdoch describes it', Antonaccio MPI 48 n5. Unfortunately, Antonaccio does not explore further this similarity as she is preoccupied with making Murdoch's liberalism compatible with her alleged Platonism. My claim is that it might have been a better interpretative strategy to question Murdoch's alleged Platonism.

[38] I have explored the analogy between this conception of objectivity and the one defended by Kantian constructivism in RLA.

depth of some experiences. Having experience requires that we articulate reality through the thickness of our concepts.

The chief experience in morality is the recognition of others and it is an experience of attention and suffering (MGM 415).[39] Through this experience, we learn what morality is about and we appreciate the need of moral concepts, e.g. the concept of good. Since this concept is urged on us by experience, it is already cognitively laden, contrary to what the non-cognitivist supposes. And yet to deploy the appropriate moral concepts is not merely a cognitive improvement consisting in making available a reality which is already there, as the standard realist claims. It is a moral effort.

The interpretation of Murdoch's meta-ethics which I am proposing is particularly useful regarding her late work MGM. One of the main philosophical endeavors of this complex and suggestive text is to look at individuals both from the political and the moral perspective. This is generally taken to be the dubious attempt at reconciling Platonism in morality with Liberalism in politics.[40] In my view, there is no incompatibility between the moral and the political strands of Murdoch's philosophy. Murdoch borrows from Plato the language and the metaphors for the exploration of moral life. But this is not enough to make her a Platonist in metaphysics, that is, a realist.

---

[39] In this passage, Murdoch refers to Wittgenstein's remarks on the concept of God: 'Life can educate one to believe in God. And experiences too are what bring this about; but I do not mean visions and other forms of sense experience which shows us "the existence of this being", but e.g. sufferings of various sorts. These neither show us God in the way a sense impression shows us an object, nor do they give rise to *conjectures* about him. Experiences, thoughts—life can force this concept on us', Wittgenstein, *Culture and Value* (Oxford: Blackwell, 1980), 85–6. Murdoch interprets the ontological proof as an argument from experience, and treats the necessity of the concept of God as the necessity of morality, See MGM Ch. 13. To the extent that respect is partly an experience of suffering, humiliation, and frustration, the argument from experience can be traced also back to Kant. For Murdoch the argument from experience establishes that through experiences of suffering we gain a certainty about the existence of God that is the subjective equivalence of its necessity (MGM 426). Analogously, for Kant the objectivity of morality is established by the fact of reason, that is by the subjective certainty felt under the guise of respect (Bagnoli, RLA). However, this claim can be understood more generally as a claim about conceptual norms. In this more general sense, it would be more fruitful and revealing to trace Murdoch's position back to Hegel (rather than to Plato or Kant), as I will argue in section 5. As a general claim about concepts, the view is that their authority is established through reciprocal recognition and that there is no distinction between the institution and administration of concepts. This view is Hegel's, see Robert Brandom, 'Some Pragmatist Themes in Hegel's Idealism. Negotiation and Administration in Hegel's of the Structure and Content of Conceptual Norms' [SPTHI], *European Journal of Philosophy*, 7 (1999).

[40] A perceptive reader of Murdoch such as Antonaccio writes: 'Murdoch's mature position was unique in that it sought to accommodate a liberal respect for the individual within the framework of an essentially Platonic metaphysics. As a Platonist, Murdoch urged liberalism toward a theory of personality that could take seriously the inner life of persons and the idea of transformation of consciousness; yet as a liberal, she refrained from seeking to impose on the individual any single notion of the good', Maria Antonaccio MPI 24. This reconciliation sounds like an improbable undertaking insofar as Murdoch has been led astray by Plato and is 'looking for unity where only a plurality is to be found', Stuart Hampshire, 'The Pleasures of Iris Murdoch', *New York Review of Books*, vol. 48 n. 18 (15 November 2001), 24. A similar worry is voiced by Alan Jacobs, 'The Liberal Neoplatonist?', *First Things*, 89 (January 1999), 58. Addressing this worry, Antonaccio argues that Jacobs and Hampshire appreciate a genuine problem but fail to see how Murdoch purports to solve it, namely, by appealing to J. S. Mill's classical Liberalism. My alternative suggestion is that this is not a genuine problem.

In fact, as I noticed above, she offers a non-standard interpretation of Platonic metaphysics in commenting on the workings of the Demiurge. This suggests that we should take carefully her allegiance to Plato: it is meant as a polemical way to set a philosophical agenda. From Plato she recuperates moral psychology, a topic which had been neglected because of the neo-positivist distrust of metaphysics. Hence, to this extent, to defend the possibility of moral psychology as a department of philosophy amounted to the possibility of making metaphysics a legitimate philosophical domain. But this does not amount to a defense of a realistic kind of metaphysics.

Contrary to the standard realist, for Murdoch there is nothing outside the picture which we make of reality that makes the picture normative. However, this is not to say that we are the source of such normativity; we do not create value from nothing, although we make a picture of the world anew. In this connection, it is important to notice how Murdoch's view of the fact/value distinction depends on her claims about the scope of deliberation. Her preoccupation is not to establish whether facts and values are distinct, but to investigate how the distinction came about by relating it to moral deliberation.[41] Realists and naturalists hold that facts and values are not logically separable, and thus, deliberation should take moral facts as starting points. Non-cognitivists claim that there is a logical gap between facts and values, and thus deliberation is a matter of deciding, given the facts at hand. The crucial question (and the matter of contention with realists, naturalists, and non-cognitivists) concerns the bounds of deliberation. In contrast to non-cognitivism, Murdoch holds that facts are impregnated with value. Rather than appealing to prefabricated moral facts (as realists and naturalists do), she argues that moral facts are of our own making, that is, the result of a piecemeal and pervasive activity of description and redescription. To acknowledge that we can be active while contemplating reality, by describing reality, is to make a claim about the scope of deliberation.

5 Individual moral visions

Murdoch deploys the metaphor of vision in a way that seems to lead to a rather idiosyncratic picture of morality. On her view, individuals may have radically different moral visions and use concepts in ways that are not transparent to others. Sometimes, if we do not share the same contexts, we fail to grasp each other's meaning. Hence, while Murdoch claims that understanding the moral life is a legitimate philosophical task, she also admits that understanding is not always possible. Indeed, there are cases in which understanding must be withheld,[42] and others where it is simply unachievable, and

---

[41] On the difference between Murdoch's argument for rejecting the fact/value dichotomy, and the arguments produced by analytical philosophers, see Diamond WPM. What I am suggesting in this section is compatible with Diamond's reconstruction of the dispute and it owes much to her fine analysis, but it is meant to direct us toward a different conclusion about the scope of deliberation.

[42] 'It is very well to say that one should always attempt a full understanding and a precise description, but to say that one can always be confident that one has understood seems plainly unrealistic. There are even moments when understanding *ought* to be withheld', VCM 50/90.

then concepts and attitudes such as hope and faith become appropriate (VCM 50/90). By allowing for these cases, Murdoch seems to concede that to account for moral disagreements in terms of differences in vision and insight might foreclose the possibility of resolving them rationally.

Non-cognitivism discards the intuitionist metaphor of vision out of dissatisfaction with Moore's failed attempt to capture the nature of moral judgments and ethical disagreements. The non-cognitivist formula, as e.g. Hare deploys it, might be seen (and certainly is proposed as) as having an advantage over the metaphor of vision in that it suggests that moral disagreements can be settled rationally, by facts-specifying arguments.[43] But facts-specifying arguments are successful only if people are not represented as picturing the world in different ways. Thus, if we agree with Murdoch that moral disagreements fundamentally depend on differences in visions, then we cannot make much use of facts-specifying arguments as non-cognitivists do. Moreover, it is not obvious what else we could do to prove that e.g. one vision is more accurate than another, to convince our interlocutor that she is misperceiving reality, or to expose her misperception. Which kinds of rational arguments can we offer to one another, aside from the protest that our interlocutor is morally blind? This question puts Moore in trouble, and it motivates non-cognitivists to provide an alternative account of moral disagreement.

Murdoch is aware that to insist on differences in vision suggests that moral disagreements are more radical and pervasive than non-cognitivism allows for, but she does not think that it posits a threat to rationality. Rather, her point is that we should rethink the structure and scope of moral rationality, and consequently the purposes of ethical theory. It is not much use to adopt a normative theory that succeeds in resolving moral disagreements only by abandoning any attempt at understanding their nature. Non-cognitivists conceive of moral disagreement as disagreement in the facts or in choices of values. Murdoch's point is not only that we differ in more radical ways than the non-cognitivist allows for, and that we have to accept with humility that there are some moral disagreements that we cannot overcome. More importantly, she wants to emphasize that failures of communication and failures in reaching agreement are common experiences, and ethical theory best serves its purposes when it makes us understand the nature and significance of these failures. In some cases, people might just agree to disagree, if the disagreement neither undermines any cooperative enterprise nor affects the nature of their personal relation. In other cases, the attempt to overcome disagreement is not legitimate; e.g. it seems wrong to suppress ethical disagreement about life styles that are different but morally permissible.[44]

---

[43] Murdoch addresses especially Hare when she attacks the oversimplification of moral disagreement that results from adopting the non-cognitivist formula. But I think the same can be said about Stevenson, EL.

[44] These remarks on the nature of moral conflicts are further argued and developed by Bernard Williams; see 'Conflicts of Values', in his *Moral Luck* (Cambridge: Cambridge University Press, 1981), 72, 81, and *Ethics and the Limits of Philosophy* [ELP] (Cambridge Mass.: Harvard University Press, 1985), 133 ff. Williams endorses also Murdoch's critique of the non-cognitivist treatment of disagreement (and the related view of

However, when resolving moral disagreement is a morally legitimate purpose, we can do more than offering facts-specifying arguments, as non-cognitivism suggests. I think this is an important yet neglected feature of Murdoch's account of ethical disagreement, which is related to her sophisticated understanding of moral language. Moral language is assertoric (rather than prescriptive or expressive) and, in virtue of this feature, it carries representations of reality, which are more or less appropriate and accurate (VCM 51/91–92).[45] We should conceive of our attempt to resolve moral disagreements as an attempt to reach a new understanding by restoring moral concepts (such as love, and hope) to our impoverished vocabulary, but also by stretching the usage of ethical concepts and extending our categories to new phenomena. By moving the boundaries of such categories, we become appreciative of new realities.[46]

This emphasis on the imaginative and creative usage of language points out that there are resources for treating disagreements, to which non-cognitivists cannot avail themselves. They can appeal only to facts-specifying arguments to rationally resolve disagreement. But the language of morals is neither only expressive and prescriptive nor only representational; it is also metaphorical and symbolic.[47] Ideals, stories, fables, and parables are part of morality and can be used as aids to talk about morality, and as instruments to frame disagreement and, possibly, to reach agreement.[48]

Therefore, the metaphor of vision (in virtue of the conception of moral language that it conveys) complicates the account of moral disagreement, but it also enriches the account of what we can and should do in order to overcome disagreements. It encourages us to conceive of morality as a multifaceted practice continuous with other cognitive activities, rather than as a special sector of reality, or a special domain of objects. Undertaking the task of seeing reality appropriately and *becoming* objective are the moral phenomena that call for philosophical investigation.[49]

concepts), see Williams, ELP 141; Williams acknowledges Murdoch's pioneering work on this subject, see Williams, ELP 218 n. 7.

[45] For this reason, this creative usage of language should not be confounded with propaganda or with Stevenson's persuasive definitions (although Stevenson claims that persuasive definitions are not irrational, but non-rational), compare Stevenson, EL.

[46] This kind of stretching the boundaries is not done at random or arbitrarily. Likewise, the imaginative usage of language is not completely free, and there are varieties of constraints. Hepburn, to whom Murdoch responds, insists on various limitations on the creative usage of language; see R. Hepburn, 'Vision and Choice in Morality', *Proceedings of the Aristotelian Society*, Supplementary Volume 30 (1956), 17–9. Murdoch also thinks that there are more or less accurate representations that fables and metaphors as well as visions can convey; this is why there is a path toward objectivity, which she recommends. This latter claim will be discussed in the next section.

[47] We invoke metaphorical descriptions not for lack of better ways to convey our representations, but because metaphors are the best ways to convey representations of the moral life. They are rich, flexible, and truthful forms of representation. See Murdoch, TL 39–40 and NP 47, 51.

[48] See Murdoch's comments to Hepburn on the role of fables, VCM 32–4 (mostly omitted from the reprint at E&M 76–7). Murdoch is careful to notice that the appeal to fables and metaphors does not constitute an alternative philosophical model of morality, but it urges us to reconsider the bounds of the moral.

[49] 'Moral philosophy is the examination of the most important of all human activities, and I think that two things are required of it. The examination should be realistic. Human nature, as opposed to the nature of

6 On becoming objective

Murdoch seeks to provide the means for reflecting upon the nature of a variety of moral phenomena. To this purpose, the metaphor of vision offers an important advantage over the metaphors of movement and choice: success, failure, and differences in choice can be explained in terms of vision but not vice versa (SG 45/336). In this section, I intend to show how the metaphor of vision is deployed to explore phenomena such as change and progress. These phenomena are crucial not only because they require the mind to be taken into account but because they necessitate a different view of moral concepts and suggest that we reconsider the configuration of the moral domain. To account for the life of the mind, we need concepts that can articulate and convey moral experience.

What is a moral change? Although a moral change is cognitive, it is not a change in beliefs; although it is affective, it is not a change of heart. Murdoch qualifies the change in moral vision as a change in mind, and this qualification is appropriate not only because such a change belongs in the mind of the agent, but because of some other features, which I am about to illustrate. Let us return to the example of the mother-in-law (M). M is described as imaginative and reflective. Her problem is that she is dissatisfied with D's undignified manners, but more importantly, she is dissatisfied with her own dissatisfaction. M conducts herself impeccably, so that no one can guess from outside her hostility. M's hostility is, in an important sense, a private reality, and M's own problem. Likewise, the deliberation she sustains and her final vision of D are peculiarly her own. The question is what kind of change M undergoes.

M's change is a change in mind, and not all alterations constitute a change in mind (SG 20/314–5).[50] M ends up regarding D as gay rather than bumptious, and refreshingly simple rather than unpolished. Her change is slow, gradual, and uneventful from the outside. It does not have anything momentous, dramatic, or radical, and in this sense, it is not akin to an epiphany or a conversion. M is depicted as a very decent person who always behaves properly. Her deliberation does not make her discover or recover a new value; thus, her change is not to be characterized as a switch of values.

Let's introduce some variations. If M discovers that D acts in an unpolished manner just in order to infuriate her, and at the end of her deliberation, M regards D as brash *and* naughty, this redescription would not count as a change in mind. A change in mind is not simply a revision of the facts one knows about the case, and it is not

---

other hypothetical spiritual beings, has certain discoverable attributes, and these should be suitably considered in any discussion of morality. Secondly, since an ethical system cannot but commend an ideal, it should commend a worthy ideal', SG 78/364. See also SG 45/335–6, 52/342. One should not expect Murdoch to offer a detailed account of moral ideal. Her picture of the moral ideal does not have a peculiar content just because morality is not a specific domain of objects, and because the list of virtues that we might be called to develop is open-ended, see SG 56–7/345–6, 101/383.

[50] Murdoch so characterizes it. As for delineating the contrast between change of mind, and change of heart, and change of beliefs, I profited from Annette Baier, 'Mind and Change in Mind', in *Postures of the Mind* (Minneapolis: University of Minnesota Press, 1985), 51–73.

issued by a supply of relevant information previously unavailable. In the original example, M is not simply acquiring new facts about D during her reconsideration of the situation, but she makes an effort to look at things differently, that is, justly and lovingly.

Alternatively, suppose that M confides in her friend and such friend manipulates her into believing that her hostility derives from unhealthy attachment to her son. M becomes very ashamed of herself, and shame replaces hostility. This is an alteration of M's mind, but it does not count as a change in mind because it is the result of manipulation, rather than the product of her own activity. Similarly, if M's son decided to divorce D, and suddenly D's manners stopped bothering M, this would not count as M's change of mind. What is interesting about M in the original example is that she performs a silent and private activity, which is neither necessitated by an external authority nor by the circumstances.

In this process of deliberation and change, M does not use new methods of reasoning. What makes M change her mind about D? She simply looks at D, attends to D, and focuses her attention. It is the quality of her imagination that makes her change in vision possible (SG 22/317). What goes on in M's mind is some thinking, more precisely, re-thinking, re-considering, conceiving differently, perceiving previously unnoticed features of the situation or looking at them afresh. Yet, this novel appreciation does not amount to simply acquiring new information or revising one's beliefs; nor can it be described as the application of a novel method of reasoning, which changes the problem before the agent's eyes. Rather, the change in mind occurs against a stable background of information and methods: it is a new resolution to an old problem.

By characterizing M's case as a change in mind, we gain an understanding of moral activity which is neither reducible to acting on the basis of true beliefs nor acting out of an appropriate desire. This moral activity is at the same time a cognitive and affective activity, and therefore cannot be fruitfully analyzed according to the non-cognitivist formula.[51] But why is it a *moral* activity? Why should we characterize M's change in mind as a moral change? To answer these questions, it is not enough to exploit M's characteristics of being reflective and imaginative; we also need an account of the obstacles she is fighting and of the nature of her achievement.

The upshot of M's activity is not simply a change in her beliefs about D; she also achieves a just and loving attitude toward D, that is, a focused and objective perception of how D really is. This achievement is nothing like mirroring things as they are independently of our minds, as the realist has it. Nor is it like producing value independently of reality, by an act of will, as the non-cognitivist thinks. The new vision, prompted by reflection, is accurate and loving, clear and just.

---

[51] For the same reason the desire/belief model is inappropriate; see McDowell, TSN.

We should say that before her change in mind, M's vision of D was obfuscated, and her judgment was clouded or that she did not see the situation clearly. Failures to conduct a proper appreciation of the situation are due to selfish fantasies, tired habits and practices, philistine rules, apathy, lack of imagination, thoughtlessness, carelessness, obliviousness, and inconsiderateness (Cf. Austin, EP 194).[52] Murdoch's conviction is that these failures are rooted in a natural tendency to be distracted from reality by our selfishness. By nature, we are selfish and egocentric, and thus it takes us an effort to acquire an unselfish regard of others. This is the source of the hindrances to morality: 'the enemy in morality is personal fantasy: the tissue of self-aggrandizing and consoling wishes and dreams which prevents one from seeing what is there outside one' (SG 59/ 347–8).[53] While fantasy is the instrument for escaping the world, we use imagination to join it. Imagination is a mode of attention; we focus our attention on others when we look away from ourselves.[54]

In this picture, attention is both the instrument and the outcome of this moral growth. It is the instrument because we grow by paying attention to reality: we grow by looking. In this sense, attention is the continuous and sustained effort of counter-acting the products of egocentric and selfish fantasies. But focused attention is also the kind of attitude of which we are capable when the illusions of the self have vanished. In this second sense, attention is the moral achievement, a loving regard, and a humble and compassionate form of discernment, the imaginative recognition of and respect for otherness.[55]

Murdoch's account of this moral achievement and of its pursuit bears a striking resemblance to Kant's account of respect. On Kant's view, respect is the moral feeling that emerges from the contemplation of the moral law. It thwarts and checks our desires, strikes down our arrogance, and confines our self-love within the bounds of the acknowledgement of other people's claims. By screening our desires, respect elicits a painful feeling of humiliation, and points at the frailty of our will. But in mastering the force of natural desires, and constraining the maxims, respect is also the inspiring awareness of the strength of rational will.[56] Murdoch thinks of the experience of morality as a struggle, which starts with a Kantian conception of the hindrances to

---

[52]   Interestingly, Austin draws a very similar list of failures when he accounts for the stage of appreciation of the situation, but Murdoch tracks these failures down to some natural propensities we have.

[53]   'We are anxiety-ridden animals. Our minds are continually active, fabricating an anxious, usually self-preoccupied, often falsifying *veil* which partially conceals the world', SG 84/369. These claims might be taken as an indication of Murdoch's interest in Freud rather than Kant. This would be a topic worth investigating, which unfortunately I cannot pursue. In this respect, it should be interesting to explore Murdoch's relation to John Wisdom. On the feature of restlessness of the mind, see SG 78/364, and compare Jonathan Lear, 'Restlessness, Phantasy, and the Concept of the Mind', in his *Open Minded*, (Cambridge Mass.: Harvard University Press, 1998), 80–122.

[54]   'The exercise of overcoming one's self' is equated to 'the expulsion of fantasy', see S&G 216; and cf. SG 90/374.

[55]   'Love is this imaginative recognition of, that is respect for, this otherness', DPR 216.

[56]   Kant, *Critique of Practical Reason*, transl. and ed. M. Gregor, (Cambridge: Cambridge University Press, 1997 [1788]) Akademie edn. V 78. Compare SG 39–40/330–32, DPR 216.

morality (our selfish natural dispositions), and accepts a Kantian conception of the achievement (a self-less regard for others).[57] Respect for others is shown in the way we conquer our selfish tendencies. Murdoch herself acknowledges that her conception of attention 'is very like *Achtung*' (E&M 216). Murdoch quite perceptively regards the undertaking of the moral ideal as the 'endless aspiration to perfection which is characteristic of moral activity', which is both humbling and thrilling (SG 31/324).[58]

Despite this profoundly Kantian picture of the experience of morality, Murdoch argues that the Kantian framework is ultimately inadequate to account for moral phenomenology: 'The crucial step towards the phenomenological viewpoint is made when we leave Kant and turn to Hegel' (NM 102).[59] That is, the project of exploring the subjective experience of morality cannot be fully carried on with Kantian means. The thrust of the argument is, in my view, that Kant's characterization of the struggle is static: like Sisyphus, the agent fights the same selfish inclinations and thoughts all over again. The agent's history has no impact on the nature and significance of such obstacles to the moral ascent. Because of our natural, hence inextirpable, propensity to evil, the effort to undertake morality as a driving ideal must always be renewed, and it is hardly cumulative: 'virtue is always in progress and yet always a beginning from the beginning' (Kant, MPV 409).[60]

Murdoch, too, thinks that undertaking the moral ideal of purity of thought (in which virtue consists) is an endless task. But unlike Kant, she does not think that it is endless because we have a natural and inextirpable propensity to evil, but because we are living individuals, who fail and progress over time, thereby displaying their history. Murdoch's claim is that an adequate account of the moral pursuit requires that change, failure, and progress be explained from within the life of the person. The resources for this developmental conception of agency cannot be found in Kant, however, because on his view agents have no history, their effort is at any moment in time solitary and radical. This feature of Kant's account of moral change prevents one from understanding progress.

For the sake of the argument, I shall take these criticisms for granted, and instead of offering a rejoinder to them, I shall try to explain how they shape Murdoch's own

---

[57] This is at odds with some readings of Murdoch, see e.g. Laurence Blum, 'Iris Murdoch and the Domain of the Moral' [IMDM], *Philosophical Studies* 50 (1986) 343–67, and Laurence Blum, 'Moral Perception and Particularity' [MPP], *Ethics* 101 (1991), 701–25. But for an argument that establishes an important similarity between Murdoch's attention and Kant's respect, see David Velleman, 'Love as a Moral Emotion' [LME], *Ethics,* 109 (1999), 338–74, and Bagnoli, RLA. Against this Kantian reading, see Elijah Millgram, 'Kantian Crystallization', *Ethics* 114 (2004) 511–3.

[58] Murdoch often blames contemporary ethical theorists for having forgotten their role in proposing worthy ideals, see SG 78/364. See also SG 45/335–6, 52/342.

[59] Throughout this paper, I used 'moral phenomenology' as equivalent to the subjective experience of morality. This is in accord with the understanding of phenomenology that Murdoch attributes to Hegel, see NM 103. Murdoch also uses (rather disparagingly) another definition of 'phenomenological', which refers to the literary style exemplified in the 'phenomenological novels' of Sartre, Camus, and Beauvoir, see NM.

[60] Kant, *Metaphysical Principles of Virtue* [MPV] (pt. II of *The Metaphysics of Morals,* 1797), in I. Kant, *Ethical Philosophy,* transl. J. W. Ellington (Indianapolis, Hackett, 1983), Akademie edn. VI 409.

project. To this purpose, I shall focus on another metaphor, which Murdoch devises in order to highlight the contrast with the behaviorist model of agency: that of 'the fabric of being' (SG 22/316). This metaphor makes us appreciate that our thoughts display a sense of direction, which are indicative of the kind of persons we are. This is not to say that such direction is consciously endorsed; on the contrary, Murdoch insists that this direction is not always under our control, it is not always captured by our conscious mind, and it can be obscure to us (NP 48–49, 52). This does mean that such phenomena are not intelligible, but that they have 'a life of their own' (NP 48), and that we should search for their intelligibility.

By placing weight solely on the executive aspect of agency, the behaviorist model represents agents as mere strings of overt choices (VCM 39/80). There is no need for anything more complicated because there is no continuity between action and other cognitive activities such as theorizing, thinking, and imagining. On Murdoch's account, the Kantian model makes choices similarly radical and non-cumulative because of the assumption about our natural propensity to evil.[61] The agent's thoughts and her actions are not seen as forming a continuous fabric of being; rather 'personality dwindles at the point of pure will' (SG 16/311, 22/316–7). But what makes us individuals, separate and distinct from one another, is our distinctive fabric of character, the peculiar way in which our actions are linked to traits, thoughts, and cognitive activities; so Murdoch argues.[62] Failure to account for character is tantamount to failure to accommodate differences among individuals. By misidentifying the locus of agency with the executive stage of action, the behaviorist model reduces individual personalities to discrete acts of will.[63] Thus, the behaviorist model of agency fails to support mutual recognition and prevents us from relating to others as individuals.[64]

[61] 'It is always in progress because, considered objectively, it is an ideal which is unobtainable, while yet our duty is constantly to approximate it. That is always beginning anew has a subjective basis in human nature, which is affected by inclinations under whose influence virtue can never settle down in peace and quiet, with the maxims adopted once and for all—unless it is climbing, it inevitably sinks', Kant, MPV VI 409.

[62] Williams makes a similar objection to Kant, see especially in 'Persons, Character and Morality', in Moral Luck (Cambridge: Cambridge University Press, 1981), 5, 14. Likewise, Frankfurt remarks: 'The pure will has no individuality whatsoever', Harry Frankfurt, The Importance of What We Care About (Cambridge: Cambridge University Press, 1988), 129–41, 132. This objection is based not only on a mischaracterization, of Kant's conception of agency and freedom, but also on a misunderstanding of the relation between phenomenal and intelligible character. For an illuminating account of the complications that arise from the relation between intelligible and phenomenal character, see Henry Allison, Kant's Theory of Freedom [KTF] (Cambridge, Cambridge University Press, 1990) 32–3, Karl Ameriks, 'The Hegelian Critique of Kantian Morality', in B. den Ouden and M. Moen (eds.), New Essays on Kant (New York: Peter Lang, 1987) 155–78.

[63] On this interpretation, Kant's act of will is equated to Sartre's decision. Murdoch attacks Sartre insofar as he holds a Kantian conception of agency and freedom, see EPM 133–6. For a forceful reply on Sartre's behalf, see Moran, 'Iris Murdoch and Existentialism', this volume.

[64] In the same vein, Murdoch thinks that Kant's conception of respect fails to appropriately express mutual recognition because it is directed to a wholly abstract feature of humanity, that is, to the rationality in our breast. 'Kant does not tell us to respect whole particular tangled-up individuals, but to respect the universal reason in their breasts. In so far as we are rational and moral we are all the same, and in some mysterious sense

Crucial to her alternative account of agency is that not only do we have individual visions of reality, but also, and more importantly, individual visions are intelligible in the context of the progressive life of a person. What I intend to emphasize is not the potential idiosyncrasy of individual visions, but their constituting the fabric of moral life, by providing narratives which display a sense of direction, and show a kind of agential unity or integrity.[65] The task of undertaking morality as a subjective motive is an endless challenge because we have incessantly to construct and re-construct, shape and modify the narratives of our lives by re-orienting ourselves, and attentively re-describing and re-adjusting to reality. The struggle is endless not so much because we are imperfect as because we are live individuals.

According to Murdoch, what is distinctive of live individuals is that they perpetually engage in the activity of reassessing, redefining, and redescribing reality. This checking procedure is pervasive and continuous; and it is a function of individual history. This does not mean that M's progress is intelligible only to M herself, but that her change in vision does not mark her final and ultimate accomplishment. The story does not end there because M is in an ongoing relation with D, and her visions of D will continue to change and deepen. This continuous and pervasive changing of visions is characteristic of a live individual, a living being with a personality, dealing with other individuals.

Our descriptions of the situation change over time and display a sense of direction because our moral concepts change and deepen. On this point, Murdoch borrows from Hegel (rather than from Plato or from Kant).[66] According to Hegel, we do not merely select and apply fully formed, static, and fixed concepts. Concepts alter and develop as we use them. The use of concepts does not simply amount to their reiteration in different contexts. Conceptual content is formed in the process of applying concepts. Their content derives from the role they play in articulating experience and thus is progressively determined over time. This means that concepts have a history; they grow as living beings. For example, the conception of love one had at twenty is different than that we have at forty. But the former concept is not simply different than the latter, rather, they stand in a more intimate relation, the latter is deeper and more complicated than the former. At twenty, we have (not just a different)

---

transcend history', S&G 215, see also S&G 214. This objection echoes Hegel's critique of Kant's categorical imperative, but it emphasizes the issue of mutual recognition. For a reply, see Allison, KTF, Velleman, LME 367, Bagnoli, RLA.

[65] I use the term 'integrity' to indicate a kind of agential unity which displays a sense of direction over time, which qualifies as an individual story. This seems to me necessary to capture Murdoch's idea of progress as something that must be accounted from within the progressive life of a person.

[66] As Murdoch remarks: 'What Hegel teaches us is that we should attempt to describe phenomena.... What we are all working upon, it might be said, is le monde vécu, the lived world, what is actually experienced, thought of as itself being the real, and carrying its own truth criteria with it - and not as being the reflection or mental shadow of some other separate mode of being which lies behind it in static parallel.... To sum things up in a rather shocking way: as far as method goes, we are all Hegelians nowadays. But the spectre which haunts us is Kant', EPM 131–2. In many respects, Murdoch appropriates in a most fruitful way the Hegelian critique of Kant. I owe this interpretation of the Hegelian critique of Kant's theory of conceptual norms to Brandom SPTHI.

but a more abstract and empty concept of love than we have at forty. Life teaches us what love is, in concrete. This is not because at forty one has loved more, so to speak. The change in concepts does not occur merely because an abstract concept has been instantiated so many times. Rather, change occurs in virtue of the intimate relation that the abstract concept stands to its embodiments. Abstract and empty universals are enriched, and therefore changed, by their embodiments, that is, by the ways in which they are expressed and manifested. On this picture, moral concepts are concrete universals.[67]

This view of concepts is particularly suitable to Murdoch's philosophical projects of restoring the mind as a legitimate philosophical subject. To succeed in this project, one must not only reclaim the neglected concepts (such as love or attention), but also propose an adequate view of them. They are not neutral and static items to be selected at a whim and then applied in contexts, combined with whatever moral beliefs.[68] They change and develop in content as they are used for articulating our experience and lived by. They exhibit both authority and history. As it appears, this is not a view that can be easily classified as realistic or anti-realistic. In fact, I surmise, it is a view which supersedes the standard distinction between realism and anti-realism. The philosophical issue about moral concepts is not whether they do or do not describe a portion of reality. The issue is how they grow.

The process through which moral concepts acquire concreteness is slow and has a direction. It's not merely a temporal process; it's an historical pattern. The direction is given by the progressive life of a person. The process of progressive enrichment consists of continuous attempts to refocus one's attention, reorient and reposition oneself. Murdoch describes this process as incrementally thickening, complicating, deepening, and adding content to our concepts, and therefore, to our descriptions. The more concrete the concept becomes, the less our vision of things is empty and abstract.[69] Murdoch's recurrent remarks that we grow by looking, we learn by attending at objects in contexts, and her insistence on the varieties of visions have been interpreted as an endorsement of particularism.[70] Contrary to many, I doubt that the thesis that moral concepts are concrete universals supports particularism, however. Particularism claims that universal moral principles are dispensable in accounting both for moral

---

[67] This is Murdoch's own expression. Reference to Hegel is particularly illuminating here because the notion of concrete universals is introduced in order to account for a peculiarity of live beings. Likewise, Hegel's treatment of abstract universals privileges two models of embodiments: the pair thought/manifestation or expression, and the pair life/individual organism. See Charles Taylor, *Hegel* (Cambridge: Cambridge University Press, 1975), 112–13, 116.

[68] Recall that this is the view of concepts which Murdoch attributes to Hare, and more generally to non-cognitivism. Interestingly, this is also the view that Hegel attributes to Kant, see Brandom SPTHI.

[69] 'Private' should be understood as equivalent to 'individual', 'particular' and 'concrete'. Hegel also uses the notion of concrete both in reference to the particular (*das Besondere*) and the individual (*das Einzelne*). See Taylor, *Hegel* 112–13.

[70] See e.g. Blum IMDM and MPP, and Millgram, 'Murdoch, Practical Reasoning, and Particularism', *Notizie di Politeia* 18, 66 (2002), 64–87.

knowledge and moral reasons: such principles are epistemologically inert or simply unavailable. These claims do not follow from Murdoch's conception of concrete universals, and are not the core of her view.

The relevant progress that Murdoch underscores is not from universality to particularity, but from abstraction toward concreteness. Her suggestion is not that we should drop universals for particulars, but that we have to treat our moral concepts as concrete universals, and this requires us to pay attention to the slow historical process of learning through which we make them concrete. Moral concepts must become concrete, but they also must be deployed as universals. To say that the deployment of universals is concrete is to say that we express and manifest something particular with them. This claim is certainly radical, and rich in consequences, but such consequences are not the ones particularists have in mind.

Murdoch agrees with the particularist that we should not think of moral deliberation as a mechanical application of rules, but so might the universalist.[71] For to claim that moral reasons are universal is not to suggest that deliberation should be thought of as a deduction from a universal principle, or that moral reasons are decided by an algorithm. Reasons are designed to address ourselves as well as others in the practice of offering some considerations that count in favor for something; but in order to perform this role, they do not need to be either rule-bound or stable in a complete set of specifiable universal rules. The universalist might agree that moral reasons are not rule-bound in the sense that they do not involve the application of a general formal principle to a particular content. But she might still hold that universal principles govern the justification of moral reasons (and whether this successfully yields moral reasons is a separate issue).[72] That moral reasons are not generated by the application of an algorithm does not imply that they are not universal, intelligible as reasons, and even shareable by others. Therefore, the universalist may find unproblematic the claim that there is no codifiability in ethics.

One can certainly find in Murdoch's essays valuable resources for appreciating the role of rules in moral education, but they represent no challenge to the universalist. Rules provide guidelines for our uncertainty, and they could be superseded in moral maturity or may prove useless in trying and novel moral predicaments. The mature as well as the perplexed agent facing an unprecedented quandary rely on judgment, rather than on rules. Making a judgment is certainly a much more complicated practice than applying a rule. Quite perceptively, Murdoch insists that if our moral understanding

---

[71] In fact, the doctrine of concrete universals may well be treated as the development of Kant's insight about aesthetic judgment, which is not rule-bound in the sense that it does not involve the application of a general formal principle to a particular content, see Terry Pinkard, 'Virtues, Morality, and *Sittlichkeit*: From Maxims to Practices', *European Journal of Philosophy* 7 (1999).

[72] On the difference between rules and principles, rule-bound practices and principled justification, see Barbara Herman, *The Practice of Moral Judgment* (Cambridge: Harvard University Press, 1993). Rawls also explains that the Categorical Imperative procedure should not be regarded as a decision procedure, but rather as a device of self-representation, which indirectly selects ends for our will; see John Rawls, *Lectures on the History of Moral Philosophy* (Cambridge Mass.: Harvard University Press, 2000), 212–14, 240–52.

does not involve anything like applying a rule, the process of learning to deepen one's understanding has to be much less conscious, quick, and easy than one might have hoped. When rules have become tired practices and thoughtless habits, they can even be obstacles to our moral understanding. This notwithstanding, rules are essential to the proper functioning of moral thinking: they constitute its indispensable background.

The consequences of this view are nonetheless radical. First, it greatly emphasizes the importance of learning over time, through cumulative experience. In order to learn a moral concept, we need to learn first as an abstract and empty universal, and then over time, and through acts of attention, it becomes a concrete and personal tool for us to reconstruct and discern reality. Second, this account puts in question the assumption that to be objective is to represent the world impersonally (SG 43–45/334–6). The claim that reality is totally independent of the workings of our mind relies on a model of objectivity which is borrowed from science, and proves inadequate in ethics (SG 27/320–21).[73] Alternatively, we ought to approach reality and objectivity as tasks, which we attempt to achieve over time through our imaginative exercise of focusing attention.

As M's example shows, there are focused and unfocused visions, clouded and unclouded judgments. On Murdoch's view, moral progress is characterized by incremental unity. The many virtues one displays on particular occasions ought to be reciprocally related to compose a unified picture. Unity is, again, a moral achievement, which is afforded by a slow and piecemeal, continuous and pervasive activity. Unity is not the structural feature of our moral agency, but the mark of moral excellence.

Murdoch's reflections on unity must not be understood as an invitation to elaborate a unified and hierarchical system of principles or of virtues. On the contrary, she often urges that moral philosophy should pay attention to and account for the 'unsystematic and inexhaustible variety of the world', and she claims that it is 'impossible to foresee and limit the ways virtue is required of us' (SG 100/382, 103–104/384–5). As the moral agent should be able to see the falsity of some vacuous pictures of unity, and should not succumb to the illusions of her self, the patient moral philosopher must not yield to the temptation to produce an empty and sterile ethical system. Morality is not the exclusive prerogative of experts, but rather the humble and constant effort of ordinary people who try to make sense of themselves and of their relation to others (SG 101/383).

7 Concluding remarks

My argument has been that Murdoch's main and not yet fully acknowledged contribution to moral philosophy is to reclaim the theoretical and cognitive resources to account for the subjective experience of morality, a topic that had become outcast with

---

[73] To this extent, John McDowell bears Murdoch's legacy; see McDowell, VSQ, McDowell TSN. Compare also Wiggins, TIML.

logical positivism. Her philosophical project is to provide a conception of moral concepts that is adequate for exploring the moral life of individuals. While this project is not a retrieval of metaphysics, it requires a sophisticated sort of moral psychology capable of addressing not only phenomena such as episodic changes of beliefs or changes of heart, but also the progressive change in view, which characterizes the moral life of an individual. In proposing this agenda for moral philosophy, Murdoch perceptively points to a serious weakness in contemporary ethics, namely, the lack of a developmental conception of agency. The recovery of moral life to philosophical investigation is a Hegelian theme.[74] In offering the rudiments of a developmental account of agency, Murdoch shows appreciation of Hegel's conception of concrete universals and insists on the importance of recognizing the historical dimension of agency. This historical dimension is, for Murdoch, confined within the bounds of individuals; it concerns exclusively the mind of the person. To this extent, she does not fully exploit Hegel's main insight, which is that of relating the progressive life of a person to the communal life within the slow development of institutions, through mechanisms of mutual recognition.[75] Murdoch does not care much for investigating the institutional landscape within which the moral life takes place. Insofar as she refrains from inquiring into the background institutions and practices that allow the agent to focus and refocus her attention, and therefore to achieve objectivity, her picture of morality remains essentially Kantian—it is private as opposed to communal.

One may legitimately doubt that one could articulate a developmental conception of agency without taking into account how agency is affected, promoted, or prevented by the detail and the history of social institutions. To this extent, however inspiring, Murdoch's project remains incomplete, and we are still in need of a fully articulated developmental conception of agency. But this must not necessarily be perceived as a failure. Perhaps, her view is that philosophy cannot attain the completion of this project. The narrative of individuals is the domain of literature rather than philosophy. As philosophers, we should regard ourselves content if we have made new places for fruitful reflection, and Murdoch has certainly done so by setting for us the task of exploring the moral life.

---

[74] Murdoch EPM 131–32.
[75] See Brandom SPTHI.

6

Iris Murdoch and the Prospects for Critical Moral Perception*

Bridget Clarke

Thank God there are some people in America today who can rise above their environment, above their community, above the backward opinions of their parents, above the teaching they've been brought up under—and stand up for what is right. . . . [T]wenty-five years from now men will look back and laugh, even at segregation.—Martin Luther King Jr., February 28, 1956.[1]

1. By any account worth considering, a virtuous agent must be someone who can regard the moral status quo with a critical eye and, where appropriate, part ways with it. We expect her to be able to see, in the relevant circumstances, that 'separate' really *isn't* 'equal' or that women really *ought* to have the vote. But what is required for her to be able to assume this kind of critical stance? One might think that the only recourse for the agent is an appeal to principles that are independent of her society's moral norms. In other words, one might think that an agent must step outside of existing norms if she is to stand in a critical relationship to those norms. And then it seems that only principles that are completely independent of existing moral practices would enable her to do this.

This line of thought has led some philosophers to criticize virtue ethics for the way that it substitutes the *virtuous person* for *moral principles* as the ultimate moral standard.[2] According to this criticism, insofar as correct conduct is defined with reference to what

* Many people have helped me to write this paper. I am very grateful to Donald Ainslie, Maria Antonaccio, Justin Broackes, Paul Muench, Martha Nussbaum, and an anonymous editor from Oxford University Press for timely and incisive comments. John McDowell, Jennifer Whiting, and Iris Young made valuable suggestions on earlier drafts. Stephen Engstrom directed the dissertation from which this essay originates and has lit the way from beginning to end.

[1] Quoted in J. Bass, *Unlikely Heroes* (New York: Simon and Schuster, 1981), 65.

[2] R. Louden, 'On Some Vices of Virtue Ethics', in R. Crisp and M. Slote (eds.), *Virtue Ethics* (Oxford: Oxford University Press, 1997), ch. 10. Louden is thinking specifically of Aristotle's conception of the virtuous person as 'the standard and measure' of the good (see, e.g. *Nicomachean Ethics* 1113a33; 1170a21; 1176a16–18). For some caveats about the term 'virtue ethics' see M. Nussbaum, 'Virtue Ethics: A Misleading Category?' *The Journal of Ethics* 3 (1999): 163–201.

the virtuous person would do rather than with reference to an antecedently established set of principles, the virtuous person has no resources that would allow her to call her society's norms into question. This problem for virtue ethics is exacerbated if one ties the achievement of virtue closely to *upbringing* or *habituation*, for upbringing and habituation seem to be irreducibly linked to the existing social norms.

The problem is how the virtuous person can constitute the normative standard and yet at the same time take a critical perspective on her *own* views. For if virtue depends on upbringing, any tools she might bring to this task have been acquired through an education already governed by the very norms at issue. It thus looks as if there is nothing that would allow the virtuous agent to interrogate her own views other than the norms which are internal to her society. In particular, there are no moral principles to which the agent can appeal more fundamental than the outlook of the virtuous person. The virtuous person therefore seems destined to reproduce the views of her society even as she is supposed to provide the norm against which these same views are to be measured. By these lights, virtue ethics looks to be complicit with an uncritical social and political conservatism. I shall refer to this as 'the charge of uncritical conservatism.'[3]

In this essay, I will consider the extent to which the charge of uncritical conservatism applies to the rich and influential version of virtue ethics developed by Iris Murdoch.[4] Murdoch characterizes virtue as a capacity for a kind of *moral perception* and in this respect her account of virtue may be grouped with the Aristotelian accounts offered by John McDowell and Martha Nussbaum.[5] I shall argue that although Murdoch does not furnish the agent with a point of view entirely outside of the moral norms—the point of view an appeal to antecedently established principles is supposed to provide—she nevertheless does equip the virtuous agent with powerful critical resources. The agent's critical resources consist in habits of thought, attention, and communication which depend on some normative commitments even as they call others into question. Virtue is the perfection of these habits. And while virtue understood in this way involves

---

[3] Rosalind Hursthouse identifies something like this as *the* criticism of virtue ethics. See 'Virtue Theory and Abortion', in D. Statman (ed.), *Virtue Ethics* (Edinburgh: Edinburgh University Press, 1997), 231. Sabina Lovibond discusses the charge of uncritical conservatism in relation to non-foundational ethics generally in *Realism and Imagination in Ethics* [RIE] (Minneapolis: University of Minneapolis Press, 1983).

[4] I will cite the relevant works by Murdoch as I proceed. Most of them have been collected in *Existentialists and Mystics* [E&M], ed. P. Conradi (1997; New York: Allen Lane The Penguin Press, 1998). The main essays are abbreviated as follows. IP: 'The Idea of Perfection' (1964). OGG: 'On 'God' and 'Good'' (1969). SGC: 'The Sovereignty of Good over other Concepts' (1967). VCM: 'Vision and Choice in Morality' (1956). For IP, OGG, and SGC, I give page references both to their appearance in *The Sovereignty of Good* (London: Routledge, 1970) and to the reprintings in E&M, separated by a forward slash/. For VCM, I give page references both to the original printing (*Proceedings of the Aristotelian Society*, Supplementary Vol. 30 (1956) 32–58) and to the reprint in E&M.

[5] Most notably, Nussbaum's *Love's Knowledge* (Oxford: Oxford University Press, 1990), ch. 2 and McDowell's 'Virtue and Reason' *Monist* 62:3 (1979), 331–50. Cf. Nussbaum, 'Why Practice Needs Ethical Theory: Particularism, Principle, and Bad Behaviour', in B. Hooker and M. Little (eds.), *Moral Particularism* (Oxford: Oxford University Press, 2000), ch. 10.

principles of conduct, these principles ultimately originate and operate from within the agent's evaluative outlook.

My paper divides into four main parts. In the first part I provide an overview of the concept of moral perception more generally before turning in the second part to Murdoch's conception of moral perception. I also address in more detail in the second part of the paper the charge of uncritical conservatism, and consider a kind of misperception related to social injustice which gives the charge focus and urgency. In the third part of the paper I examine Murdoch's account of both the main obstacle to moral perception and the way around this obstacle. I conclude that Murdoch appears to overlook the way that obstacles to moral perception may arise from an agent's social context. In response, I turn in the fourth and final part of the paper to the feminist work of Marilyn Frye. I argue that Frye brings into view an implicit feature of Murdochian moral perception: the perception of social structure. I maintain that Murdoch's account stands up well to the charge of uncritical conservatism once we recognize that it possesses this social dimension. Thus enriched, Murdoch's notion of moral perception does not equip the Murdochian agent to step outside the moral norms; it shows how an agent can be truly critical without taking such a step.

The concept of moral perception

> Do we really think there are specifiable sets of neutral facts which in the light of reason give a moral direction? Is it not rather that the prime situation is already to a considerable extent 'read' (or worked upon) when the problem arises? It is certainly often worth saying: Look at the facts! ... But what we look at, and attempt to clarify and know, are matters in which value already inheres. In deciding what the initial data are we are working with values. Value goes right down to the bottom of the cognitive situation.[6]

2. If, following Socrates, we take it that virtue is knowledge, there is the question of how to conceptualize this kind of knowledge. One can, in keeping with a familiar picture of practical rationality, identify it with a set of principles from which the agent infers what to do on the basis of a rational survey of the facts (one might consider the categorical imperative or the principle of utility as the basis for such a set of principles). The concept of moral perception has been offered as an alternative to this type of principle-centered conception of virtue. The core suggestion is that the virtuous person's knowledge is akin to a kind of perceptual capacity which both enables the agent to identify the moral requirements of a situation and leads her to act accordingly. The need for the *perception* of moral requirements is supposed to follow from the way that these requirements are bound up with situational particulars, together with the thought that these particulars vary too much from occasion to occasion for any set of

---

[6] I. Murdoch, *Metaphysics as a Guide to Morals* [MGM] (1992), 384.

principles to be able to set out all of the possible variations in advance. On this account, excellent action originates in *the very way the agent sees her circumstances*, and this way of seeing does not admit of definitive codification. To have virtue is to have a reliable capacity for this kind of perception.

Given the opposition of the moral perception account to a certain identification of virtue with principles, it is sometimes suggested that principles have no intrinsic role to play in the exercise of moral perception; this suggestion is mistaken.[7] Let us think of a moral principle as a notion of some degree of generality (e.g. 'do not lie' or 'be brave') which helps the agent to identify morally relevant considerations.[8] Moral perception is guided by principles in this sense, albeit principles which require something in the way of character for their successful application.[9] Let me spell out this thought.

To speak of the proper application of a moral principle is to recognize the possibility of its *mis*application. And this is to focus attention on the fact that principles may require something on the part of the agent for their successful application. Different things might be required of an agent for the proper application of a principle; the notion of moral perception involves the thought that there are principles which depend upon the agent's *character* for their proper application.[10] I will call such

[7] Here my account of moral perception differs somewhat from that put forward by Lawrence Blum in 'Moral Perception and Particularity' *Ethics* 101 (1991): 701–25, esp. 712. It also differs from the particularist ethics advanced by Jonathan Dancy in such works as *Ethics Without Principles* (Oxford: Oxford University Press, 2004) and 'Ethical Particularism and Morally Relevant Properties', *Mind* 92 (1983): 530–47. (There is less of a contrast with Dancy's position in *Moral Reasons* (Oxford: Blackwell, 1993), esp. ch. 4, §4; but later in that work (p. 56) Dancy discourages the association of his position with a perceptual model of moral knowledge.) It is worth remarking the divergence with Dancy since some commentators have conflated his theory with the account of moral perception developed by McDowell and Nussbaum. See, for example, T. H. Irwin, 'Ethics as an Inexact Science', in *Moral Particularism*, ch. 5, esp. 102.

[8] Although the examples I have given are of first-order principles, second-order principles would also fall under the definition. The definition is also open as to whether we should think of moral principles as (necessarily) universalizable such that for an agent to have reached a moral decision he must believe that any other agent, similarly placed, ought to act likewise. Murdoch opposes the idea of universalizability on the ground that some moral decisions carry with them an irreducibly personal background. She writes that reasons 'may be reasons for a very few, and none the worse for that' (IP 33/326; see also VCM esp. 46–51/86–92). To ignore this, on Murdoch's view, is to force different kinds of moral experience into a single mold and to overlook moral outlooks which emphasize the contingency and mystery of the moral life over its comprehensibility and systematicity. It is interesting, then, that she goes on to develop a conception of virtue which centers on a universal principle, the Good. I do not think this is a contradiction, however, as much as an artful reconciliation of the universal and the particular. As we will see, the principle of the Good directs one to attend to the particularities—including the idiosyncrasies—of one's circumstances; it thus arguably does not lead to the kind of homogenization of the moral life that animates Murdoch's resistance to the idea of universalizability. Where it places her thought in relation to contemporary opponents of the idea of universalizability, such as Dancy, is a complex question I do not address here.

[9] This thesis and the account which follows are based on the first three chapters of my dissertation, 'The Lens of Character: Aristotle, Murdoch, and the Idea of Moral Perception', University of Pittsburgh, 2003.

[10] By 'character' I mean one's patterns of thought, feeling, and outward response with respect to ethical questions; one's character in this sense (a moral sense) is indicative of one's ultimate concerns and can be distinguished from one's *mere* habits, inclinations, or beliefs. I am proceeding on the assumption that recent attempts to cast doubt on the existence of character so conceived have not succeeded. See J. Sabini and M. Silver, 'Lack of Character? Situationism Critiqued', *Ethics* 115 (2005): 535–62; R. Kamtekar, 'Situationism and Virtue Ethics on the Content of our Character', *Ethics* 114 (2004): 458–91.

principles 'character-dependent' (or 'dependent') and I will designate as 'character-independent' (or 'independent') those principles which can be perfectly applied *irrespective* of the agent's character. In order to understand this distinction, it is important to see the difference between *applying* and *observing* a principle.

To apply a principle correctly is to *ascertain* what it requires one to do in a particular case. Whether one goes on to *do* what the principle requires is another matter, the matter of *observing* the principle. An *independent* principle, as I define it, can be correctly *applied* irrespective of one's character. The most obvious examples are non-moral, e.g. 'Put 'i' before 'e' except after 'c' when spelling English words,' or 'Keep your eye on the ball.' Barring strange background conditions, there is no correlation between one's ability to apply such rules—to see what they require one to do on a given occasion—and one's character. Traffic rules are for the most part also independent; it takes nothing in the way of character to grasp what 'Drive 55 mph' requires a person to do here and now, though of course qualities of character (e.g. recklessness) could keep one from observing such a principle.[11]

The way to begin to understand the idea of a character-dependent principle is to see that it does not allow one to identify an agent's ability to *apply* the relevant principles correctly with a purely *cognitive* disposition while, at the same time, one identifies her character with a purely *motivational* disposition to *observe* (or not) the corresponding requirements. Her character informs her ability to apply the principle as well as to observe it.[12]

The underlying idea is that the character one has influences the way that one sees the world. To have achieved perfected character—virtue—is to see the world, in its moral aspect, with surpassing clarity. On this view, perfected dispositions of feeling, thought, and motivation are what enable one to see what, say, mercy requires; the person who lacks the relevant virtues cannot necessarily make things out in quite the same way. That is, imperfections in character lead not only to incorrect action but *also* to failures to grasp what would constitute the correct course of action in the first place.

3. An example of a character-dependent principle may be found in the opening chapters of Jane Austen's *Sense and Sensibility*.[13] A gentleman of the Dashwood family leaves most of his estate to his grandson, John Dashwood, who is already very well provided for. John's father, Henry, is distressed because the will overlooks three daughters he had by a later marriage who are not nearly as well off as his son. Henry learns that his own death is imminent before he can shore up the finances of his

[11] One should not be misled by these examples to think that independent principles must be easy to apply. Their application may require quite specialized knowledge; it is just that the knowledge required will not be indexed to the character of the agent.

[12] I reserve for another time the question of the *bindingness* of dependent principles. I believe that for Murdoch (and others) such principles are meant to be binding on all agents even if not all agents are in a position to see what they require. See B. Clarke, 'Virtue and Disagreement', *Ethical Theory and Moral Practice* 13 (2010): 273-91.

[13] Jane Austen, *Sense and Sensibility* (New York: Alfred A. Knopf, 1992 [1811]). Hereafter [S&S].

daughters. He therefore makes it his last request to John to look after them. The verbal indefiniteness of Henry's request is important to how the story unfolds. As John explains to his wife, Fanny: 'He did not stipulate for any particular sum ... he only requested me, in general terms to assist them, and make their situation more comfortable than it was in their power to do' (S&S 8–9).

John, we are told, is rather 'cold-hearted' and 'selfish' but nevertheless dependable when it comes to the discharge of his ordinary duties. Accordingly, he has every intention of making good on his promise to his father; indeed, he takes some genuine pleasure in the thought of fulfilling the promise generously. The only question is *what* exactly this requires. John begins with the idea that he will give his sisters £1000 each; he considers this a generous sum which he can easily spare. However, this plan does not meet with the approval of Fanny, who reasons that to give such a sum to the sisters and their mother would be to rob their own child in the interest of 'mere half-bloods'. John sees her point and then proposes half of the original sum, which would mean £500 for each of his sisters. Fanny argues that this much is unnecessary given that the sisters stand to receive an inheritance upon the death of their mother. John is again persuaded. After several more rounds of such deliberation John concludes that Henry Dashwood surely had not meant for him to give his sisters money at all; he had meant for John to provide them with neighborly assistance such as helping them move into a new house, and sending them occasional presents of fish and game. 'I clearly understand it now', John says, 'and I will strictly fulfil my engagement by such acts of assistance and kindness to them'—anything more would be 'absolutely unnecessary, if not highly indecorous' (S&S 12–13).

I will keep my analysis of this example simple for the purposes of illustration. We could say that John's promise commits him to a certain principle, that of 'looking after' his sisters (where this principle falls somewhere between the principles of benevolence and fairness) and that his deliberations seek to specify what this requires of him in the circumstances. I think it is clear, and will take it for granted, that John's application of the principle is wide of the mark.[14] To the extent that the principle of 'looking after' is a dependent principle, John's misapplication of it cannot be separated from his cold-heartedness and selfishness (and the way that these dispositions are helped along by Fanny, who herself is, Austen tells us, 'a strong caricature' of John). In these terms, it is not that his deliberations are sound and that his selfishness merely keeps him from being *motivated* to act on the requirements they disclose; it is rather that his selfish character keeps him from arriving at these requirements in the first place. This is to suggest that John would have needed to be, or at least to have been helped by, a more generous

---

[14] I doubt any reader would seriously query this. But perhaps Austen was thinking of such a reader when she had John and Fanny, in a sort of coda to their deliberations, entertain the idea of 'adding' some china which belongs to the sisters, and is presently in between places, to their own collection on the grounds that there is far too much of it for any place the sisters could now afford to move into—plus it is too nice (S&S 12–13).

person in order to see that giving £3000 of the inheritance away would *not* be 'robbing' his son, even though it would mean less for him, or, similarly, that it is irrelevant to the question of what his sisters should receive that they are 'half' sisters. To this way of thinking, and in essence, John needed to be able to *care about* his sisters and his father more (or more adeptly) than he did in order to see what his promise to 'look after' his sisters required. His overriding concern for his own comfort—part of what is meant by 'selfishness'—hindered him from seeing what providing for the comfort of the sisters involved. And his good intentions and extensive deliberations could not make up for this deficiency in his character. To this extent, the principle of 'looking after' is operating as a *dependent* principle; good character is required for its successful application.

Murdoch's conception of moral perception and the charge of uncritical conservatism

4. As I have explained it, the exercise of moral perception does not amount to seeing what to do in the absence of principles of conduct. It is rather a matter of seeing what to do in the light of principles of conduct which, however, make demands on the agent's character. In these terms, to say the virtuous agent is distinguished by a reliable capacity for moral perception is to imply that the agent is guided by principles. But given the character-dependent nature of the principles conceded, their guiding the agent will hardly secure the perception account from the charge of uncritical conservatism. For that charge rests on doubts about the ability of any agent to negotiate the complexities of real-life moral judgment without an *independent* principle.[15] Barbara Herman states the basic problem this way:

Much moral work can be done by a sensitivity that is both world-regarding and motivationally set. Agents are able to determine what is to be done through an appreciation or reading of what is morally salient in their circumstances. . . . What seems to me matter for concern [however] is the apparent absence, in such a conception . . . of a way to criticize the sensitivity itself—for it to take itself as the object of its own critical regard.[16]

---

[15] Nothing in my analysis rules out that independent principles have *some* place in the virtuous person's outlook but it would have to be a secondary place, and we can think of the charge as registering a concern with this fact.

[16] B. Herman, 'Making Room for Character,' in S. Engstrom and J. Whiting (eds.), *Aristotle, Kant and the Stoics: Rethinking Happiness and Duty* (Cambridge: Cambridge University Press, 1996), 56. Related criticisms have been raised in R. Jay Wallace, 'Virtue, Reason, and Principle', *Canadian Journal of Philosophy* 21:4 (1991): 469–95; S. Blackburn, 'Reply: Rule-Following and Moral Realism', in S. Holtzman and C. Leich (eds.), *Wittgenstein: To Follow a Rule* (London: Routledge and Kegan Paul, 1981), esp. §2. All of these (Herman included) are directed specifically at McDowell's reading of Aristotle. It might seem inappropriate, then, to focus on Murdoch's virtuous agent in this connection, but given their shared emphasis on moral perception, there is plenty of warrant for an investigation of the charge with respect to Murdoch.

Lovibond *has* discussed conservatism in connection with Murdoch (RIE, esp. §§44–5). Her analysis rests on an entirely different basis, however, than a skepticism about the ability of an agent to get by without

More precisely, if I have understood her correctly, Herman worries that without recourse to a principle that stands outside the ambit of character and its deliverances (e.g. the categorical imperative), the agent may have no way to check those deliverances and thus may be forced to rely unduly on the moral status quo.[17] The question is whether there is anything internal to the capacity for moral perception that would enable its possessor to critically assess the deliverances of that perception in the absence of an independent principle.

In considering this, it is helpful to distinguish between two problems an agent could face. The first problem is that of *complacency*. A complacent agent, in the sense intended, would lack any awareness of defects, or potential defects, in her perceptions; she would never see the need to revise or even inspect them (think of someone who never senses that they are spelling words incorrectly).[18] The second problem concerns an agent who recognizes the need to critically check or revise her perceptions, but who lacks the resources to do so (think of someone who senses they are misspelling words but lacks a dictionary). Call this the problem of *wherewithal*. At issue is whether Murdoch's agent is susceptible to either of these problems.

In discussing this question I will focus on a kind of misperception related to racial prejudice because I think this promises to engage the charge of uncritical conservatism especially well. For one, race-related misperceptions have often had the support of a corrupt status quo.[19] Moreover, it is commonly assumed that racist attitudes have a way of *pervading* an agent's whole outlook, distorting her perception of individual cases across the board. That is, an agent's perceptions of *all* of the individuals of a given race may be distorted—and mutually supporting. In such a case, it is especially difficult to see how anything within the individual's outlook might correct for the errant perceptions; for the outlook as whole seems to be infected.[20] Misperceptions linked to racial

---

independent principles and so is better addressed elsewhere. See B. Clarke, 'Iris Murdoch and the Politics of Imagination', *Philosophical Papers* 35 (3) (2006): 387-411.

[17] One might wonder what is supposed to lead the agent to *accept* such a principle given that it stands outside the agent's evaluative outlook. The idea is that independent principles appeal to the agent's rationality, narrowly conceived. This is why, in principle, *any* rational agent can apply independent principles well and why all rational agents can be expected to recognize the authority of such principles; failure to do so impugns one's rationality.

[18] As Flannery O'Connor put it in a letter to a friend: 'I have always been a very innocent speller. I never sense that I am spelling something incorrectly and so don't look up the words' (*The Habit of Being: Letters of Flannery O'Connor*, ed. S. Fitzgerald (New York: Random House/Vintage Books, 1980), 69).

[19] Bass's *Unlikely Heroes* does an excellent job of conveying just how widespread the support for segregationist policies in the American South was through a history of the Fifth Circuit Court of Appeals in the late 1950s and 1960s.

[20] We might liken this global kind of misperception to a form of blindness, and its local counterpart to an optical illusion. Whereas one overcomes an optical illusion by drawing on the deliverances of the very faculty which has been taken in, blindness does not seem to permit of this kind of solution; the blind person has no *good* deliverances of a given kind with which to correct *bad* deliverances of that same kind. Thanks to Donald Ainslie for this point.

prejudice would thus seem to provide a particularly good test of the critical powers of Murdoch's agent.[21]

5. I begin with the striking opening passage of Ralph Ellison's *Invisible Man*.

I am an invisible man. No, I am not a spook like those who haunted Edgar Allan Poe; nor am I one of your Hollywood-movie ectoplasms. I am a man of substance, of flesh and bone, fiber and liquids—and I might even be said to possess a mind. I am invisible, understand, simply because people refuse to see me . . . . When they approach me they see only my surroundings, themselves, or figments of their imagination—indeed, everything and anything except me. Nor is my invisibility exactly a matter of biochemical accident to my epidermis. That invisibility to which I refer occurs because of a peculiar disposition of the eyes of those with whom I come in contact. A matter of the construction of their *inner* eyes, those eyes with which they look through their physical eyes upon reality.[22]

The subsequent course of the novel makes clear that the failure of others to 'see' the speaker is a failure to see him *as a person*. The (pointedly nameless) speaker pretty well sums it up in a later passage when he notes that most people see him purely in terms of how he fits into their plans, as if he had no plans of his own. The speaker is African-American and the novel clearly argues the point that his 'invisibility' is bound up with the traditional status of African-Americans in American society as less than full persons.

Let me now supplement the Ellison passage we are considering with a more recent remark by Patricia Williams.

My parents were always telling me to look up at the world; to look straight at people; particularly white people; not to let them stare me down. . . . They told me that in this culture you have to look people in the eye because that's how you tell them you're their equal. . . . The cold game of equality staring makes me feel like a thin sheet of glass: white people see all the worlds beyond me but not me. They come trotting at me with force and speed; they do not see me.[23]

I don't think either speaker is asking us to think that they don't register on the white field of vision in *any* sense.[24] The point is that they don't register in the *right* way, in the way that befits the human individuals they are. 'They don't see *me*', both speakers note.

Indeed, in both cases the speakers also experience a heightened *visibility* of a sort. Ellison's man feels constantly under surveillance by whites at the same time that he feels invisible to them. After arriving in New York, for instance, he feels watchful eyes upon him everywhere, as if he were a criminal on the run.[25] Similarly, Williams connects not

<hr/>

[21] Of course a virtuous agent will, by definition, perceive correctly. So in what follows I am not considering a kind of misperception to which a virtuous agent would be susceptible; strictly speaking, there is no such thing. I am considering a kind of misperception to which an *otherwise* virtuous agent might be susceptible. I am trying to get at whether Murdoch's good agent would *really* be good, would be able to 'rise above [his] environment, above [his] community . . . and stand up for what is right'.

[22] Ralph Ellison, *Invisible Man* (New York: Random House/Vintage Books, 1989 [1947]), 3.

[23] P. Williams, *The Alchemy of Race and Rights* (Cambridge, Mass.: Harvard University Press, 1991), 222.

[24] Strictly speaking, the problem is not for either writer unique to the *white* field of vision, but it is most in evidence there.

[25] 'I looked to see if there were policemen or detectives with drawn guns following, but there was no one. Or if so, they were hidden in the hurrying crowd. . . . This was Wall Street. Perhaps it was guarded, as I had

being seen by whites with the experience of being stared down by them; white people will stare her down if she lets them—even as they don't see her. Together, these considerations suggest that the invisibility Ellison and Williams draw our attention to has as its other side a *supervisibility*.[26] Let's turn now to consider whether Murdoch's agent has the resources to altogether avoid, or correct for, this kind of misperception; to make matters difficult for the agent, I will assume that the agent is white.

6. For Murdoch, moral perception consists in, and results from, efforts of 'attention'. To attend to something is to approach it with a 'just and loving' eye and therewith to perceive it in its unbounded particularity and complexity and so as it truly is. In Murdoch's view, attention never fully exhausts its object, so it is never fully successful; to attend is to undertake an infinitely perfectible activity (IP 28/321).[27] Attention issues in (more or less) veridical perceptions of its objects based upon the exercise of virtues of character such as love, justice, honesty, courage, humility, and tolerance. At the same time, attention is guided by, and secures the application of, the principle of the Good. The Good is a second-order principle which prompts one to seek a perfect perception of the objects one encounters; to attend is to approach such a perception. To attend, then, is to see the world clearly in its moral aspect on the basis of qualities of character and at the same time to realize that one has not seen as clearly or deeply as one might. And it is this way of looking at the world which secures the application of the principle of the Good.[28]

Murdoch's account of attention can be made more concrete. Murdochian attention always takes an 'independent reality' for its object, where this refers to anything that has

---

been told post offices were guarded by men who looked down at you through peepholes in the ceiling and walls, watching you constantly, silently waiting on the wrong move. Perhaps even now an eye had picked me up and watched my every movement. Maybe the face of that clock set in the gray building across the street hid a pair of searching eyes' (*Invisible Man* 165).

[26] Consider also this observation by a journalist: 'Many whites seem captivated by an optical illusion: as they gaze out over a vast dining hall of all-white tables, their eyes are drawn to a black group sitting together. They see the blacks separating themselves; they rarely see that the whites have separated themselves as well.' D. Shipler, *A Country of Strangers: Blacks and Whites in America* (New York: Alfred A. Knopf, 1997), 27.

[27] Notwithstanding the way that even the most successful of efforts to attend leave room for improvement, I do not think we should equate attending with the *mere effort* to attend. Some degree of success seems to be implied in the term, such that if one tried to see another in the light of love and justice but failed abysmally, it would have to be said that one had not succeeded in attending to the other. This is not to suggest that one's attempt to attend was in vain; it is arguably a feature of the way Murdoch conceives of attention that all genuine efforts to attend issue in moral progress. But, if one is sufficiently benighted, one may need quite a bit of progress before one approaches 'a refined and honest perception of what is really the case' (IP 38/330). Along these lines, Lawrence Blum (during the proceedings of the Murdoch Conference at Brown University, 22–23 April 2001; cf. 'Visual Metaphors in Murdoch's Moral Philosophy', this volume) has proposed distinguishing between (a) unreflective takes on a situation; (b) reflective takes on a situation which are nevertheless unsuccessful; and (c) reflective takes on a situation which are successful—and then equating Murdochian attention with (c). This is helpful, but it must be admitted that Murdoch's language sometimes points the other way, as when she describes attention as 'the *effort* to counteract states of illusion' (IP 37/329, emphasis added). In this essay, I will equate attention with efforts to see clearly that are successful, but the issue deserves closer consideration.

[28] This very compressed analysis is based on the third chapter of my dissertation, note 9, above.

an existence outside the mind of the perceiver. Individual *persons* are, for Murdoch, the independent realities par excellence and they will be my focus here. Consider that any two persons are similar in some respects and different in others and that at any given time certain similarities and differences will be more relevant than others in reaching an appreciation of the other person. I want to suggest that for an agent to attend to another person in the Murdochian sense, the agent must grasp both the relevant *similarities* and the relevant *differences* which obtain between himself and the individual to which he attends. In these terms, to attend is to walk the fine line between overestimating and underestimating the continuities between oneself and others. Thus attending to Ellison's invisible man will entail grasping the senses in which he is genuinely and relevantly similar to oneself (e.g. in his basic needs and hopes for a good life, in his fear of dependence) *and* genuinely and relevantly different from oneself (e.g. in his experience of racism or of indigence, in his love of animals) at any given time. The appreciations of similarity crystallize in the recognition that he is as *real* as oneself. The appreciations of difference crystallize in the recognition that he is *separate* from oneself. And this, I want to suggest, is another way to understand what it means to perceive another justly and lovingly, in all his particularity and complexity, i.e. in the light of the Good as Murdoch conceives it.[29]

7. This line of exposition indicates that one way to fail to attend, in Murdoch's sense, is to possess a distorted conception of the similarities and differences that obtain between oneself and another. We can apply this thought to the example at hand: simplifying, we might say that the present cases of invisibility/supervisibility involve giving undue emphasis to select terms of difference with the result that African-Americans are seen as excessively 'other' or unlike the white perceiver.[30] And in this case at least, the failure to grasp differences accurately is *bound up with* the failure to grasp similarities accurately. It is not that one grasps the relevant similarities and simply exaggerates the differences: it is that one's exaggeration of differences rests on a neglect of relevant similarities and vice versa. The problem has to do with an exaggeration of differences in the context of deep, albeit not fully acknowledged, similarities.

It may be helpful to indicate, very briefly, how one seen as 'other' in the stipulated sense might well be (and so feel) at once supervisible and invisible. To begin with, the

[29] One might query whether I am right to suppose that Murdoch places so much emphasis on the relation of others to *oneself* in her conception of attention given that she links virtue to a kind of selflessness (especially in SGC). In response, I would argue that she considers one's own experience of *oneself* qua individual reality as a crucial element in the recognition of *others* qua individual realities, and that this need not stand in the way of an agent's achieving the particular kind of selflessness she associates with virtue. Though I cannot develop this argument here, I would point to passages such as the following in support of this reading: 'The more the separateness and differentness of other people is realized, and the fact seen that another man has needs and wishes as demanding *as one's own*, the harder it becomes to treat a person as a thing' (OGG 66/353–4, emphasis added).

[30] Note that the over-emphasis on some terms of difference (such as 'race') is quite consistent with the neglect of other terms of difference (such as 'the experience of racism'); one need not exaggerate differences *simpliciter*.

one *seen* is bound to be an object of heightened interest (and so a kind of spectacle) to the one he is seen *by* insofar as the latter exaggerates the differences between the two. Think of the prurient kind of interest which things supposedly 'exotic' tend to attract. This is the general way in which 'otherness' comports with supervisibility. As for the connection between otherness and *in*visibility, let's listen again to Ellison's man:

I am invisible, understand, simply because people refuse to see me.... When they approach me they see only my surroundings, themselves, or figments of their imagination—indeed, everything and anything except me.

'People refuse to see me.' Bearing in mind the way that attention rests on an acknowledgement of relevant differences and similarities, we could read this as a refusal by the perceivers to acknowledge some fundamental ways in which they are not so different from—evince similarities to—the one perceived. 'I might even be said', Ellison's man says, 'to possess a mind', as if he were without that most universal of human features.

Obviously enough, one seen as 'other' in this sense is not seen as he really is, and this recalls at least two features of Murdoch's *own* characterization of attention, bringing us full circle. Most straightforwardly, it recalls Murdoch's equation of attention with 'a refined and honest perception of what is really the case' (IP 38/330). To attend *just is* to counteract states of illusion that obscure reality, particularly individual realities; it is, within the limits already noted, to see others as they really are. Less conspicuously, it recalls Murdoch's equation of attention with seeing an object in all of its (significant) particularity. If to see one as 'other' is to fail to attend to him, then it is to fail to appreciate what is particular to him. In such a case, many of the distinguishing features (physical and otherwise) of one seen as 'other' will likely be overlooked. Thus, to cite a real life example, authorities repeatedly failed to distinguish a homeless African-American named Kerry Sanders from another African-American named Robert Sanders, who happened to be a convicted felon. The misidentification led to two years in a high security facility for Kerry Sanders despite the fact that the two men do not resemble one another.[31]

Summarizing: I have identified the act of attending, which Murdoch deems the characteristic mark of virtue, with a grasp of the relevant differences and similarities between the perceiver and the perceived. Because this grasp rests on qualities of character and the motivational propensities they entail, it has a practical purchase.[32] I then showed how the invisibility example betokens shortcomings in this very kind of

[31] B. Weiser, 'My Name is not Robert' *The New York Times Sunday Magazine* (6 August, 2000): 30–63.

[32] Blum, 'Moral Perception and Particularity', has argued that Murdoch's conception of moral perception (as distinct from the Aristotelian conception) is not intrinsically tied to the production of right action. I would argue that Murdochian perception is so tied, but that Murdoch rightly expands our sense of what *counts* as an action. Murdoch wishes to say that M's attention to D, though not observable, is itself a kind of action. In this way, she seeks to encourage the idea that 'one does not have to choose between activism or inwardness or feel that one is bound to swallow the other' (MGM 362).

grasp and thus, if my exposition is sound, in the act of attention. But Herman's worry can allow for the idea that the invisibility at issue is well-described as a failure of Murdochian perception. The critical point was that the agent of this misperception, the agent who is 'not seeing', will need an independent principle to right her perceptions—and I have claimed that Murdoch's agent has no such principle.[33] That agent's primary principle is the Good, and while it enjoins one to seek a perfect perception of individual realities, it provides no litmus test for the recognition of such perception; that is a part of the sense in which it is a *dependent* principle.

I will begin to respond to this point by identifying what Murdoch takes to be the principal obstacle to correct perception. I will then be in a better position to identify and assess the resources Murdochian perception contains within it to overcome this obstacle.

Murdochian moral perception: obstacle and antidote

8. Murdoch combines elements of Freud with elements of Plato and Christianity to yield a picture of the human individual as egotistical yet redeemable and of singular importance. From Freud she takes the idea of the individual self as naturally dominated by the ego and the ego as beholden to self-serving fantasy (OGG 51–52/341–342). For Murdoch, the egotistical nature of the self means that the self is inclined to be self-aggrandizing and correspondingly under-appreciative of everything that is not self. In this way, egotism severely compromises one's epistemological capacities, one's ability to *know* anything; it is thus the principal obstacle to correct perception. And it is a formidable obstacle, according to Murdoch, because the proclivity to egotism runs deep: 'It would be hard to exaggerate our capacity for egoistic fabrication. The mind is indeed besieged or crowded by selfish dream life' (MGM 317). As a result, she writes, 'it is *a task* to come to see the world as it is', and the task is a moral one (SGC 91/375, emphasis added).

For Murdoch, egotism almost always involves an *overestimation* of one's (moral) understanding of other beings. An unwarranted confidence in one's moral judgments follows naturally from the way in which egotism, as she conceives it, glorifies the self and diminishes everything else. Crudely put, egotism leads one to suppose that others are much simpler than oneself, and therefore more easily comprehended. Though Murdoch herself does not advert to it, there is a Socratic theme here: to be good is to recognize the limits of one's moral knowledge. Insofar as one fails to recognize these limits, one is unable to see others as they are.

We are absolutely prone, in Murdoch's view, to see things through the distorted lens of the ego; it is constantly at work, exerting a gravitational-type pull (MGM 51). This

---

[33] But see note 15, above.

means that we are also prone, by Murdoch's lights, to misperceive the world around us. And this makes Herman's concern appear all the more pressing.

9. At this point, we would do well to revisit the distinction between the problem of complacency and that of wherewithal. These are problems that vex an agent's ability to correct existing defects in her perception. To address the problem of *complacency* in the present context, we must suppose that the misperceiving agent hasn't a clue, a glimmering, that something is awry in her perception of African-Americans. Let us suppose further that she is not an outright racist, one who espouses doctrines of racial superiority, but someone whose perceptions unwittingly belie her garden-variety liberal doctrines.[34] In such a case, the problem of complacency would be this: the agent's perceptions are errant, and yet, since the only principles she has to go by are dependent, i.e. *presuppose* something in the way of character (and so something in the way of correct perception) for their proper application, she may not have any way to become so much as aware of the problem. Her perceptions, such as they are, are conditioned by her character, such as it is, and there is no principle to which she can appeal that would altogether bypass her character and any false sense of security it may provide with respect to the fitness of her perceptions. She may very well consider herself a model liberal and there is nothing in her moral equipment, so to speak, to tell against this.

It should be clear from the preceding section, however, that Murdoch's conception of moral perception (and so virtue) leaves no room for complacency. The picture on offer, as she puts it, 'has *built in* the notion of a necessary fallibility' (IP 23/317, emphasis added). Given the relentless machinations of the ego, the Murdochian agent must be ever vigilant, ever questioning the credibility of her perceptions and endeavoring to perfect them. By these lights, virtue indicates a 'perpetual effort', an effort simply 'to join the world as it really is' (MGM 268; 93). Virtually all of an agent's perceptions stand to come under scrutiny on this picture (albeit not all at once). If anything, such an account is liable to be called too demanding in view of the ceaseless self-monitoring it requires.

If there is a challenge to Murdoch's picture, then, it comes from the problem of *wherewithal*. To get the measure of this challenge, we must suppose that the (Murdochian) agent gets a glimmering that he is not seeing all there is to see. He is, say, aware of vague feelings of discomfort around African-Americans, and this leads him to query the veracity of his perceptions of them from time to time. Herman's question is: what resources does this agent have to check and correct any perceptions he considers suspect? For Murdoch, both check and corrective ultimately rest in the practice of attention.

In section six we saw that attention consists in a 'just and loving' gaze directed upon an individual reality, most especially another *person*. It results in a true perception of

[34] For further discussion of this phenomenon, see Adrian S. Piper, 'Higher-Order Discrimination', in O. Flanagan and A. O. Rorty (eds.), *Identity, Character, and Morality* (Cambridge, Mass.: MIT, 1990), ch. 13.

that individual, one which does justice to that individual's unlimited particularity and complexity, albeit one that can always be improved. This is a function of the way that the virtues of justice and love, for Murdoch, imply a standard of perfection to which the agent holds his perceptions accountable. We now need to consider how attention might entail a capacity for self-criticism.

On this point, it is crucial to note that attending involves a reflexive inspection of one's thoughts, feelings, and motives. This is manifest in Murdoch's most famous example of attention, the example of M and D (IP 17–23/312–318). 'M, a mother, feels hostility to D, her daughter-in-law. M finds D unpolished and lacking in dignity and refinement. . . . sometimes positively rude, always tiresomely juvenile. M does not like D's accent or the way D dresses. M feels that her son has married beneath him' (IP 17/312).

However, M attends to D, and over time this brings her to a different view of D: 'not vulgar but refreshingly simple, not undignified but spontaneous . . . not tiresomely juvenile but delightfully youthful, and so on' (IP 17–18/313). Murdoch is careful to specify that D really *is* delightful, and so that M's change of view is one we would approve of. As for what M is *doing* when she attends, Murdoch says, 'M *looks* at D . . . she focuses her attention. M is engaged in an internal struggle. She may for instance be tempted to enjoy caricatures of D in her imagination' (IP 22/317). Instead, 'M tells herself: "I am old-fashioned and conventional. I may be prejudiced and narrow-minded. I may be snobbish. I am certainly jealous. Let me look again" ' (IP 17/313). M's ability to attend to D clearly entails a capacity for self-criticism. M first saw D as frivolous, but she also sensed that this might be unfair. She checked this initial perception by inspecting her own habits of mind: she found that she was likely to be jealous, that she was old-fashioned, and so on. Having observed this about herself, she then looked at D again, with a clearer view. M will need to do this repeatedly over time, for though her view is now clearer, it is not definitive: 'M confronted with D has an endless task' (IP 28/321). M's task is endless because it is guided by an idea of perfection and because D, no less than M herself, is infinitely complex. M can never rest easy with her perceptions of others.

It is important to see how the principle of Good is supposed to be involved in this process of self-correction. I think that Murdoch herself is a bit elusive on this point because she is at pains to respect what she takes to be the genuine elusiveness of the Good itself. The Good, in her view, is a principle at once ubiquitous in human consciousness and yet indefinable.[35] 'It is in its nature', she writes, 'that we cannot get it taped. . . . It lies always beyond' (OGG 62/350). Without gainsaying this important feature of the Good, I suggest that we can, intuitively, think of its role in M's deliberations in the following way. Simply, the Good furnishes M with appropriately critical questions to ask about herself and her perceptions of D ('Is she *really* juvenile?'

---

[35] I have benefited from the account of the Good developed in Maria Antonaccio, *Picturing the Human: The Moral Thought of Iris Murdoch* (Oxford: Oxford University Press, 2000), ch. 5.

'Am I being old-fashioned, jealous?'). It does this in virtue of the way that it embodies an idea of perfection. To furnish these questions is not, of course, to provide the correct answers to them. Insofar as the Good is a dependent principle, the ability to *answer* these questions correctly requires goodness of character. But furnishing the right questions is arguably an indispensable element in the development of the character that is needed to return the correct answers. (Think of how we learn in other contexts.)[36] This is particularly so if we count it as part of what it is for M to be guided by the Good that she herself *realize* that the principle is dependent, i.e. that she realize that she is dealing with questions that may require much more than basic rational capacities if they are to be answered well.[37] To this extent, M will take care to check that her own moral defects do not lead her to a false picture. And of course this is just what M does: she considers the possibility that she may be failing to see D clearly *because* she is jealous, old-fashioned, and so on.

One might wonder why Murdoch wishes to postulate a *principle* to account for the introduction of such questions into M's stream of thought; and then one might wonder why she calls the principle at issue 'the Good'. I can address these questions only very briefly here. For Murdoch, the principle of Good indicates the common source of one's attempts to see individual realities clearly, over and against one's egoistic impulses, however different the content or details of these attempts might be; it is that in the light of which they hang together as instances of a kind of moral activity. Without the principle of Good, as Murdoch sees it, the order that obtains among the good person's efforts of attention would be lost from view. Whether one is trying to understand another language or another person, on her account, one is guided by the sense that there is something *beyond* what one's current lights reveal to one, that there is more to be understood. With a nod to Plato as well as to G. E. Moore, Murdoch identifies this sense of perfection with a principle of Good that is both elemental and indefinable. She believes that 'Good' is the least corruptible term for that which unites an agent's efforts of attention (SGC 90ff./374ff.). And though Murdoch herself does not make this point explicitly, it is plain to see that without some such principle, it would be difficult to tie the virtuous agent's understanding of what to do *here and now* (in a range of cases) to a *general* understanding of the virtues, and so to identify virtue with knowledge in a compelling way.

---

[36] I am told that in order to swim freestyle correctly, I must 'lead with my elbow'. As I move through the water, I then ask myself (in a manner of speaking) whether I *am* leading with my elbow. Initially it is hard or impossible to tell, but with enough practice and feedback, I come to recognize when I am in fact doing so. The process by which I come to recognize this just is the process of becoming a better swimmer. I need to be a good swimmer to answer the question properly, in other words, but the posing of the question is an integral part of becoming (and perhaps remaining) a good freestyle swimmer.

[37] I intend this as a familiar idea. One of the reasons we may fear being wrong about certain moral judgments (especially in the presence of others) is precisely because we feel that this error reflects poorly upon the kind of person we are, not just upon our intellect.

Of course, as I have noted, asking the right questions about one's perceptions is not the same as answering such questions correctly. M might have queried the veracity of her initial perception of D only to return with a ringing endorsement of them ('Jealous—me? Never!'). This points up the sense in which the Good is character-dependent. M had to be somewhat honest and courageous to recognize that she was being jealous and old-fashioned. I have suggested that Murdoch in effect sees what I have analyzed out as the ability to ask the right questions and the ability to answer these questions as reciprocally related: one develops the ability to answer the questions in part by asking the questions in the first place, and one's proclivity to ask the right questions deepens with one's ability to answer the questions. The character which returns the correct answer and the principle which introduces the right questions reinforce one another in an ever deepening dialectic.

This is an important picture of how one might come to correct errant perceptions, but I wouldn't expect Herman to be satisfied by it. For one thing, she would surely press the question of how the agent could ever *know* when she registered a correction. How does M, for example, know that her revised view of D is more accurate than her initial one? Murdoch herself stresses that M's checking procedure is 'a function of an individual history' and so cannot be codified in the way one might hope (IP 26/320). Furthermore, the checking procedure M devises will probably not be much better than M herself, for it will rely on M's *grasp* of her individual history. In a sense, then, M has nothing but her own self-awareness to guide her. And Murdoch herself has shown how rare and elusive genuine self-awareness is.

It might seem that Murdoch provides a way out of this predicament by furnishing the agent with 'duties' and 'axioms'.[38] For Murdoch, duties and axioms both indicate requirements, or sources of requirements, that may go against the grain of the agent's sensibility. Duty represents 'something alien, the outer not the inner', something 'not to be absorbed into, or dissolved in, the vast complexities of moral feeling and sensibility' (MGM 302). It betokens an impersonal and inflexible demand (such as 'Do not lie') and so, she says, 'can appear when moral instinct and habit fail, when we lack any clarifying mode of reflection, and seek for a rule felt as external' (MGM 302). Axioms, for Murdoch, stand at an even greater remove from the agent's particular sensibility. They represent the outermost limits of acceptable conduct and are grounded in (or indicate) self-standing or 'intuited' norms of *political* morality, such as 'life, liberty, and the pursuit of happiness' (MGM 493). Axioms are the basis of human rights; they indicate what is most categorical and impersonal in morality. It would seem, then, that duties and axioms furnish the agent with just the kind of corrective he needs in times of uncertainty, one that does not depend upon the deliverances of his own sensibility.

---

[38] Murdoch develops these concepts throughout MGM; I have drawn in particular from chapters 10, 12, and 17.

I think duties and axioms cannot play this role for two reasons. First, duties and axioms themselves may stand in need of revision (or rejection). They are, for Murdoch, historically and socially conditioned norms, not infallible edicts from a metaphysical beyond (MGM 493). So while duties and axioms can, and doubtless do, check the agent's impulses, perceptions, and reflections, the question is how the virtuous person can ever check *them*. The problem was made vivid in *The Adventures of Huckleberry Finn*. There, as Jonathan Bennett has reminded us, it was Huck's *duty* by the moral code of the antebellum American South to turn his slave friend Jim into the authorities.[39] When Huck acted otherwise, it was with the understanding that he was doing wrong, and this understanding was correct by the lights of the status quo; the inflexibility of duties and axioms should not be mistaken for infallibility. The second point is this: even where axioms or duties are beyond reproach, questions of what counts as a correct application of them are, by Murdoch's own lights, bound to arise. It is one thing to know that all humans deserve equal treatment under the law, or that human rights should always be respected, but quite another to know what equal treatment or (even) human rights amounts to in the new or complicated case. Murdoch, it seems, would be one of the last to hold that a simple rational survey of the facts will always suffice for such judgments; her longstanding rejection of the fact-value distinction suggests, to the contrary, that the agent who would act under a duty or axiom will often have to rely on his perception of the 'facts' of the case where this perception is evaluatively-inflected.[40] And this brings us right back to the problem from which we began: how to check the veracity of one's perceptions. This is not the end of the matter, but we are now in a position to see what is most valuable in Herman's criticism.

10. The question of how one knows when one's perceptions of others are sound takes on special urgency when one considers that the sort of misperceptions of African-Americans at issue, like a number of other misperceptions, finds support in American society. The series of prison-workers who dealt with Kerry Sanders were backed by deeply entrenched preconceptions about homeless people and black men when they didn't bother to 'look again'. These preconceptions can tacitly shape one's perceptions, whatever one's avowed principles. We can take Herman's point to be that where

---

[39] Jonathan Bennett, 'The Conscience of Huckleberry Finn', *Philosophy* 49 (1974), 123–34.

[40] It might seem that this is inconsistent with (*inter alia*) the eloquent argument Murdoch gave in the early 1960s against English laws that criminalized homosexuality ('The Moral Decision about Homosexuality' *Man and Society* 7 (1964): 3–6). There she states that 'the facts we need to know about [the legalization of homosexuality] are quite ordinary facts which are accessible to the observation of ordinary people' (3). What she means, however, is that the question can be settled without recourse to sociological or psychological experts, not that it can be settled without recourse to the moral sensitivities that enable us to know what other human beings are like. 'What is needed is not more science', she concludes, 'but just more humane and charitable recognition of our right to differ from one another' (6). I don't want to overstate the amount of moral sensitivity she took to be required for such a judgment; she thinks it very small indeed ('simple decency', one might say) and that *is* part of her point, but that is not enough for my imagined opponent's purposes.

such preconceptions abound, one may need more than a capacity to face unpleasant truths about oneself and to see the best in others in order to see clearly.

More specifically, the suggestion might be that some misperceptions have roots in deeply entrenched prejudices which are part of the *social* fabric, not just the fabric of the soul, so to speak. By 'entrenched' I mean that they have a hold on a lot of people, for a long time, and that they are supported by structures of power—legal, economic, political, linguistic. By 'prejudice' I mean that they embody views which conflict with some of the defining norms and ideals of the society (e.g. the ideal of equality) with the result that they may be hidden from conscious view even as they shape perceptions. Consider the way that the economic and political dominance of whites in the US has at times helped to entrench invidious distinctions between blacks and whites, making these distinctions a part of the currency, conscious and (perhaps largely) unconscious, of American society.

What this suggests is that one may be rendered susceptible to misperceptions by things quite outside of one's internal make-up. There may be prevalent theories and images and stories and the like to lead one, wittingly or not, to the misperceptions one holds. Indeed, these external shaping forces can be so strong that the initial uprooting of misperceptions may occasion a feeling of insanity or vertigo in the perceiver.[41] So the perceiver-agent has to learn how to think around and past these forces if she is to keep her perception clear.[42] And this may take some different skills from those required for virtue in the absence of such difficulties. Indeed this, we could say, is part of Herman's worry. If virtue is not conceptualized with such difficulties in mind, the virtuous agent may well not be equipped to deal with such difficulties.[43]

While I think Herman is right to draw our attention to socially-rooted obstacles to perception, I also think that Murdoch's virtuous agent *does* in fact have resources for dealing with this kind of obstacle; these resources simply need to be made more explicit. To this end, I turn to a recent feminist study in perception, and then make a final return to Murdoch. The feminist work brings into view an aspect of Murdochian attention which we might otherwise overlook, but which must be taken into account if we are to appreciate its full critical potential.

---

[41] Alison Jaggar refers to such feelings as 'outlaw emotions' ('Love and Knowledge: Emotion in Feminist Epistemology', in A. Garry and M. Pearsall (eds.), *Women, Knowledge, and Reality* (New York: Routledge, 1996), ch. 8, especially 144).

[42] I am not referring to a manipulation of the environment which is so thoroughgoing that it would be irrational for the agent to perceive in what is the correct way. I am referring to a world where critical thought is possible, if not easy.

[43] This of course presumes that misperceptions supported by entrenched prejudices are a different kettle of fish, requiring different remedial measures, than those otherwise supported. I cannot defend this presumption here, but I think that its intuitive plausibility is enough to enable me to proceed.

The social dimension of Murdochian moral perception

11. Feminist philosophers have long explored the grip that sexism can have on one's perceptions of self and others and the resources one has for extricating oneself from this grip.[44] Some of the best discussions of these matters comes from the work of Marilyn Frye.[45] Frye has argued that in order to break sexism's grip on one's perceptions—in order to perceive individuals or situations clearly—one must be careful to relate the particulars of the moment, such things as the individual man's conscious intentions and the individual woman's conscious perception of the event, to larger, systematic patterns of behavior and meaning.[46] She identifies the discovery and articulation of such patterns as the principal aim of feminist philosophy.[47]

The patterns to which Frye refers are principally patterns of *oppression*, where these are often invisible to the untutored eye. 'Oppression' as she uses the term denotes a network of social forces and barriers which are systematically interrelated in such a way as to limit the autonomy of select members of society in pervasive yet subtle ways (PR 10–11).[48] In the case of women these factors may include, for example, economic dependence, disproportionate parenting responsibilities, and 'catch-22' attitudes about their sexuality. To see how the relevant factors regularly join up to limit one's movements—and the movements of others like one in select respects—is to discern a *pattern* of oppression. For Frye, the relevant factors are always social and general in that oppression only ever affects persons qua members of socially designated groups or 'types'. One is not oppressed as a unique individual, but as a person of color, a muslim, etc. The perception she describes is thus structured to be responsive to socially-rooted obstacles to perception.

I think that the kind of perception Frye is delineating forms an implicit part of Murdochian moral perception, a part which needs to be made explicit if Murdoch's agent is going to appear capable of clearsightedness in a world where racism, sexism, and the like have a pervasive presence. I want to argue that this mode of perception

---

[44] A rough and ready definition of sexism: a complex of attitudes and institutional arrangements which work together to support disproportionate power, benefits, and privileges for men.

[45] Marilyn Frye, *The Politics of Reality: Essays in Feminist Theory* [PR] (Trumansburg, NY: The Crossing Press, 1983); *Willful Virgin: Essays in Feminism* [WV] (Freedom, CA: The Crossing Press, 1992).

[46] One might query the shift here from a problem concerning race to a solution based on studies of sexism. I do not wish to suggest that race and gender are altogether isomorphic domains of enquiry, but I think the extrapolation in the present case is not unwarranted, and I find Frye's exposition especially clear on relevant points.

[47] 'Our game is pattern perception; our epistemological issues have to do with the strategies of discovering patterns and articulating them effectively, judging the strength and scope of patterns, properly locating the particulars with reference to patterns, understanding the variance of experience from what we take to be a pattern' (WV 66).

[48] Iris Marion Young has developed this conception of oppression as a *structural* phenomenon, one whose causes are dispersed throughout the norms, institutions, habits, symbols, and images of a society and whose manifestations may therefore be hard to identify. See *Justice and the Politics of Difference* (Princeton: Princeton University Press, 1990), especially 41 and *Responsibility for Justice* (Oxford: Oxford University Press, 2011).

promises to do at least some of the critical work Herman suggests the virtuous agent might be ill-equipped to carry out.

12. Frye is concerned with how patterns of oppression become visible, particularly to those oppressed by them. As an example, she considers the pattern whereby men interrupt women more frequently in conversation than the reverse. She notes that this pattern of behavior is sometimes accompanied by certain feelings in women—feelings of vague or unfocused frustration or anger—when talking to men. Suppose a woman has these feelings and wants to justify them, to make sure it makes sense to have them. Frye's point is that if the woman considers the conversations she has with men in isolation from one another or from the conversations other women have with men, the feelings may well appear entirely unjustified. No *one* conversation will necessarily be self-justifying in terms of the feelings it generates.

What Frye suggests is that women must take a broader view of the dynamics of their conversations with men in order to discover the rationale, if any, for their feelings. If one sees that *for the most part*, men interrupt women disproportionately, and that this is simply the latest such episode, one's feelings begin to make sense.[49] To fully make sense of these feelings, one needs to connect this pattern of interruption to other patterns and social practices. An individual woman's case can then fall into place as part of a pattern of behavior which is disrespectful to women more generally by virtue of a whole host of meanings we attach to speaking, listening, men, women, and the relations among all these. Similarly, in the Jim Crow South, if one looked at individual cases of segregation in isolation from one another and from other social practices, one might in principle agree with the Court's decision in *Plessy v. Ferguson* that there is nothing intrinsic to the act of segregation which implies inferiority.[50] But when one connects the instances of segregation to one another and to other features of the social landscape, such as concurrent economic discrimination against blacks, it becomes clear that segregation did, in the context, imply inferiority.

Frye's notion of pattern-perception thus points up the need to see particulars in perspicuous relation to the complex network of social meanings and forces which constitute their backdrop. Particulars which might have appeared innocuous when considered on their own (say, one's conversation with a given individual) turn out to be problematic. Or, conversely, particulars which might have appeared problematic (say, one's apparently unjustified feelings of anger) turn out to be instructive. And this little epiphany can precipitate others, because it is an insight into how things hang together at a systematic level: 'The pattern of conversational interruption readily suggests itself as a simile for the naming of other abridgements' (WV 66).

---

[49] 'We do not say that every man in every conversation with any woman always interrupts. . . . What we do is sketch a schema within which certain meanings are sustained' (WV 65).

[50] 'We consider the underlying fallacy of the plaintiff's argument to consist in the assumption that the enforced separation of the two races stamps the colored race with a badge of inferiority. If this be so, it is not by reason of anything found in the act, but solely because the colored race chooses to put that construction upon it'; *Plessy v. Ferguson*, 163 U.S. 537 (1896).

Frye recognizes a variety of strategies for discovering patterns, but she treats as a paradigm a particular form of conversation among women that is officially termed 'consciousness-raising'.[51] Consciousness-raising starts with the idea that women may (and do) find a great deal of their own experience anomalous and unintelligible as a function of their oppression in society. Consciousness-raising conversations occur when women discuss these apparent anomalies with other women. These conversations have two main elements. First, they occur in a setting in which the interlocutors feel relatively safe telling the truth about their experience. Second, within that setting, the interlocutors compare experiences with one another and discover 'that similar "anomalies" occur in most of their lives and that those "anomalies" taken together form a pattern, or many patterns' (WV 59–60). If someone feels a certain unease when her male boss does *x* and her interlocutor says, 'funny, I feel that way too', she is alerted to something that would be very hard and perhaps impossible to detect without the help of another.[52] Of course her interlocutor's experience might be quite divergent from her own experience, and that too can be informative. Patterns are general, on Frye's account, but they do not depend on women's experiences being homogeneous (WV 66).

Note that on this account social factors figure equally in the cause and in the correction of misperception. On the one hand, it is a complex of social factors, precisely those factors represented by the word 'sexism' as I have used the term, that alienates women from a grasp of their own experience and the experience of others. On the other hand, it is a different configuration of social forces which restores this grasp to them, or perhaps provides it for the first time. More precisely, this account suggests that where certain misperceptions have the backing of society, an individual needs to form her own community of perceivers in order to right her perception. Left to her own devices, she might never discern a pattern of interruptions. Or she might discern one, but then assume that there is something specific to herself which explains these. But when she finds out that lots of women, from all walks of life, experience something similar, she is poised to see the particulars and patterns for what they are. The underlying epistemology this view proposes will come under consideration shortly, when I assess this as a response to Herman. First, however, I want to formulate more exactly the relation of Frye's pattern-perception to the perception of individual realities which Murdoch stresses in her account of virtue.

13. I have claimed that the perception of individual realities which Murdoch identifies with virtue just is, on her account, perception undertaken in the light of a principle, namely 'the Good'. Now to perceive in the light of a principle *is* to perceive a pattern.

---

[51] I assume that this kind of conversation can happen among members of other groups, but my discussion of it will follow Frye's in representing the interlocutors as women.

[52] The basic idea echoes Socrates' gloss on a line of Homer ('Going in tandem, one perceives before the other.' *Iliad* x.224) in the *Protagoras*. 'Human beings are simply more resourceful this way in action, speech and thought', Socrates says. 'If someone has a private perception, he immediately starts going around and looking until he finds somebody he can show it to and have it corroborated' (348d).

It is to recognize how one course of action hangs together with others as instances of, say, courage. The idea of pattern-perception is already present in Murdoch, then, in view of the way she equates the veridical perception of individual realities with perception in the light of the Good. To attend is to secure the application of the Good, and this is to recognize how different things hang together as 'individual realities'—infinitely complex entities which invite and reward our attempts to 'pierce the veil of selfish consciousness' and respond to the world as it is. What Frye brings to the table, then, is not the notion of pattern-perception per se, but the idea that some of the relevant patterns will be patterns of *oppression*, i.e. patterns in the way that various social forces interact to limit the autonomy of select members of society. To grasp *these* patterns requires insight into social structure, insight of a sort that gets very little mention in Murdoch's writings. There is, simply put, a markedly individualistic cast to Murdoch's portrayals of the effort to see clearly. As Nussbaum has written:

[Murdoch] seems almost entirely to lack interest in the political and social determinants of a moral vision and in the larger social critique that ought . . . to be a major element in the struggle against one's own defective tendencies.[53]

Nevertheless, I think that the materials for Frye's pattern-perception are implicit in Murdochian perception. This is a function of the fact that all agents live in societies (and imperfect ones at that).

Admittedly, there is a difference in the points of view at play here which may seem to stand in the way of the progress of my argument. We began with a Murdochian agent who needs to correct her unjust perception of others, and we shifted to agents who need to right their *self*-perceptions and who are themselves, ostensibly, victims of the unjust perception of others. Can Frye's pattern-perception, modeled as it is on *victims* of unjust perception, offer any assistance to *agents* of unjust perception? There is no difficulty here once we recognize that there is no hard and fast distinction between the misperceptions of self that oppression can help to generate, and the misperceptions of others it can also help to generate.[54] Women who perceive themselves as 'irrational' for feeling anger in certain situations will, presumably, be inclined to perceive other women (or at least that subset of women with whom they identify) in the same way. Ellison's man was as invisible to some of his fellow African-Americans as they were, in turn, to many whites. This is not the facile claim that everyone is alike both a victim and an agent of oppression, nor is it to deny important differences between the viewpoints of agents of injustice and the victims of it. It is just to say that where

---

[53] M. Nussbaum, 'When She Was Good', Review of Peter J. Conradi, *Iris Murdoch: A Life* in *The New Republic* (31 December, 2001), 32.

[54] Franklin Gamwell has suggested that Murdoch herself would allow 'that human illusions can take the form of debasement as well as aggrandizement of self, as, for instance, in the possibility that victims of racism internalize the prejudice of their victimizers and, insofar, see the world with the same debasement of themselves' ('On the Loss of Theism', in M. Antonaccio and W. Schweiker (eds.), *Iris Murdoch and the Search for Human Goodness* (Chicago: University of Chicago Press, 1996), 175).

misperceptions of self and other share a cause—forces of oppression—they may also share remedies.

I have claimed that Frye's socially-sensitive pattern perception is a tacit aspect of Murdochian perception. This amounts to the idea that true (Murdochian) perception of individuals involves understanding the past and present position of those individuals within the larger social structure. In this sense, to attend to someone involves what Maria Lugones has termed 'traveling to their world', seeing with their eyes and witnessing their own sense of self from within their world, insofar as this is possible, and recognizing when it is not.[55] 'World-traveling' includes grasping the socially-constituted patterns, oppressive and otherwise, which inform the lives of others. To attend to one's father may involve grasping the way in which being lower-class, or upper-class, shaped or shapes him; discerning the pattern that links some of his life-experience to those of others by virtue of their common class membership will be part of seeing him in his full particularity.[56]

If this seems an uneasy combination, it is due to the fact that Murdoch's attention takes the *particular* individual for its object, while pattern-perception takes the individual qua member of a *group* (e.g. woman, poet, mother) for its object. However, there is no contradiction here. For one is not *reducing* the individual to a member of a group, one is simply including the fact of her membership in certain groups in one's overall view of her. This is perfectly appropriate because this is how we find people: they *are* instances of types and we cannot but see them as such, yet they are not exhausted by those types. To return to Murdoch's example: M's awareness of D *as* her daughter-in-law helped M to suspect that she might have been jealous and thus unfair to D. And the confirmation of this suspicion helped her to see D as a particular person. It was part of the process of 'looking again'.

In fact, when we consider the example of M and D in this light, we can see that Murdoch has, after all, given us an agent with some insight into social structure—the structure of the social unit of the family. We need, then, only extend M's insights to social configurations that lie beyond the family to arrive at pattern-perception of the sort Frye identifies. Or do we? On second thought, it is clear that M has already done as much when she shifts from a description according to which her son has married 'a silly vulgar girl' who is '*beneath*' him' to a description in which invidious class distinctions play no part (IP 17/312, emphasis added).[57] This makes it all the more plausible to claim that the materials for Frye's pattern-perception are implicit in Murdochian perception, needing only to be made more explicit. If this is correct, then attending to an individual

[55] M. Lugones, 'Playfulness, "World-Traveling", and Loving Perception', in A. Garry and M. Pearsall (eds.), *Women, Knowledge, and Reality* (New York: Routledge, 1996), ch. 17.

[56] Murdoch writes, 'We learn through attending to contexts, vocabulary develops through close attention to objects, and we can only understand others if we can to some extent share their contexts. (Often we cannot.)' (IP 32/325).

[57] It is no accident that M initially dislikes D's *accent* and her *clothing*—two major indicators of class. Thanks to Maria Antonaccio for pointing out the class-inflectedness of M's initial descriptions.

will include being aware of the ways in which social forces may work to distort one's perceptions of that individual.

14. This paper began with the worry that the capacity for moral perception which Murdoch and others equate with virtue does not furnish the agent with a self-critical perspective. It is time to assess how well I have met this challenge with respect to Murdoch.

I discussed the corrective capacities internal to Murdochian attention and concluded that it appeared insensitive to misperceptions which are rooted in social structure. I then argued that this appearance is removed if we recognize that the perception of social structure that Frye delineates is actually an implicit part of Murdochian attention.

However, this may not cut much ice with the critic. For Frye's pattern-perception arguably stands in need of a 'check' at least as much as the Murdochian perception it is supposed to shore up. Who is to say, after all, that the pattern one 'cottons onto' in one's consciousness-raising group is the real pattern, or that there is any pattern at all? How does one check the veracity of the patterns one thinks one perceives? Who is to say those patterns are not the function of exactly the sorts of prejudice that pattern-perception is supposed to help one break free from? Murdoch herself might have pressed just this kind of question. As Maria Antonaccio has noted, Murdoch's concern to safeguard a liberal conception of the individual led her to be 'wary of appeals to consensus or community as an easily corruptible standard for moral claims' (*Picturing the Human*, 11).

Frye herself is no stranger to these questions: the credibility of many of the 'discoveries' of consciousness-raising groups has been forcefully called into question within the feminist community itself. Some of the patterns supposedly discovered about women, for instance, turn out to be indicative of *white middle-class* women rather than of most women. In response, Frye stresses that patterns, like metaphors, have limits and that they lose their power to illuminate when those limits are exceeded. She notes further that neither patterns nor metaphors specify their own limits. 'They work until they don't work. You find out where that is by working them until they dissolve' (WV 42). A person finds out when these patterns and metaphors are and are not working through *communication* with others, particularly others who belong to sub-groups (e.g. white) of the general group at issue (women). The testing of pattern recognition 'involves many inquirers articulating patterns they perceive and running them by as great a variety of others as possible. The others will respond by saying something like "yes, that makes sense, if you're not talking about me"' (WV 42). In other words, the process by which pattern-perceptions are checked is a variation on the process by which perceptions themselves are checked. People create a setting in which they feel able to speak truthfully and then they compare their *pattern*-perceptions. If an individual discerns a pattern whereby men interrupt women disproportionately, and her friend tells her that where she's from it's nothing like this, then she must revise the scope of the pattern. Upon closer inspection it might fall by the wayside altogether. The critical promise of the process lies in the understanding of the perceivers that the patterns they put forward are defeasible—the best sense they can make of things so far—and in their willingness to communicate with others to test the limits of their grasp.

The same thing may be said of Murdoch's agent. For Murdoch, the conditions of agency foster self-criticism in that the agent is guided by the principle of the Good and the standard of perfection it entails. This means that the agent will always have the opportunity to recognize, like M, that her perceptions are not definitive. Frye helps us to see that there are contexts in which consultation with others is an indispensable aid to self-criticism. Admittedly, consultation requires trust in the perceptions of others, but such trust need not betoken a loss of the individual's ability to be critical in any respect; indeed it is arguably a condition thereof.[58] We can agree with Murdoch, then, that the agent's critical capacities need not be supplied from without in the form of an independent principle—one whose dictates are transparently open to view—without supposing that these capacities need not be supplied from without in any sense. For Murdoch as for Frye, the agent needs to look beyond her own experience.[59]

The more general point is that one way in which the critical spirit can manifest itself in the virtuous agent is in her proclivity to revise her standing perceptions in light of considerations she finds compelling. This proclivity is part of what it *is* to be virtuous and, if I am right, it is closely tied to the primacy of dependent principles in the agent's outlook.[60] Admittedly, everything will rest on what the agent does or does not *find* compelling in her deliberations. And Herman would stress that what the agent finds compelling may be determined by the status quo. This is precisely the problem of wherewithal. The attraction of an independent principle is that it stands outside the potentially vicious circle of the agent's perceptions and her perception-laden judgments about those perceptions (and yet speaks to the agent in virtue of its appeal to her rationality). In this way it promises to ensure that what the agent finds compelling really is compelling, whatever deficiencies in character the agent may suffer and for whatever reason.

Notwithstanding its appeal, I think that neither Murdoch nor any of the advocates of moral perception fasten upon the idea of an independent principle, because none of them believes that goodness has much to do with such principles. And further, I think

---

[58] For one such argument, see N. Scheman, 'Feeling Our Way to Moral Objectivity', in L. May, M. Friedman and A. Clark (eds.), *Mind and Morals*, (Cambridge, Mass.: MIT, 1996), ch. 12, esp. §3. K. Jones has defended the role of trust in the acquisition of moral knowledge for all agents, including the virtuous agent, in 'Second-Hand Moral Knowledge', *The Journal of Philosophy* 96:2 (1999), 55–78.

[59] This result need not contradict the Aristotelian conception of the virtuous person as the moral standard. Following Jones *op. cit.*, I would argue that the virtuous person's fitness to serve as a standard stems in part from her knowledge of when to trust the moral knowledge of others.

[60] Provided we grant a thesis I introduced in §9—that it is part of what it is to be guided by a dependent principle that one realize *that* the principle is dependent and thereby subject to misapplication on the basis of defects of character.

they believe that if goodness did turn on such principles, moral reality would be radically different from what it actually is. In particular, they would contend that such a state of affairs would make goodness much *easier* than it actually is. Yet none of them would backpedal from the idea of moral objectivity or the importance of reason, properly understood, to moral life. This is manifest in their commitment to principles which guide perceptions and which, notwithstanding their dependence on the agent's character, are nevertheless subject to being properly or improperly grasped. As I read Murdoch and moral perception theorists more generally, it is not that reason provides no guidance to the moral agent, it is simply that it does not disclose itself to us in the form of a principle capable of making the necessary discriminations when things get complicated. In the practical sphere (at least), reason discloses itself to us in our distinctively human practices of thought and feeling and in a language with which to communicate these to others. Virtue is the perfection of these practices, or some of them. And while there is no end to the corrections these practices can occasion and incorporate, there is also nothing outside them that certifies their results once and for all.[61]

My objective in this paper has not been to defend Murdoch's virtuous person from the charge that she lacks critical capacities but to explore the nature and measure of these capacities, such as they are, in light of that concern. How extensive one finds these capacities to be will depend in large part on one's conception of moral philosophy. If one expects moral philosophy to articulate independent principles, one may very well be disappointed. The alternative sketched here does not so much answer to the desire for such principles as it indicates how moral agency can go on without them.

---

[61] This general line of thought has been argued in well-known terms by S. Lovibond, RIE and *Ethical Formation* (Cambridge, Mass.: Harvard University Press, 2002); J. McDowell, *Mind, Value, and Reality* (Cambridge, Mass.: Harvard University Press, 2001); M. Nussbaum, 'Aristotle on Human Nature and the Foundations of Ethics', in J. E. J. Altham and R. Harrison (eds.), *World, Mind, and Ethics* (Cambridge: Cambridge University Press, 1996), ch. 6; H. Putnam, *Realism with a Human Face* (Cambridge, Mass.: Harvard University Press, 1990), chs. 8–12; and C. Taylor, *Sources of the Self* (Cambridge, Mass.: Harvard University Press, 1989), Part I.

7

Social Convention and Neurosis as Obstacles to Moral Freedom*

Margaret Holland

> Obsession, prejudice, envy, anxiety, ignorance, greed, neurosis, and so on and so on *veil* reality. The defeat of illusion requires moral effort. (F&S 426)[1]

> A mediocre man who achieves what he intends is not the ideal of a free man. To be free is something like this: to exist sanely without fear and to perceive what is real. (DPR 201)

Iris Murdoch describes her philosophical work as 'putting up an abstract structure to edify, explain, and provoke reflection' (SBR 270). An examination of how good conduct can be achieved, a portrayal of moral change and improvement, and an investigation into the possibility of purifying consciousness are, Murdoch thinks, the proper endeavors of moral philosophers (MGM 293, F&S 457, SGC 78/364). In much of her writing Murdoch makes suggestive comments that provoke reflection, yet she often does not provide a thorough analysis of her insights. Consider, for example, her claim that, 'If I attend properly I will have no choices and this is the ultimate condition to be aimed at' (IP 40/331). In the context of contemporary philosophy and modern democracy, this may seem a jarring assertion. Furthermore, though it appears that

* I am grateful to Kelly Blake, Justin Broackes, Newton Garver, John Kronen, Laura Ruoff, and an anonymous reviewer for the press for their comments on earlier drafts of this essay. I thank the Graduate College at the University of Northern Iowa for awarding me a Summer Fellowship in 2002 for this project. Ann Stokes provided a lovely place for me to work.
[1] Murdoch's main philosophical books are abbreviated here as follows: E&M: *Existentialists and Mystics*, ed. P. J. Conradi (1997). MGM: *Metaphysics as a Guide to Morals* (1992). SG: *The Sovereignty of Good* (1970). Abbreviations for smaller works are as follows. AD: 'Against Dryness' (1961). DPR: 'The Darkness of Practical Reason' (1966). F&S: *The Fire and the Sun* (1976). HT: 'A House of Theory' (1958). IP: 'The Idea of Perfection' (1964). NM: 'The Novelist as Metaphysician' (1950). M&E: 'Metaphysics and Ethics' (1957). OGG: 'On "God" and "Good"' (1969). SBR: 'The Sublime and the Beautiful Revisited' (1959). S&G: 'The Sublime and the Good' (1959). SGC: 'The Sovereignty of Good over other Concepts' (1967). VCM: 'Vision and Choice in Morality' (1956). Page references are given to the reprintings in E&M, or (in the case of the essays that make up *The Sovereignty of Good*) to both SG and E&M, with a forward slash/to separate the two numbers.

Murdoch holds that proper attention both reduces choices and increases freedom, she does not discuss the relation between these ideas.

In this essay I pursue Murdoch's suggestion that an important part of any system of ethics is a portrayal of moral reflection and improvement, beginning with an analysis of obstacles to moral awareness (F&S 457). I do this by examining her scattered comments about social convention and neurosis as barriers to understanding (SBR 268). If, in order to act and live well, one must see moral reality clearly, then one must overcome obstacles to clear vision. Moral attention is directed toward the outer world, but engaging in the task of attentive discernment requires addressing tendencies one has to impose distorting preconceptions on external reality. By exploring how social convention and neurosis constitute obstacles to moral attention and understanding, I hope to begin to make explicit some of the implications of Murdoch's suggestions concerning the need for inner moral work. Finally, I hope to shed light on her comments about freedom and choice.

The first main section of the essay examines social convention and neurosis. It is followed by a brief discussion of Murdoch's view of the influence of fantasy and imagination on the quality of moral awareness. In sections on choice and freedom, I then examine Murdoch's suggestion that a better quality of consciousness—one that combines fewer distorting conventional beliefs and neuroses with attentiveness—is freer and reduces choices.

Since Murdoch's writing on these topics is scattered, I will proceed by presenting relevant passages from her work and then explaining how I think the cited ideas may best be understood within the larger context of Murdoch's philosophical commit-ments. The interpretations which I present are extrapolations based on my understand-ing of her work as a whole. To supplement Murdoch's work, particularly in the discussion of neurosis, I draw on other thinkers. I assume that the reader is familiar with Murdoch, and summarize below the aspects of her work which are most salient for the purposes of this essay.

Criticism of philosophy's neglect of the role of inner moral activity in moral life is among Murdoch's most significant contributions to the discipline. Her work on moral consciousness includes the following complex of ideas: moral life goes on continuously; moral awareness can be of variable quality; the quality of awareness serves as the source for the quality of conduct; an effort must be made to recognize the obstacles—egoism, neurosis, fantasy, social convention—to improving the quality of one's awareness and to pursue their defeat; seeing reality accurately, particularly seeing other persons, is a primary goal in moral life.[2] Murdoch suggests that the struggle to see

---

[2] Murdoch uses the phrase 'the quality of attention' (OGG 69/356) when discussing techniques for improving moral attention. She uses the term 'quality' to refer to the degree to which attention is oriented toward the real or is selfish or is clear. I understand her to be referring to a set of variable characteristics of moral awareness. Any instance of moral attention will be more or less distorted, just, loving, accurate, selfish. The more just, loving, accurate, unselfish attention is, the more clearly one sees and understands the object of attention. I use the term 'quality' to refer to these variable characteristics of moral attention.

moral reality has the potential to improve perception and to yield an increase in freedom. She is not, however, optimistic about either our tendency to want to engage in this struggle or the likelihood of permanent success.

Plato's influence on Murdoch can be seen in the implied contrast between appearance and reality, as well as in her discussion of the arduous task of seeing the real, the ease of comfortably settling down in the realm of appearances, and the notion that one not only sees different things but sees things in a different way as one's understanding increases. Furthermore, Murdoch's Platonism is evident in her view of the relation of understanding to freedom. As in the allegory of the Cave, Murdoch suggests that understanding and freedom go hand in hand and are achieved by degrees. When one's sight is dimmed by illusion, one lacks understanding and one's freedom is diminished.[3]

1 Social convention and neurosis

I take the general consciousness today to be ridden either by convention or by neurosis (SBR 270).

The enemies of art and of morals, the enemies that is of love, are the same: social convention and neurosis. One may fail to see the individual . . . because we are ourselves sunk in a social whole which we allow uncritically to determine our reactions, or because we see each other exclusively as so determined. Or we may fail to see the individual because we are completely enclosed in a fantasy world of our own into which we try to draw things from outside, not grasping their reality and independence, making them into dream objects of our own. (S&G 216)

1.1 Overview

Murdoch's references to convention and neurosis appear in a number of her philosophical works, including 'The Sublime and the Good' and 'The Sublime and the Beautiful Revisited', as well as The Sovereignty of Good and The Fire and the Sun. 'The Sublime and the Beautiful Revisited' contains one of Murdoch's more extended discussions of convention and neurosis. In that article she uses these terms to describe deficiencies in conceptions of the individual found in philosophy, literature, and the general consciousness. Murdoch argues that linguistic empiricism and existentialism suffer from inadequate theories of personality, and that their inadequacies may be traced to views about the individual which are, respectively, conventional and

---

[3] Though clear vision of moral reality is of central importance to both Plato and Murdoch, Murdoch's understanding of this task is not identical to Plato's. For example, Plato and Murdoch both believe that reality is transcendent, but not precisely in the same way. For Plato, to say that reality is transcendent is to say that what is real is not part of the world of appearances, but is rather eternal and immutable; reality transcends the world of matter and beliefs. When Murdoch discusses transcendence she suggests that goodness requires reaching out toward non-self aspects of the world, particularly other persons. She discusses the struggle to see the real, and focuses on the difficult task of seeing other persons and the circumstances of their lives, as they actually are. Murdoch also discusses the question of whether there is a separate form of goodness that exists beyond all particular instances of good conduct. She argues that the idea of perfection serves as a magnet in moral life. Murdoch holds that the idea of perfection transcends experience and remains mysterious.

neurotic. In her discussion of linguistic empiricism Murdoch is concerned with the then current trend to reduce moral philosophy to an analysis of the meaning of moral concepts used within the context of choice and action (SBR 267). The individual is conceived of solely as a being who uses language, makes choices and acts. 'Ordinary Language Man' is pictured as immersed in a structure—the social world, particularly language—which is not of his own making. Murdoch writes: 'Ordinary Language Man is too abstract, too conventional: he incarnates the commonest and vaguest network of conventional moral thought' (SBR 269). Murdoch faults this conception of the person because it conceives of the individual as existing within social and language systems which confine moral thought and awareness to commonly articulated concepts and familiar problems. The conventional conception of the individual omits from its portrayal of moral life the need to acquire moral knowledge, as well as the difficulty of acquiring this knowledge. In other words, it ignores obscure, demanding, and ineffable aspects of moral life.

Her criticism of existentialism is similar, though the existentialist conception of the individual differs somewhat from the empiricist conception. Rather than recognize the need to pursue moral knowledge, existentialism views such a search as an expression of bad faith. Existentialism portrays the individual as utterly alone, needing to make choices but lacking any foundation on which to base decisions. According to existentialism, anxiety in the face of this radical freedom gives rise to bad faith when individuals respond by fearing contingency and seeking necessity. The existentialist conceives of the individual as solitary, caught up in an on-going crisis, barely cognizant of the existence of other persons and their subjectivity. It is these features which lead Murdoch to describe existentialists' depiction of the individual as neurotic.

Murdoch argues that the inadequacies of these two conceptions of the person are 'intimately connected, both as cause and as effect, with the decline of our prose literature' (SBR 270). Citing the plays of Shakespeare as well as the novels of Tolstoy and George Eliot as exemplars of literary prose, Murdoch suggests that much of contemporary literature is inferior to these earlier works. The criteria by which she evaluates literature focus on the author's successful portrayal of a variety of independent and realistic characters, as well as the complex social world within which these characters live. Great literature does not, Murdoch suggests, suffer from convention or neurosis. Rather, in great literature:

The social scene is a life-giving framework and not a set of dead conventions or stereo-typed settings inhabited by stock characters. And the individuals portrayed . . . are free, independent of their author, and not merely puppets in the exteriorisation of some closely locked psychological conflict of his own. (SBR 271)

Literature which is inhabited by characters who lack psychological depth, who differ from each other only by virtue of their social roles and positions, who are not portrayed as possessing unique inner lives, and whose inner lives are not shown as mediating their interpretations of the social world, fit Murdoch's category of the conventional.

Neurotic literature, on the other hand, lacks insight into varieties of character because its characters serve as placeholders for the author's exploration of personal myths, psychological problems or anxiety about the human condition. By contrast, through the creation of characters who are separate from the author, the greatest literary writers show the reader the variety of human personality, the interaction between social world and individual lives, as well as the always approximate understanding individuals have of others.

Murdoch then argues that seeing this deficiency in literature is useful because it is parallel to the failure of philosophy to describe adequately human personality and moral life. In this regard, what philosophy and literature have in common is what they overlook: conventional thinking as well as egoism can obscure and distort perception of external reality, moral life requires recognizing the reality of other persons but the variety of the human world contributes to the difficulty of comprehending others, understanding is mediated by the social background.

Both convention and neurosis contribute to a failure to perceive the obscure and complex nature of persons. Hence, Murdoch argues, convention and neurosis have the potential to undermine both art and morality. It is because Murdoch conceives of art and morals as requiring undistorted insight that she links them with love. Murdoch holds that the essence of art, love, and morals is the same, i.e. 'the perception of individuals' and 'the extremely difficult realization that something other than oneself is real' (S&G 215). Consequently, Murdoch suggests that convention and neurosis are the enemies of both art and morals.

1.2 Social convention[4]

In 'A House of Theory' Murdoch lists the following items as falling within the category of convention: the father figure in his many guises, sexual taboos and restrictions, the subjugation of women (HT 172). Also, as I will discuss shortly, Murdoch's most famous example of inner moral work is, in large part, an example of the distorting power of social convention and a subsequent effort to check it.

Murdoch does not suggest that it would be desirable to eliminate all social conventions. There is no doubt that some social conventions are necessary and useful. Her concern is that certain conventional assumptions subtly structure conceptions of the person in a manner which is not morally innocuous and which often escapes moral reflection. Murdoch's focus on improving moral awareness seeks, among other things, to bring attention to the way conventional beliefs influence perception. Conventions

---

[4] Murdoch does not mention John Stuart Mill as an influence on her thinking about convention. However, in *On Liberty*, Mill discusses the pernicious effect of social convention on the freedom to think and live as one sees fit. While Mill focuses on the social atmosphere in democracies and Murdoch focuses on the relation between inner moral life and public action, both Mill and Murdoch see social convention as a potential threat to freedom and understanding.

can be examined, criticized, recognized for what they are (rather than, say, seen as natural) and, if need be, rejected.

Murdoch's various uses of the term 'convention' all involve the idea that a formulaic description is being substituted for a more demanding exploration of the nature of human life and individual persons. Conventional descriptions omit or obscure features of the world which Murdoch takes to be of paramount importance, e.g. that there is no prefabricated harmony in human life, that other persons are infinitely difficult to understand but the effort to understand is indispensable to moral life (S&G 216–17). Her famous example of moral attention is an illustration of this last point.

Murdoch provides the following example: a mother-in-law (M) re-examines her impression of her daughter-in-law (D). M initially feels hostility toward D, sees D as 'unpolished', 'rude', 'lacking in dignity and refinement', and 'insufficiently ceremonious'. M dislikes D's accent and feels that 'her son has married beneath him'. However, M is capable of self-reflection, she recognizes that she is 'conventional' and 'may be prejudiced', 'narrow-minded', and 'snobbish'. She knows she is 'jealous'. M reflects deliberately about D. Eventually she comes to see D as she really is: 'simple', 'spontaneous', and 'youthful' (IP 17–18/312–313, 37/329).

The purpose of Murdoch's example is to illustrate the possibility of inner moral activity which does not issue in public conduct; Murdoch stipulates that M behaves well toward D throughout their relationship. Also, while M's impression of D improves upon reflection, as Murdoch has set up the example, it is not the case that M simply is being more optimistic or is adopting a positive attitude. Certainly persons can decide to see things in a more favorable light, but Murdoch's point is that moral reality is difficult to see clearly, not that one should be optimistic or that when one sees clearly what one sees is good. As a matter of fact, Murdoch suggests that optimism can be one cause of the failure to see evil; if one sees clearly, what one sees will not always be good, and optimism can aid one in avoiding that which is painful (AD 294). One purpose of the M and D example is to show that persistent background beliefs, prejudices, and preoccupations influence how one reads other people. By both acknowledging her prejudices and engaging in attentive discernment, M comes to see D more accurately, not just more agreeably.

The value terms which M initially uses to describe D are laden with the prejudices of a particular social class, reflecting the way members of that class conceive of attractive behavior. By 'value terms' I have in mind words such as 'rude', 'unpolished', 'dignity', etc. 'Jealous' is not a value term and may, in this context, refer to an emotion which is related to a neurosis. Each value term reveals an aspect of the social conventions of M's world. It seems plausible that some of the values that are expressed by these terms would be more likely than others to survive critical reflection. One might, for example, hold the view that to be genuinely rude (leaving aside how that might be fleshed out), indicates a failure to respect persons and is a character flaw, while being unpolished is of no deep significance. Hostility toward someone because her accent reflects a lower class background cannot bear sustained examination.

Murdoch stipulates that part of what M recognizes about herself—and in part it is this recognition which makes it possible for her to be attentive—is that she is conventional and that her conventional values may be distorting her impression of D. Murdoch does not draw out the example in a manner which indicates how thorough a re-evaluation of her values M pursues. The M and D example illustrates the passage cited at the beginning of this section; M initially fails to see D because M is sunk in a social whole which she allows uncritically to determine her reaction. Moral attention, the effort to see moral reality justly and accurately, requires the discovery and revision of assumptions which may lead one to interpret and assess individuals by following formulas that obscure rather than illuminate them.[5]

Social conventions cannot be eliminated or avoided; it is difficult to imagine what life would be like without them. While some social conventions are innocuous and ease social life in a helpful and unproblematic manner, others cast a veil over individuals and circumstances. Examining one's orientation toward social conventions is one way to begin to work on the quality of one's perception. As Murdoch suggests, we need to ask ourselves: 'Are we accepting too readily the standards of our society or of our church?' (NM 105).

1.3 Neurosis

Conventional beliefs are but one aspect of consciousness which can veil reality. Murdoch indicates that neurosis can lead one to inhabit a fantasy world in which things from the outside are made into dream objects, their reality and independence denied (S&G 216). Murdoch most commonly uses the term 'neurosis' to refer to problems of self-centered egoism, anxiety, and obsession. She is not, I believe, using the term in a clinical sense, or in a solely Freudian sense. However, she is well-acquainted with Freud's work and familiar with his analysis of the causes, symptoms, and cures for neurosis.

According to Freud, both neurosis and psychosis disturb the individual's relation to reality.[6] In cases of neurosis, a part of reality is avoided. Furthermore, in neurosis, the

---

[5] Murdoch writes of the need to confront and dismantle inner barriers in order to achieve a quality of consciousness which will provide a suitable foundation for good conduct. These same barriers can, I believe, interfere with how one conceives of oneself and one's own possibilities, as well as with how one perceives other persons. A discussion of how conventional beliefs may distort one's self-conception can be found in Virginia Woolf's essay 'Professions for Women', in M. Barrett (ed.), *Women and Writing* (New York: Harcourt Brace Jovanovich, 1979), 57–63.

[6] Sigmund Freud, *The Question of Lay Analysis* (1926), chapter 3 (New York: W. W. Norton & Company, 1978), 22–9; 'Neurosis and Psychosis' (1924) and 'The Loss of Reality in Neurosis and Psychosis' (1924); all reprinted in Anna Freud (ed.), *The Essentials of Psycho-Analysis: The Definitive Collection of Sigmund Freud's Writing* (London: Penguin Books, 1991), 21–6, 563–7, 568–72. According to Freud, psychosis is the result of a conflict between the id and the ego in which the ego recognizes that reality will not accommodate the drive of the id. In the case of psychosis the ego is not strong enough to overrule the id. Instead, the ego is overcome by the id, torn away from reality, and psychotic symptoms develop. According to Freud, neurosis is the result of an ineffective response on the part of the ego to a demand made by the id. The ego seeks to satisfy the id, taking into account the requirements of the real world. When the id makes a demand which the ego, given its

subject develops a fantasy world in which to take refuge. The fantasy world provides an alternative which is more satisfying since it does not involve the constraints of the actual world. Freud believes that neurotics cannot be sharply differentiated from normal persons, that most people are somewhat neurotic, that everyday mental lapses (e.g. forgetting, misspeaking) are symptoms of neurosis, and that the severity of a neurosis is a matter of degree and can be measured by whether the symptoms interfere with important aspects of life.[7]

While Murdoch does not define 'neurosis' or state explicitly that she subscribes to Freud's view, her writing about neurosis is consistent with aspects of Freud's work. She refers approvingly to Freud's understanding of neurosis as representing 'the refusal of reality in favor of magical self-deception' (F&S 420). Murdoch cites obsession as an example of a neurosis, and writes about anxiety as another likely candidate. She repeatedly associates neurosis with fantasy, as contrasted with imagination. The deployment of energy to protect the ego from unpleasant aspects of reality results, Murdoch suggests, in a distorted picture of oneself as well as diminished engagement with the actual world. Murdoch conceives of neurosis as related to excessive self-preoccupation which diverts attention away from the external world (NM 105). Moreover, she believes that attraction to illusion is a common, even a natural, human tendency (OGG 51/341; SGC 78–9/364).

The work of David Shapiro, a contemporary psychotherapist, helps to illustrate the relation between neurosis and diminished moral attention. Shapiro, building on Freud's work, develops a conceptualization of neurosis which places the neurotic condition within the context of the entire personality. The title of his book, *Neurotic Styles*, refers to his claim that neurosis often functions as an organizing feature of an individual's personality; by 'style' he intends to convey how specific neuroses are related to subjective experiences such as thinking, perceiving, and experiencing emotion, and also to kinds of behavior.[8] His study of the characteristic features of obsessive-compulsive and paranoid individuals sheds light on Murdoch's suggestions concerning neurosis as an obstacle to moral insight.

Shapiro describes obsessive-compulsive neurosis as characterized by two features: intellectual rigidity and loss of reality. An obsessive-compulsive neurotic 'misses certain aspects of the world' because his or her attention, while sharply focused, has limited mobility and range (NS 27–8). Such an individual is 'actively inattentive' to

understanding of reality, recognizes as inappropriate or impossible to satisfy, then the ego represses the unrealizable desire. In some cases, in an effort to flee the inappropriate desire, the ego walls off part of the id, which then becomes inaccessible. That part of the id, however, is not effectively silenced. Rather, it still exerts pressure on the ego, but through indirect means. Since the id is no longer accessible to the ego, the ego looses power and influence over that part of the id. The neurotic symptoms are the revenge that the frustrated id takes on the ego which has not satisfied its desires. Types of neuroses discussed by Freud include: hysteria, obsession, narcissism, anxiety, and melancholy.

[7] Freud, *The Standard Edition of the Complete Psychological Works of Sigmund Freud* (London: Hogarth Press) vol. 6 (1959), 278–9; vol. 9 (1959), 210.
[8] David Shapiro, *Neurotic Styles* [NS] (New York: Basic Books, 1965), 1.

new ideas, is dogmatic, and lacks interest in the real truth. He or she is convinced of the beliefs that are aspects of the neurosis and avoids new information (NS 30, 51). These attitudes prevent the individual from 'seeing things in their real proportions' (NS 52). The paranoid individual, like the obsessive-compulsive, looks at the world with fixed and preoccupying expectation (NS 56). He or she ignores what does not confirm the expectation (NS 57). According to Shapiro, '[n]o such person can afford or tolerate the attitude of uncertainty, not to speak of open-mindedness or receptivity, which the unexpected or unusual . . . demands' (NS 62).

Shapiro articulates the mechanism of obscuring part of reality through fantasy which can be observed in individuals who are diagnosed as neurotic. The preoccupations of neurotic individuals actively filter and distort their perceptions of the outer world. What is seen is seen as fitting into a preconceived pattern, what does not fit the pattern is not noticed. The experience of surprise is avoided (NS 105). Shapiro's description of the effects of neurotic symptoms supports Murdoch's claim that neurosis tends to veil reality. Murdoch is concerned with how, in the ordinary individual, egoism, anxiety, and obsession tend to diminish perception and insight in moral life. Clearly, such truncated vision is more pronounced in some individuals. Shapiro's description of the influence of neurosis on individuals in whom neurosis interferes with ordinary life allows us to see the effects of this problem on a larger scale.

1.4 Neurosis and social prejudice

Murdoch offers no extended illustrations of neurosis, though if M's jealousy in regard to D stems from an obsessive attachment to her son, it may be a symptom of neurosis. In Murdoch's 1964 article 'The Moral Decision about Homosexuality' she states that the hostile reaction which the 'mere idea of homosexuality often encounters' is caused by irrational fears which also often govern reactions to black men and Jews.[9] She indicates that scientific study of the psychology of these fears would be useful.

Murdoch's purpose in her article on homosexuality is to examine arguments which are advanced by persons who find homosexuality morally problematic. She explicitly sets aside arguments which rely on religious beliefs; she focuses on arguments which assert that homosexuality is unnatural, unusual, or a disease. Murdoch shows that these arguments rely on either false empirical claims or conceptual confusion, e.g. 'natural' remains both undefined and assumed to be morally proper. She examines the view that homosexuals are promiscuous and that homosexual relationships are unstable. Murdoch notes that heterosexual promiscuity is not viewed as bringing the entire category of heterosexual relationships into moral doubt, and states that homosexuals have not been shown to be a great deal more promiscuous than heterosexuals. She acknowledges that since homosexual relationships do not result in children, are not legally sanctioned and often are kept secret, these relationships may be less stable than

---

[9] Murdoch, 'The Moral Decision about Homosexuality', [MDH] Man and Society, 7, Summer 1964, 3.

heterosexual relationships. However, with the exception of the conception of children, the causes of instability are not inherent in homosexuality. Murdoch's examination of common arguments against homosexuality reveals that these arguments lack substance and are expressions of prejudice. The use of the term 'natural' in arguments such as these is a good illustration of Murdoch's insight that social convention, ordinary language, and norms interact in a manner which obscures the variety of the human world and discourages reflection.

Murdoch states that hostility toward homosexuals is caused by irrational fears and she shows that common reasons given in support of hostile attitudes cannot withstand scrutiny. She does not examine causes for the fear or discuss how conventional beliefs about homosexuals may be related to neurosis. However, her claim that irrational fear is the origin of at least some of the hostility points in the direction of neurosis. I believe her ideas can be developed along the following lines. It may be that the hostility to which Murdoch refers is evoked by a sense that homosexuals cast doubt on traditional views about masculinity and femininity, making these views appear as conventions rather than expressions of nature. Since standard notions about sex and gender form part of most persons worldview and identity, practices which call these assumptions into question may be perceived as threatening to identity. The irrational fears to which Murdoch refers are, then, perhaps the result of a perception of a threat to a fundamental aspect of identity. If something along these lines is the case, it follows that hostile attitudes toward homosexuals are, at least in some cases, an expression of both social convention and neurosis, i.e. anxiety about the certainty and stability of identity gives rise to the relevant conventional beliefs. Social conventions, particularly when their status as conventions is obscured by the assumption that they are natural, provide a basis for beliefs about identity, appropriate behavior, and worthwhile ways of life. Perceived challenges to the conventions serve as oblique reminders of underlying uncertainty. By claiming that one expression of sexuality is natural and the other is not, the dominant group attempts to settle definitively the question in its own favor. Murdoch concludes her essay on homosexuality by suggesting that what is needed is a 'more humane and charitable recognition of our right to differ from one another'. (MDH 6).

1.5 Summary

Social convention and neurosis constitute internal obstacles to moral perception when they restrict understanding. They provide self-protective and easy formulas which reduce the need to do the work of discerning attention. One can use social convention to escape into a predetermined structure, thereby allowing unexamined assumptions to provide ready-made descriptions which obscure the difficulty of understanding particular persons and circumstances. Neurosis allows one to evade the same difficulties by taking refuge in egoism and projecting one's psychological dramas onto outer reality. Murdoch suggests that social convention and neurosis reduce imaginative engagement with moral reality. Instead, they provide comforting and untaxing fantasies which diminish or pre-empt insight. The contrast between fantasy and imagination helps to illuminate why Murdoch thinks that some conventional beliefs and neuroses reduce freedom.

2 Fantasy and imagination

The idea of moral freedom may ... be defined in terms of the triumph of imagination over fantasy. (MGM 326)
Imagination is a kind of freedom, a renewed ability to perceive and express the truth. (E&M 255)[10]

2.1 Fantasy

Some people use the words 'fantasy' and 'imagination' interchangeably, and the distinction between them can be difficult to appreciate. Murdoch uses these two terms to designate different qualities of consciousness. 'Fantasy' refers to consciousness which is egotistical and self-obsessed, perhaps even taken up with delusions of grandeur and revenge. It can, she suggests, 'imprison the mind, impeding new understanding ... possibilities of fruitful and virtuous action'. (MGM 322). Fantasy is the chief enemy of excellence in moral life because it is used to escape the world (OGG 59/347–8).

At first glance one might think that Murdoch is too severe in her criticism of fantasy and, in some circumstances, one might want to defend the use of fantasy to escape the world. However, I believe Murdoch's concern is that through fantasy one not only escapes the world but replaces the world with a self-satisfying creation of one's own. One may then fail to acknowledge that the fantasized (and more gratifying) world is a fabrication which occludes the actual world, including much within it that is obscure, demanding, and ungratifying. Moral attention can find no purchase in such an arrangement. A fantasy world, in Murdoch's sense, cannot serve as a reliable basis for good conduct.

2.2 Imagination

In contrast to 'fantasy', Murdoch uses the term 'imagination' to designate a 'moral discipline of the mind', an 'effortful ability to see what lies before one more clearly, more justly, to consider new possibilities' (MGM 322). To be imaginative is to engage in an effort, whereas to fantasize is undemanding. Through the exercise of imagination one has the opportunity to perceive experiences which are unlike one's own, as well as to perceive persons who are unlike oneself (MGM 322). Murdoch discusses the role of imagination in art, in politics ('to imagine the consequence of policies, to picture what it is like for people to be ... unemployed, persecuted, very poor') and in morals (MGM 322).

---

[10] Murdoch, 'Art is the Imitation of Nature' (1978), in E&M, 243–57.

One of Murdoch's great insights is that moral life goes on all the time, and is not limited to moments of public action. This insight is not a denial of the crucial importance of public conduct. Rather, it is a recognition of the fact that ongoing moral awareness provides the context out of which decisions about public action develop: 'I can only choose within the world I can *see, in the moral sense of "see"* which implies that clear vision is a result of moral imagination and moral effort' (IP 37/ 329). Murdoch's discussion of fantasy and imagination serves to indicate the variability of the quality of moral awareness, and the manner in which this variability is likely to influence what are conceived of as possible choices. So, for example, if I perceive the world through unexamined conventional beliefs which set up formulas that encapsulate other persons before I encounter them, or if neurotic preoccupations filter and structure my reading of the world, fantasy will influence what I conceive of as my choices.

Moral attention involves an attitude of imaginative receptivity and engagement with non-self parts of the world. This attitude itself requires engaging in the self-critical work of diminishing distorting conventional beliefs and neurotic tendencies to which one is prone. Murdoch sees a connection between the reduction of fantasy, the activity of imagination, and an increase in freedom. Her view indicates that one becomes freer by eliminating distorting conventional beliefs and neuroses.

3 Freedom and choice

The technique of becoming free is ... difficult ... [T]he assumption that we are all rational and totally free, engenders a dangerous lack of curiosity about the real world, a failure to appreciate the difficulties of knowing it. (AD 293)

Liberty, like the cure of the neurotic, lies at the level of total understanding. (SRR 62/96/124)[11]

3.1 Freedom

The conception of freedom about which Murdoch most often writes is unlike the notions of freedom which are commonly discussed in politics or much of contemporary philosophy. Murdoch is concerned primarily neither with the question of how far the state may go in regulating the behavior of its citizens, nor with traditional philosophical arguments about freedom and determinism. She takes issue with philosophers who portray freedom as the exercise of the will and as unencumbered choice (IP 23/317; OGG 53–4/343–4, 67/354). 'We are not', she writes, 'isolated free choosers' (AD 293). Philosophy's portrayal of humans as 'isolated free choosers' is, Murdoch suggests, misleading and dangerous. It ignores the ongoing need to reach out imaginatively toward what is real, as well as the social and cognitive background out of

---

[11] Murdoch, *Sartre: Romantic Rationalist* [SRR] (1953, 1987). I give references in turn to the first edition (1953, 78 pp.), the Fontana pbk (1967, 128 pp.), and the Penguin edition (1989, 158 pp.).

which public action develops. It overlooks the need for choice to be guided by understanding, as well as the difficulty of achieving understanding. The first passage cited above is an example of Murdoch's criticism of the portrayal of freedom as the exercise of the choosing will in a situation of minimal constraint. The situations in which human beings find themselves are not, Murdoch believes, empty of moral demands which properly serve to guide the will.

Murdoch refers to the type of freedom on which she focuses as moral freedom (DPR 201; MGM 326). She views moral freedom as a matter of disentangling oneself from illusions in order to see clearly the external world; in this sense, freedom is the result of understanding which is derived from clear vision. Murdoch views freedom as an incremental achievement, as an ideal toward which to strive. Rather than conceive of persons as free (or not) by nature, Murdoch views persons as more or less free depending on the quality of our engagement with 'things quite other than ourselves'. (SBR 284) Disciplined attention increases freedom by increasing understanding (M&E 70). Such disciplined attention and freedom is an ongoing and piecemeal task. It requires a two-way movement: countering inner obstacles combined with apprehension of external reality. In order to be free, fantasy, including certain conventional beliefs and neuroses, must be defeated so that imagination can engage in the effort of discernment.

The influence of Plato on Murdoch is evident here. As one acquires greater understanding one becomes freer. One moves from illusion toward understanding through a disciplined, and perhaps not entirely natural, effort to see reality. When enclosed in fantasy or illusion one does not genuinely understand either oneself or one's surroundings. Obstacles to freedom are often internal. For Plato, the appetitive and spirited parts of the soul constitute obstacles when they struggle against or dominate reason. For Murdoch, various types of comforting illusions constitute obstacles when they obscure the need for more effortful engagement with reality. For both Plato and Murdoch, freedom is release from illusion; as this release is achieved one gradually sees more accurately, and within context, both oneself and the wider world. This is, I believe, what Murdoch has in mind when she says, 'liberty, like the cure of the neurotic, lies at the level of total understanding' (SRR 124). Liberty is release from distorted conceptions of oneself and of the world; one becomes freer as one gains an increasingly accurate and comprehensive vision of reality.

Corresponding to the two-way movement—the attempt to both diminish inner obstacles and to perceive external reality—is the implication of a negative and a positive sense of freedom. The effort to examine and reduce the influence of inner obstacles can be understood as a type of negative freedom in that one strives to be unconstrained by such influences. Negative freedom involves inner moral work and creates conditions which are conducive to positive freedom.

Positive freedom may be understood as the experience of clear insight into moral reality. One is sufficiently aware so that one has not overlooked features of the situation—facts as well as relevant values—that should guide one's orientation and conduct.[12] Positive freedom involves understanding the circumstances one confronts and knowing how to conduct oneself in a manner which is appropriately responsive. Such insight may be achieved as the result of willed effort. Murdoch suggests one has some control over the direction and focus of one's vision in the sense that one can choose to engage in the inner moral work of purifying consciousness, as well as in the effort to see external reality clearly (OGG 75/361). One cannot, however, simply decide on the spot, as it were, to have sufficient insight and clarity of vision. Persistent effort is required. The quality of the background out of which public conduct develops depends on whether or not one pursues the struggle for clear vision.[13] As I mentioned earlier, Murdoch is not optimistic about our inclination to engage in this struggle. On her view, we tend to prefer consoling fantasies, particularly those which gratify our self-image, to imaginative engagement with reality.

Freedom is, then, difficult to achieve both because there are multiple internal obstacles and because other persons are obscure to us. Certain conventional beliefs and neuroses constitute internal barriers because they restrict understanding. The result is restraint on the development of freedom. When we combine the reduction of internal obstacles with a receptive discernment of others, we achieve some understanding of moral reality. One is free when one understands how things stand with others in their own right. I believe Murdoch conceives of the free individual as cognizant of moral duty, non-dogmatic, perceptive, flexible, responsive. Freedom is something like the ability to take-in the unforeseen, to move within the world in an aware and agile manner. If one is free, one is not restricted by predetermined formulas.

3.2 Choice

If I attend properly I will have no choices and this is the ultimate condition to be aimed at. (IP 40/331)

In this passage Murdoch suggests that the work of moral attention eliminates alternatives, and, ideally, a single choice presents itself as definitively compelling. As I have shown, she also suggests that freedom is achieved through proper attention. If one

---

[12] Murdoch challenges the fact-value distinction. She suggests that '[v]alue goes right down to the bottom of the cognitive situation' (MGM 384). Removing the values (if this were possible) would not leave the facts behind and unaltered. One's reading of the world is, Murdoch argues, inherently value-laden. The essential task of the moral agent is to employ imagination to read the world, to have an accurate and just vision of reality. See especially VCM 95; DPR 201. See also Cora Diamond ' "We are Perpetually Moralists": Iris Murdoch, Fact, and Value', in Maria Antonaccio and William Schweiker (eds), *Iris Murdoch and the Search for Human Goodness* (Chicago: University of Chicago Press, 1996).

[13] However, while the ongoing quality of consciousness provides the background out of which insight develops, and effortful engagement with the external world is needed to lay the foundation for insight, it is also the case that when no specific willed effort is exerted insight may occur as a kind of gift. I use the term 'gift' not to suggest that the insight will be welcome; seeing things as they are may well be painful. Rather, by 'gift' I mean to indicate the experience of unanticipated disclosure of how things stand. The likelihood of such insight is largely determined by the ongoing quality of awareness. Whether insight is sought or simply arrives, for Murdoch clarity of perception is an aspect of moral freedom.

combines these features of her thinking, one is led to the conclusion that, on her view, attention reduces choices and increases freedom; the more one understands, the freer one is and the fewer choices one has.

In order to examine this view, I begin with some general background. On the issue of the unity of moral life, Murdoch writes: '[p]hilosophers have sought for a single principle upon which morality may be seen to depend. I do not think that the moral life can be in this sense reduced to a unity' and, '[t]he scene remains disparate and complex beyond the hopes of any system, yet . . . the concept Good stretches through the whole of it and gives it the only kind of shadowy unachieved unity which it can possess' (MGM 492; SGC 97/380). So she is, at a minimum, skeptical about both the unity of moral life and philosophy's ability to systematize moral life. Moral attention can lead to the elimination of choices, but not because there is a single principle which, once grasped, provides the fulcrum upon which correct choice depends.

While Murdoch rejects the unity provided by philosophical theories based on a single principle or a set of duties, she does suggest that there is a kind of unity in moral life: 'reflection rightly tends to unify the moral world, and . . . increasing moral sophistication reveals increasing unity' (OGG 57/346–7). She finds unity present in moral life in two related ways. Murdoch endorses Plato's depiction of the journey of the soul through the realm of appearances and its ascent to the Form of the Good; she claims that the understanding which comes from insight into the Good provides a kind of unity to all the experienced phenomena. Developing comprehension of the Good contributes to understanding things in their context and giving them their proper value. This is one way in which unity may be perceived in moral life. Furthermore, Murdoch suggests that the virtues are related to each other. In connection with this view, Murdoch states that, '[i]t would be impossible to have only one virtue unless it were a very trivial one such as thrift' (SGC 95/378). Perhaps an example might be that as one matures one recognizes that a full understanding of truthfulness includes seeing its relation to courage, and a genuinely truthful individual is likely to be courageous. Increasing understanding of the virtues deepens understanding of moral life by revealing the connections among seemingly disparate character traits and indicating their proper place in a good life. This sort of reflection helps to organize one's thinking about how to live.

However, Murdoch recognizes that the conception of moral life as unified can be enormously attractive because it can provide a false sense of certainty. 'The notion that . . . "there is a best decision here", preserves from despair: the difficulty is how to entertain this consoling notion in a way which is not false' (OGG 56–57/346). Murdoch is suggesting, I believe, that the desire to come to a decision and to avoid doubt, can lead one to embrace reductive decision-making processes. Though she believes that there often is a best possible decision, the tendency to want to avoid the effort required to discover that decision contributes to reliance on views and methods which make moral life less demanding.

Murdoch suggests that moral life should combine deepening reflection on moral values with attention to the details of external reality. Ultimately, if one sees it all clearly, Murdoch thinks, 'a kind of "necessity"' will emerge and the best way to act will be clear (IP 40/331). When this clarity is achieved it involves a combination of a broad and deep view of the circumstances with a sharp perception of the relevant values: '[t]he good man knows whether and when art or politics is more important than family' (SGC 95/378). No set of rules or single principle will provide this knowledge. No one of these values—art (work), politics, family—is always the most important, so one must understand the wider context of the circumstances, as well as the consequences of the various options, in order to make a good choice. When Murdoch suggests that the complexity of the scene cannot be captured in a philosophical system, that the Good provides it with a kind of unity, and that the good person knows which choice to make, she is indicating that the unity moral life does possess cannot be formulated in a principle or articulated in a system. Yet the concept of Good is experienced as an ideal which, developed out of an intuited sense of transcendent perfection, relates the virtues to each other and provides organization in moral life (MGM 507). The person who achieves this understanding has a grasp on relevant values and contingent factors, as well as a broad sense of what a good life entails so that the area—art, politics, family—most in need of active involvement receives it. Murdoch is suggesting that increased awareness brings clearer perception of the suitability of various options. Greater degrees of insight show the shortcomings of particular options. Sometimes, 'ultimately' as Murdoch says, one choice stands out as superior to the rest.

Murdoch's sense of the disparate and complex nature of moral life is part of the basis for her skepticism about philosophical systems which distil morality to a single principle or set of duties. However, Murdoch's view of the shortcomings of conceiving of morality as consisting of duties does not lead her to reject duties as unimportant either in philosophical conceptions of moral life or in moral life itself. Rather, her view is that the concept of duty, while an 'indispensable' part of morality, must be seen in a 'wider landscape' (MGM 302–3). Duty is useful particularly when morality is being taught, as a check on egoism, 'when moral instinct and habit fail' (MGM 302). Duty must not be dispensed with, yet when moral philosophy focuses exclusively on duty much of moral life is left out of its theories. Certainty about how to act may come through a recognition of duty. However, the certainty that comes from the force of duty is not what Murdoch is referring to in the passage cited at the beginning of this section.

When Murdoch states that one will have no choices, she is claiming neither that there will be a lack of alternatives in the factual sense, nor that one will be unaware of alternatives. She is suggesting that a persistent, disciplined dedication to both the quality of one's awareness and to the conditions of other persons' lives is the approach which is most likely to provide a solid foundation for good conduct. As understanding deepens, the alternatives to which one is drawn will be increasingly limited, yet one will be free because one is uninfluenced by distorting beliefs and one is cognizant of the factors relevant to a good choice. On these occasions, one's perception of the situation is such that one is compelled to see it, and respond to it, in a particular manner because one is compelled by the facts. One sees alternatives as falling short to such an extent that one is not drawn to them.

Murdoch's claim that proper attention ultimately yields a single choice which appears as a kind of necessity, connects with and relies upon other aspects of her moral philosophy. One relevant feature is her stipulation that she is using the concept of attention to refer to the search for a just and loving perception of reality (IP 23/317). 'Reality' can best be understood as the genuine conditions of the lives of other persons and the wider world, e.g. what it is like to be poor, what D is actually like. Murdoch adds to this the claim that when one attends properly to others one has a sense of the direction in which truth lies; one is guided by a sense of perfection which provides a magnetic pull. As one engages in attentive discernment one is likely to characterize what one sees using what Murdoch refers to as 'secondary specialized terms', such as 'decent', 'cowardly', 'honest', as well as terms such as those used in the M and D example (IP 42/333). On Murdoch's view, action 'follows naturally' from the reality which is seen, hence the importance of the quality of perception (IP 42/333). 'I would be prepared to imply that one who perceives what is real will also act rightly. If the magnetic field is right our movements within it will tend to be right' (DPR 201). For example, having perceived something as 'the decent thing to do', all things being equal, one will act accordingly.

As Murdoch describes it, proper attention seeks truthful understanding. As one searches for improved understanding, one intuits and is drawn to a reality which transcends what is already understood. Experience of imperfection helps one understand perfection (MGM 427). This may sound esoteric, but learning to play a musical instrument or learning a new language are familiar experiences which follow a similar pattern. Effort is directed to closing the gap between one's current understanding and a more or less remote standard which transcends one's present level of accomplishment. The standard is intuited as 'beyond' and serves to focus and discipline one's energies. This is similar to the magnetic attraction of perfection to which Murdoch refers.

A sense of the unity of moral life develops from attentive reflection in the course of ordinary life (E&I 92).[14] Increasing understanding sheds light on the interrelation of values and shows greater order. The activity of imagination is crucial here. Murdoch writes: 'Imagination suggests the searching, joining, light-seeking, semi-figurative nature of the mind's work, which prepares and forms the consciousness for action' (E&I 91). One way to understand Murdoch's view is that the inner work of diminishing fantasy eliminates options and the initial imaginative exploration of moral reality presents new alternatives. When this initial imaginative exploration develops into proper attention, some alternatives are recognized as unsuitable and so set aside. Attention is a refined perception which reveals increasingly adequate responses. Ideally,

---

[14] Murdoch, 'Ethics and the Imagination' [E&I], *Irish Theological Quarterly*, vol. 52, 1986, 81–95.

the best course of action, with all of its advantages, is recognized; the suitability of this course of action is so compelling that alternatives cannot stand against it. It is important to note that Murdoch describes the condition of having no choices as what is ultimately to be aimed at; it is an ideal.[15]

Moral freedom is then the result of a mode of reflection which, when achieved, allows one to reorganize or change the moral concepts one uses to interpret the world; it deepens insight into moral reality (VCM 95). The power of insight is such that one is compelled by what one sees to follow the course of action most suitable to the circumstances. Quieting the distractions of the ego in all their permutations (neurosis), and avoiding the temptation to take refuge in pre-established structures and undemanding formulas (convention) provides part of the foundation for moral engagement.[16]

My concern here has been to show that Murdoch's comments about social convention and neurosis can be understood by placing them within the wider context of her work. Her focus on the quality of moral consciousness stresses the need to examine internal obstacles to moral vision in order to be attentive to others. Social convention and neuroses can constitute obstacles which diminish and distort awareness of moral reality. They thereby obscure choices which would do justice to moral reality if it were more clearly understood. Moreover, Murdoch's insistence that moral insight is an ongoing task which requires the exercise of imagination at the expense of consoling fantasy, is parallel to her conception of freedom as increased through the acquisition of greater understanding. For Murdoch, to be free is not to exercise one's will in a situation of minimal constraint, but rather to have an astute awareness of oneself and

[15] Murdoch's view is reminiscent of Aristotle's. In the *Nicomachean Ethics* Aristotle uses the metaphor of hitting a target in his discussion of virtuous action. He points out that there are many ways of going wrong, but only one way which is right. In order to perform a virtuous action in a virtuous manner, one needs an understanding of the relevant principle, a discerning perception of the particulars, the proper motive, correct timing and manner, and a good character. Despite such demanding criteria, Aristotle portrays the self-controlled individual as not only capable of hitting the target, but as possessing unwavering focus on virtuous conduct, undistracted by inclination or pleasure. It would seem that Aristotle's self-controlled individual, like Murdoch's properly attentive person, has no choice. Murdoch sets this up as an ideal, the ultimate achievement at which to aim, as does Aristotle. In her article 'Asymmetrical Freedom' Susan Wolf argues that an agent who performs a bad action and whose action is determined is not blameworthy, whereas an agent who performs a good action and whose action is determined is praiseworthy. This is the asymmetry referred to in her title. Wolf argues that a morally praiseworthy agent may be psychologically determined to act well because his character is such that he sees the reasons for the action and is compelled by the reasons. The agent could not do otherwise *because* there are good and sufficient reasons to perform the virtuous action, he recognizes those reasons, and the reasons are decisive for him. Had there not been good and sufficient reasons he could have acted otherwise. It is the reasons, which he does not create but recognizes, which determine his action. The agent has no choice, yet is free because in the absence of the grounds for his choice he could act differently. Susan Wolf, 'Asymmetrical Freedom', in D. Pereboom (ed.), *Free Will*, (Indianapolis, IN: Hackett Publishing, 1997).

[16] Despite the apparent and significant differences between Murdoch and Kant, it is possible to hear an echo of Kant in Murdoch's discussion of freedom and choice. Kant portrays the free person as governed by reason, undistracted by inclination or prudence. Such a person is free when he or she does what reason requires; freedom is lost when inclination or hypothetical commands provide the basis for action.

others which gives each its proper value. As understanding deepens one is more capable of perceiving the relative merits of various ways of construing the moral world, as well as the adequacy of various responses. As a result, the options to which one is drawn become increasingly adequate to the circumstances one faces.

Murdoch's philosophical work merits attention from contemporary thinkers because she both continues certain aspects of philosophical analysis and brings new insight to the problems she addresses. Her continuation of philosophical thinking can be found not only in the influence of Plato on her work, but also in the way she takes up and re-orients features of Aristotle's and Kant's work. For example, Murdoch's discussion of having no choice is similar to Aristotle's discussion of the demanding set of criteria—right principle, motive, manner, action—met by the self-controlled person. Her notion that genuine freedom requires understanding and the absence of internal obstacles is reminiscent of Kant's idea that the free individual is guided by reason and undistracted by inclination or prudence. Murdoch's insight that moral life is on-going, that one's ordinary awareness and construal of reality is the foundation for conduct, and that persistent effort is required in order to see and act well, focus attention on the demanding nature of moral life. Murdoch sets out an ideal in her description of moral engagement, but she sets out the ideal without being idealistic about our inclination to pursue this work. Her writing both points out gaps in the philosophical tradition and reminds the reader of the mundane demands of moral life.

8

Iris Murdoch on Nobility and Moral Value*

Roger Crisp

There are many strands in the philosophical work of Iris Murdoch, woven into a colourful and complex tapestry rather than bound tightly into a rope. In this essay, I wish to draw out one of these strands, in the hope of showing that Murdoch is better able than the dominant forms of contemporary ethical theory to make room for and offer an account of a certain paradigmatic kind of moral value.

Why did Murdoch not develop a 'moral theory', as did so many of her contemporaries? She believed that attending to detail, and bringing out the nuances of what was observed, was the way to truth:

Here it is especially important to attend to the initial delineation of the field of study, observing where and in what way moral judgements may be involved, and then to consider the relations between the selected phenomena and the philosophical technique used to describe them. A narrow or partial selection of phenomena may suggest certain particular techniques which will in turn seem to lend support to that particular selection; and then a circle is formed out of which it may be hard to break. It is therefore advisable to return frequently to an initial survey of 'the moral'. (VCM 76)[1]

If we do not stop to look, we may fail to understand not only the world, but ourselves, and value may be lost:

* For comments on previous drafts I am grateful to participants at the conference *Iris Murdoch, Philosopher* held at Brown University, 20–21 April 2001, especially to my commentator Julia Driver, and to Brad Hooker, Jeremy Watkins, and an anonymous reader for the Press. I owe a special debt to Justin Broackes, whose many penetrating remarks greatly improved the arguments of the paper.
[1] 'Vision and Choice in Morality' (1956) [VCM]. Page references to this and certain other essays of Murdoch's are to the reprintings in *Existentialists and Mystics* [E&M], ed. P. J. Conradi (1997). Cf. 'Dominant metaphors in metaphysics have large implications. By looking at something, by *stopping* to look at it, we do not selfishly appropriate it, we understand it and let it be' (*Metaphysics as a Guide to Morals* [MGM] (London: Chatto & Windus, 1992), 462); and 'Metaphysics and Ethics' (1957), E&M 75.

To do philosophy is to explore one's own temperament, and yet at the same time to discover the truth. It seems to me that there is a void in present-day moral philosophy. Areas peripheral to philosophy expand (psychology, political and social theory) or collapse (religion) without philosophy being able in the one case to encounter, and in the other case to rescue, the values involved. (OGG 46/337)[2]

Murdoch's emphasis here on the importance of attention to the phenomenon under examination must be right. As human beings we live first, and then do philosophy about things we have met in our lives. In the case of moral philosophy, then, we ought to try to understand what morality is, how it is lived and experienced, what it seems to us to be and not to be, before offering any kind of theory about it. In 1967, Murdoch said, critically: 'Recent philosophers . . . prefer to talk of reasons rather than experiences' (SGC 84/369). That claim remains true. Of course we need to understand reasons; but if we are interested in moral reasons we must first understand morality as we experience it. And 'morality is, in the human world, something unique, special, *sui generis*, "as if it came to us from elsewhere" . . . The interpretation of such phrases . . . should be a main activity of moral philosophers' (MGM 26).

So I am not going to begin my argument with any a priori or abstract moral principle (though this is not to say that that is not where an argument may respectably end). Rather, I shall begin with an example.[3] I was tempted to use Murdoch's own famous case of the mother-in-law who changes her attitude towards her daughter-in-law through sensitive attention to the facts (IP 17–18/313), but felt that she is better seen as an illustration of the importance of vision, rather than as an object of scrutiny herself. So consider the case of Magda Trocmé, the wife of the pastor André Trocmé, of Le Chambon, a French Huguenot village in Vichy France.[4] During the Nazi occupation, the village, under André Trocmé's guidance, protected about 3,000 refugees. It was as obvious to the Trocmés as it is to us what the Nazis would have done to them had they been discovered. Here is a passage from a letter André Trocmé wrote in 1943:

[2] IP, OGG, and SGC are used to abbreviate 'The Idea of Perfection' (1964), 'On "God" and "Good"' (1969) and 'The Sovereignty of Good Over Other Concepts' (1967), the three essays that make up *The Sovereignty of Good* [SG] (1970). Page numbers, separated by a forward slash/, refer to *The Sovereignty of Good* and to the reprintings in *Existentialists and Mystics* (1997). Cf.: '[P]art of what is disappearing is both the occurrence of certain experiences, and also of our tendency to *notice* them and, instinctively or reflectively, to lend them moral or religious meaning. A lack of Eros' (MGM 307).

[3] 'All one can do is to appeal to certain areas of experience, pointing out certain features, and using suitable metaphors and inventing suitable concepts where necessary to make these features visible. No more, and no less, than this is done by the most empirically minded of linguistic philosophers' (SGC 74–5/361). Cf. also the beginning of 'The Sublime and the Good' [S&G] (1959): Murdoch insists, against Tolstoy, that we begin not with a 'definition of true art' and then judge works of art in accordance with it. Instead 'our direct apprehension of which works of art are good has just as much authority . . . as our philosophical reflections upon art in general' (E&M 205).

[4] Discussed illuminatingly in Lawrence Blum, 'Moral Exemplars: Reflections on Schindler, the Trocmés, and Others', *Ethical Theory: Character and Virtue, Midwest Studies in Philosophy* 13 (Notre Dame: Notre Dame University Press, 1988), ed. P. French, T. Uehling, and H. Wettstein, 196–221.

[I]n the course of this summer we have been able to help about sixty Jewish refugees in our own house; we have hidden them, fed them, plucked them out of deportation groups, and often we have taken them to a safe country. You can imagine . . . what real dangers this means for us: threats of arrest, submitting to long interrogations . . . I used to turn our dining room into a waiting room during the summer. Now it is a waiting room all year round.[5]

Later I shall say a little about my own response to this example, a response which I trust is not unusual. But let me assert for the moment that we have here a clear case of what I shall call 'nobility', a kind of admirable 'moral goodness' or 'moral value' which a moral theory should be able to offer some account of. I shall now consider utilitarianism, Kantian ethics, and Aristotelian virtue ethics in the light of this explanatory requirement.[6]

1 Utilitarianism

Utilitarianism, by which I shall mean act-utilitarianism, like all plausible moral theories, approves Magda Trocmé's actions—indeed, it could be argued, it requires them. Further, there are certain not unattractive elements in utilitarianism, such as its strict impartiality, which I shall suggest in my final section Murdoch herself recognized. My question in this section, however, is whether utilitarianism can make sense of the moral value in what Magda Trocmé did.

By helping to save so many Jews from the holocaust, Magda Trocmé undoubtedly prevented a great deal of suffering, and replaced that suffering with happiness. But the mere fact that she promoted happiness in this way fails to explain our response. The appropriate reaction to the promotion of happiness is gladness, as can be seen in the case of natural disasters. When we hear, for example, that the inhabitants of a certain village were warned of an impending earthquake and managed to avoid being buried alive, we are glad. And, undoubtedly, one is glad that Magda Trocmé did what she did, and glad at its successful outcome. But this is not the full story, and, I suggest, this is something which Murdoch recognized: 'What [utilitarianism] lacks, and needs . . . is a positive conception of virtue'.[7]

---

[5]   Quoted in P. Hallie, *Lest Innocent Blood be Shed: The Story of the Village of Le Chambon and how Goodness Happened There* (New York: Harper and Row, 1979), 147–8.

[6]   I select these three as the dominant lines of thought in contemporary ethics, not because I believe they have any special claim to greater plausibility than, for example, contractualism, rule-utilitarianism, or Rossian intuitionism. But to my knowledge none of these other theories is (yet) in a better position to explain the value of nobility than those I discuss.

[7]   MGM 47. Utilitarianism 'nullifies the inner', though such nullification 'receives understandable lay support from those who hold that "soul-talk" is a luxury in a world where action to relieve suffering is our main duty' (MGM 348). Murdoch believed that the *Zeitgeist* of her time was utilitarian (MGM 493) and that this led 'people with high motives into a "specialised" fragmented morality. In extreme situations of this sort, which may seem to young people the only "moral" situations with which they can engage, the idea of the virtuous individual tends to vanish. A cynic . . . might say of our age that it is the end of the era of "the virtuous individual"' (MGM 427).

Utilitarianism is evaluatively reductive, in so far as it suggests that the *only* value is well-being, and all other purported values must be made sense of within this framework. This leads to various apparent distortions of our ordinary conceptions of value. What is said to be valuable about art, for example, is not its intrinsic aesthetic quality, but the experience or enjoyment of art by human beings. But it might seem that one can make sense of the content of aesthetic experience only on the assumption that art confronts us with a value independent of our own well-being.[8] The difficulty is again one of conceptual narrowness:

A new unity, involving perhaps a new dichotomy, is likely to lose, make ineffable or conceptually inaccessible, visions and values which were elsewhere evident, and indeed the eclipse of these may have been one of the aims of the metaphysician. The rulers in Orwell's *1984* alter the language so as to make certain things unsayable. Consider what values Marxism squeezed out of view, or how a strict pietistic Kantianism excludes the generality of a Benthamite outlook, while on the other hand utilitarianism lacks a detailed picture of virtue. Ideas about beauty and virtue expressed in terms of quality of consciousness or quality of happiness find no appropriate vocabulary in many recent styles of moral philosophy (MGM 84; cf. 365).

So utilitarianism, in so far as it cannot attach value in itself to an agent's character or virtue, or indeed action, will find it hard to provide a comprehensive account of the kind of moral value exemplified in nobility. For, in the case of Magda Trocmé, it is her virtuous action, or the character to which it points, in which we locate moral value. Especially significant, as can be seen from my example, is a readiness to make a great sacrifice for the sake of others. I could now pick up a telephone and, using my credit card, save as many lives as Magda Trocmé, at little cost to my own well-being. Were I to do this, it would of course be admirable, but my action would fail to exemplify moral value in the same way. There appears to be value in character, and especially in weighty self-sacrifice, which utilitarianism cannot capture.

One move the utilitarian might make would be to allow for whatever non-welfarist conception of moral value is causing the problem here, but to insist that the criterion of right action is nevertheless strictly welfarist. But the introduction of such non-welfarist value—even if we allow the view that results to be described as utilitarian—deprives utilitarianism of some of its immediate attractiveness (based on the idea that, when it comes down to it, the only thing that really matters is how well the lives of individual beings actually go), as well as introducing a hostage to other theories: If there is room for non-welfarist values, then what is to stop the anti-utilitarian claiming that such value can be found in the actions she is recommending?

A second move might be to seek a place for moral value not as non-welfarist but as a constituent of welfare itself, to see virtue as 'part of happiness', as J. S. Mill put it.[9] Mill

---

[8] I try to make a similar case in connection with the notion of accomplishment in 'Utilitarianism and Accomplishment', *Analysis* 60 (2000), 264–8.

[9] J. S. Mill, *Utilitarianism*, ed. R. Crisp (Oxford: Oxford University Press, 1998 [1861]), ch. 4, para. 5, line 28.

seems to offer an account of the 'moral quality' (MGM 47) of certain higher pleasures, speaking of the pleasures of the 'moral sentiments' of a 'person of feeling and con-science', and explaining that such a person will not surrender these pleasures because of their 'sense of dignity'. Their object is what is 'noble', and their characters are themselves 'noble' (*Utilitarianism*, 2.4.18–19; 2.6.7–8; 2.7.10; 2.9.6). Might we, then, use the notion of nobility as a constituent of well-being to explain the value of nobility?

It seems not. Even if Magda Trocmé's nobility were somehow a constituent of her own well-being, it is hard to see our response to it as to this particular aspect of it. But, anyway, it is her willingness to *sacrifice* herself which partly explains why we attribute moral value to her action in the way we do.

The most common way for utilitarians to explain the value we attribute to the virtues and virtuous actions is to instrumentalize them: The possession and exercise of virtue is to be encouraged and admired, but only because of the effects of the virtues on the well-being of the agent or others.[10] As we see in Hume, the result of such instrumentalization is that the distinction between the moral virtues and other useful qualities breaks down:

They are both of them mental qualities: And both of them equally produce pleasure; and have of course an equal tendency to procure the love and esteem of mankind . . . Since then natural abilities, tho', perhaps, inferior, yet are on the same footing, both as to their causes and effects, with those qualities which we call moral virtues, why shou'd we make any distinction betwixt them?[11]

Indeed, on this view, these useful qualities need not be qualities of persons alone, as Adam Smith noticed: '[I]t seems impossible . . . that we should have no other reason for praising a man than that for which we commend a chest of drawers'.[12]

I believe Hume is right to suggest that the boundaries between the moral virtues and natural abilities are more blurred than is often thought. In particular, the 'esteem' we have for certain largely 'involuntary' qualities—such as, for example, an equable temper which has been present from a person's earliest days—often involves an attitude which might be reserved for cases of genuinely voluntarily acquired virtue, or virtuous action. But there seems nevertheless to be a huge difference between our attitude to Magda Trocmé's actions on the one hand, and on the other to, for example, the efficacy of some life-saving drug, even though both are equally productive in terms of

---

[10] See J. Driver, *Uneasy Virtue* (Cambridge: Cambridge University Press, 2001).

[11] D. Hume, *A Treatise of Human Nature*, ed. L. Selby-Bigge, 2nd edn., rev. P. H. Nidditch (Oxford: Clarendon Press, 1978 [1739–40]), bk. 3, pt. 3, sect. 4, 606–7.

[12] A. Smith, *The Theory of the Moral Sentiments*, ed. D. D. Raphael and A. L. Macfie (Oxford: Clarendon Press, 1976 [1759]), 188. Hume appears to be responding to this kind of criticism in *An Enquiry Concerning the Principles of Morals*, ed. T. L. Beauchamp (Oxford: Oxford University Press, 1998 [1751]), sect. 5, pt. 1, n. 17; but he does not go far beyond merely recognizing the problem. Cf. *Treatise* 3.3.5, 617: 'There is something very inexplicable in this variation of our feelings.'

overall human happiness. And we should not conclude that this difference is 'inexplicable' until we have tried seriously to explain it.

Of course, the utilitarian may seek to explain it by reference to human psychology: There would be little point in morally praising some drug, whereas we know that praising human beings can steer their behaviour towards greater overall happiness. Likewise, we do not need to ascribe any very great value to actions which benefit others at little cost to the agent, since the obstacles placed by self-interest in the way of performing such actions are smaller. But in the case of actions such as those of Magda Trocmé it makes sense to apply a stronger form of social pressure than is usual.

On this 'multilevel' view, quite standard within the utilitarian tradition, there is indeed a right thing to do, namely, to maximize well-being, expected well-being, or whatever; but what we in fact praise and blame will be actions in some different class, because such practices of praising and blaming will themselves be more productive of well-being.[13]

These accounts of virtue and moral value, however, suffer from instability. On the one hand, they take our notion of moral value or moral rightness, as it usually understood, and attach the notion of rightness to utility-maximizing actions rather than those to which common-sense morality attaches it. But on the other they attempt to characterize the practice of moral praise or blame as essentially based on a fiction— that the actions praised have moral value or disvalue. But why should the fiction not extend to the notion of moral value itself, given that the practice of accepting it and acting as if there were such a thing might be productive of well-being overall?

At this point, the utilitarian may seek to instrumentalize the very institution of morality itself. Mill, following Alexander Bain, sought to explain the essence of morality in a paragraph of *Utilitarianism* which has recently received a good deal of attention from interpreters:

We do not call anything wrong, unless we mean to imply that a person ought to be punished in some way or other for doing it; if not by law, by the opinion of his fellow creatures; if not by opinion, by the reproaches of his own conscience . . . [W]e call any conduct wrong . . . according as we think that the person ought, or ought not, to be punished for it. (5.14)

Mill goes on to suggest that this desire to punish wrongdoers rests on sympathy with all sentient beings, and a natural sentiment of resentment:

[T]he natural feeling tends to make us resent indiscriminately whatever any one does that is disagreeable to us; but when moralized by the social feeling, it only acts in the directions conformable to the general good. (5.21)

For one's resentment to be moral, one has to feel that one is 'asserting a rule which is for the benefit of others as well as for [one's] own' (5.22). The story about moral value,

[13] See e.g. P. Railton, 'Alienation, Consequentialism, and the Demands of Morality', *Philosophy and Public Affairs*, 13 (1984), 134–71.

as opposed to disvalue, could, presumably, be told in the same way: We wish to reward those who follow principles that are for the general good, and so we praise them.

Much more needs to be said, of course, about the nature of blame and praise, as well as about guilt (the 'punishment' arising from blame) and about whatever the reward of being praised is. If the utilitarian can offer us a plausible account of these notions, then she is well on the way to offering us an account of moral value.[14] It does seem to me that Locke, Bentham, Hume, Mill, and others in the utilitarian tradition have made a serious start on the project of providing an instrumentalist account of morality,[15] but as things stand quite a lot more is required before utilitarianism has an answer to Bernard Williams's question: '*[B]y what right* does it legislate to the moral sentiments?'.[16]

2 Kantian ethics

'Nothing in the world—indeed nothing even beyond the world—can possibly be conceived which could be called good without qualification except a GOOD WILL' (FMM 393).[17] Kant's focus on the inner, we might expect, is likely to be a richer source of understanding of moral value than utilitarianism.

But well-known difficulties arise when we begin to examine just what it is to possess, and to exercise, a good will. Because of Kant's metaphysics, and in particular his view of the self, any action—or piece of behaviour—that arises out of sympathy or concern for others can only be praised or encouraged, not esteemed (FMM 398). In this sense, then, like Hume and other utilitarians, Kant sees no important distinction between traits such as kindness and others such as cleanliness or an ability to act well.

Now imagine what is far from the truth,[18] that Magda Trocmé, though dutiful, had little sympathy for others, and was naturally

cold and indifferent to the sufferings of others . . . —would not she find in herself a source from which to give herself a far higher worth than she could have got by having a good-natured

---

[14] Of course, any moral theorist should be prepared to offer such an account.

[15] See e.g. my 'Hume on Virtue, Utility, and Morality', in S. Gardiner (ed.), *Virtue Ethics, Old and New* (Ithaca: Cornell University Press, 2005), 159–78.

[16] B. Williams, 'Preface', *Moral Luck* (Cambridge: Cambridge University Press, 1981), x.

[17] I. Kant, *Foundations of the Metaphysics of Morals* [FMM] (1785), in *Foundations of the Metaphysics of Morals and, What is Enlightenment?*, trans. L. W. Beck (Indianapolis: Bobbs-Merrill/New York: Liberal Arts Press, 1959). Page references are to the Prussian Academy edition.

[18] In fact Magda Trocmé was a deeply caring person, and it was this characteristic that first drew her husband's attention to her, as he thought, 'Here is a person who cares for others on their own terms, not in order to parade her own virtues, but in order to keep them well. In the many years to follow, he would see how poignantly Magda felt the cold in the bodies of others, and how she would spend much of their lives covering or uncovering children' (Hallie, *Lest Innocent Blood Be Shed*, 64–5). Indeed her view of morality contrasted with that of her husband, who allowed for sheer moral authority as a source of reasons: 'Magda Trocmé believes that something is evil *because* it hurts people. Hers is an ethic of benevolence: she needed only to look into the eyes of a refugee in order to find her duty. But her husband . . . believed that something is evil both because it hurts somebody *and* because it violates an imperative, a commandment given us by God in the Bible and in our particular hearts . . . she recognized no imperatives from above: she saw only another's

temperament? This is unquestionably true . . . for it is just here that the worth of character is brought out, which is morally the incomparably highest of all: she is beneficent not from inclination, but from duty.[19]

Myself, I can detect no moral worth in the actions of the indifferent Magda Trocmé. Indeed, I find her a rather terrifying character, since, if we accept the standard objection to Kantian formalism that it puts no serious constraints on what can be willed, it is purely contingent that her conception of duty happens to chime with what is required by the virtue of kindness. (As is well known, at his trial in Jerusalem, Adolf Eichmann claimed that the Categorical Imperative supported his actions.) As R. M. Hare was aware, without assistance from some other theory (in his case, of course, utilitarianism), the possibility of Kantian fanaticism cannot be ruled out.[20]

Christine Korsgaard has recently attempted to rehabilitate Kant's account of moral worth in the *Foundations*.[21] She suggests that the person of good will (that is, the dutiful person) and the sympathetic (or compassionate) person may have the same purpose (FD 206)—to help others—and that we may understand Kant as offering us a 'double-aspect' account of motivation, according to which motivation involves (i) an 'incentive', that presents the action and its end as worthy of choice, and (ii) the principle of volition that governs the actual choice of the agent to act on the incentive in question (FD 208). Kantian moral value, she suggests, lies in the principle of volition, in that the person of good will 'chooses helping as her purpose *because* that is what she is required to do. Kant takes this to be equivalent to being moved by the thought of the maxim of the action, the principle of doing it, as a kind of law' (FD 207). The compassionate person, however, has a quite different principle of volition: it is 'the principle of doing what he likes to do' (FD 208).

Thus, she suggests, if we compare the reflective dutiful person with the reflective compassionate person, we can identify a special moral worth or value in the action of the former. For 'the agent who consciously employs the principle of self-love in his choice does seem to look to himself; in fact he seems to choose beneficence as one might choose a hobby' (FD 209). And the unreflective compassionate person is merely 'allowing his choices to be governed by his natural inclinations, and so is simply following where nature leads' (FD 210).

Kant's own ethics, of course, is underpinned by his metaphysics, but Korsgaard does not appeal explicitly to the noumenal/phenomenal contrast to make what appears to be a case for the plausibility of Kant's understanding of moral motivation. Nevertheless,

---

need, and felt only a need to satisfy that need as best she could' (ibid., 161). Note that this need is described entirely without reference to duty.

[19] FMM 398–9. I have of course changed the subject's gender.

[20] R. M. Hare, *Moral Thinking: Its Methods, Level, and Point* (Oxford: Clarendon Press, 1981), ch. 10.

[21] C. Korsgaard, 'From Duty and for the Sake of the Noble: Kant and Aristotle on Morally Good Action' [FD], in S. Engstrom and J. Whiting (ed.), *Aristotle, Kant, and the Stoics: Rethinking Happiness and Duty* (Cambridge: Cambridge University Press, 1996), 203–36.

her defence rests on the two-tier account of motivation, and that does seem a product of Kantian metaphysics, in which 'nature' causes in us 'incentives' on the basis of which a free and independent reason can make choices.

If we distance ourselves from Kantian metaphysics, an alternative to the two-tier account emerges. The compassionate person is not just driven along blindly by whatever desires she happens to have. Rather, she sees others in need, feels compassionate concern for them, and is moved to assist. This is 'unreflective' compassion. If asked to reflect, she would say something like: 'The reason for helping those people was that they were in need.' No reference to her own likes, desires, or happiness is required. This kind of motivation is, I think, what we see in the case of Magda Trocmé.[22]

What about a dutiful person? She may also feel compassionate concern, but in her case she must not allow that concern to move her to action. Rather, if she does act, she must act on her sense of duty, and when asked to justify her action, must say: 'My reason for helping is that I was required to do so.' In other words, she cannot recognize the needs of others as themselves providing reasons for action. It may be claimed that the requirement itself rests on the fact that someone was in need of help, so that both need and duty can provide reasons.[23] But the reason-giving force of need is entirely funnelled through that of duty: Need itself can provide no motivation for the dutiful person except in so far as it affects duty itself. The dutiful person is both alienated from others, and neurotically fixated on duty. If we must speak of duty here, we should say that it is her duty to help *because* these people are in need. Its being a duty cannot in itself constitute a reason for action (and so, I suggest, we could quite easily do without the notion of duty in moral philosophy).

I am here echoing certain criticisms of Kant and moral theory in general made by several modern writers such as Elizabeth Anscombe and Bernard Williams, who were themselves, whether consciously or unconsciously, echoing those of Arthur Schopenhauer in his *On the Basis of Morality* of 1841.[24] Murdoch herself takes much from Schopenhauer, speaking approvingly of his notion that exercising our capacity for compassion and identifying with others can weaken our egoistic impulses, and she links this with Simone Weil's thought that these impulses themselves constitute an obstacle to knowledge of the reality of the world, including the people within it (MGM 52–3). But, unlike Schopenhauer and Weil, Murdoch sees a place for duty in morality:

---

[22] See n. 18 above.

[23] This point was made to me by Justin Broackes.

[24] See especially G. E. M. Anscombe, 'Modern Moral Philosophy', *Philosophy* 33 (1958), 1–19; B. Williams, *Ethics and the Limits of Philosophy* (London: Fontana, 1985), ch. 10; A. Schopenhauer, *On the Basis of Morality*, trans. E. Payne (Providence, RI: Berghahn, rev. edn. 1995). I provide further commentary on Anscombe in particular in 'Does Modern Moral Philosophy Rest on a Mistake?', in A. O'Hear (ed.), *Modern Moral Philosophy* (Cambridge: Cambridge University Press, 2004, 75–93).

One might say that morality divides between moral obligation and spiritual change. The good life becomes increasingly selfless through an increased awareness of, sensibility to, the world beyond the self. But meanwhile requirements, which we still recognise abstractly and as it were externally, demand to be met. (MGM 53)

Note, however, that the role of duty here is merely preliminary, and that any reasons it provides are derivative. Murdoch's ideal is one of selflessness (compare Kant's own claim that the divine will is not constrained by any imperative—though of course he leaves no room for compassion (FMM 414)).

So duty has nothing to do with the moral value of Magda Trocmé's actions. There are three qualities which seem to me to ground their moral worth. First, they were motivated by genuine concern for others. Secondly, they had the potential to be hugely costly to her. And, finally, they were voluntary. If we were to find that Magda Trocmé's actions were the result of some bizarre experiment in hypnotism, and that other aspects of her life, both past and present, suggested strongly that without the hypnotism she would not have helped the refugees, that would deprive her action of the value of nobility (though of course the action could still be said to be right). This leads us into virtue ethics, for did Aristotle not make room for the feelings in his account of the virtues, speak of the noble sacrifices made by the virtuous person for others, and insist on voluntariness as a condition for moral praiseworthiness?

3 Aristotle and virtue ethics

Aristotle did of course allow for the feelings in his theory: The virtuous person is the person who has the right feelings, as well as performing the right actions. If we wish to make room for compassion, however, there is a problem. Compassion, kindness, benevolence—none of these is an Aristotelian virtue. But he does recognize the general concern that each human being has for another,[25] and we can anyway adapt his general account of virtue to fit our modern attitudes.

But there are deeper problems.[26] The first concerns the cost-to-the-agent criterion, which seems so important in elucidating our response to the case of Magda Trocmé. According to Aristotle, there is no such thing as rational or admirable self-sacrifice:

It is true also of the good person that he does a great deal for his friends and his country, and will die for them if he must; he will sacrifice money, honours, and in general the goods for which people compete, procuring for himself what is noble . . . They will also sacrifice money on the condition that their friends gain more; while the friend gets money, he gets what is noble, and

---

[25] Aristotle, *Nicomachean Ethics* [NE], bk. 8, ch. 1, 1155a19–22. There is also a greater place for beneficence in Aristotle's account of virtue in *Rhetoric*, 1.9. But I doubt whether this should be taken as a primary source for understanding Aristotelian ethics: See n. 29 below.

[26] I defend the following egoistic interpretation of Aristotle further in 'Socrates and Aristotle on Happiness and Virtue' in R. Heinaman (ed.), *Plato and Aristotle's Ethics* (Aldershot: Ashgate, 2003), 55–78.

therefore assigns himself the greater good . . . In all praiseworthy actions, then, the good person is seen to assign himself the larger share of what is noble.[27]

It is true that this passage allows that what we would ordinarily describe as self-sacrifice is, so to speak, its own reward. It is not valuable purely instrumentally—because of its leading to heavenly reward, for example. But what it does not allow is that such behaviour is a sacrifice overall from the point of view of the agent's happiness. Further, it is not clear that this egoistic aspect of Aristotle's view can be detached without excessively distorting his account. We might attempt, for example, to claim that he is right about what virtue consists in (right action and right feeling), and that this position can be grafted onto a standard moral principle requiring someone to be virtuous, even if it is a cost to her overall. But leaving behind the noble and the role it plays in the virtuous person's happiness would be to forget one of Aristotle's main aims: to close the gap between happiness and virtue.

Aristotle's egoism also allows him to see moral motivation as peculiarly self-conscious, and here he runs into problems similar to those faced by Kant. According to Aristotle, the virtuous person acts 'for the sake of the noble' (see e.g. NE 3.7, 1115b12–13), and as we saw in the quotation above this is not a mere side-effect of action for the sake of others. The virtuous person 'assigns himself' the greater share. Acting for the sake of the noble is equivalent to 'rational choice of the action for its own sake'.[28] The virtuous person's motivation, that is to say, is always shaped by her own conception of her own happiness, and the significant role played in that conception by the noble.[29]

---

[27] NE, trans. R. Crisp (Cambridge: Cambridge University Press, 2000), 9.8, 1169a18–1169b1. Korsgaard ('From Duty and for the Sake of the Noble', 222–3) argues that Aristotle is 'more honest' at NE 3.9, 11117a33-b20, where he 'firmly repudiates the Stoic view that virtue is sufficient for happiness', allowing that the virtuous person feels pain at the prospect of death in battle, 'for life is best worth living for such a man, and he is knowingly losing the greatest goods'. But losing (some of) 'the greatest' (or 'very great'—Aristotle does not in fact use the article) goods is consistent with one's acquiring a greater good in nobility. For further arguments against non-egoistic readings of Aristotle, see my 'Kraut on Aristotle on Happiness', *Polis* 10 (1991), 129–61.

[28] Ibid.2.4, 1105a32. Korsgaard ('From Duty and for the Sake of the Noble', 216) argues that Aristotle's claim at NE 6.13, 1144b26–7, that 'it is not merely the state in accordance with right reason, but the state that implies the presence of right reason, that is virtue' suggests that 'Aristotle thinks a good action is one whose agent *sees it as* the embodiment of right reason, just as Kant thinks that a morally worthy action is one whose agent sees it as an embodiment of the very form of law' (my italics). And she later concludes that acting from duty, especially in difficult circumstances, is to 'display that special form of moral worth that Aristotle calls nobility' (ibid., 218). But the second half of this sentence from 6.13 in Aristotle's text makes it clear that he is claiming here that the exercise of virtue involves practical wisdom (*phronesis*), of which Aristotle never offers the construction attributed to him here by Korsgaard. Practical wisdom enables the virtuous person to see the reasons for certain actions, in the light of her understanding that acting on these reasons would be virtuous, hence noble, and hence constitutive of her own happiness.

[29] Aristotle does describe a model of moral motivation in which nobility consists in the agent's unself-consciously acting for the sake of others at *Rhetoric*, 1.9, 1366b36–1367a6 (see Korsgaard, 'From Duty and for the Sake of the Noble', 217). But it is not unlikely that this part of the *Rhetoric* is early. If so, it may represent Greek common sense of the time (much the same in this respect, it turns out, as our common sense). Compare also Aristotle's description in this chapter of greatness of soul as 'the virtue which disposes us

What does Aristotle mean by 'the noble'? The primary sense of the word '*kalos*' is 'beautiful': 'beautiful, of outward form', as Liddell and Scott put it.[30] Aristotle was not the first to use it in its moral sense—indeed it is used by Homer in that way. But that moral sense seems always to have involved the notion of how one might appear to others. The opposite of '*kalos*' is '*aischros*': 'ugly', and in the moral sense 'dishonourable', i.e. 'such as to be held in dishonour'. If one wishes oneself, or one's actions, to be noble, then, one is concerned about their reputation. Indeed it is the response of others that distinguishes the noble from other goods: 'the noble is that which is both desirable for its own sake and also worthy of praise'.[31]

This quasi-aesthetic concern for how one appears to others emerges most clearly, perhaps, in Aristotle's discussion of 'greatness of soul'—which is, he says, 'a sort of crown of the virtues, because it makes them greater and does not occur in isolation from them' (NE 4.3, 1124a1–3):

If, then, he thinks himself worthy of great things—and above all the greatest—and if he is indeed so, he will be concerned with one thing in particular. Worth is spoken of with reference to external goods; and the greatest external good we should assume to be what we render to the gods, the good most aimed at by people of worth, the prize for the noblest achievements. Such is honour, since it is indeed the greatest external good . . . It is primarily with honours and dishonours, then, that the great-souled person is concerned. (NE 1123b15–21; 1124a4–5)

It is also characteristic of a great-souled person to ask for nothing, or almost nothing, but to help others readily; and to be dignified in his behaviour towards people of distinction or the well-off, but unassuming towards people at the middle level. Superiority over the first group is difficult and impressive, but over the second it is easy, and attempting to impress the first group is not ill-bred, while in the case of humble people it is vulgar, like a show of strength against the weak . . . [T]he actions he is inclined to perform are few, but great and renowned. (1124b17–26)

Aristotle does indeed make room for voluntariness in his ethics. But there is a large gap in his account of moral value. In the sort of cases of self-sacrifice we have been considering, Aristotle's virtuous person seems to have the wrong priorities, being concerned about the responses of others, and not their needs—the latter concern being the one which others take themselves to be responding to in him. Giving one's life for others can indeed in certain circumstances be noble and praiseworthy, but it is so because the person is (a) concerned for others, and not for honour, and (b) genuinely sacrificing herself. We are still lacking an account of ethics which allows for moral value in voluntary action that issues from compassion, and includes self-sacrifice as a conceptual possibility.

---

towards doing great kindnesses' (1366b17) with the account in the *Ethics* discussed in my text below. Note further the similarities between the Aristotelian conception of nobility as a part of happiness and Mill's view of virtue as a part of happiness (one of many Aristotelian echoes in Mill's essay).

[30] H. G. Liddell and R. Scott, *Greek-English Lexicon* (Oxford: Clarendon Press, 1940), s.v.

[31] Aristotle, *Rhetoric*, trans. W. Rhys Roberts, reprinted in *The Complete Works of Aristotle*, ed. J. Barnes (Princeton: Princeton University Press, 1984), vol. 2, 1.9, 1366a33–4.

It might now be suggested that modern proponents of virtue ethics can avoid the criticisms I have made of Aristotle. For, first, they need not be egoists, and can allow for self-sacrifice. And, second, they need not see the motivation of the virtuous person as a concern for honour, but can allow for genuine other-regarding concern.

This suggestion seems to me right. But, as in the case of utilitarianism, a certain amount of work remains to be done by proponents of virtue ethics to explain the kind of moral value we find in noble self-sacrifice. Much of virtue ethics, over the last forty years, has consisted in critiques of utilitarianism and Kantian ethics, while as a positive view it has come to be seen primarily as a third account of what makes actions right, the right action in any circumstances being that which the virtuous person would perform in those circumstances.[32]

As we have seen, it is Magda Trocmé's virtue to which we seem, at least in part, to be responding when we attribute moral value to what she did. So virtue ethics certainly has an advantage here. In the final section of my paper, I shall suggest that Murdoch— often seen, plausibly enough, as a 'virtue ethicist'[33]—does have more to say than most about the nature of the moral value in nobility.

4 Murdoch on moral value

Murdoch understands the unattractiveness of the aesthetic ideal, especially from a point of view involving a concern for the well-being of others, such as utilitarianism: 'Besides, a utilitarian might add to the argument,[34] ought we not to be primarily employed in removing the misery of others without bothering about our own virtue?' (MGM 352). 'Imaginative reflection upon a moral choice can become too aesthetic, can tempt us to be stylish rather than to be right' (MGM 335). The virtuous person, in other words, will be someone who looks out rather than in.

---

[32] See e.g. M. Baron, P. Pettit, M. Slote, *Three Methods of Ethics: A Debate* (Oxford: Blackwell, 1997); R. Hursthouse, *On Virtue Ethics* (Oxford University Press, 1999), ch. 1.

[33] See Thomas Norgaard, 'Murdoch, Iris', in E. Craig (ed.), *Routledge Encyclopedia of Philosophy*, online version (www.rep.routledge.com).

[34] Murdoch's open-mindedness in connection with utilitarianism is in striking contrast to that of most modern non-utilitarians: 'We should reflect . . . upon the durability and value of utilitarian moral philosophy as an independent stream of thought' (MGM 4); '[U]tilitarian insights . . . must always travel with us' (ibid., 47); 'In a (since television even more manifestly) suffering world utilitarian ideas and projects make evident sense and can always win respect. How refreshing it is to turn from the nightmarish schemata of deconstructionist thought to the open meditative pages of John Stuart Mill, who really seems to be *thinking* about recognisable human beings' (ibid., 168); 'Modern "green" politics, ecology, care for wild life, is a welcome extension of utilitarianism in the direction of everything' (ibid., 299); 'Imagination in politics: to imagine the consequences of policies, to picture what it is like for people to be in certain situations (unemployed, persecuted, very poor), to relate axiomatic moral ideas (for instance about rights) to pragmatic and utilitarian considerations' (ibid., 322). See also MGM 365; 493. Given that utilitarianism is benevolence writ large, Murdoch's response to utilitarianism—that it contains part of the truth—is a reasonable one for a virtue ethicist, being quite in line with the dialectical attitude taken by Aristotle to the thoughts of others, an attitude surprisingly rare among modern 'neo-Aristotelians'.

How will she see the world, and in particular her relationship to the people in it? Utilitarianism involves an extreme conception of impartiality, according to which my good counts no more than anyone else's, and modern proponents of the virtues tend not to advocate this. But Murdoch does. Her ideal of impartiality is one of pure 'selflessness'. Schopenhauer is 'right . . . to indicate the multiform workings of compassion' (MGM 300), and such compassion involves forgetting the fantasies of the selfish ego and attending to the reality of the suffering of others:

[T]rue vision occasions right conduct . . . The more the separateness and differentness of persons of other people is realized, and the fact seen that another man has needs and wishes as demanding as one's own, the harder it becomes to treat a person as a thing. (OGG 66/353–4)

The self, the place where we live, is a place of illusion. Goodness is connected with the attempt to see the unself, to see and respond to the real world in the light of a virtuous consciousness. (SGC 93; see IP 38; SGC 90; S&G 215)

Why should we not be repeatedly told that we are ruthless egoists and that the world which we take as all-important and *real* is a valueless and *unreal* world? (MGM 72)

There are at least two ways in which one might interpret Murdoch's conception of selflessness. On one, nicely articulated by Lawrence Blum, 'Murdoch's position . . . bids us to focus on others not at the *expense* of the self, but, so to speak, without considering the self at all'.[35] This interpretation may be supported, for example, by reference to the claim at the end of SGC that '[t]he humble man, because he sees himself as nothing, can see other things as they are' (SGC 104/385). On this view, then, '[t]he moral task is not self-negation but self-transcending' (IMDM 362), and benefiting others in any way, at any cost to oneself, is virtuous.

On a second interpretation, which I myself prefer, the agent does not entirely forget her own interests. Rather, as the quotation from OGG above puts it, she sees that others have needs as demanding as her own. The self does not disappear from view entirely, but is seen in proper proportion:

Self is as hard to see justly as other things, and when clear vision has been achieved, self is a correspondingly smaller and less interesting object. . . . In reality the good self is very small indeed. (OGG 67–8/355)

The self-transcendent interpretation has the advantage, noted by Blum, that it allows for what Michael Slote has called the 'self-other asymmetry' of common-sense morality, according to which there is moral value in benefiting others at a cost to oneself that, from the impartial point of view, fails to outweigh the benefit provided.[36] But this advantage strikes me as outweighed by the disadvantage, also pointed out by Blum (IMDM 367, n. 37), that it leaves no room for the self-regarding virtues, and attaches

[35] L. Blum, 'Iris Murdoch and the Domain of the Moral' [IMDM], *Philosophical Studies* 50 (1986), 343–67, at 362.
[36] IMDM 361–2. M. Slote, *Common-sense Morality and Consequentialism* (London: Routledge, 1985), ch. 1.

value to what might appear to be servility or self-abasement. Further, given the importance to Murdoch, evident in the quotations above, of *seeing correctly*, it is hard to see how a complete blindness to one's own genuine needs could be what she had in mind. 'Humility', as she puts it, 'is not a peculiar habit of self-effacement, rather like having an inaudible voice, it is selfless respect for reality and one of the most difficult and central of all virtues' (SGC 95/378).[37] So her claim that the humble man sees himself as nothing is perhaps best understood not as the expression of an ideal of self-transcendence but as an attempt to capture the humble man's unselfishness and lack of concern for himself in the ordinary cases of helping others Murdoch describes.

On the self-transcendent interpretation, genuine self-sacrifice evades conceptual grasp. But on the impartialist conception of Murdoch I have recommended, because each individual *has* a good, the natural thought is that she can sacrifice it for others. There is no attempt in Murdoch's work to provide an ultimately egoistic justification for self-sacrifice, and we are entitled to conclude that there is room for compassionate self-sacrifice in Murdoch's ethics.[38]

We have seen above that utilitarianism, because of its welfarism, is hard put to it to explain the nature of the value of nobility. But there is more to Murdoch's ethics than an impartial account of the relation of the self to others. Murdoch does suggest various lines of thought in connection with the notion of moral value, most of them Platonist in inspiration, and in certain important respects they seem to me to have a lot going for them, though I would want to distance myself from the notion that goodness is somehow 'transcendent' and 'not in this world' (OGG 59–60/348–9). (I suggest—though I have no strong evidence for this—that Murdoch herself may have seen the Form of the Good, as also perhaps the apparatus of religion, as useful metaphors for a more mundane, but nevertheless important, notion of moral value.)

First, moral value is not, for her, reducible to, or comprehensible in terms of, other kinds of value—aesthetic, welfarist, or whatever: '[M]orality is, in the human world, something unique, special, *sui generis*, "as if it came to us from elsewhere".'[39] Like great art, 'it is separate, it is for nothing, it is for itself' (MGM 8).

---

[37] For this reason, I cannot accept Sabina Lovibond's complaint that Murdoch's focus on 'simple' people suggests that limits are being placed on the development of the moral imagination, since such development 'can only result in their becoming less simple, with consequences no one can predict' (*Realism and Imagination in Ethics* (Oxford: Blackwell, 1983), 199). What Murdoch commends in people such as the 'inarticulate, unselfish mothers of large families' (OGG 53/342) is not their inarticulateness but their unselfishness, because in their unselfishness they are seeing (that part of) the world as it is. There may be political aspects of their position of which they remain unaware, but their humility as understood in cognitive terms by Murdoch could only be—in that respect—advanced by enlightenment.

[38] Peter Conradi speaks of the 'oft-repeated, unascribed quotation from Iris's journals, "I would go into the dark, if it meant light for you"' (*Iris Murdoch: A Life* (London: Harper Collins, 2001), 256). See also Murdoch's aunts, below.

[39] MGM 26; cf. OGG 53–4/343. Peter Conradi kindly drew my attention to the following from Murdoch's journal of 17 November 1949: 'Called on E[lizabeth] Anscombe last night... She read out bits from the end of the *Tractatus* and said this means to me sheer despair. One might read this and kill oneself. I said I thought the remark about there being no value in the world was the beginning of real thinking about

Second, it matters a great deal: 'The only thing which is of real importance is to see it all clearly and respond to it justly which is inseparable from virtue' (SGC 87/372). 'Only' is an exaggeration: Virtue is not, as Murdoch claims, 'the only thing of worth' (SGC 99/381). Nor could she seriously have thought it was, given the concern of the virtuous person with the needs of others.

Third, this conception of moral value in selfless impartiality constitutes a powerful ideal, an ideal of perfection: 'We look at Christ (or Buddha or the Form of the Good) and are magnetically attracted' (MGM 24). What of Magda Trocmé? Murdoch denies that 'ordinary' mortals cannot provide us with inspiration: 'The aunt may be the selfless unrewarded doer of good. I have known such aunts. In the activity of such workers egoism has disappeared *unobtrusively* into the care and service of others.'[40] How much more distant could one be from Aristotle's ideal of the great-souled man? 'At the highest level this is *practical* mysticism, where the certainty and the absolute appear incarnate and immediate in the needs of others' (MGM 430). This ideal is one which Mill was only too aware could be appealed to in connection with utilitarian impartiality:

In an improving state of the human mind, the influences are constantly on the increase, which tend to generate in each individual a feeling of unity with all the rest; which feeling, if perfect, would make him never think of, or desire, any beneficial condition for himself, in the benefits of which they are not now included. If we now suppose this feeling of unity to be taught as a religion . . . I think that no one, who can realize this conception, will feel any misgiving about the sufficiency of the ultimate sanction for the Happiness morality. (*Utilitarianism* 3.10.53–63)

Murdoch was not a utilitarian, but she took the same view of the importance of the self vis-à-vis others as utilitarianism. Because her view does not rest for its plausibility on welfarism, she finds no difficulty in incorporating the three elements I have claimed to be important in grounding the moral value of actions such as Magda Trocmé's: voluntariness, compassion, and self-sacrifice. 'Iris'—the rainbow—is aptly named indeed.

We have seen, then, that the three main ethical traditions currently under discussion— utilitarianism, Kantianism, and Aristotelian virtue ethics—find it hard to accommodate or to provide an account of the kind of moral value expressed in noble self-sacrifice for others. Murdoch not only recognizes such nobility, but goes some way towards sketching out an account of its nature as a moral value—though once again we have to admit that there is much more to be said. One central issue requiring urgent attention is the nature of morality as an institution. On the one hand, we have the broadly utilitarian

---

ethics.' Only the beginning, of course, for one should end with the thought that there is moral value in the world, constituting an independent kind. Virtue is 'pointless' (SGC 99/381) in so far as it has 'unique value' (SGC 104/385) in itself.

[40]   MGM 429. See also e.g. OGG 53/342, discussed in n. 37 above.

instrumentalist conception of morality, according to which our emotional reactions and evaluative attributions have their origins in social and cultural evolution, and are to be assessed solely by their contribution to well-being (after all, what else could matter?). On the other hand, we have Murdoch's modest platonism, suggesting that our reactions to cases such as those of Magda Trocmé constitute insight into a self-standing realm of moral value. We need to understand much more about the origin of morality and its nature—to stop and look, with whatever assistance may be available from anthropology, psychology, history, and sociology—before we can understand nobility and moral value properly. And, I might add in conclusion, one place in which it is always going to be profitable to look for illumination and insight is the work of Iris Murdoch.

9

'For every Foot its own Shoe': Method and Moral Theory in the Philosophy of Iris Murdoch*

Julia Driver

The significance of Iris Murdoch's work against the backdrop of analytic moral theorizing is just recently beginning to garner the attention it deserves. Roger Crisp's excellent essay in this volume points to the impact her writing has had on criticisms of traditional moral theorizing. Specifically, she was part of a group of philosophers committed to criticizing the predominant ethical theories of the 20th century. Her work, along with that of some of her contemporaries, gave impetus to the development of *particularism*. There are many varieties of the view, but many particularists, very broadly, hold that general rules and principles are insufficient to capture what is important to morality. Here I am reminded of a story I came across in Montaigne's essays, in which he declaims against those who would try to constrain experience, and try to formulate policies that cover all of our experience:

Nature always gives us happier laws than we give ourselves ... Witness ... some who employ, as the only judge in their quarrels, the first traveler passing through their mountains. And these others on market day elect one of themselves who decides all their suits on the spot ... What would be the danger in having our wisest men settle ours in this way, according to the circumstances and at sight ... ? For every foot its own shoe ...

  Who has seen children trying to divide a mass of quicksilver into a certain number of parts? The more they press it and knead it and try to constrain it to their will, the more they provoke the independence of this spirited metal; it escapes their skill and keeps dividing and scattering in little particles beyond all reckoning.[1]

* I would like to thank Justin Broackes and an anonymous referee for their very helpful comments on an earlier draft.
[1] Montaigne, from his essay 'Of Experience', in *The Complete Essays of Montaigne*, translated by Donald M. Frame (Stanford, CA: Stanford University Press, 1958), 816.

Montaigne is speaking against the attempt at formulating general policies to guide moral or political decisions and action, in favor of a methodology that gives preference to the perceptions of those with the experience to make the right decisions, or the appropriate disinterest in deciding among people who disagree. Montaigne thus might be seen as advocating a particularist approach to both moral decision-making and the understanding of moral phenomena, or what I view as a particularist methodology. Central to this methodology is the idea that experience is crucial—not sufficient, of course, but nevertheless, crucial—in training up a judger's sensibilities so that he or she can detect the morally relevant or salient features, of a given situation. This strategy goes against general theorizing, it would seem, at least of the sort that one sees in Utilitarianism and Kantian ethics. And, as Crisp points out, Iris Murdoch was concerned that people attend to the details of that experience, something that is frequently overlooked in theory with its emphasis on generalities and universal principles. A narrow diet of examples, gleaned from a narrow experience, can at best deliver only one aspect of the truth. And, as Murdoch writes, 'The authority of morality is the authority of truth, and that is of reality' (SGC 90/374).[2] Of course, there is a difference between believing that experience is the precursor to doing theory, and believing that experience replaces the genuine need for a theory.

My claim in this essay is that there is much insight in Murdoch's criticisms of principle-based ethics—her main target being Hare's universality in ethics.[3] Murdoch did believe that ethics was more closely affiliated with aesthetics, and so she rejected the scientific paradigm for philosophy. In fact, she may have viewed principle-based ethics as an illegitimate attempt to bring ethics into the science camp. Ever since Hume, however, this has been viewed as problematic due to the normative leap to be made between fact and value. However, she is famous for the rather different task of having rejected the non-cognitivist view that there is no truth in ethics (unlike physics), since normative discourse is just an expression of taste. Murdoch is seen as resisting the rejection of speculative metaphysics in ethics. This also explains her interest in religion and the good, since religion was one of those areas rejected by the Logical Positivists— relegated to the realm of bad metaphysics.

However, my view is that a substantive form of particularism is the wrong lesson to take away from the important concerns she raises. Her criticisms of theory, which Crisp expresses some sympathy for, are criticisms of theorizing in an antiseptic and overly streamlined way. Murdoch, echoing the concerns of other writers critical of the way analytic moral theorizing has developed, called for a moral philosophy which connects with the reality of human psychology, and which reflects human experience

---

[2] I shall refer to the three papers that make up Murdoch's *The Sovereignty of Good* [SG] (London: Routledge, 1970/New York: Schocken Books, 1971) as IP, OGG, and SGC—to abbreviate 'The Idea of Perfection', 'On "God" and "Good"', and 'The Sovereignty of Good Over Other Concepts'. Page numbers refer to the original book printing and (after a forward slash/) to the reprints in Iris Murdoch, *Existentialists and Mystics* [E&M], ed. P. J. Conradi (London: Chatto and Windus, 1997).

[3] See 'Vision and Choice in Morality', [VCM], reprinted in E&M.

(OGG 46/337). Experience of morally charged situations offers a mechanism for developing tools of ethical reflection. But 'experience' doesn't actually mean one has to live through situations fraught with moral overtones. One simply has to be faced with possibilities for imaginative reflection—and literature, history, the lives of one's friends, and so forth can all provide this, as well as the situations one confronts in one's own life. Before we actually set about confidently making moral judgments, we must be sure that we are basing our capacity to make them on wide rather than narrow experience. Literature and imagination, are, of course, elements on this experience, as is history, which offers us a more detached mode of evaluation.[4] We can all broaden our affective experience by reading history and literature. Again, this is one of Murdoch's themes, that 'We use our imagination not to escape the world, but to join it . . .' (SGC 90/374). Indeed, consideration of history and literature makes us better able to arrive at objective truth since it is abstracted—or at least more abstracted—from our own idiosyncratic emotional responses, from our self-serving and egoistic reactions. She's right that ethical reflection is not egoistic. But my view is that she goes wrong if what she claims is the particularist claim that there are aspects of morality, or moral reasons, which have no *general* significance. This is to be distinguished from the claim they have no *universal* significance. I will claim that the evidence for Murdoch's particularism is mixed, and that it is not clear that she was a substantive particularist—that is, a particularist about moral metaphysics. However, I do believe that the evidence is clear that she was a methodological particularist—that is, a particularist about moral theorizing.

Some writers have pointed out that the demand for generality in ethics is linked to its role in moral justification. The idea—perhaps not well defended in the literature—is that general principles such as the Utilitarian principle 'Maximize the Good' provide a superior form of justification *because* they are general—because they cover a host of cases that are quite disparate at the specific, *particular*, level.[5] But generality needs to be distinguished from universality. Generality is thought to be a degree concept in that it involves ' . . . a measure of the relative range of application of a moral principle'.[6] Thus, 'Don't Kill' is more general than 'Don't kill except in self-defense'. Universality, on the other hand, is different. One can hold a principle to be universal ' . . . if it can be stated without the use of any proper names or indexicals'.[7] As Don Loeb notes, this usage is attributed to Hare. It will be remembered that Hare is one of Murdoch's targets. Murdoch is also familiar with the distinction, though her use of it seems rather confusing. She argues that universality is mistaken because it fails to consider the point of view of those who view the world as mysterious and morality as ' . . . the

---

[4] See the really wonderful discussion in Murdoch's essay 'Morals and Politics', in *Metaphysics as a Guide to Morals* [MGM] (1992; New York: Penguin, 1993), at 389.

[5] See Don Loeb's 'Generality and Moral Justification', *Philosophy and Phenomenological Research* 56 (March 1996), 79–96. Loeb attempts to argue against this privileged role for generality.

[6] Ibid. 80–1.

[7] Ibid. 81.

exploration of that mystery in so far as it concerns each individual' (VCM 88). My claim is that a universalist will just come back and say that she is utterly mistaken here. It may be a hard task to refine principles and norms but it can be done, and, indeed, we have a good idea of what some would look like—'torturing animals just for the fun of it is wrong' is true, no matter who the particular agent is. Of course, this is not a very general claim. Fine and well.

However, there are other well known passages where Murdoch seems to embrace either generality or universality, as when she claims that one thing the utilitarians got right is the importance of happiness: '. . . utilitarian considerations are in general *prima facie* relevant because we all understand the importance of happiness. It is always *a*, not necessarily final, argument against doing something to someone that it will reduce his happiness' (MGM 365). One can find support for a variety of views in her writings, and it is quite possible that she simply did not clearly delineate the different positions in her own writings.

It seems that though Murdoch recognizes the distinction it turns out to be mis-understood in relation to many arguments purporting to establish particularist claims. Universality is not a degree concept. One principle is not more universal than another, though one principle may be more general than another. Many complaints about universality really boil down to complaints about generality.[8] This is a point to be returned to later.

With this in mind, how is Murdoch thought to be a particularist? This widely held view about Murdoch appears in various commentators. Alison Denham, for example, writes that particularism, and Murdoch's view, is:

the view that ethical properties are properties of particular actions and persons rather than classes or kinds. A correlate of this view is . . . that general principles and codifiable rules will often mislead us in ethics, we do better always to consider the context and detail of the specific case. . . . For Murdoch, scrutiny of the relevant phenomena, alertness to specifics, sensitivity to subtle differences—these are the characteristics of proper attention that must underpin reliable moral judgement.[9]

Of course, Murdoch is a complex figure. The evidence for a particularist position is much stronger in 'Vision and Choice' than in, for example, *Sovereignty of the Good*. However, it is certainly the case that recent writers, inspired by Murdoch, have taken her to be a particularist and at the very least it seems reasonable to view her work as an important source for particularism. For example, Lawrence Blum views Murdoch's work as calling to the particularity of moral perception, which is crucial to morality but separate from moral judgment. He believes that Murdoch's emphasis on love, for example, demonstrates a central place for concern for a *particular* other person, and this

[8] Russ Shafer-Landau, 'Moral Rules', *Ethics* 107 (July 1997), 584–611.
[9] See her 'Envisioning the Good: Iris Murdoch's Moral Psychology', *MFS Modern Fiction Studies* 47 (Fall 2001), 621.

is inimical to the impartialist case of much contemporary ethical theory. He writes that certain prominent ethicists (e.g. Williams, Nagel, and Sheffler)

accept an identification of morality with an impartial, impersonal, and objective point of view. These writers all give the impression that the sole or major issues of personal conduct concern the clash between personal and impartial reasons for action, between an impersonal "right" and a merely personal "good." Nowhere . . . is articulated the Murdochian moral task of caring for or attending to particular other individuals.[10]

For Blum, expanding on this Murdochian insight calls into question principle-based moral systems.[11] Principle-based moral systems, such as Utilitarianism and Kantianism, seem to be one of the primary targets of the particularist. They offer universal principles which also tend to have a high degree of generality.

Murdoch can be viewed as a particularist at several levels, and one of my aims in this paper is to spell out the different sorts of particularist attitude her philosophical work expounds. Denham's characterization conflates several senses, though it must be noted Murdoch herself isn't very clear on separating her claims.

(1) Substantive particularism
  (1a) metaphysical particularism
  (1b) particularism about reasons (or 'considerations that serve as reasons')
  (1c) particularism about rules or principles
(2) Epistemological particularism
(3) Methodological particularism[12]

These claims will be distinct, though related in various ways. In the case of (1a) the particularist believes that there is no pattern of subvening non-moral properties which underlie moral properties. This is not a version I will explicitly be discussing here, but will simply note that this version has a connection with (1b) in the following way: I can have the property of 'having a reason' to avoid, let's say, a particular action in virtue of that action having a certain 'grounding' property—e.g. it is a cruel action. There is plenty of evidence that Murdoch was committed to something like (1a) since she criticizes those who are against a metaphysical ethics. Critics of a metaphysical ethics often proceed by noting that moral terms must always be reducible to non-moral. This would mean that there is nothing 'moral' that fundamentally underlies moral terms. Murdoch was against this reductionist view. Instead, she seems to suggest that moral perception picks up on the moral reality, and that there are no patterns or generalities that are being picked up on instead (VCM). However, the view that there is no pattern

---

[10] Lawrence Blum, *Moral Perception and Particularity* (New York: Cambridge University Press, 1994), 16.
[11] Lawrence Blum, 'Moral Perception and Particularity', *Ethics* 101 (July 1991), 701–25.
[12] Walter Sinnott-Armstrong makes similar distinctions amongst types of particularism, though his use of 'methodological particularism' differs slightly from my own. See his 'Some Varieties of Particularism', *Metaphilosophy* 30 (January/April 1999), 1–12.

of non-moral properties that underlie the moral has been effectively criticized by Frank Jackson, Philip Pettit, and Michael Smith.[13] One couldn't educate others without such patterns out there to recognize. Of course, this says nothing about perception. One could agree with the view that a perceptual sensitivity is necessary to pick up on these patterns, but this by itself does not commit one to (1a). How do we square this with her realism? After all, she did write that morality is a form of realism. But again, this all by itself does not commit her to (1a) since she simply believed a kind of formal realism, a conceptual connection between truth and knowledge. In this respect her view is realist because committed to the view that there is truth in morality—it's just that the truth of moral claims citing moral properties cannot be reducible to the physical.[14] So evidence for her views on (1a) is mixed. (1b) and (1c) will be discussed shortly. (2) holds that we can only come to know moral properties by contact with particular instances; and that a priori reflection on generalities is not a route to moral knowledge. (3) holds that the methodology used in contemporary moral theorizing is flawed because it does not deal with specific cases, and instead utilizes cases which have been stripped down to isolate what is 'morally relevant'. One can see in Murdoch's work, and in particular 'Vision and Choice', a commitment to all of these claims, in one form or another. My argument will be that all of them have serious problems—however (3) does expose one problem with a popular methodological tool used in moral philosophy.

Some might argue that Murdoch couldn't possibly be committed to (2) since she places enormous weight on exposure to literature and history in developing moral sensitivity, and one of the main objections to (2) is that it doesn't account for the role imaginary cases play in reasoning. But what Murdoch could argue is that contact can be made imaginatively, as long as there's enough detail—as long as the specificity is such as to make the case seem real, and this is the work of the novelist, and, one would suppose, the gifted historian.[15] But this observation doesn't rebut the generalist position, since he or she could maintain that this method works precisely because there are true generalities. Note that there could be generalities even if a reasoning method using them doesn't work, or is misleading in some way. And this will get us to (3), methodological particularism.

There is also substantial evidence that she endorsed some version of both (1b) and (1c). She frequently condemned the rule-oriented approach to moral philosophy prevalent at the time she was writing. To her, the focus on rules was just an attempt to develop some kind of crutch, and attempt to fend off the essential 'ambiguity of the world' (VCM 90). However, it is important to note that even in making these sorts of

---

[13] F. Jackson, P. Pettit, and M. Smith, 'Ethical Particularism and Patterns', in *Moral Particularism* ed. by Brad Hooker and Margaret Olivia Little (Oxford: Clarendon Press, 2000), 79–99.

[14] OGG 60/349, where she notes that the certainty and permanency of goodness is not reducible to psychology.

[15] As she writes at OGG 65/353, when we look at great works of art, or read great literature, we learn 'about the real quality of human nature, when it is envisaged, in the artists' just and compassionate vision, with a clarity which does not belong to the self-centred rush of ordinary life'.

criticisms of the rule approach, she doesn't totally condemn them; she is simply claiming that rules cannot exhaust all there is to morality: 'this cannot be taken as the only structural model for morality'. Note the word 'only'.

One can be a particularist about reasons without being a particularist about rules or principles.[16] To quote Dancy on (1b):

The leading thought behind particularism is that the behavior of a reason (or a consideration that serves as a reason) in a new case cannot be predicted from its behavior elsewhere. The way in which the consideration functions *here* either will or at least may be affected by other considerations here present. So there is no ground for the hope that we can find out here how that consideration functions *in general*, somehow, nor for the hope that we can move in any smooth way to how it will function in a different case.[17]

One clarificatory comment on the terms: note that Dancy writes of 'a reason (or a consideration that serves as a reason'). Again, to bring this in conformity with other discussions in the literature one should note that a grounding property could offer a consideration that serves as a reason. This gets us into many complexities that I'd like to ignore in this paper—though they would benefit from further investigation.[18]

Elijah Millgram uses the following illustration of the particularist insight on reasons: 'That a company is your employer is a reason not to leak its confidential documents to the press, but when its employees are being pressed to become complicit in its misdeeds, that you are an employee becomes precisely a reason to leak.'[19] And, as Dancy notes, all kinds of reasons function this way. That a blouse is pretty may be a reason for wearing it to a party but be a reason for not wearing it while mopping the floor. The particularist about reasons, in the (1b) sense, is just pointing out that moral reasons function like other reasons. To Dancy, this is not a surprising claim at all. Indeed, the contrary would be more surprising.

Millgram refers to this as 'the defusing move'—the original reason is 'defused' as opposed to 'overridden' in the new context. Others refer to these reasons as underminers. We can note that there are two sorts of defusers or underminers—there are ones that neutralize and ones that reverse the normative force of the reason. Some underminers, however, are stronger—as when *x* is a reason to do *y* in one context, but a reason not to do it in another context. When conditions change, the reason takes on a different normative quality. Thus, the argument goes, one can't generalize about morally relevant reasons for action. And it also shows that moral norms do not apply

---

[16] Jonathan Dancy, for example, is a particularist about reasons but does not embrace particularism about rules. *Moral Reasons* (Oxford: Blackwell, 1993).

[17] Dancy, 60.

[18] For example, one can draw another sort of distinction between a sort of metaphysical particularism and another epistemological form. This would then bring in the difference between internal and external reasons. However, this investigation isn't necessary for the purposes of this paper. The same qualms about one variety could be raised for the other.

[19] See Elijah Millgram, 'Murdoch, Practical Reasoning, and Particularism', *Notizie di Politeia* 18 (2002), 69–70.

universally. This in turn is taken to show that rules and generalizations are useless. As Millgram points out, however, the main evidence used by the particularists simply seems to establish that what counts as a good reason will vary from context to context—that this is a context-sensitive issue. That isn't to say that generalizations can't be made, and certainly not that they are useless. Indeed, numerous writers have pointed out that they are critical in moral argumentation.[20]

Russ Shafer-Landau notes, for example, that Dancy's cases all involve cases where the purporting grounding properties are described in extremely general terms. Once narrowed, universal relevance can be re-established. Shafer-Landau's cases include factors such as taking pleasure in another's pain (this is bad), or being cruel (this is also bad): 'There may be very rare circumstances where such action is, all-things-considered, justified, but its permissibility must be a matter of overriding the wrong-making features present in each such action.'[21]

Roger Crisp has, further, pointed out that the particularist thesis about reasons suffers from being either trivial or false.[22] Crisp makes a distinction between ultimate and non-ultimate reasons. Ultimate reasons ground actions, provide some fundamental justificatory basis for them, non-ultimate reasons provide a kind of justification in particular cases, but a justification understood in terms of some other ultimate reason. This is like Shafer-Landau's account of grounding properties (though, of course, here we're talking about reasons). In ordinary circumstances I should return to you the book I borrowed, but if I find out that you in fact stole the book, then I should not return it, because *that* would be unjust. The cases that work for Dancy, that illustrate the defusing move, all involve non-ultimate reasons. And this makes the particularist thesis trivial— as Crisp notes, even a universalist such as an act utilitarian who employs a highly general criterion for rightness, will note that a non-ultimate reason will act as a justificatory reason in one case and not in another—because the ultimate aim will be served differently in different circumstances. But this doesn't entail the particularist thesis about ultimate reasons. And, indeed, we have a great many reasons to prefer the generalist thesis about ultimate reasons, since that assumption underlies a good deal of our moral methodology. But it is this very methodology that I think Murdoch wanted to call into question. However, one can raise questions about the methodology without being committed to particularism about reasons.

Murdoch, against universality, writes:

A man may penetrate his life with reflection, see it as having a certain meaning and a certain kind of movement. Alternatively . . . a man may regard himself as set apart from others, by a superiority which brings special responsibilities, or by a curse, or some other unique destiny. Both these fables may issue in practical judgments, possibly of great importance. Now does the question

---

[20] See Millgram; also see Sinnott-Armstrong.

[21] Op.cit., 590.

[22] Roger Crisp 'Particularizing Particularism', in *Moral Particularism* ed. by Brad Hooker and Margaret Olivia Little (Oxford: Clarendon Press, 2000), 37.

whether these are moral decisions really depend on the answer to the question: would you wish anyone else so placed to act similarly? If faced with this somewhat surprising query, the fable-makers might reply, 'Yes, I suppose so'; or possibly they might reply . . . 'But nobody could be in *this* position without being *me,'* . . . My point is that here the 'universal rules' model simply no longer describes the situation. (VCM 86)

In this passage she criticizes the relevance of the universalizability test employed in Kant's ethics. In the context of how ethics has developed over the last half century, some of Murdoch's remarks—such as this one—can be read as feeding into the widespread dissatisfaction with principles, such as the principle of utility and the categorical imperative. In trying to decide on an appropriate course of action some-times people find themselves in unique situations. Trying to figure out what to do based on a universal standard that applies to everyone fails to accurately model that uniqueness. But this does not get us all the way to substantive particularism since this is compatible with there being plenty of situations which are relevantly similar. General criteria might still apply.

What valuable lessons can be taken away from reading Murdoch on the issue of particularism? My view is that she has targeted a methodology common to analytic philosophy, at least, in analytic moral theory—a methodology she finds to be distorting of moral experience.

And here we get to (3), *methodological* particularism, which makes a point about the sort of methodology employed by moral philosophers, and is opposed to the use of reflective equilibrium and the contrastive method. The contrastive method assumes the 'ubiquity' thesis: that 'if variation in a given factor makes a difference *anywhere*, it makes a difference *everywhere*'.[23] But, as Shelly Kagan points out, even if one believes the contrastive method fails because the ubiquity thesis is false, this does not mean that principle-based moral theory is false. Indeed, principle-based moral theory may be all the more needed to ground our moral judgment since it is intuition that fails, in that it cannot capture all the subtleties and nuances when factors interact in a given context. However, in contrast to this view is a Murdochian one, picked up by Nussbaum and others, that properly cultivated perception can pick up on the nuances and can form the basis of reliable moral judgment. But the point is to get away from the contrastive method, which strips down cases to isolate the essential features, and then hold some constant while testing our intuitions about the difference that variability makes. Like some contemporary writers, I believe she displays a concern that the use of something like the contrastive method really just boils down to a description of our intuitions about cases—so—why not just go with those intuitions? Why not look at the cases as singularities, and judge them on the basis of the complex process of imaginative

[23] Shelly Kagan, 'The Additive Fallacy', *Ethics* 99 (1988).

reflection? The *principles* that one derives are just a fifth wheel, with no prescriptive force whatsoever and also woefully inadequate even as mere descriptions (because they lack the richness of actual cases). But the lessons she draws from this are far different from the lessons someone like Kagan draws. For Kagan the remedy is a greater reliance on foundational moral theory. For Murdoch, it is a rejection of such a theory since the theory cannot be a satisfactory replacement for moral perception. Perhaps she is a substantive particularist—the evidence exists for either interpretation. But I do believe there is good evidence that she is a methodological particularist, holding the view that we must consider cases in detail in making moral judgments, and we consider them as singularities:

> Philosophers have been misled, not by a rationalistic desire for unity, but also by certain simplified and generalised moral attitudes current in our society, into seeking a single philosophical definition of morality . . . Why should philosophy be less various, where the differences in what it attempts to analyse are so important? . . . For purposes of analysis moral philosophy should remain at the level of differences, taking the moral forms of life as given, and not try to *get behind them* to a single form. (VCM 97)

Methodological particularism challenges the role of *abstract* intuitions in moral decision-making—that is intuitions about a certain choice made outside of the context of the choice itself, for example. The agent in a specific situation where moral judgment is called for will be faced with truly unique circumstances; and one where imaginative reflection is called for in making a truly reliable moral judgment, one devoid of self-serving and egoistic motivations.

This, I take it, is one of the points behind the famous case of M and D, presented in 'The Idea of Perfection':

> A mother, whom I shall call M, feels hostility to her daughter-in-law, whom I shall call D . . . M feels that her son has married beneath him. Let us assume for purposes of the example that the mother, who is a very 'correct' person, behaves beautifully to the girl throughout, not allowing her real opinion to appear in any way. (IP 17/312)

But M is also someone who is 'capable of giving careful and just attention to an object which confronts her'. And, she does just that with D. By careful attention to detail, she comes to change her view of D. This has no effect on her behavior, it is purely attitudinal—it is a change not in behavior but judgment. This example is often cited in support of Murdoch's view that moral vision is relevant to moral theory, as opposed to a simple focus on conduct and behavior.[24] It also gives an example of moral reflection, and how it works. Attention to detail gets us further at the truth. But we have to approach such cases with mental descriptions that are general, and then search for more detail.

---

[24] See Maria Antonaccio, *Picturing the Human* (Oxford University Press, 2000), 89.

This is imaginative engagement:

Imagination is an (inner) activity of the senses, a picturing and a grasping, a stirring of desire. At a more explicitly reflective level, in everyday moral discussion as well as metaphysics, we deploy a complex densely textured network of values round an intuited centre of 'good'. We imagine hierarchies and concentric circles, we are forced by experience to make distinctions, to elaborate moral 'pictures' and a *moral vocabulary* . . . so we may talk and think, constantly examining and altering our sense of the order and interdependence of our values. The study of this interweaving *is* moral reflection, and at a theoretical level makes intelligible places for defining and understanding central concepts which may have become isolated and attenuated in our argumentative and emotional use of them: happiness, freedom, love. (MGM 325–6)[25]

Of course, this 'interweaving' is enormously complex. It isn't to be expected that the person's knowledge can therefore be communicated. The reflection may not be replicable. A standard in science cannot be met here—that results be replicable. This is because imaginative reflection in ethics is a singularity.

But, again, as far as particularism is concerned, one feature to be stressed is the idiosyncrasy of the moral experience or moral judgment itself that characterizes Murdoch's views. Consider again one of the things she says about the case of M: 'M's activity is peculiarly *her own*. Its details are the details of *this* personality; and partly for this reason it may well be an activity which can only be performed privately. M could not *do this* thing in conversations with another person' (IP 23/317). This may be because we are aware of the reasons, but not able to articulate them, but it also may be due to the fact that there are reasons that move us and that we respond to that we aren't even fully aware of. In 'Vision and Choice' she also writes, as part of her criticism of Hare et al.: 'There are situations which are obscure and people who are incomprehensible, and the moral agent, as well as the artist, may find himself unable to describe something which in some sense he apprehends' (VCM 90). Thus, I agree with Millgram's view that Murdoch is best read as offering an 'idiosyncrasy' account—but, even more than this, view her as being open to the view that persons can be moved by reasons that they aren't able to articulate because they aren't even fully aware of what the reasons are that they are responding to. This would explain her view that the inarticulate are virtuous, and those who are naturally good may be responsive to reasons that they cannot represent to themselves—if they could describe them internally then presumably they would be able to describe them externally. Joseph Raz nicely presents this in his discussion of particularism (though he is not discussing Murdoch):

We may be unaware of our own reasons. We act for reasons we know of, be it through our general stock of beliefs, or through what we come to believe about the situation we are in at the time of action. Either way we know more than we can articulate. No one can spell out all that he knows, and no one can detail all that he perceives, or even just sees at any moment. There may be

---

[25] From 'Imagination'.

nothing we know that cannot be stated, and nothing we see which cannot be described. But it does not follow that we can state all that we now, and all that we see. . . . We can rationally respond to what we see and act as we do because of what we know, without being aware of that knowledge at the time.[26]

Raz is pointing out that some of the force of the defusing move is due to our inability to fully articulate our reasons for actions. We may be responsive to grounding reasons, but have some difficulty either identifying them, articulating them, or both. This may be especially true as the degree of generality is reduced. But note, these reasons are universal.

So these cases don't seem to bear the weight that some particularists place on them. Millgram believes that particularists need to adopt a Murdochian approach in order to be truly distinctive. And, on his view, the Murdochian adopts a kind of idiosyncrasy approach to moral justification. Moral justification is based on individual perception; which at the most precise level of detail cannot be articulated to others. One can privately justify some moral judgments that may not be publicly justified. It's worth noting here that if this thesis is correct there is a crucial difference between public and private moral justification. Ironically, this is something the Utilitarians were criticized for, since some argued that it may not maximize utility to make public the Utilitarian rationales for various policies. However, for Murdoch, unlike the Utilitarian, the private nature of at least some instances of moral reflection and justification is essential, it is not a matter of secrecy. Even if one wanted to make it public one could not do so.

This inarticulacy of reasons isn't particularism—it is simply the view that we cannot articulate all that we do know. Some people are better at this than others, but in the end even the most articulate are at a loss for words. Of course, a rejection of codifiability of some sort does not imply particularism. Nor does a rejection of reducibility imply particularism, nor a rejection of the truth or usefulness of rules. This is because one could also deploy these considerations to argue for moral skepticism.[27]

But this is clearly not the direction Iris Murdoch would pursue. It's not that there isn't any moral truth; rather, moral truth is rich and complex. Perhaps one doesn't follow rules (though at places she claims rules are very useful) and perhaps morality isn't codifiable.

Thus, it seems a genuine methodological insight that traditional theories give the impression that detail is ignored, is irrelevant. And sometimes it is. Killing an innocent person for no good reason is wrong, and the detail of what color shirt he or she happens to be wearing matters not at all. To use an example from Loeb, the claim that it is permissible to eat potatoes but not beans is absurd. Even though potatoes and beans are different, and certainly have many different properties, they are not different in any morally relevant way. The challenge for a methodological particularist is to argue that

---

[26] Joseph Raz, 'The Truth in Particularism', in *Moral Particularism* edited by Brad Hooker and Margaret Olivia Little (Clarendon Press, 2000), 48–78.

[27] See Sinnott-Armstrong, op. cit.

in all cases exhaustive detail is relevant, and not just relevant, but crucially important to arriving at a reliable or true judgment.

Also, a danger of a particularist methodology, and one that Murdoch does not dwell on, is that it ends up providing another kind of distortion. It is the sort of distortion that Hume wanted to guard against by requiring that moral judgment take place from 'the general point of view'. If one attends to the details of a case and looks at things from the perspective of a protagonist in a novel, or the perspective of an historical figure, and so forth, one runs the risk of making judgments that are biased or prejudiced. True, they will tend not to be biased in the ways that Murdoch was primarily concerned with— i.e. in the egoistic way which she feels is the enemy of the moral perspective. However, an *empathic* engagement with an historical character such as Brutus, or a literary figure such as Madame Bovary, runs the risk of leading us astray as well. But I believe that what Murdoch wants is a balance between considering questions at a high level of generality as well as detail. That's how this danger can be avoided. My reading of her is therefore the more moderate reading in which she is advocating a particularist methodology because it has been ignored, but which does not reject a crucial role for considering things in general *as well*.[28]

But what of Murdoch's reservations regarding the tendency we seem to have, to try to focus on some single aspect of the good, isolate it, and make a principle out of it? Are we doomed to be like Montaigne's children, engaged in the impossible task of bending moral experience to our theoretical wills? I don't think so. The fact that modern Utilitarians have taken the criticisms of virtue ethics seriously shows that the reality of our moral experience has an impact on the development of the theory. And, as Crisp notes, there are aspects of this approach that are appealing to Murdoch—the impartiality of morality, for example, the cleanness of the moral vision, and the fact that it gets us away from our egoistic preoccupations. For Murdoch, the good may be indefinable, but we can still know it through our experience of life and art. And, it is a testament to the force of Murdoch's work—as well as that of Anscombe and Foot and, of course, Professor Nussbaum—that current moral theorists are taking this experience seriously and attempting to accommodate it. It may be that for every foot its own shoe—all situations are different, and deciding in advance a formula for resolving them does seem like the hopeless task of Montaigne's children. But, as Murdoch also points out, this need not rule out a unified vision of the Good, of Love, which can inform our moral perceptions and help us to appreciate the moral significance of details that all too often get lost in the theorizing.

---

[28] To me this comes out most clearly when she is discussing other views. For example, in 'Morals and Politics' she writes:

A 'sense of duty' may be a sensibility to general rules or an active creation or discovery of detailed ones. Reason seems to dart from the outside into specific situations with an eagle glance which sets all in order. (MGM 384)

10

Visual Metaphors in Murdoch's Moral Philosophy*

Lawrence Blum

Iris Murdoch famously proffers vision as a metaphor for morality, as a counterpoint to what she sees as an excessive emphasis on will in the Existentialist and British moral philosophies of the 1950s and 1960s.[1] The focus on the will, leaping about undetermined (as in Sartre's philosophy), or affirming values through choice in a world of neutral facts (as in British linguistic philosophy), omitted, says Murdoch, the essential idea of a moral reality external to the agent. For Murdoch, choice takes place only against the backdrop of the world of value, and *seeing* that world should be the prime task of the individual moral agent.

In elaborating this alternative conception of morality and moral agency, Murdoch employs several distinct visual metaphors—perceiving, looking, seeing, vision, and attention. I will argue that these metaphors refer to some importantly distinct moral phenomena but that Murdoch's vocabulary does not consistently mark nor articulate those distinctions. In addition, even once we disaggregate the distinct phenomena that can be grouped under the various visual metaphors, they are nevertheless not, as a totality, adequate to Murdoch's own larger aspiration to articulate a fuller picture of moral agency that she finds absent in her contemporaries.

* I am grateful to David Wong, Justin Broackes, Nicole Saunders, and members of the Philosophy Department at Brandeis University in 2003 (especially Jacqueline Taylor and Marion Smiley) for very helpful feedback on earlier drafts of this paper.
[1] The exploration of the various metaphors of vision is most prominent in Murdoch's collection of three essays from the 1960s, *The Sovereignty of Good* (1970; New York: Schocken, 1971). Her 1956 essay 'Vision and Choice in Morality' does so as well, though not nearly as extensively as the *Sovereignty* essays. Her later views in *Metaphysics as a Guide to Morals* (1992; Penguin, 1993 [based on the Gifford Lectures of 1982]) are not inconsistent with those in *Sovereignty* on the character or moral agency and the role of vision, perception, seeing, attention, and the like therein; but there is less direct concern with such issues. I will focus my attention on the *Sovereignty* essays. I shall abbreviate 'The Idea of Perfection' and 'On "God" and "Good"' as IP and OGG, followed by page references both to *The Sovereignty of Good* (1970) and (after a forward slash/) to the reprints in Iris Murdoch, *Existentialists and Mystics* (1997), ed. P. J. Conradi.

Murdoch's highlighting of the role of the visual in the moral life, and her inconsistencies in its articulation are well-illustrated in an oft-cited passage from 'The Idea of
Perfection', her essay with the fullest discussion of moral vision.

I can only choose within the world I can see, in the moral sense of 'see' which implies that clear
vision is a result of moral imagination and moral effort. There is also of course 'distorted vision,'
and the word 'reality' here inevitably appears as a normative word . . . If we ignore the prior work
of attention and notice only the emptiness of the moment of choice we are likely to identify
freedom with the outward movement since there is nothing else to identify it with. But if we
consider what the work of attention is like, how continuously it goes on, and how imperceptibly
it builds up structures of value round about us, we shall not be surprised that at crucial moments
of choice most of the business of choosing is already over . . . The moral life, on this view, is
something that goes on continually, not something that is switched off in between the occurrences of explicit moral choices . . . I would like on the whole to use the word 'attention' as a
good word and use some more general term like 'looking' as the neutral word. (IP 37/329)

Let us leave aside for the moment the themes of freedom, and of choice, focusing on
the four visual words used in the passage—see, vision, attention, looking.[2] 'See' is first
used to mark the way the world presents itself to an individual agent, especially at a
moment of choice. Murdoch includes in 'the seen' not only what the agent literally
sees visually, but also the behavior of other persons as viewed through moral or morally
informed categories. Suppose Jane sees Kendra and Juan arguing, and sees certain facial
and bodily movements of Kendra's in response to Juan. If Jane does not, however, see
that Kendra's behavior suggests that she is feeling humiliated and psychically battered
by Juan's words and behavior, Jane will have missed seeing something morally important in the situation.

In addition, I think we will want to include in the 'seen', in Murdoch's sense here,
not only what is *present* to the agent at any level of awareness, but also what is *salient*
to the agent. Suppose, to vary the example slightly, that Jane does see Kendra's
humiliation but it remains at the fringes of Jane's take on the situation; it does not
become salient to her. It will then not become part of the moral characterization of
the situation—the 'world Jane can see'—within which Jane contemplates choosing
and acting. Although the seen and the salient are not coextensive, it is the salient that
is operative in characterizing the subjective world within which the agent chooses
to act.

---

[2] Regarding the issue of freedom, Murdoch is criticizing a view she finds in Sartre and in some ways in
philosophers such as R. M. Hare, in *The Language of Morals* (Oxford: Oxford University Press, 1952) and
Freedom and Reason (Oxford: Oxford University Press, 1963) (although Hare is not mentioned by name in the
Sovereignty essays), according to which freedom is identified with the unconstrained or only formally
constrained (e.g. by a universalizability requirement) operation of the choosing will. Murdoch aims to
replace this with a view of freedom as a kind of obedience to moral reality. However, one can decouple
Murdoch's view of the human agent from further claims about the nature of freedom. I am not here
interested in freedom per se but only in Murdoch's conception of moral agency.

1 Attention and looking

So the visually and morally present, and the salient, are all part of the 'seen' to which Murdoch wishes to call attention when she says we choose within the world we see, and I will refer to this phenomenon as the 'subjectively perceived'. Murdoch also refers in the same first sentence to 'distorted vision', implying that the subjectively perceived may nevertheless be *untrue* to the situation at hand; it may omit morally important features of the situation confronting the agent, and include features not actually present. For example, Jane may see Juan as a confident and commanding individual; she may have gotten that picture of Juan in her mind, but it may not be at all what Juan is like. Jane may fail to see Juan's shaky confidence underneath his superficial bravado, and his failure to get others to pay much heed to what he says. What she 'sees' in the sense of 'subjectively perceives' is confidence, and she acts toward Juan accordingly. Thus the idea of 'presentness to an agent' is epistemologically, and in a sense morally, neutral or uncommitted.[3] It refers simply to how a situation presents itself subjectively to the agent, with no implication of veridicality.

The contrast between *accurate* or *just* perception and mere subjective perception seems to be what Murdoch means in the last sentence of the IP passage, about 'looking' as the 'neutral word'—neutral in that perceiving is going on but not necessarily that moral reality is being grasped in that perceiving. Here Murdoch has shifted from 'see', used at the beginning of the passage in the same neutral sense, to 'look'. 'Look' is indeed a better choice than 'see', since 'see' is generally (though not always) used as a success verb; it implies not only that an agent has a certain take on a situation, but that the take is in some way *accurate*, which for Murdoch implies that the effort to grasp, to see, has been informed by justice, love, moral imagination, and a related form of attentiveness (suggested by the reference to 'moral imagination and moral effort' in the first sentence). By contrast, 'look' carries no implication that the looking succeeds in grasping the reality before the agent. Murdoch's terminology is not entirely consistent, then, since 'choosing within the world I can see' uses 'see' to mean what she means by 'look' in the last sentence.[4]

So Murdoch is correct to distinguish between a morally-implicated visual term connoting success in grasping moral reality, and a non-morally-implicated one.[5] But

[3] I speak here of 'presentness to an agent' but this use of 'agent' is potentially misleading. An 'agent' is the human person in her capacity for acting; but it is Murdoch's deep insight that our moral capacities are not exhausted by the capacity for action. The value-infused reality subjectively present to the individual person is of moral significance not only in regard to her *agency* but to her *moral being more generally*, including perception, imagination, emotions, and so on. This is very much Murdoch's point. But no alternative single term seems to me to capture this complex truth, and so I will have to make do with 'agent', with the understanding that this is to encompass the moral person in the fullness of her moral capacities. (This issue is discussed below, 314–15.)

[4] Nicole Saunders suggests that 'looking' is not generally used as a 'neutral' term by Murdoch, but tends to imply a 'just and loving gaze' (personal communication).

[5] In her excellent article on these issues in Murdoch, Margaret Holland uses 'perception' as the neutral term and 'attention' as the morally infused one. See 'Touching the Weights: Moral Perception and Attention', *International Philosophical Quarterly*, vol XXXVIII, no. 3, Issue 151 (September 1998): 299–312.

there is a second contrast at work in this passage. Murdoch says that the 'good', morally infused, term is 'attention'. Drawn from Simone Weil, Murdoch does generally use that term to mean something like 'a just and loving gaze directed upon an individual reality outside the self' (IP 34/327, 36/328). Attention thus involves not only a grasp of a moral reality but a grasp that is the product of a deliberate putting forth of a certain kind of attentiveness or focus.[6] Not all conscious and deliberate *attempts* to grasp a reality outside the self actually *succeed* in doing so; not all focusings of one's consciousness in a certain direction manage to grasp the reality that lies in that direction. Some focusings may be entirely misdirected. Jane may focus on Juan, genuinely attempting to understand him; but she may be so 'locked in' to her view of him as a confident and commanding person that she interprets what emerges from that focus so that it confirms that false view of him. Indeed, this missing of what other people are actually like, in spite of attempting to understand them, is a phenomenon Murdoch generally wishes to highlight, in her novels as well as her philosophical essays. She frequently notes the fantasies we have about other persons close to us (and not close to us as well) that block our grasp of their reality, of what is going on with them and what they are like.

But if attempts at focusing on others can misfire, then there must be a psychic activity of focusing, independent of whether it is successful or not, as well as the morally successful focusing, here called 'attention'. No distinct term seems to have been selected for the neutral activity. But might not 'looking' do, in the way Murdoch uses it in the last sentence of the passage (' "looking" as the neutral word')? Indeed, it could so serve; but not if it means what we took it to mean above (p. 309), namely the (epistemologically and morally) neutral manner in which a situation presents itself to an individual agent, i.e. the 'subjectively perceived'. The difference between the two is this. The way a situation appears or presents itself to an individual agent does not consist solely in what the agent intentionally *focuses* on in the situation. Generally, situations contain at least some elements which force themselves on our awareness, unbidden by us. A baby's cry in the seat behind me forces itself on my attention as I sit in my airplane seat; I may even try to concentrate on the book I am reading as a way to keep the baby's cry from becoming part of my 'take' on my situation, and I may be either successful or unsuccessful in doing so. Elements of a situation that emerge through deliberate focus are, then, a subset of all features that present themselves to me. It is the latter, the totality of the subjectively perceived, that we initially called the 'seen' in Murdoch's neutral sense. But it is the former, the deliberate focus, that contrasts most directly with the morally-laden notion of 'attention'. The contrast here is between a more general category and a specific instance of it; attendings comprise the more general category and morally successful attendings (Murdoch's 'attention') the specific instances. Attention is a deliberate effort that succeeds in grasping a moral reality; so we need another word for a deliberate effort to grasp, independent of whether that

---

[6] Murdoch sometimes understands this focus or attentiveness as a kind of receptiveness, an idea she draws from Simone Weil.

effort is successful. In fact, 'look' seems a better choice for the neutral 'effort-to-grasp' than it does for the neutral 'subjectively perceived'. For 'look' generally implies a deliberate focusing.

It is perhaps worth mentioning two distinct ways an attempt to focus on an individual reality—a 'looking'—can (for Murdoch) go wrong, that is, can fail to apprehend moral reality. First, the agent could be interested in knowing about the other person with a view to doing the person harm; she would focus on the other, and perhaps grasp some genuine truths about the individual (e.g. she seems very insecure about her appearance), but would not have a 'just and loving' attentiveness to her that would yield a fuller and truer picture of that person. Some persons are quite perceptive about other people's vulnerabilities that can be exploited for personal gain or maliciousness. Second, a person could genuinely attempt a true, even loving, understanding of the individual, yet be so misled by her fantasies and deluded views of that individual that she misses his reality.

Murdoch recognizes the distinction between neutral, and morally directed and successful, attempts to understand another person, although she does not consistently use terminology that marks this difference. In the long passage cited earlier, for example, although she says that she is going to use 'attention' only for the 'good' effort, the earlier phrase 'If we ignore the prior work of attention . . .' uses it in the neutral sense, since that attention can be well- or ill-directed. In her essay 'On "God" and "Good"', she says, '[O]ur ability to act well "when the time comes" depends partly, perhaps largely, upon the quality of our habitual objects of attention' (OGG 56/ 345). Those objects of attention can be either morally good or morally bad or mediocre; so 'attention' is used here also in the neutral, rather than good (i.e. morally successful), sense. By and large, however, Murdoch generally uses 'attention' in a way that implies moral success.

I would suggest that Murdoch's failure consistently to mark the distinction between efforts to focus on the reality of others that succeed ('attention') and those that do not necessarily ('lookings') is not a mere confusion or oversight on her part. There is a countervailing strand in Murdoch's work that mitigates against her making much of this distinction. In a Platonic spirit, she sees The Good as exerting a 'magnetic pull' on a moral agent. In a sense, according to this strand in her thinking, the reality of another person—a central element of the Good for Murdoch—draws the focus of the agent toward itself. In this sense there is a sort of tendency, Murdoch implies, for outward focus to become attention—to successfully grasp another's reality—rather than remaining a neutral looking. To put it another way, there is a strand in Murdoch's thinking that involves the idea that there is tendency for efforts of attention to be successful. Her uses of the word 'attention' reflect the Simone Weilian meaning Murdoch gives it. In the earlier IP quote—'if we consider what the work of attention is like'—the context is neutral (building up subjective structures of value), but Murdoch slides easily into the honorific use of 'attention' in the later part of the passage, in which it implies the openness, receptiveness to reality, and other-directed-ness built into her Weilian understanding of 'attention'.[7]

So there is a tension between two distinct and important strands in Murdoch's thought, that bear on the distinctions among visual metaphors. One is the magnetic pull of the Good. The other is the human tendency, which Murdoch regards Freud as having been the premier thinker to have explored but whose roots go back to Plato, toward personal self-centeredness, fantasy—what at one point she calls 'the tissue of self-aggrandizing and consoling wishes and dreams which prevents one from seeing what is there outside one' (OGG 59/348).[8] This ever-present and difficult-to-control tendency may block even our best efforts at grasping the reality of other persons. It means that efforts at focus may well be unsuccessful (leaving aside for the moment the additional implication that such fantasy often prevents persons from even attempting the work of seeing the reality of others). The Platonic strand may be contributing to Murdoch's failure to consistently mark the distinction between successful and unsuc-cessful 'lookings', a distinction of which the Freudian strand makes her acutely aware.

1.1 Perception, looking, and the structures of value

Returning to the passage from 'Idea of Perfection' quoted at the beginning of this essay, we can see a further unclarity attending Murdoch's visual metaphors. We have glossed 'the world we can see' as 'the world that is present to the individual agent', or 'the subjectively perceived'. Murdoch implies later in the passage that this 'world'—the subjective structures of value that provide the setting for the agent's moral activity broadly construed—is created or built up through the prior activity of looking (called 'attention' in this passage and said to 'imperceptibly build up structures of value round about us'). If Joe, a member of an English Department at a university, perceives his colleagues primarily as rivals in a contest for honor and recognition, rather than co-workers in a collective enterprise in which each is to be honored for doing his part, this is (Murdoch implies in the passage just quoted) because Joe has built up this competi-tive view of them through prior lookings and focusings that have eventuated in his constructing them as rivals.

Murdoch frequently propounds such a view. One example: 'Innumerable "look-ings" have discovered and explored a world which is now (for better or worse) compulsively present to the will in a particular situation' (IP 39/330).[9] Two quite

---

[7] Justin Broackes has suggested to me that the idea of 'the magnetic pull of the Good' can be understood differently, as implying that once one grasps moral reality, one will be inclined to act accordingly in light of it (personal communication). I agree that this recognizably Platonic idea is present in Murdoch; but I think the idea that the Good also draws the focus of agents towards itself prior to activity is also present in Murdoch's idea of the magnetic pull of the Good.

[8] See also 'fantasy, the proliferation of blinding self-centered aims and images, is itself a powerful system of energy' (OGG 67/354)

[9] See also '[T]he task of attention goes on all the time and at apparently empty and everyday moments we are "looking", making those little peering efforts of imagination which have such important cumulative effects' (IP 43/334). Note also the confused use of 'attention' in this passage. It certainly is not true that

distinct phenomena are conflated here—presentness to the agent ('subjective perceiv-ing'), and looking. If we ask the question what is it that shapes the subjective structures of value and meaning that are present to an agent (in a situation), the answer is a wide array of factors. For example, one reason Joe may see his colleagues as rivals is a deep insecurity Joe has about his own professional value and standing, which leads him to see professional honor as a kind of zero-sum game: If the colleagues are honored, then he is not. Perhaps this insecurity itself has deep psychic roots in his childhood—an absence of unconditional love from his parents—or perhaps in the culture of his professional training. In either case, Joe's view of his colleagues as rivals is *not* a product of his prior 'lookings'. It is not that Joe has, for example, paid attention to his colleagues' professional honors and successes rather than their contributions to their shared institutional or intellectual work, and this has *resulted in* his seeing them as rivals. The causality is more likely to have gone in the other direction: Joe's already-settled view of them as rivals has led him to focus on their professional achievements rather than their contributions to his and their shared enterprises of creating a good English program at the university. An alternative psychic scenario is that Joe's view of them as rivals has caused him to *view* their accomplishments as accumulated points in a competition rather than as contributions to a shared enterprise.

What we subjectively perceive, what is present to us, is formed by a myriad of factors in our lives—personal, social, cultural, and so on. These factors shape the character, quality, and incidence of our lookings, at least most of the time. And indeed this truth seems itself in one sense an entirely Murdochian insight. It is she who (as remarked above) so often emphasizes how personal fantasy shapes the way we view others, where personal fantasy is by no means something constructed out of deliberate efforts to understand others ('lookings').

Why then does Murdoch neglect this insight when discussing subjective perceivings and the structures of value within which we exercise choice, and imply that it is the mental activity of focusing that builds up the subjectively perceived? One reason may be rooted in the Sartrian existentialism and, even more, the British analytical ethics of the 1950s and 1960s, that form the philosophical backdrop of Murdoch's essays in *The Sovereignty of Good*. What Murdoch has, with great insight, seen in these philosophies— insight that she works out in 'The Idea of Perfection' in a detailed exploration of Stuart Hampshire's *Thought and Action*, the most sophisticated and interesting of the works in this tradition—is a particular conception of the moral life. It is one in which the moral life consists in the agent's choices, exercisings of the will, in moral situations; what goes on in between these choices is not part of the moral life. Against this picture Murdoch wants to emphasize that the moral life goes on all the time, that valuings are an inevitable and constant part of living, that the world that is present to us at all times is infused and suffused with moral valuings, that it is therefore not only in overt action

people are *in fact* engaged in just and loving attentiveness to others, or even that they are attempting to do so, 'all the time'. See also (OGG 46/337, 67/354).

that we express our moral character but in these often tacit and barely conscious valuings. Of course Murdoch also wants to emphasize that this continual valuing *bears on* choice and action too; choices arise in settings constructed from valuings, so the morality of our choices is very much affected by our valuings. Indeed, as some of the passages cited above suggest, Murdoch often goes so far as to say that these choices are almost entirely determined by the structures of value that we have formed for ourselves. (We will return to this point below.)

In emphasizing this continual character of the moral life, I think Murdoch slips into thinking of this character as solely a manifestation of our moral *agency*. In perhaps the most famous example in her philosophical work, Murdoch describes a woman, 'M', attempting to see her daughter-in-law, 'D', justly and accurately. The daughter-in-law will not know of the results of M's effort; Murdoch imagines D long since departed, perhaps dead. M's efforts will have no effect on the world, result in no action. M attempts to view D accurately in her own mind and, Murdoch implies, is successful in doing so (IP 17f./312f.).

Murdoch is concerned to show that M's efforts constitute a form of moral *activity* even though they have no effect on outward *behavior*. This construal contributes to Murdoch's argument about the moral importance of the inner life of consciousness, in contrast to her stalking horse of morality as the exercise of will. Highlighting inner as a complement to outer moral activity strongly supports Murdoch's case; we can see M engaged in a deliberate moral enterprise, attempting to see her daughter-in-law in a more just, loving, and charitable manner.

However, the moral dimension of inner consciousness is not exhausted by actual *activity*. What we feel, what we habitually tend to see in situations, what we find amusing, what we fantasize about, and so on, are *also* dimensions of our moral being.[10] Yet these items of our consciousness are not, or at least not generally, manifestations of moral activity in the way lookings or attention are. (Perhaps we can *sometimes* choose what to fantasize about.) Compassion for a humiliated acquaintance or envy of a favored colleague are *reactions*, not forms of activity; and yet they reflect on us morally. They are part of our moral being.

Indeed, these reactive or non-activity-based dimensions of our moral being are part of what Murdoch must be referring to when she speaks of the moral life going on all the time, providing the setting within which our choosings of external actions arise. We react to things, in a passive mode, and these reactings contribute to, reflect, and partly constitute our valuings. Joe envies his colleague because he views her as a competitor, but one way that his so viewing her expresses itself is in his envy of her.

---

[10] Murdoch says something like this in her early essay on these topics, 'Vision and Choice in Morality': '[W]hen we apprehend and assess other people ... we consider something more elusive which may be called their total vision of life, as shown in their mode of speech or silence ... what they think attractive or praiseworthy, what they think funny' (in *Existentialists and Mystics*, 80–1). This passage is not, however, aimed at showing that our moral being goes beyond the results of our moral activity, but that it transcends our overt actions in specified situations.

As Murdoch herself frequently points out, we have but slight control over our reactions and emotions of this sort; Joe cannot just choose to stop envying his colleague, just as (to take one of Murdoch's frequent examples) one cannot choose not to be in love. Yet these reactions are very much part of our moral being.

Thus, when Murdoch says that the structures of value that provide the setting for our choices are built up out of our lookings, she is omitting much of what actually goes into creating those structures of value, perhaps because her emphasis on the existence of non-behavioral moral activity leads her temporarily to forget the reactive character of our moral being, hence of some of the important sources of our subjective structures of value.

Perhaps Murdoch should not be construed as claiming that our subjective structures of value are themselves actual *forms* of moral activity, of looking—but rather that they are *products* of such moral activity. She implies as much when she says '[I]f we consider what the work of attention is like, how continuously it goes on, and how impercept-ibly it builds up structures of value round about us' (IP 37/329, from the passage at beginning of this essay). Here Murdoch implies that lookings construct the subjective structures of value. I confess to not understanding how Murdoch can say this, and she gives no further explanation. We are affected in our subjective structures of value by so many factors other than what we choose to focus on, and our focusings themselves are deeply shaped by our prior valuings, that it just seems implausible to see the lookings as the sole factor building up the subjective structures of value.

2 The social sources of subjective structures of value

If lookings are not the only source of the subjective structures of value—of how the world presents itself to an individual agent—what does shape these structures? We can glean one answer to this from the Freudian strand in Murdoch's thinking, illustrated in our example above of Joe who views his colleagues as rivals because of a deep insecurity stemming from how he was treated as a child. Murdoch calls 'fantasy' the distorted views we have of others, whose sources lie deep in our individual psychic make-up. These distortions can apply to persons close to us, to strangers, and to those in-between. For example, a father can fail to see that his child would be happy and live a meaningful life as a social worker with a modest income, because the father has fixed an image in his mind that the child can be happy only if she lives a life devoted to the accumulation of great wealth. Perhaps on a deep level this fantasy is an unconscious product of the father's disappointment about how his own life has turned out. In any case, it entirely blocks the father from truly seeing his daughter in relation to her own genuine values and abilities.

Similarly, a person of modest but steady income may perceive persons receiving public assistance, but personally unknown to her, as being lazy and undeserving. This image of persons 'on welfare' might be a product of the individual's own personal fears of losing her tenuous grip on financial security, and a consequent need to distance herself psychically from those receiving public assistance.

However, personal fantasy, which Murdoch emphasizes, is not the only source of distortion in the views we have of other persons. Often there is a social or cultural source of distorted images of others. The example of persons on welfare just given illustrates this point well. Although my description emphasizes the personal and individual source of the image of welfare recipients as lazy and undeserving, the latter image is, independent of this, a very culturally salient one in the United States. Moreover, again in the United States, that image is deeply racialized and gendered; most White Americans think of the paradigm welfare recipient as a Black woman.[11] These social categories in turn reinforce the 'lazy and undeserving' image of the welfare recipient; they draw on long-standing images of Blacks reaching back to the slavery era. Both the character and the salience of these images in a society result from an interplay of various social and cultural forces. A given White American's susceptibility to such images need not be explained by any personal psychic difficulty or pathology. Indeed, what requires explanation is why a given White American is *not* so susceptible, given the cultural salience of the images.

One might think that the kind of distorted images provided by the larger society do not have the kind of psychic deep-rootedness that Murdoch is concerned to articulate concerning our fantasies. But it is not clear that this is relevant, and also not clear that it is true. On the former point, there may indeed be some culturally salient distorted images of groups of persons that, for some particular individual, are not very deeply rooted. Some people overcome particular stereotypes and even prejudices relatively easily, upon being presented with counter-evidence or greater familiarity with members of the group in question. Still, until corrected, these distorted images may block a true appreciation of the reality of another person; and so they should figure into any general understanding of the range of factors that create distorted images and thus block a grasp of moral reality.

Conversely, some distorted images whose source is personal rather than social may not be very deeply psychically rooted either. The way Murdoch describes the mother-in-law in her famous example exemplifies this. Although M is described as having held a view of D as juvenile, rude, and common for quite a long time—perhaps as long as she has known D—she manages to rid herself of this distorted image fairly readily. 'I assume that M observed D or least reflects deliberately about D, until gradually her vision of D alters...D is discovered to be not vulgar but refreshingly simple, not undignified but spontaneous, not noisy but gay...and so on' (IP 17–18/313). Murdoch is right to imply here that a long-standing distorted personal image need not

---

[11]   On the racial and gender dimensions of White Americans' images of persons receiving public assistance, see Dorothy Roberts, *Killing the Black Body: Race, Reproduction, and the Meaning of Liberty* (New York: Vintage, 1998), and Thomas and Mary Edsall, *Chain Reaction: the Impact of Race, Rights, and Taxes on American Politics* (New York: Norton, 1992).

be deeply psychically rooted. It might be relatively amenable to correction, as are some social prejudices and stereotypes.

On the other point, not all, or even most, *social* prejudices and stereotypes are readily amenable to change in a given individual. Certain stereotypes are quite deeply lodged in the culture of a given society. They are 'potent cultural imagery', as Diana T. Meyers says.[12] This is arguably true, in the US, of images relating to 'welfare'. The form of individualism connected with the powerfully resonant idea of 'the American Dream' is, for example, a deep feature of American political culture; and that individualism strongly contributes to the distorted image of welfare recipients mentioned above. Anyone who teaches about welfare in American universities knows that despite exposing students to wide-ranging data showing the myriad of factors (vagaries in job availability, weak skills because of poor schooling, child care responsibilities) outside the particular welfare recipients' control that lead to her requiring public assistance, it is very difficult to dislodge in one's students the image of welfare recipients as lazy and undeserving.

Another example frequently noted in the American context is the image that Whites, and other non-Black groups, often have of Black people, and especially of African-Americans. Violent, lazy, angry, intellectually weak, good at sports—these are stereotypes affecting the reactions of Whites (and other non-Blacks) to Blacks, especially those not well-known to them, but sometimes also affecting the way friends and acquaintances are seen. Stereotypes of various significant social groups—ethnic, racial, religious, cultural, sexual, national, economic—have a substantial effect on the moral lives of Americans. Through providing images of groups, they affect people's relation to various issues of social justice. It is widely and plausibly argued, for example, that White Americans' acceptance of the weakest welfare state in the advanced industrial world is deeply shaped by stereotypes of two overlapping groups as undeserving— Blacks, and poor people.[13] These stereotypes can also affect our personal relationships with particular other persons. They affect our ability to have and show respect, care, love, admiration, appreciation of others as individuals, and recognition of the common humanity of those of other races.

Murdoch's moral philosophy shows very little appreciation of the social and cultural forms of the distorting images that block an appreciation of the humanity and the individual reality of other human beings. Murdoch confines her rich insights into the myriad ways, neglected by so many other moral philosophers, that self-centered energy and personal fantasy subtly and not-so-subtly block such appreciation. An analogous

---

[12] Diana T. Meyers, *Subjection and Subjectivity: Psychoanalytic Feminism and Moral Philosophy* (New York: Routledge, 1994), 52. Meyers's analysis of how culturally salient stereotypes can be powerful yet unrecognized is quite insightful. '[P]eople can be inducted into culturally normative prejudice . . . without explicit instruction . . . Culturally entrenched figurations are passed on without obliging anyone to formulate, accept, or reject repugnant negative propositions about any group's standing' (53).

[13] On the impact of stereotypes of Blacks and poor people on White people's support for social provision, see Edsall, *Chain Reaction.*

analysis could have been given, and could be given, of the operations of entrenched social and culturally-generated stereotypes, but Murdoch does not recognize this as a task relevant to her moral philosophy.

The world of Murdoch's novels is similarly confined. There is virtually no recognition of racial difference as a significant fault line in British society, a recognition that might have led Murdoch to explore the myriad ways that racial 'fantasy' blocks the perception of common humanity and of individuality. Indeed, there is also very little recognition of class as an important differentiating factor in the world of her characters, who are largely confined to artists, intellectuals, academics, and other generally comfortably placed persons. Murdoch was for a time a socialist, and her 1958 essay 'A House of Theory' is recognizably socialist.[14] She was clearly conversant with Marxist and socialist theory and history, and Marxism as an intellectual approach plays a non-trivial role in *Metaphysics as a Guide to Morals*, and is occasionally mentioned in the essays in *The Sovereignty of Good*. Nevertheless, society as class-divided does not inform the moral world of her novels, and class as a source of the forces that block an appreciation of the reality of other persons is neither articulated within her moral philosophy nor portrayed more than peripherally in the novels.[15]

As my analysis above suggests, it is not only the case that the socio-cultural and the personal are two distinct sources of morality-occluding imagery but in addition are, or can be, deeply intertwined with one another. Ironically, Murdoch's own example of M and D illustrates this intertwining quite nicely. Although Murdoch presents the *personal* dimension of M's distorted view of D, that view is in fact deeply *social* in character. M is basically a social snob about her son's wife—'M feels that her son has married beneath him'. 'M does not like D's accent or the way D dresses' (IP 17/312). The characterizations through which M perceives D are all deeply class and status linked: 'pert and familiar', 'insufficiently ceremonious', 'vulgar'. It is not as if M has generated these distorted images from an idiosyncratic personal deficiency. We can make sense of the moral character of M as Murdoch has described her only because we recognize the sense of class superiority that it presupposes.

One of Murdoch's lasting contributions to moral philosophy has been to frame the question of how we can morally improve, how we can become better people, as a distinctly philosophical one, and to suggest a way of thinking about the obstacles to moral improvement that provides a particularly fruitful way into this philosophical

---

[14] Murdoch was a member of the British Communist Party from the late 1930s until 1942 and perhaps the winter of 1944–45, and held views sympathetic to Communism for a number of years later. See Peter J. Conradi, *Iris Murdoch: A Life* (London: HarperCollins, 2001), 76, 87, 128, 210–11.

[15] Martha Nussbaum makes a similar point in an essay prompted by Peter Conradi's biography of Murdoch: 'There are major gaps in Murdoch's philosophical vision. She seems almost entirely to lack interest in the political and social determinants of a moral vision, and in the larger social criticism that ought, one feels, to be a major element in the struggle against one's own defective tendencies. Her examples, and her characters, are almost always undone by something universal about the ego and its devious workings, almost never by prejudice or misogyny or other failings endemic to a particular society at a particular time.' 'When She Was Good', *The New Republic*, 31 December 2001.

inquiry. I do not think that contemporary moral theory has yet caught up to this insight. Even virtue theory—certainly the most hospitable home for this sort of inquiry—has not yet fully engaged in it. By and large, virtue theorists have not systematically posed the question, What is that makes it difficult for us to be virtuous? Perhaps contemporary moral philosophy has not seen how philosophy (rather than psychology) can approach that question in a systematic fashion. Murdoch's idea of the tissue of personal fantasy and, somewhat more generally, the egoistic system of energy that makes it so hard for us to see individual other persons is a vital contribution to the way that philosophy can appropriate a psychological idiom to begin to answer the question how we can morally improve.

But Murdoch's focus on individual psychology is clearly a deeply incomplete answer to that question. We live in worlds shaped by social, political, economic, and cultural forces, often, though not only, bound up with various sorts of social inequalities, that generate (while also reflecting) distorted pictures of various social groups. These distorted images, in addition to those arising from individual psychologies, are a major force in shaping our subjective structures of value—and in blocking the agent's seeing the human and individual reality of other human beings, as individuals and as groups.

3 Will and vision: limitations of Murdoch's conception of moral agency

Let us return to the conception of the moral agent to which Murdoch wishes her exploration of perception, attention, looking—of the visual—to contribute. In her critique of the overemphasis on the choosing will in moral action, Murdoch moves toward the idea that 'at crucial moments of choice most of the business of choosing is already over' (IP 37/329), and 'by time the moment of choice has arrived the quality of attention has probably determined the nature of the act' (OGG 67/354). The way we see our situation is already so suffused with value that what we regard as appropriate action is implied by our subjective perception of the situation. This is a *descriptive* point about the character of moral agency and the role of subjective perception in it. This philosophical critique of the conception of moral agency that Murdoch finds in dominant philosophies of her time permeates *Sovereignty* and 'Vision and Choice in Morality'. However, in addition, she regards the absence of a certain kind of freedom of will in action as a moral *ideal*: 'If I attend properly I will have no choices and this is the ultimate condition to be aimed at' (IP 40/331). If the agent fully grasps the moral reality before him, it will be obvious what is the right action to take. Murdoch portrays what is clearly meant to be an example of this ideal in her novel *A Fairly Honourable Defeat*.[16] In a Chinese restaurant, a Jamaican man is being assaulted and insulted by a

---

[16] Iris Murdoch, A *Fairly Honourable Defeat* (1970; London: Penguin, 1972).

group of five young White louts. Simon, a central character in the novel, witnesses this incident, is distressed, concludes that there is nothing for him to do, then, a moment later, ineffectually and feebly protests the action to the youths. Axel, Tallis, and Julius, three other central characters in the novel, arrive at the scene (they are to meet Simon). Axel begins to remonstrate with the leader of the thugs, receiving a threat in return. Julius relishes the scene; it would not occur to him to attempt to intervene. It is Tallis's actions that illustrate Murdoch's ideal:

Tallis moved in from behind Julius and before anyone could shift or cry out he had struck the youth very hard across the side of the face. He stuck him with the flat of his hand but with such violence that the boy staggered against his companions and almost fell to the floor. (*A Fairly Honourable Defeat*, 241)

The thugs—their dominance of the situation broken—leave the restaurant. Axel comments (to Julius), 'My God, it was impressive. Do you know, we all acted characteristically. Simon intervened incompetently, I talked, you watched, and Tallis acted' (241). Tallis is clearly, in the novel, a 'good' character, a moral exemplar.[17] He does not need to ruminate, to decide or choose; he goes straight for the right thing to do, because of the way (it is implied) that he sees the situation in the first place (not that his way of doing so is ever independently articulated in the book). Tallis exemplifies the Platonic idea that if a situation is seen rightly, right or good action follows almost automatically.

Murdoch's attachment to an example of this sort as allegedly paradigmatic of moral action is revealing of the limitations of the conception of moral agency that she proffers in her philosophical writings. Tallis's action carries a moral authority with it that, the novel implies, is part of why it is effective in breaking the thugs' command of the situation. It is not only, though it is partly, that, in contrast to Simon and Axel who approach the thugs with words, Tallis uses the only language they understand, that of violence. There is a further implication that because Tallis did not have to deliberate and think about alternatives—because it was so obvious what should be done—his action altered the perceived moral character of the situation even for the thugs; evil was no longer dominant, good reigned. ('Five violent men can paralyse a much larger group of ordinary citizens', the author observes as Simon perseverates, implying that breaking the mood that constitutes this paralysis is integral to what will constitute the right form of intervention.)

Yet, were such a situation to obtain in real life, it is far from clear that an action such as Tallis's would be the right one. The youths had a bicycle chain and a piece of iron piping, and Tallis's action could well have eventuated in a brawl in which more

---

[17] In her commentary on *Fairly Honourable Defeat*, Elizabeth Dipple sees Tallis as exemplifying an unself-conscious goodness. (E. Dipple, *Iris Murdoch: Work for the Spirit* (Chicago: University of Chicago, 1982), 19.) Peter Conradi sees him as a Christ-like figure, and the restaurant incident as a turning point in the book, a defeat of evil by good. Peter Conradi, *The Saint and the Artist* (London: HarperCollins, 2001), 204, 208.

innocent people would be hurt. A conscientious moral agent would have to make some sort of assessment of the likelihood of this outcome, reflecting on other possibilities, such as trying to protect the Jamaican man without inviting further violence by the thugs. Some sort of deliberation seems called for, even if it would have to be carried out in very short order. I suggest that Murdoch has conflated two aspects of moral situations such as this one—the recognition of need for a decisive action, and discerning the specific decisive action that would produce the required outcome or otherwise be the right thing to do. Tallis is the only person who clearly perceives the necessity for decisive action, and, as Murdoch portrays it, he hits upon the right such action. But in many situations, these are two very different matters. There could have been a character in the situation as described who was quite clear that some decisive action had to be taken, but was entirely unsure what it should be. An Aristotelian would see lighting on the appropriate action, following the *prior* determination of the need to act, as an exercise in a distinctive kind of moral judgment or discernment—discerning the best action once the moral character of the situation is taken as given. In theory, one can imagine someone who did not immediately see the need for decisive action, but who, upon such need's being brought to his attention, would be good at figuring out what that action should be. In any case, grasping the need for decisive action, and discerning what that action ought to be, seem to be two distinct moral 'operations', neither of which psychically guarantees the other in the psychology of a given moral agent.

To put this point another way: Murdoch often implies that the moral capacities or operations that are other than the choosing will are somehow all the same, or constitute a psychic or moral unity—they are what enable us to perceive right action, hence to act well. But this is not correct. Those capacities are multiple, not unitary. Our previous discussion of visual metaphors has already disaggregated at least two such capacities or operations—attention as the loving gaze successfully directed at an individual reality, and subjective perception as the totality of forces that determine an agent's take on a situation. And we saw that the agent's subjective take is itself composed of a myriad of factors, from personal fantasy or pathology to socio-cultural images and stereotypes. So personal self-scrutiny and certain kinds of social critique become part of the arsenal of moral operations or capacities required for moral action and response, and more general improvement of character.

The example from *A Fairly Honourable Defeat* suggests some other capacities or psychic operations as well. There is, first, the accurate initial perception of the moral character of the given situation (e.g. that a Black man is being beaten by White men out of racism).[18] Second is the recognition that the situation so perceived calls for the

---

[18] Both Jacqueline Taylor and Marion Smiley have suggested to me that moral awareness, including knowing the right thing to do once one has an adequate moral take on a situation, sometimes requires a kind of specialized knowledge that Murdoch tends not to recognize. For example, we might fail to understand what is going on because we are unfamiliar with the cultural context of the situation. Taylor suggests that

given agent to do something. Obviously not every morally significant situation requires every person present to intervene; sometimes intervention by a particular agent may undermine the autonomy of the aggrieved party to the situation.[19] Knowing when it is appropriate to engage one's agency in the face of an already-determined moral characterization of a situation itself constitutes a type of moral judgment, which can be equated neither with the original insight into the situation's moral character, nor with the subsequent discernment of the appropriate action. Knowing that I should act is not (or not always) the same as knowing *what* I should do.

Generally, knowing what one should do, once one knows what is morally going on and judges that one should act, requires *deliberation*—a consideration of alternative courses of action and a selection of what one takes to be the best one. Moral philosophers have much analyzed the character of deliberation, or at least assumed that it must be present in morally good acting. Murdoch gives no attention to deliberation and focuses on situations in which she takes the right action to be manifest to an agent who perceives accurately, who sees reality, and thus who does not need to deliberate. This remains a central moral ideal for her. The centrality of the visual as the favored alternative to the volitional perhaps contributes to masking the importance of the deliberative.

I will not further discuss whether Murdoch is right to think that deliberation is not necessary in the cases she mentions, such as the restaurant incident in *A Fairly Honourable Defeat*. I want only to note that deliberation is a moral capacity, power, or operation distinct from two others that deliberation *presupposes*—accurate perception of the moral features of a situation, and judgment whether it is appropriate or required for one to act—and (subsequent to deliberation) actually acting, that is, exerting one's will to choose the action in question. It is this last step that Murdoch recognizes in her 'will and perception' picture, although she does not give the obstacles or barriers to a successful exertion of will much attention.[20]

These brief remarks are not meant as a complete account of our moral powers related to agency, much less the broader set of moral capacities involved in right attitude, emotion, and response. But it does suggest the limitations of Murdoch's

---

certain kinds of what has been called 'cultural competence' may be necessary to gain an accurate read on a situation. Smiley suggests that, more generally, Murdoch fails to explore the substantive psychic wherewithal that an agent must bring to a situation in order to perceive it accurately or justly. Murdoch highlights the obstacles to perception, but not the requisites of perception (other than saying they involved a just and loving gaze, and the like). (Personal communication.)

[19] The ways that beneficent interventions can undermine autonomy is explored by Lisa Rivera 'Harmful Beneficence', *Journal of Moral Philosophy*, Volume 8, Issue 2 (2011), 195–220.

[20] This discussion of distinct moral capacities and operations is drawn from Lawrence Blum, 'Postscript to "Moral Perception and Particularity"', in *Moral Perception and Particularity* (Cambridge, UK: Cambridge University Press, 1994), 57–61. In that article, I also discuss bringing principles to bear on particular situations as part of engaging in right action, and various models for understanding this, including Henry Richardson's discussion of 'specification' in 'Specifying Norms as a Way to Resolve Concrete Ethical Problems', *Philosophy and Public Affairs*, vol. 19: 279–310. (Richardson's views are further developed in *Practical Reasoning About Final Ends* (New York: Cambridge University Press, 1994).)

picture of moral agency when she implies that it is comprised of perception and will, or perhaps perception, attention, and will. Murdoch is right to bring perception and attention into a conception of moral agency as a corrective to the overemphasis on will, and this insight has been far from exhausted in contemporary moral philosophy. But Murdoch does not go far enough in correcting that conception, though she points in directions that would supply the broader picture. I have suggested that Murdoch's failure to do so may lie in part in her being overenamored of situations in which the agent can immediately see both the need for her to act and what act she should perform. More fundamentally, however, her focus on the visual (perception, attention, seeing) might be blinding her to other aspects of moral being (deliberation, agency engagement, and response).

11

Psychopathy, Empathy, and Moral Motivation*

A. E. Denham

Introduction

I can remember the first time in my life when I began to suspect I was a little different from most people. When I was in High School my best friend got leukaemia and died and I went to his funeral. Everybody else was crying and feeling sorry for themselves and as they were praying to get him into heaven I suddenly realized that I wasn't feeling anything at all. He was a nice guy but what the hell. That night I thought about it some more and found that I wouldn't miss my mother and father if they died and that I wasn't too nuts about my brothers and sisters for that matter. I figured there wasn't anybody I really cared for but, then, I don't need any of them anyway so I rolled over and went to sleep.[1]

These remarks were recorded by psychologist Elton McNeil in his case study of Dan, a personal friend and prominent community figure. Dan enjoyed a successful media career, a high social profile, and a reputation for being lively and entertaining—'a great character'. McNeil, like many others, had initially been charmed by him. Over time, however, McNeil began to notice that Dan possessed some disturbing qualities: a lack of empathy for others' concerns, chronic deceitfulness, insusceptibility to shame or remorse or regret, manipulativeness, a grandiose self-image, and strangely superficial relations with even his closest associates. In short, Dan exhibited the hallmarks of psychopathic personality disorder.[2] At the same time, McNeil observed, Dan could easily assume the surface demeanour of a caring and trustworthy friend: he 'talked the talk' of everyday, conventional morality, even while his conduct revealed him to be

* This research was generously supported by the *Centre de recherche en Sens, Ethique, Société* (CERSES) of the CNRS (UMR 8137), Paris V.

[1] E. McNeil, *The Quiet Furies* (Englewood Cliffs, New Jersey: Prentice-Hall, 1967), 87.

[2] See the 'Psychopathy Checklist' in R. D. Hare, T. J. Harpur, R. A. Hakstian, A. E. Forth, S. D. Hart, et al. 'The Revised Psychopathy Checklist: Reliability and Factor Structure', *Psychological Assessment* 2 (1994), 338–41.

utterly unmoved by its requirements. Like most psychopaths, Dan 'knew the words of morality but did not hear its music'.[3]

Psychopathy provides for moral theory a paradigm of amoral agency, combining intellectual and rational competence with a profound indifference to the claims of morality. Unlike psychotic subjects who suffer from delusions or other defects in their cognitive functioning, the psychopath appears to think clearly and to understand well both the rules of morality and their implications for particular cases, whilst failing regularly and systematically to be guided by them in his practical judgements. For this reason, some theorists have proposed that psychopathy offers an empirical vindication of anti-rationalist, non-cognitivist accounts of moral motivation. After all, if the psychopath understands moral requirements as well as you or I, and if his deliberative procedures are as rational as yours or mine, then what remains to explain his conduct save a pathology of his affective constitution—his Humean sentiments? And is there not then good reason to suppose that we non-psychopaths, too, owe our moral natures to our affective ones?

This prospect sits uneasily with Iris Murdoch's conception of moral motivation. The essays collected in *The Sovereignty of Good*, in particular, feature two recurrent ideas which, if correct, would require a different analysis of both psychopathic disorder and of ordinary moral motivation. The first idea is that our ability even to discern what morality requires—the ability to form accurate moral beliefs—is of a piece with a capacity for a 'just and loving' attentiveness to other persons' inner lives, an empathic attentiveness that Murdoch sometimes calls 'compassion'.[4] 'It is in the capacity to love, that is to *see*', she wrote, 'that the liberation of the soul from fantasy consists... [F]reedom from fantasy... is the realism of compassion' (OGG 66–7/354). At one point, Murdoch even suggests that empathic love is the essence of moral knowledge: the central concept of morality is 'the individual thought of as knowable by love' (IP 30/323). Accurate perception does not float free of compassionate attention: a loving attention to others plays, for Murdoch, an ineliminable role in the very understanding of moral requirements.

At the same time, Murdoch did not construe moral judgements as disguised desires or other emotions. The second recurring theme in *The Sovereignty of Good* is that 'true vision occasions right conduct'[5] (OGG 66/353); moral knowledge consists not only in

---

[3] J. H. Johns and H. C. Quay, 'The effect of social reward on verbal conditioning in psychopathic and neurotic military offenders', *Journal of Consulting Psychology*, 26 (1962), 207–20.

[4] I abbreviate the titles of Murdoch's three essays 'The Idea of Perfection' (1964), 'On "God" and "Good"' (1969), and 'The Sovereignty of Good Over Other Concepts' (1967) as IP, OGG, and SGC respectively. Page references are given both to their appearance in *The Sovereignty of Good* (1970) and to the reprintings in *Existentialists and Mystics* [E&M], ed. P. J. Conradi (Allen Lane Penguin Press: New York, 1997), separated by a slash /. The phrase 'just and loving' attention occurs within Murdoch's discussion of her well-known example of the resentful mother-in-law (M) and her son's high-spirited wife (D). Cf: 'I can only choose within the world I can see, in the moral sense of "see" which implies that clear vision is a result of moral imagination and moral effort.... When M is just and loving she sees D as she really is' (IP 37/329).

[5] See also 'Vision and Choice in Morality' [VCM] (1956), reprinted in *Existentialists and Mystics*, 76–98, *passim*.

perceiving others accurately and compassionately, but accurate perception ensures proper motivation.[6] Murdoch's picture of moral awareness as a kind of cognitive 'vision' resolutely characterizes it as a genuine belief-state directed on a real object of knowledge—the Good. A properly informed view of the Good carries with it a compelling attraction—an intrinsic motivational force. Once we perceive what morality requires of us we are drawn to it, even if the power of its attraction does not always suffice to defeat our other desires.

These two ideas taken together yield the unremarkable conclusion that a well-functioning moral personality will both be compassionately aware of others' concerns and interests and be moved by this awareness. The psychopath, by contrast, is notoriously indifferent to others' welfare; other people principally concern him as instruments of his own wants and needs. He might be described as an affective solipsist: while aware that other persons have aims and purposes, and while often aware too, in a particular case, of just what those purposes are, the psychopath does not typically regard them as providing *him* with reasons for action. Indeed, it is not easy to grasp in what his 'understanding' of others consists. On the one hand, it may be tempting to say that the psychopath possesses a relatively normal ability to identify others' inner lives but simply fails to be moved by what he sees. (A number of Murdoch's fictional protagonists seem to be like this—for instance, Julius Kahn in *A Fairly Honourable Defeat*.) On the other hand, we may baulk at the suggestion that someone could genuinely understand others' mental states, and particularly their states of suffering, without being moved by them in any way.

These alternative descriptions of the psychopath's dysfunction parallel a different, but related distinction between externalist and internalist accounts of moral motivation. On the externalist view, moral motivation is extrinsic to the cognitive appreciation of moral requirements. Externalists typically follow Hume in insisting that beliefs alone move no one; if an agent's representation of a moral requirement does motivate him, it does so by way of some further passion or desire. Those externalists who (unlike Hume) take moral judgements to be fully cognitive normally try to account for their apparent power to move us by associating them with an independent conative state, e.g. a general desire 'do the right thing' or a more specific wish to be kind or just or sincere, or a particular inclination to help one's child or to relieve a colleague's distress. The internalist, by contrast, holds that our moral convictions are intrinsically motivating: internalism maintains that one cannot fully grasp the content of a moral claim while remaining indifferent to it. If the internalist is also a cognitivist, his position is particularly delicate, for he must maintain that at least some beliefs—namely, moral beliefs—are intrinsically motivating. This seems to have been Murdoch's own position. Murdoch did not deny, of course, that emotions and desires play a role in our moral psychology. They plainly do. Rather, Murdoch's internalism is articulated at the

---

[6] See, for instance, OGG, *passim.*

conceptual level: motivation is part of *what it is* to genuinely essay a moral belief. Understanding entails willing on this view, even when one's will is ultimately too weak to move one to do the right thing. The dispute between the externalist and the internalist so described is an a priori one concerning concept possession—concerning, that is, the conditions under which it is true that a subject possesses a given moral concept and, derivatively, the conditions under which it is true that someone sincerely holds a given moral belief.

My aim in this paper is to test a broadly Murdochian account of moral perception against the findings of recent empirical studies of psychopathy. In particular, I will argue that the structure of psychopathic thought does *not* disprove the kind of internalism Murdoch had in view. To the contrary, we will see that the anomalies of the psychopathic mind actually lend empirical support to Murdoch's idea that while our moral attitudes comprise genuine beliefs (not merely disguised feelings), they also have intrinsic motivational force: the contributions of emotion and cognition in moral judgement cannot be segregated. In Part 1 I set out Murdoch's account of moral perception, focusing on her idea that moral experience features a quasi-experiential phenomenology analogous to sensory (and particularly visual) perception. I compare Murdoch's phenomenology to the experiential phenomenology of other, more familiar kinds of properties which, like moral ones, can only be detected by subjects who possess specific experiential abilities. In Part 2 I turn to the psychopath, asking whether, as some have claimed, the anomalies of his psychology undermine the kind of internalism this phenomenology suggests.

Part 1: Moral rules and moral aspects

1.1 Moral experience

Murdoch's writings venture into the territory of traditional, a priori metaphysics and epistemology, but their beating heart is her exercises in descriptive, experiential phenomenology, where she explores the detail of what it is like to engage seriously with ethical problems from a first-person, experiential point of view. Even where Murdoch focuses on metaphysical claims about the nature of moral properties—for instance, the Platonic nature of the Good—these claims almost always arise from and find their justification in her phenomenological observations. This method in part drives Murdoch's objections to philosophical moral theories which neglect the experiential dimension of moral deliberation and conceive of moral knowledge as 'theoretical'—as a set of impersonal directions or rules a grasp of which might suffice to guide one's day-to-day evaluations.[7] Against such views, Murdoch argues that moral understanding is *essentially* first-personal: like having a headache or bearing a grudge or becoming

---

[7] See VCM. cf. 'The insistence that morality is essentially rules may be seen as an attempt to secure us against the ambiguity of the world . . . There are times when it is proper to stress, not the comprehensibility of the world, but its incomprehensibility' (VCM 90).

infatuated, moral insight is not to be had from a wholly impersonal point of view.[8] Moral belief is not solely a matter of registering the truth of certain propositions; it is also a matter of experiencing the conditions which make those propositions true.[9] This is why universal or highly general moral statements about kinds of characters or actions largely miss their mark; seeing that a person's actions are loving or wicked or noble or base requires that one *respond* to them as such, and categories and kinds are not apt objects for the requisite responses.

Murdoch's moral phenomenology is thus congenial to some version of particularism— roughly, the view that ethical properties are properties of particular actions and persons rather than of classes or kinds. The particularist usually holds, *inter alia*, that general principles and codifiable rules will often mislead us in ethics; we do better to consider the context and detail of the specific case. 'False conceptions are often generalized, stereotyped and unconnected', Murdoch writes. 'True conceptions combine just modes of judgment and ability to connect with an increased perception of detail' (SGC 96/379). For Murdoch, scrutiny of the relevant phenomena, alertness to specifics, and sensitivity to subtle differences must underpin reliable moral judgement. Of course, rules have their place: we could scarcely survive without them. As Murdoch notes, we need to know why and when to pay the bills. But we need not deny this to appreciate that a simple and straightforward appeal to general normative principles cannot accommodate the complexities of human experience. In real life we need, she says, to return to the beginning and inspect the details of the case.

Should a retarded child be kept at home or sent to an institution? Should an elderly relation who is a trouble-maker be cared for or asked to go away? Should an unhappy marriage be continued for the sake of the children? Should I leave my family in order to do political work? Should I neglect them in order to practise my art? The love which brings the right answer is an exercise of justice and realism and really *looking*. (SGC 91/375)

Murdoch's particularism is thus of a piece with her experience-based conception of moral understanding: we can only properly understand the moral nature of an act— say, an act of betrayal—by attending to its detail and experiencing its character from

---

[8] See IP.

[9] An analogy may help to make this point, and we find one ready in Kant's account of aesthetic judgement. Kant argues that aesthetic judgements are necessarily singular in form, and never universal. If we are judging the beauty of a thing, he says, then that thing must be *perceptually* present to us (or at least present to us through the remembering or imagining of a perceptual state). This is because what it is to judge that a thing is beautiful is in part just to respond to its sensible presentation in a particular way, and to express that response in the form of a judgement. If one says of some item 'X is beautiful' in the absence of any perceptual engagement with X (whether present or past) then one is not essaying an aesthetic judgement proper. Hence one cannot properly judge that, for instance, *all* roses are beautiful (for one cannot perceptually engage with and respond to all roses). One can only judge that *this* (demonstratively identified) perceived rose is beautiful. This analogy should not be taken too far: I do not think that Murdoch anywhere says that universal judgements fail—by definition—to be moral judgements at all, and in this respect her account differs from Kant's account of aesthetic ones. At the same time, Murdoch sometimes seems to endorse the epistemic claim that if one is to judge *correctly* in moral matters one should proceed on a case-by-case basis.

within, and this requires that we attend to the particular instance, not merely to the general features of most or all acts of betrayal. Indeed in many cases we might be unable to decide that a particular action *counts* as a betrayal until we have inspected and internalized the particular details of the case.

1.2 Aspectual properties and 'deep configurations'

Murdoch's recommendation that we attend to the particular case and experience value from within is intuitively attractive, but what exactly is it to 'experience' an evaluative feature of the world? Kant and others have argued that certain *aesthetic* values (especially beauty) are perceptible ones, and these claims gain some credibility from the fact that we sometimes seem literally to see the beauty or ugliness of an object. However, the counterpart idea of perceiving a moral property—Murdoch's talk of 'moral vision'— is more mysterious. The metaphor of vision on its own tells us little more than that our observations of moral properties are in some sense experience-based. What would moral properties have to be like to be both experience-based and intrinsically motivating?

In answer to that question, I will introduce a term of art, naming a certain category of properties: 'aspectual properties', or 'aspects'. Aspects are ubiquitous in everyday experience. One of their distinguishing features is that they are supervenient in the sense that they are uni-directionally dependent on certain subvenient base properties: any alteration in the aspectual property requires an alteration in its subvening ones, but not vice versa. A second feature of aspects is that they can only be detected by those who possess an appropriate sensitivity in their responses to the base properties on which they depend.[10] By the same token (thirdly) aspectual properties are 'autonomous' or unanalysable independently of the responses of those able to detect them. In particular, they cannot be fully elucidated in terms of the non-aspectual, base properties on which they supervene. Finally, aspectual properties are organizational or 'pattern' properties—what Murdoch referred to, in the vocabulary of her time, as *Gestalt* properties, or properties possessed by a thing as a whole in virtue of the relations of its component parts.[11]

Many of our everyday observations target properties which exhibit these four characteristics. Consider our judgements of visible, pictorial aspects—the depictive properties which one targets when one judges, for instance, that a portrait depicts its sitter, or that a still life depicts a bowl of apples and pears.[12] In the ordinary case, we do not identify pictorial properties by learning a 'theory of depiction'—a set of norms or rules prescribing how to translate two-dimensional planes of lines and colours into representations of three-dimensional objects. It is of course true that we arrive at our

---

[10] Colour properties, although not aspectual ones, are like this: they can only be seen by those whose optical and cognitive systems are sensitive to the reflectancy properties of visible objects. The colours presented directly in experience are 'supervenient' properties, and the base properties on which they depend (reflectancy properties) are 'subvenient'.

[11] For a more detailed discussion of aspectual properties, see my *Metaphor and Moral Experience* (Oxford: Oxford University Press, 2000) Chapter 5, *passim*.

[12] See my discussion of pictorial aspects in my *Metaphor and Moral Experience*, 144–7.

pictorial judgements by way of seeing lines and colours on a two-dimensional surface; were the lines and colours invisible to us, so too would be the pictorial aspects we find in them. But at the same time the pictorial properties are themselves visible aspects that we detect directly, not via a rule-directed *inference* from our experience of the lines and colours. When we look at a painting, we perceive it as already organized into intelligible, coherent patterns, configurations which present items in the visible world (a landscape, a bowl of fruit). There is nothing particularly mysterious about this everyday skill: when we say that someone is able to discern pictorial aspects—that he possesses 'pictorial competence'—we are not imputing to him any special visual or cognitive faculty. We just take him to have acquired, in the normal course of his development, an ability to discern pictorial aspects by looking at the properties on which they supervene.

Of course one could, in principle, generate pictorial judgements in other ways. Suppose an individual were unable to perceive a two-dimensional image as a depiction of a three-dimensional object (as sometimes happens as a result of right-hemisphere brain lesions). This subject could be taught to 'read' simple images by calculating the geometric relations of the visual-field properties of the objects they depict. For instance, he could learn to generate pictorial judgements by referring to a 'picture-reading' rule book listing visual-field properties of various familiar objects—e.g. trees and flowers and bowls of fruit—described in terms of locations on a grid of Cartesian coordinates. The book would, to be sure, need to be a very long one if he were to use it to interpret more than a few very standard images, but it matters here only as a hypothetical possibility. Pictorial judgements made in this way would be straightforwardly inferential ones. However, normal pictorial judgements—call them *basic* pictorial judgements—are typically non-inferential, or direct.[13] Like inferential, rule-driven ones, basic pictorial judgements arise by way of one's responses to the subvenient, non-pictorial features of the canvas. In basic pictorial judgement, however, one responds to those subvenient features very differently. Although in both cases the perceiver is looking at a surface which possesses those features, and in both cases his experience is caused by them, in the basic case the content of his experience is an organized, pictorial aspect: he sees a ☖ or a ✳. By contrast, in the inferential, rule-book case *the content of the perceiver's experience does not go beyond the subvenient lines and colors.* Rule-book generated judgements of pictorial aspects are not perceptual judgements as such: they would be justified by and inferred from perceptual experience, of course, but the pictorial aspects would not be themselves perceived. There is a further difference between the inferential case and the basic case. In both, the content of the subject's experience provides him with reasons for thinking that the surface has certain pictorial

---

[13] As I am using the terms 'inference' and 'inferential', they apply to beliefs or judgements which follow from other, independently justified beliefs and which have no other justification save that relationship. A belief or judgement is, by contrast, 'direct' just in case it is somehow justified, but not inferentially. Perceptual judgements are paradigmatically direct ones, as are (arguably) certain logical and mathematical beliefs. See C. Wright, *Truth and Objectivity* (Oxford: Oxford University Press, 1994), 151.

properties. Yet only in the basic case does it also *cause* him to see those properties. If a subject is pictorially competent, looking at the lines and colours does not merely justify his judgement that it represents a tree, a bowl of fruit, and so on; it also features in its causal explanation.

Consider another, non-visual type of aspectual property: musical aspects such as the melodic, the rhythmic, the dissonant, the harmonious. We arrive at judgements of these aspects by way of hearing sequences of sounded tones, but the musical aspects are not inferred from these sequences. Anyone familiar with such musical forms spontaneously organizes the sounded tones into coherent configurations or patterns that are directly experienced as melodies, rhythms, and the rest. Moreover, just as pictorial competence does not require any special visual faculty beyond a quite ordinary capacity for pictorial 'seeing-as', so musical competence does not require any special aural faculty; it issues from a quite ordinary capacity for aural 'hearing-as'—for discerning pattern properties of sounds by hearing them. Special training can of course refine one's ability to discern specifically musical properties. That is a matter not of creating some new faculty, however, but of developing the exercise of one we already possess.

Again, one might in principle learn to generate something like judgements of musical aspects in other ways. For instance, a person who is unable to perceive a major triad as consonant could be taught a rule: when the tonic, third, and fifth are sounded simultaneously, the combination of tones is consonant. Rules such as this could, in principle, be compiled in a 'tone-reading' rule book which listed the musical properties of different combinations and sequences of notes. (Beginning composition students use books more or less like this, although to different ends, and the software for some computer synthesizers is effectively a rule-book of this kind.) The tone-reading book, like the picture-reading one, would need to be very long were we to use it to interpret more than a few very standard musical features. But all that matters here is that it is empirically possible for a subject to identify musical properties in this way. The resulting musical judgements would be paradigmatically inferential ones, whereas a normal musical judgement—call it a basic musical judgement—is non-inferential, or direct. In both cases, one is hearing pitched sounds and is affected aurally by sound waves. But only in the basic case is the content of one's experience an organized, musical aspect—a lilting melody, or a pounding bass beat, or an harmonious sequence of chords. Inferential, rule-book generated judgements of musical aspects would not be basic: they would derive from one's perceptual experience of pitched tones, of course, but the subject would not *hear* the musical aspects themselves as would a musically competent subject who hears the pitched tones *as* melodious, in 3/4 waltz rhythm, and so on.

These two cases illustrate, *inter alia*, how our normal, basic judgements of pictorial and musical aspects identify and individuate those properties directly, by way of perceptual experience: they can only be properly understood and by someone acquainted with the characteristic, first-personal phenomenology of their referents. So what do our judgements of such aspects have to do with our moral beliefs? On my interpretation of Murdoch, she holds that an analogous phenomenology underpins our judgements of value generally and our moral judgements in particular. To see why, consider first the ordinary trajectory of moral education. When small children first begin to acquire a moral vocabulary, their assertions are very often a matter of reiterating the verdicts they have been taught by adults: 'This is naughty; that is nice.' Notably, while a child may have learned that these are the right things to say, that knowledge does not always translate into an understanding of what to *do*: the verdicts do not on their lips always carry the normative force which is part of their full import. He is simply echoing some familiar phrases. But as the child's command of moral concepts develops, he normally proceeds to something like a rule-book stage, and is able to venture genuine judgements of novel situations. For instance, he is able to judge that an act should be called right or wrong because it has certain standard features: it annoys Mummy, or it makes the baby cry, or it creates a frightful mess. At this stage the child, like the tone-deaf judge of musical properties, may *infer* that something merits a certain moral predicate because it satisfies some other, non-moral description. But is he making a genuine moral judgement thereby? Is there not some missing *experience* that parallels the ability to perceive musical patterns or to see colours?

There is of course no discrete faculty of moral perception to parallel the visual faculty by way of which we see pictures or the aural faculty by way of which we hear melodies and harmonies. Nonetheless, there surely is a kind of responsiveness that is absent in the case of the child who knows how to label a range of actions with moral predicates—who knows the rules—but who applies them, as it were, merely compliantly. Admittedly, even in the fully developed, morally literate adult it sometimes happens that nothing more than a kind of rule-book calculation lies behind particular moral assertions; that is, it sometimes happens that one is simply echoing learned platitudes, as in condemning dishonesty and cruelty and commending charity and courage. (Just think of the moral rhetoric of politicians: it is not for nothing that we often call it 'empty'.) But it is crucial that not all of one's moral assertions are of this kind. Genuine participation in moral life requires that at least some of our assertions express basic moral judgements—judgements which, like basic pictorial and musical judgements, arise from our experience of con-figured aspects of value (Murdoch's 'deep configurations of the world'), and occur by way of our responsiveness to the subvenient features on which those aspects depend.[14]

Saul Kripke suggests that something like this thought extends to our understanding of others' suffering: 'I, who have myself experienced pain and can imagine it', he writes, 'can imaginatively put myself in place of the sufferer, and my ability to do this gives my attitude a quality that it would lack if I had merely learned a set of rules as to when to attribute pain to others and how to help them'.[15]

---

[14] See my 'Motivation, Representation and Basic Moral Judgments', unpublished draft. Basic moral judgements a) are produced non-inferentially, b) are judgements of aspectual properties, c) are descriptive rather than expressive, d) describe the objects, not the subject who assents to them, e) describe the subject's experience of the aspects judged.

[15] Ibid. The quotation is from Saul Kripke, *Wittgenstein on Rules and Private Language* (Oxford: Blackwell/ Cambridge, Mass.: Harvard University Press, 1982), 140, emphasis in original removed.

Direct, non-inferential, and sensitive judgements of suffering depend on our first-person acquaintance with the features of experience subvening them.

Murdoch's notion of moral vision is compatible with a conception of moral properties as aspectual ones, on analogy with pictorial and musical aspects. Perhaps the most abstract, 'thin' moral properties—good, evil, right, wrong, and so forth—are not best conceived in aspectual terms. Nonetheless it seems that the properties picked out by many thick moral concepts are good candidates. When we regard a character as cruel or kind, a remark as undignified or an act as generous or malicious, we are not discerning simple, unanalysable, unitary phenomenal properties such as colours, nor experience-independent ones such as weight and size, nor natural-kind categories which might be reductively analysed in scientific terms. Rather, we are targeting complex, pattern properties by organizing an array of indefinitely many subvenient characteristics under an evaluative description identifying aspects of the whole.

What, in the moral case, might those subvenient features be? Again, Murdoch's observations of everyday moral phenomenology point us in the right direction, for among the best and most obvious candidates surely are persons' concerns and interests—the wants, needs, and purposes of other subjects of experience. We discover what we ought to believe, ethically speaking, and how we ought to act in part by attuning ourselves to the claims of other human beings. The subvening base properties of many thick moral concepts clearly include such familiar human concerns and interests, particularly the concepts featured in our 'other-regarding' moral judgements targeted on the *welfare* of other persons. Let us say that a moral belief or correlative imperative is an 'other-regarding' one just if the welfare of another person or persons is its primary and principle justification e.g. 'If a small child is suffering, it is unkind not to console him', or 'A loyal friend should not abandon you in times of need.'[16] Because other-regarding moral judgements (hereafter moral^{o-r} judgements) supervene quite directly on persons' concerns and interests, we decide their truth in part by attuning ourselves to others' ends. To put the point in Murdoch's terms, proper moral attunement is of a piece with learning to love other individuals, where loving someone implies that one acknowledges his concerns (SGC 102–3/384). If a suitably sensitive, properly attuned moral subject attends to anothers' ends—to their hopes, fears, needs—and if he sees them clearly and correctly, he will see actions affecting them as manifesting certain moral aspects: as just, loving, malicious, disloyal, kind, and the rest. And then, all things being equal, he will be in a position to essay a *basic* moral^{o-r} judgement.

This conception of moral properties as aspectual ones also harmonizes with several meta-ethical commitments to which Murdoch repeatedly alluded. First, it recognizes that moral properties are not fully analysable in terms of their subvenient base properties. What it is to be, say, cowardly or kind cannot be fully analysed in terms of some other, non-evaluative base properties such as an agents attitudes, aims, and intentions or

---

[16]   The categorization is not wholly satisfactory, but it is important in this context, for it is with respect to the psychopath's personal relations and conduct towards others that he behaves so aberrantly.

the consequences of his actions. This is not because aspects fail to constitute genuine properties on par with natural ones. ('Melodic' names a perfectly good property; so does 'malicious'.) Rather, it is because mention of our experiential responses is essential to any correct elucidation of what it is to be, say, melodic or malicious.[17] The analogy also suggests, secondly, that, as Murdoch put it, moral values are *'deep configurations'*. They are not unitary, sensible, and simple like colours and odours; they are organized forms that emerge within highly complex relations of entities within the human world. In a well-known passage, Murdoch describes a mother-in-law struggling to see her son's wife as vivacious rather than undignified, and as unaffected rather than common. Her struggles are an attempt to perceive one evaluative *pattern* rather than another in the same natural facts, to configure her observations in accordance with different moral categories and concepts or, as I have put it, to discern different moral aspects.

Thirdly, the analogy supports the idea that moral understanding is not only a matter of learning the rules—learning a normative theory—but also involves learning how to look, to see, and to respond to particular cases. Rules can take us a certain distance, of course: in music, for instance, we can expect a sequence of pitched tones within a given key to be resolved only by a return to the tonic, and in morals we can expect an action which causes gratuitous pain to be forbidden. But rules alone cannot enable one to hear the resolution of a melodic variation, nor to be moved by another's suffering.

1.3 Internalism again

This sketch of moral properties as aspects supports a hybrid model of moral experience and thought, combining cognitive and affective-motivational functions in a way that renders them conceptually *and* causally interdependent. Likewise, it implies an internalist interpretation of what it is to properly understand moral^{o-r} requirements. In fact, in respect of basic moral^{o-r} judgements it implies both a conceptual and an empirical version of the internalist thesis. It is a conceptual truth that basic moral^{o-r} judgements are intrinsically motivating because those judgements are defined in part in terms of their etiology, an etiology according to which they inherit the intrinsic motivational force of our responses to other persons. And it is an empirical truth that an individual who properly understands moral^{o-r} requirements (who understands them by way of this normal etiology) will, as a matter of fact, be moved by the moral significance of others' concerns, interests, and other salient states. Conceptual internalism builds motivation directly into the possession conditions of basic moral^{o-r} beliefs: the aversion we direct at moral^{o-r} transgressions and the pleasure we take in moral^{o-r} achievements are part of

---

[17] A given concept—say, the concept associated with the predicate 'M'—is experience-dependent just if it is true a priori that for some item x, x is M if x is such as to elicit experiential responses of kind E in (substantially specified) suitable subjects S under (substantially specified) conditions C. Experience-dependent concepts often pick out properties that I shall call *empirically experience-dependent:* The property associated with the predicate 'M' is empirically experience-dependent just if it is true, as a matter of fact, that for some item x, if x is M then x is such as to elicit experiential responses of kind E in (substantially specified) suitable subjects under (substantially specified) conditions C.

what it is to possess such beliefs at all. Empirical internalism builds moral motivation directly into the causal conditions of basic moral^{o-r} beliefs—it says that individuals who have such beliefs will, as a matter of fact, experience some motivation to act on them, even if that motivation is often insufficiently weak relative to other competing ones.

Now suppose that we add a further, stronger claim, namely, that a capacity for basic moral^{o-r} judgements is a necessary condition of mature moral competence: what it is to possess a genuine, fully-fledged understanding of moral requirements requires, *inter alia*, a capacity for experience-led, basic moral judgements. (Or correlatively: moral competence requires a capacity to directly recognize moral^{o-r} aspects, a capacity that rests, in turn, on a natural tendency to resonate, affectively and motivationally, with other persons.) Internalism would then be true, not only of basic moral^{o-r} judgements but of competent moral judgement quite generally.

Is the stronger claim true? Is it a fact that anyone who is competent to understand moral norms is also sensitive to their motivational force? Several theorists have claimed that the phenomenon of psychopathy disproves that thesis. Shaun Nichols, for instance, claims that the psychopath's moral beliefs are motivationally, but not cognitively impaired; he is unmoved by moral requirements, but he has no difficulty in understanding them. Nichols holds that 'the psychopath's deficit in moral judgment depends on a deficit in an affective mechanism, not on deficits in rationality. The evidence on psychopaths thus seems not to support cognitivist and rationalist accounts at all, but rather their rival, sentimentalism.'[18] If Nichols is right, then empirical internalism is false: understanding moral requirements does *not* reliably cause subjects to be moved by them, because the rational mechanisms required to grasp moral norms are, in the case of psychopaths, dissociated from the affective mechanism which confers on them their motivating force. Moreover, if the psychopath can understand moral judgements without being moved by them, then it must be logically possible for *anyone* to understand moral judgements without being moved by them. Hence conceptual internalism would be false as well, if unobviously so. Note, however, that Nichols's argument only works by assuming the truth of externalism in the first place. That is, only if we accept an externalist interpretation of the *psychopath's* defects do those defects provide evidence for externalism more generally. But ought we to adopt an externalist interpretation of psychopathy? That is the question to which I now turn.

[18] S. Nichols, 'How Psychopaths Threaten Moral Rationalism, or Is it Irrational to Be Amoral?', *The Monist*, 85 (2002), 285–304. At this point Nichols is specifically discussing what he calls 'Empirical Rationalism'. Earlier in his article, however, he has entered similarly motivated objections against other versions of internalism, including those which, like my own, appeal to some kind of ability for perspective-taking. Nichols dismisses the latter on the ground that Blair's studies have shown that psychopaths suffer no deficits in perspective-taking abilities. Closer inspection of Blair's studies, however, reveal that they show no such thing, and that the experimental design does little to test the kind of empathic, perspective-taking skills to which I appeal. The most one can conclude from Blair's studies is that psychopaths do not show any deficits in quite basic TOM (theory of mind) skills.

Part 2 The Realism of Compassion

There are certain moral dispositions such that anyone lacking them could have no duty to acquire them. These are *moral feeling, love of one's neighbor, and reverence for oneself* (self-esteem). There is no obligation to have these, because they lie at the basis of morality . . . All of them are natural dispositions of the mind (*praedispositio*) to be affected by concepts of duty—antecedent dispositions on the side of feeling. To have them is not a duty: every man has them and it is by virtue of them that he can be obligated.

Kant, *Doctrine of Virtue*, Sec. 59

2.1 The Psychopath: Unfeeling or ill-informed?

Our ordinary sense of ourselves as moral agents depends, as Kant says, on certain familiar features of our psychologies. For example, an ordinary moral agent will be subject to moral feelings or emotions such as shame, guilt, and remorse. He will also be capable of and disposed towards attachment to and respect for others: he will not be loveless or ruthless. Finally, he will be aware that he, like others, possesses value: as a person, he too is deserving of respect. The psychopath, by contrast, is arguably deficient in all three of these qualities, and some have argued that he does not possess them at all.[19] As Robert Hare has commented, psychopaths are

---

[19] The precise nature of psychopathic disorder has proven difficult to pin down with any precision, and clinical and research efforts continue to be hampered by definitional uncertainties. All are agreed that it should be characterized as a 'construct' or constellation of several co-existing features, but inconsistencies vitiate the way those features are identified and organized in the professional literature. First, there are terminological inconsistencies in the uses of the terms 'psychopathic disorder', 'sociopathic disorder', and 'anti-social personality disorder' (APD). Secondly, there are substantive disagreements about the specific characteristics criterial of each (and particularly those criterial of psychopathy as opposed to APD). Finally, there are radically different diagnostic instruments in use to identify psychopathic subjects—instruments which can yield strikingly different diagnoses. This is all bad news for any theorist attempting meta-analyses of past research and clinical records.

In the past decade R. D. Hare's 'Psychopathy Checklist' (PCL), has become generally (but not unreservedly) accepted as a reliable measure. The PCL was first designed and tested by Hare in 1980 as a list of 22 items. It was revised in draft form in 1985 and, after scrupulous testing for inter-rater reliability and item-reliability, saw official publication in 1991 as a checklist of twenty items: the 'Hare PCL-R'. The highest possible score is thus 40, and a subject is typically classified as psychopathic if he receives a scoring of 30 or above. Perhaps the most influential achievement of the new PCL-R was that it introduced the critical distinction between 'Factor 1' items correlated to interpersonal/affective/trait characteristics and 'Factor 2' items correlating to social deviance characteristics. The resulting checklist, including 'Factor 1' items (1–8) and 'Factor 2' items (9–20) is:

1. Glibness/superficial charm.
2. Grandiose sense of self-worth.
3. Need for stimulation/proneness to boredom.
4. Pathological lying.
5. Conning/manipulative.
6. Lack of remorse or guilt.
7. Shallow affect.
8. Callous/lack of empathy
9. Parasitic lifestyle.
10. Poor behavioral controls.

social predators who charm, manipulate, and ruthlessly plow their way through life, leaving a broad trail of broken hearts, shattered expectations, and empty wallets. Completely lacking in conscience and empathy, they selfishly take what they want and do as they please, violating social norms and expectations without the slightest sense of guilt or regret.[20]

What explains these extraordinary moral defects? Is the psychopath unable properly to understand moral norms proscribing harming others (harm-based moral^{o-r} norms)? Or does he simply fail to care about them? It is widely recognized that psychopaths have a good command of the moral vocabulary and a good grasp of the norms that *others* in his community typically endorse: he can 'talk the talk' of morality well enough. But this hardly settles the matter for, we have seen, there is more than one way to become conversant in a discourse which targets aspectual properties. In the arena of moral discourse it is not enough to learn the rules of concept application: a capacity for *basic* moral judgement requires that one be able to exercise those concepts by way of the right experiential route. Hence in order to decide whether or not the psychopath 'understands' moral^{o-r} norms, we need to decide a further question: is the psychopath's facility with moral discourse merely rule-driven, or does it reflect a genuine capacity for basic moral judgement?

To answer this further question, we need to know whether the psychopath's competence with moral discourse is appropriately related to an awareness of others' ends—their concerns and interests. If it is, then we will have reason to think he understands moral^{o-r} norms as well as anyone else; if it does not, then we will have reason to think that his facile talk masks some cognitive defect at a deeper level, for

11. Promiscuous sexual behaviour.
12. Early behaviour problems.
13. Lack of realistic, long-term plans.
14. Impulsivity.
15. Irresponsibility.
16. Failure to accept responsibility for own actions.
17. Many short-term marital relationships.
18. Juvenile delinquency.
19. Revocation of conditional release.
20. Criminal versatility

The division between Factor 1 and Factor 2 has subsequently served (in practice) to mark the distinction between *psychopathic disorder* proper, and APD, where the latter is normally identified solely by behaviourally-manifested criteria indicative of 'inadequate socialization'—for instance repeated law-breaking, aggressiveness, irresponsibility (as evidenced, for instance by employment history) and impulsivity. The label 'APD' thus serves better to reflect the anti-social, but not the interpersonal/emotional factors of the PCL. As it happens, however, almost all current research recognizes that there exist in fact two independent (if frequently co-morbid) disorders—the first, psychopathy, delineated roughly by the PCL-R, and the second delineated only by the *Diagnostics and Statistics Manual*'s behavioural indicators of APD. APD is not unrelated to the psychopathy, of course: most (but not all) subjects classified in accordance with the latter also satisfy the former. It is significant, however, that in forensic populations the prevalence of APD is two or three times higher than the prevalence of psychopathy, as measured by the PCL-R. Most offenders with a high PCL-R score meet the criteria for APD, but the converse does not hold, for APD subjects often fail to manifest the PCL-R's Factor 1 items.

[20] R. D. Hare, *Without Conscience: The disturbing world of the psychopaths among us* (New York: Pocket Books, 1993); p. xi.

instance, a defect involving his ability to identify others' morally salient psychological states. I have already intimated that a 'proper awareness' of others' morally salient psychological states is itself intrinsically motivating. Is that true? Here again we must decide between an externalist and an internalist answer. The externalist will say that a cognitive grasp of others' morally salient experiential states—detecting and individuating them—entails nothing about motivation: a subject may judge them correctly, even proficiently, yet remain unmoved by them. The internalist, by contrast, will say that a genuine understanding of, e.g. others' hopes, fears, joys, and sorrows cannot but move us, at least to some extent and in at least many cases. Framing the dispute in this way, it is easy to see why psychopathy counts as an important test case for theories of moral motivation. The externalist has no difficulty explaining how a psychopath can understand moral[o-r] beliefs while being unmoved by them: he is systematically unresponsive to the action-guiding significance of these beliefs precisely because he is motivationally indifferent to the concerns, interests, needs, etc. of other people. He perceives others' salient psychological states as well as the rest of us do, but he lacks the additional desires which, in the normal case, prompt us to respond to them in action. Beliefs alone never constitute a reason to do anything, the externalists will say: desires alone can motivate. And the desires that drive the rest of us to think of others' ends as reasons for action are desires the psychopath does not have. The externalist view implies, therefore, that the psychopath is what I will call a *desiderative egocentrist:*[21]

Desiderative Egocentrism A subject is a desiderative egocentrist just if none or few of his desires concerning others are directed at satisfying *others'* morally salient ends—satisfying their needs, relieving their suffering, etc. The desiderative egocentrist's desires are always or almost always driven by his own interests, purposes, etc. Others' ends only concern the desiderative egocentrist insofar as he believes that addressing them will instrumentally serve some end of his own.

The internalist should of course reject this analysis of psychopathy, for it leaves open the possibility that the psychopath's moral beliefs are in good order. He may instead propose that the psychopath is unresponsive to the moral significance of others' morally salient states because he does not properly register those states themselves. The internalist view suggests, that is, that the psychopath is a kind of *mindreading egocentrist:*[22]

---

[21] This distinction is in part owed to Shaun Nichols. See his 'Mindreading and the Cognitive Architecture underlying Altruistic Motivation', *Mind and Language*, 16 (2001), 425–55.

[22] Some theorists (so-called 'theory theorists') have argued that 'mind-reading' or 'mentalising'—the ability to discern others' mental states—issues from a process of theory acquisition: the theory is an inductively acquired set of general principles or laws which relate mental states to one another and to external stimuli as input, and to speech and action as output. Others (the 'simulation theorists') have argued that the ability to mentalise is less a matter of possessing a theory than it is a matter of possessing an ability—the ability to imaginatively simulate others' circumstances and psychologies, and by doing so to play out in our own minds the processes to which they are subject and the resulting mental states. I will not engage with that debate here, but in due course it will be clear to the reader that I hold with the simulationists with respect to *affectively and*

Mindreading Egocentrism A subject is a mindreading egocentrist with respect to some psychological (or psychophysical) state just if he is unable to correctly identify that state in others.

Which of these two 'diagnoses'—desiderative egocentrism or mindreading egocentrism—best describes the psychopath? Is he simply unmoved by others' inner lives, or is he somehow defective in his ability to correctly understand them?

Nichols argues that mindreading egocentrism cannot explain psychopathic disorder, because the psychopath exhibits no noteworthy mindreading dysfunctions.[23] In support of this thesis Nichols turns to psychologist James Blair's studies of criminal psychopaths. Blair's studies purported to show, *inter alia*, that psychopaths exhibit no significant cognitive defects with respect to their abilities to represent others' mental states and that they do not differ significantly from normal controls in respect of their theory of mind (TOM) abilities.[24] As Blair describes his results, psychopaths appear to be able to infer the 'full range of mental states (beliefs, desire, intentions, imagination, emotions, etc.) that cause action: the psychopath is as able as a normal subject to reflect on the contents of his own and other's minds'.[25] All is not well in with the psychopath in other ways, however: psychopaths *are* dysfunctional in their emotional and motivational responses to others. Psychopaths exhibit vivid deficits in their autonomic responses to others' mental states, and specifically to others' states of psychological and psychophysical distress, e.g. fear, sorrow, and pain. Psychopaths also show significantly reduced physiological indications of affective responses (tested by skin-conductance, heart-rate variations) to images, narratives, and speech representing others in threatening, painful, and otherwise adverse circumstances. (In controls, these same autonomic responses are strongly correlated with self-reports and other evidence of emotional-affective engagement.)[26]

---

motivationally characterized psychological and psychophysical states such as grief, joy, anxiety, fatigue, nausea, etc. Many propositional attitudes such as believing, intending, and even desiring need not exhibit any occurrent phenomenology, however, and I am content to leave these to the theory theorists.

[23] Shaun Nichols, *Sentimental Rules* (Oxford: Oxford University Press, 2004) Chapters 1 and 2, *passim*. See also J. Kennett, 'Autism, Empathy and Moral Agency', *Philosophical Quarterly* Vol. 52, No 208, July 2002, 340–57.

[24] Blair's selection criterion was a score of 30 or higher on Hare's PCL-R, and scoring was not sensitive to the distinction between Factor 1 and Factor 2 criteria. All subjects (both psychopathic and non-psychopathic controls) were incarcerated for life, all had been incarcerated for at least eighteen months, and all save one were incarcerated for either murder or manslaughter. (Life sentences in the UK are mandatory for murder; for manslaughter they are discretionary but are typically given when there are no mitigating reasons for the act.) All were male and white. Subjects were matched for average IQ (90's range), average age (early to mid 30's) and social class (D/E). Some studies have used as few as ten subjects in each category (psychopath and normal control) and some used as many as thirty.

[25] R. J. R. Blair, C. Sellars, I. Strickland, F. Clark, A. Williams, M. Smith, and L. Jones, 'Theory of mind in the psychopath', *The Journal of Forensic Psychiatry* 7, 15–25 (1996).

[26] R. J. R. Blair, L. Jones, F. Clark, and M. Smith, 'The psychopathic individual: a lack of responsiveness to distress cues?' *Psychophysiology* 34 (1997), 192–8; R. J. R. Blair, D. G. V. Mitchell, R. A. Richell, S. Kelly, A. Leonard, C. Newman, and S. K. Scott, 'Turning a Deaf Ear to Fear: Impaired Recognition of Vocal Affect in Psychopathic Individuals', *Journal of Abnormal Psychology* 111 (2002), 682–6; R. J. R. Blair, E. Colledge,

This combination of cognitive competence and affective deviance seems to provide good empirical evidence for motivational externalism. That is the conclusion both Nichols and Blair draw from Blair's findings.[27] If correct, the Nichols-Blair analysis of the psychopath would cast him as a desiderative egocentrist—as an able enough mind-reader burdened by a dysfunctional motivational system. And that diagnosis of the psychopath would in turn give us reason to favour an externalist account of moral[o-r] judgements quite generally, for it suggests that the cognitive grasp of others' concerns and interests underpinning such judgements can float free of their affective-motivational force. Moral belief and moral feeling, on this account, could each exist independently of the other.

2.2 The moral/conventional distinction and the sympathetic autistic

Nichols argues that the externalist thesis finds further support from studies of high-functioning autistics. The pervasive image of the autistic depicts him as unresponsive to socio-affective cues of others, lacking emotional warmth, and incapable of empathy. The image is not without some justification, and there is ample evidence that autistics suffer from TOM defects: most have real difficulty representing others' beliefs and intentions, and even quite high-functioning autistics characteristically fail very simple false-belief tests and other tests of an ability to 'mentalise'.[28] Autism clearly carries with it an impaired ability to deploy psychological concepts in predictions and explanations of others' speech and behaviour. Whatever the right explanation of this deficiency, all sides are agreed in their diagnosis of the autistic as to that extent an impoverished

---

L. Murray, and D. G. Mitchell, 'A selective impairment in the processing of sad and fearful expressions in children with psychopathic tendencies' *Journal of Abnormal Child Psychology* 29 (2001), 491–8.

[27] See R. J. R. Blair, 'A Cognitive developmental approach to morality: Investigating the psychopath', *Cognition* 57, (1995), 1–29. Blair's specific proposal was that the psychopath's defects in empathy and in his moral[o-r] beliefs are owed to the failure of a dedicated 'violence inhibition mechanism'—VIM—which plays a solely motivational role. The notion of VIM was inspired by the ethologist Konrad Lorenz's observation that in many species (for instances wolves and lions) an aggressing animal will withdraw his attack if a con-specific victim displays submission-behaviour. A submitting wolf, for instance, may 'collapse his posture', tuck his tale between his legs, and slowly retreat; a lion will sometimes lie on its back and bare its throat. Blair hypothesized that the aggressor's withdrawal is activated by a VIM mechanism, which causes an aversive response in him. Extending this idea to humans, Blair proposed that VIM causes *normal* subjects to experience distress when confronted with others' negative-affect states—i.e. states of either physical and emotional suffering such as pain or fear. He then appeals to VIM to argue that normal subjects' grasp of the distinction between moral and conventional norms occurs by way of a four-stage process: (1) Perception of a distress cue in another person; (2) Aversion/withdrawal response; (3) A stage (somewhat obscure) of 'meaning-analysis' whereby one correlates one's aversion to the other's distress with characteristic causes of that aversion (e.g. our aversion to another's physical pain is correlated with the assaulting actions which caused it); (4) We identify the characteristic causes as distinctively moral transgressions, our prohibitions against which are justified post-facto by appeal to others' welfare; transgressions of other kinds are conventional ones. Philosophers will be familiar with Hume's very similar account of the 'natural' vs. the 'artificial' virtues in his *Treatise on Human Nature*. In Hume, of course, the mechanism of 'sympathetic resonance' takes the role Blair assigns to VIM, and differs from VIM too in causing in the subject an 'echo' of the same or a similar *kind* of distress as he has perceived in the other.

[28] S. Baron-Cohen, A. M. Leslie, and U. Frith, 'Does the Autistic Child Have a "Theory of Mind"?', *Cognition* 21 (1985), 37–46.

342 A. E. DENHAM

mindreader.[29] And if the autistic is impaired in that way, there is good reason to expect that he will also be impaired in his capacity to form accurate beliefs about others' interests and welfare. It seems to follow that he should be poorly placed to form basic moral[o-r] judgements.

However, several studies of autistics suggest that in many respects they are as morally responsive as normal subjects. In particular, James Blair's studies indicate that autistic children (already evaluated as TOM-defective) performed well on two critical tasks which play an important role in moral judgement. The first task was to distinguish between transgressions of 'moral' versus 'conventional' requirements. The moral/conventional distinction, although fraught with ambiguities, is now a commonplace in experimental moral psychology.[30] Roughly speaking, a moral requirement is one which is directly justified by considerations of others' welfare—their pains, pleasures, desire, fears, and so on. A conventional requirement is not so justified (or at least not directly), but rather serves to maintain social conformity and order. Hence the requirement that we refrain from causing gratuitous physical pain is a moral requirement, whereas the prohibition against wearing pyjamas to a professional seminar is a conventional one. By the same token, moral requirements do not depend on the say-so of any authority: they hold (more or less) no matter what, and their normative force cannot be rescinded by the dictates of some individual or community. Conventional requirements, however, are 'authority-dependent'—they only hold relative to some individual or social authority, without which they would carry no normative force. Certain rules of etiquette are clearly conventional in this way: if one is a guest in a community in which it is usual to eat with one's hands, the requirement to use a knife and fork lapses. Likewise, certain institutional rules, e.g. not laughing aloud in a place of worship, are also conventional: if the Rabbi tells a good joke the requirement lapses. Finally, transgressions of moral requirements are, for obvious reasons, typically viewed as more serious and less permissible than conventional ones. Of course, the moral/conventional distinction, thus defined, will (and should) strike most philosophers as both implausible and crude.[31] Nonetheless, as an experimental device for probing and categorizing levels of moral competence it has proven to be surprisingly robust.

---

[29] See S. Baron-Cohen, *Mindblindness* (Cambridge, MA: MIT Press, Bradford Books, 1995).

[30] The population from which Blair's subjects were selected adds procedural difficulties to the conceptual ones: all had been incarcerated within a highly punitive institutional setting for many years (Broadmoor Special Hospital and Wormwood Scrubs Prison, on high-security wards), subjected to a highly regimented daily routine in which, for example, the 'lights-out' curfew and the dress code are as strictly enforced as the requirement to refrain from violent physical assaults on staff. It is easy to see how such a setting might lead one to construe context-dependent conventional rules as on par with context-independent ones. This kind of setting positively discourages independent thought about the rationale for behavioural requirements. (I owe this observation to Terry O'Shaughnessy.) On the other hand, the 'normal' controls were drawn from the same population and setting and matched to the psychopathic subjects for gender, age, IQ, and social class.

[31] Philosophically, the moral/conventional distinction is a Pandora's box of conceptual worries and does not survive well under pressure or in marginal cases. For instance many seemingly conventional rules (when in England, drive on the left) find their ultimate justification in moral ones (respect the lives and well-being of other drivers). Conversely, it can happen that merely conventional rules come to be regarded as carrying

When Blair tested autistics for their performance on the moral/conventional distinction, he found that autistic children show a sensitivity on par with normal children to the distinction between moral and conventional transgressions in response to narratives detailing acts of both kinds.[32] In a second set of studies, Blair tested the same group of autistics for their autonomic responses to visual images of others in various states of pain and distress. The test procedures paralleled those in the studies run on psychopathic subjects, recording electrodermal skin-conductance and heart-rate variations while viewing the images. His results again favoured his hypothesis that autistic's TOM deficits did *not* render them insensitive to considerations of others' suffering. Specifically, Blair found that measures of autistics' psycho-physiological responsiveness to images of human *distress* is not deficient; autistics who tested as TOM-defective exhibited virtually normal physiological responses to visual distress cues, although they were unable either to describe or initiate appropriate actions in response to them.[33] The fact that the (apparently) *pre*-cognitive responsiveness of autistics to others' distress appears to be intact helps to make sense of their good performance on the tests for the moral/conventional distinction.[34] No-TOM autistics do not typically display compassion or empathy in their verbal and other behaviour, and yet Blair's experiments reveal that they *do* show the usual physiological symptoms of empathic responses, despite their putative incompetence as mindreaders. This fact combined with the autistic's robust sensitivity to the moral/conventional distinction suggests that responding to others in the ways that matter to morality might well be a

independent moral force: consider the indignation with which some react to infractions of institutional protocol (e.g. failing to follow proper procedure in a committee meeting, or to respect the norms of 'impersonal' conversation at a College dinner). None the less, there are enough clear and central cases to make the distinction a useful one for certain experimental purposes in developmental psychology: it is fairly easy to determine whether a subject falls below statistical norms in his sensitivity to the distinction even if, from a philosophical point of view, it is by no means clear in just what the distinction actually consists.

[32] R. J. R. Blair, 'Psychophysiological Responsiveness to the Distress of Others in Children with Autism', *Personality & Individual Differences* 26 (1999), 477–85 Moral transgressions were represented by acts the consequences of which directly affected the welfare or rights of others (e.g. hitting a child or stealing valued property), and conventional transgressions threatened the social order (e.g. a boy wearing a dress or a child talking in the library).

[33] Ibid. In interpreting these results, Blair cites Mandler's suggestion that an emotion state can be broken down in two components: 'the autonomic nervous system response and the cognitive appraisal, where the cognitive appraisal of the autonomic response gives rise to the experienced emotion'. From a philosopher's point of view, this yields a fairly crude view of what it is to experience an emotion, and yet there is no doubt some truth in it.

[34] Both sets of results should be surprising, for at least two reasons. First, it was long believed that autistics simply did not recognize their common humanity with other persons in any way at all: as Kanner described them in 1943, 'people figure [for the autistic] in about the same manner as does the desk, the bookshelf, or the filing cabinet'. As recently as 1994, Sigman found that autistic children were *behaviourally* unresponsive to adults showing distress, fear, and discomfort in semi-naturalistic settings. Secondly, as Gillberg observes, 'if you do not even *understand* that other people have, as it were, inner worlds, how can you be expected to show compassion or empathy?' See C. Gillberg, 'Outcome in autism and autistic-like conditions', *Journal of the American Academy of Child and Adolescent Psychiatry* 30 (1991), 375–82.

job allocated to a discrete, affective-motivational system or mechanism, just as Nichols and other externalists have claimed.

Even worse news seems to await the internalist when we turn to Blair's studies of the psychopath's grasp of the moral/conventional distinction. In this series of studies, both psychopathic and control subjects were presented with brief narratives involving transgressions of both kinds of requirements, further dividing moral requirements into 'positive act'/helping requirements (e.g. sharing some new possession or assisting with a task) and 'negative act'/harming prohibitions (e.g. refraining from hitting a child).[35] Blair subjected the resulting data to a range of ANOVAs (analyses of variables), exploring his subjects' sensitivity to the moral/conventional distinction across three dimensions: the relative permissibility of a transgression, its relative seriousness, and whether or not the transgressed rule is authority-dependent (its modifiability).[36] Finally, Blair analysed the subjects' perceptions of *why* a given transgression was impermissible (its justification category). The results again appeared to support the idea that psychopaths suffer from some kind of desiderative egocentrism. Blair's control group (non-psychopathic, convicted criminals) revealed a clear tendency to respect a distinction between the two categories for *both* positive and negative requirements in all dimensions. The control subjects' responses to narratives clearly indicated that they view some requirements (e.g. do not wear a clown suit to court) as wholly authority-dependent, and others (e.g. do not humiliate a disabled person) as authority-independent. Moreover, transgressions of moral requirements were judged appropriately as less permissible, and more serious and were specifically justified by consideration of the victim's welfare. By contrast, the psychopathic subjects scored poorly in two ways. First, they showed a marked propensity to treat all requirements as moral ones: they more often treated conventional requirements as if they were authority-independent ones, transgressions of which were as impermissible, unmodifiable, and serious as moral ones.[37] Secondly, on the justification dimension of the distinction psychopathic subjects were significantly less likely to recognize that the rationale for the negative-act/harming requirements had to do with the pain or other distress of others, and they often failed to cite others' welfare as a justification when doing so required them to recognize and respond to negative states in others. They tended instead to justify harm-based moral prohibitions in very

---

[35] R. J. R. Blair, L. Jones, F. Clark, and M. Smith, 'Is the Psychopath "Morally Insane"?', *Personality and Individual differences* 19 (1995), 741–52.

[36] The dimensions were tested by putting the following questions:

Questions: (1) Was it OK for X to do Y? (permissibility) (2) Was it bad for X to [the transgression]? And on a scale of one to ten, how bad was it for X to do [the transgression]? (seriousness) (3) Why was it bad for X to do [the t]? (justification categories) (4) Would it be OK for X to Y if the teacher/librarian/policeman says X can? (authority jurisdiction).

[37] One sometimes reads that the psychopathic subjects in these experiments treated moral requirements as if they were conventional. This is misleading. Only in respect of the justification category do they 'conventionalize' the moral, usually by failing to mention others' suffering as a reason for some prohibition. In respect of the other three categories, psychopaths actually tended to treat transgressions of conventional requirements as being as impermissible, serious, and independent as moral ones.

inappropriate terms, often appealing to seemingly arbitrary norms (e.g. 'that is just not the done thing', or 'no one is allowed to do that') and social disorder ('doing that would disrupt the class' or 'doing that would cause too much trouble').

The results of Blair's different studies of psychopaths and autistics, taken together, seem to deliver an empirical argument that spells doom for the friend of internalism. The argument runs as follows: Psychopaths possess an intact TOM, but they are deficient in their pre-cognitive/autonomic responses to others' distress. Psychopaths are also defective with respect to the moral/conventional distinction and to the justificatory role of other's interests. Therefore, mindreading abilities are not a *sufficient* condition of moral competence. Moral motivation requires an independent desiderative mechanism which psychopaths lack: they are desiderative egocentrists.[38] Autistics, by contrast, lack an adequate TOM. They nonetheless have a good command of the moral/conventional distinction and their responsiveness to distress (on autonomic measures) is near-normal. Therefore mindreading abilities also are no *necessary* condition of moral responsiveness. Moral responsiveness requires some affective, desiderative mechanism—a source of motivation that is quite independent of a grasp of moral norms and of others' psychologies. Externalism, this argument suggests, is true of our judgements of *both* moral[o-r] norms and of other persons' morally salient psychological states.

2.3 Problems for externalism

In its strongest form the argument set out above moves from premises concerning only the deviant sub-populations of psychopaths and autistics to a conclusion concerning the causal basis of moral responsiveness in normal, non-deviant subjects. In that form, it is unsound. But might not a less ambitious argument go through—say, an argument concluding only that the *psychopath* is a cognitively competent, desiderative egocentrist whose anomalies are owed to some kind of pre-cognitive, affective-motivational dysfunction? Do not the contrasting results for autistics and psychopaths at least establish that the disorder of the latter is causally independent of his cognitive grasp of others' salient psychological states? This suggestion initially looks promising, but it turns entirely on the truth of two premises. The first premise is that autistics lack all but the most minimal mindreading abilities, and hence that mindreading plays no role in their responsiveness to others. The second premise is that the mindreading/TOM abilities of psychopaths are *not* impaired. The foregoing argument for externalism relies entirely on these two premises. There is, however, good reason to question both.

With respect to the first premise, it overstates the case to say that autistics are unable to identify and understand others' inner lives. They are not, in fact, mindreading egocentrists with respect to any and all mental states, let alone all of those directly

---

[38] See Shaun Nichols 'Norms with feeling: Towards a psychological account of moral judgment', *Cognition* 84 (2002), 221–36. For a different interpretation of the data see my *Metaphor and Moral Experience* [M&ME] (Oxford: Oxford University Press, 2000), 150–80.

relevant to moral judgement. First of all, many autistic children (at the same functional level as Blair's own subjects) use a range of propositional-attitude terms appropriately—particularly those relating to states of desire ('want', 'need').[39] They also frequently master terms reporting experiential states ('see', 'hurt', 'nice', 'sad', 'happy') and they are capable of attributing simple desires and emotions to others.[40] Simon Baron-Cohen observes that most autistics even understand that different people have different desires and can identify causal relations between desires and emotional states, e.g. 'that someone who gets what he wants will feel happy, and someone else who does not get what he wants will feel sad'.[41] If the capacity for attributing some intentional states—and particularly desires—is reasonably well intact in most autistic children, then the idea evaporates that their facility with the moral/conventional distinction must be independent of a capacity for mindreading of some kind.

Moreover, mindreading is almost certainly not an 'all or nothing' ability: it is important to distinguish different mindreading targets. The ability to attribute emotions—so important to the formation of other-regarding moral beliefs—appears to depend on different neurological substrates from those underpinning the ability to attribute beliefs (an arena in which autistics are notably weak). In fact, the research indicates that the *only* mindreading ability at which autistics systematically fail is the ability to attribute false beliefs. Therefore neither Nichols nor Blair are entitled to conclude that the ability to mark the moral/conventional distinction is independent of mindreading skills generally (or even independent of all but the most 'minimal' mindreading skills, as Nichols puts it). They are only entitled to the much less exciting claim that this ability is dissociable from the ability to attribute false beliefs. Further, the Nichols-Blair observation that autistics exhibit normal autonomic responses to images of others in distress tells us little about the relation of those responses to mindreading skills, and there is very considerable evidence that autism leaves intact a significant attentional, verbal, and behavioural sensitivity to others' distress, discomfort, and fear.[42] If that is so, it should be no surprise that autistics' autonomic responses follow suit.

Nichols's second premiss—that psychopaths evidence no TOM deficits and hence are able mindreaders—also distorts the wider evidence. Standard TOM tests typically present subjects with scenarios for verbal interpretation and pose questions which directly or indirectly require them to make attributions of propositional attitudes.[43]

[39] H. Tager-Flusberg, 'What language reveals about the understanding of minds in children with autism', in S. Baron-Cohen, H. Tager-Flusberg, and Donald Cohen (eds.) *Understanding Other Minds: Perspectives from Autism* (Cambridge University Press Cambridge, 1993).

[40] J. Tan and P. Harris, 'Autistic children understand seeing and wanting', *Development and Psychopathology*, 3 (1991), 163–74.

[41] S. Baron-Cohen, *Mindblindness*, Cambridge (MA: MIT Press, Bradford Books, 1995), 63.

[42] See S. Nichols and S. Stich, *Mindreading* (Oxford: Oxford University Press, 2004).

[43] I will not discuss Blair's experimental procedures in detail here, but they are not without their difficulties. His subject pools were limited in both size and scope: most experiments featured fewer than twenty-five subjects in each category (psychopathic/non-psychopathic controls). Moreover, there are arguably serious procedural difficulties in identifying and classifying subjects by the 'file only' method on

These tests are confined to 'cool' mental states such as beliefs, intentions, and desires, rather than states such as grief, rage, joy, embarrassment, physical pain, and fear which feature a rich phenomenology and are high in motivational charge. The claim that psychopaths are not TOM-impaired thus fails to reflect their mindreading deficits with respect to some of the very experiential states which are most likely to be morally salient. Moreover, the procedure of relying on verbal self-report measures may mask a difference between psychopaths and normal controls in their TOM processing. After all, there are more ways than one to identify others' mental states, and the same verbal reports may issue from two etiologically distinct kinds of judgements. This is more than a mere possibility: several studies have shown that even where the *verbal* responses of psychopaths to a presented image or scenario mirror those of normal controls, significant differences in their simultaneous autonomic responses betray the fact that the same words are masking very different global psychophysical states.[44]

These doubts about the 'normal TOM' diagnosis for psychopaths find support in the fact that in studies specifically targeting their ability to detect the *morally salient* emotions psychopaths perform much less well than controls. In particular, psychopaths who rate high on an 'emotional detachment' scale are very significantly impaired in their attributions to others of the moral emotions of shame, guilt, and remorse.[45] Further studies by Blair's own research group show that many psychopaths have difficulty recognizing sad facial expressions and sad vocal tones. Likewise, they appear to be sub-normal in their ability to detect fear, distress, and sadness in visual and auditory representations (videos, pictures, and voice recordings).[46]

which Blair often relies. The first worry is that the selection features sometimes overlap with the target features (i.e. subjects who are described in their files as possessing little empathy are tested and found to be wanting in empathy). A further cause for concern is the fact that files are created in part by a process of 'inherited descriptions'. Particularly in the case of repeat offenders, files stand to be a history written by overworked and underqualified penal officers whose views have been influenced by judges armchair assessments, whose views in turn have been swayed by penal psychiatric staff, whose views may be influenced by overworked and underqualified penal officers, and so on.

[44] Repeated studies have shown that psychopaths exhibit markedly diminished physiological responses (skin-conductance and heart-rate variations) to pictorial representations of persons in motivationally-charged circumstances (e.g. a man cowering in terror before a gun, a child cornered by a snarling wolf). These diminished responses were not mirrored in the psychopathic subjects' verbal judgements, however: like normal controls, they described the images as disturbing or frightening or distasteful. Psychopaths likewise exhibited diminished physiological responses to narrative representation of others' 'negative' states (e.g. descriptions of grief, anxiety, and pain), while again their was no discernible difference in their verbal *reports* of the events described. What are we to make of these results? Of course there is much more to possessing normal empathic reactions to others than undergoing physiological responses. But these findings suggest that there is at least a stable correlation between the absence of such responses in psychopaths *coinciding* with an ability to linguistically evaluate the targets in much the same terms as do normal controls.

[45] R. J. R. Blair, 'A Cognitive Developmental Approach to Morality: Investigating the Psychopath', *Cognition* 57 (1995), 1–29.

[46] R. J. R. Blair, D. G. V. Mitchell, K. S. Petschardt, E. Colledge, R. A. Leonard, J. H. Shine, L. K. Murray, and D. I. Perrett, 'Reduced sensitivity to others' fearful expressions in psychopathic individuals', *Personality & Individual Differences* 37 (2004), 1111–22; R. J. R. Blair, E. Colledge, L. Murray, and D. G. Mitchell, 'A selective impairment in the processing of sad and fearful expression in children with psychopathic tendencies', *Journal of Abnormal Psychology* 29 (2001), 491–8; R. J. R. Blair, D. G. Mitchell, R. Richell,

Finally, recall that psychopathic subjects underperformed specifically in their appreciation of the moral nature of harm norms; it is with respect to transgressions of this kind (rather than transgression of rules enjoining positive-act/helping behaviour) that psychopaths most significantly failed to recognize the moral/conventional distinction and failed to appreciate that the rules in question are justified by others' welfare. The psychopath's judgement seems to let him down specifically with respect to actions producing pain, fear, grief, and other states of distress: despite his superficial facility with moral talk, it seems that he does not understand the rational implications and distinctive status of human suffering.

2.4 Distress egocentrism

These considerations suggest that the standard TOM tests conducted by Blair and others do not target some of the mindreading abilities most salient to moral judgement. A psychopathic subject could be expected to pass those tests with flying colours, but such success tells us little about his ability to detect and interpret the conditions informing everyday, other-regarding moral judgements. Hence the psychopath is not, on the evidence in hand, a walking vindication of the independence of thought and feeling in moral judgement generally. Instead, it appears that psychopathy features a highly complex, symbiotic interaction of affect and cognition.

We know that psychopaths are defective in their identifications of others' states of fear, sadness, and perhaps other kinds of distress. We have also seen that psychopaths are particularly impaired in their understanding of harm norm transgressions. The coincidence of these two results reinforces the idea that the motivational force internal to moral[o-r] requirements in *normal* subjects is of a piece with their natural disposition to advert, dispel, and console others' distress. To put the point in terms of my distinction between rule-book and basic moral judgements, the psychopath's normative judgements are often of the rule-book kind: he is able to correlate the descriptive features of a situation with this or that normative requirement, but he is unable to make certain *basic* moral judgements by way of attending to and reflecting on the subvenient features of persons' concerns and interests, and particularly to their susceptibility to distress. If he is unable to attend to those features and to represent them in his thought, he will also fail to perceive the moral aspects they manifest; he will be as blind to these aspects as is the pattern-blind subject to the images in a portrait or a landscape. The analogy is not perfect, of course: while the pattern-blind subject is unable organize the subvenient lines and colours into a coherent image, he is at least able to identify them. The psychopath, however, does not even see the 'lines and colours' subvening moral aspects—the affective and motivational features of others' experience from which some of our most fundamental moral aspects are composed.

This is not to say that the psychopath is altogether unware of the fact that others are capable of suffering. He is clearly able in some sense to recognize and attribute such states to others. But he fails to represent these states empathically—as from an experiential perspective possessing the aversive motivational force they carry for those who suffer them.[47] He is unable to represent others' experience as from their point of view, and so is less likely to be moved by it when generating his normative judgements. This empathic dysfunction typically manifests itself in a quite specific distortion in his understanding of normative requirements, namely a distortion in his moral[o-r] beliefs involving harm to others. Indeed, the psychopath's cognitive grasp of harm norms is defective in a quite dramatic and telling way in this arena: by failing to recognize the moral/conventional distinction and to recognize others' welfare as a reason for action, he shows that he does not properly understand the distinctive basis of an important and primitive category of moral requirements: the badness of the suffering of other persons.

The non-pathological, 'ordinary' empathizer represents others' distress as from a point of view which is, in its affective force, partially isomorphic with that of the subject whose states they are.[48] This shift in perspective not only brings to his attention certain facts which are only available from within an experiential, first-person point of view, but carries some part of the associated motivational force. The psychopath, by contrast, may be described as a 'distress egocentrist':

---

[47] The psychopath's disability, so described is neither a strictly affective nor strictly cognitive one: we may want to say that he does not perceive certain moral aspects *because* he does not respond to others as he should, but that is not to say that the seeing is conceptually distinct from the responding.

[48] What is it to represent an experiential state 'as from the perspective of the other'? Experiential states (as I have been using that phrase) have both content and phenomenological character. An empathic representation 'as from the perspective another' is a kind of quasi-experience: it is a representation of another's state which features to some degree and in some part the very phenomenological features presented to the individual whose state it is. Where the target state is an emotion of some kind, these features typically will be affective and motivational ones. (For other targets, different phenomenological features may be involved, as in the case of empathically representing another's feelings of physical pain.) Affective character and motivational force, like the perspectival features of visual experience, can only be captured in this way: one has to participate, sometimes by way of an exercise of memory, but often by way of an exercise of imagination, if one is to understand these dimensions of others' experiential states. In this respect the notion of empathy at work here may be better captured by the German '*Einfühlung*—literally, 'in-feeling', as in feeling 'in' with or attuned to another's state of mind. Roger Scruton, in his account of musical experience, appeals to an analogy with *Einfühlung* to describe our natural responsiveness and receptiveness to expression in music—a form of expression which is most often elucidated in terms of human emotions. Scruton writes: 'When you move to music, the music takes charge of your response to it—you are being *led* by it, from gesture to gesture, and each new departure is dictated by the musical development... You are *in the hands of* the music; your sympathetic response moves in parallel to the musical development.' This responsiveness, Scruton says, is not altogether unlike the natural responsiveness of one sympathetic human being to another: Observing a gesture or expression we may have the experience of *Einfühlung*, or 'knowing what it's like', whereby the gesture becomes, in imagination, our own. We then feel it, not from the observer's, but from the subject's point of view. This experience may provide an intimation of a whole state of mind, regardless of whether the state can be described;... It is a creation of the imagination, prompted by sympathy. Roger Scruton, *The Aesthetics of Music* (Oxford: Clarendon Press, 1997), 358.

Distress Egocentrism A subject is a distress egocentrist with respect to some affectively and motivationally characterized state of suffering just if his representations of that state in other subjects systematically exclude its characteristic, first-person phenomenology.

The psychopath's particular form of distress egocentrism is that his attributions of suffering feature none of the *motivations* it carries for the person whose suffering it is. A distress egocentrist may, of course, succeed in correctly identifying many cases of that experience-type in others and he may form rule-directed beliefs about those states. (He might even pass standard verbal tests for recognizing instances of that experience-type, as many psychopaths do.) However, the distress egocentrist will not be moved by his attributions of the experience to others, and if he judges that another is, for instance, suffering, he does so as a non-partisan observer: he does not register, as Nagel puts it, a 'pained awareness of their distress as something to be relieved'.[49]

The distress egocentrist's blindness to human suffering thus excludes him from participation in some of our most fundamental moral practices, for he is unable to form many of the basic *judgements* in which they consist. Of course, his failing is not one of rationality in the sense of a failure to reject contradiction, inconsistency, or arbitrariness: the psychopath can be perfectly consistent in refusing to harmonise his beliefs and actions with others' purposes. But he nonetheless suffers from a cognitive defect in so far as he fails to perceive and believe all that he might—indeed all that he must if he is to form true, other-regarding, basic moral beliefs. Moreover, what is missing from his understanding of other persons is not something arcane or exotic: he misses out certain wholly ordinary and pervasive facts about their everyday psychological states, as those states are presented to the persons subject to them. And in so far as these states subvene and give rise to moral aspects, he misses out the moral facts as well.

It may be tempting to insist that the distress egocentrists' cognitive failings are *caused* by this affective and motivational ones. But we must tread carefully here lest we falsify the phenomenology, and so falsify the nature of the relation between responding to and representing another's psychology. The thought that an affective deficit causally explains a cognitive one might suggest that these two capacities are, in Hume's words, 'distinct existences', and that the former has some kind of temporal priority. However, I have argued (Part I) that this does not correctly capture the phenomenological relation between empathic response and accurate representation: it may be that one manages accurately to represent another's point of view because one feels with and for him, but it is also true that one feels with and for another because one has managed accurately to represent his point of view. Our empathic responses to another's suffering, for instance, are not normally independent of our belief that he is suffering—and *vice versa*. One may, of course, essay the belief in the absence of the

---

[49] T. Nagel, *The Possibility of Altruism* (Princeton: Princeton University Press, 1970), 80 n.1.

responses, but that is just to say that in some cases such beliefs are essayed for different reasons and by way of a different (and derivative) route of thought. In a *basic* moral judgement, your 'pained awareness' of another's distress is at once a matter of responding to this state and detecting that he is subject to it. Of course your propensity to respond empathically may be a necessary condition of your ability to represent his psychology as accurately as you do, and your responses may in part rationally justify your psychological attributions. It does not follow, however, that these responses are empirically distinct existences—empirically independent occurrent states. As Murdoch insisted, our attunement to and perception of another, if the perception is just and true, will be at once a state of knowledge and a state of the will. And so too will be the basic moral judgements to which it gives rise.

Endnote: Configurations of love

Sed trahit invitam nova vis, aliudque cupido. Mens alius suadet: video meliora proboque deteriora sequor.
(Some strange power draws me on against my will. Desire persuades me one way, reason another. I see the better course and approve it, [but] I follow the worse.)

Ovid, *Metamorphoses*, VII, 19–21

All of us at times have acted against our better moral judgement. This may have been because we felt ourselves compelled by motives we did not respect, but were powerless to resist. Or we may simply have found ourselves indifferent and unmoved by considerations of right and wrong—perhaps because we were too worn with fatigue or overwhelmed by cares. On such occasions, it undoubtedly can be helpful to advert to a 'rule-book' knowledge of morality to steer our practical reasoning, and at least to this extent general moral principles will be indispensable both as a guide to and explanation of our conduct. Murdoch was right to observe, however, that rules cannot be the whole of morality; the messy and complicated cases of day to day life require an experiential engagement sensitive to particular details and differences and responsive to the individuals whose welfare is at stake. Murdoch argued for this type of particularism in concert with two further commitments: an epistemological commitment to the robust cognitive content of moral requirements and a phenomenological commitment to their intrinsic motivational force.

The first commitment, I have argued, fits well with a conception of moral properties as aspectual properties on analogy with other 'deep configurations' of reality, such as pictorial and musical aspects. This conception invites an experiential account of our awareness of moral requirements according to which the subject's first-personal responsiveness to others is a necessary condition of his capacity to essay certain basic moral judgements. Murdoch's second commitment—her internalist thesis—is closely related. That thesis, we saw, features both a conceptual component (the thought that motivational force is built into the meaning of moral concepts) and an empirical component (the thought that affect and motivation are empirically necessary conditions of competence in moral reasoning). I have focused here principally on the empirical claim, arguing that in the case of psychopathic disorder—a paradigm of moral *in*competence—the psychopath's blindness to states of suffering and distress renders him unable to represent accurately certain crucial human concerns, and so unable properly to grasp a range of fundamental moral requirements. The psychopath's disorder, in short, is just as Murdoch's phenomenology of 'moral vision' would predict: it is at once a failure to feel properly and a failure to judge correctly.

The experimental studies discussed here also connect in an interesting way with Murdoch's emphasis on the role of love in moral development. She frequently suggests that sensitivity to the Good is of a piece with our capacity for love, and she develops this point in both a metaphysical and a psychological dimension. The metaphysical dimension leads her to endorse Plato's thought that knowing the Good and loving it are unified aspects of our perception of a transcendent moral ideal. The psychological dimension is less exotic, but no less important: it is that our ability to understand what morality requires of us in specific, ordinary cases is bound up with an ability to regard others lovingly. The phenomenon of psychopathy lends support to this idea: two defining features of the psychopath's disorder are his incapacity for deep attachments to others—for persisting love—and the solipsistic, emotional isolation that follows on love's absence. In Murdoch's *A Fairly Honourable Defeat*, she herself constructs a striking profile of a personality disfigured in these ways in the novel's anti-heroic protagonist, Julius King. King is revealed to be a sometime camp-survivor, Julius Kahn, and his personality is morally and emotionally dysfunctional in ways that vividly reflect the cold and calculating nature of the psychopath. His personal history, too, is marked by many of the events characteristically associated with that disorder: the childhood loss and abandonment, the social exclusion, and the exposure to radical brutality he suffers are all common features of the often tragic biographies of psychopaths. I doubt that Murdoch intended to construct a fictional instantiation of any particular psychopathology, but we nonetheless find in Kahn a striking portrait both of the lovelessness and its origins that are the hallmarks of the psychopath's inner life. Perhaps as we come better to understand the nature and causes of psychopathy we will also grow to appreciate more deeply the importance of our ability to respond to one another with love. For there is surely something correct in Murdoch's claim that 'even partially refined [love] . . . is the energy and passion of the soul in its search for Good, the force that joins us to Good and joins us to the world' (SGC 103/384).

Bibliography

Aldwinckle, Stella, *Christ's Shadow in Plato's Cave: A Meditation on the Substance of Love* (Oxford: Amate Press, 1990).

Allison, Henry, [KTF] *Kant's Theory of Freedom* (Cambridge: Cambridge University Press, 1990).

Altorf, Marije, 'Iris Murdoch and the Art of Imagination: Imaginative Philosophy as Response to Secularism'. (Ph. D. thesis, Centre for Literature, Theology and the Arts, University of Glasgow, 2004.)

Altorf, Marije, *Iris Murdoch and the Art of Imagining* (London: Continuum, 2008).

Ameriks, Karl, 'The Hegelian Critique of Kantian Morality', in B. den Ouden and M. Moen (eds.), *New Essays on Kant* (New York: Peter Lang, 1987), 155–78.

Anscombe, Elizabeth, 'Modern Moral Philosophy', *Philosophy* 33 (1958), 1–19; repr. in Roger Crisp and Michael Slote (eds.), *Virtue Ethics* (Oxford: Oxford University Press, 1997), 26–44.

Anselm, St. *Anselm's Proslogion*, transl. M. J. Charlesworth (Oxford: Clarendon Press, 1965).

Antonaccio, Maria, 'Form and Contingency in Iris Murdoch's Ethics', in Maria Antonaccio and William Schweiker (eds.), *Iris Murdoch and the Search for Human Goodness* (Chicago: University of Chicago Press, 1996), 110–37.

Antonaccio, Maria, 'Moral identity and the good in the thought of Iris Murdoch' (Ph. D. thesis, University of Chicago Divinity School, 1996).

Antonaccio, Maria, 'Imagining the Good: Iris Murdoch's Godless Theology', *Annual of the Society of Christian Ethics* 16 (1996), 223–42.

Antonaccio, Maria, 'Moral Change and the Magnetism of the Good', *Annual of the Society of Christian Ethics* 20 (2000), 143–64.

Antonaccio, Maria, [PH] *Picturing the Human: The Moral Thought of Iris Murdoch* (New York/ Oxford: Oxford University Press, 2000).

Antonaccio, Maria, 'The Consolations of Literature', *Journal of Religion* 80.4 (October 2000), 615–44.

Antonaccio, Maria, 'Picturing the Soul: Moral Psychology and the Recovery of the Emotions', *Ethical Theory and Moral Practice* 4 (2001), 127–41.

Antonaccio, Maria, [MPI] 'The Moral and Political Imagination of Iris Murdoch', *Notizie di Politeia* XVIII, 66 (2002), 22–50.

Antonaccio, Maria, and William Schweiker (eds.), [SHG] *Iris Murdoch and the Search for Human Goodness* (Chicago: University of Chicago Press, 1996).

Aquinas, Thomas of, *Summa Theologiae*. Vols. 4–12 (1888–1906) of: *Opera omnia iussu impensaque Leonis XIII P.M. edita* (Romae: Ex Typographia Polyglotta S. C. de Propaganda Fide, 1882–).

Aristotle, *Rhetoric*, trans. W. Rhys Roberts, repr. in *The Complete Works of Aristotle*, J. Barnes (ed.) (Princeton: Princeton University Press, 1984), vol. 2.

Aristotle, *Nicomachean Ethics*, trans. R. Crisp (Cambridge: Cambridge University Press, 2000).

Augustine, *Confessions*, trans. Henry Chadwick (Oxford: Oxford University Press, 1992).

Augustine, *The Essential Augustine*, V. J. Bourke (ed.) (Indianapolis: Hackett, 1964, 1974).

Austen, Jane, [S&S] *Sense and Sensibility* (New York: Alfred A. Knopf, 1992 [1811]).

Austin, J. L., [PE] 'A Plea for Excuses', in *Philosophical Papers* (Oxford: Clarendon Press, 1961, 1970, 1979), 175–204.

Ayer, A. J., *Language, Truth, and Logic* (London: Victor Gollancz, 1936; 2nd edn. 1946).

Backus, Guy, *Iris Murdoch: The Novelist as Philosopher, the Philosopher as Novelist; 'The Unicorn' as a Philosophical Novel* (Berne/Frankfurt am Main/New York: Peter Lang, 1986).

Bagnoli, Carla, [MC] 'Moral Constructivism: A Phenomenological Argument', *Topoi* 21 (2002), 125–38.

Bagnoli, Carla, [RLA] 'Respect and Loving Attention', *Canadian Journal of Philosophy* 33 (2003), 483–516.

Baier, Annette, 'Mind and Change in Mind', in *Postures of the Mind* (Minneapolis: University of Minnesota Press, 1985), 51–73.

Barnes, J., *Early Greek Philosophy* (Harmondsworth: Penguin, 1987).

Baron, Marcia, Philip Pettit, and Michael Slote, *Three Methods of Ethics: A Debate* (Oxford: Blackwell Publishers, 1997).

Baron-Cohen, S., *Mindblindness* (Cambridge, Mass.: MIT Press, Bradford Books, 1995).

Baron-Cohen, S., A. M. Leslie, and U. Frith, 'Does the Autistic Child Have a "Theory of Mind"?', *Cognition* 21 (1985), 37–46.

Bass, Jack, *Unlikely Heroes: the dramatic story of the Southern judges of the Fifth Circuit who translated the Supreme Court's Brown decision into a revolution for equality* (New York: Simon and Schuster, 1981).

Benhabib, Seyla, *Situating the Self: Gender, Community and Postmodernism in Contemporary Ethics* (New York: Routledge, 1992).

Bennett, Jonathan, 'The Conscience of Huckleberry Finn', *Philosophy* 49 (1974), 123–34.

Blackburn, Simon, 'Reply: Rule-Following and Moral Realism', in S. Holtzman and C. Leich (eds.), *Wittgenstein: To Follow a Rule* (London: Routledge and Kegan Paul, 1981), 163–87.

Blackburn, Simon, 'Errors and the Phenomenology of Value', in Ted Honderich (ed.), *Morality and Objectivity* (London: Routledge and Kegan Paul, 1985), 1–22.

Blackburn, Simon, 'Must we weep for sentimentalism?', in James Dreier (ed.), *Contemporary Debates in Moral Theory* (Oxford: Blackwell, 2006), 144–59.

Blair, R. J. R., 'A cognitive developmental approach to morality: Investigating the psychopath', *Cognition*, 57 (1995), 1–29.

Blair, R. J. R., 'Psychophysiological Responsiveness to the Distress of Others in Children with Autism', *Personality & Individual Differences* 26 (1999), 477–85.

Blair, R. J. R., 'Responsiveness to distress cues in the child with psychopathic tendencies', *Personality and Individual Differences* 27 (1999), 135–45.

Blair, R. J. R., E. Colledge, L. Murray, et al. 'A selective impairment in the processing of sad and fearful expressions in children with psychopathic tendencies', *Journal of Abnormal Child Psychology* 29 (2001), 491–8.

Blair, R. J. R., D. G. V. Mitchell, R. A. Richell, et al. 'Turning a Deaf Ear to Fear: Impaired Recognition of Vocal Affect in Psychopathic Individuals', *Journal of Abnormal Psychology* 111 (2002), 682–6.

Blair, R. J. R., C. Sellars., I. Strickland, et al. 'Theory of mind in the psychopath', *The Journal of Forensic Psychiatry* 7 (1996), 15–25.

Blair, R. J. R., L. Jones, F. Clark, et al. 'Is the Psychopath "Morally Insane"?', *Personality and Individual Differences* 19 (1995), 741–52.

Blair, R. J. R., L. Jones, F. Clark, et al. 'The psychopathic individual: a lack of responsiveness to distress cues?' *Psychophysiology* 34 (1997), 192–8.

Blair, R. J. R., D. G. V. Mitchell, K. S. Petschardt, et al. 'Reduced sensitivity to others' fearful expressions in psychopathic individuals', *Personality & Individual Differences* 37 (2004), 1111–22.

Blum, Lawrence, [IMDM] 'Iris Murdoch and the Domain of the Moral', *Philosophical Studies* 50 (1986), 343–367; repr. in Blum, *Moral Perception and Particularity*, 12–29.

Blum, Lawrence, 'Moral Exemplars: Reflections on Schindler, the Trocmés, and Others', *Ethical Theory: Character and Virtue, Midwest Studies in Philosophy* 13 (Notre Dame: University of Notre Dame Press, 1988), P. French, T. Uehling, and H. Wettstein (eds.), 196–221; repr. in Blum, *Moral Perception and Particularity*, 65–97.

Blum, Lawrence, [MPP] 'Moral Perception and Particularity', *Ethics* 101 (1991), 701–25; repr. in Blum, *Moral Perception and Particularity*, 30–63.

Blum, Lawrence, 'Postscript to "Moral Perception and Particularity"', in *Moral Perception and Particularity* (Cambridge: Cambridge University Press, 1994), 59–63.

Blum, Lawrence, *Moral Perception and Particularity* (New York: Cambridge University Press, 1994).

Blum, Lawrence A., and Victor J. Seidler, *A Truer Liberty: Simone Weil and Marxism* (New York: Routledge, 1989).

Boghossian, Paul, and Christopher Peacocke (eds.), *New Essays on the A Priori* (Oxford: Clarendon Press, 2000).

Botting, Douglas, *Gavin Maxwell: A Life* (London: HarperCollins, 1993).

Bradley, F. H., *Ethical Studies* (London: Henry S. King, 1876), (2nd edn. Oxford: Oxford University Press, 1927).

Brandom, Robert, [SPTHI] 'Some Pragmatist Themes in Hegel's Idealism: Negotiation and Administration in Hegel's Account of the Structure and Content of Conceptual Norms', *European Journal of Philosophy* 7 (1999), 2, 165–91.

Brewer, Bill, 'Externalism and A Priori Knowledge of Empirical Facts', in Paul Boghossian and Christopher Peacocke (eds.), *New Essays on the A Priori* (Oxford: Clarendon Press, 2000), 415–32.

Byatt, A. S., *Degrees of Freedom: The Novels of Iris Murdoch* (London: Chatto & Windus/New York: Barnes & Noble, 1965); rev. edn. with addition of later reviews and pamphlets: *Degrees of Freedom: The Early Novels of Iris Murdoch* (London: Vintage, 1994).

Canetti, Elias, *Die Blendung: Roman* (Wien; Leipzig; Zürich: Herbert Reichner, 1936, *c.*1935).

Canetti, Elias, *Auto da fé*, translated from the German under the personal supervision of the author by C. V. Wedgwood (London: Jonathan Cape, 1946).

Canetti, Elias, *The Tower of Babel*, trans. C. V. Wedgwood (New York: A. A. Knopf, 1947).

Canetti, Elias, *Masse und Macht* (Hamburg: Claassen, 1960).

Canetti, Elias, *Crowds & Power*, trans. Carol Stewart (London: Gollancz, 1962).

Canetti, Elias, *Die Provinz des Menschen: Aufzeichnungen 1942–1972* (Munich: Hanser, 1973).

Canetti, Elias, *The Human Province,* trans. J. Neugroschel (New York: Seabury, 1977; Picador, 1986).

Cavell, Stanley, 'Must We Mean What We Say?', in Vere Chappell (ed.), *Ordinary Language* (Englewood Cliffs: Prentice Hall, 1964), 75–112.

Cavell, Stanley, *The Claim of Reason: Wittgenstein, skepticism, morality, and tragedy* (Oxford: Oxford University Press, 1979).

Clarke, Bridget Joy, 'The Lens of Character: Aristotle, Murdoch and the Idea of Moral Perception'. (Ph. D. thesis, University of Pittsburgh, 2003).

Clarke, Bridget Joy, 'Virtue and Disagreement', *Ethical Theory and Moral Practice* 13 (2010), 273–91.

Collingwood, R. G., *The Principles of History and Other Writings in the Philosophy of History*, ed. W. H. Dray and W. J. van der Dussen (Oxford: Oxford University Press, 1999).

Conradi, Peter J., 'Platonism in Iris Murdoch', in Anna Baldwin and Sarah Hutton (eds.), *Platonism and the English Imagination* (Cambridge: Cambridge University Press, 1994), 330–42.

Conradi, Peter J., *Iris Murdoch: The Saint and the Artist* (London: Macmillan, 1986; 2nd edn. 1989).

—— *The Saint and the Artist: A Study of the Fiction of Iris Murdoch* (3rd edn. London: Harper-Collins, 2001).

Conradi, Peter J., *Iris Murdoch: A Life* (London: HarperCollins, 2001; New York: W. W. Norton, 2001).

Cooperman, D., and Walter, E. V., *Power and Civilization: Political Thought in the Twentieth Century* (New York: Crowell, 1962).

Crary, Alice, 'The Happy Truth: J. L. Austin's *How to Do Things with Words*', *Inquiry* 45 (2002), 59–80.

Crisp, Roger, 'Kraut on Aristotle on Happiness', *Polis* 10 (1991), 129–61.

Crisp, Roger, 'Particularizing Particularism', in B. Hooker and M. O. Little (eds.), *Moral Particularism* (Oxford: Clarendon Press, 2000), 23–47.

Crisp, Roger, 'Utilitarianism and Accomplishment', *Analysis* 60 (2000), 264–8.

Crisp, Roger, 'Socrates and Aristotle on Happiness and Virtue', in R. Heinaman (ed.), *Plato and Aristotle's Ethics* (Aldershot: Ashgate, 2003), 55–78.

Crisp, Roger, 'Does Modern Moral Philosophy Rest on a Mistake?', in A. O'Hear (ed.), *Modern Moral Philosophy* (Cambridge: Cambridge University Press, 2004), 75–93.

Crisp, Roger, 'Hume on Virtue, Utility, and Morality', in S. Gardiner (ed.), *Virtue Ethics, Old and New* (Ithaca: Cornell University Press, 2005), 159–78.

Dancy, Jonathan, 'Ethical Particularism and Morally Relevant Properties', *Mind* 92 (1983), 530–47.

Dancy, Jonathan, 'Two Conceptions of Moral Realism', *Proceedings of the Aristotelian Society*, suppl. vol. 60 (1986), 167–87.

Dancy, Jonathan, *Moral Reasons* (Oxford: Blackwell Publishing, 1993).

Dancy, Jonathan, *Ethics Without Principles* (Oxford: Oxford University Press, 2004).

Dante Alighieri, *The Purgatorio: a verse translation for the modern reader by John Ciardi*, introd. by Archibald T. MacAllister (New York: New American Library, 1961).

Davidson, Donald, 'Mental Events', in L. Foster & J. W. Swanson (eds.), *Experience and Theory* (Amherst: U. of Massachusetts Press, 1970), 79–101; repr. in Davidson, *Essays on Actions and Events* (Oxford: Clarendon Press, 1980).

Davies, Martin, 'Externalism and Armchair Knowledge', in Paul Boghossian and Christopher Peacocke (eds.), *New Essays on the A Priori* (Oxford: Clarendon Press, 2000), 384–414.

Denham, A. E., *Metaphor and Moral Experience* (Oxford: Oxford University Press, 2000).

Denham, A. E., 'Envisioning the Good: Iris Murdoch's Moral Psychology', *MFS Modern Fiction Studies* 47 (Fall 2001), 602–29.

Descartes, René, [AT] *Œuvres de Descartes*, Ch. Adam & P. Tannery (eds.), rev. ed., Paris: Vrin/C.N.R.S., 1964–76.

Descartes, René, [CSM] *The Philosophical Writings of Descartes*, trans. J. Cottingham, R. Stoothoff, D. Murdoch, 2 vols. (Cambridge: Cambridge University Press, 1984–85).

Diamond, Cora, 'Losing Your Concepts', *Ethics* 98 (1988), 255–77.

Diamond, Cora, [WPM] ' "We are Perpetually Moralists": Iris Murdoch, Fact and Value', in Maria Antonaccio and W. Schweiker (eds.), *Iris Murdoch and the Search for Human Goodness* (Chicago: University of Chicago Press, 1996), 79–109.

Dipple, Elizabeth, *Iris Murdoch: Work for the Spirit* (Chicago: University of Chicago Press, 1982).

Dooley, Gillian, ed., [FTC] *From a Tiny Corner in the House of Fiction: Conversations with Iris Murdoch* (Columbia, South Carolina: University of South Carolina Press, 2003).

Dostoevsky, Feodor, *Crime and Punishment: The Coulson Translation; Backgrounds and Sources; Essays in Criticism*, ed. George Gibian (New York: W. W. Norton & Co., 1964, 1975, 1989).

Dover, K. J., *Greek Homosexuality* (London: Duckworth/Cambridge, Mass.: Harvard University Press, 1978; rev. edn. with new postscript, Harvard University Press, 1989).

Driver, Julia, *Uneasy Virtue* (Cambridge: Cambridge University Press, 2001).

Dummett, Michael, 'Nominalism', *Philosophical Review* 65 (1956), 491–505; repr. in *Truth and other Enigmas* (London: Duckworth, 1978), 47–65.

Dummett, Michael, *Frege: Philosophy of Language* (London: Duckworth, 1973, 2nd edn. 1981).

Dummett, Michael, *Frege: Philosophy of Mathematics* (London: Duckworth, 1991).

Edsall, Thomas and Mary, *Chain Reaction: the impact of race, rights, and taxes on American politics* (New York: Norton, 1992).

Ellison, Ralph, *Invisible Man* (New York: Random House/Vintage Books, 1989 [1947]).

Findlay, J. N., *Hegel: A Re-Examination* (London: George Allen & Unwin, 1958).

Fletcher, John, and Cheryl Bove, *Iris Murdoch: A Descriptive Primary and Annotated Secondary Bibliography* (New York: Garland, 1994).

Flew, Anthony, *Hume's Philosophy of Belief* (London: Routledge and Kegan Paul, 1961).

Foot, Philippa, 'The Philosopher's Defence of Morality', *Philosophy* 27 (1952), 311–28.

Foot, Philippa, 'When is a Principle a Moral Principle?', *Proceedings of the Aristotelian Society*, suppl. vol. 28 (1954), 95–110.

Foot, Philippa, 'Free will as Involving Determinism', *Philosophical Review* 66 (1957), 439–50; repr. in Foot, *Virtues and Vices*, 62–73.

Foot, Philippa, 'Moral Arguments', *Mind* 67 (1958), 502–13; repr. in Foot, *Virtues and Vices*, 96–109.

Foot, Philippa, 'Moral Beliefs', *Proceedings of the Aristotelian Society* 59 (1958–59), 83–104; repr. in Foot, *Virtues and Vices*, 83–104.

Foot, Philippa, 'Goodness and Choice', *Proceedings of the Aristotelian Society*, suppl. vol. 35 (1961), 45–60; repr. in Foot, *Virtues and Vices*, 132–147.

Foot, Philippa, 'Hume on Moral Judgment', in David Pears (ed.), *David Hume: A Symposium* (London: Macmillan, 1963), 67–76; repr. in Foot, *Virtues and Vices*, 74–80.

Foot, Philippa, 'The Problem of Abortion and the Doctrine of Double Effect', *Oxford Review* 5 (Trinity 1967), 5–15; repr. in Foot, *Virtues and Vices*, 19–32.

Foot, Philippa, 'Morality and Art', *Proceedings of the British Academy* 56 (1970), 131–44.

Foot, Philippa, (ed.), *Theories of Ethics* (Oxford: Oxford University Press, 1967).

Foot, Philippa, 'Morality as a System of Hypothetical Imperatives', *Philosophical Review* 81 (1972), 305–16; repr. in Foot, *Virtues and Vices*, 157–173.

Foot, Philippa, *Virtues and Vices and Other Essays in Moral Philosophy* (Oxford: Blackwell, 1978).

Foot, Philippa, 'Does Moral Subjectivism Rest on a Mistake?' *Oxford Journal of Legal Studies* 15(1) (1995), 1–14.

Foot, Philippa, *Natural Goodness* (Oxford: Clarendon Press, 2001).

Frankfurt, Harry, *The Importance of What We Care About: Philosophical Essays* (Cambridge: Cambridge University Press, 1988).

Frege, Gottlob, *Die Grundlagen der Arithmetik* (Breslau: W. Koebner, 1884); repr. with parallel trans. by J. L. Austin, as *The Foundations of Arithmetic* (Oxford: Basil Blackwell, 1950, 1953).

Frege, G., *Translations from the Philosophical Writings of Gottlob Frege*, P. T. Geach and M. Black (eds.) (Oxford: Basil Blackwell, 1952, 1960, 1980).

Freud, Sigmund, 'Creative Writers and Day–Dreaming' (1908), Standard Ed. 9: 143–53.

Freud, Sigmund, 'Formulations on the Two Principles of Mental Functioning' (1911), Standard Ed. 12: 218–26.

Freud, Sigmund, *Introductory Lectures on Psycho–Analysis* (1915–16 (Pts. I–II), 1917 (Pt. III)), Standard Ed. vols. 15 and 16.

Freud, Sigmund, 'Beyond the Pleasure Principle' (1920), Standard Ed. 18: 7–64.

Freud, Sigmund, 'Neurosis and Psychosis' (1924, Standard Ed. 19:149–54), repr. in Anna Freud (ed.), *The Essentials of Psycho-Analysis: The Definitive Collection of Sigmund Freud's Writing* (London: Penguin Books, 1991), 563–7.

Freud, Sigmund, 'The Loss of Reality in Neurosis and Psychosis' (1924, Standard Ed., 19:183–90), repr. in Anna Freud (ed.), *The Essentials of Psycho-Analysis: The Definitive Collection of Sigmund Freud's Writing* (London: Penguin Books, 1991), 568–72.

Freud, Sigmund, *The Question of Lay Analysis* (1926, Standard Ed. 20, 177–258) (New York: W. W. Norton & Company, 1978).

Freud, Sigmund, [GW] *Gesammelte Werke*, 17 vols. (London; Imago, 1940–1952; Frankfurt am Main: S. Fischer, 1968–78, with additional vol. 18).

Freud, Sigmund, [SE] *Standard Edition of the Complete Psychological Works of Sigmund Freud*, ed. James Strachey, 24 vols. (London: Hogarth Press, 1953–1966).

Freud, Sigmund, *The Essentials of Psycho-Analysis*, with introduction and commentaries by Anna Freud (London: Hogarth Press/Harmondsworth: Penguin, 1986).

Frye, Marilyn, [PR] *The Politics of Reality: Essays in Feminist Theory* (Trumansburg, New York: The Crossing Press, 1983).

Frye, Marilyn, [WV] *Willful Virgin: Essays in Feminism* (Freedom, Calif.: The Crossing Press, 1992).

Gamwell, F., 'On the Loss of Theism', in M. Antonaccio and W. Schweiker (eds.), *Iris Murdoch and the Search for Human Goodness* (Chicago: University of Chicago Press, 1996), 171–89.

Geach, P. T., 'Good and Evil', *Analysis* 17 (1956), 33–42.

Gellner, E. A., 'Ethics and Logic', *Proceedings of the Aristotelian Society* 55 (1954–55), 157–78.

Gibieuf, Guillaume, *De libertate Dei et creaturae libri duo* (Paris, 1630).

Gillberg, C., 'Outcome in autism and autistic-like conditions', *Journal of the American Academy of Child and Adolescent Psychiatry*, 30 (1991), 375–82.

Gilson, Étienne, *Index Scolastico-Cartésien* (Paris: Félix Alcan, 1913); 2nd ed. (Paris: Vrin, 1979).

Gilson, Étienne, *La liberté chez Descartes et la théologie* (Paris: Félix Alcan, 1913).

Glover, Jonathan, *Humanity: A Moral History of the Twentieth Century* (New Haven: Yale University Press, 2000).

Gordon, David J., *Iris Murdoch's Fables of Unselfing* (Columbia, Missouri: University of Missouri Press, 1995).

Grene, Marjorie, (ed.), *The Anatomy of Knowledge: Papers presented to the Study Group on Foundations of Cultural Unity, Bowdoin College 1965 and 1966* (London: Routledge & Kegan Paul/ Amherst: Univ. of Massachusetts Press, 1969).

Grimaldi, Nicolas, *Six études sur la volonté et la liberté chez Descartes* (Paris: Vrin, 1988).

Hallie, P., *Lest Innocent Blood be Shed: The Story of the Village of Le Chambon and how Goodness Happened There* (New York: Harper and Row, 1979).

Halperin, David, 'Plato on Erotic Reciprocity', *Classical Antiquity* 5 (1986), 60–80.

Hampshire, Stuart, [TA] *Thought and Action* (London: Chatto and Windus, 1959).

Hampshire, Stuart, 'Disposition and Memory'. Ernest Jones Lecture, British Psycho–Analytic Association, *International Journal of Psycho–Analysis* 43 (1962), 59–68; repr. in S. Hampshire, *Freedom of Mind, and other essays* (Princeton: Princeton University Press, 1971; Oxford: Clarendon Press, 1972), 160–182; repr. with revisions, in R. Wollheim & J. Hopkins (eds.), *Philosophical Essays on Freud* (Cambridge: Cambridge University Press, 1982), 75–91.

Hampshire, Stuart, *Freedom of the Individual* (London: Chatto & Windus, 1965; 2nd ed., 1975).

Hampshire, Stuart, 'The Pleasures of Iris Murdoch', *New York Review of Books*, vol. 48 n. 18 (15 November 2001), 24–6.

Hare, R. D., *Without Conscience: The disturbing world of the psychopaths among us*, (New York: Pocket Books, 1993).

Hare, R. D., T. J. Harpur, R. A. Hakstian, et al., 'The Revised Psychopathy Checklist: Reliability and Factor Structure', *Psychological Assessment*, 2 (1994), 338–41.

Hare, R. M., 'Imperative Sentences', *Mind* 58 (1949), 21–39.

Hare, R. M., [LM] *The Language of Morals* (Oxford: Oxford University Press, 1952).

Hare, R. M., 'Universalisability', *Proceedings of the Aristotelian Society* 55 (1954–55), 295–312; repr. in Hare, *Essays on the Moral Concepts* (London: Macmillan, 1972), 13–28.

Hare, R. M., *Freedom and Reason* (Oxford: Clarendon Press, 1963).

Hare, R. M., *Moral Thinking: Its Methods, Level, and Point* (Oxford: Clarendon Press, 1981).

Harpham, Geoffrey, *Getting it Right: Language, Literature, and Ethics* (Chicago: University of Chicago Press, 1992).

Hauerwas, Stanley, *Vision and Virtue: Essays in Christian Ethics* (Notre Dame: University of Notre Dame Press, 1974).

Hauerwas, Stanley, 'Murdochian Muddles: Can we get through them if God does not exist?', in M. Antonaccio and W. Schweiker (eds.), *Iris Murdoch and the Search for Human Goodness* (Chicago: University of Chicago Press, 1996), 190–208.

Hegel, G. W. F., *System der Wissenschaft: erster Theil, Die Phänomenologie des Geistes* (Bamberg & Würzburg: bey Joseph Anton Goebhardt, 1807).

Hegel, G. W. F., *Phenomenology of Spirit*, trans. J. B. Baillie (London: S. Sonnenschein, 1910); 2nd ed., rev. (London: George Allen & Unwin, 1931).

Hegel, G. W. F., *Phenomenology of Spirit*, trans. A. V. Miller, with analysis of the text and foreword by J. N. Findlay (Oxford: Oxford University Press, 1977).

Heidegger, Martin, *Sein und Zeit*, Erster Hälfte. *Jahrbuch für Philosophie und Phänomenologische Forschung*, Band VIII (1927), also issued as a separate volume. 2nd ed (Halle: Max Niemeyer, 1929).

—— *Sein und Zeit*, 7th edn (Tübingen: Max Niemeyer, 1953).

Heidegger, Martin, *Being and Time*, trans. John Macquarrie & Edward Robinson (London: SCM Press, 1962; New York, Harper & Row, 1962).

Held, Virginia, 'Whose Agenda? Ethics versus Cognitive Science', in Larry May, Marilyn Friedman, and Andy Clark (eds.), *Mind and Morals: Essays on Ethics and Cognitive Science* (Cambridge, Mass.: MIT Press, 1996), 69–87.

Hepburn, R. W., 'Vision and Choice in Morality', *Proceedings of the Aristotelian Society*, suppl. vol. 30 (1956), 14–31.

Herman, Barbara, *The Practice of Moral Judgment* (Cambridge, Mass.: Harvard University Press, 1993).

Herman, Barbara, 'Making Room for Character', in S. Engstrom and J. Whiting (eds.), *Aristotle, Kant and the Stoics: Rethinking Happiness and Duty* (Cambridge: Cambridge University Press, 1996).

Hesiod, *Theogony*, ed. with prolegomena and commentary by M. L. West (Oxford: Clarendon Press, 1966).

Heusel, Barbara Stevens, *Patterned Aimlessness: Iris Murdoch's Novels of the 1970s and 1980s* (Athens, Georgia: University of Georgia Press, 1995).

Holland, Margaret, 'Touching the Weights: Moral Perception and Attention', *International Philosophical Quarterly*, vol XXXVIII, no. 3, Issue 151 (September 1998), 299–312.

Hooker, Brad, and Margaret Olivia Little (eds.), *Moral Particularism* (Oxford: Oxford University Press, 2000).

Hume, David, *A Treatise of Human Nature*, L. Selby-Bigge (ed.), 2nd edn., rev. P. H. Nidditch (Oxford: Clarendon Press, 1978 [1739–40]).

Hume, David, *An Enquiry Concerning the Principles of Morals*, T. L. Beauchamp (ed.) (Oxford: Oxford University Press, 1998 [1751]).

Hursthouse, Rosalind, 'Virtue Theory and Abortion', in D. Statman (ed.), *Virtue Ethics: A Critical Reader* (Washington, DC: Georgetown University Press, 1997), 227–44. (First publ. in *Philosophy and Public Affairs* 20 (1991), 223–46.).

Hursthouse, Rosalind, *On Virtue Ethics* (Oxford: Oxford University Press, 1999).

Huxley, T. H., *Method and Results: Essays* (London: Macmillan, 1893).

Irwin, T. H., 'Ethics as an Inexact Science', in B. Hooker and M. Little (eds.), *Moral Particularism* (Oxford: Oxford University Press, 2000), 100–29.

Jackson, Frank, Philip Pettit, and Michael Smith, 'Ethical Particularism and Patterns', in B. Hooker and M. O. Little (eds.) *Moral Particularism* (Oxford: Clarendon Press, 2000), 79–99.

Jacobs, Alan, 'The Liberal Neoplatonist?' (Review of Iris Murdoch, *Existentialists and Mystics*) *First Things* 89 (January 1999), 57–61.

Jaggar, A., 'Love and Knowledge: Emotion in Feminist Epistemology', in A. Garry and M. Pearsall (eds.), *Women, Knowledge, and Reality: Explorations in Feminist Philosophy* (Boston: Unwin Hyman, 1989; 2nd ed, New York: Routledge, 1996), 166–90. (First publ. in *Inquiry* 32 (1989), 151–76.).

James, William, *The Varieties of Religious Experiences, A Study in Human Nature: Being the Gifford Lectures on Natural Religion delivered at Edinburgh in 1901–1902* (New York/London: Longmans, Green, 1902).

Jansenius, Cornelius, *Augustinus* (Louvain, 1640), 3 tomes in 1 vol., folio.

Johns, J. H., & H. C. Quay, 'The effect of social reward on verbal conditioning in psychopathic and neurotic military offenders', *Journal of Consulting Psychology* 26 (1962), 217–20.

Jones, K., 'Second-Hand Moral Knowledge', *The Journal of Philosophy* 96:2 (1999), 55–78.

Kagan, Shelly, 'The Additive Fallacy', *Ethics* 99 (1988), 5–31.

Kamtekar, R., 'Situationism and Virtue Ethics on the Content of our Character', *Ethics* 114 (2004), 458–91.

Kant, Immanuel, *Critik der reinen Vernunft* (Riga: Johann Friedrich Hartknoch, 1781; 2nd edn. 1787).

Kant, Immanuel, [GMS] *Grundlegung zur Metaphysik der Sitten* (Riga: Johann Friedrich Hartknoch, 1785, 2nd edn. 1786).

Kant, Immanuel, [KpV] *Critik der practischen Vernunft* (Riga: Johann Friedrich Hartknoch, 1788).

Kant, Immanuel, *Critik der Urtheilskraft* (Berlin: Lagarde und Friederich, 1790, 1793).

Kant, Immanuel, *Metaphysik der Sitten* (Königsberg: F. Nicolovius, 1797).

Kant, Immanuel, [Ak.] *Gesammelte Schriften herausgegeben von der Königlich Preußischen Akademie der Wissenschaften.* Division I: 9 vols. (Berlin: G. Reimer, 1902–1923).

Kant, Immanuel, *The Critique of Judgement*, trans. J. C. Meredith (Oxford: Clarendon Press [1928], 1952).

Kant, Immanuel, *Immanuel Kant's Critique of Pure Reason*, trans. Norman Kemp Smith (London: Macmillan, 1929, 1933).

Kant, Immanuel, *The Moral Law, or, Kant's Groundwork of the Metaphysic of Morals*, trans. and analysed by H. J. Paton (London: Hutchinson University Library, 1948).

Kant, Immanuel, *Critique of Practical Reason*, trans. Lewis Beck ([1949]; New York: Liberal Arts Press, 1956, 3rd edn. 1993).

Kant, Immanuel, [FMM] *Foundations of the Metaphysics of Morals* (1785), in *Foundations of the Metaphysics of Morals and What is Enlightenment?*, trans., with introduction by Lewis White Beck (Indianapolis: Bobbs-Merrill/New York: Liberal Arts Press, 1959).

Kant, Immanuel, *Ethical Philosophy: the complete texts of Grounding for the Metaphysics of Morals, and Metaphysical Principles of Virtue, part II of the Metaphysics of Morals*, trans. James W. Ellington; introduction by Warner A. Wick (Indianapolis: Hackett, 1983).

Kant, Immanuel, *The Metaphysics of Morals*, trans. Mary Gregor (Cambridge: Cambridge University Press, 1991).

Kant, Immanuel, *Critique of Practical Reason*, trans. and ed. Mary Gregor (Cambridge: Cambridge University Press, 1997).

Kant, Immanuel, *Critique of the Power of Judgment*, trans. Paul Guyer and Eric Matthews (Cambridge: Cambridge University Press, 2000).

Katznelson, Ira, 'From the street to the lecture hall: The 1960s', *Daedalus: Proceedings of the American Academy of Arts and Sciences*, Winter 1997, 126 [1], 311–32.

Kearney, Richard, *The Wake of Imagination: Toward a Postmodern Culture* (Minneapolis: University of Minnesota Press, 1988).

Kearney, Richard, *Poetics of Imagining: Modernity to Postmodernity* (New York: Fordham University Press), 1998.

Kennett, J., 'Autism, Empathy and Moral Agency', *Philosophical Quarterly*, vol. 52 (2002), 340–57.

Kerr, Fergus, 'The Self and the Good: Taylor's Moral Ontology', in Ruth Abbey (ed.), *Charles Taylor* (Teddington: Acumen, 2000), 84–104.

Kierkegaard, Søren, *The Journals of Søren Kierkegaard: a selection*, ed. and trans. Alexander Dru (London: Oxford University Press, 1938).

Kierkegaard, Søren, *Fear and Trembling: A Dialectical Lyric by Johannes de Silentio*, trans. Robert Payne (London: Oxford University Press, 1939).

Kierkegaard, Søren, *The Sickness unto Death*, trans. Walter Lowrie (Princeton: Princeton University Press, 1941).

Kierkegaard, Søren, *Either/Or*. 2 vols. Vol. 1 trans. David F. Swenson and Lillian Marvin Swenson; vol. 2 trans. by Walter Lowrie (Princeton: Princeton University Press, 1944); with revisions and foreword by Howard A. Johnson (Garden City: Doubleday, 1959).

Kierkegaard, Søren, *Kierkegaard's Writings*, ed. & trans. Howard V. Hong & Edna H. Hong (Princeton: Princeton University Press, 1978–2000, 26 vols.).

Köhler, Wolfgang, *The Place of Value in a World of Facts* (New York: Liveright, 1938).

Kojève, Alexandre, *Introduction à la lecture de Hegel; leçons sur la Phénoménologie de l'esprit, professées de 1933 à 1939 à l'École des hautes-études*, réunies et pub. par Raymond Queneau (Paris: Gallimard, 1947; 2nd ed., 1968).

Kojève, Alexandre, *Introduction to the Reading of Hegel*, Allan Bloom (ed.), trans. James H. Nichols (New York: Basic Books, 1969).

Korsgaard, Christine, [FD] 'From Duty and for the Sake of the Noble: Kant and Aristotle on Morally Good Action', in S. Engstrom and J. Whiting (eds.), *Aristotle, Kant, and the Stoics: Rethinking Happiness and Duty* (Cambridge: Cambridge University Press, 1996), 203–36.

Krikpe, Saul, *Wittgenstein on Rules and Private Language: An elementary exposition* (Oxford: Blackwell/Cambridge: Harvard University Press, 1982).

Larson, Kate, *"Everything Important is to do with Passion": Iris Murdoch's Concept of Love and its Platonic Origin* (Ph. D thesis, Uppsala: Dept. of Philosophy, Uppsala University, 2009).

Laverty, Megan, 'Narrative and the unity of a life: the ethical significance of Kant's *Critique of Judgement*' (Ph. D thesis, University of New South Wales, 2000).

Laverty, Megan, *Iris Murdoch's Ethics* (London: Continuum, 2007).

Lear, Jonathan, 'Restlessness, Phantasy, and the Concept of the Mind', in his *Open Minded: Working out the Logic of the Soul* (Cambridge, Mass.: Harvard University Press, 1998), 80–122.

Leibniz, G. W., *Philosophical Essays*, ed. & trans. R. Ariew & D. Garber (Indianapolis: Hackett, 1989).

Liddell, H. G., and R. Scott, *Greek-English Lexicon* (Oxford: Clarendon Press, 1843; 9th edn., rev. H. S. Jones, 1940).

Lloyd, A. C., 'Thinking and Language', *Proceedings of the Aristotelian Society* Supplementary vol. 25 (1951), 35–64.

Loeb, Don, 'Generality and Moral Justification', *Philosophy and Phenomenological Research* 56 (March 1996), 79–96.

Louden, R., 'On Some Vices of Virtue Ethics', in R. Crisp and M. Slote (eds.), *Virtue Ethics* (Oxford: Oxford University Press, 1997), 201–16. (First publ. in *American Philosophical Quarterly* 21 (1984), 227–36.).

Lovibond, Sabina, [RIE] *Realism and Imagination in Ethics* (Oxford: Basil Blackwell/Minneapolis: University of Minneapolis Press, 1983).

Lovibond, Sabina, *Ethical Formation* (Cambridge, Mass.: Harvard University Press, 2002).

Lugones, M., 'Playfulness, "World-Traveling," and Loving Perception', in A. Garry and M. Pearsall (eds.), *Women, Knowledge, and Reality: Explorations in Feminist Philosophy* (Boston: Unwin Hyman, Inc., 1989; 2nd ed., New York: Routledge, 1996), 419–33. (First publ. in *Hypatia* 2(2) (Summer 1987), 3–19.)

Mackenzie, N., (ed.), *Conviction* (London: MacGibbon & Kee, 1958).

Mackie, J. L., *Ethics: Inventing Right and Wrong* (Harmondsworth: Penguin, 1977).

MacKinnon, Donald M., 'Things and Persons', *Proceedings of the Aristotelian Society*, suppl. vol. 22 (1948), 179–89.

MacKinnon, Donald M., *A Study in Ethical Theory* (London: Adam & Charles Black, 1957).

MacKinnon, Donald M., *The Problem of Metaphysics* (Gifford Lectures 1965 & 1966) (Cambridge: Cambridge University Press, 1972).

MacKinnon, Donald M., *Borderlands of Theology and other Essays*, ed. G. W. Roberts and D. E. Smucker (London: Lutterworth/Philadelphia & New York: J. B. Lippincott, 1968).

Marcel, Gabriel, *Être et avoir* (Paris: F. Aubier, Éditions Montaigne, 1935).

Martin, Priscilla, and Anne Rowe, *Iris Murdoch: A Literary Life* (Basingstoke/New York: Palgrave Macmillan, 2010).

Marx, Karl, *Das Kapital. Kritik der politischen Oekonomie*, vol. 1 (Hamburg: O. Meissner, 1867, 1872); vol. 2, ed. Friedrich Engels (Hamburg: O. Meissner, 1885); vol. 3, ed. Friedrich Engels (Hamburg: O. Meissner, 1894).

Marx, Karl, *Grundrisse der Kritik der politischen Ökonomie (Rohentwurf) 1857–1858* (Moskau: Verlag für fremdsprachige Literatur, 1939).

Marx, Karl, *Grundrisse: Foundations of the Critique of Political Economy (Rough Draft)*, trans. Martin Nicolaus (Harmondsworth: Penguin, 1973).

Marx, Karl, *Early Writings*, trans. R. Livingstone & G. Benton (Harmondsworth: Penguin, 1975).

Marx, Karl, *Capital: a Critique of Political Economy*, 3 vols, trans. B. Fowkes (Harmondsworth: Penguin, 1976–1981).

Mathewes, Charles T., 'Agency, Nature, Transcendence, and Moralism: A Review of Recent Work in Moral Psychology', *Journal of Religious Ethics* 28, 2 (Summer 2000), 297–328.

McDowell, John, *Plato: Theaetetus*, trans. with notes by John McDowell (Oxford: Clarendon Press, 1973).

McDowell, John, [AMR] 'Are Moral Requirements Hypothetical Imperatives?', *Proceedings of the Aristotelian Society*, suppl. vol. 52 (1978), 13–29; repr. in McDowell, *Mind, Value, and Reality*, 77–94.

McDowell, John, [VR] 'Virtue and Reason', *The Monist* 62 (1979), 331–50; repr. in McDowell, *Mind, Value, and Reality*, 50–73.

McDowell, John, 'The Role of Eudaimonia in Aristotle's Ethics', in A. O. Rorty (ed.), *Essays on Aristotle's Ethics* (Berkeley: Univ. of California Press, 1980); repr. in McDowell, *Mind, Value and Reality*, 3–22.

McDowell, John, [NCRF] 'Non-Cognitivism and Rule-Following', in S. Holtzman & C. Leich (eds.), *Wittgenstein: to Follow a Rule* (London: Routledge & Kegan Paul, 1981), 141–62; repr. in McDowell, *Mind, Value, and Reality*, 198–218.

McDowell, John, [AVO] 'Aesthetic Value, Objectivity, and the Fabric of the World', in Eva Schaper, (ed.), *Pleasure, Preference, and Value* (Cambridge: Cambridge University Press, 1983), 1–16; repr. in McDowell, *Mind, Value, and Reality* (1998), 112–130.

McDowell, John, 'Wittgenstein on Following a Rule', *Synthese* 58 (1984) 325–63; repr. in McDowell, *Mind, Value, and Reality* (1998), 221–62.

McDowell, John, [VSQ] 'Values and Secondary Qualities', in Ted Honderich (ed.), *Morality and Objectivity* (London: Routledge, 1985), 110–29; repr. in McDowell, *Mind, Value, and Reality*, 131–150.

McDowell, John, 'Critical Notice of Bernard Williams, *Ethics and the Limits of Philosophy*', *Mind* 95 (1986), 377–86.

McDowell, John, *Mind and World* (Cambridge, Mass.: Harvard University Press, 1994).

McDowell, John, 'Might there be External Reasons?', in J. E. J. Altham and R. Harrison (eds.), *World, Mind, and Ethics: Essays on the Ethical Philosophy of Bernard Williams* (Cambridge: Cambridge University Press, 1995); repr. in McDowell, *Mind, Value & Reality*, 95–111.

McDowell, John, [TSN] 'Two Sorts of Naturalism', in R. Hursthouse, G. Lawrence, and W. Quinn (eds.), *Virtues and Reasons: Philippa Foot and moral theory: Essays in honour of Philippa Foot* (Oxford: Clarendon Press, 1995) 149–79; repr. in McDowell, *Mind, Value and Reality*, 167–97.

McDowell, John, [SIA] 'Some Issues in Aristotle's Moral Psychology', in Stephen Everson (ed.), *Ethics* (Cambridge: Cambridge University Press, 1998), 107–28; repr. in McDowell, *Mind, Value, and Reality* (1998), 23–49.

McDowell, John, [MVR] *Mind, Value, & Reality* (Cambridge, Mass.: Harvard University Press, 1998).

McDowell, John, Response to Crispin Wright, in 'Responses', in Nicholas H. Smith (ed.), *Reading McDowell on Mind and World* (London: Routledge, 2002), 269–305.

McGuinness, Brian, *Wittgenstein, A Life: Young Ludwig (1889–1921)* (London: Duckworth, 1988).

McGuinness, Brian, and Charlotte Vrijen, 'First thoughts: An unpublished letter from Gilbert Ryle to H. J. Paton', *British Journal for the History of Philosophy* 14 (2006), 747–56.

McKinsey, Michael, 'Anti-individualism and privileged access', *Analysis* 51 (1991): 9–16.

McLean, Mark, 'On Muffling Murdoch', *Ratio* 13 (2000), 191–8.

McNeil, E., *The Quiet Furies* (Englewood Cliffs, New Jersey: Prentice-Hall, 1967).

Mehta, Ved, *Fly and the Flybottle* (London: Weidenfeld & Nicolson, 1963; Harmondworth: Penguin, 1965).

Meyers, Diana T., *Subjection and Subjectivity: Psychoanalytic Feminism and Moral Philosophy* (New York: Routledge, 1994).

Meyers, Jeffrey, *Privileged Moments: Encounters with Writers* (Madison: University of Wisconsin, 2000).

Midgley, Mary, 'Is "Moral" a Dirty Word?', *Philosophy* 47 (1972), 206–28.

Midgley, Mary, 'The Objection to Systematic Humbug', *Philosophy* 53 (1978), 147–69.

Midgley, Mary, *The Owl of Minerva: A Memoir* (London & New York: Routledge, 2005).

Migne, J.-P., [Patrologia latina] *Patrologiae cursus completus: sive biblioteca universalis, integra, uniformis, commoda, oeconomica, omnium SS. Patrum, doctorum scriptorumque eccelesiasticorum...* 221 vols (Paris: Migne, 1844–55).

Mill, J. S., *Utilitarianism*, ed. R. Crisp (Oxford: Oxford University Press, 1998 [1861]).

Millgram, Elijah, 'Inhaltsreiche ethische Begriffe und die Unterscheidung zwischen Tatsachen und Werten', in C. Fehige and G. Meggle (eds.), *Zum moralischen Denken* (Frankfurt am Main: Suhrkamp, 1995), 354–88.

Millgram, Elijah (ed.), *Varieties of Practical Reasoning* (Cambridge, Mass.: MIT Press, 2001).

Millgram, Elijah, 'Murdoch, Practical Reasoning, and Particularism', *Notizie di Politeia* 18 (66) (2002), 64–87; repr. in Millgram, *Ethics Done Right* (Cambridge: Cambridge University Press, 2005), 168–197.

Millgram, Elijah, 'Kantian Crystallization', *Ethics* 114 (2004), 511–3.

Millgram, Elijah, *Ethics Done Right: Practical Reasoning as a Foundation for Moral Theory* (Cambridge/New York: Cambridge University Press, 2005).

Mitchell, Basil, *Morality: Religious and Secular: The Dilemma of the Traditional Conscience* (Oxford: Clarendon Press, 1980).

Molina, Luis de, *Concordia liberi arbitrii cum gratiae donis...Ludovico Molina auctore* (Olyssipone [i.e. Lisbon]: Apud Antonium Riberium, 1588–89).

Montaigne, Michel de, 'Of Experience', in *The Complete Essays of Montaigne*, trans. Donald M. Frame (Stanford: Stanford University Press, 1958), 815–57.

Moore, G. E., *Principia Ethica* (Cambridge: Cambridge University Press, 1903).

Moore, G. E., 'Replies to my Critics', in P. A. Schilpp (ed.), *The Philosophy of G. E. Moore* (Evanston, Chicago: Northwestern University, 1942), 535–677.

Morgan, David, *With Love and Rage: A Friendship with Iris Murdoch* (Kingston: Kingston University Press, 2010).

Mulhall, Stephen, 'Constructing a Hall of Reflection: Perfectionist Edification in Iris Murdoch's *Metaphysics as a Guide to Morals*', *Philosophy* 72 (1997), 219–39.

Mulhall, Stephen, 'Misplacing Freedom, Displacing the Imagination: Cavell and Murdoch on the fact/value distinction', in A. O'Hear (ed.), *Philosophy, the Good, the True and the Beautiful: The 1998–9 Royal Institute of Philosophy Annual Lectures* (Cambridge: Cambridge University Press, 2000), 23–34.

Mulhall, Stephen, ' "All the world must be 'religious' "': Iris Murdoch's Ontological Arguments', in Anne Rowe (ed.), *Iris Murdoch: A Reassessment* (London: Palgrave Macmillan, 2006).

Murdoch, Iris, [NM] 'The Novelist as Metaphysician', *The Listener* vol. XLIII no. 1103 (16 March 1950); repr. in E&M 101–107.

Murdoch, Iris, [EH] 'The Existentialist Hero', *The Listener* vol. XLIII no. 1104 (23 March 1950); repr. in E&M 108–115.

Murdoch, Iris, [T&L] 'Thinking and Language', *Proceedings of the Aristotelian Society* suppl. vol. 25 (1951), 25–34; repr. in E&M 33–42.

Murdoch, Iris, [NP] 'Nostalgia for the Particular', *Proceedings of the Aristotelian Society* 52 (1951–52), 243–60; repr. in E&M 43–58.

Murdoch, Iris, [EPM] 'The Existentialist Political Myth', *Socratic Digest* 5 (Oxford: Basil Blackwell, 1952); repr. in E&M 130–145.

Murdoch, Iris, [SRR] *Sartre: Romantic Rationalist* (London: Bowes and Bowes/New Haven: Yale U. P., 1953, 78pp.); paperback with revised bibliography and biographical note (Glasgow: Fontana/Collins, 1967, 128pp).

—— 'Second edition' [but with text identical to 1953 edn.] under title *Sartre: Romantic Realist* (Sussex: Harvester Press/New York: Barnes & Noble, 1980, 78 pp.).

—— *Sartre: Romantic Rationalist* [with new introduction] (London: Chatto & Windus/NY: The Viking Press, 1987, 158 pp); paperback (Penguin, 1989).

Murdoch, Iris, [UN] *Under the Net: A Novel* (London: Chatto & Windus, 1954; Penguin, 1960).

Murdoch, Iris, et al. 'Philosophy and Beliefs: A Discussion between four Oxford Philosophers' (1955): *see under* Quinton, A.

Murdoch, Iris, [FFE] *The Flight from the Enchanter* (London: Chatto & Windus, 1956; Penguin, 1962).

Murdoch, Iris, [VCM] 'Vision and Choice in Morality', *Proceedings of the Aristotelian Society*, suppl. vol. 30 (1956), 32–58; repr. with omissions in E&M 76–98.

Murdoch, Iris, [KV] 'Knowing the Void', Review of *The Notebooks of Simone Weil*, 2 vols., trans. and ed. Arthur Wills (1956), *The Spectator* no. 6697 (2 November 1956), 613–14; repr. in E&M 157–61.

Murdoch, Iris, [M&E] 'Metaphysics and Ethics', in D. F. Pears (ed.), *The Nature of Metaphysics* (London: Macmillan, 1957), 99–123; repr. in E&M 59–76.

Murdoch, Iris, [HMD] 'Hegel in Modern Dress', Review of J.-P. Sartre, *Being and Nothingness*, trans. Hazel E. Barnes (1957), *New Statesman and Nation* (May, 1957); repr. in E&M 146–150.

Murdoch, Iris, [HT] 'A House of Theory', in N. Mackenzie (ed.), *Conviction* (London: Mac-Gibbon & Kee, 1958); repr. in *Partisan Review* 26.1 (Winter 1959), 17–31; and in *Power and Civilization: Political Thought in the Twentieth Century*, D. Cooperman and E. Victor (eds.) (New York, 1962), 442–55; repr. in E&M 171–86; first 3 paragraphs repr. in *The Daily Times* (Pakistan), November 18, 2003.

Murdoch, Iris, [B] *The Bell* (London: Chatto & Windus, 1958; London: Penguin, 1962); with an introduction by A. S. Byatt (London: Vintage, 1999).

Murdoch, Iris, [S&G] 'The Sublime and the Good', *Chicago Review* (Autumn 1959), 42–55; repr. in E&M 205–221.

Murdoch, Iris, [SBR] 'The Sublime and the Beautiful Revisited', *Yale Review* 49 (2) (December 1959), 247–71; repr. in E&M 261–286.

Murdoch, Iris, 'Words and Ideas' (Review of Ernest Gellner, *Words and Things*), *Partisan Review* 27 (Spring 1960), 348–53.

Murdoch, Iris, [AD] 'Against Dryness: A Polemical Sketch', *Encounter* 16 (1) (January 1961), 16–20; repr. in E&M 287–295.

Murdoch, Iris, [U] *The Unicorn* (London: Chatto & Windus, 1963; Harmondsworth: Penguin, 1966).

Murdoch, Iris, [IP] 'The Idea of Perfection', *The Yale Review* LIII (3) (March 1964): 342–380; repr. in *The Sovereignty of Good*, 1–45, and in E&M 299–336.

Murdoch, Iris, [MDH] 'The Moral Decision about Homosexuality', *Man and Society* 7 (1964), 3–6.

Murdoch, Iris, [DPR] 'The Darkness of Practical Reason', review of Stuart Hampshire, *Freedom of the Individual* (1965), *Encounter* 27 (1) (July 1966), 46–50; repr. in E&M 193–202.

Murdoch, Iris, [SGC] *The Sovereignty of Good over other Concepts: The Leslie Stephen Lecture 1967* (Cambridge: Cambridge University Press, 1967); repr. in *The Sovereignty of Good*, 77–104, and in E&M 363–385.

Murdoch, Iris, [NG] *The Nice and the Good* (London: Chatto & Windus, 1968; Harmondsworth: Penguin, 1969).

Murdoch, Iris, [OGG] 'On "God" and "Good"', in Marjorie Grene (ed.), *The Anatomy of Knowledge* (1969), 233–58; repr. in *The Sovereignty of Good*, 46–76, and in E&M 337–362.

Murdoch, Iris, [SG] *The Sovereignty of Good* (London: Routledge & Kegan Paul, 1970; New York: Schocken, 1971).

Murdoch, Iris, [FHD] *A Fairly Honourable Defeat* (London: Chatto & Windus, 1970; Penguin, 1972).

Murdoch, Iris, 'Existentialists and Mystics', in W. W. Robson (ed.), *Essays & Poems Presented to Lord David Cecil* (London: Constable, 1970); repr. in E&M 221–34.

Murdoch, Iris, [SW] 'Salvation by Words', *New York Review of Books*, June 15, 1972 (part of the Blashfield Address to the American Academy of Arts and Letters, 17 May 1972); repr. in E&M 235–42.

Murdoch, Iris, [BP] *The Black Prince* (London: Chatto & Windus, 1973; Penguin, 1975); with an introduction by Martha C. Nussbaum (New York: Penguin, 2003).

Murdoch, Iris, [SPLM] *The Sacred and Profane Love Machine* (London: Chatto & Windus, 1974; Penguin, 1976).

Murdoch, Iris, [F&S] *The Fire and the Sun: Why Plato Banished the Artists* (Oxford: Clarendon Press, 1977); repr. in E&M 386–464.

Murdoch, Iris, *The Sea, The Sea* (London: Chatto & Windus, 1978; Harmondsworth: Penguin, 1980); with an introduction by Mary Kinzie (New York: Penguin, 2001).

Murdoch, Iris, *Acastos: Two Platonic Dialogues* (London: Chatto and Windus, 1986); repr. in E&M 464–531.

Murdoch, Iris, [E&I] 'Ethics and the Imagination', *Irish Theological Quarterly*, 52 (1986), 81–95.

Murdoch, Iris, [MGM] *Metaphysics as a Guide to Morals* (London: Chatto and Windus, 1992; New York: Allen Lane, 1993; London: Penguin, 1993).

Murdoch, Iris, [JD] *Jackson's Dilemma* (London: Chatto & Windus, 1995; London: Penguin, 1996).

Murdoch, Iris, [E&M] *Existentialists and Mystics: Writings on Philosophy and Literature*, Peter J. Conradi (ed.), foreword by George Steiner (London: Chatto & Windus, 1997; New York: Allen Lane The Penguin Press, 1998; Penguin, 1999).

Murdoch, Iris, *A Writer at War: Letters and Diaries 1939–45* (i.e. 1938–46), ed. & introduced by Peter J. Conradi (London: Short Books, 2010).

Murdoch, Iris, 'Postscript on Politics' [unpublished Postscript (1966) to 'On "God" and "Good"'], *Iris Murdoch Review* (forthcoming, 2011).

Murphy, J., 'Moral Death: A Kantian Essay on Psychopathy', *Ethics* 82 (1972), 284–98.

Nagel, T., *The Possibility of Altruism* (Princeton: Princeton University Press, 1970).

Nichol, Bran J., *Iris Murdoch: The Retrospective Fiction* (New York: Palgrave Macmillan, 2004).

Nichols, Shaun, 'Mindreading and the Cognitive Architecture underlying Altruistic Motivation', *Mind and Language*, 16 (2001), 425–55.

Nichols, Shaun, 'How Psychopaths Threaten Moral Rationalism, or Is it Irrational to Be Amoral?', *The Monist* 85 (2002), 285–304.

Nichols, Shaun, 'Norms with feeling: Towards a psychological account of moral judgment', *Cognition* 84 (2002), 221–36.

Nichols, Shaun, *Sentimental Rules* (Oxford: Oxford University Press, 2004).

Nichols, Shaun, and S. Stich, *Mindreading* (Oxford: Oxford University Press, 2004).

Norgaard, T., 'Murdoch, Iris', in E. Craig (ed.), *Routledge Encyclopedia of Philosophy*, online version www.rep.routledge.com, 2002.

Nussbaum, Martha, *The Fragility of Goodness: Luck and Ethics in Greek Tragedy* (Cambridge: Cambridge University Press, 1986, rev. edn. 2001).

Nussbaum, Martha, 'Reply to David Halperin', *Proceedings of the Boston Area Colloquium in Ancient Philosophy* 4 (1989), 53–72.

Nussbaum, Martha, *Love's Knowledge: Essays on Philosophy and Literature* (New York/Oxford: Oxford University Press, 1990).

Nussbaum, Martha, 'Beatrice's "Dante": Loving the Individual?', in *Virtue, Love, and Form: Essays in Memory of Gregory Vlastos*, Terence Irwin and Martha Nussbaum (eds.), (Edmonton: Academic Printing & Publishing, 1993); =*Apeiron* 26 (1993), numbers 3 and 4, 161–78.

Nussbaum, Martha, 'Eros and the Wise: the Stoic Response to a Cultural Dilemma', *Oxford Studies in Ancient Philosophy* 13 (1995), 231–67.

Nussbaum, Martha, *Poetic Justice: The Literary Imagination and Public Life* (Boston: Beacon Press, 1995).

Nussbaum, Martha, 'Love and Vision: Iris Murdoch on Eros and the Individual', in *Iris Murdoch and the Search for Human Goodness*, M. Antonaccio and W. Schweiker (eds.), (Chicago: University of Chicago Press, 1996), 29–53.

Nussbaum, Martha, 'Aristotle on Human Nature and the Foundations of Ethics', in J. E. J. Altham and R. Harrison (eds.), *World, Mind, and Ethics* (Cambridge: Cambridge University Press, 1996), 86–131.

Nussbaum, Martha, 'Platonic Love and Colorado Law', in M. Nussbaum, *Sex and Social Justice* (New York: Oxford University Press, 1999), 299–331. (Abridgment of article first publ. in *Virginia Law Review* 80 (1991), 1515–651.)

Nussbaum, Martha, 'Virtue Ethics: A Misleading Category?' *The Journal of Ethics* 3 (1999), 163–201.

Nussbaum, Martha, 'Why Practice Needs Ethical Theory: Particularism, Principle, and Bad Behaviour', in B. Hooker and M. Little (eds.), *Moral Particularism* (Oxford: Oxford University Press, 2000), 227–55.

Nussbaum, Martha, *Upheavals of Thought: The Intelligence of Emotions* (Cambridge: Cambridge University Press, 2001).

Nussbaum, Martha, 'When She Was Good', Review of Peter J. Conradi, *Iris Murdoch: A Life*, *The New Republic* (31 December, 2001), vol. 225 issue 27/28, 28–34.

O'Connor, F., *The Habit of Being: Letters of Flannery O'Connor*, S. Fitzgerald (ed.) (New York: Random House/Vintage Books, 1980).

O'Connor, Patricia J., 'The Moral Philosophy of Iris Murdoch' (Ph. D. thesis, University of Exeter, School of English, 1990).

O'Connor, Patricia J., *To Love the Good: The Moral Philosophy of Iris Murdoch* (New York: Peter Lang, 1996).

O'Neill, Onora, *Towards Justice and Virtue: A Constructive Account of Practical Reasoning* (Cambridge: Cambridge University Press, 1996).

Pascal, Blaise, *Opuscules et pensées*, ed. Léon Brunschvicg (6th edn., Paris: Hachette, 1912).

Paton, H. J., 'The Alleged Independence of Goodness', in P. A. Schilpp (ed.), *The Philosophy of G. E. Moore* (Evanston, Chicago: Northwestern University, 1942), 111–34.

Pears, D. F., (ed.), *The Nature of Metaphysics* (London: Macmillan, 1957).

Pears, D. F., (ed.), *David Hume: A Symposium* (London: Macmillan, 1963).

Pears, D. F., (ed.), *Freedom and the Will* (London: Macmillan, 1963).

Phillips, D. Z., 'Does it pay to be good?' *Proceedings of the Aristotelian Society* 65 (1964–65), 45–60.

Pincoffs, Edmund L., 'Quandary Ethics', *Mind* 80 (1971), 552–71.

Pinkard, Terry, 'Virtues, Morality, and *Sittlichkeit*: From Maxims to Practices', *European Journal of Philosophy* 7 (1999), 217–38.

Piper, Adrian, 'Higher-Order Discrimination', in O. Flanagan and A. O. Rorty (eds.), *Identity, Character, and Morality* (Cambridge, Mass.: MIT, 1990), 285–309.

Plato, *The Collected Dialogues of Plato*, Edith Hamilton and Huntington Cairns (eds.)(New York: Pantheon Books, 1961; Princeton: Princeton University Press, 1963).

Plato, *Theaetetus*, trans. with notes by John McDowell (Oxford: Clarendon Press, 1973).

Plato, *Complete Works*, John M. Cooper (ed.), D. S. Hutchinson assoc. ed. (Indianapolis/Cambridge: Hackett, 1997).

Price, A. W., *Love and Friendship in Plato and Aristotle* (Oxford: Clarendon Press, 1989).

Proust, Marcel, *Remembrance of Things Past*, trans. C. K. Scott Moncrieff and Terence Kilmartin (London: Chatto & Windus/New York: Random House, 1981, 3 vols).

Purton, Valerie, *An Iris Murdoch Chronology* (Basingstoke: Palgrave Macmillan, 2007).

Putnam, Hilary, 'The Analytic and the Synthetic' (1962), repr. in *Mind, Language, and Reality* (Cambridge: Cambridge University Press, 1975), 33–69.

Putnam, Hilary, *Philosophical Papers*, vol. 2 *Mind, Language, and Reality* (Cambridge: Cambridge University Press, 1975).

Putnam, Hilary, 'The Place of Facts in a World of Values', in D. Huff and O. Prewett (eds.), *The Nature of the Physical Universe: 1976 Nobel Conference* (New York: John Wiley, 1979), 113–40; repr. in H. Putnam, *Realism with a Human Face* (1990), 142–62.

Putnam, Hilary, 'Objectivity and the Science/Ethics Distinction', in H. Putnam, *Realism with a Human Face* (1990), 163–78.

Putnam, Hilary, *Realism with a Human Face*, J. Conant (ed.) (Cambridge, Mass.: Harvard University Press, 1990).

Putnam, Hilary, *The Collapse of the Fact/Value Dichotomy and other Essays* (Cambridge, Mass.: Harvard University Press, 2002).

Queneau, Raymond, *Pierrot mon ami, roman* (Paris: Gallimard, 1943).

Quinton, Anthony, Stuart Hampshire, Iris Murdoch, Isaiah Berlin, 'Philosophy and Beliefs: A Discussion between four Oxford Philosophers', *The Twentieth Century* (Formerly *The Nineteenth Century and After*) vol. clvii Number 940 (June 1955), 495–521.

Railton, P., 'Alienation, Consequentialism, and the Demands of Morality', *Philosophy and Public Affairs* 13 (1984), 134–71.

Raine, Kathleen, *Autobiographies* (London: Skoob, 1991).

Raphael, Frederic, (ed.), *Bookmarks* (London: Jonathan Cape, 1975).

Rawls, John, *Lectures on the History of Moral Philosophy*, Barbara Herman (ed.) (Cambridge, Mass.: Harvard University Press, 2000).

Raz, Joseph, 'The Truth in Particularism', in B. Hooker and M. O. Little (eds.), *Moral Particularism* (Oxford: Clarendon Press, 2000), 48–78.

Rhees, Rush, (ed.), *Recollections of Wittgenstein* (Oxford: Oxford University Press, 1984). (First publ. under the title *Ludwig Wittgenstein: Personal Recollections* (Oxford: Basil Blackwell, 1981).)

Ricciardi, Mario, 'Philosophy, Literature, and Life', *Notizie di Politeia* 66 (2002), 5–21.

Richardson, Henry, 'Specifying Norms as a Way to Resolve Concrete Ethical Problems', *Philosophy and Public Affairs* 19 (1990), 306–31.

Richardson, Henry, *Practical Reasoning About Final Ends* (New York: Cambridge University Press, 1994).

Roberts, Dorothy, *Killing the Black Body: Race, Reproduction, and the Meaning of Liberty* (New York: Vintage, 1997).

Robjant, David, 'The River as a Guide to Iris Murdoch'. (Ph. D. thesis, University of Wales, Lampeter [now University of Wales Trinity St David], 2008.)

Robjant, David, 'As a Buddhist Christian: The Misappropriation of Iris Murdoch', *Heythrop Journal*, forthcoming.

Robjant, David, 'Is Iris Murdoch a Closet Existentialist? Some Trouble with Vision, Choice and Exegesis.', *European Journal of Philosophy*, forthcoming.

Rowe, Anne (ed.), *Iris Murdoch: A Reassessment* (London: Palgrave Macmillan, 2007).

Ryle, Gilbert, *The Concept of Mind* (London: Hutchinson, 1949; Harmondsworth: Penguin, 1963).

Ryle, Gilbert, 'Thinking and Language', *Proceedings of the Aristotelian Society* suppl. vol. 25 (1951), 65–82.

Ryle, Gilbert, *Dilemmas* (Cambridge: Cambridge University Press, 1954).

Sabini, J., and M. Silver, 'Lack of Character? Situationism Critiqued', *Ethics* 115 (2005), 535–62.

Sale, Kirkpatrick, *SDS* (New York: Random House, 1973; Vintage Books, 1974).

Sartre, J.-P., *L'être et le néant* (Paris: Gallimard, 1943).

——. *Being and Nothingness: An Essay on Phenomenological Ontology*, transl. with introduction by Hazel Barnes (New York: Philosophical Library, 1956; London: Methuen, 1958). UK paperback with introduction by Mary Warnock (London: Methuen, University Paperbacks); new edn. (London: Routledge, 2003).

——. (US paperback:) *Being and Nothingness: A Phenomenological Essay on Ontology*, trans. with introduction by Hazel E. Barnes (New York: Washington Square Press, 1966).

Scheman, N., 'Feeling Our Way to Moral Objectivity', in L. May, M. Friedman, and A. Clark (eds.), *Mind and Morals* (Cambridge, Mass.: MIT, 1996), 221–36.

Schopenhauer, A., *On the Basis of Morality*, trans. E. Payne ([1965]; rev. edn., Providence, RI: Berghahn, 1995).

Schweiker, William, *Responsibility and Christian Ethics* (Cambridge: Cambridge University Press, 1995).

Schweiker, William, 'Consciousness and the Good: Schleiermacher and Contemporary Theological Ethics', *Theology Today* 56.2 (July 1999), 180–96.

Scruton, R., *The Aesthetics of Music* (Oxford: Clarendon Press, 1997).

Sekida, Katsuki, *Zen Training: Methods and Philosophy*, A. V. Grimstone (ed.) (New York: Weatherhill, 1975).

Shafer-Landau, Russ, 'Moral Rules', *Ethics* 107 (July 1997), 584–611.

Shafer-Landau, Russ, *Moral Realism: A Defence* (Oxford: Clarendon Press, 2003).

Shapiro, David, [NS] *Neurotic Styles* (New York: Basic Books, 1965).

Shipler, D., *A Country of Strangers: Blacks and Whites in America* (New York: Alfred A. Knopf, 1997).

Sibley, F. N. 'Aesthetic Concepts', *Philosophical Review* 68 (1959), 421–50.

Sinnott-Armstrong, Walter, 'Some Varieties of Particularism', *Metaphilosophy* 30 (January/April 1999), 1–12.

Slote, M., *Common-sense Morality and Consequentialism* (London: Routledge, 1985).

Smith, Adam, *The Theory of the Moral Sentiments*, D. D. Raphael and A. L. Macfie (eds.) (Oxford: Clarendon Press, 1976 [1759]).

Smith, Nicholas H., (ed.), *Reading McDowell on Mind and World* (London: Routledge, 2002).

Steiner, Franz Baerman, *Selected Writings*, ed. and with introduction by Jeremy Adler and Richard Fardon (New York: Berghahn Books, 1999).

Stevenson, C. L., 'The Emotive Meaning of Ethical Terms', *Mind* 46 (1937), 14–31.

Stevenson, C. L., [EL] *Ethics and Language* (New Haven: Yale University Press, 1944).

Tager-Flusberg, H., 'What language reveals about the understanding of minds in children with autism', in S. Baron-Cohen, H. Tager-Flusberg & D. Cohen (eds.), *Understanding Other Minds: Perspectives from Autism* (Cambridge: Cambridge University Press, 1993) 133–58.

Tan, J., and P. Harris, 'Autistic children understand seeing and wanting', *Development and Psychopathology* 3 (1991), 163–74.

Taylor, Charles, *Hegel* (Cambridge: Cambridge University Press, 1975).

Taylor, Charles, *Language and Human Agency: Philosophical Papers* vol. 1 (Cambridge: Cambridge University Press, 1985).

Taylor, Charles, [PHS] *Philosophy and the Human Sciences: Philosophical Papers* vol. 2 (Cambridge: Cambridge University Press, 1985).

Taylor, Charles, [SS] *Sources of the Self: The Making of the Modern Identity* (Cambridge: Cambridge University Press/Cambridge, Mass.: Harvard University Press, 1989).

Taylor, Charles, 'Iris Murdoch and Moral Philosophy', in M. Antonaccio and W. Schweiker (eds.), *Iris Murdoch and the Search for Human Goodness* (Chicago: University of Chicago Press, 1996), 3–28.

Tertullian, *de Carne Christi Liber, Tertullian's Treatise on the Incarnation. The text edited with an introduction, trans., and commentary* by Ernest Evans (London: SPCK, 1956).

Toulmin, Stephen, *An Examination of the Place of Reason in Ethics* (Cambridge: Cambridge University Press, 1950).

Trunski, Slavcho, *Grateful Bulgaria* (Sofia: Sofia Press, 1979).

Velleman, J. David, [LME] 'Love as a Moral Emotion', *Ethics* 109 (1999), 338–74.

Vermazen, B., and M. B. Hintikka, (eds.), *Essays on Davidson: Actions and Events* (Oxford: Clarendon Press, 1985).

Waismann, Friedrich, *Wittgenstein and the Vienna Circle, conversations recorded by Friedrich Waismann*, ed. Brian McGuinness, trans. J. Schulte and B. McGuinness (Oxford: Blackwell, 1979).

Wallace, R. J. 'Virtue, Reason, and Principle', *Canadian Journal of Philosophy* 21 (1991), 469–95.

Warnock, Mary, *Ethics Since 1900* (London: Oxford University Press, 1960, 1966).

Warnock, Mary, *The Philosophy of Sartre* (London: Hutchinson, 1965).

Warnock, Mary, *An Intelligent Person's Guide to Ethics* (London: Duckworth Overlook, 1998).

Warnock, Mary, *Mary Warnock: A Memoir: People and Places* (London: Duckworth, 2000).

Weil, Simone, *La pesanteur et la grâce*, avec une introd. par Gustave Thibon (Paris: Plon, 1948).

——, trans. by Arthur Wills, as *Gravity and Grace* (London: Routledge & Kegan Paul/New York: Putnam, 1952).

Weil, Simone, *Attente de Dieu: Lettres et réflexions*, introd. et notes de J. M. Perrin (Paris: La Colombe, 1950).

——, trans. Emma Craufurd as *Waiting on God* (London: Routledge & Kegan Paul, 1951). Also issued in U.S.A. as *Waiting for God*, with introduction by Leslie A. Fiedler (New York: Putnam, 1951).

Weil, Simone, *La connaissance surnaturelle* (Paris: Gallimard, 1950).

Weil, Simone, *Cahiers* (Paris: Plon, 3 vols., 1951, 1953, 1956).

Weil, Simone, *Notebooks*, trans. Arthur Wills, 2 vols. (London: Routledge & Kegan Paul/New York: Putnam, 1956).

Weiser, B., 'My Name is not Robert', *The New York Times* Sunday Magazine (6 August, 2000), 30–63.

Widdows, Heather, 'The Relationship of Morality and Religion: An investigation of the issue in modern anglophone philosophy.' (Ph. D. thesis, University of Edinburgh, 1999.)

Widdows, Heather, *The Moral Vision of Iris Murdoch* (Aldershot: Ashgate, 2005).

Wiggins, David, [TIML] 'Truth, Invention and the Meaning of Life', *Proceedings of the British Academy* 62 (1976), 331–78; repr. in *Needs, Values, Truth* (London: Blackwell, 1987), 87–138.

Wiggins, David, *Sameness and Substance* (Oxford: Basil Blackwell, 1980).

Williams, Bernard, 'Conflicts of Values', in *Moral Luck* (Cambridge: Cambridge University Press, 1981), 54–74.

Williams, Bernard, 'Persons, Character and Morality', in *Moral Luck* (Cambridge: Cambridge University Press, 1981), 1–19.

Williams, Bernard, *Moral Luck: Philosophical Papers, 1973–1980* (Cambridge: Cambridge University Press, 1981).

Williams, Bernard, [ELP] *Ethics and the Limits of Philosophy* (London: Fontana/Cambridge, Mass.: Harvard University Press, 1985).

Williams, Patricia J., *The Alchemy of Race and Rights* (Cambridge, Mass.: Harvard University Press, 1991).

Winch, Peter, *Simone Weil: "The Just Balance"* (Cambridge: Cambridge University Press, 1989).

Wisdom, John, *Philosophy and Psychoanalysis* (Oxford: Basil Blackwell, 1953).

Wittgenstein, Ludwig, *Tractatus Logico-Philosophicus*, trans. C. K. Ogden, with introduction by Bertrand Russell, F. R. S. (London: Routledge & Kegan Paul, 1922).

Wittgenstein, Ludwig, [PI] *Philosophical Investigations*, ed. G. E. M. Anscombe and R. Rhees, trans. G. E. M. Anscombe (Oxford: Basil Blackwell, 1953, 1958, 1968).

Wittgenstein, Ludwig, *Remarks on the Foundations of Mathematics*, ed. G. H. von Wright, R. Rhees, and G. E. M. Anscombe, trans. G. E. M. Anscombe (Oxford: Basil Blackwell, 1956, 1964, 1978).

Wittgenstein, Ludwig, 'Lecture on Ethics', *Philosophical Review* 74 (1965), 3–12.

Wittgenstein, Ludwig, *Lectures and Conversations on Aesthetics, Psychology & Religious Belief*, ed. Cyril Barrett (Oxford: Basil Blackwell, 1966).

Wittgenstein, Ludwig, *On Certainty*, ed. G. E. M. Anscombe and G. H. von Wright, trans. D. Paul and G. E. M. Anscombe (Oxford: Basil Blackwell, 1969).

Wittgenstein, Ludwig, *Culture and Value*, ed. G. H. von Wright in collaboration with H. Nyman, trans. Peter Winch (Oxford: Basil Blackwell, 1980).

Wolf, Susan, 'Asymmetrical Freedom', *Journal of Philosophy* 77 (1980), 151–66; repr. in Derk Pereboom (ed.), *Free Will* (Indianapolis: Hackett Publishing, 1997).

Wolf, Susan, *Freedom Within Reason* (New York: Oxford University Press, 1990).

Woolf, Virginia, 'Professions for Women', in M. Barrett (ed.), *Women and Writing* (New York: Harcourt Brace Jovanovich, 1979). (First publ. in Woolf, *The Death of the Moth and Other Essays* (1942).)

Wright, Crispin, *Frege's Conception of Numbers as Objects* (Aberdeen: Aberdeen University Press, 1983).

Wright, Crispin, *Truth and Objectivity* (Oxford: Oxford University Press, 1994).

Young, Iris Marion, *Justice and the Politics of Difference* (Princeton: Princeton University Press, 1990).

Zuba, Sonja, 'Iris Murdoch and the Contemporary Retrieval of Platonic Themes' (Ph. D. thesis, Katholieke Universiteit Leuven, Hoger instituut voor Wijsbegeerte, 2007).

Zuba, Sonja, *Iris Murdoch's Contemporary Retrieval of Plato; The Influence of an Ancient Philosopher on a Modern Novelist* (Lewiston, NY: Edwin Mellen Press, 2009), with foreword by William Desmond.

Index

Lightning Source UK Ltd.
Milton Keynes UK
UKOW03f0326250714

235738UK00002B/4/P